Behavioral Health
Response to Disasters

Behavioral Health Response to Disasters

Edited by
Julie L. Framingham
Martell L. Teasley

CRC Press
Taylor & Francis Group
Boca Raton London New York

CRC Press is an imprint of the
Taylor & Francis Group, an **informa** business

CRC Press
Taylor & Francis Group
6000 Broken Sound Parkway NW, Suite 300
Boca Raton, FL 33487-2742

© 2012 by Taylor & Francis Group, LLC
CRC Press is an imprint of Taylor & Francis Group, an Informa business

No claim to original U.S. Government works

Printed in the United States of America on acid-free paper
Version Date: 20120322

International Standard Book Number: 978-1-4398-2123-7 (Hardback)

Visit the Taylor & Francis Web site at
http://www.taylorandfrancis.com

and the CRC Press Web site at
http://www.crcpress.com

In loving memory of
Charles M. Kimber, Shelli Plotkin, and Brian McKernan,
who left us too soon and will always be missed.

Contents

PART I Overview of the History and Fundamental Concepts behind Disaster Behavioral Health

PART II Organizational Response to Disasters and Key Partners

PART III Psychological Resilience and Pathological Responses to Disaster

PART VI   Disaster Behavioral Health Interventions

PART VII   Leaving a Legacy: Training and Community Empowerment

Foreword

Behavioral Health Response to Disasters

Disaster behavioral health has come a long way in a short amount of time. The book you hold in your hands (or perhaps view on your Kindle e-reader) encompasses an array of topics almost unimaginable even 25 years ago. It covers the roles and responsibilities of government and non-governmental organizations and the integration of behavioral health into public health preparedness and response. There are separate chapters on children, adolescents, older adults, and racially and ethnically diverse populations. Other chapters address secondary trauma in disaster workers and assessing local disaster vulnerability. The list goes on, including dealing with school systems, long-term care, behavioral health in shelters, treatment for disaster survivors, disaster substance abuse services, culturally competent case management, response team training, and building community resilience. A simple perusal of the table of contents serves as an illustration of the way that attention to disaster behavioral health has grown exponentially in research, policy, and practice communities.

It was not always so. When I began graduate training in the mid 1980s, to my knowledge disaster mental health was not part of any graduate school curriculum. A small subset of clinical psychologists and other mental health professionals had some training in crisis mental health, but it was optional, and it carried a different and much more specific meaning. Crisis mental health in those days typically meant: (1) working with people who were in acute crisis, (2) working with victims of extreme circumstances using models derived from the military and trauma research, and/or (3) community crisis intervention.

The individual-focused training usually emphasized working with individuals in an acute crisis and often conceptualized the crises as primarily psychiatric in nature—for example, schizophrenics having an acute episode. The focus with these cases was de-escalation and/or restraint, and often led to a reductionistic approach, reinforcing a "medical model" of focusing on individual pathology.

Some research and training did address victims of extreme circumstances, relying on principles of trauma research or individual crisis management. These models acknowledged that the trigger for the crisis was not necessarily intrinsic to the individual, nor was it the fault or responsibility of the individual. Instead, it was understood that crises could stem from events outside the individual's control. Research and training for this work built on the vast military experience with shell shock, battle fatigue, and other syndromes, as well as emerging research on child abuse, domestic violence, and sexual assault. While these models could sometimes still be pathologizing, the interventions were less so, often focusing on reinstating people's coping or developing new coping as a way to manage the current crisis.

Community crisis mental health response, building on the work of pioneers such as Gerald Caplan, also provided a model for intervention that further emphasized individual coping. This training was very valuable. I highly respect the work that was done at the outpatient community crisis clinic where I trained, and I remain grateful for the excellent supervisors who educated me in crisis response models and facilitated the assistance we offered to thousands of community members annually. This learning experience significantly helped trainees understand trauma and stress reactions, but it was necessarily incomplete. Because it was primarily clinically focused, this training could not always take into account the complexities of disaster response and the ways in which some trauma is, in words that became almost a mantra later, "a normal reaction to an abnormal event."

So, is training in acute crisis, trauma, and community crisis valuable? Absolutely. Does it prepare the clinician or the researcher to understand all the issues involved in disaster behavioral health? No. This is not an indictment of clinical training models, but rather a reflection of the state of mental health training in the past and, sadly, in the present. Our students and our licensed professionals are seldom required to have more than a passing understanding of trauma and crisis intervention, although they may seek it out. Training in disaster behavioral health is an even rarer commodity.

But the times are a-changin'. The approaches I mentioned before are important aspects of education in behavioral health. They are also precursors for understanding the field of disaster behavioral health. But they are not the same as disaster behavioral health. Disaster behavioral health is now emerging as its own field, with distinct interventions and its own empirical literature. Progress in research, practice, and theory has multiplied exponentially in the last 20 years, and the reader of this book has the opportunity to benefit from this progress. There now exist continuing education programs, courses, and even graduate certificates in disaster mental health. The American Red Cross and other organizations have developed cadres of mental health professionals with valuable specialized skills in responding to the needs of the general population in a disaster context. At the same time, researchers sponsored by the National Institutes of Health, the U.S. Department of Veterans Affairs, and the U.S. Department of Defense have made significant strides in understanding how disasters impact people differentially. This work has included studies on how that impact may differ across individuals and communities and what clinical responses make sense, ranging from psychological first aid to cognitive-behavioral interventions for posttraumatic stress disorder.

As you will see from reading this book, disaster behavioral health is a field with multiple foci, including emergent behavioral health needs, exacerbation of prior conditions, and responder support. The authors of these chapters represent some of the best and brightest in the field, with collective experience that encompasses many years of practice, research, and national advisory board service for disaster behavioral health. The reader is in good hands with these authors and the topics they have chosen. It is my hope that this volume will not only help the reader understand critical issues in disaster behavioral health, but that each reader will also reflect on how he or she can participate in this endeavor and continue to advance the field. Who knows where we may be in another 25 years?

Daniel Dodgen, PhD
Director, Division for At-Risk Individuals, Behavioral Health, and Community Resilience
Office of the Assistant Secretary for Preparedness and Response, Office of the Secretary
U.S. Department of Health and Human Services

Acknowledgments

An enormous undertaking such as this text could never have been completed without the assistance and support of others. We are especially indebted to our friend and colleague Dr. Lisa M. Brown at the University of South Florida for her constant encouragement, advice, and support in the development of this text. We are also grateful to work with such a fine group of contributing authors. They were very understanding and gracious about meeting timelines and requests for additional information and extremely patient as we experienced obstacles and delays. Importantly, they were committed to expanding the field of disaster behavioral health by lending their vast knowledge and expertise to contribute to the literature on this important subject. Their dedication to improving the lives of survivors after disaster strikes is evident in their comprehensive, thought-provoking coverage of crucial issues and creative solutions to identified challenges. We consider ourselves fortunate to have the guidance and assistance of CRC Press senior editor Mark Listewnik. He patiently guided us through the manuscript development process and provided extensive advice and feedback about our work. His patience knew no bounds—it was truly a pleasure to work with him! Likewise, we appreciate the kind assistance and support of Jennifer Ahringer, our copy project coordinator at CRC Press.

Our immediate families were a bastion of support throughout the preparation of this text, and we take this opportunity to say a loving "thank you" to all of them: Robert (Bob), Tyler, and Savanna Framingham for being so understanding about the many hours and months taken away from them while this book was being completed, and especially to Bob for lending a hand when assistance was needed most; and Tanya Dunlap-Teasley, Aura Teasley, and Taylor Collins, whose support and understanding allowed Martell the time to work on this project.

Editors

Julie L. Framingham, MSW, has an extensive background in writing disaster grants and managing large federally funded disaster behavioral health recovery projects that have provided crisis counseling, clinical interventions, and case management services for hurricane and tornado survivors. She was the director of the SAMHSA-funded Project Recovery and the FEMA-funded Project H.O.P.E. (Helping Our People in Emergencies) in Florida from 2005 through 2008. Each of the programs managed represented either new approaches to supporting survivors or a paradigm shift toward more evidenced-based technologies for dealing with the reactions to traumatic events. She has made numerous presentations at state and national conferences on disaster behavioral health, and she has served as a consultant and trainer for the Substance Abuse and Mental Health Services Administration's Disaster Technical Assistance Center. Ms. Framingham also has collaborated with the National Center for Posttraumatic Stress Disorder, the National Child Traumatic Stress Network, and the Administration for Children and Families to develop new approaches to mental health intervention and case management services for disaster survivors.

Martell L. Teasley, PhD, is an associate professor and chair of the Social Work and Disaster Recovery Certificate Program at Florida State University College of Social Work. Part of his research agenda includes a focus on disaster relief and recovery with a particular emphasis on cultural competence and vulnerable populations. Dr. Teasley works with several faith-based organizations in educating and training disaster case managers and paraprofessionals. This includes the evaluation of case management practices and emergency management organizational readiness assessments. He has served as a consultant for the Administration for Children and Families on the development of national case management standards and presented both nationally and internationally on disaster planning, relief, and recovery.

Contributors

Erin Barnett, PhD, is a psychologist and education specialist at the National Center for Posttraumatic Stress Disorder and a Research Associate at the Dartmouth Trauma Interventions Research Center. Dr. Barnett's interests are in developing educational products related to PTSD and providing, disseminating, and evaluating evidence-based trauma treatments for traumatized children, adults, and families. She assists with numerous research studies related to interventions for trauma and PTSD, provides trainings on trauma and PTSD to community organizations, and facilitates a Trauma Seminar for psychology interns.

Mari C. Bennasar, PsyD, is a multicultural clinical psychologist with a psychodynamic background and specialty training and experience in behavioral medicine. Dr. Bennasar owns a diverse private practice in Southborough, Massachusetts, and has been the associate director of the Center for Multicultural Training in Psychology since 2001. Dr. Bennasar's primary areas of interest include multicultural counseling, multicultural competencies, and diversity education and mentoring. Dr. Bennasar has conducted cultural competence research as part of the Department of Social Medicine at Harvard University Medical School. Dr. Bennasar has been providing mental health disaster services to survivors and Psychological First Aid trainings to providers since 2001. She is bilingual (Spanish/English) and bicultural (a native of the Dominican Republic).

Lisa M. Brown, PhD, is a clinical psychologist and an associate professor in the School of Aging Studies, College of Behavioral and Community Sciences, at the University of South Florida, Tampa. Dr. Brown's clinical and research focus is on aging, disasters, health, vulnerable populations, and long-term care. Since 2004, Dr. Brown has studied the acute and long-term psychosocial reactions and consequences of natural and human-caused disasters. Her research efforts focus on disaster mental health literacy, psychological first aid, access and use of disaster mental health services, and the effects of disasters on vulnerable populations.

Carol Bryant, PhD, is a Distinguished USF Health Professor and codirector of the Florida Prevention Research Center at the University of South Florida, College of Public Health. For 20 years, she has directed social marketing research on a wide variety of public health projects. Her work in social marketing has been acknowledged with the Philip Kotler Social Marketing Distinguished Service Award. She is also the founding editor of the *Social Marketing Quarterly* and Social Marketing in Public Health Conference.

Melissa J. Brymer received her PhD and PsyD in clinical psychology from Nova Southeastern University. She is director of Terrorism and Disaster Programs at the UCLA/Duke University National Center for Child Traumatic Stress in the Department of Psychiatry and Biobehavioral Sciences at UCLA. Her research interests include evaluating child and adolescent disaster behavioral health programs, postdisaster interventions and treatment outcome among traumatized youth, and the psychological impact of school shootings on youth.

Tracy Cooper, PhD, is an assistant professor at the University of South Florida. Her research interests include interorganizational network leadership, the third sector and its grassroots capabilities, nonprofit organizations in disaster management, and international development. She has experience working with nonprofit organizations on leadership and management issues.

Kermit A. Crawford, PhD, is a licensed psychologist and designated forensic psychologist. An associate professor of psychiatry, he is director of the Center for Multicultural Mental Health at the Boston University School of Medicine/Boston Medical Center. Dr. Crawford has expertise in cross-cultural competencies and professional practice in mental health, disaster behavioral health, and workforce development. He is principal investigator on state and federal grants and has published in refereed journals. He is recipient of the Commissioner's Excellence Award and the 2011 APPIC Excellence in Diversity Training Award. In addition to his earned doctorate from Boston College, he is recipient of an honorary doctoral degree of humane letters from the Massachusetts School of Professional Psychology. He has conducted consultations with and evaluations of mental health service systems and provided disaster behavioral health training across the nation. He serves on several mental health advisory committees and is a psychologist with the New England Patriots of the National Football League.

Elizabeth A. Davis, JD, EdM, is an emergency management consultant focusing on inclusive emergency management, marginalized population planning, disaster human services, and related issues through her firms EAD & Associates, LLC, and the National Emergency Management Resource Center (NEMRC). She began public service with the NYC Mayor's Office for People with Disabilities as assistant to counsel and senior policy advisor and later became the first director of the National Organization on Disability's Emergency Preparedness Initiative (EPI). Ms. Davis is also an advisor to DHS and FEMA, sits on many research review boards, and serves on several national advisory boards, including as the chair of the National Hurricane Conference Health Care/Special Needs Committee; chair of the International Association of Emergency Managers Special Needs Committee; and as a founding board member of Emergency Preparedness Initiative Global.

David Dosa, MD, MPH, is a practicing geriatrician and Associate Professor of Medicine and Community Health at Brown University in Providence, Rhode Island. Dr. Dosa is a funded researcher with grants from the National Institute on Aging, the California Health Care Foundation, and the Veterans Administration. He jointly conducts his research through Brown University's Center for Gerontology and the Providence VA Medical Center's Research Enhancement Award Program. His current research interests include nursing home quality improvement, nursing home response to hurricane disasters, nursing home infections, and medication errors in the elderly. He is also the *New York Times* bestselling author of *Making Rounds with Oscar: The Extraordinary Gift of an Ordinary Cat* (Hyperion, 2010).

Angela M. Eikenberry, PhD, is an associate professor in the School of Public Administration at the University of Nebraska at Omaha. Her main research interests include philanthropy and non-profit organizations and their role in democratic governance. She has published articles in numerous academic journals, and her research has been featured on National Public Radio's *All Things Considered* and in the *Stanford Social Innovation Review.* Her book *Giving Circles: Philanthropy, Voluntary Association, Democracy* (Indiana University Press, 2009) won the CASE 2010 John Grenzebach Research Award for Outstanding Research in Philanthropy, Published Scholarship.

Diane L. Elmore, PhD, MPH, is the Associate Executive Director of the Public Interest Government Relations Office at the American Psychological Association (APA) and Director of the APA Congressional Fellowship Program. In this role, she is responsible for health and social policy initiatives related to trauma and abuse, emergency preparedness and response, health and aging, caregiving, intergenerational issues, and the health and well-being of military service members, veterans, and their families. Dr. Elmore is also an adjunct professor in the School of Public Affairs at American University.

Maggie Gibson obtained her PhD from the University of Western Ontario. She is a psychologist with the Veterans Care Program, St. Joseph's Health Care London; an adjunct clinical professor in the Department of Psychology, University of Western Ontario; and an associate investigator at the Lawson Health Research Institute, London, Ontario, Canada. She collaborates on knowledge translation and exchange projects sponsored by the Canadian Coalition for Seniors Mental Health, the Alzheimer Society of Canada, the International Psychogeriatric Association, and the Public Health Agency of Canada, for whom she co-chairs an international working group that is focused on building capacity to address the needs of older adults in emergency and disaster situations.

Christine Haley is director of wellness for a real estate company specializing in developing active adult retirement communities and a current doctoral candidate in the School of Aging Studies at the University of South Florida. Her professional experience includes wellness positions in the corporate, collegiate, continuing care, and active adult community environments. Ms. Haley's research interests include promoting positive health behaviors among older adults and the relationship between physical activity and cognitive function. She has a BS in human nutrition and foods and a MSS in fitness management.

Jessica L. Hamblen, PhD, is the deputy director for education at the National Center for Posttraumatic Stress Disorder (PTSD) and an assistant professor of psychiatry at Dartmouth Medical School. Dr. Hamblen's interests are in developing, disseminating, and evaluating cognitive behavioral treatments for PTSD and related conditions. She has written articles for more than 30 publications, presents regularly at national conferences, and provides training nationwide on PTSD and postdisaster interventions. She was principal author of a 12-session cognitive behavioral intervention for postdisaster distress that was in New York after 9/11, Florida following the hurricanes of 2004, and Baton Rouge, Louisiana, after Hurricane Katrina. Dr. Hamblen is currently evaluating the intervention in a randomized controlled trial with survivors of Hurricane Ike.

Rebecca Hansen, MSW, has been working in the field of emergency management for nearly 15 years. Through her career she has focused on improving the integration of diverse and underserved populations into emergency management programs. Currently with EAD & Associates, LLC, Ms. Hansen brings her experience as an emergency manager and planner together with her social work background to encourage and support individual and community resiliency to disasters.

Elizabeth Harris holds both a BS and MA in political science from Oklahoma State University, with concentrations in public administration, public policy, and emergency management. After completing her MA, she served in the National Preparedness and Response Corps through AmeriCorps at the Tulsa Area Chapter of the American Red Cross. She currently serves as the research associate in the Innovation Lab at Community Action Project of Tulsa County.

Kathryn Hyer, PhD, MPP, is the director of the Florida Policy Exchange Center on Aging and an associate professor in the School of Aging Studies, College of Behavioral and Community Sciences, at the University of South Florida, Tampa. Since 2004, Dr. Hyer has studied the impact of natural disasters, especially hurricanes, on elders residing in nursing homes, assisted living facilities, and in the community. Her research is on the organizational and health systems policies associated with quality of care for elders and disabled people receiving long-term care services.

Jessica Love is a graduate student in the Fire and Emergency Management Program at Oklahoma State University, where she is pursuing a master's degree. Ms. Love has worked on projects concerning functional needs populations and sheltering issues. She has also interned with the Oklahoma State Office of Homeland Security.

Brian McKernan, MEd, ACADC, had a background providing substance abuse and mental health treatment for adolescents and adults in a variety of public and private inpatient and outpatient settings, including culturally competent care for rural and LGBT populations. Mr. McKernan also managed the Whitman-Walker Clinic's Scott-Harper Recovery House, one of only four programs of its kind in the nation for HIV-positive or LGBT clients. His clinical work included the provision of long-term counseling for those with mental health and substance abuse disorders who were impacted by the events of September 11, 2001. From 2005 to 2011, he provided disaster behavioral health technical assistance to states, territories, local communities, and tribes at the SAMHSA Disaster Technical Assistance Center. He supported SAMHSA's Hurricane Katrina response by organizing deployment of three consecutive crisis-counseling teams to coastal Mississippi. His on-site technical assistance included providing consultation to the California Department of Mental Health regarding the California wildfires disaster of 2007 and the Iowa flooding disaster of 2008, in addition to grantee federal site visits. He provided extensive guidance on Crisis Counseling Assistance and Training Program (CCP) data collection and evaluation. In addition, he worked with the National Center for Child Traumatic Stress and the National Center for Posttraumatic Stress Disorder to increase collaborations with these valuable SAMHSA partners. He also presented internationally on disaster substance abuse, and nationally on opioid treatment provider preparedness, stress management, the CCP, and the behavioral health impact of pandemic influenza. Mr. McKernan was thrilled to have just accepted a position to become a project officer with SAMHSA to continue his work supporting the CCP when he died suddenly in a motor vehicle accident in September 2011.

Lauren M. B. Mizock is currently completing her predoctoral American Psychological Association internship at the Center for Multicultural Training in Psychology at Boston Medical Center, affiliated with Boston University. In addition, she is working at the Child and Adolescent Psychiatry Department at Boston Medical Center, where she provides child and family therapy. Her current research is investigating many topics of culture, including rates of transgender veterans, multiracial identity constructs, and culturally sensitive disaster mental health treatment. Ms. Mizock also received a graduate student research award from the psychology department at Suffolk University in 2008 and 2009. Her experience as an Outreach Fellow and Diversity Committee member has been invaluable to supporting her continued commitment to clinical work, research, and teaching in the areas of underserved and marginalized populations.

April Naturale is a traumatic stress specialist who obtained her MSW from Columbia University and her PhD in clinical social work from New York University. Dr. Naturale was the statewide director for the New York 9/11 response, Project Liberty, as well as the 9/11 10th anniversary Healing and Remembrance program. In 2004, she helped launch the National Suicide Prevention Lifeline; in 2006, the *In-Courage* program after Hurricanes Katrina and Rita in Louisiana; and more recently, the BP Oil Spill Distress Helpline. Her dissertation research studied the levels of PTSD and Secondary Traumatic Stress in social workers who responded to the terrorist attacks in New York City. Over the past 10 years, Dr. Naturale has continued to provide disaster mental health preparedness and response training, consultation, and field assistance throughout the United States and internationally. Dr. Naturale currently works with ICF International where her primary responsibility is as a Senior Advisor to the Substance Abuse and Mental Health Services Administration's Disaster Technical Assistance Center.

Anthony T. Ng, MD, is medical director of the Acadia Hospital Psychiatric Emergency Services. He is an assistant professor of psychiatry at the Uniformed Services University of Health Sciences and the George Washington University School of Medicine. He is also the immediate past president of the American Association of Emergency Psychiatry. Dr. Ng has worked extensively in several disasters and various major crisis responses, including the El Salvador earthquakes in 2001, the September 11th terrorist attacks in New York in 2001, the anthrax mental health responses at NBC and ABC networks, the crash of AA Flight #587, Hurricane Katrina in 2005, and the Amish school shooting in 2006. He has also provided consultations in various other disasters, including the Asian tsunamis disaster in 2004 and the Virginia Tech shooting in 2007. Dr. Ng was chair of the New York City chapter of Voluntary Organizations Active in Disaster (NYCVOAD), a coalition of disaster human services agencies. He was a member of the American Psychiatric Association (APA) Committee on Psychiatric Dimensions of Disaster (CPDD) and was the past chair of the committee that he led between 2003 and 2006. He was recognized by the APA for his work in Hurricanes Katrina and Rita with a Special Presidential Commendation.

Fran H. Norris, PhD, is a community psychologist and a research professor in the Department of Psychiatry at Dartmouth Medical School, where she is affiliated with the National Center for Posttraumatic Stress Disorder (PTSD) and the National Consortium for the Study of Terrorism and Responses to Terrorism (START). She is also the director of the NIMH-funded National Center for Disaster Mental Health Research. Her research interests include posttraumatic stress, postdisaster mobilization of social support, and community resilience.

Dee S. Owens, MPA, is the director of the Alcohol-Drug Information Center at Indiana University and is currently on leave serving as a special expert on the Deepwater Horizon Data Coordination Project at SAMHSA. She has nearly 30 years of experience in the substance abuse/mental health field. Working as the Deputy Commissioner for Substance Abuse Services for the State of Oklahoma during the Murrah Federal Building bombing in Oklahoma City and serving on the disaster management team, she learned about the paucity of substance abuse services after disaster. Ms. Owens served on the consensus panel of CSAT's Treatment Improvement Protocol, "Substance Abuse and Trauma." For the New York Office of Alcoholism and Substance Abuse Services, she interviewed survivors, program and agency staff, and clients in New York City, Westchester County, and Albany, and coauthored "The Impact of the World Trade Center Disaster on Treatment and Prevention Services for Alcohol and Other Drug Abuse in New York: Immediate Effects, Lingering Problems, and Lessons Learned" in 2002. She was also on the governor's Emergency Management Assistance Compact (EMAC) Team as part of the medical effort to respond to destruction from Hurricane Katrina in Biloxi, Mississippi, assisting the state mental health agency with its immediate needs. She serves on the Indiana Division of Mental Health and Addictions All-Hazards Advisory Council and lectures internationally on substance abuse services, disaster, and planning. Her Master of Public Affairs in Policy Analysis is from the School of Public and Environmental Affairs at Indiana University.

Brenda D. Phillips, PhD, is a professor in the Fire and Emergency Management Program at Oklahoma State University. She is the author of *Disaster Recovery* (Auerbach, 2009) and the lead researcher on *Effective Emergency Management: Making Improvements for Communities and People with Disabilities* (National Council on Disability, 2009). She recently coedited *Women and Disasters: From Theory to Practice* (Xlibris, 2008) with Betty Hearn Morrow, and *Social Vulnerability to Disasters* (CRC Press, 2009) with Deborah Thomas, Alice Fothergill, and Lynn Blinn-Pike. Her published research can be found in a variety of journals, including the *International Journal of Mass Emergencies and Disasters, Disaster Prevention, Disasters, Humanity and Society, Journal of Emergency Management, Natural Hazards Review,* and *Environmental Hazards.* Dr. Phillips received the 2010 Mary Fran Myers Award from the Natural Hazards Center for her work on gender issues in disaster contexts.

John C. Pine, PhD, is director of the Research Institute for Environment, Energy & Economics (RIEEE) and professor, Department of Geography and Planning, Appalachian State University, Boone, North Carolina. He joined the Appalachian faculty after serving 30 years at Louisiana State University in Baton Rouge, where he directed the graduate and undergraduate Disaster Science and Management Program, and was a professor in the Department of Geography and Anthropology and the Department of Environmental Sciences. His research on disasters and emergency management centers on emergency planning, hazards and risk assessment, and risk management. He has worked with many federal, state, and local entities to identify strategies to enhance community preparedness and ensure the resilience of communities impacted by disasters. Dr. Pine's recent publications include *Natural Hazards Analysis: Reducing the Impact of Disasters* (Auerbach, 2009), *Technology and Emergency Management* (Wiley, 2007), and *Tort Liability Today* (National League of Cities and Public Risk Management Association, 2005). He has served on the Board of Visitors for FEMA's Emergency Management Institute in Emmitsburg, Maryland. Dr. Pine's publications have been included in: *Disasters: The Journal of Disaster Studies, Policy and Management, Journal of Race and Society, International Journal of Mass Emergencies and Disasters, Oceanography, Journal of Emergency Management, Natural Disaster Review, Journal of Environmental Health,* and *Journal of Hazardous Materials*. He received his doctorate in higher education administration and public administration from the University of Georgia, Athens, in 1979.

Mary L. Pulido, PhD, currently serves as the executive director of The New York Society for the Prevention of Cruelty to Children. She is a consultant, lecturing and training nationally on the prevention and management of secondary traumatic stress. She has also developed a protocol, entitled Restoring Resiliency Response, for crisis debriefing following child fatality that is currently utilized throughout New York City for child protective services staff. She is president-elect of the American Professional Society on the Abuse of Children – New York (APSAC-NY), and is an adjunct assistant professor at the Silberman School of Social Work at Hunter College in New York City.

Gilbert Reyes earned his PhD in clinical psychology from the University of Colorado. He is a licensed clinical psychologist and associate dean in the School of Psychology at Fielding Graduate University, in Santa Barbara, California. Dr. Reyes specializes in disaster psychology and psychological trauma, and has consulted and participated in projects with organizations including the American Red Cross, the American Psychological Association, and the National Child Traumatic Stress Network. He has contributed to the development of a variety of training materials, and frequently trains mental health workers and others who serve their communities in disasters.

Kelly Rouba is an accomplished journalist and public speaker. Among the publications she currently writes for are *Life in Action* magazine, ThisAbled.com, and GalTime.com. She is also the author of *Juvenile Arthritis: The Ultimate Teen Guide* (Scarecrow Press, 2009). A children's book on disabilities that she coauthored with her brother Kevin will be released soon. Ms. Rouba works full time as a Communications & Emergency Management Specialist for the State of New Jersey and is also a DAE/Special Needs Specialist with the Department of Homeland Security/FEMA Region II. She is a member of the Patient Advocacy Institute, the American Society of Journalists & Authors, Hamilton YMCA's Advisory Board, Mercer County's Disability Advisory Council, Hamilton Township's Special Needs Commission, and the board of e-Quality Productions. She also serves as 2nd vice president of the Board of the Arthritis National Research Foundation, which named an annual grant of $75,000 in her honor called The Kelly Award for Juvenile Arthritis Research. She previously served on the boards of Enable, Inc., and Project Freedom, and on the NJ Independent Living Council. Ms. Rouba was diagnosed with juvenile rheumatoid arthritis at the age of two and later became an advocate for those living with all types of disabilities. She held the title of Ms. Wheelchair New Jersey from December 2006 to February 2008 and has been featured in numerous news publications and shows, from ABC's television show *Perspective New Jersey* to the *Wall Street Journal*.

Raymond Runo, MPA, is the president of Preparedness & Response Partners, LLC. He has an extensive background in law enforcement, occupational health and safety, human resources, and more than 25 years of experience in emergency management. From 2004 through 2010, he managed the State of Florida's public health and medical response system through 10 hurricanes, 16 tropical storms, other natural and manmade disasters, and in 2009/10 served as the Incident Commander for Florida's response to pandemic influenza. During this period, he managed the development of a comprehensive and integrated public health and medical response system, which has been recognized as a national model. This included working with public and private partners in the development of a statewide disaster behavioral health preparedness and response system. In 2006, Mr. Runo initiated the development of the Unified Planning Coalition, which integrated and coordinated the public health and medical response for nine southern states (FEMA Region 4). His masters in public administration is from Florida State University. He has served on a number of national committees and panels and is recognized as a national expert on emergency management preparedness and response issues.

Josef I. Ruzek, PhD, is director of the Dissemination and Training Division of the National Center for Posttraumatic Stress Disorder (PTSD). He specializes in early intervention for trauma survivors and has been active in development and evaluation of early preventive interventions for disaster and terrorism survivors, returning Iraq War personnel, and patients seen in hospital trauma centers. He is an author of the Psychological First Aid field guide created jointly by the National Center for Posttraumatic Stress Disorder (PTSD) and the National Child Traumatic Stress Network for the SAMHSA's Center for Mental Health Services. He is also an author of *Skills for Psychological Recovery*, a manualized approach to crisis counseling. Dr. Ruzek is on the board of directors of the International Society for Traumatic Stress Studies, and is co-chair of the society's early intervention special interest group.

Richard Salkowe is a PhD candidate in the Department of Geography, Environment, and Planning at the University of South Florida. His dissertation research examines health outcomes and federal disaster declarations. He has published papers and book chapters pertaining to disaster policy, historical disaster experiences, and health care disparities. He is a podiatric physician and surgeon and serves on the Florida Department of Health Community Preparedness Target Capability Task Force and as a medical officer for the Region IV-Florida State Medical Response Team.

Patricia Santucci, MD, FAPA, FAED, is a retired associate professor of psychiatry from the Stritch School of Medicine at Loyola University Chicago. During 40 years of private clinical practice, her interests included traumatized children, adolescents, and women. As past medical director of Linden Oaks Hospital, she trained professionals in crisis intervention and emergency psychiatry, as well as developed and implemented a variety of mental health programs for the acute setting. As co-chair of the Medical Reserve Corps Mental Health Committee on Disasters, Dr. Santucci worked alongside the Center for PTSD and the National Child Traumatic Stress Network, contributing to the development of Psychological First Aid™. Promoting the integration of mental health into disaster response, she became a certified instructor for the American Medical Association's National Disaster Life Support courses. In her present role as medical director of the SW Florida Medical Reserve Corps, Dr. Santucci provides training and program development for both the medical and behavioral health aspects of disaster. She has appeared on major media networks, lectured nationwide, testified before Congress, founded academic and advocacy organizations, and has received multiple awards, including recognition for her volunteerism and work during Hurricane Katrina.

Alan M. Steinberg received his PhD in philosophy from Cornell University. He is associate director of the UCLA/Duke University National Center for Child Traumatic Stress in the Department of Psychiatry and Biobehavioral Sciences at the University of California, Los Angeles. His areas of interest include the development and validation of instruments to evaluate traumatized and bereaved children and adolescents, and public mental health approaches to postdisaster recovery programs for children and families.

Jeannie Straussman, MSW, clinical social worker, formerly was a regional director and clinical coordinator for Disaster Mental Health for the New York State Office of Mental Health. She has been an active long-term member of the American Red Cross as a disaster mental health responder for local and national disasters. Currently, Ms. Straussman is a consultant at the State University of New York at New Paltz – Institute for Disaster Mental Health, the College of St. Rose, Albany, New York, and the National University of Singapore.

Bruce H. Young, LCSW, is a health science specialist for the Dissemination and Training Division of the National Center for Posttraumatic Stress Disorder (PTSD). He specializes in disaster mental health in the areas of organizational planning and policy, practice guidelines, as well as field, classroom, and online training programs. He continues to be a major contributor and author in the development of Psychological First Aid and emergency responder self-care guidelines. He also is a coauthor of *The Readiness-To-Deploy Survey.* Mr. Young is chair of the Veterans Health Administration (VHA) Emergency Mental Health Steering Committee, and a mental health consultant for the VHA's Office of Emergency Management and Disaster Emergency Medical Personnel System. He serves on the VHA's National Emergency Medical Field Advisory Committee and the California Disaster Mental Health Coalition. Since 1989, he has been a first responder to numerous natural and human-caused disasters.

Michael J. Zakour earned an MA in anthropology (1980) from Pennsylvania State University, and an MSW (1984) and PhD in social work (1988), both from the Brown School of Social Work at Washington University in St. Louis. He is currently an associate professor at West Virginia University in the School of Social Work, where he serves as director for the NOVA Institute, a research and education institute focusing on nonprofit organizations, volunteers, and disaster social work. He teaches courses on social welfare, community organization theory and practice, and management. Dr. Zakour has published in a variety of journals including *Social Work Research, Nonprofit and Voluntary Sector Quarterly, Journal of Social Service Research,* and *Social Development Issues.* In 2000, he was editor of the monograph *Tulane Studies in Social Welfare: Disaster and Traumatic Stress Research and Intervention.* He has published numerous chapters on social work in disasters, traumatic stress, and community disaster vulnerability. He is the founder (1995) and original chairperson of the Disaster & Traumatic Stress Track/Symposium at the Council on Social Work Education Annual Program Meetings.

Introduction

Until the mid- to late 1990s, homeland security and emergency management professionals had focused primarily on the physical consequences of natural and human-caused disasters. Disasters in the United States have become more prevalent within the past decade, a fact that has not escaped the attention of the American public. Indeed, catastrophic disasters such as Hurricane Katrina and the 9/11 terrorist attacks have left an indelible mark on our society and the public psyche of America. Media coverage of disasters, as well as the grim spectacle of new and emerging hazards like pandemic influenza, which have the potential to cause thousands, and perhaps millions, of people to become ill or die, to disrupt businesses, schools, and essential services, further incite the public's fears of such events. Given these contingencies, a focus on the adverse physical impacts of disaster is obvious. Although in research and practice the field of disaster behavioral health is a relative newcomer to the scene of emergency management and homeland security preparedness and response, it has garnered serious interest from governmental and nongovernmental agencies, researchers and academicians, and behavioral health services providers who realize that restoring people's psychological well-being is as vital to restoring community functioning as restoring critical infrastructures, homes, and basic human needs. Intensive media coverage of the high rates of posttraumatic stress disorder, depression, and substance abuse after events like Hurricane Katrina has served to illustrate to the world the need to protect people from physical harm and the adverse psychological consequences of a disaster occurrence.

Large-scale disasters like Hurricane Katrina also illustrate one of the greatest challenges facing disaster behavioral health services providers—delivering appropriate services to diverse cultural groups and ethnic minorities who are among the most vulnerable and are already marginalized in our society, which places them at greater risk to suffer from the adverse psychological impacts of disasters and potentially in grave need of assistance in the recovery process. Coupled with growing class and economic stratification, the concept of disaster vulnerability has the potential to take on many new and dynamic dimensions that should be the subject of research and education and training programs for disaster management professionals. The increasing frequency and intensity of disasters warrants greater attention and focus on the development of modalities for prevention and intervention.

Supported by research in multiple domains, the underlying assumption of disaster behavioral health is to anticipate and provide immediate and appropriate services for emotional and physical symptoms and cognitive dysfunction that may occur. While stress and anxiety are normative responses for people who are exposed to disaster, disasters can cause long-term disruptions to the routines of individuals and communities, which can place individuals at greater risk of developing serious behavioral health disorders that require treatment. According to the U.S. Department of Health and Human Services, Substance Abuse and Mental Health Services Administration, disaster behavioral health services assist survivors by providing emotional support, normalizing stress reactions, assessing recovery options, encouraging adaptive coping, and connecting survivors to community resources that aid the recovery process. By providing such services, individual distress may be mitigated and potentially adverse long-term psychological outcomes may be avoided. Appropriately used, behavioral health intervention can facilitate individual, family, and community resiliency in the postdisaster environment. A central aim of behavioral health intervention is the reduction of costly and inappropriately used community resources such as hospitals, psychiatric facilities, and personnel who provide professional medical and behavioral health treatment.

This book brings together multidisciplinary scholars and expert field practitioners to review and discuss key topics in disaster behavioral health. These professionals have collaborated to produce a single text that covers the wide variety of issues in the emerging field of disaster behavioral health response. Two central themes are embedded within the authors' collective work: a focus on evidence-based practice and cultural competence. Evidence-based practice is the process of identifying, critically appraising, and documenting the best available evidence from empirical research to guide practice. It requires critical thinking in its application and the continuation of research to validate its utilization. And while the empirical evidence on disaster behavioral health planning, response, and recovery is still evolving, there is a growing field of research literature on disaster behavioral health that guides scholars and practitioners to develop and implement promising interventions and services.

Given the growing diversification of the United States, including gross disparities in wealth and assets, culturally competent disaster relief and recovery is an area of great need for research and the subsequent development of evidence-based practices. Culturally competent disaster behavioral health is the process of transitioning specific knowledge of one's own practices, beliefs, values, preferences, and biases while most effectively providing immediate and appropriate services to others for the distress and cognitive dysfunction that may occur as a result of a disaster occurrence. This need is captured within the research literature and the general media through a multiplicity of examples of problematic approaches to disaster planning, relief, and recovery as it concerns minority populations, transgender groups, women and children, the elderly and disabled, immigrants, and the poor—the traditional recipients of high disaster vulnerability and poor postdisaster outcomes. As a whole, this text unfolds an expanding field of behavioral health research and the ongoing challenges that competent behavioral health professionals need to understand.

Part I introduces the subject of disaster behavioral health. It consists of two chapters. Using a purposive sample of historical literature, Chapter 1 presents a selected historical account of behavioral responses to disaster preparation and relief. Richard Salkowe demonstrates how social and cultural factors influence individual and group behaviors to disaster preparation and the need for interventions to help survivors cope with and recover from the adverse psychological consequences of disaster. A salient point in the chapter is how socially endorsed prejudice and ill attitudes toward racial and ethnic groups are used to justify postdisaster discriminatory practices. Factors identified as critical in the consideration of an overall approach to disaster relief and recovery identified from the study are individual levels of risk perception for disaster exposure, the manifestation of individual behaviors based on the geographical prevalence of a disaster occurrence, the response of multitiered support mechanisms (private, parochial, and public), and the need for culturally competent practice.

Chapter 2 distinguishes between traditional behavioral health treatment and interventions commonly used in disaster behavioral health. Julie L. Framingham contrasts and compares both approaches through review of relevant literature on the intervention setting, outreach to diverse populations, service referrals, methods for community outreach, counseling strategies, and postdisaster social support. Cultural competence is stressed throughout the chapter as critical to appropriate behavioral health response in areas such as the response team composition, identification of volunteer workers, inclusion of indigenous workers, and the personal qualities of outreach workers.

Part II consist of three chapters and is an overview of organizational response in the development of policies and programs that address disaster behavioral health. The roles and responsibilities of key governmental and nongovernmental partners at the federal, state, and local levels will help readers to understand how behavioral health services are implemented after disaster. Chapter 3 unfolds the historical progression of government involvement in disaster behavioral health policy. Acknowledging the role of nongovernmental entities in disaster preparation and response, Richard Salkowe and Julie L. Framingham discuss specific national governmental responsibilities, measures, and mandates that guide state and local operationalization of behavioral health services. First established in 1979, the Federal Emergency Management Agency continues to consolidate and coordinate disaster response efforts. Created in 1988, the Stafford Act gave presidential authority to the determination of federal declaration of a disaster area. Disaster planning and coordination at the state and local levels were further embellished with the development of the Disaster Mitigation Act of 2000. The Post-Katrina Emergency Management Reform Act of 2006 marks the advent of federal involvement in long-term recovery support, technical assistance, and improved coordination of governmental and nongovernmental response entities. The authors demonstrate that behavioral health guidelines based on best practices are woven throughout the federal disaster agency framework. As a balance, the latter part of the chapter articulates research finding on the advantages and shortcomings of federal guidelines in state and local behavioral health response to disasters. Recommendations for improving the federal and state governments' roles in disaster behavioral health planning and response policy are suggested.

It is important for behavioral health professionals and practitioners to understand how nongovernmental organizations respond to a disaster environment. In Chapter 4, Angela M. Eikenberry and Tracy Cooper provide an overview of key types of nongovernmental organizations that generally respond to disaster along with recommendations for improving future response. The roles of nongovernmental organizations such as the American Red Cross, the Salvation Army, and the National Voluntary Organizations Active in Disaster are discussed along with their coordination of services with the Federal Emergency Management Agency and other governmental entities. In recent years, the White House Office of Faith-Based and Neighborhood Partnerships has expanded the capacity and coordination of disaster response services between the federal government and nongovernmental organizations. The multiple challenges that confront appropriate planning and preparation (e.g., organizational distrust, fear and competition, leadership issues, and lack of agency coordination) are addressed along with suggestions for overcoming these challenges.

Focusing on public health in planning and the postdisaster environment, Anthony T. Ng and Jeannie Straussman discuss in Chapter 5 why disasters are public health emergencies and need comprehensive prevention planning to avoid behavioral health complications. An important aspect in the planning process is to understand community and individual reaction to a disaster occurrence. Concurrently, consideration is given to the impact of social, psychological, economic, and health policies on individual stress and coping in the postdisaster environment. Disasters have reverberating effects—those who first present as victims of a disaster occurrence are only the "tip of the iceberg," as many others are affected by the losses of primary disaster victims.

Part III has two chapters and moves into the area of psychological challenges and response to individuals who have been impacted by a disaster occurrence. In Chapter 6, Michael J. Zakour reviews available evidence on disaster vulnerability and adaptive behaviors for effectively coping with traumatic loss and death during disaster. Given the multiple ways in which loss occurs from disaster, Zakour conceptualized a multidimensional approach to understanding the formation of individual, family, and community vulnerability based on existing research. Levels of risk for poor behavioral health outcomes, due to traumatic loss after a disaster experience, are based on vulnerability and biopsychosocial susceptibility and their intersection with the severity of individual and family experiences; closeness to the loss; stage in the life cycle of survivors; the appropriateness of behavioral health response; and the degree of individuals and familial resilience—all of which are factors. Research demonstrates that individual behavioral health outcomes due to experiencing loss from a disaster are heavily impacted by environmental antecedents to stress, trauma, and coping. Protective factors in the form of social support, stress and coping, preventive mental health, health care access, formation of social capital, and individual empowerment are demonstrated as methods to facilitate individual resilience.

Chapter 7 by clinical psychiatrist Patricia Santucci consists of two parts. The first focuses on the mental health of adult survivors of disasters and terrorist attacks. Research findings on behavioral changes due to stress and maladaptive behaviors during the postdisaster environment are identified. This includes data on behavioral health risk after the September 11, 2001, World Trade Centers terrorist attack. In general, when a disaster occurs, those who have preexisting stressors and health challenges (e.g., substance and alcohol abuse, tobacco use, prescription and nonprescription drug use) may relapse as a method of coping with the aftermath of a disaster experience. Similarly, marital conflict, domestic violence, spousal and emotional abuse, child abuse, and health issues such as anxiety, depression, cardiovascular disease, chronic pain, and physical distress are discussed for their prevalence in the postdisaster environment. The chapter's second part focuses on why people develop posttraumatic pathology. A detailed overview of acute stress disorder and posttraumatic stress disorder is discussed along with information on behavioral health challenges based on the geographical locale of disaster survivors. Risk and protective factors are identified along with coping strategies and behavioral health diagnostic issues.

Part IV is comprised of five chapters dedicated to a review of research findings on at-risk populations that experience disasters and risk factors that contribute to individual and community vulnerability. In Chapter 8, Melissa J. Brymer, Gilbert Reyes, and Alan Steinberg provide an overview of the literature on the effects of disasters on children and adolescents, with a particular focus on risk and resilience. A three-tiered public health model of postdisaster is presented, along with an in-depth description of recommended preparedness, response and recovery activities to address the varied behavioral health challenges that children and their families experience after a disaster. Stressing that more research is needed, the authors give examples of how to work with children and adolescents during disaster response and recovery. Implications for training, planning, and working with diverse children and youth using behavioral health interventions are discussed.

Chapter 9 by Lisa M. Brown, Maggie Gibson, and Diane L. Elmore examines disaster behavioral health readiness and response for older adults in the United States and Canada. The challenge of disaster preparation for intervention with members of the baby boomer generation has emerged as a major topic in disaster research literature. Demographic trends in both countries dictate the necessity for disaster planning, relief, and recovery operations to address the age-related physiological and chronic health challenges of disaster survivors. Yet, Brown and associates maintain that the education and training of emergency management response and recovery professionals and paraprofessionals has in the past neglected geriatric issues for disaster planning and preparation. This chapter demonstrates areas of needed improvement in future education and training programs and stresses the importance of social networks, planning for caregiving issues, and appropriate considerations for social, economic, and cultural factors related to disaster vulnerability for aging adults.

While there is scant research on culture competence and disaster intervention, the need for such research seemingly grows with the passing of each disaster occurrence. Historically, ethnic and cultural minorities have experienced significant disparities in postdisaster behavioral health utilization. As such, in Chapter 10, Kermit A. Crawford, Mari C. Bennasar, and Lauren M. B. Mizock stress using the foundational components of cultural competence—awareness, knowledge, and skill development—as methods of engaging in restructuring cognitive schema through experiential learning for responders and other emergency management personnel. This is illustrated within the chapter through the use of narratives from the authors' personal experiences in responding to the behavioral health needs of racial and ethnic minority clients who have been exposed to disasters.

Chapter 11 focuses on the psychological challenges faced by disaster responders who provide behavioral health support and counseling to disaster survivors. Although expressed within research literature by various conceptual approaches, *secondary traumatic stress* is the emotional consequence resulting from responders' knowledge of a traumatizing event through helping or wanting to help those who have experienced a disaster. April Naturale and Mary L. Pulido discuss the signs of secondary traumatic stress, including information on burnout, psychological and physiological responses to traumatic stress, and cognitive and behavioral reactions to trauma. Risk factors contributing to secondary traumatic stress for disaster responders are addressed along with guidelines for monitoring and assessing levels of secondary traumatic stress, burnout, and satisfaction with work. Importantly, behavioral health training for disaster responders at all levels is suggested with a specific focus on organizational, professional, and personal interventions.

Chapter 12 examines the issue of climatic, geographic, and topographic considerations in the assessment of disaster vulnerability. John C. Pine reviews dimensions of community vulnerability such as social, economic, ecological, and environmental. Environmental analysis is necessary in the estimation of global, national, regional, and community disaster vulnerability. This includes the maintenance, planning, and safeguarding of the infrastructure of a given society. Thus, a large portion of community vulnerability and resilience is based on planning and environmental stewardship. Community planning for a disaster must include risk analysis in the assessment of known structural and environmental hazards. Likewise, understanding and assessing social and economic conditions, cultural norms such as coping strategies, communication channels, transportation management, population dynamics, and household structures must be part of risk analysis and preparation of a disaster occurrence.

Part V of this book addresses barriers to behavioral health response within systems of care. Because they are away from their families, school children and youth may experience high levels of stress and anxiety during a disaster occurrence. Chapter 13 by Martell L. Teasley reviews research on school readiness for disaster intervention with a focus on behavioral health for children and youth. Existing evidence on school vulnerability based on geographic location, school size, and building construction is discussed in connection with disaster planning, readiness, and risk factors that impact behavioral health outcomes. Low-income minority school-aged children, particularly those in urban communities, often experience greater disaster vulnerability and therefore reciprocally experience poorer disaster outcomes. Additionally, rural areas consistently lack necessary infrastructure and resources that facilitate youth resilience in the aftermath of a disaster occurrence. Cultural competence in this arena requires assessment and planning for specific geographic locations and for diverse populations of school children. National guidelines for school readiness are presented along with the current state of school disaster readiness, as articulated from a review of research literature. Broad dissemination of behavioral health intervention information through education and training, parental involvement, and social support have been demonstrated to be effective in the reduction of poor behavioral health outcomes for school-aged children exposed to a disaster.

A significant challenge in the development of the planning for behavioral and medical health care in the postdisaster environment is the issue of long-term care. Chapter 14 by David Dosa, Kathryn Hyer, and Lisa M. Brown is an overview of issues and challenges identified within research literature on residents of long-term care facilities such as nursing homes and assisted living facilities. Aging and disabled residents living within such facilities are, in general, at a state of high risk and vulnerability when there are catastrophic events such as disasters. The challenge of a chaotic environment after a disaster, where normalcy and routine activities of daily living are interrupted, can result in adverse outcomes for aging adults with physical and mental conditions that require skilled professional attention. Stress, depression, and other behavioral health challenges in the postdisaster environment are all noted within the research literature. Research demonstrates that the transfer of frail and disabled nursing home patients, for example, must be carefully planned with detailed considerations for physical and behavioral health care. Recommendations for improving behavioral health service delivery for residents of long-term care facilities during a disaster are provided. As an evidence-informed method of engaging in behavioral health intervention for those impacted by a disaster, the use of psychological first aid is highly suggested. Training in psychological first aid should be offered to all nursing home staff as part of predisaster training, and to all personnel who may come into contact with long-term-care-facility patients.

The need for evacuating populations to find safe haven during an impending disaster occurrence is an enormous challenge for public shelters and the personnel providing services. Chapter 15 by Brenda D. Phillips and colleagues is a thorough overview of functional shelter provisions that must be considered in emergency planning. For example, public health issues, shelter management, location options, size, spatial arrangements, management and operations, population and group nutritional needs, and animal management must all be considered. Special provisions for pediatric and geriatric care, the disabled, pregnant women, and those with medical needs are further logistical considerations and resources demands for a functional shelter. Topics from shelter staffing, security needs, and case management, to discharge planning and family reunification are presented.

Part VI details disaster behavioral health interventions in the form of disaster case management, crisis counseling, and long-term mental health treatment for survivors. In Chapter 16, Julie L. Framingham presents the multiple contingencies that crisis counseling programs face in response to individual and community needs in the postdisaster environment. The Crisis Counseling Assistance and Training Program (CCP) is a provision that follows the presidential declaration of a disaster area. The CCP is jointly administered by the Federal Emergency Management Agency (FEMA) and the U.S. Department of Health and Human Services, Substance Abuse and Mental Health Services Administration. The critical role that state agencies play in facilitating services to disaster-stricken communities is examined. Detailed information on the functional use of community needs assessments in the determination of behavioral health needs is discussed. Using Florida's experience in the aftermath of Hurricane Charley and subsequent disasters from the period of 2004 to 2007, the author focuses on the challenges faced in the design, implementation, and administration of crisis counseling programs. In the end, lessons learned from this experience are identified and discussed.

There is a clear and present need to address the long-term behavioral health concerns of adult disaster survivors. In Chapter 17, Jessica L. Hamblen, Erin Barnett, and Fran H. Norris take on the task of reviewing the available evidence on long-term mental health treatments for adult disaster survivors. Conditions such as substance abuse, depression, and grief are addressed. Barriers to care are identified, particularly as they pertain to those of low socioeconomic status and cultural orientation. For those who experience posttraumatic stress, cognitive behavioral treatments can help address maladaptive thinking through psychoeducation, anxiety management, exposure, and cognitive strategies. Recommendations for reducing barriers to treatment and strategies for improving behavioral health intervention for adult survivors are suggested.

The subject of substance abuse in the postdisaster environment is a continuing thread throughout this textbook. Chapter 18 by Dee S. Owens, Brian McKernan, and Julie L. Framingham examines the growing evidence on disaster survivor use and abuse of alcohol and other drugs in the postdisaster environment. Research has demonstrated higher rates of postdisaster substance use among the general population exposed to a disaster. Findings from postdisaster research, including the attack on September 11, 2001, and Hurricanes Katrina and Rita in 2006, illustrate higher substance use among adults who were displaced from their homes and communities. Anxiety, depression, and posttraumatic stress disorder are among associated mental health challenges. Those most at risk for substance abuse in the postdisaster environment are former users who are in recovery, survivors experiencing disaster-related mental health symptoms, first responders, and adolescents. Problems are exacerbated when community substance abuse treatment centers are not available to treat survivors. Field case studies are provided with examples of how federal- and state-organized recovery efforts aimed at substance abuse intervention can be effective. The authors make suggestions for future planning, preparation, and training based on lessons learned from the past experiences of federal and state agencies participating in postdisaster substance abuse intervention.

Chapter 19 is an overview of research on disaster case management and its role in assessment, referral, and treatment of behavioral health challenges related to a disaster occurrence. Martell L. Teasley explains the process in which disaster case management guidelines were developed by FEMA in collaboration with nonprofit organizations. There have been several demonstration projects organized and funded by federal agencies for the purpose of documenting the characteristics and scope of disaster case management. Research on disaster case management heavily focuses on specific populations or tasks. One impediment to research on disaster case management is that there are numerous and competing models. The literature review reveals several documented challenges in the federal government's efforts and lessons learned for future disaster case management research.

Part VII is committed to disaster preparedness through responder training, using social marketing to build community resiliency, and behavioral health planning. In Chapter 20, Bruce H. Young and Josef I. Ruzek explain important considerations related to postdisaster services implementation. The chapter delineates content and process in the training of managers, supervisors, service practitioners, and teams. This includes information on the scope of agency operations, the scope of service provisions, staffing issues, and preparation and sustainability of training. Research findings on staff training issues such as stress and coping, face-to-face meetings with clients, relaxation techniques, cognitive behavioral techniques, and disaster counseling are examined for evidence of the benefits and shortcomings. Detailed guidelines for staff training and development are recommended. In particular, behavioral health intervention and training based on psychological first aid is considered state of the art and a best practice. Since federal governmental agencies provide online options for training in psychological first aid, responders and other emergency management personnel can benefit from this.

In Chapter 21, Lisa M. Brown, Christine Haley, and Carol Bryant conceptualize the idea and role of social marketing in the development of disaster behavioral health programs. The basic premise here is that since nationally declared disaster areas often encounter significant challenges in delivering behavioral health services, even to those that need them the most, social marketing can reduce the underutilization of services. The authors note that underutilization of disaster crisis counseling is often attributable to a variety of institutional factors that consistently hinder appropriate and accessible behavioral health intervention—all of which, social marketing and outreach can substantially resolve. Similarly, the historic constraints of minority communities concerning behavioral health challenges can be addressed through marketing strategies like consumer product orientation, product promotion, and continuous monitoring and improvements. Brown and associates contend that culture not only influences how disasters affect populations, it likewise influences how program administrators and clinicians interact with the general public. The chapter provides an array of marketing strategies all aimed at improving disaster behavioral health service utilization and client satisfaction.

The primary purpose of disaster planning is to identify potential community hazards and vulnerabilities, assess the community's capacity to respond efficiently and effectively, and enhance disaster response and recovery efforts through improved integration and coordination of community resources and external partners. In the final work of this collection, Chapter 22, Raymond Runo and Julie L. Framingham discuss the underlying assumptions of disaster planning and how they impact decision making. Several federal initiatives are reviewed to include the National Response Framework and the Comprehensive Preparedness Guide. The benefits of effective planning for behavioral health services delivery include increased flexibility and adaptation, collaboration, and meeting the needs of underserved, at-risk groups. It is important to note that emergency operations plans should follow the commonly accepted model for all-hazards response and use the standard terminology and components found in other local, state, and federal plans to facilitate integration and coordination of emergency response efforts.

To our knowledge, there is currently no other comprehensive text that addresses such a wide range of disaster mental health and substance abuse subject matter, nor is there one that systematically examines the impact of culture on service delivery to ameliorate the adverse psychological effects of disaster within diverse populations. Given the gravity of such outcomes for individuals, communities, and service systems, disaster behavioral health merits consideration of best practices for assessment, referral, and treatment of postdisaster behavioral health outcomes. It is essential for disaster responders, government officials, and others desiring to be of service to survivors to understand the complex network of federal, state, and local resources for dealing with disasters. Finally, we hope to promote understanding of the growing reality and dynamics of disaster vulnerability and its dimensionality in order to more efficiently identify and reach out to marginalized and underserved populations that may need extra assistance after a disaster.

Part I

Overview of the History and
Fundamental Concepts behind
Disaster Behavioral Health

1 Past Disaster Experiences and Behavioral Health Outcomes

Richard Salkowe

CONTENTS

1.1 INTRODUCTION

Disasters have been defined as events in which a society "undergoes severe danger and incurs such losses to its members and physical appurtenances that the social structure is disrupted and the fulfillment of all or some of the essential functions of the society is prevented" (Fritz 1961, 655). In this context, it is clearly evident that disasters represent much more than a quantifiable compromise to the economic value of the natural and built environment. The postdisaster fragmentation of a community's social structure is represented by the loss of places of work and worship; by the places of safety, sanctuary, and solace; and ultimately by the places of contentment and emotional well-being that are the markers of a healthy society.

In 1954, the National Opinion Research Center (NORC) at the University of Chicago produced a seminal report regarding the behavior of individuals in disasters entitled "Human Reactions in Disaster Situations" (Marks and Fritz 1954; Quarantelli 1988). This study revealed that while the majority of disaster survivors suffer from negative psychological effects, there is a low incidence of "incapacitating or behaviorally dysfunctional consequences" (Quarantelli 1988, 305). The report also indicated that widespread looting is an infrequent finding in most disasters in the United States, postdisaster community volunteerism is common, and social capital is a major factor in determining individual behavior. This research provided some of the earliest insight into postdisaster behavioral outcomes, and most of the NORC findings remain consistent with more recent disaster analyses. There are multiple aspects of individual and community capacity that may affect the recovery from the adversities of disasters. Tierney (2007, 512) informs us that "disasters are occasions that can intensify both social solidarity and social conflict," and prior research has emphasized the importance of cultural competency in disaster response to address the varied needs of a diverse group of survivors (SRA International, Inc. 2008). The risk of adverse behavioral health outcomes after disasters is influenced by the social, cultural, economic, and political dynamic of afflicted populations and the concomitant interplay between these factors and the type, severity, and frequency of the disaster event. The psychosocial consequences of disasters may take an insidious toll on individuals and communities, and the relationship between the social stressors that are inherent to disaster scenarios and varied aspects of physical and behavioral well-being have been well established in several prior studies of postdisaster health outcomes (Madakasira and O'Brien 1987; Norris and Murrell 1988; Lutgendorf et al. 1995; Norris, Phifer, and Kaniasty 2001; Norris, Friedman, and Watson 2002; Norris, Friedman, Watson, et al. 2002; Reacher et al. 2004; Bland et al. 2005; Burton et al. 2009).

This chapter utilizes a purposive sample of historical texts and journals to examine narrative accounts of disaster events ranging from the eruption of Mt. Vesuvius and the destruction of Pompeii in 79 CE to the Buffalo Creek flood of 1972. Many of these events precede the timeframe of formal structured disaster research and, as such, they are not intended to provide a quantitative measure of behavioral well-being after disasters. Instead, the perspectives of the survivors of these unfortunate occurrences are considered with the intent to provide additional foundation for an understanding of the importance of behavioral health intervention with particular attention to the support structures, or lack thereof, that were historically available to assist in the psychosocial recovery from disasters. The use of temporal context serves an integral role in disaster research as it provides a perspective to frame and substantiate the more recent analyses of behavioral health outcomes after disasters. This study attempts to clarify the similarities and differences in our perceptions of disaster scenarios over varied periods of time and, in so doing, provides us with an opportunity to reassess our progress regarding the response to and recovery from disastrous events.

1.2 HISTORICAL APPROACHES TO BEHAVIORAL HEALTH IN DISASTERS

1.2.1 Background: The Eruption of Mt. Vesuvius and the Destruction of Pompeii

Nothing, then, was to be heard but the shrieks of women, the screams of children, and the cries of men; some calling for their children, others for their parents, others for their husbands, and only distinguishing each other by their voices; one lamenting his own fate; another that of his family; some wishing to die, from the very fear of dying.… Among these were some who augmented the real terrors by imaginary ones; and made the frighted multitude falsely believe that Misenum was actually in flames.

Pliny the Younger

These words, retrieved from a letter written to Tacitus, the Roman senator and historian, several years after the eruption of Mt. Vesuvius in 79 CE, represent Pliny the Younger's recollection of the scene during the Pompeii disaster, which resulted in the estimated death of more than 10,000 people. Pliny the Younger, who later achieved acclaim as an author, lawyer, and magistrate in ancient Rome, was 17 years old at the time of the eruption of Pompeii, and he witnessed the devastation and ensuing chaos, first hand, from the town of Misenum on the Bay of Naples. His uncle, Pliny the Elder, the Roman naturalist and philosopher, had succumbed to respiratory complications from the inhalation of volcanic ash fall during an attempt to provide support to the citizens of Pompeii. Similar vivid accounts of disasters have been retold in varied forms throughout history after events ranging from the Antioch earthquake in 526 CE to the Indian Ocean tsunami of 2004. Although there are unique aspects associated with each disaster occurrence, there is some degree of consistency with respect to the range of human emotions and behaviors that are evident during the response and recovery phases of disasters. Pliny the Elder died in a heroic attempt to provide aid to the people of Pompeii. Pliny the Younger maintained an extensive set of letters that provided details of Roman life during the first century CE, and he had sufficiently recovered from the mental duress associated with his exposure to the devastation of Mt. Vesuvius to pursue a career as an attorney in 80 CE, the year after the Pompeii disaster. The citizens who had lost family, friends, and neighbors exhibited an array of stress-related responses, and the role of emotional comfort and community support after the disaster inevitably played a substantial role in the recovery process. This is represented in a correspondence to Pliny the Younger from a friend of his uncle:

> At this point, my uncle's friend from Spain spoke up still more urgently; if your brother, if your uncle is still alive, he will want you both to be saved; if he is dead, he would want you to survive him—why put off your escape? We replied that we would not think of considering our own safety as long as were uncertain of his. (Sigurdsson and Carey 2002, 40)

These sentiments are indicative of the mutual concerns that are shared by survivors of disasters and the potential to ameliorate the adverse effects of disaster events by support mechanisms ranging from individual aid to government intervention. Community support was not limited to individual outreach after the eruption of Vesuvius in 79 CE. The news of the disaster traveled rapidly to Rome, and Emperor Titus Flavius acted rapidly to provide relief to disaster survivors. Titus Flavius had become emperor two months before the eruption of Vesuvius, and upon learning of the disaster, he immediately left Rome for the region of Campania where he organized aid and reconstruction efforts (Sigurdsson and Carey 2002; Suetonius 2007). The emperor used the funds obtained from the value of estates belonging to deceased disaster victims without heirs to assist in the reconstruction efforts, and he supplemented the necessary disaster relief with his own personal accounts. Suetonius (2007, 326), the Roman historian, informs us that "with regard to the public buildings destroyed by fire in the City, he (the Emperor Titus) declared that nobody should be a loser but himself." Survivors from the devastated areas of Pompeii and surrounding communities fled the area and sought refuge in other cities. Titus Flavius provided special privileges to the cities that were willing to accommodate the survivors of the disaster (Sigurdsson and Carey 2002). Titus Flavius returned the following year to evaluate the reconstruction efforts in Campania, and during his travels, there was a devastating fire and a resultant plague in Rome. Once again, the emperor provided relief to the afflicted citizenry and "for the relief of people during the plague, he employed in the way of sacrifice and medicine, all means both human and divine" (Suetonius 2007, 326). These extensive measures of government support were undoubtedly integral to the well-being of the populace that was affected by the event. The actions undertaken by Titus Flavius in response to the Pompeii disaster are consistent, in many aspects, with present-day federal disaster policy and protocols in the United States.

It is worth noting that the Roman Empire in 79 CE had a social structure that was based on several classes of citizenry, with slaves residing at the lowest end of the social ladder. Approximately 40 percent of the population of Pompeii was estimated to be slaves. Many of the slaves were unable to leave the city during the disaster because they did not own horses or carriages; some were found chained to wheat grinders along with mules in the archaeological excavation of the ruins of Pompeii (Dyson 2006). The benefits of government intervention and community support were not as easily accessed by the slave class. Pliny the Younger unintentionally attests to the differential status of slaves in describing the death of his uncle, Pliny the Elder:

> Upon this, an outbreak of flame and smell of sulphur, premonitory of further flames, put some to flight and roused him. With the help of two slave-boys he rose from the ground, and immediately fell back, owing (as I gather) to the dense vapour obstructing his breath and stopping up the access to his gullet, which with him was weak and narrow and frequently subject to wind. When day returned.... his body was found whole and uninjured, in the dress he wore; its appearance was that of one asleep rather than dead. (Lewis 1890, 194)

The unanswered question is: What became of the slave-boys? While it is understandable that Pliny the Younger's recollection of the tragic events of the day were focused on his uncle's suffering and heroic efforts, the reality of the situation reveals the fact that the slave-boys who attended to Pliny the Elder were exposed to the same risk, and their story remains untold. These selective and abridged recounts of disaster scenarios are common in historical writings with respect to the misfortune of the underclass, as will be seen in narratives from disasters in the United States during the late 19th and early 20th centuries. The concept of culturally competent intervention after disasters is antithetical to the plight of those groups that were disenfranchised from the equitable consideration of suffering and, in some cases, blamed for the social unrest that ensued after the crisis.

Nearly two millennia removed from the Pompeii disaster, we are able to see the similarities between this historically tragic event and present-day disaster interventions that are designed to improve psychosocial well-being. The past can serve as a prologue to the future with respect to behavioral health outcomes after disasters. The letters of Pliny the Younger and the findings of the excavation of Pompeii reveal a story of emotional comfort, community support, and government intervention, albeit selective, to assist in postdisaster recovery. The following analysis of historical events provides additional insight into the perceptions and behaviors of individual actors, the role of government and community support, and the necessity for cultural competence in disaster response and recovery.

1.2.2 RISK PERCEPTION AND BEHAVIOR IN DISASTERS: A HISTORICAL PERSPECTIVE

1.2.2.1 Risk Perception

Disasters are inherently full of uncertainty, and the processes of decision making under the dynamics of uncertainty demand a broad consideration of various factors that influence human behavior. Those of us who are not directly exposed to the disaster scene often wonder why the victims and survivors of these events did not pursue more purposeful actions to protect themselves and their families. The behaviors that are prevalent in disaster environments are often associated with limits on human cognition that constrain the capacity to consider all relevant choice options in a given scenario. This concept of limitations in rational thought with respect to decision making (Simon 1957) during disasters may be associated with stress-related physiological compromise and/or the constraints that exist with respect to insufficient time, knowledge, and resources to make optimal decisions (Gigerenzer 1997). Evacuating from a disaster scenario may not be practical if there are limitations in available transportation or if the perception of risk to family and personal possessions compromises the willingness to leave the area. Additionally, the role of disaster-related emotional arousal has been acknowledged as a source of bounded rationality (Kaufman 1999).

Historical accounts of disasters provide valuable information regarding the vulnerabilities of populations that settle in hazard-prone areas. The tendency for human habitation in areas that are associated with a high risk of hazard exposure and subsequent disaster is often a result of the land use and transportation amenities that exist in these same places. Regions that are prone to flooding and volcanic eruption are also associated with fertile plains and hillsides that yield bountiful food crops. Places that are prone to hurricanes, typhoons, and tsunamis are also places of commerce, trade, and transportation where population density became centralized during historical periods of settlement. The benefits of the land and waterways far exceeded the risk of infrequent disaster, and we have constructed a world of high-risk cities, seemingly unaware of the inevitable outcome.

Smith (1992) describes three forms of risk perception that people exhibit in order to cope with the potential danger associated with natural hazards: determinate perception, dissonant perception, and probabilistic perception. Determinate perception involves the assumption of predetermined regularity or repetition of disaster events and is often utilized by individuals who assume that structural mitigation and technological advancements have removed the hazard risk. Dissonant perception encompasses the denial of risk and danger associated with hazardous events. Probabilistic perception acknowledges the random nature of natural disasters but may be associated with a loss of the sense of responsibility to prepare for disasters as they are attributable to the forces of nature. Risk perception in the late 19th and early 20th centuries was affected, in part, by limited prior experience with the hazards that existed in particular geographic locales and the nascency of valid geophysical and meteorological warning systems. Recent settlement and high rates of immigration often resulted in lack of familiarity with potential local hazards. This is a problem that persists in regions of the world where migration has exposed socially marginalized people to high risk from natural hazards. Violent conflict and the demise of rural agrarian lifestyles led to an influx of immigrants to the coastline of Thailand prior to the 2004 tsunami. The individual lack of familiarity with the type of natural hazard risk in this area played a significant role in the ultimate death toll (Wisner and Walker 2006).

The attachment to places ranging from the Mississippi flood plain to Port-au-Prince, Haiti, is often created out of necessity, and the acceptance or denial of risk becomes a valid coping mechanism. The industrial mill towns of Pennsylvania and West Virginia, during the mid-20th century, were representative of areas where known hazards were considered to be an acceptable risk in return for the benefit of stable employment. In 1948, a temperature inversion trapped poisonous fumes from the local zinc smelter over Donora, Pennsylvania, resulting in 25 deaths and illness in an estimated 43 percent of the 13,600 residents (Townsend 1950). Quarantelli (1988) notes that personnel from the Army Chemical Center who were evaluating the community after the event noticed that some citizens who were not exposed to the poisonous fumes exhibited physical symptoms similar to those individuals who suffered direct exposure. This was considered to be an early indicator of psychosocial factors affecting behavioral health after a disaster. Although there was limited crisis intervention capacity at this point in the response to disasters, the Donora event did lead to the passage of the federal Air Pollution Control Act in 1955.

While some risk-related decision-making processes are based on the necessities of livelihood, other choices are made out of dissonant disregard for potential danger due to the perceived advantage of the particular amenities of land and sea (Salkowe, Tobin, and Bird 2006). Garesche (1902, 97) describes the prevailing attitude in Martinique prior to the eruption of Mt. Pelée in 1902:

That a disaster such as this would at some time occur in this volcanic region had frequently been predicted. The group of islands to which Martinique belongs is wholly of volcanic origin, and there has never been lacking proof of the thinness of the earth's crust or evidence that nature's great fires had not been wholly extinguished. Geologists who had made a careful study of the region had time and again declared that Mt. Pelee was liable to burst forth in eruption at any time.... Men had no fear of it. They even dared to toy with it and on its sides, nearly half-way to its dangerous mouth, built a pleasure resort, and there many of the wealthy people had erected handsome homes, where they resided nearly all the year.

In reference to the 1906 San Francisco earthquake, Banks and Read (1906, 186) state:

The fate that befell San Francisco had long been expected by scientists. The city's location was more dangerous than that of any other large city in the United States and often had its destruction by earthquake been predicted. But the warnings of geologists and of nature were alike unheeded by the devoted city. Its people went on erecting palatial buildings and beautiful residences, growing happier, more prosperous and more gay year by year, ever trusting that their glorious city would be spared serious damage in the future as it had been in the past.

Willis Fletcher Johnson (1889, 34–35) quotes an inhabitant of Johnstown after the flood of 1889:

We were afraid of that lake seven years ago....People wondered, and asked why the dam was not strengthened, as it certainly had become weak; but nothing was done, and by and by they talked less and less about it, as nothing happened, though now and then some would shake their heads as if conscious the fearful day would come some time when their worst fears would be transcended by the horror of the actual occurrence.

Lake Pontchartrain's levees evoked similar concern from citizens, hazard experts, and government officials for years prior to their failure during Hurricane Katrina in 2005. Many of the inhabitants of Saint-Pierre, Martinique; San Francisco; and Johnstown were obviously aware of the dangers associated with their chosen location and ignored the known risk based on the infrequency of its occurrence and the preferential aspects of living in these areas.

Supernatural and deistic powers were often associated with disaster causality in the historical literature (Salkowe, Tobin, and Bird 2006). The Lisbon earthquake of 1755 has been referred to as the first modern disaster due to the extensive emergency management measures that were put into place by the government in response to this event. This earthquake was also unique in European disaster history because it was the one of the earliest recorded events where "natural" rather than "supernatural" causality was offered as an explanation for the disaster (Dynes 1997; Alexander 2002). After the Mt. Pelée eruption on Martinique, the Reverend G. Scholl of Chicago stated:

> The scientists of Martinique, on the day before the horrible catastrophe, according to official and press reports, met and declared that all was well and safe at St. Pierre. The next day the hand of God was upon the place and their lips are now silenced as to their explanation. We firmly believe the trembling of the earth, the volcanic eruptions and misfortunes which are still growing, are sure signs of the coming end and are just what the Bible sets forth with reference to the approaching end of the world and the second coming of Christ. The Galveston disaster was likewise considered by us as a punishment meted out by God and as a warning. (Garesche 1902, 222)

Marshall (1913, 13), in addressing the Dayton flood of 1913, states:

> There is no sure definition of the course of the earthquake, the path of the wind, the time and place of the storm-cloud. Science has its limitations. Only the Infinite is the master of these forces. In the legal parlance of the practice of torts such occurrences as these are known as "acts of God." Theologians who attempt to solve the mysteries of Providence have found in such occasions the evidence of Divine wrath and warning to the smitten people.

The attribution of natural disasters to a higher authority remains present in today's society, and the recent 2010 earthquake in Haiti has been associated with a "pact with the devil" (ABC News 2010). Drinker (1918, introduction), in review of the 1913 Dayton flood, makes a salient point that transcends the timeframe from the secular interpretations of the Lisbon earthquake of 1755 to the present day:

> In the presence of such a fearful disaster there are few persons who will say, but there are some who will think, that this is in some manner a visitation decreed upon the communities which suffer. The very magnitude and superhuman force of it will suggest to many minds the thought of an ordered punishment and warning for offenses against a higher power. Such a concept, happily more rarely held now than in earlier times, is, of course, revolting to sober judgment and to the instincts of religious reverence. For it would imply that multitudes of the innocent should suffer indescribable cruelty; it would attempt the impossible feat of justifying the smiting of Dayton, where all the inhabitants lived lives of peaceful, helpful industry, and the sparing of communities where men serve the gods of dishonest wealth and vicious idleness. This was no vengeance decreed for human shortcomings. It was superhuman, but not supernatural. It was but a manifestation of the unchangeable, irresistible forces of nature, governed by physical laws which are inexorable.

1.2.2.2 Individual Behavior

Individual behaviors after disasters range from selfless acts of heroism to dysfunctional panic. Prior research has noted differences in postdisaster measures of stress, well-being, and resiliency based on factors including age, race, marital status, and prior disaster experience (Kilijanek and Drabek

1979; Norris and Murrell 1988; Ferraro 2003). The work of the National Opinion Research Center (Marks and Fritz 1954) and subsequent studies have revealed that the great majority of disaster-affected individuals exhibit highly adaptive behavioral characteristics and are able to recover from the event without incapacitating consequences. Historical accounts of prior disasters address these findings:

> For two days after the great catastrophe the people of the city of Galveston were stunned. They seemed to be dazed. It is a remarkable thing that there were no signs of outward grief in the way of tears and groans to mark the misery that raged in the breasts of the people. Only when some person who was thought to have been dead appeared to a relative living, who had mourned for him or her, were there any tears. There was a callousness about all this that attracted the attention of those who had just come to the unfortunate place. There was a stoicism in it, but it was unexplainable. It indicated no lack of appreciation of what had occurred. It demonstrated no lack of affection for those who had gone. Nature, generous in this instance, came to their relief in a way and made them dull to the seriousness of what had occurred to an extent which prevented them from becoming maniacs, for if the grief which comes to a mortal when he loses a dead one had come to his whole community the island would have been filled with raving maniacs. In case of individual losses there is always someone near to give consolation. Had the grief come to the whole island there could have been no consolation, for every soul on it had lost in some way that which was dear to it. (Green 1900, 102–103)

Similar descriptions of the emotions of disaster-stricken individuals were described in recounts of the aftermath of the 1972 Buffalo Creek dam collapse and flood disaster in West Virginia. Two years after the dam's collapse, persistent traumatic stress reactions affected 80 percent of the population (Titchener and Kapp 1976). Erikson (1976, 157) provides a telling recollection of the emotions of a disaster survivor:

> I think we will have to leave Buffalo Creek before we can get any peace. I have been a resident of this place for forty-five years and now I am unhappy, dissatisfied, and disturbed. The disaster has left me very nervous. When something like that happens and all the friends you had down the years—some are living and some are dead and some you don't know where they're at—you don't forget something like that. As we stood in the rain and snow and saw what we saw coming down the hollow—houses washing down Buffalo Creek, people crying and getting out of the creek naked and almost frozen to death, people begging for help which we could not give, I had about twenty or more of my kin killed in the disaster, and if these things won't crack a person up they sure are strong people.

The findings of posttraumatic stress in the Buffalo Creek flood survivors highlight the need for crisis intervention and behavioral first aid after disaster events. Emotion-focused and problem-focused coping mechanisms (Brown, Shiang, and Bongar 2003, 435–437) were exhibited in reports of personal reconciliation with the consequences of the Johnstown flood and in the heroic acts of individuals after the San Francisco earthquake:

> Just below Johnstown, on the Conemaugh, three women were working on the ruins of what had been their home. An old arm-chair was taken from the ruins by the men. When one of the women saw the chair, it brought back a wealth of memory, probably the first since the flood had occurred, and throwing herself on her knees on the wreck she gave way to a flood of tears. "Where in the name of God," she sobbed, "did you get that chair? It was mine—no, I don't want it. Keep it and find for me, if you can, my album. In it are the faces of my husband and little girl." (Johnson 1889, 112)

> To stand clear-headed and observant while the world seems on the edge of utter ruin, one must be either a very great or a very depraved soul. Nero fiddled while Rome was burning. It was the crowning act of the world's supreme pessimist. But the San Francisco earthquake discovered men and women actuated by the most sublime motives, who not only looked with cool judgment upon "the wreck of matter and the crash of worlds" but went down into the seething furnace and remained on duty there in order that

the world might know something of what was taking place in that ruined and burning city. (Banks and Read 1906, 115)

1.3   GOVERNMENT AND COMMUNITY SUPPORT: A HISTORICAL PERSPECTIVE

Lofland (1998) describes three realms of social interaction—private, parochial, and public—that are particularly relevant to the consideration of support mechanisms after disasters. The private realm is represented by family and kinship networks; the parochial realm is represented by neighbors and acquaintances; and the public realm is the "world of strangers" (Kusenbach 2006). Each of these spheres defines a portion of our social capital. Historically, the recovery from disasters was primarily dependent on the support of the private and parochial realms. In the United States, there was no well-defined structured intervention from the "world of strangers" until the formation of the American Red Cross in 1881. Federal disaster relief was not mandated until 1950 in the United States, and government assistance was distributed on a case-by-case basis without any assurance of support on a national level. However, prior accounts of governmental and nongovernmental intervention after disasters substantiate the importance of the public realm in postdisaster behavioral health and community well-being.

Several nongovernmental organizations were involved in disaster response during the late 19th through early 20th centuries. Communities damaged by the Florida hurricane of 1926 benefited from the efforts of the American Red Cross, the Masonic Service Association, citizens' committees, and various clubs and fraternities (Sturges 1931). Medical care was surprisingly efficient as numerous references to sanitation protocols and disease-spread warnings are referenced in the literature, including recommendations for boiling water, malaria prevention, and receiving typhoid immunizations (Marshall 1913; Johnson 1927; Russell 1913; Simpich 1927). A rapid return to some semblance of normal routine was encouraged. During the New England floods of 1927, the public sector intervened to make certain that mail was delivered by rowboat and horse when washed-out roads prevented delivery by truck or automobile (Pease 1928).

At the age of 79, Clara Barton, president of the American Red Cross, departed for Galveston in 1900 to assist in the support of disaster survivors. She issued the following appeal:

> The American National Red Cross at Washington, D.C., is appealed to on all sides for help and for the privilege to help in the terrible disaster which has befallen Southern and Central Texas. It remembers the floods of the Ohio and Mississippi, of Johnstown and Port Royal, with their thousands of dead, and months of suffering and needed relief, and turns confidently to the people of the United States, whose sympathy has never failed to help provide the relief that is asked of it now. Nineteen years of experience on nearly as many fields render the obligations of the Red Cross all the greater. The people have long learned its work, and it must again open its accustomed revenues for their charities. It does not beseech them to give, for their sympathies are as deep and their humanity as great as its own, but it pledges to them faithful old-time Red Cross relief work among the stricken victims of these terrible fields of suffering and death. (Green 1900, 136)

Although no formal federal disaster relief policy existed during the late 19th through early 20th centuries, the United States government and nongovernmental organizations were responsive to major disasters. More than $1.5 million ($38 million, 2009 inflation adjusted; Lerner 1975; U.S. Census Bureau 2009) in relief aid was provided by cities and states throughout the United States after the Galveston hurricane in 1900. Twenty-five million dollars ($589 million, 2009 inflation adjusted; Lerner 1975; U.S. Census Bureau 2009) was raised by relief agencies within seven days of the 1906 San Francisco earthquake (Tyler 1906), and temporary shelter was provided for 300,000 homeless people (Banks and Read 2006). The United States Congress authorized $200,000 ($4.9 million, 2009 inflation adjusted; Lerner 1975; U.S. Census Bureau 2009) for the relief of the citizens of Martinique within four days of the Mt. Pelée eruption in 1902 and adopted the following resolution:

To enable the President of the United States to procure and distribute among the suffering people of the islands of the French West Indies such provisions, clothing, medicines, and other necessary articles and to take such other steps as he shall deem advisable for the purpose of rescuing and succoring the people who are in peril and threatened with starvation. (Garesche 1902, 119)

Federal government intervention after the San Francisco earthquake has been critiqued due to the inordinate authority that was granted to the military. However, the presence of federal troops provided the mayor with the power to order the disbandment of self-constituted citizen vigilante committees. Mayor Eugene Schmitz of San Francisco stated, "Causes of friction thus being removed and tangles straightened out, the mighty task of bringing order out of chaos went forward smoothly and rapidly" (Banks and Read 1906, 88).

1.4 CULTURAL COMPETENCE: A HISTORICAL PERSPECTIVE

The differential implementation of governmental policy regarding the distribution of relief aid to groups based on race, ethnicity, disability, and socioeconomic status was pervasive during the late 19th through early 20th centuries in the United States. The concept of the importance of cultural competence in disaster behavioral health has a foundation that is built upon the observations of centuries of inequitable outcomes and compromise to the well-being of marginalized populations. Banks and Read (1906, 84) inform us of the following:

The care of the Chinese colony received special attention. President Roosevelt asked that the Chinese be given relief, as well as other nationalities, and a separate camp was established for the Orientals, where their peculiar needs were given attention, under the direction of their leading representatives.

At the time of the disaster event, this action was interpreted as culturally enlightened intervention. Decades later, research has revealed that the treatment of the Chinese after the San Francisco earthquake was associated with a derisive policy of culturally insensitive segregation that undermined the representation of an egalitarian approach to governmental support after disasters (Bancroft Library 2006). The Chinese evacuees settled at a compound near the Presidio, but local residents complained that "they did not want to live downwind of the odors of the encampment," and the Chinese were forced to move at least four additional times by city and military officials (Bancroft Library 2006). Approximately 45,000 Chinese lived in the Chinese quarter in 1906 (Banks and Read 1906, 157). After the evacuation of Chinatown, there were reports of National Guard troops looting the area (National Park Service 2007), and city officials recommended against resettling the local population in the Chinatown area due to the presumed commercial development value of the real estate. Tyler (1906, 311–312) indicated that during the 1906 San Francisco earthquake and subsequent fire, "Chinamen of the lower class … sat behind barred windows and guarded their poultry and smoked fish until they themselves were smoked to death." Morris (1906, ch 5), in referencing the same disaster, notes the slums of Chinatown, the ruin of the Italian tenements, and the flight and panic that ensued during the earthquake and subsequent fires:

Here on one side dwelt 10,000 Chinese, and on the other thousands of Italians, Spaniards and Mexicans, while close at hand lived the riff-raff of the "Barbary Coast." Seemingly the whole of these rushed for that one square of open ground, the two streams meeting at the centre of the square and heaping up on its edges. There they squabbled and fought.

These conceptualizations of "foreigners" as more prone to violence and less capable of rational action provided false justification for aggressive action and supported further misrepresentations of blame with respect to looting and social unrest. Criminal acts were disproportionately attributed to "foreigners" and "negroes" in review of the historical disaster literature (Salkowe, Tobin, and Bird 2006). There was evidence of looting, but it was sparse, and the media coverage aggrandized the events based on race and ethnicity. Green (1900, 164–165), reporting on the 1900 Galveston hurricane, quotes from the *Galveston News*:

> One soldier at guard reported that he had been forced to shoot five negroes. They were in the act of taking jewelry from a dead woman's body. The soldier ordered them to desist and placed them under arrest. One of the number whipped out a revolver and the soldier shot him. The others made for the soldier and he laid them out with four shots.

Halstead (1900, 176–177) quotes observers of criminal activity during the aftermath of the Galveston hurricane of 1900: "I saw a negro woman carrying a large basket of silver that was not hers.... Upon all hands this horrible work is going on. The offenders are usually negroes. As soon as the storm subsided the negroes stole all the liquor they could get, and, beastly drunk, proceeded with their campaign of vandalism." Marshall (1913, 90) reveals that after the 1913 Dayton flood, "Nine colored men and one white man were added to the seven suspected looters shot and killed since martial law was proclaimed." Garesche (1902, 414) reports on the Galveston hurricane of 1900, "Tuesday night ninety negro looters were shot in their tracks by citizen guards. One of them was searched and $700 found, together with four diamond rings and two water soaked gold watches. The finger of a white woman with a gold band around it was clutched in his hands." Johnson (1889, 239), in review of the Johnstown flood of 1889, quotes a correspondent who said, "Last night a party of thirteen Hungarians were noticed stealthily picking their way along the banks of the Conemaugh toward Sang Hollow. Suspicious of their purpose, several farmers armed themselves and started in pursuit. Soon their most horrible fears were realized. The Hungarians were out for plunder."

The vulnerability of the poor, the ethnically disenfranchised and racial minorities was evident in late 19th through early 20th century disaster reports. Everett (1913, 85) informs the reader that "Governor Cox stated, 'The crowded north side of the river, where there may be thousands of foreigners dead and dying, lay far beyond reach. No one speaks of it, the immediate needs of the known survivors calling for every attention.'" Regarding the Mississippi flood of 1927, Sturges (1931, 180) states:

> Thousands of refugees, white and colored together, crowded the levee tops.... At first there were no shelters and but little food; the levee tops were concentration camps of misery and disease.... Relief was hampered, in spite of money and willingness, by lack of sufficient motor boats, difficulties of navigation, and the constantly spreading flood waters which turned the safe ground of today into the flooded area of tomorrow.

However, Barry (1998, 320) writes that a letter from a black Republican activist at the time of the flood stated:

> It is said that many relief boats have hauled whites only, have gone to imperilled [sic] districts and taken all whites out and left the Negroes; it is also said that planters in some instances hold their labor at the point of a gun for fear they would get away and not return. In other instances, it is said that mules have been given preference on boats to Negroes.

Du Bois (1928, 5) indicates that "in the white camps transportation on the river boats was issued to individual refugees at their request." Evidently, blacks were only allowed to leave the camps when the owners of the land on which they sharecropped requested their return. Although Mississippi state law canceled all tenant indebtedness for sharecroppers during time of flood disaster, the black sharecroppers were effectively bound to the plantation by the inability to obtain equitable access to evacuation from the flood-ravaged area. (Du Bois 1928).

Simpich (1927, 265) writes, "On the levees, fighting now to save their homes and their lives, white men and negroes work side by side." However, Du Bois (1928, 7) states, "The work on the Vicksburg levee was entirely the enforced labor of Negro refugees, superintended by armed guardsmen. This was done by order of General Green, the labor to be brought from the colored refugee camps." Similar historical representations of racial harmony in the response to disaster events are countered by accounts of forced labor and selective punishment. Green (1900, 177) reports the following:

> Galveston shall be rebuilt. Galveston shall be the greatest of towns. Hurrah for Galveston! Thus they talked and went about the work of throwing up breastworks against disease by cleaning the town. Thousands of people, negroes as well as whites, went about the work of burning the dead and cleaning away the debris. They asked nothing about wages, even those who had no property. They had begun the fight. It was evident that they intended to keep it up.

In contrast, Everett (1913, 302) describes the following scene in Cairo, Illinois, after the 1913 flood:

> A strange parade was held Tuesday when 100 militiamen marched through the thoroughfares in charge of nearly 600 colored men, whom they had dragged from their homes to act as laborers. The negroes had not responded to the call for help and had to be "gone for." Although their wives, in some instances, falsified blithely and earnestly from the front door steps, the searches usually were rewarded by discovering the recalcitrants in bed—if not in fact under the bed—endeavoring to avoid service at the levee.

After the 1928 Florida hurricane, it was reported that "Negroes ordered to load bodies at Pahokee and other Everglade towns were forced to do so at the point of a gun. One negro in town was shot for disobeying. They were better then" (Kleinberg 2003, 187). The mass burial of deceased black hurricane victims in the pauper's cemetery at West Palm Beach stood out as a marker of racial injustice after this hurricane disaster. These opposing representations of equity in the treatment of marginalized individuals after disasters are indicative of the overt cultural insensitivity that existed during this period in history.

The problems associated with the institutionalization of the mentally ill were exacerbated by disaster events, and cultural insensitivity to the plight of the disabled was exemplified in Morris's recount (1906):

> Outside this town ... was Agnew's State Hospital for the Insane, which was reduced to an utter ruin, a large number of the inmates being killed or injured, while those unhurt escaped and roamed about the country, to the terror of the people.... The main building of the hospital collapsed, pinioning many of the insane under the debris. The padded cells had to be broken open and the more dangerous patients tied to trees out on the lawn, in lieu of a safer place.

Clara Barton, founder of the Red Cross, was a strong advocate of culturally competent disaster support and behavioral intervention. Turner (2000, 2) indicates that "in her dealings with city officials, she carefully crafted a socially progressive role for middle-class white women, attempted to set a more positive example for race relations, and, after her vast experience with disaster survivors, introduced concepts of permanent individual housing for the homeless." Given the option of providing supplementary goods or money to the African American citizens of Galveston, Barton elected to distribute money directly to the African American Red Cross so that this organization could appropriately determine the needs of its own community and utilize the funds accordingly. Most of the money was saved to build a "Home for Indigent Colored People" and for Bibles and books for schoolchildren. Barton's role in providing relief to the Sea Island, South Carolina, African American community after the 1893 hurricane was instrumental at a time when the federal government showed little interest in the community. Barton was warned by "locals and by other philanthropists that the Red Cross relief efforts would create a class of dependents because everyone knew that blacks would not work where there were rations given out" (Turner 2000, 10). The African American community on Sea Island rebuilt their homes and replanted their fields, recovering sufficiently by 1900 to provide a donation to the Red Cross for the relief effort in Galveston (Pryor 1988).

1.5 CONCLUSION

Historical accounts of disasters from the destruction of Pompeii in 79 CE to the Buffalo Creek flood of 1972 reveal consistencies and variations in postevent behavioral health outcomes based on factors ranging from the severity of the event to individual response capacities and community support. The need for crisis intervention and behavioral first aid has been highlighted in this review by considering the narratives of individuals who experienced these historical events and who suffered the personal consequences of a disaster. The importance of culturally competent disaster support is evident in the retrospective consideration of outcomes that are associated with inequities in access to community resources and behavioral health intervention. Historical perspectives provide an opportunity to reflect upon our progress and to move forward with an agenda that seeks to improve behavioral health outcomes after disasters.

REFERENCES

ABC News. 2010. *Pat Robertson blames earthquake on pact Haitians made with Satan.* http://blogs.abcnews.com/politicalpunch/2010/01/pat-robertson-blames-earthquake-on-pact-haitians-made-with-satan.html.

Alexander, D. 2002. Nature's impartiality, man's inhumanity: Reflections on terrorism and world crisis in a context of historical disaster. *Disasters* 26(1): 1–9.

Bancroft Library. 2006. *The 1906 San Francisco earthquake and fire.* The Regents of the University of California. http://bancroft.berkeley.edu/collections/earthquakeandfire/exhibit/room04_item04.html.

Banks, C., and O. Read. 1906. *The Complete History of the San Francisco Disaster and Mount Vesuvius Horror-Death and Ruin by Eruption, Earthquake and Fire.* Chicago, IL: C. E. Thomas.

Barry, J. M. 1998. *Rising Tide: The Great Mississippi Flood of 1927 and How It Changed America.* New York: Touchstone.

Bland, S. L., L. Valoroso, S. Stranges, P. Strazzullo, E. Farinaro, and M. Trevisan. 2005. Long-term follow-up of psychological distress following earthquake experiences among working Italian males: A cross-sectional analysis. *Journal of Nervous and Mental Disease 193*: 420–423.

Brown, L. M., J. Shiang, and B. Bongar. 2003. Crisis intervention. In *Handbook of Psychology: Volume 8: Clinical Psychology*, eds. G. Stricker and T. A. Widiger, 435–437. Hoboken, NJ: John Wiley and Sons, Inc.

Burton, L. C., E. A. Skinner, L. Uscher-Pines, R. Lieberman, B. Leff, R. Clark, Q. Yu, K. W. Lemke, and J. P. Weiner. 2009. Health of Medicare plan enrollees at 1 year after hurricane Katrina. *American Journal of Managed Care 15*(1): 13–22.

Drinker, F. E. 1918. *Horrors of Tornado, Flood and Fire.* Harrisburg, PA: The Minter Company.

Du Bois, W. E. B., ed. 1928. The Flood, the Red Cross and the National Guard. *The Crisis: A Record of the Darker Races.* New York: National Association for the Advancement of Colored People.

Dynes, R. 1997. *The Lisbon earthquake in 1755: Contested meanings in the first modern disaster.* Preliminary Paper #255. University of Delaware, Disaster Research Center.

Dyson, M. E. 2006. *Come Hell or High Water: Hurricane Katrina and the Color of Disaster.* New York: Basic Civitas Books.

Erikson, K. 1976. *Everything in Its Path: Destruction of Community in the Buffalo Creek Flood.* New York: Simon and Schuster.

Everett, M. 1913. *Tragic Story of America's Greatest Disaster—Tornado, Flood and Fire in Ohio, Indiana, Nebraska and Mississippi Valley.* Chicago: J. S. Ziegler Company.

Ferraro, R. F. 2003. Psychological resilience in older adults following the 1997 flood. *Clinical Gerontologist* 26(3): 139–143.

Fritz, C. 1961. Disasters. In *Contemporary Social Problems*, eds. R. K. Merton and R. A, 651–694. Nisbet. New York: Harcourt Brace.

Garesche, W. A. 1902. *Complete Story of the Martinique and St. Vincent Horrors.* L. G. Stahl.

Gigerenzer, G. 1997. Bounded rationality: Models of fast and frugal inference. *Swiss Journal of Economics and Statistics 133*(2): 201–218.

Green, N. C. 1900. *The Story of the Galveston Hurricane.* Baltimore: R. H. Woodward Co.

Halstead, M. 1900. *Galveston: The Horrors of a Stricken City.* Chicago: American Publishers Association.

Johnson, L. B. 1927. *Floodtide of 1927.* Randolph, VT: Roy L. Johnson Company.

Johnson, W. F. 1889. *History of the Johnstown Flood.* Edgewood Publishing Co.

Kaufman, B. E. 1999. Emotional arousal as a source of bounded rationality. *Journal of Economic Behavior & Organization 38*: 135–144.

Kilijanek, T. S., and T. Drabek.1979. Assessing long-term impacts of a natural disaster: A focus on the elderly. *The Gerontologist 19*(6): 555–565.

Kleinberg, E. 2003. *Black Cloud: The Deadly Hurricane of 1928.* New York: Carroll & Graf Publishers.

Kusenbach, M. 2006. Patterns of neighboring: Practicing community in the parochial realm. *Symbolic Interaction 29*(3): 279–306.

Lerner, W. 1975. *Historical statistics of the United States, Colonial times to 1970. Part 1.* Bureau of the Census. http://purl.access.gpo.gov/GPO/LPS55561.

Lewis, J. D., trans. 1890. *The Letters of the Younger Pliny.* London: Kegan Paul, Trench, Kubner & Co., Ltd.

Lofland, L. 1998. *The Public Realm: Exploring the City's Quintessential Social Theory.* Piscataway, NJ: Aldine Transaction.

Lutgendorf, S. K., M. H. Antoni, G. Ironson, M. A. Fletcher, F. Penedo, A. Baum, N. Schneiderman, and N. Klimas. 1995. Physical symptoms of chronic fatigue syndrome are exacerbated by the stress of Hurricane Andrew. *Psychosomatic Medicine 57*: 310–323.

Madakasira, S., and K. F. O'Brien. 1987. Acute posttraumatic stress disorder in victims of a natural disaster. *Journal of Nervous and Mental Disorders 175*: 286–290.

Marks, E. S., and C. E., Fritz. 1954. *Human Reactions in Disaster Situations.* Chicago: University of Chicago, National Opinion Research Center.

Marshall, L. 1913. *The True Story of Our National Calamity of Flood, Fire and Tornado.* L. T. Myers.

Morris, C. 1906. *The San Francisco Calamity by Earthquake and Fire.* Philadelphia: The John C. Winston Co.

National Park Service. 2007. *1906 earthquake: Chinese displacement.* http://www.nps.gov/prsf/historyculture/1906-earthquake-chinese-treatment.htm.

Norris, F. H., F. J. Friedman, and P. J. Watson. 2002. 60,000 disaster victims speak: Part II. Summary and implications of the disaster mental health research. *Psychiatry 65*(3): 240–260.

Norris, F. H., F. J. Friedman, P. J. Watson, C. M. Byrne, E. Diaz, and K. Kaniasty. 2002. 60,000 disaster victims speak: Part I. An empirical review of the empirical literature, 1981–2001. *Psychiatry 65*(3): 207–239.

Norris, F. H., and S. A. Murrell. 1988. Prior experience as a moderator of disaster impact on anxiety symptoms in older adults. *American Journal of Community Psychology 16*(5): 665–683.

Norris, F. H., J. F. Phifer, and K. Kaniasty. 2001. Individual and community reactions to the Kentucky floods: Findings from a longitudinal study of older adults. In *Individual and Community Responses to Trauma and Disaster*, eds. R. J. Ursano, B. G. McCaughey, and C. S. Fullerton. Cambridge: Cambridge University Press.

Pease, S. J. 1928. *Mail Story of the Flood.* Concord: Concord Press.

Pliny, and W. Melmoth. 1809. *The Letters of Pliny the Consul with Occasional Remarks by William Melmoth, Esq.* Boston: E. Larkin, No. 47, Cornhill.

Pryor, E. B. 1988. *Clara Barton: Professional Angel.* Philadelphia: University of Pennsylvania Press.

Quarantelli, E. L. 1988. The NORC research on the Arkansas tornado: A fountainhead study. *International Journal of Mass Emergencies and Disasters 66*(3): 283–310.

Reacher, M., K. McKenzie, C. Lane, T. Nichols, I. Kedge, A. Iversen, P. Hepple, T. Walter, C. Laxton, and J. Simpson. 2004. Health impacts of flooding in Lewes: A comparison of reported gastrointestinal and other illness and mental health in flooded and non-flooded households. *Communicable Disease and Public Health 7*(1): 1–8.

Russell, T. H. 1913. *Story of the Great Flood and Cyclone Disasters.* T. H. Morrison.

Salkowe, R., G. A. Tobin, and S. E. Bird. 2006. Calamity, catastrophe & horror: Representation of natural disaster 1885–2005. *Papers of the Applied Geography Conferences 29*: 196–205.

Sigurdsson, H., and S. Carey. 2002. The eruption of Vesuvius in A.D. 79. In *The Natural History of Pompeii*, eds. W. F. Jashemski and F. G. Meyer, 37–64. Cambridge: Cambridge University Press.

Simon, H. 1957. A behavioral model of rational choice. In *Models of Man, Social and Rational: Mathematical Essays on Rational Human Behavior in a Social Setting*, ed. H. Simon, 241–260. New York: John Wiley and Sons, Inc.

Simpich, F. 1927. The great Mississippi flood of 1927. *National Geographic Magazine 52*(3): 243–289.

Smith, K. 1992. *Environmental Hazards: Assessing Risk and Reducing Disaster.* London: Routledge.

SRA International, Inc. (2008). *Cultural competency in disaster response: A review of current concepts, policies, and practices.* Report prepared for the Office of Minority Health. Rockville, MD: SRA International, Inc. https://www.thinkculturalhealth.org/ccdpcr/documents/EnvironmentalScan.pdf.

Sturges, G. R. 1931. *United Masonic Relief.* Washington, DC: The Masonic Service Association of the United States.

Suetonius. 2007. *The twelve Caesars*, trans. A. Thomson. Digireads.com.

Tierney, K. J. 2007. From the margins to the mainstream? Disaster research at the crossroads. *Annual Review of Sociology 33*: 503–525.

Titchener, J. L., and F. T. Kapp. 1976. Disaster at Buffalo Creek. Family and character change at Buffalo Creek. *American Journal of Psychiatry 133*: 295–299.

Townsend, A. 1950. Investigation of the smog incident in Donora, PA and vicinity. *American Journal of Public Health 40*: 183–189.

Turner, E. H. 2000. *Clara Barton and the formation of public policy in Galveston, 1900*. The Rockefeller Archive Center Publications Conference Proceedings. http://www.rockarch.org/publications/conferences/turner.pdf.

Tyler, S. 1906. *San Francisco's Great Disaster—Earthquake, Fire and Volcano in California and at Vesuvius*. Philadelphia: P. W. Ziegler Co.

U.S. Census Bureau. 2009. *Statistical abstracts of the United States*. http://www.census.gov/compendia/statab.

Wisner, B., and P. Walker. 2006. Getting tsunami recovery and early warning right. *Open House International 31*(1): 54–61.

2 Disaster Behavioral Health Outreach

A Nontraditional Approach to Assisting Survivors

Julie L. Framingham

CONTENTS

A therapist or traditional mental health person sees the mud covered survivor and … is gonna say, "Gee, how does that mud feel?" and the disaster mental health person sees that [same person] and says, "Let's get that mud off of you."

Elrod, Hamblen, and Norris (2006, 160)

2.1 INTRODUCTION

Disasters may vary by type, speed of onset, and extent of damages, but they share the potential to threaten the prosperity of communities and the lives of their residents. Disasters can cause physical, emotional, cognitive, and behavioral consequences such as stress, anxiety, grief, anger, interpersonal problems, insomnia, hopelessness, depression, acute stress and posttraumatic stress disorders, which may fluctuate over time (Ruzek et al. 2004; SAMHSA nd). Displacement, prior trauma experience, and loss of employment, transportation, and social support networks can greatly intensify disaster-related distress (Norris et al. 2002; Acierno et al. 2007). Disasters may also contribute to increased use of tobacco, alcohol, or other substances (Ruzek et al. 2004).

Various internal and external factors may influence the extent to which an individual may develop postdisaster distress, including one's sense of optimism and self-efficacy and social support (Bourque et al. 2006). The goal of disaster behavioral health is to prevent or lessen the adverse psychological effects of disaster by offering interventions or services that will foster adaptation, resiliency, and improved coping to return individuals and communities to predisaster levels of functioning (SAMHSA nd; Bulling and Abdel-Monem 2009; Young et al. 1998). While many individuals may already possess good coping skills to deal with the adverse impacts of disaster, certain survivors may require a helping hand. Disaster behavioral health emphasizes the provision of practical assistance, empowering survivors in the recovery process by creating recovery plans based on self-identified needs, and connecting survivors to available helping resources (SAMHSA nd). Disaster behavioral health differs from traditional behavioral health in several key respects that we will discuss in the following sections.

2.2 TRADITIONAL BEHAVIORAL HEALTH PRACTICE VERSUS DISASTER BEHAVIORAL HEALTH PRACTICE

In traditional behavioral health practice, licensed professional psychiatrists, psychologists, social workers and members of other mental health–related disciplines assign diagnoses to individuals for pathological disorders after careful examination or psychological testing (Sundararaman, Lister, and Williams 2006, 13). Similar to the medical model of care, there is a defined clinician-patient (or client) relationship, and treatments for diagnosed conditions generally occur in an office setting on an outpatient basis, with or without prescription medications to help manage the patient's condition (Bulling and Abdel-Monem 2009). Additionally, some patients may be court-ordered into treatment. Personality traits and the extent to which past life experiences have led to current problems are factored into diagnosis and treatment. Treatments may be short- or long-term, individual and/or group sessions, with sessions scheduled in advance, and consist of a variety of evidence-based or evidence-informed interventions to maintain or restore the patients' equilibrium and help them achieve a higher level of individual functioning (Young et al. 1998).

While the disaster behavioral health workforce may consist of licensed behavioral health professionals, paraprofessionals, and volunteers, generally even licensed professionals do not provide treatment to survivors immediately after a disaster (Young et al. 1998; Ruzek et al. 2004; Bulling and Abdel-Monem 2009; Haskett et al. 2008). Given the brevity of assignments, frequently changing work locations, inadequate information about survivors' past trauma experiences, and numbers

TABLE 2.1

Differences between Traditional Behavioral Health and Disaster Behavioral Health

Traditional Behavioral Health	Disaster Behavioral Health
• Office-based	• Community-based
• Safe, secure environment	• Proximity to stressors
• Long-term treatment	• Short-term interventions
• Focus on diagnosis and treatment of a mental illness	• Focus on assessment of strengths and coping skills
• Affect the baseline of personality and functioning	• Restore people to predisaster levels of functioning
• Encourage insight into past life experiences and their influence on current problems	• Validate the appropriateness of reactions to the event and its aftermath and normalize the experience
• Psychotherapeutic focus	• Psychoeducational focus
• Focus on present and past	• Focus on present and future
• Conducted by behavioral health professionals	• Conducted by paraprofessionals and behavioral health professionals

Source: Based on and adapted from *Cultural Competency in Disaster Response: A Review of Current Concepts, Policies, and Practices*, SRA International, Inc., Rockville, MD, https://www.thinkculturalhealth.hhs.gov/ccdpcr/documents/EnvironmentalScan.pdf, 2008.

of survivors needing help, therapeutic treatment is usually not feasible in the immediate postdisaster context (Haskett et al. 2008).

Licensed mental health professionals comply with state laws regarding practice ethics, including regulations concerning patient confidentiality and consent to treatment. Breach of state professional practice statutes could result in serious consequences, such as loss of licensure and criminal and/ or civil penalties (Sundararaman, Lister, and Williams 2006; Bulling and Abdel-Monem 2009). Records such as psychosocial assessments, treatment plans, and progress notes are maintained to record the services provided and the patients' progress toward achieving identified treatment goals (Young et al. 1998; Sundararaman, Lister, and Williams 2006; SAMHSA nd). Records are also required for billing. In disaster behavioral health, services are typically free of charge and records of individual survivors are not maintained. Collecting personally identifying information on numerous survivors who may not be seen more than once or twice would be problematic and, in some organized programs, not permitted (SAMHSA nd).

Table 2.1 identifies and describes some of the primary differences between traditional behavioral health and disaster behavioral health.

2.3   DISASTER BEHAVIORAL HEALTH OUTREACH

Active outreach to impacted communities is perhaps the most significant function and unique aspect of disaster behavioral health services. Unlike traditional behavioral health practice, outreach occurs in diverse community settings to help individuals who might otherwise be neglected or who are unable to access recovery services on their own. Disaster behavioral health outreach workers assess survivors' psychological and social functioning and promote use of human and disaster relief services. Outreach workers help survivors through harm reduction by screening survivors for distress symptoms, and partner with numerous community agencies to provide referrals and resources to meet survivors' basic human, as well as emotional, behavioral or psychological needs (Bulling and Abdel-Monem 2009; Rosen, Matthieu, and Norris 2009). Outreach is typically short-term. Various outreach methods are used to help survivors cope with their postdisaster circumstances, while ameliorating current distress in order to restore them to predisaster levels of functioning.

2.3.1 Outreach and Cultural Competence

To be effective, disaster behavioral health services need to reflect the culture, beliefs, and practices of the community's various populations because they influence help seeking and accepting disaster behavioral health services (Goodman and West-Olatunji 2009). Personal barriers to accepting health-related services include past trauma experience and history of oppression (Goodman and West-Olatunji 2009). Disaster behavioral health services that are culturally sensitive have a greater chance of getting survivors to accept assistance. Therefore, services should be attuned to the culture and language of survivors, and disaster behavioral health workers should appropriately mirror the demographic makeup of the impacted communities (SRA International 2008). Furthermore, disaster behavioral health workers need to appreciate the cultural, social, and historical background of the survivors' problems to comprehend their needs, correctly evaluate their current situations, and develop effective interventions (Goodman and West-Olatunji 2009). Such outreach to diverse populations can increase cultural competence and decrease cultural bias (Goodman and West-Olatunji 2009, 87).

2.3.2 Outreach to At-Risk Populations

Strategic and effective outreach has improved outcomes for diverse social and health-related problems (Blodgett et al. 2008). The outreach process includes finding survivors who need assistance, evaluating needs, connecting them to necessary services, and referring individuals to professional behavioral health treatment as the need arises. Outreach strategies have been effective in assisting many underserved vulnerable groups (Blodgett et al. 2008).

Some disaster survivors may be reluctant to seek out or accept help—never having needed behavioral health services previously—and may be fearful of being labeled mentally ill (Young et al. 1998; Wang et al. 2007). Given this stigma regarding behavioral health and the assumption that many survivors will not seek out services, vigorous, proactive outreach to impacted communities is crucial (Norris and Rosen 2009).

Additionally, certain ethnic groups may see little value in traditional office-based services and thus fail to access them (Weems et al. 2010). Outreach may be more effective in assisting certain vulnerable groups such as ethnic minorities or isolated older adults. Such groups may not be easy to persuade to access office-based services or have the ability to reach providers on their own (Weems et al. 2010, 50; Brown 2007). Care must be taken, however, to tailor outreach strategies to gain access to different cultural groups since what works for one population may be ineffective with others (Elrod, Hamblen, and Norris 2006).

Some individuals are at greater risk for postdisaster distress than others, including children, highly exposed survivors, members of minority populations, and individuals of low socioeconomic status (Norris et al. 2002). Regarding children and adolescents, it is crucial for disaster behavioral health providers and organizations to establish partnerships with school systems, preferably predisaster, to have greater access to children and their families (Elrod, Hamblen, and Norris 2006).

This is not always easily accomplished, however, since students may prefer assistance from their peers rather than teachers, counselors, or strangers (Tatar and Amram 2007). Moreover, school administrators may deny access to schools in impacted communities for various reasons. For example, they may wish to avoid interrupting students' schedules, they may question disaster workers' qualifications to provide assistance, or they may be fearful that discussion of disaster-related information may intensify students' apprehensions (Elrod, Hamblen, and Norris 2006). Equally, if not more, problematic is how to provide outreach to children when schools are out of session, a season when disasters frequently occur (Elrod, Hamblen, and Norris 2006, 164).

Likewise, difficulties engaging or serving older adults have also been reported. Gaining access to senior communities is not always easy. Once workers are successful in locating older survivors who need assistance, information or education should be geared to their cognitive and physical abilities (Brown et al. 2007).

2.3.3 OUTREACH SETTINGS

Outreach may take place in diverse community settings including shelters, family assistance centers, community centers, homes, workplaces, and churches (SAMHSA nd; Elrod, Hamblen, and Norris 2006). Some of these locations may be noisy and lack privacy, especially in the immediate aftermath of disaster when most outreach services will be conducted at Disaster Recovery Centers,[a] family assistance centers, or other places where large numbers of survivors congregate to obtain recovery information and assistance (Young et al. 1998; SAMHSA nd).

Outreach workers frequently labor in places without air-conditioning, assisting survivors by answering questions and offering refreshments while they wait in long lines in the hot sun; these workers may be needed to help clean facilities and unload supply trucks; and they often assist survivors in completing applications for financial assistance (Haskett et al. 2008). Most survivors need information about how to satisfy basic human needs such as places to obtain temporary housing, food, clothing, or medication refills, or they may require assistance with housing repairs and debris removal. However, disasters frequently exhaust available community resources, so, in some cases, the workers themselves can become frustrated in their attempts to find helping resources. Faith-based organizations have been cited as particularly reliable sources for survivors to obtain the assistance they need after disaster (Haskett et al. 2008; Elrod, Hamblen, and Norris 2006).

2.3.4 OUTREACH STRATEGIES

Disaster behavioral health outreach programs employ a number of strategies to identify and engage survivors who need assistance. Various media outreach frequently includes information to help survivors identify common disaster-related stress reactions, enhances positive coping methods, and provides helping resources when survivors are ready to seek out behavioral health services. Public education seminars or workshops are not only effective in targeting specific groups such as families, first responders, or high school students, but also beneficial for creating opportunities to work with community partners such as public libraries, civic groups, senior centers, and so forth. Informational materials such as flyers, door hangers, and brochures, in languages commonly spoken in the impacted communities, are an effective and relatively low-cost means of providing outreach. Depending on the size of the organization's budget, advertising program services through television and radio commercials is an excellent way to reach large numbers of residents in a community.

Developing engagement strategies is a great way to utilize team talents and creativity to help survivors recognize their need for and encourage them to access services. For example, Project Liberty in New York after 9/11 reported success in engaging survivors in behavioral health services through advertising on dinner placemats in restaurants and bar coasters in local drinking establishments (Naturale 2006). At other times, however, the intended targeted audience might not be engaged successfully by the particular methods used (Kestin 2006a). Additionally, misunderstanding of engagement methodologies has led to some programs being criticized as wasteful expenditures of taxpayer monies. Such was the case in Florida and in certain other states where programs employed certain outreach strategies that invited congressional scrutiny (Kestin 2006a; Kestin 2006b). However, simply lecturing to survivors about mental health problems is not likely going to encourage them to access services. According to one federal disaster behavioral health project officer, Linda Ligenza, with the Substance Abuse and Mental Health Services Administration:

"We know certainly that it's not helpful to stand up in front of a group, for instance, and talk about reactions," Ligenza said. "It's much more advantageous, certainly in working with children, in working with elderly, to use some kind of engagement strategy like puppets or bingo to really engage people in a less threatening, fun, acceptable manner." (Kestin 2006a)

No research has been conducted on the use and success of outreach strategies (Naturale 2006). Consequently, engagement strategies merit careful consideration and field testing. When program managers become cognizant of strategies that are failing to reach their intended audiences or are misunderstood, they should be modified or retired in favor of alternative methods.

2.3.5 Survivor Contacts

Contacts with survivors are typically quite brief, sometimes just a few minutes, and each contact should be considered a stand-alone visit since workers may be reassigned repeatedly (SAMHSA nd; Young et al. 1998). In fact, workers may speak with hundreds of disaster survivors in the immediate postdisaster phase in frequently changing locations and range from a few minutes to an hour to resolve urgent basic human or psychological needs (Young et al. 1998; Haskett et al. 2008). In such circumstances, it is difficult to establish rapport, and the worker must quickly assess whether the individual needs referral to other services (Young et al. 1998).

2.3.6 Canvassing and Service Intimacy[b]

Later in the recovery period, behavioral health workers may attempt to conduct widespread community outreach and door-to-door canvassing to identify survivors and help connect them to needed services, as well as offer to engage them in brief counseling (Norris, Hamblen, and Rosen 2009). Workers partner with many community agencies, such as the United Way, Catholic Charities, homeless coalitions, Councils on Aging, churches, and schools, to provide public education and locate survivors in need of services. Some partners have been willing to help promote behavioral health services through the local media (Brown et al. 2007).

Canvassing and home visitation allow time for workers to conduct more protracted in-home or other private-setting counseling visits. Longer-term disaster behavioral health programs, such as the federally funded Crisis Counseling Assistance and Training Program (CCP; U.S.C. 42 § 5183), typically incorporate extensive community outreach and engagement techniques, including canvassing, as a means to identify survivors who might benefit from brief counseling and need assistance connecting to sources of help for any unmet instrumental or psychological needs (SAMHSA nd).

Although staffing and funding may preclude extensive outreach and canvassing, research conducted by Norris and colleagues suggests that counseling locations that offer some degree of privacy and put the survivor more at ease about sharing information is an important factor in how well services are perceived. Further, longer visits and repeat visits contribute to greater survivor-perceived benefits (Norris, Hamblen, and Rosen 2009).

Workers sometimes canvass very devastated areas and areas known for high poverty, crime, and lack of resources to locate survivors who may be unable to obtain services without assistance (Brown et al. 2007, 25). Since some people may not see the value of outreach services, they may not feel comfortable speaking with behavioral health workers. Some survivors may consider canvassing as intrusive (Brown et al. 2007, 25). Their feelings should be respected if they choose to use alternative means of support (Wessely et al. 2008). Unfortunately, there have been occasions when workers have encountered resistance or even hostility in their canvassing efforts; therefore, workers should be adequately trained and take appropriate safety precautions (Elrod, Hamblen, and Norris 2006).

2.3.7 Disaster Behavioral Health Services Organizations

After disasters, there are many organizations and agencies that may offer behavioral health outreach services, including governmental (e.g., city, county, state, and federal, as well as community behavioral health centers contracted by governmental providers) and nongovernmental providers such as the American Red Cross, the National Organization for Victim Assistance (NOVA), the Salvation Army, the United Methodist Committee on Relief (UMCOR), the International Association of Trauma Counselors, and faith-based groups, among many others.

Without clear state or federal guidelines for designating a lead agency for delivering behavioral health services after a disaster, there may be confusion about which agency is in charge of providing services, which may increase distress among survivors and workers (Gard and Ruzek 2006, 1030). Sometimes the state behavioral health agency may be appointed as the lead agency after disaster, and sometimes a city government may be appointed (Gard and Ruzek 2006, 1030). However, when an aviation accident happens, federal law designates the American Red Cross as the lead agency for all mental health response (Gard and Ruzek 2006; Jacobs and Kulkarni 1999). Therefore, workers should be cognizant of the structure of local organizations and how they interact to bridge gaps in services while avoiding duplication, which calls for synchronized efforts (Gard and Ruzek 2006).

Within organized disaster behavioral health programs, clearly defined roles, administrative procedures, and treatment/services protocols need to be in place prior to program onset to minimize worker confusion and frustration. Without such planning, there is the potential for misinformation, communication breakdowns, or confusion about service parameters (Brown et al. 2007).

2.3.8 CRISIS INTERVENTION

While a variety of strategies are available to assist survivors, ensuring the safety of survivors and mitigating additional harm is of paramount concern for disaster behavioral health workers. Workers must determine the need for crisis intervention when individuals present with extreme stress reactions. Studies support that crisis intervention can assist individuals experiencing distress and lessen potential harm in a variety of crisis contexts and can be effective in both face-to-face and telephone counseling sessions (Bobevski and McLennan 1998; Blodgett et al. 2008; Shelby and Tredinnick 1995). Further, brief crisis intervention can have long-lasting positive effects (Shelby and Tredinnick 1995). The effectiveness of the counseling experience depends in part on the dynamics of the counselor-survivor intercourse; understanding survivor needs, empathy, and good communication between the counselor and the survivor is key (Bobevski and McLennan 1998). Through practical assistance, crisis intervention can help survivors satisfy immediate basic human needs, restore emotional stability and interrupt longer-term psychological sequelae, and help identify individuals in need of ongoing professional behavioral health treatment (Blodgett et al. 2008).

This kind of counseling calls for workers to think quickly on their feet and react appropriately to clients' expressed or unintentional cues. The reasons for this include the fact that the individual's problems are often unclear, complicated, interconnected, and difficult to work out (Bobevski and McLennan 1998, 50). Thus, it is incumbent upon disaster behavioral health workers to deduce survivors' strengths and coping processes as they discuss their trauma-related experiences, which, in turn, can be used to build self-efficacy (Haskett et al. 2008). Such crisis counseling has been described as a "… complex, dynamic decision process" (Bobevski and McLennan 1998, 48). One must also understand that counseling practices that reflect understanding of how culture influences the coping strategies survivors rely upon can increase their effectiveness (Goodman and West-Olatunji 2009).

2.3.9 NONTHERAPEUTIC APPROACHES TO CARE

While "there are no universally accepted standards of care in disaster behavioral health services" (Bulling and Abdel-Monem 2009, 761), many agencies prefer to use crisis counseling or psychological first aid,[e] which, contrary to traditional behavioral health practice, are nonclinical approaches to the care of disaster survivors (Chapter 10, this volume). These methods of care aim to restore the individual's predisaster level of functioning by validating and normalizing the disaster experience; providing psychoeducation to recognize symptoms of unresolved distress and thwart the onset of more serious mental health problems; improving coping and stress management skills; and connecting survivors to recovery resources (Young et al. 1998; Ruzek et al. 2004; Elrod, Hamblen, and Norris 2006; SAMHSA nd; Haskett et al. 2008; Soliman, Lingle, and Raymond 1998). Identifying survivors' strengths and building resilience may be especially helpful interventions to lessen dysfunction, interpersonal conflict, and severe psychological symptoms (Wieling 2008). Thus, successful postdisaster adjustment may depend on the disaster worker's ability to help survivors recognize their inner strengths and understand available recovery options to make wise decisions (Soliman, Lingle, and Raymond 1998).

Designated State Mental Health Authorities (42 U.S.C. § 201) may also offer more prolonged crisis counseling services after presidentially declared disasters through the CCP. Instead of therapy, crisis counseling emphasizes active listening, encouragement, connecting survivors to helping community resources, and linking them to support systems (Elrod, Hamblen, and Norris 2006).

2.3.10 CLINICAL APPROACHES TO CARE IN COMMUNITY-BASED SETTINGS

Over the past decade, Jessica Hamblen and colleagues from the National Center for Posttraumatic Stress Disorder and other research institutions have also developed brief, manualized, cognitive behavioral therapies designed to be an intermediate intervention, between crisis counseling and longer-term clinical treatment, and delivered by licensed behavioral health professionals to ameliorate postdisaster distress. Outreach workers typically identify and refer survivors who might potentially benefit from cognitive behavioral interventions, which can be delivered in office- or community-based settings, including survivors' homes. Unlike crisis counseling programs where anonymity makes assessing intervention effectiveness difficult, individuals participating in these clinical treatments agreed to participate in the research, which made program evaluations possible (Elrod, Hamblen, and Norris 2006; Norris, Hamblen, and Rosen 2009; Drury, Scheeringa, and Zeanah 2008). Findings from these studies have been very promising for lessening postdisaster distress (Hamblen et al. 2009; Hamblen et al. 2006). However, cognitive behavioral therapies may not be appropriate for survivors immediately after a disaster (U.S. Department of Veterans Affairs, National Center for Posttraumatic Stress Disorder 2010).[c]

Another approach to care, critical incident stress debriefing (Mitchell 1983),[d] which can be offered in a variety of community locations, has historically been endorsed by a number of organizations for several years. More recently, however, disaster behavioral health researchers have questioned the efficacy of this intervention specifically with disaster survivors, and some have suggested that psychological first aid might be a more appropriate response to this population (Rose et al. 1999; Mayou, Ehlers, and Hobbs 2000; Rose et al. 2001; Litz et al. 2002; NIMH 2002).

2.3.11 THE IMPORTANCE OF SOCIAL SUPPORT

As stated earlier in this chapter, certain conditions can place individuals at greater risk for developing postdisaster distress than others. In the aftermath of disaster, people normally seek out family, friends, peers, and religious advisors, among others, for instrumental and/or emotional support. Social embeddedness and social support, actual or perceived, are protective factors and exert tremendous influence on the recovery process (Norris et al. 2002; Wessely et al. 2008; Acierno et al. 2007). Disasters, however, can temporarily interrupt social networks. In the case of Hurricane Katrina in 2005, some survivors were separated for weeks or even months without word about the fate of their loved ones and friends. In many instances, survivors did not have any family or friends to whom they could turn (Bourque et al. 2006). Disaster behavioral health workers will need to identify survivors who lack social support and provide them with brief counseling, education, and other supports to reduce distress (Acierno et al. 2007). Additionally, workers should offer survivors referrals to helping community resources until they can be reconnected to their own support systems or, when these are absent or permanently disrupted, to connect them to helping resources.

2.3.12 PSYCHOEDUCATION

Psychoeducation is a crucial component of disaster outreach because it helps survivors understand "…the causes of and contributors to stress and the cognitive, emotional, behavioral and physical effects of stress" (Steinhardt and Dolbier 2008, 446). Sharing information about disasters' potential psychological effects, through public educational seminars or in other media community-wide, may have the potential to promote empathy and compassion with residents who were not directly impacted by the disaster (Marbley 2007). Psychoeducation helps to normalize survivors' reactions to disaster and engages those who may need additional assistance (Naturale 2007; Elrod, Hamblen, and Norris 2006). In particular, symptom information may be helpful in reducing trauma-related avoidance behaviors (Kilpatrick, Cougle, and Resnick 2008).

Rather than simply provide survivors with an inventory of adverse postdisaster symptomatology, which may lead survivors to believe they should expect adverse psychological outcomes, disaster behavioral health programs should ensure that psychoeducation is constructed in ways that foster resiliency (Wessely et al. 2008). Psychoeducation that also includes information about adaptive coping strategies promotes resiliency and may help mitigate the stigma concerning help-seeking (Jacobs, Vernberg, and Lee 2008). In an ideal world, community agencies would provide such education predisaster to build community resiliency.

Studies have linked the use of psychoeducation with various populations posttrauma to a reduction in posttraumatic stress disorder symptoms and other posttrauma reactions (Leitch, Vanslyke, and Allen 2009), including children dealing with school- or war-related trauma (Brown et al. 2006; Layne et al. 2008), college students (Steinhardt and Dolbier 2008), substance use disorders (Ford, Russo, and Mallon 2007), and disaster workers (Naturale 2007). Psychoeducation may be especially beneficial for adults who sometimes neglect their own needs while caring for their families postdisaster (Madrid and Grant 2008).

Psychoeducation often includes handouts explaining common stress reactions and strategies for enhancing individual coping (Naturale 2007). However, care must be taken to provide linguistically and educationally appropriate informational materials (Elrod, Hamblen, and Norris 2006). Predominant class assumptions that fail to consider cultural and linguistic differences may not only heighten distress in minority group survivors, but erode their sense of control and self-respect when they cannot obtain the information they need (Shelby and Tredinnick 1995, 496).

2.3.13 REFERRALS

Besides referrals for basic human needs and financial assistance, disaster workers are expected to refer survivors to ongoing professional behavioral health services when they present with symptoms of extreme or unresolved disaster-related distress and when brief nontherapeutic interventions fail to help (Elrod, Hamblen, and Norris 2006). Therefore, workers should be able to recognize and assess survivors' needs and decide if they might benefit from a referral. Evidence of suicidal or homicidal ideation, inability to function, alcohol dependence, and exacerbated preexisting mental illness are "red flags" for workers, and these cases should be referred immediately to professional treatment services in the community (Elrod, Hamblen, and Norris 2006, 161; Gard and Ruzek 2006). Disaster-related losses and degree of trauma exposure may also be compelling indicators for the need to refer survivors to professional treatment services (Rosen, Matthieu, and Norris 2009).

2.3.13.1   Referrals and Minorities

Some research has also shown that white survivors receive referrals more frequently than survivors from minority groups, which might be attributed to personal bias, survivor inclinations toward informal forms of assistance, or a lack of culturally appropriate behavioral health providers (Rosen, Matthieu, and Norris 2009, 193). This is disturbing since research suggests that minorities often have unmet instrumental and psychological needs predisaster, have greater difficulty accessing help- ing resources, and suffer greater adverse psychological outcomes postdisaster than whites (Norris and Alegria 2005; Wang et al. 2007). Thus, extra consideration should be given to ensure that these minority populations have the same quality of services and level of assessment, and opportunities from treatment, as any other.

2.3.13.2   Timing of Referrals

Most behavioral health referrals occur several months after brief nontherapeutic interventions have been attempted and workers have had time to identify survivors who are truly in need of professional services (Gard and Ruzek 2006). Analysis of referral frequency may reveal how well workers are examining survivors' needs. Further, research has demonstrated that higher referral frequency in counties resulted in increased survivor-perceived benefits from the counseling experience (Norris, Hamblen, and Rosen 2009, 183).

At times, disaster workers may be unsure exactly when to refer survivors for professional ser- vices even though many disaster behavioral health programs provide staff with referral guidelines. In some cases, survivors may be referred to treatment after accessing disaster behavioral health services several times. Even with guidelines, however, confusion has been noted within programs regarding the exact number of visits that should prompt a referral (Elrod, Hamblen, and Norris 2006). Thus, it is important for responder organizations to establish written protocols that clearly define such issues and provide adequate training and clinical supervision to achieve consistency in services throughout the programs' duration.

2.3.13.3   Referrals and Community Resources

Workers should be familiar with available community resources that can assist survivors and be able to motivate them to accept referrals (Rosen, Matthieu, and Norris 2009). Some studies have shown that there are higher frequencies of referrals in urban areas, which may mean workers are aware of more resources in those environments (Norris, Hamblen, and Rosen 2009; Rosen, Matthieu, and Norris 2009).

Frustration concerning the lack of community resources is a common problem after disaster. Most community mental health centers are overburdened and underfunded, with long waiting lists of individuals who need help (Elrod, Hamblen, and Norris 2006). Disasters can flood community mental health centers with countless new applicants requesting assistance, which may force them to reject new clients (Rosen, Matthieu, and Norris 2009). Therefore, workers must also be careful to make judicious use of referrals to ensure that community resources are reserved for those who have the greatest need (Gard and Ruzek 2006).

Although many disaster behavioral health programs do not retain personally identifying survivor data, which makes subsequent follow-up problematic, developing some means of contacting certain higher-risk survivors at a later time might reduce the number of unnecessary referrals (Norris, Hamblen, and Rosen 2009; Gard and Ruzek 2006).

2.3.14   THE OUTREACH WORKFORCE

One of the greatest sources of contention and controversy in disaster behavioral health is the com- position and qualifications of its workforce. According to Bulling and Abdel-Monem (2009, 762), "The current lack of accepted standards for preparation of a disaster mental health workforce, both clinical and indigenous, is a glaring gap in the development of organized disaster mental health response."ᵉ Since many disaster workers, including behavioral health professionals, have no prior disaster experience or training, these deficits in taxonomy and norms have led many organizations to create a variety of approaches to training workers (Bulling and Abdel-Monem 2009, 761; Goodman and West-Olatunji 2009).

2.3.14.1 Team Composition

Disaster behavioral health programs generally employ a mix of professionals, paraprofessionals, and volunteers. How to deal with spontaneous groups of volunteers after disaster is generally problematic for local emergency managers and any designated lead agencies for behavioral health response (Elrod, Hamblen, and Norris 2006; Bulling and Abdel-Monem 2009). Aside from spontaneous volunteers, however, many licensed clinicians are volunteers in organized relief efforts such as the Medical Reserve Corps and the American Red Cross. Volunteer status offers them a degree of immunity from civil suits, provided there is a declared emergency, since the federal government and most of the states have enacted laws to protect disaster volunteers during response (Bulling and Abdel-Monem 2009; Hodge, Jr. 2006). This may be important for workers who are deployed to another state where their health care licensure would not normally be recognized (Hodge, Jr. 2006).

Concern has been expressed about the ability of nonclinical responders to provide disaster behavioral health services effectively and safely (Kestin 2006a and 2006b). However, there may not always be sufficient numbers of licensed clinicians available or willing to assist in organized response efforts. They may also be equally affected by disaster and consequentially unable to participate in response efforts.

Even when sufficient numbers of clinical staff are available, one should not assume that clinicians make good supervisors. As one disaster behavioral health team leader stated, "…just because you're a therapist does not mean you know how to set up a program and know how to run a program" (Brown et al. 2007, 22). Therefore, necessity often dictates the composition of teams to include a variety of licensed clinicians, paraprofessionals, and volunteers (Cohen 2002). Factors such as the response duration, culture, assistance from external organizations, and availability of professional workers impact job functions and how work tasks are distributed within response teams (Bulling and Abdel-Monem 2009, 762). Given appropriate supervision and training of paraprofessionals, however, it is possible to provide disaster behavioral health services that are based on sound crisis theories and strategies (Cohen 2002).

2.3.14.2 Indigenous Workers

Some studies have shown that paraprofessionals, indigenous or from external sources, can indeed effectively provide disaster behavioral health services given appropriate training. Their ability to focus on the community and help change community systems for the better makes them desirable in disaster programs (Soliman, Lingle, and Raymond 1998). Teams that include workers with diverse knowledge, skills, and abilities may be more capable of problem solving survivors' sundry needs (Soliman, Lingle, and Raymond 1998; Brown et al. 2007). It is also possible that a sharing of common values helps sustain the vision and energy required in challenging response work (Haskett et al. 2008).

Many governmental and nongovernmental organizations make a concerted effort to hire indigenous members of disaster-stricken communities since they are familiar with the community's populations, resources, and social and political compositions (Soliman, Lingle, and Raymond 1998). Indeed, the ability of impacted communities to contribute to their own recovery should not be overlooked in favor of external resources. Indigenous workers have the advantage of being known within the community and therefore are more likely to be trusted (Bulling and Abdel-Monem 2009). They may be more capable of penetrating community locations that have suffered the greatest devastation and thus help create community resilience (Elrod, Hamblen, and Norris 2006; Bulling and Abdel-Monem 2009). In particular, minority indigenous workers may generate greater trust and rapport with similar members of the impacted community due to shared or assumed understanding of their backgrounds and experience (Haskett et al. 2008).

2.3.14.3 Educational Background

Research by Norris, Hamblen, and Rosen (2009) conducted on the educational backgrounds of a number of disaster workers revealed that those with advanced degrees were perceived by survivors to be more helpful, at least in part, because they provided greater service intensity and more referrals to professional psychological services in the community. Another study by Soliman, Lingle, and Raymond (1998) found that, regardless of the level of education, workers with degrees in the social sciences reported more positive perceptions after performing disaster work than their colleagues with different educational backgrounds. Further, females generally reported more positive perceptions about their experience in disaster relief than their male counterparts.

2.3.14.4 Prior Work Experience

The amount of work experience an individual has may also influence worker perceptions. Soliman, Lingle, and Raymond's study (1998) suggests that individuals with longer experience in human services were more positive about the impacts of relief work on their personal and professional growth, particularly their ability to remain calm under pressure, to act rationally in disaster conditions, enhance communications abilities, and expand their knowledge about disaster-related problems (Soliman, Lingle, and Raymond 1998). Less experienced workers may suffer more from secondary traumatic stress than experienced workers; albeit, strong team bonding may mitigate stress and heighten positive perceptions about the work (Elrod, Hamblen, and Norris 2006; Soliman, Lingle, and Raymond 1998). Organizational obstacles like caseload, paperwork, finding survivors, and lack of interest in services may contribute to an erosion of quality in services and job satisfaction (Soliman, Lingle, and Raymond 1998). This underscores the importance of adequately preparing outreach workers to respond to their own and others' physical and psychological problems (Connor, Foa, and Davidson 2006).

2.3.14.5 Personal Qualities of Outreach Workers

Some researchers have suggested that there are certain personal qualities that may make some individuals more suited to performing disaster behavioral outreach irrespective of their education and past experience. As Haskett and colleagues (2008) note, "This type of service requires far more than simply the possession of a professional license and training in disaster relief" (94). Disaster outreach requires workers who can endure adverse physical and psychological conditions for days or weeks at a stretch—individuals who are flexible to frequently changing conditions and the resources with which to work and can deal with rapid turnover in staff or knowledge that the duration of one's work is uncertain (Haskett et al. 2008).

Therefore, workers should be realistic in self-appraisals that they can endure such conditions because, once thrust into the often chaotic world of disaster response, they may become anxious and inattentive to the needs of survivors if they realize too late they are unsuited to this kind of work. In crisis response, self-management skills are crucial for maintaining control and making effective decisions (Bobevski and McLennan 1998). Workers must constantly process incoming information about the individual in need of help while simultaneously deciding how to respond (Bobevski and McLennan 1998, 50).

Strong communication skills, and awareness of how ethnicity and culture influence survivors' decision making and willingness to accept disaster behavioral health services, are necessary to assist survivors effectively (Cohen 2002). Therefore, individuals who desire to work in this field should be mature, motivated, and able to make effective decisions quickly, because they may only get one chance to help a survivor (Connor, Foa, and Davidson 2006; Bobevski and McLennan 1998; Soliman, Lingle, and Raymond 1998).

Individuals who typically react with less anxiety and deal with survivors' stories of trauma and loss in a compassionate and appropriate manner may be highly effective in disaster situations (Connor, Foa, and Davidson 2006). In turn, workers with such qualities may benefit from their work experience by getting more in tune with own feelings and learning that they are actually capable of helping others to come through tough times (Soliman, Lingle, and Raymond 1998).

Some prior counseling experience would enhance workers' personal attributes (Cohen 2002). Therefore, potential workers in organized programs should be carefully screened and given suitable training and close supervision throughout their service (Connor, Foa, and Davidson 2006; Cohen 2002).

2.3.14.6 Clinical Supervision

Legitimate concerns about the ability of paraprofessionals or other nonclinical workers to provide services effectively and safely stress the importance of close, ongoing clinical supervision. Organized programs should hire sufficient numbers of clinical staff to provide such support to nonclinical staff and follow up with those survivors who have been identified by nonclinical staff as in potential need of professional treatment (Norris, Hamblen, and Rosen 2009). Further, clinical supervisors need to ensure that nonclinical staff clearly understand their mission parameters to prevent them from attempting to use clinical treatments that they are not qualified to perform (Elrod, Hamblen, and Norris 2006). Consequently, this may help alleviate any concerns that clinical supervisors may have regarding liability for the actions of team members (Bulling and Abdel-Monem 2009).

2.4 CONCLUSION

This chapter provides a brief overview of disaster behavioral health outreach, its primary functions, and how disaster behavioral health differs from traditional behavioral health practice. Disaster behavioral health is a flourishing field that offers many opportunities for research and practice. Clearly, there are certain aspects of disaster behavioral health outreach that could benefit from future research. Emerging knowledge should be incorporated into practice to improve interventions for, and delivery of, services to survivors suffering from postdisaster distress and other significant psychological outcomes.

NOTES

a. See FEMA's website at http://www.fema.gov/assistance/opendrcs.shtm.
b. Norris and colleagues (2009) use the term *service intimacy* to describe the depth and quality of worker–survivor interactions in private settings. See reference list for the complete citation on their research.
c. See Chapter 17, this volume, for additional information about recent efforts to develop cognitive behavioral therapies for disaster survivors.
d. See Mitchell, J. T. 1983. When disaster strikes… The critical incident stress debriefing process. *Journal of Emergency Medical Services 8*: 36–39.
e. The word *indigenous* is sometimes used in the literature to refer to nonclinicians, minority group members of a community, or any member of a community.

REFERENCES

Acierno, R., K. J. Ruggiero, S. Galea, H. S. Resnick, K. Koenen, J. Roitzsch, M. de Arellano, J. Boyle, and D. G. Kilpatrick. 2007. Psychological sequelae resulting from the 2004 Florida hurricanes: Implications for postdisaster intervention. *American Journal of Public Health 97*(S1): S103–S108.

Blodgett, C., K. Behan, M. Erp, R. Harrington, and K. Souers. 2008. Crisis intervention for children and caregivers exposed to intimate partner violence. *Best Practices in Mental Health 4*(2): 74–91.

Bobevski, I., and J. McLennan. 1998. The telephone counseling interview as a complex, dynamic, decision process: A self-regulation model of counselor effectiveness. *Journal of Psychology 132*(1): 47–60.

Bourque, L. B., J. M. Siegel, M. Kano, and M. M. Wood. 2006. Weathering the storm: The impact of hurricanes on physical and mental health. *Annals of the American Academy of Political and Social Science 604*: 129–151.

Brown, E. J., J. McQuaid, L. Farina, R. Ali, and A. Winnick-Gelles. 2006. Matching interventions to children's mental health needs: Feasibility and acceptability of a pilot school-based trauma intervention program. *Education and Treatment of Children 29*(2): 257–286.

Brown, L. M. 2007. Issues in mental health care for older adults after disasters. *Generations 31*(4): 21–26.

Brown, L., J. Syvertsen,, J. Schinka, A. Mando, and L. Schonfeld. 2007. *Project Recovery: Final Program Evaluation*. Tampa, FL: Louis de la Parte Florida Mental Health Institute, University of South Florida.

Bulling, D., and T. Abdel-Monem. 2009. Disaster mental health. In *Wiley Encyclopedia of Forensic Science, Volume 2 (C-E)*, eds. Allan Jamieson and Andre Moenssens, 760–764. http://digitalcommons.unl.edu/cgi/viewcontent.cgi?article=1051&context=publicpolicypublications.

Cohen, R. 2002. Mental health services for victims of disasters. *World Psychiatry 1*(3): 149–152. http://www.ncbi.nlm.nih.gov/pmc/articles/PMC1489840/pdf/wpa010149.pdf.

Connor, K. M., E. B. Foa, and J. R. T. Davidson. 2006. Practical assessment and evaluation of mental health problems following a mass disaster. *Journal of Clinical Psychiatry 67*(S2): 26–33.

Drury, S. S., M. S. Scheeringa, and C. H. Zeanah. 2008. The traumatic impact of Hurricane Katrina on children in New Orleans. *Child Adolescent Psychiatric Clinics of North America 17*(3): 685–702.

Elrod, C. L., J. L. Hamblen, and F. H. Norris. 2006. Challenges in implementing disaster mental health programs: State program directors' perspectives. *Annals of the American Academy of Political and Social Science 604*: 152–170.

Ford, J. D., E. M. Russo, and S. D. Mallon. 2007. Integrating treatment of posttraumatic stress disorder and substance use disorder. *Journal of Counseling and Development 85*(4): 475–489.

Gard, B., and J. I. Ruzek. (2006). Community mental health response to crisis. *Journal of Clinical Psychology: In Session 62*(8): 1029–1041.

Goodman, R. D., and C. A. West-Olatunji. 2009. Applying critical consciousness: Culturally competent disaster response outcomes. *Journal of Counseling & Development 87*: 458–465.

Hamblen, J. L., L. E. Gibson, K. T. Mueser, and F. H. Norris. 2006. Cognitive behavioral therapy for prolonged postdisaster distress. *Journal of Clinical Psychology: In Session 62*(8): 1043–1052.

Hamblen, J. L., F. H. Norris, S. Pietruszkiewicz, L. E. Gibson, A. Naturale, and C. Louis. 2009. Cognitive behavioral therapy for postdisaster distress: A community based treatment program for survivors of Hurricane Katrina. *Administration and Policy in Mental Health 36*: 206–214.

Haskett, M. E., S. Smith Scott, K. Nears, and M. A. Grimmett. 2008. Lessons from Katrina: Disaster mental health service in the Gulf Coast region. *Professional Psychology: Research and Practice 39*(1): 93–99.

Hodge, J. G., Jr. 2006. Legal issues concerning volunteer health professionals and the hurricane-related emergencies in the Gulf Coast region. *Public Health Reports 121*(2): 205–207. http://www.ncbi.nlm.nih.gov/pmc/articles/PMC1525256/pdf/phr121000205.pdf.

Jacobs, A. K., E. Vernberg, and S. J. Lee. 2008. Supporting adolescents exposed to disasters. *The Prevention Researcher 15*(3): 7–10.

Jacobs, G. A., and N. Kulkarni. 1999. Mental health responses to terrorism. *Psychiatric Annals 29*(6): 376–380. http://ehs.umbc.edu/distance/632Readings/MHRespTerror.PDF.

Kestin, S. 2006a. "Fema Spends Millions On Puppet Shows, Bingo & Yoga." *Sun-Sentinel*, October 8. http://articles.sun-sentinel.com/2006-10-08/news/0610070535_1_hurricane-bingo-windy-biggie-project-hope-wilma.

Kestin, S. 2006b. "Hurricane crisis leaders fall short." *Sun-Sentinel*, December 10. http://articles.sun-sentinel.com/2006-12-10/news/0612090460_1_project-hope-hurricane-bingo-fema.

Kilpatrick, D. G., J. R. Cougle, and H. S. Resnick. 2008. Reports of the death of psychoeducation as a preventative treatment for posttraumatic psychological distress are exaggerated. *Psychiatry 71*(4): 322–328.

Layne C. M., W. R. Saltzman, L. Poppleton, G. M. Burlingame, A. Pasalić, E. Duraković, M. Musić, N. Campara, N. Dapo, B. Arslanagić, A. M. Steinberg, and R. S. Pynoos. 2008. Effectiveness of a school-based group psychotherapy program for war-exposed adolescents: A randomized controlled trial. *Journal of the American Academy of Child and Adolescent Psychiatry 47*(9): 1048–1062.

Leitch, M. L., J. Vanslyke, and M. Allen. 2009. Somatic experiencing treatment with social service workers following hurricanes Katrina and Rita. *Social Work 54*(1): 9–18.

Litz, B. T., M. J. Gray, R. A. Bryant, and A. B. Adler. 2002. Early intervention for trauma: Current status and future directions. *Clinical Psychology: Science and Practice 9*(2): 112–134.

Madrid, P. A., and R. Grant. 2008. Meeting mental health needs following a natural disaster: Lessons from Hurricane Katrina. *Professional Psychology: Research and Practice 39*(1): 86–92.

Marbley, A. F. 2007. In the wake of Hurricane Katrina: Delivering crisis mental health to host communities. *Multicultural Education 15*(2): 17–23.

Mayou, R., A. Ehlers, and M. Hobbs. 2000. Psychological debriefing for road traffic accident victims. *British Journal of Psychiatry 176*: 589–593.

Mitchell, J. 1983. When disaster strikes: The critical incident stress debriefing process. *Journal of Emergency Medical Services 8*: 36–39.

National Institute of Mental Health (NIMH). 2002. *Mental Health and Mass Violence: Evidence-Based Early Psychological Intervention for Victims/Survivors of Mass Violence*. A Workshop to Reach Consensus on Best Practices. NIH Publication No. 02-5138, Washington, DC: U.S. Government Printing Office. http://www.nimh.nih.gov/health/publications/massviolence.pdf.

Naturale, A. 2007. Secondary traumatic stress in social workers responding to disasters: Reports from the field. *Clinical Social Work Journal 35*: 173–181.

Naturale, A. J. 2006. Outreach strategies: An experiential description of the outreach methodologies used in the September 11, 2001, disaster response in New York. In *Interventions Following Mass Violence and Disasters: Strategies for Mental Health Practice*, eds. E. C. Ritchie, P. J. Watson, and M. J. Friedman, 365–384. New York: Guilford Press.

Norris, F. H., and M. Alegria. 2005. Mental health care for ethnic minority individuals and communities in the aftermath of disasters and mass violence. *CNS Spectrums 10*(2): 132–140.

Norris, F. H., M. J. Friedman, P. J. Watson, C. M. Byrne, E. Diaz, and K. Kaniasty. 2002. 60,000 disaster victims speak: Part I. An empirical review of the empirical literature, 1981–2001. *Psychiatry 65*(3): 207–239.

Norris, F. H., J. L. Hamblen, and C. S. Rosen. 2009. Service characteristics and counseling outcomes: Lessons from a cross-site evaluation of crisis counseling after Hurricanes Katrina, Rita and Wilma. *Administration and Policy in Mental Health 36*(3): 176–185.

Norris, F. H., and C. S. Rosen. 2009. Innovations in disaster mental health services and evaluation: National, state, and local responses to Hurricane Katrina (Introduction to the special issue). *Administration and Policy in Mental Health 36*(3): 159–164.

Rose, S. C., J. Bisson, R. Churchill, and S. Wessely. 2001. Psychological debriefing for preventing post traumatic stress disorder (PTSD). *Cochrane Database of Systematic Reviews*, Issue 2. Art. No.: CD000560. DOI: 10.1002/14651858.CD000560.

Rose, S., C. Brewin, B. Andrews, and M. Kirk. 1999. A randomized controlled trial of individual psychological debriefing for victims of violent crime. *Psychological Medicine 29*(4): 793–799.

Rosen, C. S., M. M. Matthieu, and F. H. Norris. 2009. Factors predicting crisis counselor referrals to other crisis counseling, disaster relief, and psychological services: A cross-site analysis of post-Katrina programs. *Administration and Policy in Mental Health 36*(3): 186–194.

Ruzek, J. I., B. H. Young, M. J. Cordova, and B. W. Flynn. 2004. Integration of disaster mental health services with emergency medicine. *Prehospital and Disaster Medicine 19*(1): 46–53. http://pdm.medicine.wisc.edu.

Shelby, J. S., and M. G. Tredinnick. 1995. Crisis intervention with survivors of natural disaster: Lessons from Hurricane Andrew. *Journal of Counseling and Development 73*: 491–497.

Soliman, H. H., S. E. Lingle, and A. Raymond. 1998. Perceptions of indigenous workers following participation in a disaster relief project. *Community Mental Health Journal 34*(6): 557–568.

SRA International, Inc. 2008. *Cultural Competency in Disaster Response: A Review of Current Concepts, Policies, and Practices*. Report prepared for the Office of Minority Health. Rockville, MD: SRA International, Inc.

Steinhardt, M., and C. Dolbier. 2008. Evaluation of a resilience intervention to enhance coping strategies and protective factors and decrease symptomatology. *Journal of American College Health 56*(4): 445–453. http://vnweb.hwwilsonweb.com.proxy.lib.fsu.edu/hww/jumpstart.jhtml?recid=0bc05f7a67b1790ecd6c3 0ba6af0d560d4648f48a030baf4337bcde4e060289c68940d977be681ce&fmt=P.

Substance Abuse and Mental Health Services Administration (SAMHSA). nd. *Federal Emergency Management Agency Crisis Counseling Assistance and Training Program Guidance*. http://www.samhsa.gov/dtac/CCPtoolkit/pdf/CCP_Program_Guidance.pdf.

Sundararaman, R., S. A. Lister, and E. D. Williams. 2006. *Gulf Coast Hurricanes: Addressing Survivors' Mental Health and Substance Abuse Treatment Needs*. Report RL33738, ed. Congressional Research Service. Washington, DC: The Library of Congress. http://stuff.mit.edu/afs/sipb/contrib/wikileaks-crs/wikileaks-crs-reports/RL33738.pdf.

Tatar, M., and S. Amram. 2007. Israeli adolescents' coping strategies in relation to terrorist attacks. *British Journal of Guidance & Counselling 35*(2): 163–173.

U.S. Department of Veterans Affairs, National Center for Posttraumatic Stress Disorder (NCPTSD). 2010, reviewed/updated. *Cautions regarding cognitive-behavioral interventions provided within a month of trauma*. http://www.ptsd.va.gov/professional/pages/cbi-after-trauma.asp.

Wang, P. S., M. J. Gruber, R. E. Powers, M. Schoenbaum, A. H. Speier, K. B. Wells, and R. C. Kessler. 2007. Mental health service use among Hurricane Katrina survivors in the eight months after the disaster. *Psychiatric Services 58*(11): 1403–1411.

Weems, C. F., L. K. Taylor, M. F. Cannon, R. C. Marino, D. M. Romano, B. G. Scott, A. M. Perry, and V. Triplett. 2010. Post traumatic stress, context, and the lingering effects of the Hurricane Katrina Disaster among ethnic minority youth. *Journal of Abnormal Child Psychology 38*: 49–56.

Wessely, S., R. A. Bryant, N. Greenberg, M. Earnshaw, J. Sharpley, and J. Hacker Hughes. 2008. Does psycho-education help prevent post traumatic psychological distress? *Psychiatry 71*(4): 287–302.

Wieling, E. 2008. Linking human systems: Strengthening individuals, families, and communities in the wake of mass trauma. *Journal of Marital and Family Therapy 34*(2): 193–209.

Young, B. H., J. D. Ford, J. I. Ruzek, M. J. Friedman, and F. D. Gusman. 1998. *Disaster Mental Health Services: A Guidebook for Clinicians and Administrators*. White River Junction, VT: Department of Veterans Affairs. The National Center for Post-Traumatic Stress Disorder. http://www.hsdl.org/?view& doc=17822&coll=limited.

Part II

Organizational Response to
Disasters and Key Partners

3 Governmental Roles and Responsibilities in Disaster Behavioral Health Response and Recovery

Richard Salkowe and Julie L. Framingham

CONTENTS

3.1 INTRODUCTION

The role of government intervention in the response to and recovery from disasters and catastrophic events has an extensive history in the United States. Financial aid and military support has been provided for infrastructure repair, public safety, and individual assistance in response to prior disaster events ranging from the San Francisco earthquake of 1906 to the Mississippi floods of 1927 (Morris 1906; Simpich 1927), but there was no specific mandate for the distribution of federal relief in disasters until 1950. Prior to this time, disaster relief was authorized on a case-by-case basis without any guarantee of federal intervention.

Historically, nongovernmental organizations served an essential role in the provision of services after disasters and a variety of national and state Voluntary Organizations Active in Disaster (VOAD) continue to provide critical disaster relief services in the United States. Voluntary organizations such as the Salvation Army have provided support for disaster-afflicted individuals and communities dating back to the Galveston hurricane of 1900 when volunteers from across the country served "to help clean, feed and shelter the thousands of survivors, while also providing much needed spiritual and emotional support" (Salvation Army 2009). In 1900, the U.S. Congress granted the American Red Cross a federal charter to "carry on a system of national and international relief in time of peace and to apply the same in mitigating the sufferings caused by pestilence, famine, fire, floods, and other great national calamities" (American Red Cross 2010).

This amalgam of nongovernmental, quasi-governmental, and multilevel governmental responses to disasters evolved concurrent with an increased understanding of the critical role of behavioral health intervention after these extraordinary events. The observations of posttraumatic stress symptomatology in combat-exposed soldiers gradually led to an interventional model of psychological first aid after natural and technological disasters (Grob 1994; Jacobs 1995). Additionally, the findings of an increased incidence of stress-related behavioral and physiological disorders in disaster victims after events such as the Cocoanut Grove fire in 1942, the Donora "Death Fog" of 1948, the 1972 Buffalo Creek flood and Hurricane Agnes events, and the 1976 Grand Teton flood revealed a need for crisis intervention to address postdisaster psychological problems (Okura 1975; Logue, Hansen, and Streuning 1979; Jacobs 1995).

The federal government specifically addressed the need for crisis counseling services in conjunction with a variety of support mechanisms for individuals and families in disaster-affected areas of the United States by the creation of the Disaster Relief Act of 1974. In 1989, the American Red Cross formally recognized the role of a well-defined plan for the mental health needs of disaster survivors, which led to the formation of the American Red Cross Disaster Mental Health Services program (Morgan 1995; Weaver, et al. 2000). Consistent with the recognition of the importance of behavioral health services after disasters, the U.S. Department of Homeland Security and the U.S. Department of Health and Human Services have established standards for the provision of disaster behavioral health services in the National Preparedness Guidelines, the National Response Framework, Homeland Security Presidential Directive-21, the National Health Security Strategy, and in the Federal Emergency Management Agency's (FEMA) Long-Term Community Recovery initiatives (Department of Homeland Security 2007; Homeland Security Presidential Directive-21 2007; Department of Homeland Security 2008b; U.S. Department of Health and Human Services 2009; Department of Homeland Security 2009).

States, counties, and municipalities have the constitutional authority to independently establish disaster behavioral health policy in a federalist democracy, and these respective jurisdictions have undertaken a variety of approaches in an attempt to effectively respond to the needs of disaster survivors across the United States. The ongoing reformulation of disaster policy in the United States on both local and national levels has refined the role and responsibility of government with respect to disaster behavioral health. This chapter is intended to provide further insight into the specific measures and mandates that empower state and federal governmental entities to enable and operationalize behavioral health services in the response to and recovery from disastrous events in the United States.

3.2   SETTING THE STAGE: ESTABLISHING THE ROLE OF GOVERNMENT IN DISASTER BEHAVIORAL HEALTH

Establishing the current role of the government in disaster behavioral health response requires an understanding of the historical foundation of mental health policy in the United States. The perception of mental illness in this country has changed dramatically since the 1800s. Jails, almshouses, and asylums for the mentally insane were the norm in the 19th century, and a decentralized form of federalism prevailed in the United States without a recognized mandate at a national level with respect to mental health hygiene and preventive approaches to mental illness. Grob (1994, 97) references the prevailing sentiment of the executive branch during the mid-19th century with respect to the role of the federal government in the care for indigents with mental illness by quoting President Franklin Pierce:

> The fountains of charity will be dried up at home, and the several States, instead of bestowing their own means on the social wants of their own people, may themselves, through the strong temptation, which appeals to States as to individuals, become humble supplicants for the bounty of the Federal Government, reversing their true relation to this Union.

This lack of federal support for mental health services and the mounting evidence of a failure for the institutional treatment of the "insane" to result in meaningful recovery were addressed in 1909 by the formation of the National Committee for Mental Hygiene under the auspices of Clifford W. Beers. Beers (1913) revealed the inhumane treatment of the institutionalized mentally ill in his autobiography *A Mind That Found Itself,* and he was an integral force in the establishment of the National Committee. His preventive approach to mental illness via the application of mental hygiene practices would "change the face of mental health in the first half of the 20th century" (Friedman 2002, 45). The concept of mental hygiene is based on a commitment to the premise that the social environment is causal in the development of mental illness and that social support mechanisms are an integral component of mental health and well-being. Adolf Meyer, a psychiatrist and professional colleague of Clifford Beers, is considered to be instrumental in the establishment of the mental hygiene approach in the early 20th century (Dreyer 1976); the combined contributions of Beers and Myers were essential in the subsequent creation of disaster behavioral health policy in the United States.

The roots of federal government involvement and responsibility in disaster behavioral health were established in foundational legislation that established a framework for the present-day organizational flow of federal disaster support and oversight. In 1944, President Franklin Roosevelt signed the Public Health Service Act of July 1, 1944 (42 U.S.C. 201). This act consolidated and revised a significant amount of existing legislation relating to the Public Health Service and established the framework for the provision of "resources and expertise to the States and other public and private institutions in the planning, direction, and delivery of physical and mental health care services" (Department of Health and Human Services 2005). The U.S. Public Health Service via its component agency, the Substance Abuse and Mental Health Services Administration (SAMHSA), "supports the delivery of services to build resilience and facilitate recovery in communities across the United States" (National Institute of Mental Health 2010). SAMHSA is the primary agency providing technical support and administrative monitoring for the federally authorized postdisaster Crisis Counseling Assistance and Training Program (CCP) under the provisions of an interagency agreement with FEMA. In 1946, President Harry Truman signed into law the National Mental Health Act of 1946, which was legislated in response to the realization of the high incidence of stress-related illness associated with the trauma of combat exposure in soldiers returning from World War II (Herman 1995). This act led to the formation of the National Institute of Mental Health (NIMH) in 1949, which replaced the Public Health Service Division of Mental Hygiene. The NIMH remains an agency of the U.S. Public Health Service and maintains an essential mission to "transform the understanding and treatment of mental illnesses through basic and clinical research, paving the way for prevention, recovery, and cure" (National Institute of Mental Health 2010). The NIMH has supported a broad agenda of research initiatives and grant-funded projects pertaining to the consequences of stress and trauma after disasters and activated the ongoing Rapid Assessment Post Impact of Disaster (RAPID) research program that was designed to "fund new research grant applications for assessing needs, planning of services, and improving preparedness and response to disasters" (Office of the Assistant Secretary for Preparedness and Response 2008). These measures established the framework for creating an action agenda that led to existing federal policy and for the further definition of government roles and responsibilities in disaster behavioral health response and recovery.

3.3   RECOGNIZING A NEED: FEDERAL DISASTER POLICY IN THE UNITED STATES

The failure of federal policy to formally address the needs of disaster victims via established guidelines led to congressional legislation in 1950 "to provide a general congressional policy in respect to federal disaster relief" (Rubin 2007, 83). The Federal Disaster Relief Act of 1950 represents the formal initiation of federal government involvement in disaster response and recovery in the United States (Platt 1999). As previously noted, federal relief had been distributed for infrastructure repair and individual assistance prior to this legislation, but there was no specific mandate for distribution of relief aid prior to 1950, and disasters were considered on a case-by-case basis without any degree of assured government intervention at the national level. The initial federal act was intended to provide relief for public assistance projects involving infrastructure repair (Sylves and Waugh 1996). This legislation granted sole authority to the president in deciding when federal resources would be allotted in response to a request for disaster relief and required the governor of a requesting state to indicate that local resources had been sufficiently dedicated to the disaster relief effort as a precondition for federal aid. This legislation did not address the health need of individuals or communities after disasters. Extensions of the Federal Disaster Relief Act in 1970 and 1974 provided for individual assistance via temporary housing and grant programs for furniture, clothing, and essential needs in a cost-share arrangement between states and the federal government (Sylves and Waugh 1996). The Disaster Relief Act of 1970 allowed for the separate category of emergency declaration that was indicated when immediate federal intervention was required for the preservation of life and property and to lessen the threat of catastrophe. Emergency declarations require a federal cost share of not less than 75 percent of funds distributed; the financial aid is limited to $5 million, although the president may exceed this amount with congressional notification if there is a continuing threat to public safety and property. Federal aid in emergency declarations is limited to debris clearance and emergency protective measures, including, in part, technical assistance to local governments, coordination of disaster relief between government agencies, and individual and household assistance consisting of temporary housing grants and distribution of food, medicine, and consumables.

The Disaster Relief Act of 1974 emphasized an all-hazards approach in an attempt to coordinate the historically fragmented response to specific types of disasters and institutionalized the concept of mitigation in disaster management (Sylves 1998). This federal disaster policy legislated a variety of measures that were available to assist individuals and families after disasters and marked the initial authorization for the CCP. The establishment of the CCP and the extension of federal benefits under the Disaster Relief Act of 1974 were mandated in response to an understanding of the role and responsibilities of the federal government in protecting the physical and emotional well-being of disaster-afflicted individuals and communities. The findings of the National Institute of Mental Health after the devastation associated with Hurricane Agnes led to an increased understanding of the adverse psychological and physiological manifestations of exposure to emotional stressors associated with catastrophic events. In 1972, Hurricane Agnes was considered to be "the greatest natural disaster in American history" (Okura 1975, 136; U.S Department of the Army 1972), and a subsequent series of tornado events affecting 10 states and resulting in 6 federal major disaster declarations in 1974 encouraged the federal government to pass the Disaster Relief Act of 1974 (Department of Homeland Security 2003), which included the following extended provisions for individual assistance after disasters (Oregon State University 2004):

- Temporary housing
- Disaster loans
- Tax preparation assistance
- Legal services
- Consumer aid
- Disaster unemployment benefits
- Crisis counseling
- Individual and family grants
- Emergency shelter
- Emergency food
- Emergency medical assistance
- Essential repairs to homes so occupants can return
- Temporary assistance with mortgage or rental payment

FEMA was established in 1979, through an executive order by President Jimmy Carter, to "consolidate and coordinate disaster response efforts" (Downton and Pielke 2001, 158) as federal disaster relief initiatives had previously been distributed across a vast array of bureaucratic agencies. Sylves and Cumming (2004) indicate that since its inception, FEMA's jurisdictional priorities have varied from civil defense against nuclear attacks and continuity of government to natural disaster management, depending on presidential administrations and perceived dangers.

Currently, federal disaster declarations in the United States are authorized by the president under the provisions of the Robert T. Stafford Disaster Relief and Emergency Assistance Act of 1988 (Stafford Act). This act furthered the mechanisms established by the Disaster Relief Act of 1974 for the distribution of various forms of relief aid after disasters, including debris removal, temporary housing, individual and household financial assistance, infrastructure repair, emergency communications, military support for the preservation of life and property, and crisis counseling, by establishing specific cost-share requirements between states and the federal government and expanded hazard mitigation assistance (Bea 2006; Rubin 2007). A thorough analysis of the benefits and limitations of the provisions of the Stafford Act is essential to an understanding of the availability of resources for behavioral health services in the response to and recovery from disasters.

Disaster declaration requests are considered when a state or local government indicates that it has been "overwhelmed" by the effects of a disaster event and the governor of the affected state has executed the state's emergency plan and requested disaster relief from the president of the United States (Sylves and Waugh 1996; Bazan 2005). The Stafford Act gives the president permanent authority to direct federal aid to affected states, territories, and U.S. possessions (Bea 2005). The governor of a disaster-stricken state is required to declare a state of emergency, activate the state emergency response plan, and furnish information to FEMA regarding the availability of state resources that are committed to the disaster, including the ability to participate in all cost-sharing requirements contained in the Stafford Act (Bazan 2005). The president may declare a disaster without a gubernatorial request if the event pertains to federal property or involves primary federal responsibility, as was evident in the bombing of the Alfred P. Murrah Federal Building in Oklahoma City in 1995. The Catastrophic Incident Annex to the National Response Framework also provides for the deployment of federal resources, including mental health services, in times of significant disaster without requiring a gubernatorial request for assistance. Disaster declarations may provide federal support under the provisions of the Public Assistance Program and/or the Individual and Household Assistance Program based on the determined needs of the disaster-affected county or state. The Public Assistance Program may include federal support for public safety, debris removal, and infrastructure repair and replacement. The Individual and Household Assistance Program provides the previously described types of relief aid, including crisis counseling. Additionally, Hazard Mitigation Assistance grants are available to assist in reducing disaster losses and protecting life and property from future damage in areas that received major presidential disaster declarations. It is important to note that the president can selectively approve specific relief measures within the allowed provisions of Public Assistance and Individual and Household Assistance Programs. A major presidential disaster declaration does not guarantee access to crisis counseling services, and gubernatorial requests for disaster behavioral health services are dependent on the review of FEMA with technical assistance from the Substance Abuse and Mental Health Services Administration, subject to the final approval of the president.

Prior to 1999, there were no objective criteria applied to the disaster declaration determination process under the provisions of the Stafford Act, with the exception of the requirement for an affected state to show evidence of the fiscal capacity to provide 25 percent of the cost share associated with the disaster. FEMA reviews the request and makes a recommendation for disaster declaration or turndown based on several objective and subjective factors, including, as of 1999, a minimum threshold of $1 million in public assistance damages per disaster. This fiscal requirement for disaster aid was established with the assumption that even low-population states can manage the obligation for this amount of public assistance. No provision for inflation was made for this threshold (U.S. GAO 2001). In addition, a $1.00 statewide per capita critical financial threshold was established in 1999 for consideration of public assistance (U.S. GAO 2001). This is adjusted annually by the Consumer Price Index for all Urban Consumers and is $1.30 noninsured damages per capita statewide and/or $3.27 noninsured damages per capita countywide as of October 1, 2010 (Federal Register 2010b; Federal Register 2010c). Due to burgeoning costs associated with disaster relief, FEMA suggested instituting "economic capability factors" to determine eligibility for assistance in 1986, but this recommendation was not supported by Congress. The Stafford Act Amendments of 1988 specifically prohibited the use of any specific sole formula to determine eligibility for relief aid, leaving the power of determination under the sole discretion of the president of the United States. The federal share of relief aid was not to be less than 75 percent and could be up to 100 percent, including 100 percent of temporary housing costs for disaster declarations that received individual and household assistance. It was also required that states show the nature and amount of their commitment in terms of local resources. Since the West Virginia floods of 1985 there have been more than 200 cost-share waivers to the 25 percent requirement; the federal contribution has paid up to 100 percent of assessed damages for several disaster events. The 2010 threshold for seeking waivers to the 25 percent local contribution is $125 statewide loss per person, and waiver consideration is also given if there is more than one disaster in a 12-month period in a specific disaster request area (Bea 2006; Federal Register 2010a).

Localized impacts are evaluated where critical facilities are involved or local per capita impacts are high even when statewide per capita impacts do not meet the aforementioned threshold. Insurance coverage obligations are considered and assistance is decreased if mandated coverage was not maintained by the affected state (Bazan 2005). Hazard mitigation measures that have been initiated by the state are evaluated with respect to their contribution to loss reduction (Bazan 2005). Factors including recent disaster exposure, local impact, and the percentage of population that is low income, elderly or unemployed are considered when waivers or modifications in Stafford Act requirements are applied to state eligibility (Bazan 2005). Subjective criteria, including the extent of health and safety problems and the extent to which the disaster area is traumatized—such as injuries, loss of life, and disruption of normal community functions (McCarthy 2009)—are also factored into the final determination of disaster declaration or denial. There are no per capita monetary threshold guidelines for the Individual and Household Assistance Program, and FEMA's post-disaster preliminary damage assessment provides for the consideration of disaster-related emotional trauma and the needs of special populations. The approval of individual and household assistance for crisis counseling services in a major disaster declaration is dependent on the determination of a disruption of normal community function after a disaster and the behavioral health needs of the affected community. FEMA's recommendation for a disaster declaration is made when it has been determined that all other resources and authorities to meet the crisis are inadequate. The recommendation is then forwarded to the president for approval or denial of the state's request for federal disaster relief under the provisions of the Stafford Act. The capacity for selective application of the objective requirements of the Stafford Act and the broad latitude given to the president in the use of subjective criteria for disaster declaration determinations has created an environment of suspicion regarding underlying motives for marginal disaster declarations and the equitable distribution of federal relief (Downton and Pielke 2001; Garrett and Sobel 2003). However, recent research has failed to reveal significant evidence of presidential partisanship in the distribution of federal disaster declarations (Salkowe and Chakraborty 2009).

Predisaster mitigation became an area of increased emphasis in 1997 with the initiation of Project Impact, which was designed to foster community partnerships that identified hazards and vulnerability and prioritized risk reduction (Wachtendorf, Connell, and Tierney 2002). This program was discontinued in 2001 and replaced with a competitive-based predisaster mitigation grant protocol. The Disaster Mitigation Act of 2000 further amended the Stafford Act by establishing additional mitigation plan requirements that called for coordination of disaster planning and implementation activities on state and local levels (Disaster Mitigation Act of 2000). This act specifically requires that localities implement a predisaster hazard mitigation plan in order to be eligible for federal disaster mitigation funding under the provisions of the Stafford Act. The mitigation plan must include measures to reduce human health impacts in a disaster.

Additionally, in 2000, the U.S. Congress recognized the increasing role of the Department of Health and Human Services in responding to the behavioral health needs that arise as the result of both natural and human-caused emergencies and disasters by establishing Section 3102 of the Children's Health Act of 2000. This legislation amended the Public Health Services Act to allow for "emergency response" and establish mental health and substance abuse emergency response criteria. This expanded the grant assistance authority of the Substance Abuse and Mental Health Services Administration beyond the established crisis-counseling services authorized by the Stafford Act for individual and household assistance in federally declared major disasters.

Congress recognized the need to expand emergency services to include both mental health and substance abuse concerns, whether or not a presidential disaster is declared under the above authority. To help address these needs the Secretary of the U.S. Department of Health and Human Services (HHS), through SAMHSA, was given the mandate to develop a new emergency grant program subsection entitled "Emergency Response" (Federal Register 2001). This "Emergency Response" provision is included in section 3102 of the Children's Health Act of 2000 and authorizes the Secretary of HHS to use up to 2.5 percent of the funds appropriated for discretionary grants for responding to emergencies.

FEMA was abolished as an independent agency in 2003 and became part of the cabinet-level Department of Homeland Security. The U.S. General Accounting Office (GAO) acknowledged the management challenges that faced FEMA in 2003 as it merged with the Department of Homeland Security. The 2003 GAO report emphasized that FEMA must "ensure effective coordination of preparedness and response efforts, enhance the provision and management of disaster assistance for efficient and effective response, reduce the impact of natural hazards by improving the efficiency of mitigation and flood programs, and resolve financial weaknesses to ensure fiscal accountability" (U.S. GAO 2003). The goal was to provide a more comprehensive approach, including mitigation, while providing control over costs.

The Stafford Act was amended by the Post Katrina Emergency Management Reform Act (PKEMRA) of 2006, which was formulated in an attempt to improve the organization and coordination of intergovernmental and nongovernmental operations in order to provide a focus on long-term recovery in disaster scenarios. Prior to the Post Katrina Emergency Management Reform Act of 2006, the emphasis on recovery under the Stafford Act was on the repair of damaged buildings and infrastructure, debris removal, temporary housing and limited home repairs, and revenue loss loans (Bea 2005). The enactment of PKEMRA authorizes the lead federal official in presidential disaster declared areas "to activate a team of federal long-term recovery experts to offer technical assistance to States to support particularly challenged communities organize and plan for long-term recovery, as well as access coordinated Federal, State, non-governmental and private sector recovery resources" (Department of Homeland Security 2009). Section 219 of PKEMRA amends the Stafford Act as follows:

> [T]o expand the authorization for professional counseling services to victims of major disasters to include substance abuse and mental health counseling. Requires federal agencies providing mental health or substance abuse services, in coordination with state and local officials, to: (1) survey mental health or substance abuse services available to individuals affected by, and emergency responders to, major disasters; and (2) develop a strategy for the adequate provision of such services. (The Library of Congress 2006)

Additionally, in 2006, the president signed into law the Pandemic and All-Hazards Preparedness Act, which amended the Public Health Service Act by creating an Assistant Secretary for Preparedness and Response (ASPR) in the Department of Health and Human Services to focus on preparedness, planning and response, and to strengthen the capabilities of health systems in disasters. This act also established the National Health Security Strategy. The purpose of the Pandemic and All-Hazards Preparedness Act is "to improve the Nation's public health and medical preparedness and response capabilities for emergencies, whether deliberate, accidental, or natural" (Public Health Emergency 2010). This law has been integral in the distribution of hospital preparedness grants that are utilized to improve local capacity to handle hospital surge and the resultant psychological trauma associated with mass casualty events.

3.4   THE CRISIS COUNSELING ASSISTANCE AND TRAINING PROGRAM

The Crisis Counseling Assistance and Training Program (CCP) is the primary mechanism for the federal government to authorize the delivery of behavioral health services to disaster-affected communities and individuals. FEMA implements the CCP under the authority of Section 416 of the Stafford Act, which authorizes FEMA to "fund mental health assistance and training activities in areas which have been presidentially declared a disaster" (FEMA 2010). The mission of the CCP is "to assist individuals and communities in recovering from the challenging effects of natural and human-caused disasters through the provision of community-based outreach and psychoeducational services" (Substance Abuse and Mental Health Services Administration 2009). The CCP operates under the oversight of the SAMHSA, Center for Mental Health Services (CMHS), Emergency Mental Health and Traumatic Stress Services Branch, and this program provides funding for a variety of behavioral health services, including (Substance Abuse and Mental Health Services Administration 2009):

- Individual crisis counseling
- Basic supportive or educational contact
- Group crisis counseling
- Public education
- Community networking and support
- Assessment, referral, and resource linkage
- Development and distribution of educational materials
- Media and public service announcements

There are two separate programs in the CCP. The Immediate Services Program (ISP) provides funding for urgent crisis counseling services immediately after a disaster event; this program may be authorized for two months after the date of the disaster declaration date with possible extensions for pending Regular Service Program (RSP) requests. The RSP typically funds services up to nine months from the date of award notice (Department of Homeland Security 2008a). The Department of Homeland Security (2008a, 5) states the following:

> The scope of the Crisis Counseling Program is immediate, short-term, incident-specific, intervention-style crisis counseling services and support for emotional recovery to individuals adversely affected by major disasters. The Crisis Counseling Program is intended to supplement state and local mental health resources, both public and private, for the specific incident-related need, and is not meant to replace or fund existing services. Individuals identified as having needs that fall outside the scope and duration of the Crisis Counseling Program are referred to other agencies that provide mental health treatment or other appropriate types of assistance on a permanent, long-term, and regular basis.

FEMA's Disaster Financial Status Report (2008; provided by Rick Sylves) for the time period from the initiation of the Stafford Act in 1989 thru 2007 indicates that the federal government has distributed $145,230,684 for the ISP and $399,236,419 for the RSP (see Table 3.1). This federal funding distribution included 280 presidential declarations for the ISP and 152 presidential

TABLE 3.1

Disaster Financial Status Report, Crisis Counseling Program 1989–2007

Year	Immediate Services Program ($)	Regular Services Program ($)
1989	1,874,578	7,159,814
1990	2,163,331	3,222,685
1991	393,551	1,276,819
1992	10,784,866	28,632,679
1993	5,956,653	12,393,280
1994	13,931,603	23,833,582
1995	2,709,414	5,994,511
1996	4,397,031	6,496,234
1997	3,186,775	7,037,365
1998	5,605,781	8,702,279
1999	4,190,206	8,340,789
2000	797,923	1,425,700
2001	31,945,455	134,338,548
2002	3,715,789	6,261,645
2003	3,390,258	5,342,331
2004	8,935,918	19,338,242
2005	35,580,491	101,765,320
2006	3,336,056	11,047,189
2007	2,335,005	6,627,407
Totals:	**145,230,684**	**399,236,419**

Source: Adapted from Federal Emergency Management Agency, *DFSR Obligations Summary*, 2008. Courtesy of Rick Sylves.

disaster declarations for the RSP. Approximately 47 percent of all presidential disaster declarations for the Individual and Household Assistance Program received funding for ISP services, and approximately 25 percent of all presidential disaster declarations for the Individual and Household Assistance Program received funding for RSP services. Data pertaining to denials of requests for CCP funding are not available.

3.5 STATE AND LOCAL GOVERNMENTAL BEHAVIORAL HEALTH RESPONSE TO DISASTERS

Whereas the federal government has the capacity to define an emergency management structure and competencies, and distribute disaster information and funding nationally, state government must manage and distribute federal and state assets, and coordinate mutual aid and assistance, across local jurisdictions to lessen the impacts of disasters to the greatest extent possible (Donahue and Joyce 2001, 732; Butcher and Hatcher 1988). Consequently, effective disaster relief to local communities depends on the competence and intentions of the state agencies charged with leading the response (Donahue and Joyce 2001). State emergency management agencies generally mirror the federal government in organization and terminology. Despite the lawful authority to provide relief and coordinate disaster activities across local jurisdictions, state emergency management agencies vary widely in funding levels and influence over local governments in the counties and municipalities (Butcher and Hatcher 1988).

At the local level, county and municipal governments are responsible for protecting individuals and communities and are most capable of assessing needs and tailoring services for their disaster-affected communities (Donahue and Joyce 2001). Inadequate funding, however, may prompt some local leaders to rely heavily on the state for disaster relief as they focus on correcting more immediate problems or invest in revenue-generating projects instead of disaster mitigation and preparedness activities (Donahue and Joyce 2001; Bourque et al. 2006).

With few historical exceptions, the federal government has had a limited role in formulating mental health policy. Other than disaster preparedness and relief, the federal government assists state governments by providing block grant funding for mental health services and reimbursement for services rendered through Medicaid or Medicare (Mechanic and Surles 1992). Instead, mental health policy has primarily been the purview of state government, which must provide for the medical, behavioral health, and social welfare of individuals with severe mental illness (SMI; Mechanic and Surles 1992; Mazade and Glover 2007).

The State Mental Health Authority (SMHA; 42 U.S.C. § 201) is typically tasked with providing disaster behavioral health services as part of the state government's overall response to disaster. Providing behavioral health services for disaster survivors is quite challenging since state behavioral health systems are often complex, consisting of a host of local or regional governmental units, social services and community-based organizations, as well as partnerships with consumer organizations, school systems, and other groups (Elrod, Hamblen, and Norris 2006; Mechanic and Surles 1992). Emergency management frameworks imposed by federal mandates both help and hinder these systems that have preestablished responsibilities, and vary in their ability to provide disaster behavioral health services (Elrod, Hamblen, and Norris 2006). State cost-saving efforts have resulted in managed care options and privatization of some state facilities, while an increased emphasis on community-based care has also led SMHAs to contract with local agencies to provide services. Such decentralization has caused the SMHA's role to change from being the direct authority over consumer services to being the quality assurance monitor and standards and rate setter for behavioral health services delivery (Mechanic and Surles 1992; Mazade and Glover 2007). When the pools of community providers with the capacity to provide quality services are limited, or, conversely, when the state contracts with so many providers those services become overly fragmented, these systems of care may lose their ability to provide consumers with appropriate care (Mechanic and Surles 1992). Additionally, numerous contracted providers may cause uncertainty about the roles and responsibilities of the SMHA and its partners in disaster (Mechanic and Surles 1992).

From the local perspective, it may be difficult to discern which agency is in charge of the response efforts since there are few protocols for establishing a lead agency (Gard and Ruzek 2006). Moreover, federal and state guidelines compelling collaboration between community organizations and the SMHA in disaster response are lacking (Person and Fuller 2007). As a result, disputes and miscommunication between agencies can occur. In the words of one state agency director, reported by Elrod and colleagues (2006), "If someone could develop a course in how to get people to play well in the sandbox, that would have been good training" (164). Therefore, SMHAs must put forth a concerted effort to establish clear communications and partnerships with other agencies, resolve territorial disputes, and develop effective funding mechanisms to ensure seamless services delivery (Elrod, Hamblen, and Norris 2006).

In the immediate postdisaster context, however, the SMHA may be faced with competing demands to maintain routine services for consumers, ensure community safety, and apply for federal funding for provision of disaster behavioral health services such as those authorized by the CCP (Elrod, Hamblen, and Norris 2006). Funded services must be quickly incorporated into preestablished community systems of care, and culturally relevant training must be provided to disaster responders (Elrod, Hamblen, and Norris 2006). Given that SMHAs generally have an aging, largely Caucasian workforce and have found it difficult to attract younger, more diverse and multilingual workers, the need for cultural competence training is accentuated (Mazade and Glover 2007). Furthermore, private sector competition and generally low state salaries have made it difficult for many SMHAs to recruit and retain qualified staff for routine operations (Mazade and Glover 2007). Consequently, finding experienced behavioral health responders can be difficult, especially for communities with little prior experience responding to disasters. SMHAs are limited, however, in their ability to hire additional staff or purchase extra assets needed for disaster response, or to petition legislators directly for emergency dispensations (Mechanic and Surles 1992). This makes federal-funding mechanisms authorized by the Stafford Act all the more appealing, albeit receipt and distribution of such funds is not without certain inherent challenges (Elrod, Hamblen, and Norris 2006).

Without intervention, the distress from disasters can cause some survivors to develop serious psychological disorders that would require long-term treatment from an already-overburdened behavioral health system. However, the ubiquitous stigma regarding the acceptability of behavioral health services and, frequently, distrust of external resources, are significant deterrents to seeking out or accepting behavioral health services (Elrod, Hamblen, and Norris 2006). Even if they are willing to seek assistance for disaster-related distress, survivors are more likely to ask for help from their primary care physicians, clergy or traditional healers, school personnel, social services agencies, or other nonbehavioral health specialists (Siegel, Laska, and Meisner 2004; Elrod, Hamblen, and Norris 2006).

Despite these impediments, state behavioral health agencies must respond swiftly and efficiently to provide aid to impacted communities lest survivors assume an attitude of helplessness or blame the government for failure to respond appropriately (Bourque et al. 2006). Additionally, these systems are responsible for reestablishing general services for their consumers, especially for individuals with SMI who may need shelter and help securing psychotropic medications to control their conditions (Person and Fuller 2007; Gard and Ruzek 2006). As Person and Fuller (2007) aptly expressed, "Hurricane Katrina has challenged the perception that after a disaster, regional mental health services are capable of easily returning to the pre-existing level of services provided for people with SMI" (244). Catastrophic disasters such as Hurricane Katrina or 9/11 highlight that state behavioral health systems require additional resources to provide an adequate level of care and relief aid (Person and Fuller 2007; Siegel, Wanderling, and Laska 2004). Even if the SMHA receives CCP funding, federal guidelines limit how CCP funding may be used to provide services for individuals with SMI (Person and Fuller 2007). Furthermore, with an uneven distribution of funding and services operating at maximum capacity, state mental health systems struggle just trying to meet the routine needs of individuals with cognitive, behavioral, or emotional disorders (Person and Fuller 2007; Siegel, Wanderling and Laska 2004).

Thus, state behavioral health systems must be innovative in their approaches to estimating the psychological needs of current consumers and disaster survivors who may have never previously accessed behavioral health services. It is critical to identify at-risk populations within jurisdictions and to develop comprehensive plans for providing disaster relief. In particular, plans should address how to care for individuals with psychiatric disabilities and include plans for maintaining prior treatment and providing crisis intervention for illness exacerbation, sheltering, and medication management (Gard and Ruzek 2006; Person and Fuller 2007). Some state behavioral health systems might benefit from constitutional modifications to solidify their roles and responsibilities vis-à-vis local jurisdictions and other disaster response partner agencies (Mechanic and Surles 1992). Lastly, the federal government should reevaluate limitations imposed on federal crisis program funding for services for individuals with psychiatric disabilities who experience disaster (Person and Fuller 2007).

3.6 CONCLUSION

In 2007, Homeland Security Presidential Directive-21 was issued by President George W. Bush to "plan and enable provision for the public health and medical needs of the American people in the case of a catastrophic health event through continual and timely flow of information during such an event and rapid public health and medical response that marshals all available national capabilities and capacities in a rapid and coordinated manner" (Homeland Security Presidential Directive-21 2007). This directive acknowledged the obligation of the federal government to "enhance our capability to protect the physical and mental health of survivors" and called for the establishment of a Federal Advisory Committee for Disaster Mental Health to proffer recommendations for "protecting, preserving, and restoring individual and community mental health in catastrophic health event settings, including pre-event, intra-event, and post-event education, messaging, and interventions."

The Disaster Mental Health (DMH) Subcommittee of the National Biodefense Science Board was established as the Federal Advisory Committee for Disaster Mental Health under the aforementioned presidential directive. The DMH Subcommittee, in its most recent 2010 report, states that "the most pressing and significant problem that hinders integration of disaster mental and behavioral health is the lack of appropriate policy at the highest Federal level. Compounding that problem is the lack of any clear statement as to where the authority to devise, formulate, and implement such policy should reside" (Disaster Mental Health Subcommittee 2010). Concurrently, the 2010 Report to the President and Congress from the National Commission on Children and Disasters recommends the following:

- The president should accelerate the development and implementation of the National Disaster Recovery Framework with an explicit emphasis on addressing the immediate and long-term physical and mental health, educational, housing, and human services recovery needs of children.
- HHS should lead efforts to integrate mental and behavioral health for children into public health, medical, and other relevant disaster management activities.
- HHS should enhance the research agenda for children's disaster mental and behavioral health, including psychological first aid, cognitive-behavioral interventions, social support interventions, bereavement counseling and support, and programs intended to enhance children's resilience in the aftermath of a disaster.
- Federal agencies and nonfederal partners should enhance predisaster preparedness and just-in-time training in pediatric disaster mental and behavioral health—including psychological first aid, bereavement support, and brief supportive interventions—for mental health professionals and individuals, such as teachers, who work with children.
- DHS/FEMA and SAMHSA should strengthen the Crisis Counseling Assistance and Training Program (CCP) to better meet the mental health needs of children and families.

It is evident from the opinions of the DMH and the National Commission on Children and Disasters that the multiple layers of existing local, state, and federal initiatives that were designed to provide for the behavioral health needs of disaster survivors have yet to be woven into a "patchwork quilt" (Thomas and Bowen 2008) of cogent and effective disaster policy. However, as stated by the Disaster Mental Health Subcommittee (2010), "the urgent issue of high quality integrated disaster mental health and behavioral health leadership, policy, and structure" can be brought to greater attention within the federal government and the country in an effort to establish and operationalize protocols that will protect the psychological well-being of individuals affected by disasters.

REFERENCES

American Red Cross. 2010. *The federal charter of the American Red Cross*. http://www.redcross.org/museum/history/charter.asp.
Bazan, E. B. 2005. Robert T. Stafford Disaster Relief and Emergency Assistance Act: Legal Requirements for Federal and State Roles in Declarations of an Emergency or a Major Disaster. CRS Report for Congress. Congressional Research Service. Order Code RL 33090.

Bea, K. 2005. Federal Stafford Act Disaster Assistance: Presidential Declarations, Eligible Activities, and Funding. CRS Report for Congress. Congressional Research Service. Order Code RL 33053.

Bea, K. 2006. Update-Federal Stafford Act Disaster Assistance: Presidential Declarations, Eligible Activities, and Funding. CRS Report for Congress. Congressional Research Service. Order Code RL 33053.

Beers, C. W. 1913. *A Mind That Found Itself: An Autobiography,* 3rd ed. New York: Longmans, Green & Co.

Bourque, L. B., J. M. Siegel, M. Kano, and M. M. Wood. 2006. Weathering the storm: The impact of hurricanes on physical and mental health. *Annals of the American Academy of Political and Social Science 604*: 129–151.

Butcher, J. N., and C. Hatcher. 1988. The neglected entity in air disaster planning. *American Psychologist 43*(9): 724–729. http://www1.umn.edu/mmpi/Reprints/The%20neglected%20entity%20in%20air%20 disaster%20planning-%20Psychological%20services.html.

Department of Health and Human Services. 2005. *Public health service.* http://www.hhs.gov/about/opdivs/ phs.html.

Department of Homeland Security. 2003. *A citizen's guide to disaster assistance.* Federal Emergency Management Agency. http://training.fema.gov/emiweb/downloads/IS7complete.pdf.

Department of Homeland Security. 2007. *National preparedness guidelines.* http://www.dhs.gov/xlibrary/ assets/National_Preparedness_Guidelines.pdf.

Department of Homeland Security. 2008a. *FEMA's Crisis Counseling Assistance and Training Program; State of Florida's Project H.O.P.E.* http://www.dhs.gov/xoig/assets/mgmtrpts/OIG_08-96_Sep08.pdf.

Department of Homeland Security. 2008b. *National response framework.* http://www.fema.gov/pdf/emer- gency/nrf/nrf-core.pdf.

Department of Homeland Security. 2009. *The road to recovery 2008.* http://www.fema.gov/pdf/rebuild/ ltrc/2008_report.pdf.

Disaster Mental Health Subcommittee. 2010. *Integrating behavioral health in federal disaster preparedness, response, and recovery: Assessment and recommendations.* http://www.phe.gov/Preparedness/legal/ boards/nbsb/meetings/Documents/dmhreport.pdf.

Disaster Mitigation Act, Pub. L. No. 106-390 (2000).

Donahue, A. K., and P. G. Joyce. 2001. A framework for analyzing emergency management with an application to federal budgeting. *Public Administration Review 61*(6): 728–740.

Downton, M. W., and R. A. Pielke. 2001. Discretion without accountability: Politics, flood damage, and cli- mate. *Natural Hazards Review 2*(4): 157–166.

Dreyer, B. A. 1976. Adolf Meyer and mental hygiene: An ideal for public health. *American Journal of Public Health 66*(10): 998–1003.

Elrod, C. L., J. L. Hamblen, and F. H. Norris. 2006. Challenges in implementing disaster mental health pro- grams: State program directors' perspectives. *Annals of the American Academy of Political and Social Science 604*: 152–170.

Federal Emergency Management Agency. 2008. *DFSR obligations summary.* Provided by Rick Sylves, PhD.

Federal Emergency Management Agency. 2010. *Crisis counseling assistance and training program.* http:// www.fema.gov/pdf/media/factsheets/2009/dad_crisis_counseling.pdf.

Federal Register. 2001. *Substance Abuse and Mental Health Services Administration: Mental health and sub- stance abuse emergency response criteria.* Volume 66, Number 197. FR Doc No: 01-25451. http://www. gpo.gov/fdsys/pkg/FR-2001-10-11/html/01-25451.htm.

Federal Register. 2010a. *Notice of adjustment of statewide per capita threshold for recommending a cost share adjustment.* FR Doc. 20101757. http://www.thefederalregister.com/d.p/2010-01-28-2010-1757.

Federal Register. 2010b. *Notice of adjustment of statewide per capita indicator.* FR Doc. 2010-25334. http:// edocket.access.gpo.gov/2010/2010-25334.htm.

Federal Register. 2010c. *Notice of adjustment of countywide per capita indicator.* FR Doc. 2010-25332. http:// edocket.access.gpo.gov/2010/2010-25332.htm.

Friedman, M. B. 2002. The Clifford Beers story: The origins of modern mental health policy. *Mental Health News.* http://www.mha-nyc.org/media/983/cliffordbeersstory12_2008.pdf.

Gard, B. A., and J. I. Ruzek. 2006. Community mental health response to crisis. *Journal of Clinical Psychology 62*:1029–1041.

Garrett, T. A., and R. S. Sobel. 2003. The political economy of FEMA disaster payments. *Economic Inquiry. 41*(3): 496–509.

Grob, G. N. 1994. *The Mad among Us: A History of the Care of America's Mentally Ill.* New York: Simon & Schuster Inc.

Herman, E. 1995. *The Romance of American Psychology: Political Culture in the Age of Experts.* Berkeley: University of California Press.

Homeland Security Presidential Directive-21: Public health and medical preparedness. 2007. http://www.dhs. gov/xabout/laws/gc_1219263961449.shtm#1.

Jacobs, G. A. 1995. The development of a national plan for disaster mental health. *Professional Psychology: Research and Practice 26*(6): 543–549.

The Library of Congress. 2006. *Post-Katrina Emergency Management Reform Act of 2006.* http://thomas.loc. gov/cgi-bin/bdquery/z?d109:SN03721:@@@D&summ2=m&.

Logue, J. N., H. Hansen, and E. Streuning. 1979. Emotional and physical distress following Hurricane Agnes in Wyoming Valley of Pennsylvania. *Public Health Reports 94*(6): 495–502.

Mazade, N. A., and R. W. Glover. 2007. State mental health policy: Critical priorities confronting state mental health agencies. *Psychiatric Services 58*: 1148–1150. http://www.psychservices.psychiatryonline.org/ cgi/content/full/58/9/1148.

McCarthy, F. X. 2009. *FEMA's disaster declaration process: A primer.* Congressional Research Service. RL34146. http://www.crs.gov.

Mechanic, D., and R. C. Surles. 1992. Challenges in state mental health policy and administration. *Health Affairs 11*(3): 34–50.

Morgan, J. 1995. American Red Cross disaster mental health services: Implementation and recent developments. *Journal of Mental Health Counseling 17*(3): 291–300.

Morris, C. 1906. *The San Francisco Calamity by Earthquake and Fire.* Philadelphia: The John C. Winston Co.

National Commission on Children and Disasters. 2010. 2010 Report to the President and Congress. http:// archive.ahrq.gov/prep/nccdreport/nccdreport.pdf.

National Institute of Mental Health. 2010. *The National Institute of Mental Health strategic plan.* http://www. nimh.nih.gov/about/strategic-planning-reports/index.shtml.

Office of the Assistant Secretary for Preparedness and Response. 2008. *Summary of HHS disaster behavioral health assets and capabilities.* http://www.phe.gov/Preparedness/planning/abc/Documents/sum-hhs-disasterbehavioralhealth.pdf.

Okura, K. P. 1975. Mobilizing in response to a major disaster. *Community Mental Health Journal 11*(2): 136–143.

Oregon State University. 2004. *Federal Disaster Assistance Program.* http://extension.oregonstate.edu/catalog/ pdf/em/em8871-e.pdf.

Person, C., and E. J. Fuller. 2007. Disaster care for persons with psychiatric disabilities. *Journal of Disability Policy Studies 17*(4): 238–248.

Platt, R. 1999. *Disasters and Democracy—The Politics of Extreme Natural Events.* Washington, DC: Island Press.

Public Health Emergency. 2010. *Pandemic and All Hazards Preparedness Act.* http://www.phe.gov/pre paredness/legal/pahpa/pages/default.aspx.

Rubin, C. B. 2007. *Emergency Management: The American Experience 1900–2005.* Fairfax, VA: Public Entity Risk Institute.

Salkowe, R., and J. Chakraborty. 2009. Federal disaster relief in the U.S.: The role of political partisanship and preference in presidential disaster declarations and turndowns. *Journal of Homeland Security and Emergency Management 6*(1): Article 28: 1–21.

Salvation Army. 2009. *The Salvation Army disaster response history.* http://www.salvationarmyusa.org/usn/ www_usn_2.nsf/vw-text-dynamic-arrays/190F4B74F5ED5E81852574B70000119F?openDocument.

Siegel, C. E., E. Laska, and M. Meisner. 2004. Estimating capacity requirements for mental health services after a disaster has occurred: A call for new data. *American Journal of Public Health 94*(4): 582–585.

Siegel, C., J. Wanderling, and E. Laska. 2004. Coping with disasters: Estimation of additional capacity of the mental health sector to meet extended service demands. *Journal of Mental Health Policy and Economics 7*(1): 29–35.

Simpich, F. 1927. The great Mississippi flood of 1927. *National Geographic Magazine 52*(3): 243–289.

Substance Abuse and Mental Health Services Administration. 2009. *Crisis Counseling Assistance and Training Program.* http://store.samhsa.gov/shin/content//SMA09-4373/SMA09-4373.pdf.

Sylves, R. T. 1998. *Disasters and coastal states: A Policy analysis of presidential declarations of disaster 1953–1957.* DEL-SG-17-98. Newark, DE: University of Delaware, Sea Grant College Program.

Sylves, R., and W. R. Cumming. 2004. FEMA's Path to Homeland Security: 1979–2003. *Journal of Homeland Security and Emergency Management 1*(2): Article 11: 1–23.

Sylves, R. T., and W. L. Waugh. 1996. *Disaster Management in the U.S. and Canada: The Politics, Policymaking, Administration and Analysis of Emergency Management.* Springfield, IL: Charles C. Thomas Publisher Ltd.

Thomas, E. A., and S. K. Bowen. 2008. *Post-disaster reconstruction: The patchwork quilt—A creative strategy for safe and long-term post-disaster rebuilding*. National Floodproofing Conference IV, New Orleans, Louisiana.

U.S. Department of the Army. 1972. *Wyoming Valley Flood Control, Susquehanna River, Pennsylvania*. Baltimore: Corps of Engineers.

U.S. Department of Health and Human Services. 2009. *National health security strategy*. http://www.phe.gov/Preparedness/planning/authority/nhss/strategy/Documents/nhss-final.pdf.

U.S. General Accounting Office (GAO). 2001. *Report to the Subcommittee on VA, HUD, and Independent Agencies, Committee on Appropriations, U.S. Senate-Disaster Assistance: Improvement Needed in Disaster Declaration Criteria and Eligibility Assurance Criteria*. GAO-01-837. Washington, DC: United States General Accounting Office.

U.S. General Accounting Office. 2003. *Major Management Problems and Program Risks: Federal Emergency Management Agency, Performance and Accountability Series*. GAO-03-113. Washington, DC: United States General Accounting Office.

Wachtendorf, T., R. Connell, and K. Tierney. 2002. *Disaster Resistant Communities Initiative: Assessment of the pilot phase—Year 3 pilot communities report—Project # EMW-97-CA-0519*. Report to the Federal Emergency Management Agency. Newark, DE: Disaster Research Center.

Weaver, J. D., R. L. Dingman, J. Morgan, B. A. Morgan, and C. S. North. 2000. The American Red Cross disaster mental health services: Development of a cooperative, single function, multidisciplinary service model. *Journal of Behavioral Health Services & Research 27*(3): 314–320.

4 Nongovernmental Organizations Responding to Disasters in the United States

Angela M. Eikenberry and Tracy Cooper

CONTENTS

4.1 INTRODUCTION

In the last decade, disasters have occurred with increasing frequency, magnitude, destructiveness, and cost in the United States and around the world, highlighting the need for adequate preparation to respond immediately and effectively to disasters (Brough 2002). The overall goals of disaster relief are "to reduce physical, social, and economic vulnerability and to facilitate the effective provision of short-term emergency assistance and longer-term recovery aid" (Tierney, Lindell, and Perry 2001, 256). To achieve these goals, an overwhelming number of participants is often needed during disaster relief efforts: government agencies, coordinating agencies, transportation agents, freight forwarders, health personnel, donors, media, nongovernmental organizations (NGOs), and volunteers. NGOs have always played an important role in disaster relief in the United States and throughout the world; however, this role seems to have grown substantially in recent years (Coppola 2007, 390; Lewis and Opoku-Mensah 2006, 668; Özerdem and Jacoby 2006). In the United States, in particular, it appears that government has come to rely on NGOs to implement many of its programs and projects, including disaster relief efforts (Salamon 2003).

Although NGOs are diverse, they do share several characteristics. They are "voluntary in the sense that they are created, maintained, and terminated based on voluntary decision and initiative by members or a board" (Hudson and Bielefeld 1997, 32). In addition, they are typically not part of the governmental apparatus and do not distribute profits to board members or to any other stakeholders. NGOs usually are focused on addressing some community need, hence, serving a particular public good. NGOs are typically referred to as nonprofit organizations in the United States. As legal entities, nonprofit tax-exempt organizations conduct work related to the arts, education, health care, and social welfare. They are known for their independence and for being "highly practice-oriented" (Coppola 2007, 389).

It is important for behavioral health practitioners and survivors of emergencies and catastrophic events to understand how NGOs normally respond in a disaster and to have realistic expectations about the benefits and challenges of working with NGOs during these daunting situations. The focus of this chapter is to provide an overview of key types of NGOs that respond to disasters and their functions during response efforts, challenges of this response, and suggestions for improving NGO disaster response in the future. To illustrate this overview, we highlight the NGO response to Hurricane Katrina because the magnitude and wide media coverage of this disaster vividly brought to light the role of NGOs in disaster response. NGOs have almost always played a role in responding to disasters in the United States, but concentrated efforts to understand this role have largely emerged only in the decade following September 11, 2001, and after the Hurricane Katrina disaster in August 2005 (Benson, Twigg, and Meyers 2001, 200; Kapucu 2006, 206). In particular, the NGO response to Katrina took on an entirely new level of magnitude compared to 9/11 and led to an outpouring of commentary and research on NGO roles in disaster relief that we draw on to illustrate our discussion.

Many types of NGOs will and do respond to disasters in the United States, but they are often not very well coordinated and comprehensive in their response, in part because they are independent by nature and because government agencies have not fully integrated NGOs into disaster planning. Disaster preparedness planners and frontline responders may be able to help lay the groundwork for better NGO disaster response in the future.

4.2 TYPES AND FUNCTIONS OF NGOs RESPONDING TO DISASTERS

In the United States, there are five main actor groups comprising the disaster response and relief structure: (1) the Federal Emergency Management Agency (FEMA); (2) state government agencies; (3) first responders or local emergency service providers; (4) the media; and (5) NGOs that include the American Red Cross (ARC), The Salvation Army, and other key national nonprofit organization responders, local and faith-based organizations, International NGOs (INGOs), and NGO networks, such as the National Voluntary Organizations Active in Disaster (NVOAD).

FEMA is mainly a facilitating agency, coordinating "relief and assistance activities of federal, state and local governments, the ARC and The Salvation Army, as well as other voluntary relief organizations that agree to operate under FEMA's direction" (Kapucu 2006, 215). Its mission is to support first responders and citizens with all phases of disasters—preparedness, response and relief, recovery and rehabilitation, and mitigation—and is charged with helping others strengthen their disaster management capabilities. Within the National Response Framework (NRF),[a] FEMA is assigned to Emergency Support Function (ESF) 6, which handles "mass care" (emergency first aid, shelter, food, and other relief items) and long-term housing and needed human services. FEMA typically relies on the ARC and other NGOs to aid in this effort (see Section 4.2.1).

Under the Stafford Act, it is standard procedure for state governors to request assistance from FEMA before the federal agency will enter the state.[b] The U.S. Constitution "implicitly assigns health and safety to the states rather than to the national government through the Tenth Amendment, which provides that all powers not specifically assigned to the national government are reserved to the states" (Col 2007, 115). State governments are responsible for preparing for disaster situations and coordinating state resources when local governments request the state's assistance in disaster response and relief efforts.

First responders are individuals in the affected area who often work for local government. Prime local emergency services include police, fire and rescue, ambulance, and civil protection. First responders are typically responsible for evacuation, search and rescue, the security of affected areas, and casualty handling. These activities usually take place in the core perimeter where the most destruction has occurred. Local emergency crews work at the operational level and engage in the day-to-day activities needed to cope with any damages.

The media provide coverage of major disasters. Generally, the media are expected to provide necessary alert notices and warnings to the general public to help ensure safety, as well as relay the actions of the major relief organizations responding to a disaster. Often, however, "the *scope* and *intensity* of a situation are the criteria that determine [a disaster's] newsworthiness" (Hartsough and Mileti 1985, 284). As a result, media can be highly influential in determining how important a disaster is perceived by politicians, organizations, donors, and the general public. Thus, the media can have an impact on public awareness and the operations of first responders and relief organizations during disaster situations.

Finally, NGOs figure prominently in offering survivor support to relieve suffering in the aftermath of disasters, and more recently in helping to prevent disasters through developmental programs (Ahmed and Potter 2006, 40; Salamon 2003, 245; Smillie 1995, 39). NGO disaster relief often includes providing shelter, food and first aid, as well as other physical and emotional support. It is difficult to provide, with accuracy, the number of NGOs working in disaster relief in the United States. To give some idea of the numbers, as of 2008, there were 445 organizations reporting under the U.S. Internal Revenue Service's National Taxonomy of Exempt Entities – Core Code M20 (Disaster Preparedness and Relief Services; National Center for Charitable Statistics nd). However, many other NGOs, such as local faith-based organizations or human service agencies, also provide assistance when disasters occur. Testimony by the U.S. Government Accountability Office (GAO) and the final report of the U.S. House Select Bipartisan Committee to Investigate the Preparation for and Response to Katrina recognized the widespread provision of NGO assistance in response to Katrina (Fagnoni 2006; U.S. House 2006). It is estimated that a total of \$3.3 billion in private donations was raised for this response. The ARC garnered most of this (\$2.1 billion), while Mercy Corps and World Vision received \$10 million and nearly \$11 million, respectively (Kerkman 2006). NGOs have and will continue to respond to disasters, especially when disaster relief is their mission.

4.2.1 KEY NGO ACTORS

There are several key actors or types of NGOs that typically respond to disasters in the United States. On the broadest level, the ARC is engaged directly and extensively in disaster relief because of its Congressional Charter and mission. Other large, nationally focused NGOs, such as The Salvation Army, respond to disasters because of their missions. In addition, local faith-based and other NGOs often respond to disasters because of their location and intimate connection to the community. Since the response to Katrina, international NGOs have also become important actors in the U.S. disaster response arena. Finally, many NGOs have banded together at the national, state, and local levels to share knowledge and resources throughout many of the disaster phases to help disaster survivors and their communities. One example is the National Voluntary Organizations Active in Disaster (NVOAD). Each of these NGO entities is discussed in more detail in the following section.

4.2.1.1 The American Red Cross and Other National Nonprofits

The ARC is required by its Congressional Charter (since 1900) to give relief to and serve as a medium for communication between members of the American armed forces and their families and to provide national and international disaster relief and mitigation.[c] It frequently engages in disaster relief activities, such as providing feeding stations, shelter, first aid kits, clothing, and emergency transportation. For example, as soon as news of Katrina was imminent, the ARC dispatched hundreds of its disaster teams and almost 200 emergency response vehicles to the region, erecting more than 3,500 shelters in 27 states for nearly 450,000 evacuees (American Red Cross nd). One county's local chapter of the ARC in North Central Texas, where many Katrina survivors were relocated, estimated that more than 28,000 people registered at shelters—they required more than 34,000 Disaster Health Services and more than 33,000 Disaster Mental Health Services contacts (Weeks 2007).

When necessary, the ARC makes referrals to governments and other agencies offering disaster assistance and engages in long-term recovery activities if needs cannot be met locally. For instance, the ARC led the effort, less than two months after Katrina hit, to create the Greater New Orleans Disaster Recovery Partnership (GNODRP), "a collaboration of more than 52 agencies from the interfaith, nonprofit and government sectors helping to meet the needs of residents living in the Greater New Orleans area and those who have been displaced" (American Red Cross nd, 12). GNODRP was formed to address long-term recovery needs. Since Katrina, the ARC has also worked with the U.S. Department of Homeland Security to create a national preparedness campaign, Be Red Cross Ready, which encourages the general public and organizations to take specific measures to prepare for any emergency. To be prepared itself, the ARC has tripled its warehouse space throughout the country and increased its supplies to help approximately 500,000 people when the need arises (American Red Cross nd).

The ARC, because of its Congressional Charter, has a special relationship with federal and state governments. Although a private organization, the ARC functions as a support agency during disasters to FEMA in ESF-6. In this position, designated ARC staff members are at the table with FEMA and state officials to offer their expertise on mass care activities, including "planning, preparedness, and response activities" (U.S. GAO 2008, 11). Before Katrina, the ARC was expected to play a more prominent role in coordinating disaster response; however, after Katrina, "DHS [Department of Homeland Security] and the Red Cross agreed that the mass care primary agency role in the NRF should be shifted from the Red Cross to FEMA in large part because the primary agency needs to be able to direct federal resources, which the Red Cross cannot do" (U.S. GAO 2008, 4). This means that FEMA oversees the actions of any NGOs that agree voluntarily to work under the umbrella of FEMA during disaster response.

Another important national service provider responding to disasters is The Salvation Army, which provides food, temporary shelter, clothing, medical assistance, counseling services, missing person services, and referrals to other agencies for special services during disaster relief efforts. The Salvation Army assisted Katrina survivors by organizing cleanup and restoration activities, offering social service and emotional support, and giving financial aid. The organization helped 2.5 million people and donated $382 million to Katrina-related areas (The Salvation Army nd). A few other nationally focused nonprofits typically active in disaster relief efforts include: Second Harvest Food Bank, which collects, transports, stores, and distributes food for other agencies that operate feeding stations; the American Radio Relay League, whose volunteer members provide communications to all levels of government; and Volunteers of America, which addresses critical needs of survivors, especially the disabled, frail elderly, and those previously homeless before disasters strike.

4.2.1.2 Faith-Based and Community Organizations

Faith-based and community organizations frequently provide immediate relief in a disaster because of their proximity to a disaster's core area; however, because they are typically locally based, they often do not have much experience responding to disasters. Examples of faith-based organizations (FBOs) include local churches, nationally affiliated denominations, and cooperative interfaith groups, many of which are established nonprofit organizations. FBOs have received more attention as social service providers in recent years in the United States with President George W. Bush's establishment of the White House Office of Faith-Based and Community Initiatives and the Centers for Faith-Based and Community Initiatives in five federal agencies by executive orders in 2001 (Chaves and Tsitsos 2001). The initiatives sought to strengthen faith-based and community organizations and expand their capacity to provide federally funded social services. President Obama has maintained this focus, changing the name to the Office of Faith-Based and Neighborhood Partnerships.

FBOs and other local community organizations played a significant role in the response to Katrina—perhaps the largest disaster response ever from these organizations (Fagnoni 2006; Homeland Security Institute 2006; Pipa 2006; U.S. House 2006; U.S. White House 2006). Thousands of FBOs and community organizations responded to the disaster, at times sheltering as many evacuees as the ARC (Pipa 2006). According to De Vita and Kramer (2008), most FBOs that they surveyed provided immediate relief services—such as food, water, clothing, and temporary shelter—rather than long-term recovery services—such as housing rehabilitation, mental health counseling, or job training. In addition, few had worked with state or local governments previously and none of the case study organizations that were analyzed had previously engaged in disaster response planning before Katrina. Connections to traditional response or human service systems were rare or nonexistent.

4.2.1.3 International NGOs

International NGOs (INGOs) operate across multiple countries or regions rather than operating in a single country. Oxfam, Save the Children, Amnesty International, and World Relief are well-known examples of INGOs (though they do not necessarily represent the vast majority of INGOs that are smaller in size, scope, and assets). In comparison to national or local nonprofit organizations, INGOs typically serve developing countries and regions, frequently conducting work in areas related to development, humanitarian assistance, and advocacy (Anheier 2005). It is estimated that INGOs dedicated to disaster relief and development have combined expenditures totaling more than $13 billion, which nearly equaled the official aid budget of the United States in 2003 (Anheier and Cho 2005, 1).

Even though INGO relief efforts are typically conducted in developing countries and territories, the destruction caused by Katrina led more than one dozen INGOs to provide significant humanitarian assistance and relief for the first time ever in the United States. INGOs responded to Katrina in many cases by disregarding their missions and/or organizational policies and mandates (Eikenberry, Arroyave, and Cooper 2007). That is, some of these INGOs responded even though they had organizational mandates in place stating that they only work outside the United States or that they do not respond to disasters because they focus on long-term health development. For example, International Relief and Development shifted its programs to include U.S. domestic emergencies due to Hurricane Katrina (Wilhelm 2005).

4.2.1.4 National Voluntary Organizations Active in Disaster

National Voluntary Organizations Active in Disaster (NVOAD) is an association of 49 member organizations that encourages the formation of and gives guidance to state and regional voluntary organizations active in disaster relief. It provides support to its member organizations by disseminating current disaster management information and offering training and leadership development opportunities. Its aim is to provide a neutral space for organizations to come together in order to bring about cooperation in disaster response. Additionally, NVOAD serves as a national voice for its members on appropriate disaster legislation. NVOAD members seek to provide more effective, less duplicative services by getting together before disasters strike; however, once disasters occur, NVOAD (or an affiliated state VOAD) encourages members and other voluntary agencies to convene on site. NVOAD also is officially designated by the government as a support organization in ESF-6 under the NRF; that is, during major incidents, National VOAD sends representatives to FEMA's National Response Coordination Center "to represent the voluntary organizations and assist in response coordination" (U.S. Department of Homeland Security 2008, 20).

During the aftermath of Katrina, NVOAD coordinated communication among its members; yet, NVOAD's main form of coordination—conference calls—proved to be ineffective (U.S. GAO 2008, 5). To rectify this communication issue, NVOAD is looking into Web-based technology to encourage information sharing after disasters strike. In connection with this issue, NVOAD is working with NGOs to assist FEMA in standardizing terminology and resources; FEMA and NVOAD officials believe "having organizations use the same language and resources makes it easier to scale up disaster response operations" (U.S. GAO 2008, 21). Additionally, as a national voice interested in improving disaster response, NVOAD recently drafted Disaster Recovery Case Management Standards to offer quality case management services to disaster survivors and "to encourage client empowerment in recovery planning, a crucial component of healing after a disaster" (NVOAD 2009).

4.2.2 NGO Contributions in Disaster Response

NGOs bring essential benefits during disaster response. Local NGOs and FBOs often work at the grassroots level and so have the potential for greater awareness of unique local situations creating vulnerability. They are most familiar with the needs and cultures of the community (Brinkerhoff 2002, 49; U.S. GAO 2007, 6). For example, strong community ties allowed many local organizations to provide critical services following Katrina, especially in areas that were not immediately reached by FEMA or the ARC (Adams 2008, 27; Homeland Security Institute 2006). These local NGOs and FBOs were fairly effective in their response although they were not included in much of the government predisaster planning and did not have experience in prior relief efforts. They sheltered tens of thousands of evacuees, prepared and served millions of meals, and provided a broad range of services: medical care, warehousing, physical reconstruction, and more. They provided these services not only for evacuees but also for relief workers and volunteers. By hosting those who came into a community to rebuild and restore, FBOs and NGOs enabled communities to heal and return to a more "normal" condition (Homeland Security Institute 2006, 5).

NGOs and FBOs were successful in their response to Katrina because they adapted and developed effective practices to deal with limitations and challenges (Homeland Security Institute 2006). Many of these organizations specialized in one or a few services and then partnered with others that provided complementary services to meet needs. An example was an arrangement in which one FBO served as a shelter, while a community NGO prepared meals and delivered them to the shelter (De Vita and Kramer 2008, 46). Preserving family unity was a key benefit of these practices: "Shelters that strove to preserve family unity found that this practice had beneficial ramifications in shelter operations, medical services, mental health and spiritual support, children's services, and care for those with special needs" (Homeland Security Institute 2006, 2).

Because many nationally and internationally focused NGOs, through their missions, are dedicated to provide relief to survivors when disasters occur, they have the speed and flexibility to arrive on the scene quickly; they generally do not have to obtain prior consent from a board of directors or go through several levels of authority to make important decisions (Brinkerhoff 2002, 49; Edwards 2004, 80; Kapucu 2006, 214–216; Smillie 1995, 119; Smillie and Minear 2004, 50). Additionally, these NGOs have "access, either directly or through networks, to unique resources and capabilities directly applicable to the types of services needed following a disaster" (Homeland Security Institute 2006, 2). In the case of the ARC, for instance, not only does it have national and international networks, but it also has direct access to information from FEMA. Many national and international disaster relief NGOs have also integrated disaster mitigation and preparation into their organizational programs. By improving a community's mitigation and preparation activities, community members should be better able to respond to and recover, physically and psychologically, from a disaster.

4.3 CHALLENGES OF NGO INVOLVEMENT IN DISASTER RELIEF

While NGOs contribute a great deal to disaster relief efforts, there are several challenges associated with NGO involvement in disaster relief operations in the United States. Discussed next are a few of those challenges. These include general lack of NGO involvement in disaster preparedness and planning, poor coordination and collaboration among NGOs and with other agencies during disaster response, and "voluntary failure."

4.3.1 LACK OF NGO INVOLVEMENT IN DISASTER PREPAREDNESS

An important phase of the disaster response cycle is preparedness or planning. Preparedness means collaborating on a larger scale in order to be ready for any potential disasters that could affect a particular location. It requires information gathering and dissemination and working with a variety of stakeholders to discuss different viewpoints, seeking solutions to challenges so complex that it requires a group effort (Canton 2007; Gray 1991). It also requires joining efforts with first-responder emergency services (such as fire departments, police, and ambulance services) and numerous other local organizations that would typically respond to a disaster (such as social service agencies, churches, and some businesses). According to Mileti (1999), "In the absence of prior interorganizational and community planning, each affected agency will tend to perform its disaster-related tasks in an autonomous, uncoordinated fashion" (223), which leads to less effective and efficient response when disasters occur.

Although NGOs are key actors in disaster response and relief activities, they often are not included in formal planning procedures regarding disaster management policies and activities, especially at the state and local levels. While "the domestic response architecture for a disaster does try to anticipate that the charitable sector will play a major role following a disaster" (Pipa 2006, 15), disaster response would probably be most effective if state and local governments made a more concerted effort to integrate NGOs into their disaster planning decisions and training. The ARC and NVOAD are active in planning and preparedness at the national level since both are official participants working alongside FEMA under the NRF; however, local NGOs and FBOs—organizations that are likely to know the community and have some useful connections—seldom have seats at the table when it comes to decisions made by government officials, particularly decisions regarding disaster management issues (Chandra and Acosta 2009; Cutter et al. 2006, 1; Tierney, Lindell, and Perry 2001, 257; U.S. White House 2006, 49; Waugh 2006). Additionally, local NGOs and FBOs are generally not included in exercises and training events that would make them more effective in a crisis and are rarely consulted on what resources, including information, would be most helpful to them.

One reason local NGOs and FBOs are seldom included in disaster preparedness is that communities and organizations generally do not engage to the extent necessary in prior planning regarding disaster management (Dynes 1978, 59; Mileti 1999, 223). Even those who should be concerned with disaster management issues—local planners, public works engineers, other local government officials—usually place disaster preparedness as a low priority. From their research, Berke and Campanella (2006) discovered that these officials are more focused on short-term rather than long-term, possibly unlikely, events: "The importance of preparing for a disaster in the distant future and risk-averse action is likely to be eclipsed by more immediate and pressing concerns (street potholes, waste disposal, and crime) that affect people almost daily" (195).

Another possible reason that these NGOs are not invited to participate in planning is that government officials may not trust NGOs with disaster efforts. Over the years, in some cases an antagonistic relationship has existed between government and NGOs. At times, these relations are caused by politics and, at other times, by funding issues. Regardless, government officials involved with disaster management appear wary of NGOs' motives, of their safety since they may lack the necessary training and skills, and of potential liabilities (Kapucu 2005; Waugh 2000). Volunteers often just show up on the scene and local officials have no idea who they are, what their mission is, and to whom they report, if to anyone.[d] In the hours and days immediately after a disaster, officials have little time to check volunteers' credentials.

NGOs, particularly smaller organizations and those with missions that do not include disaster response and relief, also may not place disaster response as a priority. This may be due to lack of adequate funding, staff capacity, or time to plan for the unexpected or seek long-term strategic solutions when short-term ones are easier to fund and demonstrate results to donors and the general public. As Kiefer and Montjoy (2006) note, "Serious preparation is often expensive, requiring implementers to divert resources from tangible current needs and demands to prepare for something they hope will never happen" (123). Without a mission to respond to disasters, NGOs will continue to face these problems unless they adequately plan and are involved in their communities' disaster planning activities.

With the response to the Katrina disaster, lack of planning was a major challenge in at least six functional areas: shelter, medical services, hygiene, transportation management and services, children's services, and case management (Homeland Security Institute 2006). For example, emergency plans did not address emergent needs, such as pop-up shelters run by FBOs to accommodate a mass of evacuees unable to reach government or ARC shelters, or routine transportation for evacuees and relief workers and volunteers (Homeland Security Institute 2006, 23). Plans also did not involve credentialing, which caused local NGOs and FBOs to have difficulty with physical access to disaster areas and associated activities (Joint Commission 2005, 49). Without government-issued credentials identifying them as serving in some official capacity, NGO staff and volunteers were blocked from delivering resources and services. This was particularly an issue for smaller FBOs and NGOs that were not recognized at law enforcement and military checkpoints. In addition, spiritual care providers were not allowed access to some shelters (Homeland Security Institute 2006, 2). Many local NGOs responded to Katrina, in the beginning, because of the magnitude of the hurricane, but without adequate forethought to sufficient staff and funding needs to carry out operations (Pipa 2006, 32; Smith 2006, 6).

4.3.2   POOR COORDINATION AND COLLABORATION

Collaboration and coordination are the most discussed solutions in the literature for mitigating and/ or eliminating many problems encountered in disaster situations (Beristain 1999; Canton 2007; Coppola 2007; Drabek et al. 1981; Granot 1997; Gray 1991; Linden 2002; Minear 2002; Smillie 1995; Smillie and Minear 2004). Collaboration is a process of give and take that provides space for the construction of solutions no individual actor could achieve alone. It may be the best method for dealing with "complex and interrelated problems that cross … administrative and jurisdictional boundaries" (Williams 2002, 120), as is often the case in disaster response. Although the literature stresses the importance of collaboration and urges organizations to invest time and dollars in it, inadequate collaboration in disaster response remains an ongoing reality. This was certainly the case in the response to Katrina (Homeland Security Institute 2006; Smith 2006, 8; U.S. GAO 2007, 10; Waugh 2006, 15).

Numerous hurdles prevent and undermine collaboration, such as:

- Distrust among organizations (Babiak and Thibault 2009; Corbacioglu and Kapucu 2006; Linden 2002, 35; Vernis et al. 2006, 37; Waugh and Streib 2006)
- Competition among organizations (Coppola 2007; Granot 1997, 305; Linden 2002; Minear 2002, 25; Smillie 1995, 233; Smillie and Minear 2004, 200; Van de Ven and Walker 1984; Vernis et al. 2006, 69)
- Fear of a reduction in organizational autonomy and power (Babiak and Thibault 2009; Coppola 2007, 393; Minear 2002, 23; Vernis et al. 2006, 37)

Edwards (2004) suggests collaboration continues to be a challenge "because it is incredibly difficult to stick to best practice when 'all hell breaks loose around you'...; and ... because few NGOs or intergovernmental organizations are interested in co-operation when this may lose them precious opportunities for profile and publicity, the lifeblood of agencies that are competing for donations" (105). If NGOs receive significant funds, as with most catastrophic disasters, few financial incentives exist for cooperating with others. NGOs, particularly those in the same region or with similar interests, routinely vie for the same resources. Resources include not only dollars but also donor and volunteer time and media attention. In the response to Katrina, local NGOs were competing with the ARC and INGOs for resources; donors appeared to give their dollars to the more familiar, larger organizations (Pipa 2006; Smith 2006). Yet, a decision not to collaborate with others is clearly an obstacle to effective disaster relief efforts (Edwards 2004, 105; Vernis et al. 2006, 68).

Lack of agreement on how coordination structures should be devised is another reason why collaboration is stymied during disasters (Babiak and Thibault 2009; Huxham and Vangen 2005; Minear 2002, 29). NGOs hesitate to become involved in rigid bureaucratic structures because their flexibility and autonomy might be negatively affected. Indeed, as voluntary organizations, NGOs "have no obligation to coordinate with other NGOs or with official government responders" (Coppola 2007, 398). In addition, with numerous organizations responding to disasters, it is difficult to coordinate and apprise everyone of the latest status of the situation. According to Granot (1997), "Even when all participants are skilled at what they are called on to do, co-ordinating their efforts is one of the most troublesome aspects of emergency management" (305). Even when NGOs do try to cooperate, their efforts to assist may be thwarted. For instance, during Katrina, NGOs were on several occasions prevented by government officials from obtaining needed information and from entering the disaster area (Pipa 2006, 11; Waugh 2006, 21).

Throughout the response to Katrina, lack of coordination led to major limitations and challenges in at least four functional areas: shelter, medical services, physical reconstruction services, and logistics management and services (Homeland Security Institute 2006, 2). Part of the reason for this lack of coordination may be that even though the role of FEMA within ESF-6 of the NRF seemed clear, there was a good deal of uncertainty about which agency should coordinate all the relief organizations that offer their services during disaster response. During the Katrina aftermath, FEMA and state officials seemed to think that duty was assigned to the ARC. The ARC, for its part, indicated to others in the field that it viewed its job as managing its own food and shelter operations and coordinating its efforts with federal and state officials; "it did not view as its responsibility the role of establishing a central information and coordinating structure that would incorporate all responding agencies" (Pipa 2006, 16). As noted previously, this has since been clarified in the NRF.

4.3.3 Voluntary Failure

Salamon (1995, 45–47) defines voluntary failure as: philanthropic insufficiency, particularism, paternalism, and amateurism. NGOs can fail in response to problems, such as those caused by disasters, because they typically have insufficient resources on a scale that is adequate and reliable enough to cope with the magnitude of the problem; they have a tendency to focus on particular subgroups of a population and geographic area, which leads to gaps and/or duplication of efforts; they vest authority for defining community needs and response to these needs within the hands of those in command of the greatest resources, thus allocating foregone public revenues without benefit of a public decision-making process; and they frequently take an amateur approach to coping with problems.

Voluntary failures are played out in many ways in disaster relief efforts. Regarding resources, the majority of NGOs depend upon donations and contracts to implement their missions and respond to disasters. They also rely upon media to generate enough attention to a disaster that the public, businesses, and governments respond by sending donations to NGOs. Benthall (1993) claims, "The coverage of disasters by the press and the media is so selective and arbitrary that, in an important sense, they 'create' a disaster when they decide to recognize it" (11). Hundreds of disasters around the world are not given the media's spotlight. Without the media bringing attention to the situation, donations are low and, therefore, NGOs' response can be limited.

In addition, even though several NGOs have begun to see the importance of the relief-recovery-development continuum, they still are mostly particularistic in their focus. Wood, Apthorpe, and Borton (2001, 6) write:

> While most of the larger international NGOs have the capacity to work simultaneously in several sectors (such as health, shelter, food and nutrition, and water and sanitation) in large parts of the affected area, many NGOs are highly specialized, concentrating on the needs of a particular population (children, elderly, disabled) or confine their work to a particular locale.

This is similar to the challenge that NGOs face with donors. Many donors designate funds without thought to overhead expenses necessary to prepare for and respond to disaster. Donors often prefer their gifts to be used immediately for relief for assisting survivors and not for rehabilitation for long-term needs (Freemont-Smith, Boris, and Steuerle 2006, 1). According to Moore (2006, 24):

> When there are excess funds for disaster relief and inadequate funds for disaster recovery, diverting funds is tempting. But donors may contest this new, more problematic use of their money. This issue has become salient after Hurricane Katrina because the natural disaster exposed a man-made one. It is hard to draw the line between disaster relief efforts designed to restore New Orleans and much larger and more sustained efforts to improve it. And it is by no means clear which of these goals is being supported by the social response to Katrina.

Finally, many NGOs "lack the professional support or institutional memory to continually improve operations" (VanRooyen et al. 2001, 216). In particular, the high burnout rates and turnover in humanitarian relief staff, due to taxing working conditions, the urgent nature of the work, and relatively low compensation and benefits, is well documented (Lindenberg and Bryant 2001). This means that the all-important trust built up among relief workers and between relief workers and local communities continually has to be reinstituted as staff come and go (Brinkerhoff 2002, 64). The majority of NGOs also lack funds to train staff, which exacerbates the situation (Salamon 2003).

The response to Katrina revealed some of these shortcomings and weaknesses. According to Smith (2006), many nonprofit agencies in affected areas closed altogether or curtailed services because of a lack of resources. The extensive media coverage put Katrina on the top of the news list; however, the finances received were far below the amount needed to respond effectively. The amount donated in response to Katrina—$3.3 billion—was quite modest compared to the need; rebuilding, for example, has been estimated at more than $200 billion. Furthermore, voluntary and philanthropic assistance in response to Katrina concentrated on meeting immediate and basic needs. There was, and still is, a lack of resources and expertise for longer-term and complex services (such as job training, child care, mental health counseling, and abuse treatment; Smith 2006, 7). Finally, planned response by the city of New Orleans to a potential disaster relied heavily on the hope that neighbors and congregation members would voluntarily help New Orleans' immobile population leave the city in an emergency (Kiefer and Montjoy 2006). This clearly was not adequate for the catastrophe caused by Katrina.

In addition to the voluntary failures described above is the basic reality that NGOs are voluntary entities without the legal authority to coerce and, thus, without the power to address long-term and deep-seated problems that create situations conducive to disasters in the first place. According to Özerdem and Jacoby (2006), the diverse and often fragmented character of the NGO/donor sector has significant negative implications for efforts to bring relief to disaster victims, rehabilitate disaster-affected areas, and bring about reconstruction initiatives and reduce hazard vulnerability (18).

In addition, there is some question as to whether NGOs actually achieve (or even aim to achieve) building self-reliance among community members and institutions—that would enhance a community's ability to respond to disasters—or if they are allowing a community to become dependent on others to solve problems now and in the future.

4.3.4　Improving NGO Disaster Response

Because NGOs are so essential to disaster response efforts, it is imperative that policy-makers, administrators, and front-line responders work to improve NGO disaster response efforts. Following are several areas that might be addressed, including better integration of NGOs in planning for disasters, better coordination and collaboration across and among government agencies and NGOs during response, and strengthening community and NGO capacities.

4.3.4.1　Involve NGOs in Planning for Disasters

NGOs will respond to disasters. It makes sense for government agencies to acknowledge this and plan for it. Indeed, the White House report on the response to Hurricane Katrina noted that government "must recognize that NGOs play a fundamental role in the recovery efforts and will contribute in ways that are, in many cases, more efficient and effective than the government's response... [and] must plan for their participation and treat them as valued and necessary partners" (U.S. White House 2006, 63). Numerous researchers emphasize the benefits of being aware of and understanding the local culture of disaster sites to be effective in disaster management, especially in planning (Beristain 1999; Lindenberg and Bryant 2001; Minear 2002; Özerdem and Jacoby 2006; Skeet 1977; Smillie 1995). This requires obtaining information about economic status, governance structure, political situations, state capabilities, local institutions, and local needs. It requires relief workers to be aware of survivors' psychosocial needs by knowing local social norms. NGOs, especially local NGOs, are situated to know such issues since they work at the grassroots level. These NGOs should already understand the pulse of the communities in which they work and have formed relationships with local leaders, as well as with vulnerable populations (Pipa 2006). Vulnerable populations, in general, are the communities' minorities, those who are underrepresented in community issues. NGOs are potential channels to these vulnerable populations since they are the ones working at the local level. NGOs "often bring an in-depth understanding of a particular geographic area or special population and have access to underserved populations" (U.S. GAO 2007, 6).

With such knowledge, NGOs can assist emergency managers to develop better informed and more realistic crisis plans and utilize appropriate communication channels to provide essential information to survivors, to each other, and to relevant external agencies. Thus, governments should determine how NGOs can be included in disaster planning at all levels, as well as be involved in disaster simulations and training (Homeland Security Institute 2006; U.S. White House 2006, 49). To do this, state and local governments in particular must be better prepared and understand and improve upon their own capacity levels.

4.3.4.2　Improve Coordination and Collaboration Efforts

All major actors and groups in disaster response and relief should make a concerted effort to work together before disasters strike. They should work to strengthen their knowledge of each other throughout the year because they will inevitably be tested during disasters. According to Waugh and Streib (2006, 132):

> Making and maintaining the necessary linkages is a monumental challenge, and it is a necessary task when dealing with catastrophic or potentially catastrophic disasters. In other words, the capacity to collaborate effectively with the nation's disaster networks is essential. Frequent interaction, including participation in planning and training exercises, builds that capacity.

Scholars suggest improved communication as the most effective, efficient means of enhancing relationships among agencies (Beristain 1999; Drabek et al. 1981; Dynes 1978; MacCormack 2007). If communication is ongoing and information is accurate, agencies should be able to develop positive trusting relationships, thereby improving collaboration. According to Kapucu (2006), "Trust is crucial in the uncertain situations caused by an extreme event. The building of trust among public and nonprofit organizations can best be done prior to emergency situations occurring" (209).

This advice can also apply to relationships with the media. According to Minear (2002), "The media has claimed its own place in the humanitarian architecture of the future … [and] requires skillful cultivation by the humanitarian enterprise as an actor in its own right whose own constraints and agendas must be recognized" (142). Forming meaningful relationships with the media can possibly lead to more useful, accurate information disseminated to the public and on which politicians and others can make informed decisions (Coppola 2007; Drabek et al. 1981; Minear 2002). Such outreach to the media may have made a difference during Katrina when inaccurate information was often being broadcast by the various media outlets.

There is also a need for improved leadership coordination (Minear 2002, 32). It is the lack of leadership—the ambiguity of authority—during disasters that seems to most often thwart efficient response. No one organization has authority for any phase of a disaster. Some believe a single point of contact—a central coordinating body to organize disaster response—would ensure effective, efficient operations, reducing chaos and improving communication and coordination (Corbacioglu and Kapucu 2006; Drabek et al. 1981; Skeet 1977; Wise 2006, 308–310). All emergency relief operations would flow through this central coordinating body, helping to keep participating organizations well informed. One suggestion has been for the federal government to play this role.[e]

Yet, much of the disaster relief literature notes that such a top-down model is incompatible with the complexity of emergency response. As Kapucu (2006) argues, "In extreme events, standard procedures cannot be followed; such events require a dynamic system to adapt to unanticipated and rapidly changing conditions" (210). There is a need for coordination through collaborative networks, including ongoing interaction among actors leading to the development of shared goals to adequately prepare for disaster response (Dynes 2002; MacCormack 2007; Waugh and Streib 2006). Networks offer several benefits, such as division of tasks, flexibility, and an emphasis on communication (Canton 2007, 312). Benefits are derived from members who bring their skills, knowledge, and interest to networks but are also allowed to retain their independence. In addition, it is not clear that NGOs will want to participate in a plan that might constrain or seem to co-opt their own visions and missions. A comment made by an NGO disaster response staff person is enlightening here: "We typically don't like to work with big governments and we like to work with on-the-ground indigenous organizations as much as possible, because they're there for the long haul and they also know the land, the landscape the best" (Eikenberry, Arroyave, and Cooper 2007, 167). Yet, the problem still remains that "when network participants are unclear about the leadership in a particular network, the network is likely to be less effective" (Choi and Kim 2007, 205). Provan and Milward (1995) believe large networks are more productive if they are centralized. A coordinating model of disaster response in the United States would need to balance the need for centralized coordination with the nature of disaster response, including the response of NGOs—a model that addresses the tension between coordinating NGOs and other organizations while also allowing them to address the complexities of providing relief (Eikenberry, Arroyave, and Cooper 2007).

To incorporate more flexibility, Agranoff (2007) suggests the use of "collaborarchies" in disaster response. According to Agranoff, collaborarchies are "hybrids between voluntary organizations with boards and officials, and collaborative structures like work groups and committees within contemporary bureaucratic organizations" (84). Elements of bureaucracies and networks are combined for enhanced collaboration, coordination, and communication, particularly at the field level. Representatives from organizations self organize into a "pooled authority system that is based more on expertise than on position" (Agranoff 2007, 87). Such an arrangement allows for the flexibility of networks and the stability of bureaucracies. Within a collaborarchy, "communication channels substitute for the hierarchical structure in participants' home organizations. It is through this array of actors that the patterns of communication flow" (Agranoff 2007, 101). These nonlinear structures are set up to increase information sharing, which should, as a result, create a solid base for partner organizations to work toward improved planning and capacity building.

The Unified Command (UC) structure now promoted under the NRF does not yet approach a collaborarchy, but it could, over time, if the federal government can become more flexible and rely less on a command-and-control structure during response. UC is used when multiple agencies and/or multiple jurisdictions are needed to respond to a disaster; it outlines how numerous responders can coordinate and collaborate together without giving up their authority or abdicating their responsibilities (Joint Commission 2005, 28; Canton 2007, 273; U.S. Department of Homeland Security 2008, 48; U.S. White House 2006, 13). UC is meant to encourage information sharing since "jurisdictional authorities jointly determine objectives, strategies, plans, and priorities and work together to execute integrated incident operations and maximize the use of assigned resources" (U.S. White House 2006, 209). Thus, the UC concept allows NGOs to work with government without giving up their independence. UC also urges government to have a "limited preoccupation with adhering to the chain of command" (Canton 2007, 312). At this point, however, the NRF and its UC structure neither fully takes into account the extensive number of NGOs that will respond to disasters nor how best to coordinate NGO activities into the overall disaster response efforts. During Katrina, the tasks and responsibilities of NGOs were not integrated into the national plan; at times, NGO representatives were not even allowed into FEMA or state EOC meetings, undermining coordination efforts (U.S. White House 2006, 49).

Yet, attempts are under way to remedy this. The federal government acknowledges, "Effective *unified command* is indispensable to response activities and requires a clear understanding of the roles and responsibilities of each participating organization" (U.S. Department of Homeland Security 2008, 10). As a starting point to improve the situation, after Katrina, "FEMA and the Red Cross agreed that having FEMA serve as the primary agency for all four functions of ESF-6 would help ensure a unified command structure during operational response" (U.S. GAO 2008, 14). Since the UC system still does not fully incorporate NGOs into the NRF, coordination is and will be problematic until they are streamlined into the system.

Another model to consider is that used at the international level with the United Nations Office for the Coordination of Humanitarian Affairs (OCHA), which typically acts as a coordinator of humanitarian emergency response by ensuring that an appropriate response mechanism is established and as a facilitator for helping humanitarian organizations access information to understand the scope of needs in affected areas. OCHA has worked extensively with numerous INGOs and appears to have a better appreciation for the flexibility necessary to respond effectively during disasters than FEMA. For example, OCHA has a designated liaison for humanitarian organizations. It also has established direct communication mechanisms with INGOs, preidentified INGOs that will most likely respond to disasters, preidentified INGOs that will take the lead on certain issues during disaster, and incorporated INGOs into the planning process. This international humanitarian relief system is not perfect, to be sure, but it may be another way to balance the tensions noted before of loosely coordinating NGOs and other agencies while addressing the complexities of providing relief. FEMA has a similar mandate to that of OCHA, but state and local governments tend to see FEMA as a first responder rather than as a coordinator. Thus, there is an immediate, imperative need to clarify the role of FEMA (in the U.S. system and in relation to other international actors like OCHA) in disaster response and, in particular, how it might coordinate the NGO sector with government efforts. If FEMA should take on the role of NGO coordinator, staff must be open to creating a process that works for all parties involved. Regardless of the type of coordinating structure used during a disaster, Skeet (1977) aptly notes that "a certain loss of sovereignty should, during joint operations, be accepted" (24).

4.3.5 STRENGTHEN CAPACITIES

Capacity building is an effective tool in disaster mitigation and preparation (Beristain 1999; Minear 2002; Özerdem and Jacoby 2006; Paton and Johnston 2006) and can improve a community's response to a disaster. Capacity building means fortifying the social and economic aspects of a community. It offers local individuals and organizations the means to enhance quality of life, improve the surrounding environment, become self-sufficient, and be more resilient to a disaster. It involves utilizing the resources already in a community in order for that community to tackle its own problems. Local participation and local resource utilization and renewal are thus essential for building and rebuilding capacity after a disaster. According to Minear (2002), "Even in high-profile emergencies receiving massive foreign inputs, the scale of locally contributed resources may in the end be more substantial still, and certainly altogether indispensable to the process" (59).

How resilient a community is to a major disaster is determined by community members' skills and other traits, as well as by their personal and organizational relationships within the community. Strong social bonds may assist community members in resuming their way of life during and after a disaster. Relationships and partnerships, therefore, are critical to response and recovery. For NGOs to be as effective as possible in their disaster efforts, they should seek partnerships with local individuals and organizations and strive for cultural competencies in the areas they work. NGOs may need to adjust their hiring practices to focus more on local people and local resources when responding to disasters. With local citizen involvement, local norms can be understood, and relevant alternative crisis plans and solutions to local problems can emerge along with the communities' sense of ownership (Berke & Campanella 2006, 193). Paton and Johnston (2006) claim, "The quality of reciprocal relationships between communities and societal institutions will influence the quality of the community experience of recovery" (313).

NGOs should also consider strengthening their internal capacity for responding to disasters. Organizational policy adaptation is a starting point. NGOs that anticipate responding to disasters should ensure that a detailed response strategy is already in place. This strategy should include knowing what other area NGOs' capabilities are and how they may respond in relation to these. Another action to take is locating opportunities to train staff in disaster response. A possible option is FEMA's Citizen Corps, a "grassroots strategy to bring together government and community leaders to involve citizens in all-hazards emergency preparedness and resilience," which focuses on preparedness, first aid training, and volunteering to help local emergency responders (FEMA nd, para. 1). Participating NGOs will get some of the training needed, as well as have the opportunity to form relations with other community responders and FEMA contacts. Another means for NGOs to obtain funds for staff training is to work closely with donors to help them understand the importance of disaster preparedness and response training.

Finally, NGOs should consider engaging in policy making that relates to disaster response. NGOs have successfully worked together, on a global basis, to put a spotlight on corporate and government abuse. Likewise, NGOs could collaborate before and during disaster situations to change policies and bring more attention to the importance of disaster management. If NGOs can change behaviors concerning corporate social responsibility issues and government mismanagement, they may be able to push through an improved disaster management agenda to force needed changes to the system. One potential issue to tackle first is related to the Stafford Act, which states that

> Other than the American Red Cross for some shelter services, there is no provision to allow the government to contract with NGOs for services related to human recovery. Established contracts between the federal government and local NGOs are one possible mechanism for pre-positioning needed resources. Having these contracts in place could encourage a more efficient, timely, and coordinated local response. (Chandra and Acosta 2009, 10)

This could also encourage the collaboration needed to work together before disasters happen and would certainly assist in the preparedness stage.

The U.S. Department of Health and Human Services Administration for Children and Families has taken steps in this direction already with its Disaster Case Management (DCM) program. Prior to Hurricane Katrina, there was no federal authority to fund disaster case management as part of a Stafford Act declaration. In recognition of the need for this authority, Congress passed the Post Katrina Emergency Reform Act of 2006. DCM is the process of organizing and providing a timely coordinated approach to assess disaster-related needs as well as existing health care, mental health, and human services needs that may adversely impact an individual's recovery if not addressed. DCM facilitates the delivery of appropriate resources and services, works with a client to implement a recovery plan, and advocates for the client's needs to assist him or her in returning to a predisaster status while respecting human dignity (USDHHS 2009, para. 1).

4.4 CONCLUSION

It is important for behavioral health practitioners and survivors of emergencies and catastrophic events to understand how NGOs respond in a disaster environment and to have realistic expectations about the benefits and challenges of working with NGOs during these daunting situations. The focus of this chapter is to provide an overview of key types of NGOs that respond to disasters and their functions during response efforts, challenges of this response, and suggestions for improving NGO disaster response in the future. Throughout the decades in the United States, NGOs have shown their capabilities in helping those in need. They have and continue to feed the hungry, shelter the homeless, and counsel those in stressful situations.

Yet, NGOs are often not very well coordinated and comprehensive in their disaster response, in part because they are independent by nature and because government agencies have not fully integrated them into disaster planning. NGOs need assistance in strengthening their capacities to respond to survivors of disasters as was clearly shown in the response to Hurricane Katrina, but in a way that enables them to obtain their independence and allows them to stay connected to local communities. It would be beneficial if federal, state, and local agencies did more to include NGOs in their planning discussions, as well as in training activities. By inclusion, operational processes and responsibilities would become clearer to all parties. Collaboration among all agencies that will respond to disasters is essential in maximizing the help given to those adversely affected by disaster.

NOTES

a. The National Response Framework (NRF) is the United States' national plan for responding to disasters, whether natural or man-made. The NRF superseded the National Response Plan (NRP) on March 22, 2008. The NRP was the plan invoked during Hurricane Katrina, giving federal government oversight of response because both local and state governments were overwhelmed. However, the NRP was displaced by the NRF because of the experience with Hurricane Katrina and because of reorganization: the Department of Homeland Security was established in 2003 and FEMA was placed within it.

b. The Robert T. Stafford Disaster Relief and Emergency Assistance Act (Stafford Act) outlines the process of how states receive federal aid during a disaster. It gives the president the authority to declare a major disaster or emergency if he believes the state has exceeded its capacity. However, the governor must request federal assistance before the federal government, under the leadership of the Department of Homeland Security and FEMA, will provide mass care, facility and environmental restoration, financial aid to disaster survivors, and debris removal. It should be noted that the Stafford Act was amended after Hurricane Katrina. For instance, it now gives the president the authority to provide monetary assistance for case management services because of the passage of the Post-Katrina Emergency Management Reform Act of 2006.

c. Congress granted the ARC its federal charter in 1905, establishing the ARC as the organization to perform services to comply with the Geneva Convention. This included creating and maintaining a system for national and international relief during disasters and developing disaster prevention measures. Congress last amended the charter on May 11, 2007.

d. Thanks to Julie Framingham for raising this point.

e. Lutheran Disaster Response (LDR) successfully played this role of coordinating NGO/FBO response activities during the 2004 Florida hurricanes. LDR coordinated events through daily (Florida) statewide conference calls, which were hosted and initiated at LDR's headquarters in Chicago (Framingham, personal communication, March 16, 2010).

REFERENCES

Adams, L. M. 2008. Comprehensive vulnerability management: The road to effective disaster planning with the community. *Journal of Theory Construction & Testing 12*: 25–27.

Agranoff, R. 2007. *Managing within Networks: Adding Value to Public Organizations*. Washington, DC: Georgetown University Press.

Ahmed, S., and D. Potter. 2006. *NGOs in International Politics*. Bloomfield, CT: Kumarian Press.

American Red Cross. nd. *The face of recovery*. http://www.preventionweb.net/files/2720_filecont6989lang02850.pdf.

Anheier, H. 2005. *Nonprofit Organizations: Theory, Management, Policy*. New York: Routledge.

Anheier, H., and H. J. Cho. 2005. International NGOs as an element of global civil society: Scale, expressions, and governance. Paper prepared for the 6th Global Forum on Reinventing Government, Seoul, Korea, May 24–27. http://6thglobalforum.org/eng/documents/background.asp.

Babiak, K., and L. Thibault. 2009. Challenges in multiple cross-sector partnerships. *Nonprofit and Voluntary Sector Quarterly 38*: 117–143.

Benthall, J. 1993. *Disasters, Relief and the Media*. New York: I. Tauris and Company Ltd.

Benson, C., J. Twigg, and M. Myers. 2001. NGO initiatives in risk reduction: An overview. *Disasters 25*(3): 199–215.

Beristain, C. M. 1999. *Humanitarian Aid Work: A Critical Approach*. Philadelphia: University of Pennsylvania Press.

Berke, P., and T. Campanella. 2006. Planning for postdisaster resiliency. *Annals of the American Academy of Political and Social Science 604*: 192–207.

Brinkerhoff, J. M. 2002. *Partnership for International Development: Rhetoric or Results?* Boulder, CO: Lynne Rienner Publishers.

Brough, D. 2002. *Natural disasters increasing, more U.N. aid needed*. Reuters Foundation. http://www.reliefweb.int/rw/rwb.nsf/AllDocsByUNID/48f875594dea4049c1256b9f004648b1.

Canton, L. G. 2007. *Emergency Management: Concepts and Strategies for Effective Programs*. Hoboken, NJ: John Wiley & Sons.

Chandra, A., and J. Acosta. 2009. *The role of nongovernmental organizations in long-term human recovery after disaster: Reflections from Louisiana four years after Hurricane Katrina*, Occasional Paper. Pittsburgh, PA: RAND Corporation. http://www.rand.org.

Chaves, M., and W. Tsitsos. 2001. Congregations and social services: What they do, how they do it, and with whom. *Nonprofit and Voluntary Sector Quarterly 30*: 660–683.

Choi, S., and B-T. Kim. 2007. Power and cognitive accuracy in local emergency management networks. *Public Administration Review 67*: 198–209.

Col, J-M. 2007. Managing disasters: The role of local government. *Public Administration Review 67*: 114–124.

Coppola, D. 2007. *Introduction to International Disaster Management*. Boston: Elsevier.

Corbacioglu, S., and N. Kapucu. 2006. Organisational learning and self-adaptation in dynamic disaster environments. *Disasters 30*: 212–233.

Cutter, S. L., C. T. Emrich, J. T. Mitchell, B. J. Boruff, M. Gall, M. C. Schmidtlein, C. G. Burton, and G. Melton. 2006. The long road home: Race, class, and recovery from Hurricane Katrina. *Environment: Science and Policy for Sustainable Development 48*(2): 8–20.

De Vita, C. J., and F. D. Kramer. December 2008. *The Role of Faith-Based and Community Organizations in Post-Hurricane Human Service Relief Efforts*. Washington, DC: The Urban Institute.

Drabek, T. E., H. L. Tamminga, T. S. Kilijanek, and C. R. Adams. 1981. *Managing Multiorganizational Emergency Responses: Emergent Search and Rescue Networks in Natural Disasters and Remote Area Settings*. Boulder, CO: University of Colorado.

Dynes, R. 1978. Interoganizational relations in communities under stress. In *Disasters: Theory and Research*, ed. E. L. Quarantelli, 50–64. London: SAGE.

Dynes, R. 2002. *The importance of social capital in disaster response*. Preliminary Paper #327. University of Delaware, Disaster Research Center.

Edwards, M. 2004. *Future Positive: International Co-Operation in the 21st Century*. Sterling, VA: Earthscan.

Eikenberry, A., V. Arroyave, and T. Cooper. 2007. Administrative failure and the international NGO response to Hurricane Katrina. *Public Administration Review 67*: 160–170.

Fagnoni, C. 2006. Observations on charities' response to Hurricanes Katrina and Rita. In *After Katrina: Public Expectation and Charities' Response*, eds. E. Boris and C. E. Steuerle, 11–18. Washington, DC: Urban Institute. http://www.urban.org/url.cfm?ID=311331.

FEMA. nd. *Citizen corps*. http://www.citizencorps.gov.

Freemont-Smith, M., E. Boris, and C. E. Steuerle. 2006. Charities' response to disasters: Expectations and realities. In *After Katrina: Public Expectation and Charities' Response*, eds. E. Boris and C. E. Steuerle, 1–4. Washington, DC: Urban Institute. http://www.urban.org/url.cfm?ID=311331.

Granot, H. 1997. Emergency inter-organizational relationships. *Disaster Prevention and Management 6*(5): 305–310.

Gray, B. 1991. *Collaborating: Finding Common Ground for Multiparty Problems*. Oxford: Jossey-Bass.

Hartsough, D., and D. Mileti. 1985. The media in disaster. In *Perspectives on Disaster Recovery*, eds. J. Laube and S. Murphy, 282–294. Norwalk, CT: Appleton-Century-Crofts.

Homeland Security Institute. 2006. *Heralding unheard voices: The role of FBOs and NGOs during disasters*. http://www.homelandsecurity.org/hsireports/Herald_Unheard_Voices.pdf.

Hudson, B. A., and W. Bielefeld. 1997. Structures of multinational nonprofit organizations. *Nonprofit Management and Leadership 8*: 31–49.

Huxham, C., and S. Vangen. 2005. *Managing to Collaborate: The Theory and Practice of Collaborative Advantage*. New York: Routledge.

Joint Commission on Accreditation of Healthcare Organizations. 2005. *Standing together: An emergency planning guide for America's communities*. http://www.jointcommission.org/NR/rdonlyres/FE29E7D3-22AA-4DEB-94B2-5E8D507F92D1/0/planning_guide.pdf.

Kapucu, N. 2005. Interorganizational coordination in dynamic context: Networks of emergency response management. *Connections 26*: 33–48.

Kapucu, N. 2006. Public-nonprofit partnerships for collective action in dynamic contexts of emergencies. *Public Administration 84*: 205–220.

Kerkman, L. 2006. Three large charities end solicitations for Katrina relief as total tops $3-Billion. *Chronicle of Philanthropy*. http://www.mercycorps.org/aboutus/inthenews/1145.

Kiefer, J., and R. Montjoy. 2006. Incrementalism before the storm: Network performance for the evacuation of New Orleans. *Public Administration Review 66*: 122–130.

Lewis, D., and P. Opoku-Mensah. 2006. Moving forward research agendas on international NGOs: Theory, agency and context. *Journal of International Development 18*: 665–675.

Linden, R. M. 2002. *Working across Boundaries: Making Collaboration Work in Government and Nonprofit Organizations*. San Francisco: Jossey-Bass.

Lindenberg, M., and C. Bryant. 2001. *Going Global: Transforming Relief and Development NGOs*. Bloomfield, CT: Kumarian Press.

MacCormack, C. 2007. Coordination and collaboration: An NGO view. In *The Pulse of Humanitarian Assistance*, ed. K. Cahill, 243–262. New York: Fordham University Press and the Center for International Health and Cooperation.

Mileti, D. 1999. *Disasters by Design: A Reassessment of Natural Hazards in the United States*. Washington, DC: Joseph Henry Press.

Minear, L. 2002. *The Humanitarian Enterprise: Dilemmas and Discoveries*. Bloomfield, CT: Kumarian Press.

Moore, M. 2006. Disasters and the voluntary sector: Reflections on the social response to Hurricane Katrina. In *After Katrina: Public Expectation and Charities' Response*, eds. E. Boris and C. E. Steuerle, 23–28. Washington, DC: Urban Institute. http://www.urban.org/url.cfm?ID=311331.

National Center for Charitable Statistics. nd. *Public charities—NTEE = M20 (Disaster preparedness & relief services)*. http://nccsdataweb.urban.org/PubApps/showOrgsByCategory.php?ntee=M20.

NVOAD. November 4, 2009. *Disaster case management standards (draft)*. http://www.nvoad.org/Portals/0/NVOAD%20DCM%20Standards%20Draft%20Nov%203%202009.doc.

Özerdem, A., and T. Jacoby. 2006. *Disaster Management and Civil Society: Earthquake Relief in Japan, Turkey and India.* London: I. B. Tauris.

Paton, D., and D. Johnston. 2006. *Disaster Resilience: An Integrated Approach.* Springfield, IL: Charles Thomas.

Pipa, T. 2006. *Weathering the storm: The role of local nonprofits in the Hurricane Katrina relief effort.* Nonprofit Sector Research Fund Working Paper Series. Washington, DC: The Aspen Institute. http://www.nonprofitresearch.org/usr_doc/Nonprofits_and_Katrina.pdf.

Provan, K., and H. Milward. 1995. A preliminary theory of interorganizational network effectiveness: A comparative study of four community mental health systems. *Administrative Science Quarterly 40*: 1–33.

Salamon, L. M. 1995. *Partners in Public Service: Government-Nonprofit Relations in the Modern Welfare State.* Baltimore: Johns Hopkins University Press.

Salamon, L. 2003. *The Resilient Sector: The State of Nonprofit America.* Washington, DC: Brookings Institution Press.

The Salvation Army. nd. *The Salvation Army disaster response history.* http://www.salvationarmyusa.org/usn/www_usn_2.nsf/vw-search/EF30DAEC5735B889852574B40056A312?opendocument.

Skeet, M. 1977. *Manual for Disaster Relief Work.* New York: Churchill Livingstone.

Smillie, I. 1995. *The Alms Bazaar.* Ottawa, Canada: International Development Resource Center.

Smillie, I., and L. Minear. 2004. *The Charity of Nations: Humanitarian Action in a Calculating World.* Bloomfield, CT: Kumarian Press.

Smith, S. R. 2006. Rebuilding social welfare services after Katrina: Challenges and opportunities. In *After Katrina: Public Expectation and Charities' Response*, eds. E. Boris and C. E. Steuerle, 5–10. Washington, DC: Urban Institute. http://www.urban.org/url.cfm?ID=311331.

Tierney, K., M. Lindell, and R. Perry. 2001. *Facing the Unexpected: Disaster Preparedness and Response in the United States.* Washington, DC: Joseph Henry Press.

United States Department of Health and Human Services. (USDHHS). 2009. *Disaster case management overview.* http://www.acf.hhs.gov/ohsepr/dcm/dcm_overview.html.

United States Department of Homeland Security. 2008. *National response framework.* Washington, DC: FEMA Publications. http://www.fema.gov/NRF.

United States Government Accountability Office (U.S. GAO). 2007. *Nonprofit Sector: Increasing Numbers and Key Role in Delivering Federal Services*, Report no. GAO-07-1084T. Washington, DC: U.S. Government Printing Office.

United States Government Accountability Office (U.S. GAO). 2008. *National Disaster Response: FEMA Should Take Action to Improve Capacity and Coordination between Government and Voluntary Sectors*, Report no. GAO-08-369. Washington, DC: U.S. Government Printing Office.

United States House. 2006. *Select Bipartisan Committee to Investigate the Preparation for and Response to Hurricane Katrina: A Failure of Initiative*, House Report No. 109-377. Washington, DC: U.S. Government Printing Office. http://katrina.house.gov/full_katrina_report.htm.

United States White House. 2006. *The Federal Response to Hurricane Katrina: Lessons Learned.* Washington, DC: Office of the Assistant to the President for Homeland Security and Counterterrorism. http://www.whitehouse.gov/reports/katrina-lessons-learned.

Van de Ven, A. H., and G. Walker. 1984. The dynamics of interorganizational coordination. *Administrative Science Quarterly 29*: 598–621.

VanRooyen, M. J., S. Hansch, D. Curtis, and G. Burnham. 2001. Emerging issues and future needs in humanitarian assistance. *Prehospital and Disaster Medicine 16*(4): 216–222.

Vernis, A., M. Iglesias, B. Sanz, and A. Saz-Caranza. 2006. *Nonprofit Organizations: Challenges and Collaboration.* New York: Palgrave Macmillan.

Waugh, W., Jr. 2000. *Living with Hazards Dealing with Disasters: An Introduction to Emergency Management.* Armonk, NY: ME Sharpe.

Waugh, W., Jr. 2006. The political costs of failure in the Katrina and Rita disasters. *Annals of the American Academy of Political and Social Science 604*: 10–25.

Waugh, W., Jr. and G. Streib. 2006. Collaboration and leadership for effective emergency management. *Public Administration Review 66*: 131–140.

Weeks, S. M. 2007. Mobilization of a nursing community after a disaster. *Perspectives in Psychiatric Care 43*: 22–29.

Wilhelm, I. 2005. Sharing a world of experience: Foreign-aid groups offer advice in hurricanes' aftermath. *The Chronicle of Philanthropy.* October 6. http://philanthropy.com/free/articles/v18/i01/01002701.htm.

Williams, P. 2002. The competent boundary spanner. *Public Administration 80*: 103–124.

Wise, C. R. 2006. Organizing for homeland security after Katrina: Is adaptive management what's missing? *Public Administration Review 66*: 302–318.

Wood, A., R. Apthorpe, and J. Borton. 2001. *Evaluating International Humanitarian Action: Reflections from Practitioners*. New York: Zed Books.

5 Disaster Mental Health
A Public Health Paradigm

Anthony T. Ng and Jeannie Straussman

CONTENTS

5.1 WHY DISASTERS ARE PUBLIC HEALTH EMERGENCIES

The implications of disasters on communities has been an increasing component of any emergency planning for communities in recent years. Disasters often result in widespread property damages, deaths, and injuries. In recent decades, the mental health effects on population have received greater attention, in light of events such as the 9/11 terrorist attacks, the anthrax attacks, Asian tsunamis and Hurricane Katrina. Postdisaster sequelae include posttraumatic stress disorder, major depression, anxiety disorders, and substance abuse disorders (North 2003; Pfefferbaum et al. 2001; Leon 2004; Math et al. 2006; Coker et al. 2006). Such psychiatric pathology can lead to significant impairment in functioning and distress. Affected individuals may have problems with work and school. There may also be an associated increase in medical issues. In disasters that involve chemical, biological, or radiological agents, there may be few fatalities, but these events can lead to significant psychological, social, and economic harm (Hyams, Murphy, and Wessely 2002). Mass psychogenic illness has also been identified as a consequence of events stemming from these agents. This is a social phenomenon where two or more people share beliefs about a syndrome of symptoms with no identifiable etiology.

Beyond clinical diagnosis, the mental health effects of disaster can result in a variety of distresses for individuals. There is increasing focus that disasters can result in distress behaviors, that is, how individuals will behave both pre, during and post disaster. An Institute of Medicine report in 2003 highlighted the potential impact of disasters on stress behavioral changes and the implications of such behavior (Institute of Medicine 2003). Such behaviors often are not severe enough to result in a clinical diagnosis or severe impairment, but they can have ripple effects on the management of disaster plans. How decision makers and policy makers act in disaster planning and response is another good example of distress behaviors. Disaster stress behaviors may affect survivors' critical decision-making processes and thus can positively or negatively influence the course of the response to the crisis or disaster (DiGiovanni 2003; Noy 2004). For example, individuals with anxiety or concentration problems after a disaster may not be able to effectively obtain postdisaster aid, thus perhaps exacerbating the disaster response as well as the individuals' distress. And in the long run, disaster stress reactions can lead to interpersonal problems, family strain and conflict, and social support erosion (Norris et al. 2002).

Disasters can lead to a variety of effects that may result in long-term implications. There may be population shifts due to communities being uprooted and relocated. There may be the spontaneous evolution of ad hoc communities, such as family assistance shelters and refugee camps, which may have their own unique public health needs. Long-term unemployment and financial issues may complicate communities' abilities to address public health issues. There may be poor life adjustments after disasters and public health emergencies that can lead to marked loss of functional capacity, both at the individual and community level. Due to the public nature of such events, media coverage may shape public health response policies. Lastly, there may be contentions between groups, communities, and other entities that can lead to friction in the development and implementation of public health policies in response to disasters.

The direct disaster survivors are often the most noticeable in the aftermath of disasters, often the most visible recipient of mental health services as they are such a high-risk group. They are the ones with the most direct losses—deaths, injuries, and/or property losses. They certainly have tremendous psychosocial needs. They are in need of postdisaster human services such as sheltering, mass care, and financial assistance. However, as Figure 5.1 illustrates, disaster survivors are often the "tip of the iceberg." There are many others who will be affected by the losses of these primary disaster survivors. They include family members, friends, coworkers, and even the professionals (health or others) who may be in contact with them. They may be at risk of secondary trauma from experiencing the survivors' firsthand losses. Lastly, the mental health effects of these secondary survivors could perpetuate to their friends and families and the public at large.

It is because of this disaster pyramid of survivors that any health and mental health responses to disasters must be community oriented and not just focus on the sole needs of the direct disaster survivors. Disasters are as such public health emergencies. While postdisaster response to mental health needs has often focused on providing more funding or resources to deal with the direct mental health issues, decision makers and policy makers have taken a more

FIGURE 5.1   Disaster pyramid.

public health approach and have become more aware of issues that may influence public health responses to disasters. All aspects of disaster planning, response, and recovery must be public health focused to ensure a more comprehensive response. An integration of mental health with public health will provide for better assessment of community needs and, in turn, individual needs. Integration will also encourage and promote buy-in by all parties and stakeholders into both mental health and public health. As often happens in disasters, resources are limited, and the close interface between mental health and public health can ensure a more efficient allocation of resources and allow a more targeted focus on basic postdisaster human services and medical needs.

5.2 ASSESSMENT, PREVENTION, SURVEILLANCE, AND INFECTIOUS DISEASE CONTROL

In public health, interventions are conceptualized as preventions, and public health centers around three essential phases: primary, secondary, and tertiary preventions. Primary prevention is the education of populations about health risk and the encouragement and promotion of behaviors that will prevent illness. For example, a primary prevention approach to cardiac disease would be to encourage proper diet and exercise. Secondary prevention will be the acute management of diseases after diagnosis has been made, such as acute treatment for hypertension and heart attacks. Finally, tertiary prevention will include the prevention of disease progression after a diagnosis is given, such as preventing reoccurrence of heart attack with anticlotting medications and physical therapy to regain function among stroke patients. Likewise in the integration of mental health and disaster planning, a public health model of prevention will need to be appreciated. Using a preventive medicine model of mental health, mental health has significant impacts in all phases of public health prevention and can help to identify high-risk groups for surveillance and intervention (Pfefferbaum and Pfefferbaum 1998; Ursano, Fullerton, and Norwood 1995). Exposure of an entire community can lead to a large net community benefit. While the benefit per individual may be small, the sum of these benefits can be substantial across an entire community population (Engel et al. 2003).

5.3 PUBLIC HEALTH BEHAVIORS IN DISASTERS

Beyond the clinical mental health issues of anxiety and posttraumatic stress, individuals may exhibit various distress behaviors after a disaster. As described earlier in this chapter, how populations behave and react after a disaster is critical in the planning and response to disasters. Four changes in behaviors are particularly relevant to disaster planning and response for decision and policy makers: the perceptions of safety, consumer behavior, stigmatization, and trust.

5.3.1 PERCEPTIONS OF REDUCED SAFETY

After a disaster, especially one that is terrorist-related, the perception of safety by a population may be lowered. Disasters challenge the notion of social capital, which includes the values, morals, and beliefs that members of any community hold to maintain cohesion. Threat to life is probably one of the most potent of psychological stressors, especially with biological, chemical, and radiologic agents (Ursano et al. 2003). Such perceptions of danger, realistic or not, have implications for the management of disasters. Public health officials, for example, focusing on the possibility of a disease outbreak, such as the H1N1 virus, must consider how the public may perceive the threat, including disease transmission mode, acuteness and proximity of risk, and availability of interventions or mitigating factors, and whether those interventions work or not. Several studies have demonstrated that individuals assess risk and threat based on their feelings of being in control and their level of knowledge and familiarity with an event (MacGregor and Fleming 1996). The perception of safety may influence an individual's adherence to public health recommendations, including possible quarantine. Individuals and communities tend to rank risk perception on what they know, true or not, and on how close those risks may be. Decision makers should consider not only how to implement a disaster plan; they should also consider how to educate the public about the plans in order to boost their sense of safety and gain their cooperation. Additionally, the perception of safety from the responder side should also be appreciated; how that safety level is perceived may impact work performance (Lam et al. 2007). While baseline clinical knowledge and competence may be a motivating factor for responders to help, a perception of safety remains the primary determinant to whether or not a health provider will respond to a mass casualty incident (Veenema et al. 2008).

5.3.2   STRESS BEHAVIOR

With reduced perceptions of safety, the public may alter their behaviors to better protect themselves and to heighten their sense of safety from perceived threat. For example, some people may choose not to fly after an aviation accident or after an event such as the terrorist attacks of September 11, 2001. Some shunned beef during the mad cow disease outbreak. And in the case of Severe Acute Respiratory Syndrome (SARS), they avoided going to Asia or Canada, and even Asian restaurants, for fear of contracting the illness. Evacuations may also be affected due to stress behavior, with some people self-evacuating, for example, rather than following planned or organized evacuations (Soffer et al. 2008). In a potential disease outbreak, many in the community may be reluctant to go to public events and gatherings that they feel may lead to contracting the illness. At the same time, they may be more likely to go to emergency rooms and hospitals to seek medical assistance for fear that they or their family members have contracted the illness. These self-protective behaviors have implications about how, where, and when medical assistance can and will be delivered in a crisis. Plus, of course, there can be economic and social consequences to such mass changes in behavior. One study that assessed a Scandinavian population of pregnant women after the Chernobyl incident found an increase in concerns about malformation of fetuses. Nine out of 10 pregnant women made behavioral changes to reduce exposures, most commonly by avoiding locally grown vegetables (Krüger and Krüger 1995). Public health officials will need to factor in help-seeking behaviors such as these in the course of disaster planning.

5.3.3   STIGMATIZATION

Blame is often seen in disasters whereby there are perceptions that the disaster was attributed to the acts and beliefs of some entities or groups. Individuals and groups, by association, may be stigmatized after disasters. Sadly, after the September 11th attacks and the London train bombings, some members of the Muslim community around the world were victims of discrimination and hate crimes, despite the efforts of officials to stem such acts. There may also be stigmatization of those who are quarantined in an epidemic. Individuals and communities may be concerned about being marginalized for being quarantined, even when they turn out to be disease free. For example, during the SARS crisis, many associated being near Asians as a significant risk factor to contracting the illness (Person et al. 2004), and this led to individuals' decreased interactions with Asians. Also during the SARS outbreak, the public avoided health care workers who had cared for those infected with SARS because of fears that they might contract the illness from them (Koh et al. 2005). Such stigmatization observed during the SARS outbreak was in many ways similar to how HIV patients have been and, to some degree, continue to be treated (Holzemer et al. 2009).

Groups may not only be stigmatized by the general population, but they may also perceive stigmatization coming from health providers. For example, individuals from a lower socioeconomic group, such as the uninsured or an ethnic group that has been traditionally marginalized by the health care community, may be reluctant to get medical assistance, believing falsely that they may be turned away. Thus, disaster public health response planners need to appreciate the potential for stigmatization so groups will not feel marginalized or be discriminated against.

5.3.4 TRUST

How the public adheres to disaster plans and instructions depends on their level of confidence in how those plans will be carried out and in those who devised the plans. The public is more likely to have a higher level of trust in plans and directives when they have been included in the planning stages. Rumors may be present in these communities that can further reinforce the distrust of government. Many individuals may also be reluctant to seek external resources for help after a disaster, especially if these resources are government related. This may in part be due to mistrust or lack of confidence of government-related entities to adequately address their concerns. This is especially true of individuals from various cultural groups. For example, some groups, such as African Americans and Native Americans, may have historical distrust in government. Almost 60 years after the Tuskegee Syphilis Study, there remains distrust and suspicion of the government and medical profession in African American communities that has adversely impacted health education, such as HIV education (Thomas and Quinn 1991). This distrust of government can also occur in ethnic populations that have experienced distrust of their home government. Marked distrust of past and current government information about health effects was evident for many Russians who still report that they frequently think about the Chernobyl nuclear accident (Koscheyev et al. 1997). Their experiences and level of distrust could be generalized to reflect all governments, including the United States.

Unfortunately, trust in disaster response agencies, especially those from the governmental sector, was severely strained in the aftermath of Hurricane Katrina. Many affected individuals believed the government failed not only in protecting them from the hurricane but also failed to provide the necessary postdisaster aid. Even if new or revised plans attempt to address previous problems, the shadow of Katrina may cloud the public's trust in the agencies responsible for carrying out the disaster plans. In essence, the public may unrealistically raise their expectations of the government's disaster response, while also being more critical of any problems that may arise. Early detection, successful management of casualties, and effective interventions can foster and strengthen the public's sense of safety and increase confidence in institutions (Ursano et al. 2003).

5.4 MASS CASUALTY INCIDENTS

In mass casualty incidents, especially related to a pandemic outbreak, there are two important public health issues that mental health can and must closely interface with: surge capacity and risk communication.

5.4.1 SURGE CAPACITY

The impact of disasters on surge capacity has been one of the major concerns of disaster response planners and policy makers. It is a common assumption in public health disaster planning that there will be a sudden influx of casualties that will strain an already-taxed health system, thus overwhelming its scarce resources and personnel. When Iraq launched 39 Scud missiles in Israel during the first Persian Gulf War, 1,059 people presented to emergency rooms but only 232 of them actually suffered direct injuries and there were two deaths from the attacks (Karsenty et al. 1991). In the Aum Shinrikyo sarin gas attack on the Japanese subway system in 1995, more than 5,500 casualties presented at nearby area hospitals. Of those, approximately 1,000 were treated for direct exposure to sarin gas. This is a ratio of four to one psychological casualties versus physical casualties (Tucker

1996). In another study, a significant portion of mildly affected patients after an aborted terrorist attack required psychiatric evaluation (Bloch et al. 2007).

The concept of surge capacities applies not only to health systems but also to other areas of disaster response, including social service deliveries such as sheltering and aid. Family Assistance Centers (FAC) can be quickly overwhelmed. Individuals may present to health care facilities with caregivers, family members, and friends. All these individuals can quickly overwhelm a system response capability. And while much of the focus of surge capacity has been to look at the number of individuals presenting to a health care system, it is equally important to consider that many individuals may not. One study showed that 52 percent of individuals interviewed would not evacuate due to the presence of elderly relatives in the home and 44 percent would not evacuate due to the presence of children in the home (Redlener, Markenson, and Grant 2003).

Important steps by disaster public health planners can include education about disaster preparedness before disaster occurs. Communities should be given clear instructions on what they can do alone and in partnerships with local disaster response agencies to prepare their communities. There should be consistent messaging from various stakeholders, governmental and nongovernmental, public and private agencies about any information related to disaster preparedness and disaster risks. Reassurance from recognized public figures—political leaders, community leaders, or other high-profile and community-respected figures—can be extremely helpful to reinforce the efforts of disaster planning. This should be done, perhaps in town hall formats, with community input to ensure appropriate feedback and buy-in (Engel et al. 2003). The hospital systems themselves will need to develop coordinated and integrated mechanisms, both between hospitals and all departments within those hospitals to handle surge (Dayton et al. 2008). A system of follow-up services should also be planned with arrangements for families and other ancillary and extended support systems. Lastly, a volunteer management system, that is, call-up and credentialing, should be developed and strengthened. The Medical Reserve Corp (MRC) and Certified Emergency Response Teams (CERT) are two such examples.

5.4.2 RISK COMMUNICATION

Disasters can lead to intense fear and anxiety amongst the affected population. Many are afraid of the insidious nature of such events, as well as the unknown nature of it as well as the government response to these events. The most effective means of mitigating the anxiety and fear in response to disasters is the use of primary prevention, effective communication with the goals of minimizing the human loss by reducing the number of casualties (e.g., fatalities, physical wounds, and psychological injury) and lessening and even preventing the widespread sense of helplessness in the general population. Effective risk communication, with the gradual dissemination of information and guidance to the public, can empower affected populations to become active participants in this prevention effort. The public needs to be given information concerning the nature of the threat and the risks, as well as effective methods of coping with them (Noy 2004). Information will also need to be focused and nonhomogeneous as the information needed in an affected area may be different from information to a broader population (Peltz et al. 2008).

Effective risk communication is a vital component of any disaster response plan. Such communication can lessen and mitigate public anxiety, concerns, and fear related to a disaster. Effective risk communication needs to consider how such messages will be interpreted and how they will translate into the perception of risk. Not all messages will be interpreted the same by everyone in the community. One message may be benign to one group but not to another. Mental health clinicians can work closely with public health officials and community leaders to identify and craft messages that are relevant to the targeted groups. Different cultural groups utilize different media to obtain a majority of its news (Ng 2005).

How the public may perceive risk communication may be influenced by the culture of the affected population. In a study by Lasker, two-fifths of the population (and up to three-fifths of minority and low-income groups) expressed serious concerns about what government officials would say or do in a potential smallpox terrorist attack. Forty-two percent of the American population believed there was a moderate to very good chance that government officials in the United States would decide to do something in this situation that they *knew* would harm them or people like them in some way (Lasker 2004). A total of 41 percent of the population believed the government would do one or both of the above. Concern about what officials would say or do in a smallpox situation was prevalent among Hispanic (61 percent), African American (57 percent) and foreign-born (55 percent) Americans compared to 31 percent of the general population. Two-fifths of the American population was concerned that government officials would knowingly: (1) conceal or withhold information from the public; (2) lie or provide false information to the public (e.g., about the safety of the vaccine); (3) experiment on people; or (4) look after their own interests—or the interests of wealthy Caucasian Americans—at the expense of others. In terms of vaccination for a potential smallpox terrorist attack, half of the population (48 percent)—and two-thirds of African Americans (68 percent)—would be extremely or very concerned if they were asked to sign a form at the vaccination site acknowledging that the smallpox vaccine is an investigational drug that has not been completely tested (Lasker 2004).

5.5 RESPONSE TO CHEMICAL, BIOLOGICAL, OR RADIOLOGICAL HAZARDS

Disaster planning and response by the public-mental health partnership can be conceptualized from a cyclical manner that includes pre-event, acute response, and postevent phases (see Figure 5.2). While there are unique focuses to chemical, biological, or radiological events, there will be many issues and challenges that transcend all types of disasters and public health emergencies. The various phases of the cycle help define the unique reactions and needs of individuals and communities and identify the roles and responsibilities in disasters and other public health emergencies. Disaster planning along these phases can help provide a paradigm to shape and guide planning, policy development, and response implementation (Gurwitch et al. 2004).

5.5.1 PRE-EVENT PHASE

Effective disaster response needs to be approached from a public health and mental health collaborative. Much of the foundation for this collaboration is set in the pre-event stage. Mental health's role can be at the system level as well as the clinical level. At the system level, first and utmost, senior leadership within disaster planning agencies must be committed to a robust and integrated disaster

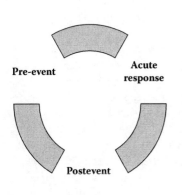

Pre-event
Create joint public health and mental health disaster response plan
Educate communities on disaster issues and disaster mental health
Identify community resilience strengths and assets
Create response structure
Disease surveillance planning
Acute response
Ensure continuity of public health/mental health operation
Provide psychological first aid
Promote responder wellness
Postevent
Promote individual and community resilience
Ongoing liaison between public health and mental health
Mental health interventions in conjunction with public health
Continue worker wellness

FIGURE 5.2 Matrix of disaster public/mental health response. (Modified from Ng, A., *Psychiatric Issues in Emergency Care Settings*, 11–18, 2005.)

response that includes mental health. Mental health must advocate actively for the role of mental health in disaster planning, including participating in the overall development of response plans in the community (Ursano, Fullerton, and Norwood 1995). An important component of disaster response is triage care. Timely and adequate preplanning can lessen the impact of surge on communities and health resources. Mental health should collaborate closely with public health to develop plans to properly refer individuals who seek help in a disaster setting, including those seeking psychological care (Gurwitch et al. 2004; Ruzek et al. 2004; Van Amerongen et al. 1993). Public health in collaboration with mental health can help plan for the presence of spontaneous volunteerism of health care workers. Often in disasters, both medical and nonmedical volunteers may present to health care facilities. Many are eager to help and have a wide range of experiences and training. But chaos ensues with too many helpers for each patient, or leaders becoming engaged in treatment and lacking familiarity with disaster response plans (Romundstad et al. 2004). Mechanisms need to be in place to determine the credentialing and the deployment of these volunteers in a manageable manner. An appreciation of the potential impacts of volunteers, including how to manage them in the response, can assist organizations to plan more effectively. For instance, what drives volunteers to come forth, what are their expertise and expectations, and how to identify barriers to volunteers are some of the questions organizations need to consider to better manage and coordinate this vital resource.

The mental health and public health partnership can help shape messages to the public as to what to do and what to expect in disasters, as such messages can alleviate psychological distress about disasters (Noy 2004). Education is an important component of disaster preparedness and mitigation, and educational messaging can alleviate anxiety about disasters. In the pre-event phase, mental health workers need to be educated about what to expect in disasters and their sequelae, the differing effects of various disasters in their communities, as well as the workers' role in the response process. Mental health staff need to develop familiarity with disasters and public health and emergency medical services (EMS) disaster responses (Garcia-Castrillo and Larcia 2003; Moles 1999; Stratton et al. 1996). Public health and mental health workers need to develop a basic understanding of disaster management issues, including familiarity with disaster management language, human services issues, disaster response, and recovery processes (Norwood, Ursano, and Fullerton 2000; Holmes 2004). In disasters, there are unique social issues that may present challenges to both public and mental health responses. There needs to be an awareness of the different impacts of disasters. Biologic, chemical, and radiological events can be either human-caused or natural. Natural disasters may raise issues that are different than those from human-caused disasters, including terrorism (Ursano, Fullerton, and Norwood 1995). Psychological effects of natural disasters can be different from those of human-caused disasters. Individuals are more likely to recover quickly from natural disasters than from human-caused disasters, including acts of terrorism. This may be related to the former event being more easily attributed as an act of God. Natural disasters often occur in areas that have been susceptible to these events in the past. Acts of terrorism will likely involve law enforcement, in which disaster victims are considered to be victims of crime. Mental health staff may be interviewing survivors, possibly subjecting disaster survivors to additional reminders of trauma, and thus increasing the likelihood of psychological distress. Such issues can present challenges to mustering a robust, integrated public health/mental health response to disasters.

Mental health workers can educate public health workers to have a greater understanding of postdisaster psychological concerns. There is a diverse spectrum of disaster stress reactions that affect individuals at various points after a disaster (Ursano, Fullerton, and Norwood 1995). These reactions can present as cognitive (e.g., problems with concentration, difficulty in making decisions, and memory), behavioral (e.g., withdrawal, mood irritability, and overwork), emotional (e.g., anger, depression, and anxiety), physical (e.g., lack of appetite, sleep disturbances, and extreme fatigue), and spiritual (e.g., intense use of prayer, loss or gain of faith, and loss or gain of trust) in nature. While many of these reactions are intense and distressing for the affected individuals, they are often transient. Many individuals do not go on to develop psychiatric disorders or have significant functional impairments. However, in more severe cases, these distresses can affect individuals' abilities to deal with postdisaster issues, including help-seeking or the processing of information. A close collaboration between mental health and public health workers can provide close community surveillance of the effects on the general population.

An integrated public health and mental health approach has a liaison role in community education, networking, and support. Community resilience assets and strengths can be identified. Mental health and public health staff can be an important interface between individuals in crisis and community resources support. In day-to-day work, mental health and public health workers are used to networking and setting up referral sources for their clients (Ruzek et al. 2004). Thus, it is vital that the two disciplines proactively engage the community in disaster–mental health planning. The public must be engaged in the planning process. Unfortunately, much of disaster planning overall has not elicited the input of the public (Lasker 2004). This can result in misallocation of resources due to inaccurate determination of needs, the promotion of distrust between the public and the disaster response structure, and the disenfranchising of the community from managing its own disaster response and facilitating community resilience. It is important that mental health and public health workers appreciate the unique needs of the community and advocate for the public participation in disaster planning. At the same time, it is important to establish links with other community partners such as social service agencies. With such formal and informal relationships established, agencies are familiar with one another and know what services each can provide when disaster strikes.

5.5.2 ACUTE RESPONSE PHASE

One of the most important aspects of disaster response is the effective use of limited resources. This is especially true with respect to mental health and its partnership with public health. It is important that mental health work toward the efficient use of its resources. There are limited mental health resources in disaster response. As such, it is important to identify what disaster issues should or should not receive direct mental health interventions. For example, individuals may be upset over a bioterrorism event, and an appropriate intervention may be for public health officials to answer their questions about the offending agent to alleviate their anxiety, rather than direct mental health interventions for their distress. Identifying and addressing the cause of distress is just as important as addressing the distress itself. Clear, consistent, and reliable information from trusted sources can also help mitigate public anxiety about disasters and public health emergencies (Noy 2004; Benedek, Holloway, and Becker 2002).

In the early acute response phase of disasters, appropriate disaster interventions require the public health system to appreciate some of the unique issues faced by individuals affected by disasters. Many of these disaster issues have direct as well as indirect psychological consequences. Individuals will present with a variety of issues after disasters (see Table 5.1). In the early acute phase of disaster, basic needs are often the main concern of those affected. These basic needs

---

TABLE 5.1

Types of Disaster Issues

Loss of family members, friends, and animals (i.e., livestock, pets)

Direct or indirect injuries (medical and psychiatric)

Loss of home/work

Displacement (i.e., evacuation or inability to evacuate)

Feelings stemming from actual event

Frustrations from response and recovery efforts (i.e., benefits, community let down)

Overall chaos caused by disaster

Source: From Ng., A., *Psychiatric Issues in Emergency Care Settings*, 11–18, 2005. With permission.

---

include food and shelter, information, and social support to assist with such issues as displacement, obtaining financial assistance, and reconnecting with families and friends. Individuals may try to discover additional information about ongoing public health risks, that is, will there be more attacks or more people stricken with illness? They may look for information about their loved ones who are hospitalized or missing (Rodoplu et al. 2004).

Some of the patients may present with physical symptoms that are secondary to psychological concerns. These physical symptoms may include back pain, flu-like symptoms, headaches, insomnia, chest palpitations, and shortness of breath. Such presentations may be especially prevalent among some cultural groups where there is greater tendency to somatize their psychological distress (Aderibigbe, Bloch, and Pandurangi 2003). Patients may also be more likely to present with physical complaints if the disaster is biological or chemical in nature (Hassett and Sigal 2002; Norwood, Holloway, and Ursano 2001). Such presentations can put further strain on postdisaster resources. By collaborating, public and mental health workers can help identify and mitigate some of these demands. This can be done through more effective triaging of individuals with psychiatric distress from truly medical concerns. Additionally, the public can be educated to take preventive measures to mitigate some of their psychological concerns, thus lessen the risk of somatization. In some instances, faith-based organizations and agencies should be used to complement mental health resources, as many individuals may seek spiritual counseling before they will seek psychological interventions (Stocks 2001).

There will be individuals who will present to health facilities after disasters seeking help for psychological distress reactions such as panic, severe anxiety, depression, or shock. As described earlier, many of these reactions, while intense, are transient. Affected individuals are often responsive to Psychological First Aid (PFA) such as support and reassurance (Ritchie et al. 2004). Other effective interventions may include helping individuals address any medical concerns, return to their routines, prioritize and problem solve, and receive appropriate referrals for disaster recovery aid (Watson et al. 2003). It is important to bear in mind that the goal of postdisaster mental health intervention is focusing on assisting and facilitating individuals to return to their predisaster functioning level. Promoting individual resilience is an important component of disaster–mental health interventions. Affected individuals should be encouraged to utilize predisaster support structures and resources.

It is important that any collaborative postdisaster response between mental health and public health services takes into account not only the individuals directly affected but also extended networks (as previously identified in the disaster pyramid). Often after disasters, individuals with health and mental health distresses will present on their own or be accompanied by family or friends. It will be important that postdisaster public health interventions include them in the acute response phase. By including this extended network of family, friends, and caregivers, they can help lessen the distress of the direct victims. Additionally, they can mitigate future stresses. Such an extended network can also aid in disease surveillance, to help identify disaster victims' current needs, and later in the postdisaster phase.

Ensuring health and mental health staff wellness in disasters is a key component of acute disaster response. Disasters affect communities, and very likely, disaster and trauma workers, such as emergency health and mental health workers, may have secondary traumatization from the care of disaster victims (Fullerton, Ursano, and Wang 2004; Palm, Polusny, and Follette 2004; Ursano et al. 1999; Van der Ploeg and Kleber 2003; North et al. 2002). The physical and psychological injuries observed by health workers in disasters are often extremely traumatic and intense. Additionally, the disaster work itself is stressful on disaster health responders. There may be conflicting demands on them, and there may be changing directions and priorities, as well as information on their roles, from leadership. Responders may need to assume multiple and unfamiliar roles. In pandemic situations, health workers are at higher risk of being in close proximity to infected patients, thus resulting in uncertainty about whether or not the workers themselves may have become infected and contagious. This concern may lead to social isolation and onset and persistence of health fears. Workers may suffer from changes in sleep and eating patterns due to irregular and intense work schedules and demands. There may be cognitive impairments as consequences to the changes in sleep and eating patterns, which potentially can impact patient care. Health workers who overwork after disasters can suffer the adverse effects of lack of sleep and subsequent negative influences on concentration.

Additionally, emergency health workers may themselves be disaster survivors. They may have lost property, or have family members and friends injured, killed, or missing. They, too, may have been displaced. They can have direct psychological distress from being the primary victims. It is therefore vital that public health and mental health workers proactively address workforce wellness to mitigate burnout issues. Interventions may include staff wellness monitoring, distress surveillance, encouraging the use of more regular schedules, assuring adequate sleep and nutrition, and promoting wellness skills. Helping to maintain communication between workers and their families can be a useful intervention. Individual and group counseling may also be necessary and should be made available, including educating providers to the needs and resiliency factors of this important population.

5.5.3 POSTEVENT PHASE

The partnership between mental health and public health must continue to have a significant role in the postevent phase of disaster response. Individuals and communities may have ongoing and persistent psychological distress, as well as new ones. Somatization of psychological symptoms may continue for some individuals to seek care. Mass psychogenic illness has also been identified as a consequence of events stemming from these agents. This is a social phenomenon where two or more people share beliefs about a syndrome of symptoms with no identifiable etiology. This has been reported after nuclear or radiological releases, excessive smog incidents, and water contamination (Boss 1997).

There needs to be an ongoing education and liaison for mental health and public health workers concerning patients presenting with psychiatric reactions and symptoms. Mental health interventions may be similar to the acute phase, with some application of psychological first aid as well as ongoing attention to basic needs issues. Additionally, as the disaster environment becomes more stable, opportunities to provide more formal psychiatric interventions, such as cognitive behavioral therapy, may be possible (Gray, Maguen, and Litz 2004; Katz et al. 2002; Ruzek et al. 2008). Educating primary care providers about this modality can be helpful as these providers may be the first point of contact of any individuals with postdisaster psychological distresses (Yehuda 2002).

Staff wellness for health workers remains an important postevent concern. Ongoing monitoring of staff burnout is necessary, as well as appropriate interventions when warranted. Postdisaster interventions include encouraging health workers to return to regular work schedules when possible, as well as the appropriate use of breaks and vacations. There needs to be ongoing education on wellness skills. Ongoing advocacy and support of programs for both staff and their families will be important. Mental health workers can also encourage public health leadership to provide clear directives for staff in ongoing disaster response, as well as ongoing recognition for the work of the health workforce. Resources and support for families of health workers should continue to be made available (Palm, Polusny, and Follette 2004). Postevent assessment of the public health response can refine the structure of response and enhance the abilities to respond to future disasters.

5.6 WORKING WITH SPECIAL POPULATIONS (PEOPLE WITH DISABILITIES AND CULTURAL GROUPS)

It is vital that any effective collaboration between population-based disaster–public health and mental health response appreciate the unique needs of special populations. While there may be many special populations that are based on professions, age, gender, and culture—all of which have unique needs and challenges in any disaster–public health response—this section will focus briefly on two important groups, those with disabilities and cultural groups. It is important to appreciate that there may be overlapping issues between special populations, as well as individuals who may belong to multiple special populations, for example, an elderly Latino or a young woman with a hearing impairment.

Most disaster plans and responses have focused on addressing the needs of a well population, including someone who can cognitively access and process information or someone without any physical impairment. However, there is a significant proportion of the community that has some degree of disability, be it physical, psychiatric, or developmental delay. These individuals have specific unique needs, and disaster–health service deliveries can pose significant challenges to public health authorities. These individuals may have difficulty following instructions regarding their care. Someone who is deaf may require sign language interpreters or additional signs that tell them what to do. People with visual impairment may need guidance. Transportation aids, such as wheelchairs or vehicles that can accommodate individuals with physical disabilities, need to be considered in disaster planning. Lastly, individuals with preexisting physical disabilities may find their disabilities exacerbated by the disaster trauma, thus further complicating their medical management.

In addition to individuals with physical disabilities, individuals with psychiatric and developmental disabilities can also present unique challenges to disaster health responders. Their disabilities may be worsened by the disaster. Some may become agitated or may have further cognitive and judgment impairments that can affect how they interact with health workers. Sleep disturbances may precipitate relapses, such as mania. Individuals with substance abuse may relapse. Disaster stresses can also lead to recurrence of symptoms in individuals with preexisting trauma and posttraumatic stress disorder (PTSD), leading to flashbacks and nightmares of past trauma. In the stress of disaster, these individuals may have disruption in their medication and other treatment regimens that can worsen their preexisting conditions. Such disruptions may include the loss of treatment facilities, medication issues, and even the ability to pay for treatment.

Individuals with disabilities may have additional issues that have direct, as well as indirect, impacts on public health response. Similar to the extended network described earlier in the chapter, these individuals may have caretakers. These caretakers can be both formal, that is, health aides, or informal, such as family members, friends, or other well-meaning individuals. Any public health response will need to make accommodations for these caretakers who can influence surge capacity. Some individuals with disabilities may not wish to be transported despite existing danger if their caretaker is not accompanying them. The transport of individuals with disabilities to health facilities in disaster may have to include these caretakers, thus influencing the ability of emergency medical services to transport additional patients. Failure by public health systems to recognize these needs will exacerbate stress and anxiety amongst not only the individuals with disabilities but also their caretakers. It will be necessary for the public health system to devise plans to address the presence of service animals, including the handling and sheltering of such animals. For example, arrangements will need to be made for such service animals in health care settings if there are mass vaccinations. Lastly, many individuals with disabilities often have special human service needs, both prior to and following a disaster, that public health systems must consider in disaster planning.

Multiple approaches are necessary for public health and mental health systems to adequately address the concerns of individuals with disabilities in disaster. Foremost is the need to have greater awareness of and education about the unique needs of individuals with disabilities in disaster and how such needs can affect the public health response. It will also be important to decrease stigmatization of these individuals by the disaster response system and to develop greater competency to provide care for these individuals in disasters. Such awareness must be achieved at two levels, the senior public health and mental health leadership and the health workers who provide direct clinical care in disasters. It is important that public health leaders assess the level of disability needs in their communities and what resources can be brought in to address those needs and to provide postdisaster clinical care. This can be done effectively in collaboration with human services agencies in the communities that provide services to individuals with disabilities, as well as the emergency management community. Outreach to this community will help to educate individuals with disabilities about what they can do to lessen and mitigate the impact of disaster stress. The use of outreach services and telephone interventions, such as hotlines, can be effective (McMurray and Steiner 2000). Lastly, the needs of individuals with disabilities should be incorporated into any drills and exercises, including tabletop, so public health personnel can learn to work comfortably with this population.

5.6.1 Cultural Groups

According to the 2000 U.S. Census, ethnic minorities were 29 percent of the U.S. population in 2000 and are projected to grow to 34 percent and 37 percent by 2010 and 2020, respectively (United States Census Bureau 2001). While the importance of cultural consideration has been emphasized in disasters (Marsella and Christopher 2004; Webb, Wachtendorf, and Eyre 2000), cultural groups do present unique issues that need to be appreciated for the effective integration of disaster mental health services with public health services. Some of those unique issues have been highlighted throughout the chapter, but there are some additional ones to bear in mind. Many members of cultural groups have past traumatic experiences, either from their home country or from historic trauma, as Native Americans and African Americans have had. A disaster can trigger past trauma, resulting in greater psychological distress (Kinzie et al. 2002). Many members of these groups may also be of lower socioeconomic status, which has been shown to increase risk of adverse psychological sequelae (Solomon and Smith 1994). The interpretation of traumatic events also varies amongst many cultural groups. For example, in some Eastern world cultures, a sense of fatalism or predestiny may be the predominant theme in the members of those cultures as they process their traumatic experience. This reflects their belief in Buddhism, as they perceive death as a natural part of and an extension of life itself (Char et al. 1996). Bereaved individuals may demonstrate symptoms that might appear to be pathologic, when in fact these symptoms may be expressions of a culturally patterned response that is thought appropriate within that person's culture. The Mu Ghayeb belief in Omani society involves a complete denial of the loss of a person for a relatively long period with the expectation of the return of the dead (al-Adawi, Burjorjee, and al-Issa 1997). In the West, hallucinations of the dead are considered to be normal for the first month or so after a death, but among the Hopi, it is not uncommon for hallucinations to continue for months or years (Matckett 1972). Disaster care workers unfamiliar with Hispanic culture may be unequipped to deal with the histrionic, seizure-like episodes of *ataque de nervios* ("attack of nerves") in response to stress (Einsenbruch 1984).

There may be different burial rituals with some culture groups. In Islam, the deceased are always buried, never cremated (Gatrad 1994). However, in disasters, such burials may not be possible. The victim may be missing or the remains may not be whole or they may be badly disfigured, thus creating distress in the Islamic family. Mental health clinicians need to have appreciation for the significance of losses amongst cultural groups. There may be gender issues where some ethnic groups may be more responsive and accepting to a provider of the same gender. Individuals of cultural groups may also not seek help from emergency rooms but instead go to traditional healers. This may be related to their distrust of the "external" system, as well as a different interpretation of disease. In an extreme example, one Khmer tribe resisted a vaccination program as a result of a serious epidemic outbreak in a refugee camp. Some people even hid from the authorities because to them, the concept of contagion was inconceivable. They believe that spirits rather than microorganisms cause illness (Bernier 1992). These cultural nuances present unique challenges to delivering response and care outside of the more familiar health and social services systems.

Today disasters have wide-ranging global impacts beyond the borders of the United States due to extensive social network overseas, increased mobility, and increased communication, including the media (Ng 2005). Any effective public health response to disasters must include the strengthening of disaster cultural competency with an appreciation to the issues associated with these diverse cultural groups.

5.7 FROM THEORY TO PRACTICE

What does the collaboration between mental health and public health services look like during the pre-, acute response, and postevent phases of disasters? The following examples were given by American Red Cross (ARC) and mental health workers in ARC chapters and county and state agencies across New York State.

Example 5.1: H1N1 Eligibility Concerns

During the beginning of the recent H1N1 vaccination clinics, the lines were long in early weeks when limited supplies of H1N1 vaccine were available and there was more nasal spray than injectable vaccine available. Both disaster mental health and health workers provided information about the two vaccines. Some people in line, in their urgency to get the vaccine, while not in the high-risk categories, apparently were believed to be lying about preexisting conditions in order to qualify for the limited supply of vaccine. Health workers discussed whether to begin further exploration of their medical conditions to determine if they were in fact eligible. Mental health workers interceded to avoid increased agitation and disruption and allowed people to self report on their preexisting conditions. Put into the role as "Ad Hoc swine flu police," it was virtually impossible to verify most of the claims and the problems were compounded by the unpredictable distribution of supplies in different parts of the country or even within the same state.

Example 5.2: Heightened Distress and Anxiety during H1N1

In central New York City, mental health workers were providing assistance both at the public health clinic and by staffing a phone hotline providing information and emotional support. In the fall, the H1N1 phone line received a call from a woman requesting information about the vaccination. She was highly anxious and had not been able to leave her home for weeks due to her increasing fear of contracting the H1N1 virus. She had no food in her home. The hotline worker spoke to her director and then called the county Department of Mental Health who, in turn, contacted the mobile emergency team. The mobile team made a home visit and subsequently helped her get both mental health services and an H1N1 vaccination. In this capacity, the disaster mental health worker provided assessment, screening, and referral services to someone demonstrating severe symptoms in the face of a health emergency.

Example 5.3: Hepatitis A in Western New York

An employee in charge of the produce department of a large supermarket in western New York was diagnosed with Hepatitis A. The County Health Department was the lead agency and offered vaccinations to anyone who might have had contact with the produce department. Two sequential vaccinations at a 4- to 6-month interval was the recommended treatment. The first injection was paid for by the supermarket chain, and more than 7,000 people received it within three days. For the second vaccination, a POD (Point of Distribution) was set up at the local community college where physicians were available to screen and ensure that individuals received the correct injection and accurate information. Public buses were parked outside the community college to keep people warm while they waited in line. Over four hundred people were able to wait within the college building with 12 to 15 buses outside filled with more waiting people. The first two days, the average waiting time was four hours with some people waiting up to seven hours. By the third day, the wait was one hour. Mental health workers were originally brought in by the health department in teams of three or four to help with people waiting in line. After "just-in-time training," they were able to provide accurate information on Hepatitis A, how it is transmitted, what the risks of the vaccine were, and the symptoms. They talked to those in line, checked on their level of anxiety and discomfort, and especially reached out to the elderly and to parents with small children who were the most distressed. They regularly went on the buses, as well as to the lines, to let people know the wait time, give them encouragement, and monitor how they were doing. The buses helped to avoid dangerous crowding and to maintain a calm, orderly process. The workers provided water and snacks both on the buses and in the building. Some of those waiting in line expressed basic vaccination anxiety reactions—fear of needles—which intensified as they waited for hours. They set up separate waiting areas for children and found that kids did not benefit by watching their parents or others get the shot. The contagion of parental anxiety at times led the workers to bring the children to a separate play area with parental permission. When one child would become distressed and start screaming, it immediately would lead to six or seven others starting to scream as well. The POD functioned for three 12-hour days with many staff working 14 hours. Mental health workers also reached out to the public health staff to ensure that they were taking breaks, eating and hydrating, and changing assignments if needed. Four months later, the county health department provided a drive-thru clinic for the second injection by appointment, with people remaining in their car and waiting for 10 minutes afterwards. The community members demonstrated a very different and highly diminished level of anxiety, and a much smaller percentage came for the second injection. Two mental health workers staffed the drive-thru clinic and primarily provided support to the staff. The success of this response to a sudden health emergency was based on the prior relationship of public health and mental health services at the county level and with the ARC chapter.

These examples reflect the critical importance of implementing key foundation pieces before a disaster occurs in order to have clear roles, relationships, and communication utilizing a shared framework at the city, county, state, and federal levels.

5.8   A PUBLIC HEALTH APPROACH

Disasters and public health emergencies pose significant public health and mental health risks due to their traumatic effects on populations (Noji 2000; Logue 1996). As distressful as the direct mental health consequences of disasters on individuals are, it is important to appreciate that mental health impact on communities as a whole. Just as important, indirect mental health consequences affect every aspect of disaster response and recovery, thus influencing community-based resilience. Thinking in terms of public health can also improve predisaster preparedness by encouraging individuals and communities to get the training they need *before* a disaster, to reduce the impact and even the likelihood of a disaster. Appreciating such issues can facilitate and lessen the traumatic impacts of disasters, thus decreasing stress and anxiety not only on affected individuals but also on whole communities. Lastly, more stringent and robust research is needed to strengthen further the knowledge base, not only in the scientific and clinical arena but also operationally, so that the integration of public health and mental health services in disaster preparation, response, and long-term recovery and resilience can be more clearly defined. Through these efforts, a comprehensive paradigm of clinical care practices can be developed to promote greater individual and community resilience in disasters.

REFERENCES

Aderibigbe, Y. A., R. M. Bloch, and A. Pandurangi. 2003. Emotional and somatic stress in eastern North Carolina: Help seeking behavior. *International Journal of Social Psychiatry* 49(2): 126–141.
al-Adawi, S., R. Burjorjee, and I. al-Issa. 1997. Mu-Ghayeb: A culture-specific response to bereavement in Oman. *International Journal of Social Psychiatry* 43(2): 144–151.

Benedek, D. M., H. C. Holloway, and S. M. Becker. 2002. Emergency mental health management in bioterror-ism events. *Emergency Medicine Clinics of North America 20*(2): 393–407.

Bernier, D. 1992. The Indochinese refugees: A perspective from various stress theories. In *Social Work with Immigrants and Refugees,* ed. A. S. Ryan, 15–30. New York. Haworth Press.

Bloch, Y. H., A. Leiba, N. Veaacnin, Y. Paizer, D. Scwartz, A. Kraskas, G. Weiss, A. Goldberg, and Y. Bar-Dayan. 2007. Managing mild casualties in mass-casualty incidents: Lessons learned from an aborted terrorist attack. *Prehospital and Disaster Medicine 22*(3): 181–185.

Boss, L. P. 1997. Epidemic hysteria: A review of the published literature. *Epidemiologic Reviews 19*(2): 233–243.

Char, D. F., K. S. Tom, G. C. Young, T. Murakami, and R. Ames. 1996. A view of death and dying among the Chinese and Japanese. *Hawaii Medical Journal 55*(12): 286–290, 295.

Coker, A. L., J. S. Hanks, K. S. Eggleston, J. Risser, P. G. Tee, K. J. Chronister, C. L. Troisi, R. Arafat, and L. Franzini. 2006. Social and mental health needs assessment of Katrina evacuees. *Disaster Management & Response 4*(3): 88–94.

Dayton, C., J. Ibrahim, M. Augenbraun, S. Brooks, K. Mody, D. Holford, P. Roblin, and B. Arquilla. 2008. Integrated plan to augment surge capacity. *Prehospital and Disaster Medicine 23*(2): 113–119.

DiGiovanni, C., Jr. 2003. The spectrum of human reactions to terrorist attacks with weapons of mass destruc-tion: Early management considerations. *Prehospital and Disaster Medicine 18*(3): 253–257.

Einsenbruch, M. 1984. Cross-cultural aspects of bereavement II: Ethnic and cultural variations in the develop-ment of bereavement practices. *Culture, Medicine and Psychiatry 8*(4): 315–347.

Engel, C. C., A. Jaffer, J. Adkins, V. Sheliga, D. Cowan, and W. J. Katon. 2003. Population-based health care: A model for restoring community health and productivity following terrorist attack. In *Terrorism and Disaster: Individual and Community Mental Health Interventions,* eds. R. J. Ursano, C. S. Fullerton, and A.E. Norwood, 287–307. New York: Cambridge University Press.

Fullerton, C. S., R. J. Ursano, and L. Wang. 2004. Acute stress disorder, posttraumatic stress disorder, and depression in disaster and rescue workers. *American Journal of Psychiatry 161*(8): 1370–1376.

Garcia-Castrillo, R. L., and M. A. Larcia. 2003. Terrorism in Spain: Emergency medical aspects. *Prehospital and Disaster Medicine 18*(2): 148–151.

Gatrad, A. R. 1994. Muslim customs surrounding death, bereavement, postmortem examinations, and organ transplants. *British Medical Journal 309*(6953): 521–523.

Gray, M. J., S. Maguen, and B. T. Litz. 2004. Acute psychological impact of disaster and large-scale trauma: Limitations of traditional interventions and future practice recommendations. *Prehospital and Disaster Medicine 19*(1): 64–72.

Gurwitch, R. H., M. Kees, S. M. Becker, M. Schreiber, B. Pfefferbaum, and D. Diamond. 2004. When disaster strikes: Responding to the needs of children. *Prehospital and Disaster Medicine 19*(1): 21–28.

Hassett, A. L., and L. H. Sigal. 2002. Unforeseen consequences of terrorism: Medically unexplained symptoms in time of fear. *Archives of Internal Medicine 162*(16): 1809–1813.

Holmes, A. 2004. System issues for psychiatrists responding to disasters. *Psychiatric Clinics of North America 27*(3): 541–558.

Holzemer, W. L., S. Human, J. Arudo, M. E. Rosa, M. J. Hamilton, I. Corless, L. Robinson, P. K. Nicholas, D. J. Wantland, S. Moezzi, S. Willard, K. Kirksey, C. Portillo, E. Sefcik, M. Rivero-Méndez, and M. Maryland. 2009. Exploring HIV stigma and quality of life for persons living with HIV infection. *Journal of the Association of Nurses in AIDS Care 20*(3): 161–168.

Hyams, K. C., F. M. Murphy, and S. Wessely. 2002. Responding to chemical, biological, or nuclear terrorism: The indirect and long term health effects may present the greatest challenge. *Journal of Health Politics, Policy and Law 27*(2): 273–292.

Institute of Medicine. 2003. *Preparing for the Psychological Consequences of Terrorism: A Public Health Strategy.* National Academies of Sciences, Washington, DC: National Academic Press.

Karsenty, E., J. Shemer, I. Alshech, B. Cojocaru, M. Moscovitz, Y. Shapiro, and Y. L. Danon. 1991. Medical aspects of the Iraqi missile attacks on Israel. *Israel Journal of Medical Sciences 27*(11-12): 603–607.

Katz, C. L., L. Pellegrino, A. Pandya, A. Ng, and L. E. DeLisi. 2002. Research on psychiatric outcomes and interventions subsequent to disasters: A review of the literature. *Psychiatry Research 110*(3): 201–217.

Kinzie, J. D., J. K. Boehnlein, C. Riley, and L. Sparr. 2002. The effects of September 11 on traumatized refugees: Reactivation of posttraumatic stress disorder. *Journal of Nervous and Mental Disease 190*(7): 437–441.

Koh, D., M. K. Lim, S. E. Chia, S. M. Ko, F. Qian, V. Ng, B. H. Tan, K. S. Wong, W. M. Chew, H. K. Tang, W. Ng, Z. Muttakin, S. Emmanuel, N. P. Fong, G. Koh, C. T. Kwa, K. B. Tan, and C. Fones. 2005. Risk perception and impact of Severe Acute Respiratory Syndrome (SARS) on work and personal lives of healthcare workers in Singapore: What can we learn? *Medical Care 43*(7):676–682.

Koscheyev, V. S., G. R. Leon, A. V. Gourine, and V. N. Gourine. 1997. The psychosocial aftermath of the Chernobyl disaster in an area of relatively low contamination. *Prehospital and Disaster Medicine 12*(1): 41–46.

Krüger, Ø., and M. B. Krüger. 1995. Pregnant women's worries and actions in a local community in response to the Chernobyl accident: A survey by general practitioners and district physicians. In *Biomedical and Psychosocial Consequences of Radiation from Man-Made Radionuclides in the Biosphere*, ed. G. Sundess, 211–216. Trondheim, Norway: Tapir.

Lam, K. W., F. L. Lau, W. K. Chan, and W. N. Wong. 2007. Effect of Severe Acute Respiratory Syndrome on bystander willingness to perform Cardiopulmonary Resuscitation (CPR)—Is compression-only preferred to standard CPR? *Prehospital and Disaster Medicine 22*(4): 325–329.

Lasker, R. D. 2004. *Redefining Readiness: Terrorism Planning through the Eyes of the Public.* New York: New York Academy of Medicine.

Leon, G. R. 2004. Overview of the psychosocial impact of disasters. *Prehospital and Disaster Medicine 19*(1): 4–9.

Logue J. N. 1996. Disasters, the environment, and public health: Improving our response. *American Journal of Public Health 86*(9): 1207–1210.

MacGregor, D. G., and R. Fleming. 1996. Risk perception and symptom reporting. *Risk Analysis 16*(6): 773–783.

Marsella, A. J., and M. A. Christopher. 2004. Ethnocultural considerations in disasters: An overview of research, issues and directions. *Psychiatric Clinics of North America 27*(3): 521–539.

Matckett, W. M. 1972. Repeated hallucinatory experiences as a part of the mourning process among Hopi Indian women. *Psychiatry 35*(2): 185–194.

Math, S. B., S. C. Girimaji, V. Benegal, G. S. Uday Kumar, A. Hamza, and D. Nagaraja. 2006. Tsunami: Psychosocial aspects of Andaman and Nicobar Islands. Assessments and interventions in the early phase. *International Review of Psychiatry 18*(3): 233–239.

McMurray, L., and W. Steiner. 2000. Natural disasters and service delivery to individuals with severe mental illness—ice storm 1998. *Canadian Journal of Psychiatry 45*(4): 383–385.

Moles, T. M. 1999. Emergency medical services systems and HAZMAT major incidents. *Resuscitation 42*(2): 103–116.

Ng, A. T. 2005. Cultural Diversity in the Integration of Disaster Mental Health and Public Health: A Case Study in Response to Bioterrorism. *International Journal of Emergency Mental Health 7*(1): 23–31.

Noji, E. K. 2000. The public health consequences of disasters. *Prehospital and Disaster Medicine 15*(4): 147–157.

Norris, F. H., M. J. Friedman, P. J. Watson, C. M. Byrne, E. Diaz, and K. Kaniasty. 2002. 60,000 disaster victims speak: Part I. An empirical review of the empirical literature, 1981–2001. *Psychiatry 65*(3): 207–239.

North, C. S. 2003. Psychiatric epidemiology of disaster responses. In *Annual Review of Psychiatry*, eds. R. J. Ursano and A. E. Norwood, 37–62. Washington, DC: American Psychiatric Association.

North, C. S., L. Tivis, J. C. McMillen, B. Pfefferbaum, E. L. Spitznagel, J. Cox, S. Nixon, K. P. Bunch, and E. M. Smith. 2002. Psychiatric disorders in rescue workers after the Oklahoma City bombing. *American Journal of Psychiatry 159*(5): 857–859.

Norwood, A. E., H. C. Holloway, and R. J. Ursano. 2001. Psychological effects of biological warfare. *Military Medicine 166*(12S): 27–28.

Norwood, A. E., R. J. Ursano, and C. S. Fullerton. 2000. Disaster Psychiatry: Principles and practice. *Psychiatric Quarterly 71*(3): 207–226.

Noy, S. 2004. Minimizing casualties in biological and chemical threats (war and terrorism): The importance of information to the public in a prevention program. *Prehospital and Disaster Medicine 19*(1): 29–36.

Palm, K. M., M. A. Polusny, and V. M. Follette. 2004. Vicarious traumatization: Potential hazards and interventions for disaster and trauma workers. *Prehospital and Disaster Medicine 19*(1): 73–78.

Peltz, R., A. S. Galit, M. Ventura-Gabay, and Y. Bar-Dayan. 2008. Differences in sources of information used by the population between the affected area and the general population during the first phase of a bird flu outbreak. *Prehospital and Disaster Medicine 23*(1): 57–59.

Person, B., F. Sy, K. Holton, B. Govert, and A. Liang. 2004. Fear and stigma: The epidemic within the SARS outbreak. *Emerging Infectious Diseases 10*(2): 358–363.

Pfefferbaum, B., C. S. North, B. W. Flynn, R. J. Ursano, G. McCoy, R. DeMartino, W. E. Julian, C. E. Dumont, H. C. Holloway, and A. E. Norwood. 2001. The emotional impact of injury following an international terrorist incident. *Public Health Reviews 29*(2-4): 271–280.

Pfefferbaum, B., and R. L. Pfefferbaum. 1998. Contagion in stress: An infectious disease model for post traumatic stress in children. *Child and Adolescent Psychiatric Clinics of North America 7*(1): 183–194.

Redlener, I., D. Markenson, and R. Grant. 2003. *How Americans Feel about Terrorism and Security: Two Years after 9/11*. New York: National Center for Disaster Preparedness, Columbia University.

Ritchie, E. C., M. Friedman, P. Watson, R. Ursano, S. Wessely, and B. Flynn. 2004. Mass violence and early mental health interventions: A proposed application of best practice guidelines to chemical, biological, and radiological attacks. *Military Medicine 169*(8): 575–579.

Rodoplu, U., J. L. Arnold, R. Tokyay, G. Ersoy, S. Cetiner, and T. Yücel. 2004. Mass casualty terrorist bombings in Istanbul, Turkey, November 2003: Report of the events and the prehospital emergency response. *Prehospital and Disaster Medicine 19*(2): 133–145.

Romundstad, L., K. O. Sundnes, J. Pillgram-Larsen, G. K. Røste, and M. Gilbert. 2004. Challenges of major incident management when excess resources are allocated: Experiences from a mass casualty incident after roof collapse of a military command center. *Prehospital and Disaster Medicine 19*(2): 179–184.

Ruzek, J. I., R. D. Walser, A. E. Naugle, B. Litz, D. S. Mennin, M. A. Polusny, D. M. Ronell, K. J. Ruggiero, R. Yehuda, and J. R. Scotti. 2008. Cognitive-behavioral psychology: Implications for disaster and terrorism response. *Prehospital and Disaster Medicine 23*(5): 397–410.

Ruzek, J. I., B. H. Young, M. J. Cordova, and B. W. Flynn. 2004. Integration of disaster mental health services with emergency medicine. *Prehospital and Disaster Medicine 19*(1): 46–53.

Soffer, Y., D. Schwartz, A. Goldberg, M. Henenfeld, and Y. Bar-Dayan. 2008. Population evacuations in industrial accidents: A review of the literature about four major events. *Prehospital and Disaster Medicine 23*(3): 276–281.

Solomon, S., and E. M. Smith. 1994. Social support and perceived controls as moderators of responses to dioxin and flood exposure. In *Community Responses to Trauma and Disaster: The Structure of Human Chaos*, eds. R. J. Ursano, B. G. McCaughey, and C. S. Fullerton, 179–200. New York: Cambridge University Press.

Stocks, K. H. 2001. Understanding the chaplain's role in an age of weapons of mass destruction. *Military Medicine 166*(12S): 55.

Stratton, S. J., V. P. Hastings, D. Isbell, J. Celentano, M. Ascarrunz, C. S. Gunter, and J. Betance. 1996. The 1994 Northridge earthquake disaster response: The local emergency medical services agency experience. *Prehospital and Disaster Medicine 11*(3): 172–179.

Thomas, S. B., and S. C. Quinn. 1991. The Tuskegee Syphilis Study, 1932 to 1972: Implications for HIV education and AIDS risk education programs in the black community. *American Journal of Public Health 81*(11): 1498–1505.

Tucker, J. B. 1996. Chemical/biological terrorism: Coping with a new threat. *Politics and Life Sciences 15*(2): 167–183.

United States Census Bureau. 2001. Table no. 15 resident population by Hispanic origin status, 1980 to 2000, and projections, 2005–2050, *Statistical Abstract of the United States: 2001*. Springfield, VA: National Technical Information Service.

Ursano, R. J., C. S. Fullerton, and A. E. Norwood. 1995. Psychiatric dimensions of disaster: Patient care, community consultation, and preventative medicine. *Harvard Review of Psychiatry 3*(4): 196–209.

Ursano, R. J., C. S. Fullerton, K. Vance, and T. C. Kao. 1999. Posttraumatic stress disorder and identification in disaster workers. *American Journal of Psychiatry 156*(3): 353–359.

Ursano, R. J., A. E. Norwood, C. S. Fullerton, H. C. Holloway, and M. Hall. 2003. Terrorism with weapons of mass destruction. In *Trauma and Disaster Response and Management*, eds. R. J. Ursano and A.E. Norwood, 125–154. *Review of Psychiatry Series*, 22(1); series eds. J. Oldham and M. B. Riba. Washington, DC: American Psychiatric Publishing.

Van Amerongen, R. H., J. S. Fine, M. G. Tunik, G. M. Young, and G. L. Foltin. 1993. The Avianca plane crash: An emergency medical system's response to pediatric survivors of the disaster. *Pediatrics 92*(1): 105–110.

Van der Ploeg, E., and R. J. Kleber. 2003. Acute and chronic job stressors among ambulance personnel: Predictors of health symptoms. *Occupational and Environmental Medicine 60*(S1): i40–i46.

Veenema, T. G., B. Walden, N. Feinstein, and J. P. Williams. 2008. Factors affecting hospital-based nurses' willingness to respond to a radiation emergency. *Disaster Medicine and Public Health Preparedness 2*(4): 224–229.

Watson, P. J., M. J. Friedman, L. E. Gibson, J. Ruzek, F. Norris, and E. C. Ritchie. 2003. Early intervention for trauma-related problems. In *Annual Review of Psychiatry*, eds. R. J. Ursano and A. E. Norwood, vol. 22, 97–124. Washington, DC: American Psychiatric Association.

Webb, G. R., T. Wachtendorf, and A. Eyre. 2000. Bringing culture back in: Exploring the cultural dimensions of disaster. *International Journal of Mass Emergencies and Disasters 18*(1): 5–19.

Yehuda, R. 2002. Post-traumatic stress disorder. *New England Journal of Medicine 346*(2): 108–114.

Part III

Psychological Resilience and Pathological Responses to Disaster

6 Coping with Loss and Overcoming Trauma

Michael J. Zakour

CONTENTS

6.1 INTRODUCTION

This chapter discusses the adaptive behaviors that individuals use to effectively cope with traumatic loss during disaster. The nature, extent of, and trends in traumatic loss in disasters will be described. Theoretical and conceptual frameworks useful for understanding loss and trauma in disasters will be presented. These frameworks include vulnerability, resiliency, stress, and posttraumatic growth theories. Next, normative responses to disaster losses, stress, and trauma will be described, with a multidimensional framework examining individual, support network, and community components of stress and coping. The components and steps of typical coping responses and behaviors will be described to suggest the most effective means of responding to loss and trauma in disasters. Finally, empowerment and strengths perspectives will be used as a foundation for understanding coping and resilience, as well as social work interventions in disasters.

6.1.1   THE NATURE OF ADVERSITY IN DISASTERS

Major disasters often involve many types of loss and trauma, including death of a close family member or friend, and serious personal injury. Accidents and hazardous environmental conditions, which continue into the rebuilding phase of a disaster, often contribute to stress from disasters. A number of illnesses, such as cardiovascular disease and respiratory illness, are exacerbated by stress (Niederhoffer and Pennebaker 2009). Environmental destruction can lead to severe health problems from accidentally inhaling or ingesting destructive chemicals, and from exposure to mosquito-borne and other contagious diseases (Bourque et al. 2007). The destruction of organizations and businesses that employ local people can lead to long-term unemployment, especially if employers permanently relocate outside of the local geographic area (Tierney 2007).

Though increased social support is needed to cope with loss and trauma, it is likely that social support networks of individuals, groups, and formal service organizations will be less accessible. The loss of human service organizations in disasters may make obtaining needed services after a disaster more difficult or impossible. Social support is the single most important determinant of well-being after a traumatic experience (Niederhoffer and Pennebaker 2009). Given the damage to social support systems in a disaster, the need for support among disaster survivors may far exceed available social support and formal services for months or even years (Norris et al. 2001).

6.1.2   THE SEVERITY AND FREQUENCY OF DISASTER TRAUMA

Major disasters involve disruption of nearly every social and physical system needed by people for survival. When these systems are disrupted, damaged, or destroyed, individuals may face injury, the death of family and/or friends, and loss of their home and sometimes neighborhood. For people affected by a disaster, these losses can be highly traumatic, extreme in scope, and life threatening. Individuals who witness the death of a loved one, a child, or the family pet are more likely to experience posttraumatic stress disorder (PTSD), particularly if the death was in horrific circumstances (Honig et al. 1999). People who are themselves severely injured are also likely to experience PTSD (Norris and Elrod 2006).

6.1.3   TRENDS IN DISASTER LOSSES AND TRAUMA

Disasters and disaster casualties have been increasing in number over the last 30 to 35 years (United Nations 2009). Since 1950, the annual numbers of disasters and economic losses in constant dollars has gradually increased (Wisner et al. 2004). During the last two decades, there has been a trend toward ever-larger numbers of people being affected by disasters each year (International Federation of Red Cross and Red Crescent Societies 2008). Hurricane Katrina in 2005, the Tsunami of 2004, the 2008 cyclone in Myanmar, and the Haiti earthquake in 2010, which collectively killed nearly 600,000 people, illustrate this recent increase in disasters and casualties. Compared to the decade of 1988–1997, the decade of 1999–2008 had 80 percent more deaths due to disasters. Though some disasters before 1950 are believed to have killed hundreds of thousands or even millions of people, most of these disasters occurred before the widespread use of early warning systems as well as electronic communications, which can facilitate more rapid disaster response. The adverse effects of disasters are also more persistent than they were in previous decades, even in developed nations like the United States. For example, only about half of the residents living in the city of New Orleans before Hurricane Katrina returned to reside in the city in the five years after Katrina destroyed nearly 80 percent of the city's buildings.

With the rise of mean sea level, and increased numbers of families with young children living on land vulnerable to flooding, the trend of increasing numbers of disasters and disaster casualties seems likely to continue for the rest of this century. Accompanying this trend is more disaster losses for greater numbers of people each year. The increase in disaster losses will likely lead to a great increase in mental health and other psychosocial problems, including PTSD (Intergovernmental Panel on Climate Change 2007). This decrease in the well-being of populations due to disasters is a global phenomenon, though disasters disproportionately strike less-developed countries and impoverished communities and regions (International Federation of Red Cross and Red Crescent Societies 2008). This was dramatically illustrated in January 2010, by the 7.0 earthquake that struck Haiti, the poorest nation in the Western Hemisphere, killing more than 200,000 people and making more than a million people homeless.

6.1.4 DEFINITION OF KEY TERMS

A disaster is defined as the disruption of community systems that are necessary for provision of resources needed by people for their survival and well-being. These resources include safety, social and emotional support, food, housing, medical care, employment, and household assets (Zakour 2008). A hazard is the physical force that triggers a disaster. Hurricanes, earthquakes, tsunamis, and wildfires are examples of hazards triggering a natural disaster. Chemical spills, explosions, and other industrial accidents are examples of hazards associated with human-caused disasters. Disaster vulnerability is the degree to which social systems are susceptible to loss and damage from disasters, relative to the level of resilience of the social system to recover after a disaster (McEntire 2007).

6.2 CONCEPTUAL AND THEORETICAL FOUNDATIONS

6.2.1 VULNERABILITY THEORY

Disaster vulnerability theory examines the factors that help determine the susceptibility and resilience of individuals, groups, organizations, and communities to losses and trauma in disaster. The degree of disaster susceptibility and disaster resilience of social systems and populations is largely determined by the nature of the local social, built, and natural environment (Zakour 2010). A basic tenet of vulnerability theory is that vulnerability to disasters, though widespread, is not fairly or randomly distributed among populations, even in the same community. Historical, political, economic, and social factors lead to uneven and unfair distribution of vulnerability, as well as environmental liabilities and capabilities that influence levels of disaster susceptibility and resilience (Oliver-Smith 2004). The specific root causes of vulnerability in a society differ by the cultural context of a population or region (Pedrotti, Edwards, and Lopez 2009). An important example of this uneven distribution of vulnerability is the migration of poor households with young children to geographic locations at high risk for disasters. These households cannot afford to own or perhaps even rent a plot of land to live on. Coastal land and/or islands in a river delta, as well as urban landfills or trash heaps, may provide these otherwise landless families in less-developed countries a place of residence, and proximity to resources for a livelihood. Social, economic, and political inequality leads to residence of poor households on marginal land that is highly susceptible to flooding, landslides, and earthquakes. Young children are at much higher risk for injury or disease after such a disaster, making these households disproportionately vulnerable to disasters (Wisner et al. 2004).

Environmental liabilities cause greater social susceptibility of people to loss and trauma in a disaster, as well as long-term health and mental health difficulties. Environmental capabilities foster disaster resilience. Capabilities in the environment can reduce susceptibility in an additive fashion, so that greater numbers and levels of resources translate directly into reduced vulnerability. It is also possible that environmental capabilities act as a buffer during a disaster, reducing vulnerability and severe stress reactions only when a hazard is present or a disaster occurs (Zakour and Gillespie 2010). This interactive effect of capabilities means that the buffering effects of environmental capabilities are greatest when disasters are most severe.

6.2.1.1 Disaster Vulnerability

Disaster vulnerability is the level of risk that people and systems experience, both in terms of the likelihood they will be affected by a disaster and the likely level of severity of disaster impact. In this definition of vulnerability, disaster vulnerability is first of all the probability that a specific category or population of individuals in a community will be affected by a disaster hazard, such as a flood or chemical spill, during any given period of time. For example, those populations residing along the central Gulf Coast of the United States on average experience hurricane-force (74 miles per hour [mph] or greater) winds once every eight years. Vulnerability is additionally conceptualized as the nature and severity of damage that is likely to occur to the functioning and well-being of people and social systems (Wisner et al. 2004). For individuals, the adverse effects on bio-psychosocial functioning may range from minimal to extremely severe, especially for those who are seriously injured during disaster. To use hurricane vulnerability again as an example, single-parent households with several young children living in a trailer near the Gulf Coast can expect a Category 1 hurricane (74–94 mph) to destroy their homes and cause serious injury to children, if the household does not evacuate. Additional losses are likely to result from lack of access to medical care, and also lack of homeowner's insurance.

6.2.1.2 Disaster Social Susceptibility

Susceptibility refers to the extent to which an individual, population, or social system is unable to resist loss and trauma during a disaster. All individuals and communities experiencing a major disaster suffer losses. It is not possible to completely prevent hazards, disasters, or their adverse effects (Zakour 2010). However, susceptibility varies widely among individuals and populations. Differences in disaster susceptibility are associated with socioeconomic status and the demographic characteristics of people. This is because the social and physical environments of people differ by their sociodemographic characteristics. The environments of low-income and socially marginalized populations have fewer resources to reduce losses in a disaster. Less-developed communities and regions tend to lack disaster mitigation projects. These communities have older and more-fragile physical infrastructures, a lower level of social resources, fewer and lower-capacity human services organizations, and lower levels of social capital (Wisner et al. 2004).

6.2.1.3 Disaster Resilience

Resilience is the ability of individuals and social systems to rapidly recover from a disaster and return to predisaster levels of functioning. The level of resilience of populations is largely dependent on the capabilities embedded in their environments. Individual characteristics and personal resources also affect resilience, though individual capabilities are in turn strongly influenced by the social and physical environment. Important resources that increase resilience are adequate levels of social support, formal education, household wealth and income, social development, and formal social services (Greene 2002). Like vulnerability, these resources are not evenly or fairly distributed among populations, communities, regions, or countries. Many social systems are highly stratified, especially in terms of socioeconomic status, social capital, and social resources. Most countries and global regions have a high internal degree of stratification in resources for disaster resilience (Oliver-Smith 2004). Populations in less-developed countries, as well as ethnic, cultural, and racial minorities, tend to have lower levels of disaster resilience than higher-status populations and developed regions and countries (Bankoff, Frerks, and Hilhorst 2004).

6.2.1.4 Environmental Liabilities

Environmental liabilities are largely responsible for disaster susceptibility in individuals and communities. Liabilities can be inherent in the social, physical, and natural environment. Some liabilities that may be ubiquitous yet nearly invisible in a society include limited access to political power, social resources embedded in networks, and tangible as well as intangible resources. Additionally, ideologies that justify political and economic inequality are among the liabilities that increase disaster susceptibility. Other more-visible liabilities include aging and unprotected physical infrastructures, lower income levels, lack of social institutions providing resources to people, and endemic disease. Less-developed communities and regions may also disproportionately suffer from social problems such as hunger, mental illness, drug and alcohol abuse, homelessness, poverty, and violence. All of these liabilities lead to a high level of susceptibility to disasters, and result in increased trauma, loss, and severe stress (Bolin 2007; Wisner et al. 2004).

6.2.1.5 Environmental Capabilities

Environmental capabilities are those phenomena in the social, physical, and natural environments that provide accessible resources needed for recovering from disaster. Ideologies promoting social justice and altruism among different countries and sociodemographic groups in a society, and the presence of institutions that reduce political and economic stratification, are examples of causes of resilience. The presence and levels of these capabilities are largely dependent on cultural context of the environment (Pedrotti, Edwards, and Lopez 2009). The presence of a strong voluntary sector, democratic governmental institutions, a vibrant economy, and high levels of social development are additional environmental capabilities that increase disaster resilience. The existence of many disaster services and emergency management organizations in a community or region, other health and social services organizations, and high levels of social capital are other important environmental capabilities that increase the resilience of local populations (Zakour 2010).

6.2.2 RESILIENCY THEORY

Resiliency theory focuses on risk and protective factors that affect the ability of individuals, groups, and communities to recover rapidly after adversity, loss, or trauma (Greene 2002). Similar to vulnerability theorists, resiliency theorists seek to understand how risk and protective factors can mediate or buffer stress, and affect long-term coping and well-being. This theory originated from research and interventions for children in stressful social and physical environments. Resiliency theorists have long sought to better understand the risk and protective factors that affect the well-being of children when they enter their teen and adult years. Recently, research on resiliency has expanded to include not only children but also individuals throughout the entire lifespan (Tedeschi and Calhoun 2004; Niederhoffer and Pennebaker 2009).

Resiliency theorists in social work have recently begun to closely examine resiliency in disasters, given that social work has historically served at-risk populations. The trauma and extreme losses characteristic of disasters represent a severe type of stressor. Social workers have also increasingly been involved in disaster mental health interventions and research (Zakour 2007). Psychologists began to emphasize a strengths and empowerment perspective, especially through research and practice in positive psychology (Diener 2009). Compared to traditional psychological approaches, positive psychology has a much greater emphasis on the assessment and use of individual and group strengths in work, family, friendship, and community contexts. Psychiatrists have begun to focus on increasing individual and community resources, strengths, and protective factors to empower people and foster resilience in disasters (North and Norris 2006; Norris and Elrod 2006). As social work has embraced a strengths and empowerment perspective, resiliency has increasingly been viewed as a process primarily determined by the capabilities in a person's environment. This represents a departure from a more medical model of resiliency, which generally postulates that psychodynamic characteristics of individuals determine level of resilience.

6.2.2.1 Resiliency as Resilience over Time

Disaster resilience is a subset of all of the types of resilience that social work, psychology, psychiatry, anthropology, and related professions and social science disciplines are concerned with (McEntire 2007). Resiliency is somewhat different from resilience because resiliency is a process, while resilience implies a state or trait at a single point in time. A shift in the focus of theories about resilience has occurred, as researchers and clinicians have realized that people's level of resilience changes over time. This change may be a result of development, an increase over time in the social and other resources that people can access, or a loss of resources because of an extremely adverse event, such as death of a family member. Disaster resilience is closely related to day-to-day resilience, and an individual's level of disaster resilience can be maintained or changed after a disaster occurs (Greene 2002; Norris et al. 2001; Norris and Elrod 2006; Wisner et al. 2004). This research suggests that disaster resiliency is an important area in disaster vulnerability research. It also means that disaster resilience must be examined longitudinally, rather than through cross-sectional designs.

6.2.2.2 Protective Factors

Protective factors are understood to be those phenomena in the social and physical environment of people and social systems that mediate the effects of stressors. Protective factors can buffer people from the worst effects of stress, or increase well-being regardless of the presence or severity of stress. As discussed earlier, protective factors were originally conceptualized as environmental influences on children that buffer the impact of severe stress and help produce positive outcomes later in life despite childhood adversity (Greene 2002). Protective factors in resiliency theory are very similar to environmental capabilities in disaster vulnerability theory. Both theories examine environmental forces that mediate stress and help produce positive outcomes despite loss or adversity.

6.2.2.3 Risk Factors

Like protective factors, risk factors are environmental phenomena or characteristics that mediate the effects of stress, adversity, or loss. Risk factors can amplify the harmful effects of adversity, interacting with adversity to multiply its negative impacts. Risk factors may also have an additive effect on negative outcomes, and affect people and their level of psychosocial functioning even when no other stressors exist in an individual's or community's environment (Norris and Elrod 2006). Risk factors in resiliency theory are analogous to environmental liabilities in vulnerability theory. Similar to liabilities in vulnerability theory, risk factors in resiliency theory are also believed to originate primarily in the social and physical environment, rather than the attributes of individuals.

6.2.2.4 Social Support and Social Resources

A focus on social support and other social resources explicitly links resiliency and vulnerability theories. Access to and mobilization of social and other resources reduces disaster vulnerability and increases the level of disaster resilience (Wisner et al. 2004). Social support and social resources are central elements in resilience and recovery from adversity (Norris and Elrod 2006; Niederhoffer and Pennebaker 2009). When social support is lacking, it is much more difficult for individuals to be resilient and recover from extreme losses and traumatic events. Though social networks are part of the individual's environment, individual attributes can affect levels of social support. The broaden-and-build theory of positive emotions posits that positive emotions help people to broaden the scope of novel thoughts, activities, and relationships. The broadening of alternatives promotes building enduring personal resources such as social support, skills, and knowledge, which leads to increased resilience. In the long-term, broadening and building enhances health, survival, and personal fulfill-ment (Cohn and Fredrickson 2009).

6.2.3 STRESS AND COPING

6.2.3.1 Adversity as Stressor

Though positive life events, such as starting a new career or caring for a newborn, may be stress-ful, traumatic stress is usually associated with extreme loss and adversity. Adversity in a disas-ter includes loss of one's home, neighborhood, or place of employment. Traumatic loss includes severe injury or death of a family member or a close friend. These kinds of adversity are extremely stressful because being homeless, unemployed, or experiencing the death of a family member can sharply reduce an individual's well-being. These examples of adversity in disaster can be particularly stressful because of the meaning people assign to loss of a spouse, home, or job (Florian and Mikulincer 2004; Niederhoffer and Pennebaker 2009). These losses are connected to the loss of an important social role giving individuals a greater sense of worth and self-esteem.

Adversity resulting from disaster is a particularly severe stressor that can take months or years to adequately cope with. Time itself does not reduce the stress of disaster adversity, particularly if the loss is permanent, such as in the death of a loved one. Disaster adversity is also likely to create multiple problems for people, because disasters simultaneously harm families, organizations, and many other social systems in a community. Particularly stressful is damage to a person's social support network. In a disaster, family members or close friends may be killed or forced to permanently relocate to distant geographic areas. When entire neighborhoods or communities are destroyed, it may be impossible for many people to return to their former community. Even if a person's friends and family return to their original neighborhood or community, they are likely to experience the same losses and collective stress that a given individual is experiencing. Finally, if disaster relief efforts are perceived to be inadequate, disorganized, or unfair, stress from the disaster can be prolonged for years or even indefinitely (Rajan 2002). Even when a community or city recovers from a disaster, its original residents and households may still be struggling to cope and recover.

6.2.3.2 Loss and Grieving

The most severe adversity in a disaster usually involves death of a close family member or friend. Bereavement includes negative emotions, such as sadness, which are appropriate for marking and fully acknowledging a loss (Cohn and Fredrickson 2009). If the death of a loved one was tragic or horrific, the survivor may not regain their predisaster level of well-being or happiness for many years, if ever. Like other kinds of adversity in disaster, the death of a loved one leads to bereavement that is not reduced solely by the passage of time. Unless the survivor gradually learns to cope more effectively with such an extreme loss, this kind of grief in a disaster can progress to complicated grief and even posttraumatic stress disorder.

6.2.3.3 Stress Reactions

Stress often refers interchangeably both to stressors, such as the disaster itself, and the stress reactions that individuals and communities experience. However, especially in a disaster, it is clear that the stressor and the stress reaction are related to each other causally, with the stressor acting as the cause of a stress reaction. The magnitude of the stressor is an important predictor of the severity of the stress reaction. Stress reactions can have physiological, cognitive, and behavioral components that interact with one another. Physiological responses include a rise in cortisol, adrenaline, blood sugar, and blood pressure, and other aspects of physiological arousal (Norris and Elrod 2006; Niederhoffer and Pennebaker 2009). Cognitive components include a rigid focus on avoiding or mitigating the stressor, a loss of self-esteem and an increase in caution, a reduced ability to make decisions, increased cognitive uncertainty, and cognitive states including mortality salience (Greenberg, Koole, and Pyszczynski 2004).

Contrary to widespread belief in a state of shock and paralysis, behavioral responses in disaster usually involve adaptive behavior (Bourque et al. 2007). Appropriate coping behavior includes survival actions, avoiding or reducing further injury, and helping young children and other dependent persons. After the threat of injury or death has been dealt with, efforts are made to reduce further loss of tangible resources, such as a home, its contents, an automobile, or vital medical equipment needed on a daily basis. These physiological, cognitive, and behavioral responses are highly adaptive and necessary for survival in a disaster. However, if the stress response is very extreme or persistent long after disaster impact, then an individual's health, mental health, and well-being is threatened (Niederhoffer and Pennebaker 2009).

6.2.3.4 Traumatic Stress and Severe Stress

Stressors are traumatic when they cause extreme damage, adversity, and loss in people and their communities. Many people report that they felt as if the world had come to an end after a regional and very destructive disaster occurred. If the impact of a disaster is horrific, and in particular leads to horrific scenes of death, the effect is more likely to be traumatic. Physical injury and witnessing the death of a close family member or friend are very likely to be highly traumatic. Seeing children who have been killed in a disaster, or being a body handler at a morgue in a disaster, can also be highly traumatic. In a disaster in which multiple family members and friends of an individual are killed the stress can be extreme. The severe stressors discussed here make it more likely that individuals will experience long-term posttraumatic stress. The resulting prevalence of PTSD in a community destroyed by a major disaster, such as New Orleans in Hurricane Katrina, is likely to be substantially higher than 8 percent of the population, which is an average rate of PTSD in nondisaster contexts (Honig et al. 1999).

6.2.3.5 Effects and Changes in Personal Worldview and Assumptions

Most people in developed countries believe that they are in control of their lives and their quality of life. In many Western nations, particularly affluent democracies, there is the worldview that the world is just, and that bad things that happen to people result from some transgression in the victim of tragedy. It is also assumed that death is something that will happen to an individual only in the future, when one is very old and "it is their time." When a person witnesses widespread, severe, and seemingly random suffering during a disaster, this Western worldview is shattered. Many disaster survivors will realize that they do not know why bad things happen to people, that there is considerably less control over events than once believed, and that death does not happen only to very old people or people seen on the nightly news (Young and Morris 2004). This shattering of assumptions is at first accompanied by an inability to make decisions, as the individual wavers between old and emerging worldviews. In order for people to cope with tragedy, their worldviews, assumptions, and values must be modified to better fit their present understanding of reality. This revision of assumptive worldviews can be idiosyncratic among individuals, and it is affected by the cultural context in which it takes place (Pedrotti, Edwards, and Lopez 2009).

6.3 NORMATIVE RESPONSES TO TRAUMATIC LOSS IN DISASTERS

In the immediate aftermath of a disaster involving traumatic losses, individuals are very likely to respond in an adaptive fashion. The great majority of people immediately protect themselves and family members from further injury (Bourque et al. 2007). Once protection has been achieved, people will help family, neighbors, and others search for and rescue people who may be trapped in collapsed or damaged buildings. Though an individual may have experienced extreme losses in the disaster, for hours or days after the loss, affected individuals often minimize thoughts about the significance or extent of their losses. By helping others, individuals can distract themselves from the reality of their loss, or deny the otherwise overwhelming nature of loss of loved ones or close friends (Kuhl and Koole 2004).

6.3.1 INDIVIDUAL-LEVEL RESPONSES

Within several days after disaster onset, after survival actions have been completed, those who have suffered extreme loss will begin the process of grieving. If a person has been badly injured, or has witnessed the severe injury or death of others, the grieving is likely to be long term. When multiple or extreme losses have occurred to a single individual or household, the loss and bereavement can become a major part of a person's or the household members' social identity. The pain that accompanies bereavement may be long lasting, and persist at some level for the rest of the disaster survivor's life. The grieving process is essential to frankly acknowledge and begin to cope with the loss and related secondary losses. Efforts to suppress memory of the loss and eliminate the pain through self-medication, psychoactive drugs, or dissociation will only be temporarily successful, and can lead to psychological problems (Niederhoffer and Pennebaker 2009), substance abuse, or PTSD (Honig et al. 1999).

6.3.1.1 Psychological: Increased Anxiety and Depressive Symptoms

Anxiety and depressive symptoms are likely to be intense as an individual begins to recognize their losses and the meaning and implications of their losses. These negative mood manifestations of loss are likely to represent adaptive coping responses rather than pathology. For weeks or months after the disaster occurred, the anxiety and depressive symptoms may appear to be indistinguishable from anxiety or depressive disorders. If the loss is extreme enough, for the first few months after a disaster, the survivor is likely to have a number of symptoms indicative of PTSD. Hypervigilance, and/or an exaggerated startle response, to cues reminding one of the disaster are associated with severe anxiety (Norris and Elrod 2006). Disengagement from others is associated with the depressive symptoms resulting from extreme loss. Disengagement includes a loss of interest in others and the world, pessimism about the future, and a decreased ability to enjoy things that were once enjoyable (Janoff-Bulman and Yopyk 2004).

6.3.2 Fight-or-Flight Response

Anxiety and hypervigilance during a disaster are adaptive reactions that are part of the fight-or-flight response triggered by threat to the individual's survival or safety. The fight-or-flight response is a survival mechanism helping individuals deal with and mitigate danger and threat. The anxiety component of the fight-or-flight response may continue long after disaster trauma and loss occurs. Increased and prolonged anxiety can be viewed as an indication that an individual is attempting to cope with a difficult and adverse situation, such as a severe loss in a disaster (Dienstbier and Zillig 2009).

6.3.2.1 Physiological Deterioration in Health Status and Sleep Patterns

Changes in a person's physiological arousal, health behaviors, sleep patterns, and mood are likely after a traumatic loss in a disaster (Norris and Elrod 2006). An increase in blood sugar and blood pressure, adrenaline and cortisol levels, immune cell activity, and psychological hypervigilance are all adaptive during a disaster or trauma. If the fight-or-flight response continues for a very long period of time after a loss in disaster, however, then the individual's health status will suffer from the chronic physiological arousal and state of readiness. Higher blood glucose and blood pressure can progress to diabetes and cardiovascular disease, or existing cardiovascular problems can be made worse. Increased immune activity and cortisol levels eventually will lead to inflammation, particularly in air passages and the respiratory system. Chronic heightened immune and inflammatory responses could make the individual more vulnerable to respiratory illness or severe asthma, as well as other disorders of the immune system. Increased adrenaline and hypervigilance can lead to sleep disorders, such as insomnia or disruption of normal sleep patterns. Exaggerated attention and worry regarding cues associated with the trauma make it more difficult for individuals to enact behaviors beneficial to health and mental health. This occurs at a time when increased attention to one's own health and mental health is necessary for recovery from loss (Norris and Elrod 2006).

6.3.2.2 Impairment of Concentration and Memory

Immediately after trauma occurs, most survivors lose some of their ability to concentrate and remember new information. In the short term, this is a trade-off that occurs when an individual mobilizes all of their attention for coping with threats to survival. Hypervigilance and heightened arousal disrupt the normal sleep architecture of light sleep, REM sleep, and deep sleep and will disrupt the ability of the hippocampus part of the brain to learn and retain new knowledge or memories. If it persists for too long, hypervigilance will eventually make it more difficult for a person to appropriately attend to information in their total environment, besides the cues associated with the traumatic loss. Prolonged anxiety or depressive symptoms will also begin to narrow the range of environmental or biological information an individual is able to process. This makes it more difficult for an individual to problem solve, which is essential for coping. The fight-or-flight response, so adaptive immediately after disaster, can eventually lead the individual to attempts to cope that are ineffective or destructive, such as drug and alcohol abuse (Cohn and Fredrickson 2009).

6.3.2.3 Personal Search for Meaning

In many developed nations, particularly those with European and neo-European cultures, among the first responses to extreme adversity is to ask the question, "Why did this happen to me?" Western cultures have a strong bias toward trying to understand cause and effect, and there is also the widespread belief that the individual is in control of their own circumstances and life events. Individuals who are able to respond to this existential question are in a position to reconstruct useful and optimistic meaning systems and assumptions about themselves, others, and the world (Kuhl and Koole 2004; Niederhoffer and Pennebaker 2009). However, if an individual's reconstructed worldview emphasizes that other people and the world are very dangerous or horribly unfair, then the individual is likely to experience heightened posttraumatic stress and even PTSD.

6.3.3 CHANGES IN IMMEDIATE SOCIAL ENVIRONMENT

Disasters are among the most severe stressors that individuals, groups, and communities are likely to experience. The severity of disaster stressors is partly the result of the damage and disruption caused to systems at all levels in a community. The family unit may be affected by the death of one of its members, similar to the situation for organizations. Communities may be unable to provide resources necessary for the survival of community members. If the disaster is widespread, such as a hurricane affecting an entire region, or a tsunami affecting many nations, then an entire society could be disrupted by disaster (Wisner et al. 2004).

6.3.3.1 Loss of Supportive Others and Relationships

Though the need for social support is critical for overcoming loss and adversity, a disaster can seriously disrupt the social support networks of survivors facing other adversity (Norris et al. 2001; Bolin 2007). An important implication of the multidimensionality of disasters is that the social support networks of disaster survivors are likely to be disrupted or damaged. If a central member of an individual's social support network is killed during the disaster, then permanent adverse changes may occur for the support network of family, friends, and neighbors. During the immediate aftermath of a major disaster, people may not know of the whereabouts or the well-being of the members of their network. When the disaster recovery period is under way, families may be split up because one member of the family is forced to relocate temporarily to a worksite outside the local area. If the recovery is a prolonged process, then the separation of family members may continue for months. If an individual had a strong support network at the workplace, the damage and/or destruction caused by a disaster at the place of employment could disrupt this network for months or years.

6.3.3.2 Reduction of Available Social Resources

Social resources, whether from informal or formal sources, may be depleted in a community as it tries to recover and respond to the needs of the many individuals affected by the disaster. Social resources are very important for individuals and groups to become and remain disaster resilient (Zakour 2010). The deleterious impact of the disaster on networks of support and the social resources embedded in these networks can severely reduce access to resources, as well as disaster and day-to-day resilience. For populations that were poor and socially marginalized before the disaster occurred, this loss of accessible social resources is likely to have a strong negative effect on resilience. If the impoverished population was close to the survival level in terms of resources, even a minor disaster could create a crisis in levels of resources needed to live (Cardona 2004).

6.3.3.3   Compassion versus Marginalization

After a disaster occurs, there is an outpouring of aid, compassion, and altruism, first from people in the disaster area, and then from people and organizations outside of the area of impact. A local manifestation of the altruistic community forms, and often those community members who have been most affected by the disaster are the first to volunteer to help other survivors (Barton 1969). State-, regional-, and national-level organizations move into the impact area, and their volunteers and paid disaster professionals begin to help victims with their needs. This compassionate and altruistic response may begin to wane after a few months to a year, particularly for outside organizations. As other areas experience a disaster, or as the media reduce or eliminate regular coverage of the disaster area, interest in helping survivors decreases. If local disaster survivors feel mistreated or neglected by homeowners' insurance companies, governmental aid agencies, or disaster relief and recovery programs, the survivors may protest this treatment and engage in litigation to gain reparations. Public sentiment may begin to change from compassion to blaming of the victims of disaster (Button 2002; Young and Morris 2004).

6.3.3.4   Socially Constructed Meaning

After a disaster in which there has been great loss, a search for meaning to understand the suffering of disaster begins. This meaning-making goes beyond individual efforts to become a collective and community effort (Greenberg, Koole, and Pyszczynski 2004). Persistent interaction and mutual support among disaster survivors, and news and commentary from the local and national media, build a shared understanding of the disaster at the community and societal level (Button 2002). Faith-based groups and organizations often are central to this effort to construct meaning out of a very adverse event, such as a disaster. Unfortunately, this process of socially constructed meaning can be driven by the same political-economic and societal forces that help to unfairly distribute disaster vulnerability and resilience (Wisner et al. 2004). While faith-based and other voluntary organizations may provide a constructive leadership role in creating meaning out of chaos, other organizations and groups may reinforce meaning that blames the victim.

6.4   COMPONENTS AND STEPS IN COPING

6.4.1   Individual Coping Behaviors

6.4.1.1   Increased Action Orientation as Defense and Survival Strategy

During disaster onset, response, and recovery, a central requirement for coping is an action orientation aimed at problem solving and adaptive instrumental behavior (Kuhl and Koole 2004). When traumatic losses have occurred, it is important that disaster survivors avoid endless worry, rumination, and anxiety that can paralyze the individual's coping ability. An action orientation is not only an appropriate response to extreme loss, but it serves as a distraction from the sometimes horrific details of the situation. Action to help oneself and others is also incompatible with paralyzing anxiety and depression. After a traumatic loss or extreme adversity, individuals tend to feel helpless, and their self-esteem often plummets. If their actions are successful in some manner to reduce loss, this usually increases the self-efficacy and self-esteem of the survivor.

6.4.1.2   Telling One's Own Story Verbally and in Writing

Many disaster survivors want to tell their own story or narrative concerning their experience in a disaster (Niederhoffer and Pennebaker 2009). Though this desire to tell one's own story may begin after their initial response to the disaster, this narrative activity can be very helpful in coping with and overcoming loss and adversity. By verbally describing the events and losses from a disaster, the aversive emotions associated with the losses can be brought under the control of words and other symbols. This process of framing the traumatic event through talking and writing can help to reduce the sadness and pain inherent in the extreme loss. By gradually reexposing oneself initially through words and symbols, the fear response to the loss diminishes. The experience is normalized by learning that others have had the same experiences and emotional reactions to the trauma. The story of the individual's losses and experience may also help others to provide social and tangible support to the survivor, and others may be in a better position to help the survivor problem solve (Niederhoffer and Pennebaker 2009).

6.4.1.3   Processing Memories and Cognitions Concerning the Traumatic Loss

It is very important for survivors of disasters and other traumatic events to gradually confront and reexperience some of the memories, emotions, and cognitions that their losses have elicited (Martin, Campbell, and Henry 2004). Any attempt to completely avoid reminders and discussions related to a traumatic loss will likely result in an increase in sadness, fear, and anxiety about the experience. Not only is emotional processing helpful in desensitizing a survivor to some of the details of their losses, but the extreme loss and trauma must somehow be integrated into a person's assumptive worldview (Niederhoffer and Pennebaker 2009). Survivors must reorganize their worldviews so that they can better accept and understand that loss and suffering is not only part of the human condition, but that it can even happen to good people, including themselves (Young and Morris 2004). Emotional processing and cognitive restructuring are needed to help reduce the intense pain and suffering accompanying extreme loss, and these processes are a foundation for rebuilding one's life and identity.

6.4.1.4   Meditation and Mindfulness

Meditation, mindfulness, and a combination of these two coping behaviors have been found to be very helpful in reducing aversive emotions and improving well-being (Shapiro 2009). This is particularly true after an extreme or very painful loss in a disaster. After a significant loss or traumatic event, it is very common for a disaster survivor to focus on the events of the recent past. This is a normative response because humans focus disproportionately on very negative events, and they quickly adapt to positive events through habituation or hedonic adaptation. It is also very difficult for grieving people to imagine the future with much optimism, given a worst-case scenario has just affected them. Meditation helps to reduce the level of anxiety and physiological arousal that are remnants of the fight-or-flight response. Mindfulness, and particularly mindfulness meditation, focuses the individual on events and experiences in the present. Both of these techniques help people to live in the here and now, and to recondition their aversive emotions to be less painful and fearful.

6.4.1.5   Rebuilding a Personal Worldview and Shattered Assumptions

A majority of people in more-developed Western countries strongly believe that their actions control their circumstances, as well as events that occur in their lives. They hold the assumption that if you are a moral, righteous, and good person then you will be rewarded with positive events, opportunities, and experiences. A disaster and its accompanying trauma and personal loss are so difficult to deny or forget that the commonly held Western beliefs about control over negative events become impossible to maintain. The denial of one's mortality will also be impossible after injury, illness, or death of a loved one. A more-realistic set of beliefs and assumptions must be fashioned from the individual's predisaster worldview (Kuhl and Koole 2004). This worldview must be able to encompass the ubiquitous nature of suffering among all people, regardless of their level of resources to control events or their moral goodness. This new and fuller understanding of the world is more realistic than the denial of mortality and suffering (Wallace 1956/2003; Niederhoffer and Pennebaker 2009). If the individual is able to rebuild their worldview so they can see new opportunities, personal strengths that they have developed or newly recognized, and new relationships with others, then the stage will be set for posttraumatic growth (Tedeschi and Calhoun 2004).

6.4.2   Reactivating Health and Mental Health Behaviors

6.4.2.1   Reducing Sleep Problems

Trauma, loss, and severe adversity generally make sound sleep much more difficult for disaster survivors. The fatigue that results from sleep disorders, however, makes it more difficult for people to effectively deal with the difficulties in living they experience. Poor sleep quality can lead to depression, weight gain, and elevated blood glucose and blood pressure (National Sleep Foundation 2010b). Immediately after disaster onset, a pattern of lighter sleep and frequent waking can be adaptive, in that the individual may be more ready to deal with dangerous and life-threatening events. However, for many people, worry about the future and sadness over the past may prolong the persistence of sleep problems for months and years. A first step to reestablishing a healthy sleep architecture is to better problem-solve and cope with the ongoing and secondary losses and difficulties in living that a person faces as a consequence of their disaster loss and trauma. Scheduling a time each day to worry and problem-solve is also very helpful by separating sleep and worry time. Other sleep hygiene behaviors, such as a regular time for sleep and waking, eliminating all behaviors except for sleep and intimacy while in bed, and physical exercise three to five hours before bedtime, can be very helpful in improving sleep (National Sleep Foundation 2010a).

6.4.2.2   Increased Physical Activity to Reduce Depression

Engaging in almost any effort to help oneself cope reduces depression levels, and regular aerobic and strength exercise can be as effective in reducing mild to moderate depression as are antidepressant drugs (Lyubomirsky 2007). Rather than having negative side effects, as drug therapies often do, exercise improves health and functioning in most people. If exercise takes place in a social setting, such as a sports team or health club, then additional socializing can occur, potentially leading to new relationships and/or friendships. Because exercise can help people improve sleep, lose weight, control metabolic conditions (such as insulin intolerance and diabetes), prevent cardiovascular disease, and reduce mortality from all causes, it is an especially useful strategy for overcoming adversity and loss.

6.4.2.3   Distraction and Mindfulness as Defense and Coping Behavior

Meditation, an action orientation, close relationships, increased physical activity, and regular exercise not only help people cope with adversity, but all of these methods serve to distract the individual from thinking about or ruminating over loss and trauma. Particularly if no additional means exist to control or change difficult circumstances, it is not helpful to ruminate or worry. Continued focus on very negative or traumatic aspects of events can lead to reconditioning so that events and things, which were once pleasant, can become painful or fear provoking. Rumination or overthinking also makes people more vulnerable to depression or anxiety disorders. Though mental health professionals tend to believe that distraction is usually a form of unhealthy denial, distraction and mindfulness can be highly adaptive and beneficial in conditions of extreme loss. Mindfulness and distraction can result in improved well-being and positive emotions after loss or adversity (Shapiro 2009).

6.4.3   Community Responses to Foster Individual Resilience

6.4.3.1   Preventive Health and Mental Health

Community responses and conditions can have a substantial effect on the health and mental health outcomes for disaster survivors. This effect is mediated by a community's efficacy in disaster recovery. If communities are able to rapidly respond to and recover from a disaster, then health and mental health outcomes will be more positive for survivors. A major predictor of a positive prognosis for disaster survivors is the rebuilding of their damaged homes and the homes of their neighbors within one year after disaster impact. If normalcy is rapidly restored at places of employment and education (e.g., local school system), the restored daily routines of survivors will positively affect both their mental health and their overall health. The return of survivors to employment, education, and other activities after a disaster will provide them with purposeful and adaptive activities. The restoration of predisaster routines also can help reduce grief reactions of survivors of traumatic loss (Rosenfeld et al. 2005).

6.4.3.2   Increasing Access to Medical and Mental Health Services

If human services can be restored in a timely fashion after a disaster, then the interruption in provision of needed social resources will be minimized. This kind of restoration limits the duration and severity of the disaster. It helps to prevent what disaster researchers have labeled the "second disaster," which results from a failed response and recovery (Rajan 2002). The rapid restoration of services will also help prevent deterioration in well-being for people who had been receiving ongoing treatment for serious health and mental health conditions before the disaster. Restoring social services can help the community return levels of social resource provision to predisaster conditions, which is critical if survivors who have experienced major losses are to recover and maintain their disaster resiliency (Norris et al. 2001).

6.4.3.3   Facilitation of Increased Social Support

After a disaster occurs, there is no shortage of volunteers who wish to help survivors. If training and planning for the use of volunteers was conducted before the disaster, then the large pool of volunteers can help fill the gaps in social support that survivors experience after traumatic loss, and particularly the injury and death of loved ones (Zakour 2010). Support may be tangible, such as help in preparing meals for households with several young children. It may be intangible, such as a willingness to listen to and reassure those survivors who have suffered from extreme losses. Volunteers can also complement the efforts of professional human service workers by working closely together to provide services to meet expanded demand after disaster. Many volunteers will be professionals, such as teachers and clergy, and these volunteers can be especially helpful by teaming up with disaster mental health professionals to provide support for survivors.

6.4.3.4   Help in (Re)building Close Relationships and Social Networks

Communities, which contain many opportunities for individuals to connect to others and to build new friendships and relationships, facilitate positive relationships and social capital among its residents and members. As discussed in the previous section, volunteering not only provides needed services and social support for survivors, but volunteer opportunities can help survivors meet new people, make new friends, and form supportive relationships with other people and with the volunteer organization itself. Other opportunities for civic engagement, group recreation activities, and new employment roles not only restore a sense of normalcy, but also provide new opportunities for forming close, supportive relationships. Particularly if a survivor has lost a job, employment in the recovery effort can provide the connections to people inherent in work, and can restore a sense of identity and worth in survivors (Rosenfeld et al. 2005).

6.5   EMPOWERMENT AND STRENGTHS PERSPECTIVES IN DISASTER

6.5.1   COMMUNITY RESILIENCE AND INDIVIDUAL EMPOWERMENT

The approach of assessing a community's strengths and fostering community disaster resilience is closely related to the empowerment approach in social work. Because a strengths perspective is needed when assessing community resources for environmental capabilities, the focus on resilience is also part of the strengths perspective. Though increasing environmental capabilities is likely to be a more productive approach than decreasing environmental liabilities, the recognition that susceptibility to disasters originates in the liabilities of environments and not individual deficits is consistent with empowerment and strengths perspectives. Interventions to foster resilience will often be community interventions, which help people to better access social capital, and to mobilize existing strengths and resources to foster their own disaster resilience (Zakour 2010).

6.5.1.1 Increasing Environmental Capabilities

Many vulnerable communities have substantial strengths, and resources exist in the social, built, and natural environments of these communities. Community strengths can be inventoried, leveraged, and expanded to foster disaster resilience. High levels of disaster resilience also result from improved access to environmental resources and protective factors, such as political influence, economic assets, and societal ideologies, which support the inherent dignity and the rights of people to enjoy a good quality of life. Environmental capabilities include (in addition to other resources mentioned earlier in this section) civil society, high levels of social development, and a vibrant voluntary sector that is well coordinated to amplify the voices of constituents. Emergency management organizations, disaster mitigation projects, and a coordinated network of disaster services organizations are other environmental capabilities, which can be developed to increase and foster resilience (Wisner et al. 2004).

6.5.1.2 Reducing Environmental Liabilities

Though an empowerment and strengths approach to fostering resilience will focus primarily on leveraging the strengths of communities, reducing environmental liabilities can be a useful approach as well (Zakour and Gillespie 2010). Environmental liabilities include lack of a strong civil society, low levels of development, and few voluntary or governmental organizations serving the community, particularly in disaster prevention and response. Other liabilities include ideologies that justify economic and political inequalities and stratification of communities by levels of available resources. The relative importance of any of these liabilities in producing disaster susceptibility will vary according to cultural context (Pedrotti, Edwards, and Lopez 2009). These liabilities are a threat to social justice, particularly distributive justice. Remedying these social injustices may involve challenging ideologies that help maintain inequality and lack of access to the resources of society. Reducing environmental liabilities, in turn, reduces levels of susceptibility of communities and people to disaster.

6.5.1.3 Formal Provision of Social Capital and Support

If organizations have a client-centered approach, and mental health and other human service professionals seek to give clients access to the resources of organizations, then clients are empowered and have greater access to social capital embedded in organizations and social networks. Case finding, outreach, brokering of services, and client advocacy are examples of client-centered service provision (Zakour 2008). Human service professionals have access to the resources of the organization they work in, and they have special expertise in helping people and humanizing social systems. These resources and knowledge often create a power differential between helper and client. Helping professionals need to use their influence to build a trusting and collaborative relationship with clients. By fostering a relationship with the client based on trust and mutual respect, the client is able to build on his or her own strengths. Through client-centered practice, the client is empowered and can exercise self-determination to recover from disaster.

6.5.1.4 Mobilization of Tangible and Intangible (e.g., Spiritual) Resources for People

Though the environments of communities and other social systems can be rich in resources, these resources are often not available to people who need them. This situation can lead to the paradox that the people who need these resources most are the very same people who have the least power to mobilize the resources to be more resilient in disasters. Related to this paradox, poor people tend to receive poor services, both day to day and during a disaster. In the United States, this difficulty in mobilizing resources is part of the ideology of local and personal responsibility. The problem with this ideology is that the communities and households that are most vulnerable to disasters also have the fewest resources to address the social problems, which disasters can cause or exacerbate. Communities with lower levels of social development have more day-to-day difficulties in living, as well as problems such as drug abuse and violent crime. The same communities, which have the most problems in living, have the fewest resources to solve these problems on their own. Social development approaches can help mobilize available resources and strengthen existing resources to make communities more resilient (Cardona 2004).

6.5.2 DEALING WITH FEAR OF DEATH AND EXISTENTIAL UNCERTAINTY

Disasters are dramatic and severe stressors—they can lead people to feel uncertain about their futures and become more aware of their own mortality. This is particularly the case for survivors who have experienced trauma, loss, and adversity in a disaster. However, people who have had a close encounter with death do not necessarily become more fearful of it. Disaster survivors who have experienced loss of a loved one and other severe losses often find the means to cope with both loss and the inevitability of their own death (Kuhl and Koole 2009). Depending on the cultural context and coping styles of individuals, a variety of strategies have been used by people to reduce and control fear of their own mortality.

6.5.2.1 Membership in Groups

Identification with the worldview and culture of a social group is an important means for reducing fear of death. Developing or emphasizing membership in a reference group can help disaster survivors not only have a greater sense of belonging and social integration, but also increase social support and feelings of safety (Greenberg, Koole, and Pyszczynski 2004). Because social support is such an important component of overcoming loss and adversity, group membership provides a greater sense of safety and certainty. Collectives, such as groups and communities of interest (e.g., faith communities), are often based on mutual aid and support, as well as reciprocity. An individual may perceive the efficacy and resources of the group as an important part of their own self-efficacy. There is also a sense that the members of the group are coping with and going through the process of recovery together, rather than alone as individuals (Niederhoffer and Pennebaker 2009).

6.5.2.2 Identification with Large Collectives and Their Cultural Value Systems

Identifying with something much larger than oneself—such as a culture, nation, religion, or social movement—can decrease the disaster survivor's fear that their physical death also means the death of their own social identity (Greenberg, Koole, and Pyszczynski 2004). One reason why death is terrifying is that it can mean that an individual will not be remembered by others. Death of the individual represents the obliteration of all the individual has worked for and aimed at for his or her entire life. A larger collective can have an existence far longer than the maximum lifespan of individuals. The collective or social system will likely continue after the death of an individual member. If the individual commits herself to shared goals and values of the collective, then the death of the individual may not mean the obliteration of her social identity.

6.5.2.3 Bolstering Culturally Constructed Self-Esteem

It is difficult for disaster survivors who have experienced traumatic loss and adversity to maintain a high level of self-esteem and self-efficacy. These survivors have likely realized that they have only limited control over adverse events, and this realization can lead to intense suffering. The illusion of complete control over life events through one's own actions, an illusion that is useful when circumstances are favorable, is shattered by extreme loss and trauma in a disaster (Kuhl and Koole 2004). Because the assumption of control is shown to be inadequate, and self-efficacy therefore limited, achievement of goals that are culturally sanctioned and approved, and socially desirable, can be a pathway to increasing self-esteem for the individual. Though control over adversity in disaster has been proven to be unrealistic and limited, it is possible for survivors to engage in roles for which they can receive positive social recognition (Niederhoffer and Pennebaker 2009). Reinforcement from others for the achievement of important culturally sanctioned goals can increase the individual's self-esteem and perception of self-efficacy.

6.5.2.4 Compassion and Generosity

An important set of socially useful strengths includes compassion and generosity toward others. These traits are valued by a large majority of traditions, religions, and cultures. The increased compassion, which may be developed by people who themselves have suffered great loss, is often recognized by disaster victims as a new strength or a strength they have begun to recognize in themselves. Compassion and generosity are behaviors that are culturally valued, reinforced, and rewarded. The exercise of these strengths tends to increase the individual's sense of well-being and happiness (Davis and Nolen-Hoeksema 2009). A focus on helping others also prevents rumination or overthinking fears of one's own death.

6.5.2.5 Intimate and Close Relationships

One of the most powerful means of decreasing one's fear of death and uncertainty in life is by developing or reemphasizing close relationships (Greenberg, Koole, and Pyszczynski 2004). These relationships may include close friendships, family ties, or romantic intimate relationships. The power of close relationships to address existential concerns is complex and multifaceted. When individuals devote their attention to the well-being of other persons, they have less time and opportunity to worry about the adversity in their own lives, or adversity that may occur in an uncertain future. Close relationships can produce positive emotions, which may be incompatible with negative emotions, such as fear or anxiety (Cohn and Fredrickson 2009). A series of close relationships may assure individuals that they have adequate social and emotional support if a future crisis or loss occurs. Finally, disaster survivors engaged in close relationships may be reassured that, even if they die in the short-term future, a number of close friends, family, or other loved ones will survive them. The survival of loved ones is also insurance against complete loss of one's social identity.

6.5.3 POSITIVE PSYCHOLOGY AND THE STRENGTHS APPROACH

Positive psychology has deep roots in social work, humanistic psychology, community psychiatry, cultural anthropology, and organizational psychology research and practice (Oliver-Smith 2004; Norris et al. 2001). Social work has long emphasized the strengths approach, and this has served as one foundation for positive psychology (Diener 2009). Humanistic theories of human behavior, including the human relations approach, have long been accepted as important for humanistic psychology and counseling, management science, and social work practice. These theories focus on what is right with people. Social work, developmental psychology, community psychiatry, humanistic psychology, and cultural anthropology have included an exploration of the strengths, resources, and capabilities of people and communities, along with assessment of protective and destructive environmental forces affecting well-being (Cardona 2004; Norris and Elrod 2006; Wisner et al. 2004). Finally, social development interventions in social work, public health, and applied anthropology have sought to foster the capacities, resilience, and well-being of communities and people (Bankoff, Frerks, and Hilhorst 2004; Greene 2002; McEntire 2007).

6.5.3.1 Signature Strengths and Increased Happiness

An individual who has experienced the death of a spouse, partner, or child is likely to have a much lower perception of well-being and happiness for at least a year after the death. This reduced level of well-being and happiness persists on average for eight years (Lyubomirsky 2007). Happiness and well-being levels may never return to the levels that existed in the first year after marriage to their spouse, or the initial year after the birth of a child. Positive psychology and the strengths approach in social work, humanistic psychology, and community psychiatry focus on recognizing and helping people frequently enact the strengths that bereaved people demonstrated while successfully coping with loss. This approach emphasizes recognition and use of the strengths of disaster survivors, and deemphasizes focusing on the most painful aspects of loss.

6.5.3.2 Forgiveness and Gratitude

If the disaster survivor has been hurt because of the negligence or malevolence of other people, the survivor may harbor strong anger toward those presumably responsible for the losses. Anger and bitterness, though common after a disaster, tend to isolate survivors from the social support they need so much. Anger and bitterness can prevent the development of new friendships and close relationships. Individuals who have experienced extreme loss and trauma may feel bitter toward others and their current life circumstances. Often the anger hurts only the person who sustained the losses. Anger and bitterness can prevent survivors from moving on with their lives, and eventually recovering (Niederhoffer and Pennebaker 2009). Forgiveness toward others, and gratitude for the good things that have happened in the past and remain in the present, can reduce anger and bitterness. Forgiveness and gratitude are positive emotions that can reduce the frequency of negative emotions accompanying loss. Both of these positive emotions improve the levels of an individual's happiness, which in turn may facilitate the development of new relationships, and reintegration into social groups and support systems (Cohn and Fredrickson 2009).

6.5.3.3 Positive versus Negative Emotions

Positive emotions include gratitude, interest, love, and joy. Rather than focusing solely on reducing negative or aversive mood states, such as sadness and hopelessness, it can also be important to increase positive emotions during the recovery stage of coping. Positive emotions are prominent in resilience and recovery from adversity, and can reduce the occurrence of negative mood states, including sadness and depression (Cohn and Fredrickson 2009). Increased occurrence of positive emotions also contributes to the individual gaining resources needed to maintain increased resilience. Such resources include social support, broadening of perceived options for problem solving, and improved health and mental health.

It is important to recognize, however, that negative emotions are very useful for coping. Negative emotions are essential for avoiding or reducing serious risks, just as positive emotions can promote resilience. Without some frequency of negative emotions it would be impossible for most people to avoid danger. Coping behaviors can be degraded if individuals are in very positive emotional states during the performance of health and coping behaviors (Cohn and Fredrickson 2009). As discussed earlier in this chapter, negative emotions, such as sadness and grief, are necessary to acknowledge the seriousness of loss of a loved one.

6.5.3.4 Meaningful Actions and Purposeful Behavior

After a traumatic event or loss occurs in a disaster, many survivors will seek meaning in the adversity as a way of reducing the suffering and sadness that is part of the loss. One aspect of meaning is comprehending why the loss and suffering happened to the survivor. If the survivor assumes that he or she is somehow responsible for the loss, this comprehension of the suffering will lead to a severe loss of self-esteem and even self-hate. This meaning of the loss is the logical outcome of believing that suffering is punishment for one's own transgressions (Martin, Campbell, and Henry 2004). Most survivors will realize that they will never know why the loss or trauma occurred to them. The meaning of the loss in terms of its comprehensibility may never be established. However, meaning in terms of what needs to be done now that the loss has occurred, or how one is to proceed in the future, may be understood, developed, and acted on by the survivor. While the question, "Why did this happen?" may be unanswerable, the question, "How do I respond to this tragedy?" cannot only be answered, but acted upon. Meaning is difficult to find in terms of comprehensibility, but meaningful actions and meaningful lives may be emphasized, recognized, or realized after a loss (Niederhoffer and Pennebaker 2009).

6.5.4   Empowerment and Posttraumatic Growth

6.5.4.1   Positive Changes in Life Priorities

One change that is related to posttraumatic growth is a change in one's values. Survivors of traumatic loss and adversity are likely to reprioritize their own goals and values as a result of their experiences. An increase in the value of relationships often occurs at the expense of materialism or a focus on wealth. There is also the recognition that simple pleasures, such as enjoying the beauty of nature or appreciating the good things in life, can abruptly come to an end if one's life were to suddenly end. Because of the acknowledgement of the impermanence of everything, the value of all aspects of life increases. Life experiences are known to be fleeting, and will come to an end one day, so their value increases (Martin, Campbell, and Henry 2004).

6.5.4.2   Greater Appreciation of Close Relationships

The newly found appreciation and value of close relationships may lead to greater happiness for survivors of disaster losses and adversity (Greenberg, Koole, and Pyszczynski 2004). Increases in wealth and salary, assumed by many to be a major route to happiness, are understood to be less important than good relationships (Lyubomirsky 2007). Close relationships are a central means to decreasing fear of death and uncertainty in life, and relationships can provide the social support that is critical for coping with severe stressors that result from disasters. Close relationships that result when others come to the aid of a bereaved person often persist long after the survivor's crisis period has passed. Closer relationships are indeed one of the benefits of coping responses to disaster losses. If the survivor places increased emphasis on relationships as a beneficial aspect of an otherwise tragic loss, and engages in further developing family relationships or friendships, this enacting of new priorities after a disaster can increase happiness (Cohn and Fredrickson 2009).

6.5.4.3   Spirituality, Nature, and the Search for the Sacred

An important type of posttraumatic growth is beginning new life projects where the goal is spiritual development. Though sacred beings and phenomena cannot be objectively studied or measured, people's perceptions of sacredness are real. Spirituality can be defined as the search for the sacred. Sacred beings or phenomena include the God of the Judeo-Christian-Muslim tradition, as well as other divine beings. These sacred beings and other sacred phenomena are thought of as transcendent, which means they are incomprehensible and beyond the realm of ordinary experience. Other beings, phenomena, and things outside of the sacred realm, but endowed with sanctity, include nature, places of worship, things believed to be created by the divine, and even people and their bodies. Since spirituality and religious beliefs are an important aspect of cultural diversity and coping in adversity, it can be very useful for mental health professionals to understand the religious and spiritual beliefs of their clients. The search for the sacred when used as a central organizing principle in people's lives can serve to increase their disaster and day-to-day resilience. To the extent their spirituality is well-integrated into many aspects of their lives, it can be very helpful in improving the ability of individuals to cope with trauma and adversity (Pargament and Mahoney 2009).

6.6   CONCLUSIONS

With the increasing frequency and severity of disasters, resilience for overcoming adversity, loss, and trauma has received renewed attention from vulnerability and resiliency theorists. Vulnerability and resiliency theory have begun to be integrated in a stress and coping framework to reduce losses in disaster and help people not only survive and recover in disasters but to experience posttraumatic growth. Disasters have multidimensional effects, potentially damaging people and systems at the individual, social network, and community levels. It is important for disaster social workers to realize, however, that individuals often have the resources to cope well with adversity, reinstate health and mental health behaviors, and reintegrate themselves into their own communities. All of these behaviors enhance an individual's ability to overcome adversity and loss.

The recognition that individuals have considerable strengths, and that environmental capabilities facilitate their resilience, is consistent with empowerment and strengths perspectives in social work, community psychiatry, humanistic psychology, and counseling. The same resources and capabilities a community has can lead to greater resilience of community members. Individuals and communities are often able to cope with mortality salience and to develop or recognize considerable strengths after a trauma such as a disaster. Not only can individuals survive disaster, but with the additional empowerment disaster social services interventions can provide, the survivors of disaster can recover and thrive even after extreme adversity. Not only can adversity and traumatic loss be overcome, but individuals can experience posttraumatic growth in their value systems, relationships, and their spiritual lives.

REFERENCES

Bankoff, G., G. Frerks, and D. Hilhorst., eds. 2004. *Mapping Vulnerability: Disasters, Development and People*. London, UK: Earthscan.

Barton, A. H. 1969. *Communities in Disaster: A Sociological Analysis of Collective Stress Situations*. Garden City, NY: Doubleday.

Bolin, B. 2007. Race, class, ethnicity, and disaster vulnerability. In *Handbook of Disaster Research,* eds. H. Rodriguez, E. L. Quarantelli, and R. R. Dynes, 113–129. New York: Springer.

Bourque, L. B., J. M. Sieger, M. Kano, and M. M. Wood. 2007. Morbidity and mortality associated with disasters. In *Handbook of Disaster Research,* eds. H. Rodriguez, E. L. Quarantelli, and R. R. Dynes, 97–112. New York: Springer.

Button, G. V. 2002. Popular media reframing of man-made disasters: A cautionary tale. In *Catastrophe & Culture: The Anthropology of Disaster* (A School of American Research advanced seminar series), eds. S. M. Hoffman and A. O. Smith, 143–158. Santa Fe, NM: School of American Research Press.

Cardona, O. D. 2004. The need for rethinking the concepts of vulnerability and risk from a holistic perspective: A necessary review and criticism for effective emergency management. In *Mapping Vulnerability: Disasters, Development & People*, eds. G. Bankoff, G. Frerks, and D. Hilhorst, 37–51. London: Earthscan.

Cohn, M. A., and B. L. Fredrickson. 2009. Positive emotions. In *Oxford Handbook of Positive Psychology*, 2nd ed., eds. S. J. Lopez and C. R. Snyder, 13–24, New York: Oxford University Press.

Davis, C. G., and S. Nolen-Hoeksema. 2009. Making sense of loss, perceiving benefits, and posttraumatic growth. In *Oxford Handbook of Positive Psychology*, 2nd ed., eds. S. J. Lopez and C. R. Snyder, 641–650. New York: Oxford University Press.

Diener, E. 2009. Positive psychology: Past, present, and future. In *Oxford Handbook of Positive Psychology*, 2nd ed., eds. S. J. Lopez and C. R. Snyder, 7–11. New York: Oxford University Press.

Dienstbier, R. A., and L. M. P. Zillig. 2009. Toughness. In *Oxford Handbook of Positive Psychology*, 2nd ed., eds. S. J. Lopez and C. R. Snyder, 537–548. New York: Oxford University Press.

Florian, V., and M. Mikulincer. 2004. A multifaceted perspective on the existential meanings, manifestations, and consequences of the fear of personal death. In *Handbook of Experimental Existential Psychology,* eds. J. Greenberg, S. L. Koole, and T. Pyszczynski, 54–71. New York: Guilford.

Greenberg, J., S. L. Koole, and T. Pyszczynski, eds. 2004. *Handbook of Experimental Existential Psychology.* New York: Guilford.

Greene, R. R., ed. 2002. *Resiliency: An Integrated Approach to Practice, Policy, and Research.* Washington, DC: NASW Press.

Honig, R. G., M. C. Grace, J. D. Lindy, C. J. Newman, and J. L. Tichener. 1999. Assessing long-term effects of trauma: Diagnosing symptoms of avoidance and numbing. *American Journal of Psychiatry 156*(3): 483–485.

Intergovernmental Panel on Climate Change. November 2007. *Summary for policymakers of the synthesis report of the IPCC fourth assessment report.* http://www.ipcc.ch/IPCC Nov17 ar4_syr_spm.pdf.

International Federation of Red Cross and Red Crescent Societies. 2008. *World disasters report 2008.* http://www.ifrc.org/Docs/pubs/disasters/wdr2008/WDR2008-full.pdf.

Janoff-Bulman, R., and D. J. Yopyk. 2004. Random outcomes and valued commitments: Existential dilemmas and the paradox of meaning. In *Handbook of Experimental Existential Psychology*, eds. J. Greenberg, S. L. Koole, and T. Pyszczynski, 122–138. New York: Guilford.

Kuhl, J., and S. L. Koole. 2004. Workings of the will: A functional approach. In *Handbook of Experimental Existential Psychology*, eds. J. Greenberg, S. L. Koole, and T. Pyszczynski, 411–430. New York: Guilford.

Lyubomirsky, S. 2007. *The How of Happiness: A Scientific Approach to Getting the Life You Want.* New York: Penguin Press.

Martin, L. L., W. K. Campbell, and C. D. Henry. 2004. The roar of awakening: Mortality acknowledgement as a call to authentic living. In *Handbook of Experimental Existential Psychology*, eds. J. Greenberg, S. L. Koole, and T. Pyszczynski, 431–448. New York: Guilford.

McEntire, D. A. 2007. The importance of multi- and interdisciplinary research on disasters and for emergency management. In *Disciplines, Disasters, and Emergency Management. The Convergence and Divergence of Concepts, Issues and Trends from the Research Literature*, ed. D. A. McEntire, 3–14. Springfield, IL: Charles C. Thomas.

National Sleep Foundation. 2010a. *Can't sleep? What to know about insomnia.* http://www.sleepfoundation. org/article/sleep-related-problems/insomnia-and-sleep.

National Sleep Foundation. 2010b. *Sleep studies.* http://www.sleepfoundation.org/article/sleep-topics/ sleep-studies.

Niederhoffer, K. G., and J. W. Pennebaker. 2009. Sharing one's story: On the benefits of writing or talking. In *Oxford Handbook of Positive Psychology*, 2nd ed., eds. S. J. Lopez and C. R. Snyder, 621–632. New York: Oxford University Press.

Norris, F. H., and C. L. Elrod. 2006. Psychosocial consequences of disaster: A review of past research. In *Methods for Disaster Mental Health Research*, eds. F. H. Norris, S. Galea, M. J. Friedman, and P. J. Watson, 20–42. New York: Guilford.

Norris, F. H., A. D. Murphy, K. Kaniasty, J. L. Perilla, and D. C. Ortis. 2001. Postdisaster social support in the United States and Mexico: Conceptual and contextual considerations. *Hispanic Journal of Behavioral Sciences 23*(4), 469–497.

North, C. S., and F. H. Norris. 2006. Choosing research methods to match research goals in studies of disaster or terrorism. In *Methods for Disaster Mental Health Research*, eds. F. H. Norris, S. Galea, J. J. Friedman, and P. J. Watson, 45–61. New York: Guilford.

Oliver-Smith, A. 2004. Theorizing vulnerability in a globalized world: A political ecological perspective. In *Mapping Vulnerability: Disasters, Development & People*, eds. G. Bankoff, G. Frerks, and D. Hilhorst, 10–24. London: Earthscan.

Pargament, K. I., and A. Mahoney. 2009. Spirituality: The search for the sacred. In *Oxford Handbook of Positive Psychology*, 2nd ed., eds. S. J. Lopez and C. R. Snyder, 611–620. New York: Oxford University Press.

Pedrotti, J. T., L. M. Edwards, and S. J. Lopez. 2009. Positive psychology within a cultural context. In *Oxford Handbook of Positive Psychology*, eds. S. J. Lopez and C. R. Snyder, 49–57. New York: Oxford University Press.

Rajan, S. R. 2002. Missing expertise, categorical politics, and chronic disasters: The case of Bhopal. In *Catastrophe & Culture: The Anthropology of Disaster* (A School of American Research advanced seminar series), eds. S. M. Hoffman and A. O. Smith, 237–259. Santa Fe, NM: School of American Research Press.

Rosenfeld, L. B., J. S. Caye, O. Ayalon, and M. Lahad. 2005. *When Their World Falls Apart: Helping Families and Children Manage the Effects of Disasters.* Washington, DC: NASW Press.

Shapiro, S. L. 2009. Meditation and positive psychology. In *Oxford Handbook of Positive Psychology*, 2nd ed., eds. S. J. Lopez and C. R. Snyder, 601–610. New York: Oxford University Press.

Tedeschi, R. G., and L. G. Calhoun. 2004. Posttraumatic growth: Conceptual foundations and empirical evidence. *Psychological Inquiry 15*(1): 1–18.

Tierney, K. J. 2007. Businesses and disasters: Vulnerability, impacts, and recovery. In *Handbook of Disaster Research*, eds. H. Rodriguez, E. L. Quarantelli, and R. R. Dynes, 275–296. New York: Springer.

United Nations. 2009. *2008 disasters in numbers.* http://www.unisdr.org/preventionweb/files/8742_2008disas tersinnumbersISDRCRED.pdf.

Wallace, A. F. C. 1956/2003. Mazeway resynthesis: A biocultural theory of religious inspiration. In *Revitalizations and Mazeways: Essays on Culture Change*, ed. R. S. Grumet, Vol. 1, 164–177. Lincoln, NE: University of Nebraska Press. Originally published in *Transactions of the New York Academy of Sciences 18*: 626–638.

Wisner, B., P. Blaikie, T. Cannon, and I. Davis. 2004. *At Risk. Natural Hazards, People's Vulnerability and Disasters.* 2nd ed. New York: Routledge.

Young, M. J., and M. W. Morris. 2004. Existential meanings and cultural models: The interplay of personal and supernatural agency in American and Hindu ways of responding to uncertainty. In *Handbook of Experimental Existential Psychology*, eds. J. Greenberg, S. L. Koole, and T. Pyszczynski, 215–230. New York: Guilford.

Zakour, M. J. 2007. Social work in disasters. In *Disciplines, Disasters, and Emergency Management. The Convergence and Divergence of Concepts, Issues and Trends from the Research Literature*, ed. D. A. McEntire, 124–141. Springfield, IL: Charles C. Thomas.

Zakour, M. J. 2008. Vulnerability to climate change in the Nile Delta: Social policy and community development interventions. *Proceedings of the 21st International Conference of Social Work: Social work and human welfare in a changeable community*, March 12–13, 2008, 425–451. Cairo, Egypt: Helwan University.

Zakour, M. J. 2010. Vulnerability and risk assessment: Building community resilience. In *Disaster Concepts and Issues: A Guide for Social Work Education and Practice*, ed. D. F. Gillespie and K. Danso, 15–33. Alexandria, VA: CSWE Press.

Zakour, M. J., and D. F. Gillespie. 2010. Recent trends in disaster vulnerability and resiliency research: Theory, design, and methodology. In *Disaster Concepts and Issues: A Guide for Social Work Education and Practice*, ed. D. F. Gillespie and K. Danso, 35–60. Alexandria, VA: CSWE Press.

7 Mental Health Outcomes of Disasters and Terrorism

Patricia Santucci

CONTENTS

7.1   RESPONSES TO DISASTER

Disasters are often life-changing events that have far-reaching mental health effects on survivors, families, friends, responders, communities, and even nations (Weisaeth and Tønnessen 2003, 69, quoted; Raphael 2000). A wide range of psychological and behavioral consequences has been reported in those who are exposed to disasters. The majority experience fear and distress; a smaller subset will respond by making behavioral changes. A substantial minority will have an onset, exacerbation, or reoccurrence of a psychiatric disorder, and 30 percent will experience chronic symptoms lasting more than a year (Shultz et al. 2007, cited Butler, Panzer, and Goldfrank 2003). This chapter will focus on the mental health outcomes of adult survivors of disasters and terrorism.

7.1.1   Disaster-Related Fear and Distress

Immediately following a disaster, most survivors show signs of fear and distress (Butler, Panzer, and Goldfrank 2003). A wide spectrum of emotional, behavioral, cognitive, physical, and spiritual responses has been identified. Acute trauma-related stress responses vary in severity from mild distress to intense posttrauma-like responses. One-third of survivors of high-impact disasters experience clinically significant distress (Friedman et al. 2004). These intense reactions immediately following an event are not considered pathological (Housley and Beutler 2006). Most survivors can be reassured that their responses are anticipated, understandable, and nearly universal, and that recovery is expected. A normal response to an abnormal event may not be the best clinical description, but it is often most calming and reassuring. A rapid decline in the rate of distress occurs in the first two weeks; it then falls by two-thirds within six to eight weeks (Whalley and Brewin 2007). For the most part, reactions are transitory and tend to dissipate with time, even without specific treatment. Most survivors develop coping strategies and social support networks leading to a natural recovery. About 60 percent of survivors display resiliency. Continued adaptation occurs within the next three to six months, with the expectation of full recovery within 6 to 16 months (NCPTSD 2010; NSW Institute of Psychiatry and Centre for Mental Health 2000). For the majority of disaster survivors, significant stress reactions are only temporary and do not result in lasting mental health implications (Vazquez, Perez-Sales, and Matt 2006). Ninety percent of Americans surveyed nationally reported at least moderate distress within three to five days after 9/11. Forty-four percent of them reported one or more substantial symptoms of severe distress (Schuster et al. 2001).

Forty-two percent of the symptoms dissipated within a month and an additional 23 percent within a year (Norris et al. 2003).

7.1.2 Behavioral Changes

For some, distress may lead to either positive or negative behavioral changes. Minor and transient behaviors, such as separation anxiety, are common. After the London bombings in 2005, 32 percent of Londoners reported behavioral changes, such as fear of travel (Rubin et al. 2005). More serious, maladaptive behavioral changes can occur and even perpetuate distress. While these responses may not warrant a psychiatric diagnosis, they are cause for concern and can become health risks, impact the utilization of the health care system, and/or create subsequent nonspecific chronic attitudes and behavioral problems (Norris et al. 2002).

7.2 MALADAPTIVE RESPONSES TO DISASTER

7.2.1 Health Risk Behaviors

Disaster situations may lead to neglect and indifference regarding self care, lack of adherence to medical recommendations, and poor eating habits. Also, risk-taking behaviors, overcommitment resulting in fatigue, exhaustion, and poor regulation of the rest/work cycle are frequent.

Sleep disturbances are among the most common complaint and may be secondary to extreme arousal, grief, anticipatory anxiety, or underlying psychiatric disorders. While restoration of sleep is essential, excessive use of substances may interrupt the normal sleep cycle. This may lead to the development of a substance-induced sleep disorder and potential dependency. Five months after 9/11, 30 percent of Americans and 39 percent of New York City residents still had difficulty getting to sleep and were twice as likely as other Americans to ask for medicine to calm down, help with sleep, or help with mood (Rasinski et al. 2002, 13).

The occasional use of alcohol is a way of coping or self-medicating in about 15 percent of people, and increases up to 40 percent in those with psychiatric illness (NCPTSD 2005, 1). After disasters, reports substantiated an increase in the use of alcohol, tobacco and other drugs (Galea et al. 2002; Vlahov et al. 2002). Post 9/11, residents from the south of 110th Street in Manhattan reported an increase in the use of the previously described substances. There remained a sustained increase six to nine months later: 24.6 percent increase in alcohol, 9.7 percent increase in tobacco, and 3.2 percent increase in marijuana (Vlahov et al. 2002). A nationwide study noted also after 9/11 an increase in the use of alcohol, tobacco, and prescription and nonprescription medications by people who may not have used these substances previously (McDuff and Ford 2005). However, these increases did not translate into new substance abuse disorders. Only 0–2 percent of new-onset substance use disorders have been reported after disasters (NCPTSD 2005, 1). Individuals with significant preexisting problems with alcohol are likely to also have them after disasters. Individuals in active addiction may increase their use. Those on the border may cross over and some in recovery may relapse (David et al. 1996; North, Smith, and Spitznagel 1994; North et al. 1999).

In disaster settings, acute intoxication, withdrawal, or drug-seeking behaviors can create problems regarding health risks and health care utilization. When supply lines are interrupted and treatment resources limited, caring for patients with substance abuse becomes an additional challenge.

Hurricanes Katrina and Rita had a huge impact on substance abuse treatment capacity because of program unavailability, damage to treatment facilities, and loss of professional staff (McKernan 2005, cited Louisiana Office of Addictive Disorders; Mississippi Department of Mental Health, Division of Alcohol and Drug Abuse). One year later, "more than 50% of new clients presented with depression and substance abuse diagnosis. These cases primarily represented people who did not have an alcohol or drug abuse/dependence diagnosis prior to Hurricane Katrina" (McKernan 2005, 15). Coastal regions reported experiencing increased use of alcohol to cope with chronic stressors. Outreach workers increasingly encountered methamphetamine labs in FEMA trailer parks. This information indicates a need for more studies on substance abuse in disasters (see Section 7.5.6.3).

Domestic violence and marital conflicts increase during disasters and are highly predictive of postdisaster symptoms. Married women represent a high-risk group. In a recent study of post-flood behavior, 14 percent of women experienced at least one act of physical aggression, and 25 percent reported emotional abuse over a nine-month period (Steury and Parks 2003, 18). Distrust, externalization of blame, and destructive venting can lead to family conflict and domestic violence. Spousal abuse calls to a community helpline after Hurricane Andrew increased by 50 percent (Laudisio 1993), and 22 percent of adult residents in the area affected by Hurricane Andrew admitted to a new conflict with someone in their household (Norris et al. 1999).

Severe child abuse may increase after a natural disaster. Traumatic brain injury (TBI) is one of the most severe forms of child abuse, often leading to hospitalization and even death. In the six-month period after Hurricane Floyd in North Carolina, the rate of inflicted TBI in children under age two showed a fivefold increase in counties severely affected by the hurricane. In counties less affected or not affected, there was no increase in the rate (WHO 2005, 1).

7.2.2 HEALTH ISSUES AND MEDICAL UTILIZATION

According to Norris's 2005 review of 225 cases and 132 events, 27 percent were identified with physical health problems or somatic concerns. Nonspecific stress, defined as psychological and psychosomatic symptoms, were reported in 35 percent of the cases.

Frequently, somatization represents underlying depression or anxiety. Patients can present with physical distress and nonspecific symptoms such as chronic pain, irritable bowel, fibromyalgia, chronic fatigue syndrome, various autoimmune disorders, and sleep disorders (Davidson et al. 2004). Evidence linking cardiovascular disease is particularly strong. In the 1995 Kobe earthquake, a three-fold increase in myocardial infarction and a doubling of strokes was reported in people living close to the epicenter (Frohlich and Schwartz 2008).

Trauma can interact with environmental exposure and exacerbate or contribute to a wide range of medical disorders (McEwen and Lasley 2002). The World Trade Center Health Registry reported new cases of both asthma and posttraumatic stress disorder (PTSD) among those who experienced intense and prolonged exposure five to six years after 9/11. This study suggested that the major health ramifications of the 9/11 World Trade Center (WTC) attack were PTS symptoms and asthma, which often occur together (Brackbill et al. 2009).

Disasters often increase medical utilization by generating new symptoms. Medically unexplained physical symptoms (MUPS) can be defined as physical symptoms that provoke people to seek care but have no clinically determined pathogenesis (Clauw 2003). Mass psychogenic illness (MPI) is defined as a cluster of patients who have a common belief regarding the etiology of their symptoms and present similar psychosomatic symptoms.

Fear of exposure can be as serious as actual exposure. The uncertainty regarding exposure and long-term outcomes can become a source of anxiety. MUPS cases emerged after WWI as "shell-shocked" soldiers returned home, and Vietnam veterans voiced concerns of exposure to Agent Orange. In the 1990s, hundreds returned from the Middle East with a wide range of symptoms known as the "Gulf War Syndrome."

MUPS may become chronic and present as a major burden to the health care system. While newly diagnosed somatoform disorders are rare, subsyndromal fears of this nature may be widespread after disaster or terrorism. The term *worried well* has often been applied to these cases. Unfortunately, this label stigmatizes individuals and gives the impression that their health concerns are not being taken seriously. It may also stop the physician from searching for potential medical problems and lead to substandard care. Butler et al. (2003) have suggested that use of the terms *high risk*, *moderate risk*, or *low risk* should be applied to those experiencing psychological distress.

A surge is essentially "a sudden increase in patient volume that would otherwise severely challenge or exceed the current capacity of the health care system" (Hick et al. 2004, 254). Following disasters there is an increase in medical utilization, and psychological causalities frequently outnumber medical causalities. A conservative estimate of the ratio of psychological to physical injuries is 4:1, but this ratio can be much higher in some types of disaster, particularly terrorist attacks involving weapons of mass destruction (Shultz et al. 2006, 24). For example, in the anthrax attacks following 9/11, the number of people who feared exposure was 1,500 times greater than the number of people who actually developed anthrax (Rundell and Christopher 2004, 90).

A surge can include medical patients, family, friends, Good Samaritans, volunteers, curious onlookers, media, and injured responders. In the 1995 Tokyo sarin gas attacks, 12 people died but more than 5,500 presented to emergency rooms. The acute demand for medical care consisted mainly of individuals who had no signs of exposure but believed they were "poisoned" (Tucker 1996). In addition, responders and hospital personnel accidently were contaminated and became additional and unexpected patients.

The dynamics of surge will be determined by the unique characteristics of the disaster (Shultz et al. 2006, 20). In response to the 2004 Madrid train bombings, the emergency medical care was handled adequately, but what was not anticipated was the surge of family members and friends searching hospitals for their loved ones. Arguments between relatives and hospital staff created frenzy as some three hundred people awaited information (Calcedo-Barba 2004).

Panic usually refers to desperate acts of self-preservation that can harm self or others. In disasters, panic is rare and altruism dominates (Steury and Parks 2003, cited Lacy and Benedeck 2003). Panic did not occur in Israel with the Scud missiles attacks, in Tokyo with sarin attacks, in the Oklahoma City bombing, or during the evacuation of the WTC on 9/11. For instance, a blind worker and his guide dog descended from the 78th floor of the WTC on 9/11. Many cheered him on and encouraged his escape (Weisaeth and Tønnessen 2003). People will usually care for others, helping those in need when possible. Panic is not widespread or contagious, with few participants and of short duration (Quarantelli 1960, 72).

Following initial impact, 75 percent of individuals appear stunned, 12–25 percent are able to analyze the dangers, formulate a plan, and act on it, and the remaining 12–25 percent may become confused, hysterical, or perhaps paralyzed by fear or anxiety (Steury and Parks 2003, cited Tyhurst 1951). Risk factors for panic include being trapped, threat of death or injury, lack of credible leadership or direction, and limited resources in which the concept of "first come, first served" prevails (Glass and Schoch-Spana 2002).

7.2.3 NONSPECIFIC ATTITUDES AND BEHAVIORS

Many individuals do not merit a psychiatric diagnosis or meet full symptom criteria, but have significant symptoms and impairment. The interpersonal, social, and occupational dysfunction experienced can be as disabling as any psychiatric disorder.

There are no rigorous studies on this broad set of pathological behavioral changes. Changes in belief systems, view of self, trust and intimacy are often difficult to measure. Guilt, shame, fear, hyperviligence, and irritability are not "diagnoses." A desire to remain withdrawn and isolated was so strong in many after 9/11 that they "might well have met the diagnosis of separation anxiety" (Ursano et al. 2007, 11). Avoidance may make returning to normal activities impossible. Occupational impairment, absenteeism, consideration of alternative careers, impaired work performance, and economic loss can be consequences of this behavior.

In addition to the primary stressor of the event, secondary stressors may continue to impact the individual, reinforce unhealthy coping mechanisms, and interfere with recovery. Common secondary stressors include financial hardship, displacement, loss of social support, and community infrastructure (Shultz et al 2007, 120).

The extensive damage of secondary stressors were noted to cause mental illness, which in and of itself, was associated with poorer physical health outcomes and many forms of illness (Anderson 2007). Stressors caused by Katrina have resulted in a significant rise in mental illness among survivors. One would expect a significant decline with approximately half of the cases resolving within the first year and the majority within the second year. Instead, two years after the disaster, the percentage of people with mild to moderate mental health problems increased from 9.7 percent to almost 20 percent and serious mental illness from 6.1 percent to 11.3 percent (Galea et al. 2007; see Section 7.5.5 for information about suicide and suicidal ideation).

7.3   ADAPTIVE CHANGES

The psychiatric consequences of disaster are not exclusively bad and most people do well. Trajectories can provide a longitudinal perspective. A minority will meet diagnostic criteria for psychiatric diagnosis. The following trajectories have been proposed by Layne et al. (2007). Shultz et al. (2007) describes these trajectories as: Stress Resistance—the ability to maintain a near steady course of highly adaptive functioning where the individual is considered "immune" to stress; Resilience—"bouncing back" after experiencing transient perturbations and rapidly reestablishing normal functioning and a stable healthy status across time; Protracted Recovery—the gradual return to normal after a notable period of dysfunction and diminished function; and Posttraumatic Growth—the positive response with emergence in an even healthier state (126).

7.3.1   Resilience

This is the most common response to disaster and is the rule rather than the exception. It has been described as "mastery against adversity" (Reissman 2006). After 9/11, rates of stress-related symptoms and PTSD soared among survivors and responders. Six months later, 65 percent of individuals living in and around New York City showed a resilient trajectory defined as having no stress-related symptoms or one symptom since the attack. Bonanno et al. (2006, 184) concluded that "even among the groups with the most pernicious level of exposure and highest probable PTSD, the proportion that was resilient never dropped below one-third."

Resiliency can be learned and enhanced, but it is not a fixed attribute (Shultz et al. 2007, cited Layne et al. 2007). Some individuals are resilient in some circumstances, but not in others (Shultz et al. 2007, cited Layne et al. 2007). A series of strategies can be employed by individuals, families, and organizations to strengthen resiliency throughout all phases of disaster (Shultz et al. 2007, 168).

Studies to date have not identified any universal resiliency factors. However, individual factors such as motivation, humor, optimism, social skills, emotional well-being, religion, and life satisfaction enable some people to mobilize protective factors (Shultz et al. 2005). Perceptions of self-efficacy may be the key, and one's ability to cope may be only as effective as he or she believes it to be (Norris et al. 2002).

7.3.2   Posttraumatic Growth

Traumatic experiences can be life-changing in positive ways, and "a traumatic experience can become the center around which a victim organizes a previously disorganized life, reorienting values and goals" (Fullerton and Ursano 1997, 6). Some will emerge from a disaster in a healthier state, with positive changes in attitude, enhanced coping skills, and improved functioning. Personal growth can come from learning about one's strengths through deeds of altruism. These experiences may result in positive changes in relationships with others, spirituality, and/or the ability to appreciate life. One survey of post-Katrina survivors revealed that 81.6 percent became closer to loved ones; 95.6 percent developed faith and the ability to rebuild life; 66.8 percent became more spiritual and religious; 75.2 percent found deeper meaning and purpose in life; and 69.5 percent discovered inner strength (Kessler et al. 2006).

7.4   MENTAL HEALTH OUTCOMES

We are just beginning to understand why some people develop posttrauma pathology and others do not. Mental health outcomes are highly variable and reflect the characteristic of the disaster, the biopsychosocial vulnerability of the individual, and the response.

No two disasters are alike. A review of 60,000 disaster victims found 67 percent of survivors exposed to mass violence were more severely impaired compared to 34 percent exposed to natural disasters (Norris et al. 2002). While terrorism may be associated with the most severe mental health consequences, the impact of natural disasters, such as the Asian tsunami and Hurricane Katrina, cannot be underestimated. Negative outcome is greatest in those who experience a perceived threat to life with low controllability and lack of predictability. In addition, high loss, injury, and exposure to death and dying increase risk (APA, 2000). The longitudinal course of recovery may be different when the community and social networks are disrupted, homes destroyed, and jobs lost. Viewing trauma survivors as one homogeneous group can lead to imprecise conclusions. Individual responses, even when exposure is the same, can vary widely. Social, cultural, and religious factors can modify the perception and influence coping strategies.

A rapidly changing clinical picture necessitates monitoring the type, severity, and duration of responses. It is a priority to differentiate *signs* of distress from *symptoms* of a diagnosis. Directing limited resources and rapidly providing services to those in need in the first few weeks postevent can lead to a sustained reduction in morbidity (Bryant 2006, 52). It remains a challenge to identify who will develop long-term problems, but early identification is often the initial step in recovery (Bryant 2006). We can then go forward and match the individual with the appropriate evidence-based and/or evidence-informed interventions at the appropriate time.

7.4.1   RISK FACTORS AND PREDICTORS

Severity of trauma, lack of social support, and adverse life stressors following trauma have been identified as key risk factors. These may have greater effect on the development of PTSD than preexisting factors such as demographics, psychiatric illness, and family history (Brewin, Andrews, and Valentine 2000). Identification of predictors and risk factors may not be consistent across all studies, but they serve as a source of information that can help us make an educated decision regarding referral and treatment (Housely and Beutler 2006, 5).

7.4.2   PREDISASTER

Female gender is a robust predictor of PTSD (10 percent in females vs. 5 percent in males) and of depression (14 percent in females vs. 6 percent in males; Kessler et al. 1995). PTSD has usually been associated with inherent biological vulnerability. Some suggest it may be the influence of varying social roles, culture, and intensity of prior trauma exposure (Breslau and Anthony 2007). Male gender is more prone to illicit drug use (11 percent in males, 6 percent in females; Anthony and Helzer 1991).

Individuals with preexisting psychiatric illness, prior trauma, limited coping skills, and neuroticism—that is, proneness to irritability, depression, anxiety—are more likely to experience psychiatric illness after disasters (North et al. 1989, 1994, 1999). Survivors of the Oklahoma City bombing with preexisting psychiatric disorders had twice the rate of PTSD

(46 percent vs. 26 percent). Preexisting illness is neither necessary nor sufficient to generate psychiatric morbidity after disasters (North 2007, 38). Forty percent of the survivors of the Oklahoma City bombing who developed PTSD or depression did not have a history of mental illness (North et al. 1999).

More than 90 percent of individuals with severe mental illness (SMI) have experienced a traumatic event and are more likely to experience multiple traumatic events (Goodman et al. 2001). People with SMI are about 20–30 times more likely to have PTSD than those without SMI. Even if coping is effective in the immediate aftermath, extremely stressful events and deteriorating resources can exacerbate symptoms. Preexisting psychiatric illness is a strong predictor in mild events or minimal exposure. With increasing severity and exposure, psychiatric history becomes less predictive (Breslau and Davis 1992).

There is evidence that susceptibility to PTSD is hereditary. In the Vietnam twin studies, genetic factors accounted for approximately one-third of the variance with regard to PTSD symptoms and exceeded trauma severity factors (True et al. 1993). A serotonin-regulating gene has been identified, with one variant associated with resiliency and the other with stress, depression, and suicide (Caspi et al. 2003). Vulnerability and resiliency are mediated by multiple neurochemical and neuroendocrine mechanisms (Charney et al. 1993). Functional neuroimaging has indicated that small hippocampal volume may be a risk factor rather than a consequence of PTSD (Gilbertson et al. 2002).

Family risk factors include being married, having children at home, and having a distressed spouse. Risk varies by age, with an increase in school age, followed by a second, more prominent increase in middle age (Norris et al. 2002). Middle-aged adults may represent the *sandwich generation* and have greater burdens before disaster strikes and assume even greater responsibilities afterwards. Prevalence of PTSD in disaster victims differs strongly within ethnic groups: Caucasian (15 percent); African American (23 percent); and Hispanic (38 percent) (Perilla, Norris, and Lavizzo 2002). This difference may be explained by such factors as low socioeconomic status, event exposure, social support, and peri-event emotional reactions. After 9/11, New York City residents of lower socioeconomic status were 2.5 times more likely to develop PTSD (Galea et al. 2002).

7.4.3 DISASTER RELATED

Fundamentally, "some disasters are more horrifying than others and are accompanied by more injury, property destruction, and threats to individuals" (Galea, Nandi, and Vlahov 2005, 84). The greater the dose of traumatic stressors, the more likely the development of higher rates of psychiatric morbidity.

Exposure, while considered to be among the highest risk predictor, is mediated by factors such as physical proximity, level of threat, severity, duration, and personal loss or injury to family or friends (Herman, Felton, and Susser 2002). Proximity has constantly been related to severity of subsequent symptoms. After 9/11, symptoms spread outward in diminishing ripple patterns concentrically from Ground Zero. Those who lived closest to the WTC had a three times greater risk of developing PTSD (Galea et al. 2002).

Those who experienced direct exposure were considered at highest risk but a substantial number of individuals indirectly exposed had disturbing levels of trauma-related symptoms (Silver et al. 2002). In some cases, repeated trauma exposure can even have a stress inoculation effect and strengthen an individual's protective factor (NCPTSD 2010).

Injured survivors may live every day with the physical and emotional reminders of the trauma and are at higher risk for increased cooccurrence of psychiatric illness. The degree of injury predicted the development of PTSD. Of the 87 percent who sustained injuries in the Oklahoma City bombing, one-third developed PTSD (North et al. 1999). Consistent predictors for PTSD included female gender, preinjury trauma, greater initial distress, and an initial higher heart rate in the emergency room (Zatzick et al. 2005).

7.4.4 POSTDISASTER

A decrease in social support and the occurrence of adverse life events are powerful predictors of mental health problems and appear to be more important than preexisting risk factors (Shalev et al. 2003, cited Brewin, Andrews, and Valentine 2000). There is substantial evidence that perceived social support buffers the effect of stress and may even offset genetic vulnerabilities (Kilpatrick et al. 2007).

Secondary stressors include loss of home and possessions, family separation, displacement, marital difficulties, loss of employment, and financial difficulties. The continued lack of control, uncertainty about safety of self or others, and the possibility that the event may reoccur result in continued high stress (Watson and Shalev 2005). These significantly impact the recovery trajectory (Grace et al. 1993).

Coping strategies assessed shortly after 9/11 were among the strongest predictors of PTS symptoms over time. Ineffective coping strategies such as giving up, avoidance, denial, or passive coping predicted adverse outcomes (Silver et al. 2002). The presence of negative perceptions of symptoms, other people's responses, catastrophic attributions of responsibility, and other dysfunctional cognitions may help determine who may be at risk (Ali et al. 2002).

Excessive peritraumatic arousal, dissociation, and depression are responses known to predict later PTSD and may be targeted for psychopharmacological intervention (Brewin et al. 1999). Genetic and biological markers, such as low cortisol and elevated resting heart rate in the acute aftermath of trauma, are under investigation as to how they can be effectively utilized (Whitehead et al. 2006).

7.4.5 DIAGNOSTIC ISSUES

Immediately post trauma, it may be impossible to select a diagnosis, beyond describing the symptoms of acute distress. The majority of survivors will have symptoms of acute distress, but few will warrant intervention in the immediate hours after the event, other than support and resources. Traditional treatment is not the appropriate intervention or goal at this point. Not everyone will need or want "Psychological First Aid ™" but components of this intervention can be offered by trained mental health and nonmental health responders (Brymer et al. 2006, 1). Recognizing that symptoms will dissipate fairly rapidly, those who are at highest risk of long-term problems are initially identified. The remainder may be eliminated from follow-up since they will most likely recover without treatment. During the early weeks there is continued informal monitoring of the severity of symptoms and the degree of impairment. Patients with persistent symptoms can receive further evaluation and treatment with evidenced-based early interventions as indicated. Then, "it is not until six to eight weeks after the incident that one can begin to identify for whom a formal diagnostic evaluation will be helpful in planning treatment" (Housely and Beutler 2006, 11). Psychiatric disorders must be determined individually and the clinical interview still remains the "gold standard" for assessment (Benedek 2007, 155). British psychiatrist Simon Wessley offered some wise words to therapists: "Once the dust has settled, literally and figuratively... access decent quality treatment" (Satel 2007, 276–277).

7.4.6 SEVERITY OF IMPAIRMENT

A rough estimate of the overall impact was studied by Norris and updated in 2005. Of the 225 samples and 132 events, 9 percent showed minimal impairment indicative of transient distress; 50 percent showed moderate impairment indicative of prolonged stress; 24 percent showed severe impairment indicative of significant psychopathology or distress; and 17 percent showed very severe impairment (Norris 2005, 4).

7.4.7 RANGE OF DIAGNOSIS

In the same study as mentioned before, Norris identified the percent of samples in which the following outcomes were assessed and observed. PTSD (74 percent) was the most commonly observed disorder, followed by depression (39 percent), somatic concerns (27 percent), anxiety (20 percent), and nonspecific distress (35 percent) (Norris 2005, 3).

PTSD is often considered the signature diagnosis of trauma, but it represents only part of the clinical picture. Assuming one diagnosis will be the standard response may lead to omission or inappropriate targeted therapy, which could compromise recovery and even exacerbate posttraumatic stress symptoms.

When acute stress disorder (ASD) or PTSD exists, it is highly probable that other psychiatric conditions exist as well. While psychiatric disorders can exist independently, there is tremendous overlap of symptoms. Comorbidity among psychiatric disorders is high, but with PTSD it appears to be the rule rather than the exception. PTSD was the primary diagnosis in 30–50 percent of men and 40–60 percent of women with comorbid disorders (Kessler et al. 1995). A lifetime history of at least one other psychiatric disorder was present in 84 percent of individuals with PTSD (Kessler et al. 1995). These disorders can develop before, during, or after PTSD, but are often the byproduct of PTSD.

While PTSD, depression, and chemical abuse are the diagnoses most often seen among postterror and posttrauma survivors (Galea et al. 2003b), mental health professionals must be aware of the presentation and complexity of the various psychiatric disorders and mental health concerns that occur following disasters.

Of those who survive a disaster, some will experience an onset, exacerbation, or recurrence of a psychiatric disorder, but only a minority will experience long-term impairment. The consequences for these individuals are the most chronic and disabling outcomes of disaster.

The following discussion is intended as an overview of common diagnoses and concerns but not a complete differential diagnosis or description of each disorder. The reader is encouraged to consult the DSM IV-TR for detailed diagnostic criteria.

7.5 OVERVIEW OF COMMON PSYCHIATRIC DIAGNOSES AND CONCERNS

7.5.1 ACUTE STRESS DISORDER/POSTTRAUMATIC STRESS DISORDER

Acute Stress Disorder (ASD) was added to the DSM-IV in 1995 to describe those individuals experiencing high magnitude and clinically significant distress within the first month of a traumatic event. In addition, it was hoped that ASD would help identify those who would subsequently develop posttraumatic stress disorder (PTSD). ASD was diagnosed in 7 to 33 percent of survivors (Friedman 2006).

7.5.1.1 ASD as a Predictor of PTSD

ASD has received a mixed reception. Some feel it is the "nucleus" from which a variety of posttraumatic symptoms evolve (Houseley and Beutler 2006, 10). As many as 70–80 percent of those with ASD will develop PTSD within six months (Ursano et al. 2007, 10). Exposed disaster workers with ASD were 7.33 times more likely to meet PTSD diagnostic criteria (Ursano et al. 2007, 9). ASD combined with a resting heart rate of 90 beats per minute had high sensitivity (88 percent) and specificity (85 percent) in predicting PTSD symptoms (Kleim, Ehlers, and Glucksman 2007, 1458). ASD may not be as reliable a predictor as one had hoped since 60 percent will have PTSD without previous ASD (Classen et al. 1998). Controversy exists over the diagnosis with some feeling that we should not use a diagnosis to predict another diagnosis and that ASD carries the potential to pathologize acute transient stress reactions.

Central to the diagnosis of ASD is dissociation, which is often considered one of the best predictors for the development of PTSD (Bryant and Harvey 1998). Continued flashbacks, periods of derealization, and depersonalization that persisted beyond two weeks characterized high risk for long-term problems (Marmar et al. 2004). Time distortion, accompanied by dissociative symptoms, indicated a four-time greater risk for chronic PTSD (Ursano et al. 2007, 10). Avoidance and numbing may be a marker for PTSD (McMillen, North, and Smith 2000). In contrast, PTSD has been reported in cases of ASD without dissociation. Dissociation is also viewed by some as an adaptive mechanism. In the immediate aftermath of trauma, it can serve by protecting against overwhelming stress, but as time goes on it can become maladaptive.

Immediately post impact, symptom severity may not predict the future course of the disorder (McNally et al. 2003). Early after disasters, two to four weeks, symptom severity appears to be a good predictor (North et al. 2004). MacFarlane (1988) noted that dissociation the day of the event did not predict PTSD, but dissociation two weeks later was predictive. Indicators of more pathological responses also include the following: continuous distress; intense recollections that are fearfully avoided; tormented or interrupted sleep; extreme social withdrawal; or inability to think about, rather than to just emotionally experience, the trauma (NCPTSD 2010).

7.5.1.2   Course of ASD

The majority of ASD symptoms usually resolve over the course of the intervening month, even without treatment. If symptoms persist for more than one month and meet full criteria for PTSD, the diagnosis is changed from ASD to PTSD (APA 2000). Patients who do not meet full criteria are diagnosed with an adjustment reaction (APA 2000).

7.5.2   PTSD

7.5.2.1   Prevalence

PTSD is the fifth most common psychiatric diagnosis in the United States and is usually assumed to be the most common after disasters. In a lifetime, 61 percent of men and 51 percent of women experience at least one traumatic event, with up to half of individuals reporting multiple traumas (Kessler et al. 1995). Ursano and colleagues (2007, 9) observed, "ASD and early PTSD may be more like the common cold—experienced at sometime by nearly all."

U.S. prevalence rates for PTSD were reported at 8–9 percent (Kessler et al. 1995). Women are twice as likely to develop PTSD despite having a lower exposure to trauma (Kessler et al. 1995). Empirical evidence suggests prevalence rates are approximately 10–20 percent among rescue workers and 30–40 percent among direct victims of disasters, but can be higher or lower for particular groups (Galea, Nandi, and Vlahov 2005, 84). Kessler and colleagues (1995) reported in the National Comorbidity Survey that 18.9 percent of men and 15.2 percent of women reported a lifetime experience of a natural disaster. The prevalence of PTSD can vary significantly. In some natural disasters, such as tornados, PTSD was reported in only 2–4 percent of survivors (North et al. 1989). Much higher rates, up to 50–100 percent, were reported for individuals who were exposed to a plane crash into a shopping mall (Newman and Foreman 1987).

7.5.2.2   Differentiation of ASD/PTSD

ASD and PTSD are very similar, but not identical. ASD requires three or more dissociative symptoms, persists for a minimum of two days and maximum of four weeks, and occurs and is resolved within four weeks of the traumatic event. After four weeks, the diagnosis of ASD is either dropped or upgraded to PTSD, if full criteria are met. Both diagnoses require: (1) that the person experience, witness, or be confronted with a stressor that involved actual or threatened death or serious injury

TABLE 7.1

Differentiation of ASD/PTSD

Reexperiencing Cluster	Avoidance/Numbing Cluster	Hyperarousal Cluster	ASD Dissociative Symptoms
ASD (≥1)	ASD marked	ASD marked	ASD (≥3)
PTSD (≥1)	PTSD (≥3)	PTSD (≥2)	
Recurrent intrusive distressing memories	Avoidance thoughts, feelings, or conversations associated with event	Difficulty with sleep	Subjective sense of numbing, detachment or absence of emotional responsiveness
Recurrent distressing dreams	Avoidance of activities, places, and persons associated with event	Irritability or outburst of anger	Reduction of awareness of surroundings (being in a daze)
Illusions, hallucinations, flashbacks; sense of reliving	Amnesia about certain aspects of event	Problems concentrating	Derealization
Intense distress on exposure	Decreased interest and participation	Hyperviligence	Depersonalization
Physiological reactivity on exposure to external or internal clues	Feeling detached, restrictive affect, sense of foreshortened future	Exaggerated startle response	Dissociative amnesia

Source: Modified from *Diagnostic and Statistical Manual of Mental Disorders*, 4th ed., American Psychiatric Association, Washington, DC, 2000. With permission.

or a threat to physical integrity of self or others, and (2) the response triggers intense feelings of fear, helplessness and horror. In addition, the three symptom clusters are shared (see Table 7.1) but the number in each category differs. PTSD does not require dissociation in the diagnostic criteria. PTSD symptoms must be new after the event, cause significant clinical impairment, continue for at least a month, and not be better accounted for by another disorder (APA 2000).

7.5.2.3 Reexperiencing Symptoms

Reexperiencing symptoms were the most commonly reported and present as intrusive and distressing memories provoking panic, terror, dread, grief and despair. Triggers can precipitate a PTSD flashback, in which there is a reliving of the traumatic experience and loss of all connection with the present. Daytime recollections and traumatic nightmares disrupt functioning and the quality of life.

7.5.2.4 Avoidance/Numbing Symptoms

Avoidance/numbing symptoms have been labeled as the "pathological part" of PTSD and are considered "markers" for PTSD (McMillen, North, and Smith 2000). Ninety-four percent of the Oklahoma City bombing survivors who met full criteria of three or more symptoms of avoidance and numbing yielded 94 percent specificity and 100 percent sensitivity for PTSD (North 2007, 32). Constant effort is made to avoid anything related to the original traumatic event, even to the point of experiencing psychogenic amnesia. Psychic numbing is the "emotional anesthesia" used to suppress all feelings, in order to block out the negative ones. While intrusive symptoms decrease, the avoidant and numbing behaviors increase in time and impair recovery and influence the development of chronic PTSD (McFarlane 2000). Avoidance does not allow an individual the opportunity to correct negative perceptions and master self-regulation. Subsequently, the world is seen as a dangerous place and survivors are left with feelings of helplessness and ineffectiveness, which furthers additional negative thoughts.

7.5.2.5 Hyperarousal

Hyperarousal symptoms are also quite common and cause difficulty with concentration, sleep, and performance of cognitive tasks. At times they may closely resemble those seen in generalized anxiety or panic disorders. Hypervigilance can be mistaken for paranoia.

7.5.2.6 Associated Clinical Features

There is the consistent association between PTSD and physical health. Many patients with PTSD will present to their primary care physician with physical rather than psychological complaints. Cardiovascular, gastrointestinal, musculoskeletal, diabetes, psoriasis, and autoimmune disorders, such as rheumatoid arthritis, have all been associated. PTSD is related to increased medical utilization, poor self-care, noncompliance with medication and even premature death (Schnurr and Green 2004).

Poor physical health may also be related to the comorbid depression, anxiety, hostility, and anger. Increased smoking and substance use are also associated with PTSD. Alcohol abuse or dependence was reported in 52 percent of men and 28 percent of women with PTSD. The abuse or dependence on other substances was reported as 35 percent and 27 percent, respectively (Kessler et al. 1995).

Additional features associated with PTSD include shame, despair, hopelessness, social withdrawal, impaired modulation of affect, survivor guilt, difficulties with interpersonal relationships, change in belief and personality, violence, impulsive, and self-destructive behaviors (Foa, Stein, and McFarlane 2006).

PTSD has been associated with unemployment and loss of productivity estimated at approximately three billion U.S. dollars annually (Greenberg et al. 1999). Many of these factors can cause clinically significant distress and impairment in the social, occupational, or other important areas of functioning (APA 2000).

7.5.2.7 Time Course of PTSD

The onset of PTSD is usually fairly rapid. Within five to eight weeks of 9/11, 7.5 percent of New York City residents developed PTSD (Galea et al. 2002). PTSD is seen by some as occurring in a series of stages and represents a failure of natural recovery (McFarlane 2000).

Duration of symptoms vary. For instance, in a study of rape victims, symptoms were transient and more than half were resolved within four to twelve weeks (Rothbaum et al. 1992). A nationwide study post 9/11 indicates that postdisaster distress was most acute in the immediate period following the event, and the majority of individuals experienced a natural recovery (Silver et al. 2002). Longitudinal studies of the cohort of New York City residents south of Canal Street demonstrated the decline of PTSD from 7.5 percent initially reported to 1.7 percent at five months and by six to nine months to 0.6 percent (Galea et al. 2003a; Galea et al. 2003b).

PTSD symptoms had resolved within one year after the attacks on the WTC in 57 percent of survivors (Galea et al. 2005). In contrast, in the Oklahoma City bombing, no cases had recovered by three months, and a year later most people with PTSD remained symptomatic (North et al. 2004).

According to the APA (2000), *acute PTSD* is defined as symptoms resolving in less than three months; *chronic PTSD* is defined as symptoms persisting for greater than three months; *delayed onset PTSD* is defined as onset of symptoms at least six months after the stressor (465).

The course of PTSD is variable and few predictors of recovery have been identified (North et al. 1994; 2004). In general, the majority will recover within a year, and the vast majority recover within two years. People who do not recover within two years typically have a chronic course without much improvement. There are some reports that there may be slight improvement up to six years (Kessler et al. 1995). An estimated 60 percent will recover, while the remaining one-third experience chronic, unremitting PTSD. Fifty percent of those who received treatment improved in about three years. It took five years for the same percentage to improve in those who did not receive treatment. The clinical picture, however, is complicated. Recurrent relapses cause overlapping of single episodes giving a persistent and chronic picture (Kessler et al. 1995).

7.5.2.8   Delayed Onset

Little is known about delayed-onset disaster PTSD. Previous evidence suggested that it is rare in comparison to child abuse (McNally et al. 2001) or PTSD related to combat (Heltzer, Robins, and McEvoy 1987; Prigerson, Maciejewski, and Rosenheck 2001). Israeli combat veterans were studied one, two, three, and twenty years post war. At the twenty-year follow up, 8.6 percent had developed new-onset PTSD (Solomon and Mikulincer 2006).

Kessler and colleagues (2008) surveyed 800 Katrina survivors in Louisiana, Mississippi, and Alabama nearly two years post event and noted a delayed onset of PTSD (increased from 16 percent to 21 percent).

Boscarino and Adams (2009) examined WTC disaster exposures and noted delayed onset PTSD can surface up to two years after the event in individuals with preexisting emotional or social problems. Analysis of the WTC Health Registry reported new diagnosis of PTSD, five to six years after the attack (Brackbill et al. 2009). Some have speculated that delayed PTSD represents a subsyndromal diagnosis within the first six months, which, if triggered by a stressful situation, surfaces later to meet full criteria (Stein et al. 1997; Zlotnick, Franklin, and Zimmerman 2002). Those who delay seeking help should not be confused with delayed onset. In addition, there is the factor of over- or underreporting in regards to disability or compensation.

7.5.3   Depression

Major depression is typically considered the next most prevalent disorder but may be more common than PTSD. Related symptoms of suicidality and remorse are increased with severity of exposure (Norris et al. 2001; Warheit et al. 1996). One to three months after the 2004 Madrid train bombings, 2.3 percent reported symptoms consistent with PTSD and 8 percent symptoms consistent with major depression (Miguel-Tobal et al. 2006, 69). Approximately 1,000 adults interviewed in New York City between one to two months after 9/11 reported symptoms consistent with the diagnosis of current PTSD (7.5 percent) and current depression (9.7 percent) (Galea et al. 2002).

Depression is relatively common six to twelve months post disaster, reflecting reactions to injuries, illness, and secondary stressors (Ursano et al. 2007, 10; Vlahov et al. 2002). After a traumatic event, about 26 percent of individuals develop depression (Maes et al. 2000). Mood disorders are a risk factor for PTSD (Brady et al. 2000) but may occur independently and need to be treated as such (Brady et al. 2000). Forty-eight percent of individuals with PTSD had a lifetime diagnosis of major depression disorder (MDD; Kessler et al. 1995). Individuals with comorbidity present with a complicated clinical picture and have greater functional impairment and are less likely to show remission of symptoms over six months (Foa, Stein, and McFarlane 2006, 23).

7.5.4   Bereavement—Complicated/Traumatic Grief

7.5.4.1   Bereavement

While loss is usually focused on death, postdisaster loss can include property destruction, sudden unemployment, and impaired physical, social, or psychological capacities (NCPTSD 2010). There is no right or wrong way to grieve and there is considerable cultural variation in the duration and expression of bereavement. Initially there may be a brief period of numbness, disbelief, and some denial. Individuals can become highly aroused, especially while waiting for body recovery or identification or upon notification of death. When physical remains are not identified, families have more difficulty in accepting the death of their loved one. Some may even place themselves in danger as they search the environment. Anger may be directed at those who are seen as responsible for the death or those who are still alive. Usually the acute distress phase settles in the early weeks and months, but the emotions and preoccupations may occur over the first year or following years. It is worth noting, "When a loved one's death is sudden, violent, random, preventable, mutilating, and associated with multiple other deaths, the grieving process is intensified and complicated" (USDHHS 2004, 13). The Haitian earthquakes of 2010 will hopefully offer clinicians a better understanding of the despair that survivors experience and use this knowledge to better serve the individual.

7.5.4.2 Complicated Grief

The diagnosis of complicated grief (CG) is being considered as a new addition to the upcoming DSM-V. It represents a more significant grief reaction that develops in about 9 percent of a normal community sample of bereaved people but is common after a major disaster (Foa, Stein, and McFarlane 2006).

CG predicts "substantial morbidity such as risk of cancer, cardiac events, increased alcohol and tobacco consumption, and suicidality ideation" (Latham and Prigerson 2004, 351). CG substantially heightens the risk of suicidality after controlling for major depressive disorder (MDD) and PTSD, indicating an independent psychiatric risk for suicide thoughts and actions (350). Complicated grief can result in difficulty with moving on with the grief process due to the preoccupation with trauma and its imagery. The continual intrusion may alternate with denial and interfere with emotional response to accommodate to the loss (Foa, Stein, and McFarlane 2006).

CG is comprised of symptoms of separation distress and traumatic distress and overlapping, but distinct, symptoms of depression and anxiety. Prigerson and others have proposed diagnostic criteria that would require intrusive thoughts, yearning, searching, and loneliness. In addition, a minimum of four of the following symptoms would need to be experienced: difficulty accepting the death; inability to trust; anger; unease about moving forward; feeling life is meaningless without the deceased; futile future; and agitation.

7.5.4.3 Differentiating Bereavement from a Major Depressive Episode

As part of a reaction to loss, some grieving individuals may present with signs of major depression (e.g., feelings of sadness, insomnia, poor appetite, weight loss). The diagnosis of depression is generally not given unless symptoms are still present two months after the loss. According to the APA (2000), the following symptoms are not characteristic of a "normal" grief reaction and include: (1) guilt about actions taken or not taken at the time of death; (2) thoughts of death other than feeling that one would be better off dead or should have died with the person; (3) morbid feelings of worthlessness; (4) marked psychomotor retardation; (5) marked functional impairment; (6) hallucinatory experiences other than thinking that one hears the voice or sees the image of the deceased person.

7.5.5 SUICIDE

The best predictor of suicide is previous suicidal attempts. Mood disorders, substance abuse, and PTSD are common diagnoses associated with suicide, and when they occur together, there is a risk for increased suicidal behavior (Oquendo et al. 2005, 560). Controversy exists as to whether this is secondary to the symptoms of PTSD or the related psychiatric conditions. There is evidence that "individuals with PTSD are six times more likely than those without PTSD to attempt suicide and that, overall, 19% of individuals with PTSD will attempt suicide" (Foa, Stein, and McFarlane 2006, 17). Complicated grief is associated with a 6.58 times greater likelihood of high suicidality after controlling for depression (Latham and Prigerson 2004, 350).

Given the link between increased mental illness and disasters and the link between mental illness and suicide, it seemed reasonable to expect the suicide rate to increase after a disaster. While several studies have shown an increased suicide risk, such as in the Bali bombings (Suryani et al. 2008), most studies revealed no change or an unexpectedly low rate of suicide.

Two studies of the New York City death records compared the suicide rate before and after the September 11, 2001, attack and concluded that the rate did not increase in the first four years before and after the event (Mezuk et al. 2009). Another study showed suicidal rates declined in New York City significantly in the first six months after 9/11 (Claassen et al. 2010). There was no evidence of increased suicides following the 1995 Oklahoma City bombing, the 1994 Northridge and 1995 Kobe earthquakes, the July 7, 2005, London bombing, or the 2004 tsunami in Sri Lanka (Krug et al. 1999; Shioiri et al. 1999; Rodrigo, McQullin, and Pimm 2009). Five to eight months post Hurricane Katrina, as expected, the prevalence of suicidal ideation had decreased, despite the doubling of mental illness. Suicidality may have been offset by protective factors such as optimism, hope, self-efficacy, and perceived social support (Benight et al. 2006).

Despite a retraction of elevated suicide rates after natural disasters (Krug et al. 1999), there remained clinical concerns. In 2006, New Orleans' annual suicide rate rose from 9 per 100,000 before the storm to 26 per 100,000 (Hudson 2009).

Rates of PTSD almost always decline in the two years following a major traumatic event. Even in cases where there is no decrease, the typical pattern is for prevalence to remain stable for some time rather than increase significantly (Norris et al. 1999). However, two years after Hurricane Katrina, Kessler and colleagues (2008) reported PTSD and mental illness increased, suicidal ideation rose from 2.8 percent to 6.4 percent and suicidal plans from 1 percent to 5 percent. In addition, it appeared that this was an "equal opportunity" disaster, not targeted at only the disadvantaged, but rather widely distributed (Kessler et al. 2008, 374).

Disasters affect whole communities and the determinants of suicide are complex. While suicide is a singular event, one must remain aware of system issues and group dynamics as well as the broader array of social, cultural, and political issues (Pandya 2009). It is important to recognize that perhaps the low prevalence of suicidality may be temporary (as in Katrina) and considered evidence of short-term postponement rather than a permanent absence of suicidality (Kessler et al. 2006).

7.5.6   OTHER ANXIETY DISORDERS: GENERALIZED ANXIETY DISORDER, PANIC DISORDER, PHOBIA

7.5.6.1   Generalized Anxiety Disorder

Generalized anxiety disorder (GAD) is less prevalent than PTSD or MDD, but "it has been diagnosed at higher than normal levels in disaster stricken populations" (Norris 2005, 3). Individuals with GAD find it difficult to control worry and are overwhelmed by generalized fearful anticipation that persists for more than six months and causes significant clinical distress and impairment. They are unable to be reassured, even when the realization that their anxiety is more intense than the situation warrants. Associated symptoms include restlessness, fatigue, muscle tension, sleep disturbances, and difficulty with concentration. GAD occurred in about 16 percent of individuals with PTSD (Kessler et al. 1995). PTSD appears to develop after GAD rather than be the primary diagnosis (Brady et al. 2000).

7.5.6.2   Panic Disorders

Panic disorders and phobias are observed occasionally in samples of disaster victims (Shultz et al. 2007, 130; Maes et al. 2000). Panic attacks are characterized by an unexpected and sudden onset of intense fear or discomfort, which usually peaks in about 10 minutes. Intense physiological responses reinforce the fear that the individual might have a heart attack, lose control, or "go crazy," leading to avoidance. Panic with agoraphobia typically involves situations such as fear of leaving home, traveling on a plane, or being in a crowd. Post 9/11, 15 percent of New York school-age children showed evidence of agoraphobia, and 12.3 percent showed separation anxiety (Hoven et al. 2005, 545). The incidence of panic disorders is about 10 percent among individuals with PTSD. The fear and avoidance in panic disorder is related to the anticipation of a panic attack, whereas in PTSD it is related to the memories of the traumatic event.

7.5.7 SUBSTANCE USE DISORDERS

There appears to be a sustained increase in substance use after disasters. North and colleagues (2004) reviewed a variety of different types of disasters and noted across the studies that 8 percent of adults met the criteria for postdisaster alcohol dependence. However, the rate of new onset alcohol use disorders was only 0 to 2 percent (North et al. 2004). There were no new onset drug problems in any of the studies. These statistics are interesting when there are recorded significant increases in PTSD and MDD.

Any increase must be differentiated from abuse or dependence. Alcoholism is the norm rather than the exception for PTSD (Creamer 2000). It has been theorized that there is a strong correlation between PTSD and substance use, such that they might be "causal in nature." Usually PTSD occurs first and is followed by substance abuse (Wilson 2004, 16). These individuals may have more severe symptoms, be less responsive to treatment, and use substances as a form of self-medication.

Alcohol is often used to cope with distress and suppress PTSD symptoms. Unanticipated withdrawal from alcohol and barbiturates needs to be identified early to prevent medical complications. During detoxification and early rehabilitation, PTSD symptoms may surface and become overwhelming to a point where they interfere with treatment (Kofoed, Friedman, and Peck 1993).

7.5.8 MED-PSYCH ISSUES

7.5.8.1 Recognition and Importance

Medical illness or injuries following a disaster or terrorist attack increase the likelihood of psychiatric morbidity. It is important to differentiate individuals with psychiatric disorders secondary to medical conditions; individuals with organic disorders and concurrent psychiatric illness; and individuals who develop psychosomatic symptoms secondary to anxiety. The psychiatrist is important in merging behavioral and medical approaches and plays an important role in triage.

7.5.8.2 Delirium

Delirium is a medical emergency requiring prompt attention in order to avoid permanent brain damage or even death. Symptoms include an acute onset with a fluctuating course of disturbance in consciousness, disorientation, global cognitive dysfunction, perceptual disturbances, agitation, and/or diminished responsiveness (APA 2000).

Delirium can develop in victims with major illnesses; injuries (head trauma, crush injuries or burns); infection; substance intoxication or withdrawal; or exposure to chemical or biological toxins. The medical community has little experience with weapons of mass destruction (WMD), which may cause a wide range of psychiatric disturbances. Atropine, which is used as an antidote for nerve agents, can precipitate an anticholinergic delirium. Other medications, such as lidocaine, epinephrine, or morphine, which are commonly used in the management of agitation, trauma, or life-saving procedures, can also have significant psychiatric side effects.

Rundell (2007, 180) states, "Differentiation of head trauma from dissociation is one of the most important roles of psychiatrists participating in large-scale triage operations following explosive terrorist events." If dissociation continues to be frequent and disabling, then consideration of a dissociative disorder may be appropriate. Severe head trauma is the most common cause of death in terrorist bombings and has been identified as major injury in more than half of those injured in such incidents (CDC 2009). Mild traumatic brain injury (TBI) can present with overlapping physical, cognitive, emotional, and behavioral complications.

7.5.8.3 Somatoform Disorders

Somatoform disorders, such as conversion reactions, have been reported especially in combat and terrorism and must be differentiated from malingering. Individuals experiencing medically unexplained physical symptoms (see MUPS) may not be easily reassured, and subsyndromal hypochondrical fears may be widespread after exposure to biological or chemical agents. Hypochondriasis is the fear of having a serious disease based on misinterpretation of bodily symptoms despite medical evaluation and reassurance. The diagnosis should be considered if significant clinical distress continues for more than six months (APA 2000).

7.5.9 ADJUSTMENT DISORDER

This diagnosis requires a change in behavior or emotion within three months of the onset of the stressor. Once the stressor is over, symptoms must not continue for more than six months (APA 2000).

7.5.10 PSYCHOTIC DISORDERS

Flashbacks in PTSD must be differentiated from illusions, hallucinations, and other perceptual disorders that can occur in schizophrenia, mood disorders with psychotic features, substance-induced disorders, and psychotic disorders due to general medical conditions.

7.6 OVERVIEW OF DISASTER OUTCOMES

Across the world, a disaster occurs almost every day. Disasters are divided into two major types: natural or human caused. Human-caused disasters can either be accidental or intentional, such as terrorism.

The variety of psychosocial outcomes and overall severity of impairment has previously been discussed. Psychiatric morbidity depends upon the nature of the disaster and its magnitude, location, timing, frequency, duration, perception, predictability, familiarity, controllability, preventability, and intentionality (Shultz et al. 2005, 34–35). The mental health impact will be the greatest when at least two of the four following characteristics of a disaster are present: widespread damage to property; serious and ongoing financial problems; human error or intent; and destruction, injuries, or threat to life (Norris et al. 2001).

Natural and accidental disasters caused similar levels of severe impairment, 39 percent and 37 percent, respectively. Mass violence and malicious intent, such as terrorism or shooting sprees, found 67 percent exposed to be severely or very severely impaired (Norris et al. 2002).

In estimating the average duration of symptoms, it was found that 70 percent declined over time; 19 percent did not change and 2 percent increased; and 9 percent of findings were mixed. According to Norris (2005, 7), "Sometimes symptoms declined at first, then stabilized; or stabilized for a while, then began a new downward trend; or showed a quadratic or cyclical pattern." Symptoms that did not decline were not related to any identifiable factors.

Several well-known U.S. disasters were broken down into events and level of impairment to determine possible common denominators. These disasters were classified as low, moderate, or high impact.

Examples of low-impact disasters included the 1989 Loma Prieta and 1994 Northridge earthquakes. Moderate-impact disasters, such as Hurricane Hugo in 1989, had low overall rates of PTSD (2–6 percent). Those with greater losses showed clinically more significant symptoms (34 percent of men and 44 percent of women) than those with fewer losses (5 percent of men and 11 percent of women) (Freedy et al. 1992).

The nuclear accident at Three Mile Island (TMI) also was classified as a moderate-impact disaster. Proximity was a predictive symptom. Rates of GAD and MDD among mothers were higher if they lived near the site (15–18 percent) than if they did not (11–17 percent). Only a minority was considered at risk for severe distress or impairment, but the population was stressed by residual uncertainty (Norris 2005).

Surprisingly, the 9/11 terrorist attacks also were rated as a moderate-impact disaster. Galea and colleagues (2002) reported a strong impact followed by a strong recovery. However, conclusions can easily be changed as new studies emerge.

Examples of high-impact disasters included Hurricane Andrew, Buffalo Creek Dam, and the Oklahoma City bombing. Hurricane Andrew created extraordinary destruction and disruption. The prevalence rates for new psychiatric disorders were 51 percent, including: 36 percent PTSD; 30 percent MDD; and 11 percent GAD. The Buffalo Creek Dam collapsed in 1972. Two years later, PTSD rates were 44 percent among adults and 32 percent among children and remained high for 14 years (Gleser, Green, and Winget 1981; Green et al. 1994). In the Oklahoma City bombing six months post event, one-third of the injured adults met criteria for PTSD and 45 percent had some postdisaster disorder. Eighteen to thirty-six months later, PTSD symptoms were still highly prevalent. In addition, new health problems were reported, worsening of preexisting medical conditions, and a change for the worse in activities of daily living (Smith et al. 1999).

7.6.1   Types of Disasters and Areas of Concern

Disasters share many issues in common that contribute to outcome. Specific types of disasters bring particular issues of concern to the forefront. These may include effects of displacement, impact on health care workers, surge in emergency rooms, public perception, and/or care of the injured.

7.6.1.1   Natural Disasters

Natural disasters—whether earthquakes, floods, hurricanes, or wildfires—are familiar and may be predictable to a certain extent. Unless there is a high number of fatalities or injuries, such as the 2004 Asian tsunami, the primary impact is centered on loss and damage to valuables, property, and community. Communities with vast destruction, especially in developing countries, are associated with worse outcomes (Ursano et al. 2007, 5).

Providing basic needs and resources, especially in geographic locations that cannot easily be reached, can be problematic. Ability to evacuate and manage displaced persons is critical. The estimated number of people who were evacuated in anticipation of or in the wake of Hurricanes Katrina and Rita ranged widely from 600,000—1.2 million. Many were unable to return home or even to their communities.

Displacement resulted in living in unfamiliar environments and separation from friends, family and community. These factors, along with homelessness, persistent uncertainty, and depression placed individuals at risk for short-term and long-term consequences (Abramson et al. 2007, 8). The 2010 earthquake in Haiti will provide additional data to study these issues.

Of all natural disasters, a pandemic is the most deadly and most likely to induce mental health problems. The 2003 SARS outbreak provided a model to look at the impact on health care providers. Twenty percent of health care workers became infected (WHO 2003). Almost two-thirds of health care providers experienced intense emotional reactions during the SARS outbreak. Distress was associated with quarantine, fear of contagion, concern for family, job stress, interpersonal isolation, perceived stigma, ethical dilemmas, grief, and exhaustion. Issues related to adequate training, assurance of safety, and resource support had a significant impact on their work performance (Maunder et al. 2003, 1247). During a biological event, either natural or terrorist related, health care providers and responders will face substantial challenges.

7.6.1.2   Human-Caused Disasters

Disasters caused by malicious human intent were more likely than any others to cause severe or very severe impairment. "Terrorism is psychological by design" and is capable of producing the deadly combinations of stressors by being "unpredictable, unfamiliar, uncontrollable and unrelenting" (Shultz et al.

2003, 234, 238). Chemical, biological, and radiological agents can produce mass destruction, but will probably be used more commonly as weapons of mass disruption (Ursano et al. 2007, 249).

7.6.1.3 Chemical, Radiological, Nuclear, and Explosive Events

Chemical events are distinguished by being local, invisible, and presenting with a rapid onset. Hospitals must prepare for the surge of psychological casualties that will present as medical problems. The SCUD missile attacks in Israel demonstrated the degree of psychological trauma that can result from a perceived chemical attack. More than 1,000 patients presented to the emergency room of which 234 (22 percent) were direct casualties and 835 (78 percent) were psychological in nature (Karsenty et al. 1991).

Radiological events are very different from nuclear explosions, but the fear of radiation is not always logical. A dirty bomb would probably cause more harm from the explosion than from the radioactivity. Even though the risk may be minimal, anything linked to radiation may be linked to death (Lifton 1967, 108). Unique to this stressor is the "future-oriented" perspective. There is no end point at which the stress is over. The likelihood of future developments of cancer, leukemia, genetic alteration, miscarriage, birth anomalies, infertility, and risk to children become highly charged issues (Lifton 1967, 130).

Society may become frightened and alienate innocent victims of radioactive contamination. Both the Chernobyl and the *hibakusha* (survivors of Hiroshima and Nagasaki) were treated as contagious carriers of radiation and faced years of stigmatization (Bertazzi 1989).

Explosives are readily available and are commonly used to not only kill but also to inflict painful injury and mutilation. The injured are at highest risk for post trauma psychopathology. The medical issues may take priority and the psychological issues may never become identified or addressed. Trauma medicine has the "golden hour" and an excellent triage system. Disaster mental health has the "golden month." New and innovative models are needed for behavioral health. Schreiber has proposed a model, Psy-START™, which provides rapid triage, identifies at-risk individuals on scene, links resources, and creates a seamless system that follows patients across the phases of response and recovery (UCLA Center for Public Health and Disasters 2009). Integration of mental health into the acute care setting provides a "surge-sort-support" approach to managing the influx of med-psych patients and their loved ones upon arrival at the hospital (Shultz et al. 2006, 3). During hospitalization, care managers can be assigned to provide early evidenced interventions and link patients to follow-up in order to avoid fragmented care (Ursano et al. 2007). With these resources in place, we can hopefully look toward improved outcomes.

ACKNOWLEDGMENTS

The author would like to thank Jeanne Hamilton and David Warren for their research and support.

REFERENCES

Abramson, D., I. Redlener, T. Stehling-Ariza, and E. Fuller. 2007. The legacy of Katrina's children: Estimating the numbers of at-risk children in the Gulf Coast states of Louisiana and Mississippi. National Center for Disaster Preparedness, Research Brief 2007:12. New York: Columbia University Mailman School of Public Health. http://www.ncdp.mailman.columbia.edu/files/legacy_katrina_children.pdf.

Ali, T., E. Dunmore, D. Clark, and A. Ehlers. 2002. The role of negative beliefs in posttraumatic stress disorder: A comparison of assault victims and non victims. *Behavioural and Cognitive Psychotherapy* 30(3): 249–257.

American Psychiatric Association. 2000. *Diagnostic and Statistical Manual of Mental Disorders,* 4th ed., text revision. Washington, DC: American Psychiatric Association.

Anderson, P. 2007. Residents hit by Hurricane Katrina suffer mental illness. *Medscape Medical News,* December 13. http://www.medscape.com/viewarticle/567426.

Anthony, J. C., and J. E. Helzer. 1991. Syndromes of drug abuse and dependence. In *Psychiatric Disorders in America*, eds. L. N. Robins and D. A. Regier. New York: Free Press.

Benedek, D. M. 2007. Acute stress disorder and post-traumatic stress disorder in the disaster environment. In *Textbook of Disaster Psychiatry*, eds. R. J. Ursano, C. S. Fullerton, L. Weisaeth, and B. Raphael, 3–27. Cambridge: Cambridge University Press.

Benight, C.C., E. Swift, J. Sanger, A. Smith, and D. Zeppelin. 2006. Coping self-efficacy as a mediator of distress following a natural disaster. *Journal of Applied Social Psychology 29*(12): 2443–2464.

Bertazzi, P. A. 1989. Industrial disasters and epidemiology: A review of recent experiences. *Scandinavian Journal of Work, Environment & Health 15*(2): 85–100.

Bonanno, G. A., S. Galea, A. Bucciarelli, and D. Vlahov. 2006. Psychological resilience after disaster: New York City in the aftermath of September 11th terrorist attack. *Psychological Science 17*(3): 181–186.

Bonanno, G. A., and A. D. Mancini. 2008. The human capacity to thrive in the face of potential trauma. *Pediatrics 121* (2): 369–375.

Boscarino, J. A., and R. E. Adams. 2009. PTSD onset and course following WTC disaster: Findings and implication for future research. *Social Psychiatry and Psychiatric Epidemiology 44*(10): 887–898.

Brackbill, R. M., J. L. Hadler, L. DiGrande, C. Ekenga, M. Farfel, S. Friedman, S. Perlman, S. Stellman, D. Walker, D. Wu, S. Yu, and L. Thorpe. 2009. Asthma and posttraumatic stress symptoms 5 to 6 years following exposure to the World Trade Center terrorist attack. *Journal of the American Medical Association 302*(5): 502–516.

Brady, K., T. Pearlstein, G. M. Asnis, D. Baker, B. Rothbaum, C. Sikes, and G. Farfel. 2000. Efficacy and safety of sertraline treatment of posttraumatic stress disorder: A randomized controlled trial. *Journal of American Medical Association 283*(14): 1837–1844.

Breslau, N., and J. C. Anthony. 2007. Gender differences in the sensitivity to posttraumatic stress disorder: An epidemiological study of urban young adults. *Journal of Abnormal Psychology 116*(3): 607–611.

Breslau, N., and G. C. Davis. 1992. Migraine, major depression and panic disorder: a prospective epidemiologic study of young adults. *Cephalalgia 12*(2): 85–90.

Brewin, C. R., B. Andrews, S. Rose, and M. Kirk. 1999. Acute stress disorder and posttraumatic stress disorder in victims of violent crime. *American Journal of Psychiatry 156*(3): 360–366.

Brewin, C. R., B. Andrews, and J. D. Valentine. 2000. Meta analysis of risk factors for posttraumatic stress disorder in trauma-exposed adults. *Journal of Consulting and Clinical Psychology 68*(5): 748–766.

Bryant, R. A. 2006. Recovery after the tsunami: Timeline for rehabilitation. *Journal of Clinical Psychiatry 67*(S2): 50–55.

Bryant, R. A., and A. G. Harvey. 1998. Relationship between acute stress disorder and posttraumatic stress disorder following mild traumatic brain injury. *American Journal of Psychiatry 155*(5): 625–629.

Brymer, M., A. Jacobs, C. Layne, R. Pynoos, J. Ruzek, A. Steinberg, E. Vernberg, and P. Watson. 2006. *Psychological first aid: Field operations guide.* 2nd ed. National Child Traumatic Stress Network and National Center for PTSD. http://ncptsd.va.gov/ncmain/ncdocs/manuals/PFA_V2.pdf.

Butler, A. S., A. M. Panzer, and L. R. Goldfrank. 2003. *Preparing for the Psychological Consequences of Terrorism: A Public Health Approach.* Washington, DC: National Academies Press.

Calcedo-Barba, A. 2004. The Madrid terrorist attacks: Chronicles from a psychiatrist on the front lines. Letter to the editor, in *International Federation of Psychiatric Epidemiology Bulletin 2*(2): 1–5. http://proj1.sinica.edu.tw/~ifpe/ifpe_bulletin/Volume2(2).pdf.

Caspi, A., K. Sugden, T. Moffitt, A. Taylor, I. Craig, H. Harrington, J. McClay, J. Mill, J. Martin, A. Braithwaite, and R. Poulton 2003. Influence of life stress on depression: Moderation by a polymorphism in the 5-HTT gene. *Science 301*(5631): 386–389.

Centers for Disease Control and Prevention (CDC). 2009. Blast injuries: Traumatic brain injuries from explosions. http://www.bt.cdc.gov/masscasualties/blastinjury-braininjury.asp.

Charney, D. S., A. Y. Deutch, J. H. Krystal, S. M. Southwick, and M. Davis. 1993. Psychobiologic mechanisms of posttraumatic stress disorder. *Archives of General Psychiatry 50*(4): 295–305.

Claassen, C. A., T. Carmody, S. M. Stewart, R. Bossarte, G. Larkin, W. Woodward, and M. Trivedi. 2010. Effect of 11 September 2001 terrorist attacks in the USA on suicide in areas surrounding the crash sites. *British Journal of Psychiatry 196*(5): 359–364.

Classen, C., C. Koopman, R. Hales, and D. Spiegel. 1998. Acute stress disorder as a predictor of posttraumatic stress symptoms. *American Journal of Psychiatry 155*(5): 620–624.

Clauw, D. 2003. Unexplained symptoms after terrorism and war: An expert consensus statement. *Journal of Occupational and Environmental Medicine 45*(10): 1040–1048.

Creamer, M. 2000. Post-traumatic stress disorder following violence and aggression. *Aggression and Violent Behavior 5*(5): 431–449.

David, D., T. A. Mellman, L. M. Mendoza, R. Kulick-Bell, G. Ironson, and N. Schneiderman. 1996. Psychiatric morbidity following Hurricane Andrew. *Journal of Traumatic Stress 9*(3): 607–612.

Davidson, J. R. T., D. J. Stein, A.Y. Shalev, and R. Yehuda. 2004. Posttraumatic stress disorder: Acquisition, recognition, course treatment. *Journal of Neuropsychiatry and Clinical Neuroscience 16*(2): 135–147

DiMaggio, C., and S. Galea. 2007. The mental health and behavioral consequences of terrorism. In *Victims of Crime*, eds. R. C. Davis, A. J. Lurigio, and S. Herman, 147–160. London: Sage Publications, Inc.

Foa, E. B., D. J. Stein, and A. C. McFarlane. 2006. Symptomatology and psychopathology of mental health problems after disaster. *Journal of Clinical Psychiatry 67*(S2): 15–25.

Freedy, J. R., D. Shaw, M. P. Jarrell, and C. Masters. 1992. Towards an understanding of the psychological impact of natural disasters: An application of the conservation resources stress model. *Journal of Traumatic Stress 5*(3): 441–454.

Friedman, M. J. 2006. *PTSD and Acute Post-Traumatic Reactions*. Kansas City: Compact Clinicals.

Friedman, M. J., J. L. Hamblen, E. B. Foa, and D. S. Charney. 2004. Commentary: Fighting the psychological war on terrorism. *Psychiatry 67*(2): 123–136.

Frohlich, E. D., and R. S. Schwartz. 2008. Stress and cardiovascular disease: Lessons from Katrina. *American College of Cardiology: Cardiosource*. http://www.medscape.com/viewarticle/569342.

Fullerton, C. S., and R. J. Ursano. 1997. The other side of chaos: Understanding patterns of posttraumatic responses. In *Posttraumatic Stress Disorder: Acute and Long-Term Responses to Trauma and Disasters*, eds. C. S. Fullerton and R. J. Ursano, 3–20. Washington, DC: American Psychiatric Press, Inc., 1997.

Galea, S., J. Ahern, H. Resnick, et al. 2002. Psychological sequelae of the September 11 terrorist attacks in New York City. *New England Journal of Medicine 346*(13): 982–987.

Galea, S., J. Boscarino, H. Resnick, and D. Vlahov. 2003a. Mental health in New York City after the September 11 terrorist attacks: Results from two population surveys. In *Mental Health, United States, 2001*, eds. R. W. Manderscheid and M. J. Henderson. Washington, DC: U.S. Government Printing Office.

Galea, S., C. R. Brewin, M. Gruber, et al. 2007. Exposure to hurricane-related stressors and mental illness after Hurricane Katrina. *Archives of General Psychiatry 64*(12): 1427–1434.

Galea, S., A. Nandi, and D. Vlahov. 2005. The epidemiology of post-traumatic stress disorder after disasters. *Epidemiologic Reviews 27*:78–91.

Galea, S., D. Vlahov, H. Resnick, et al. 2003b. Trends of probable post-traumatic stress disorder in New York City after the September 11 terrorist attacks. *American Journal of Epidemiology 158*(6): 514–524.

Gilbertson, M. W., M. E. Shenton, A. Ciszewski, et al. 2002. Smaller hippocampal volume predicts pathologic vulnerability to psychological trauma. *Nature Neuroscience 5*(11): 1242–1247.

Glass, T. A., and M. Schoch-Spana. 2002. Bioterrorism and the people: How to vaccinate a city against panic. *Clinical Infectious Diseases 34*(2): 217–223.

Gleser, G. C., B. L. Green, and C. Winget. 1981. *Prolonged Psychosocial Effects of Disaster: A Study of Buffalo Creek*. New York: Academic Press.

Goodman, L. A., M. P. Salyers, K. T. Mueser, and S. D. Rosenberg. 2001. Recent victimization in women and men with severe mental illness: Prevalence and correlates. *Journal of Traumatic Stress 14*(4): 615–632.

Grace, M. C., B. L. Green, J. L. Lindy, and A. C. Leonard. 1993. The Buffalo Creek disaster: A 14-year follow-up. In *International Handbook of Traumatic Stress Syndromes*, eds. J. P. Wilson and B. Raphael, 441–449. New York: Plenum.

Green, B. L., J. D. Lindy, M. C. Grace, et al. 1994. Buffalo Creek survivors in the second decade: Stability of stress symptoms. *American Journal of Orthopsychiatry 60*(1): 43–54.

Greenberg, P. E., T. Sisitsky, R. C. Kessler, et al. 1999. The economic burden of anxiety disorders in the 1990s. *Journal of Clinical Psychiatry 60*(7): 427–435.

Hall, R. C. W., R. C. W. Hall, and M. J. Chapman. 2004. Emotional and psychiatric effects of weapons of mass destruction on first responders. In *Bioterrorism: Psychological and Public Health Interventions*, eds. R. J. Ursano, A. E. Norwood, and C. S. Fullerton, 250–273. Cambridge: Cambridge University Press.

Heltzer, J., L. Robins, and L. McEvoy. 1987. Posttraumatic stress disorder in the general population. *New England Journal of Medicine 317*: 1630–1634.

Herman, D., C. Felton, and E. Susser. 2002. Mental health needs in New York State following the September 11th attacks. *Journal of Urban Health 79*(3): 322–331.

Hick, J. L., D. G. Hanfling, J. L. Burstein, et al. 2004. Health care facility and community strategies for patient care surge capacity. *Annals of Emergency Medicine 44*(3): 253–261.

Housley, J., and L. E. Beutler. 2006. *Treating Victims of Mass Disaster and Terrorism*. Cambridge: Hogrefe and Huber.

Hoven, C. W., C. S. Duarte, C. P. Lucas, et al. 2005. Psychopathology among New York City public school children 6 months after September 11. *Archives of General Psychiatry 62*(5): 545–551.

Hudson, A. 2009. Mental illness tidal wave swamps New Orleans. *Washington Times*, August 4. http://www. washingtontimes.com/news/2009/aug/04/mental-illness-tidal-wave//print.

Karsenty, E., J. Shemer, I. Alshech, et al. 1991. Medical aspects of the Iraqi missile attacks on Israel. *Israel Journal of Medicine and Science 27*(11-12): 603–607.

Kessler, R. C., S. Galea, M. Gruber, N. A. Sampson, R. J. Ursano, and S. Wessely. 2008. Trends in mental illness and suicidality after Hurricane Katrina. *Molecular Psychiatry 13*(4): 374–384.

Kessler, R. C., S. Galea, R. T. Jones, and H. A. Parker. 2006. Mental illness and suicidality after Hurricane Katrina. *Bulletin of the World Health Organization 84*(12): 930–939.

Kessler, R. C., A. Sonnega, E. Bromet, M. Hughes, and C. Nelson. 1995. Post-traumatic stress disorder in the National Comorbidity Survey. *Archives of General Psychiatry 52*(12): 1048–1060.

Kilpatrick, D. G., K. C. Koenen, K. J. Ruggiero, and R. Acierno. 2007. The serotonin transporter genotype and social support and moderation of posttraumatic stress disorder and depression in hurricane-exposed adults. *American Journal of Psychiatry 164*(11): 1693–1699.

Kleim, B., A. Ehlers, and E. Glucksman. 2007. Early predictors of chronic post-traumatic stress disorder in assault survivors. *Psychological Medicine 37*(10): 1457–1467.

Kofoed, L., M. Friedman, and R. Peck. 1993. Alcoholism and drug abuse in patients with PTSD. *Psychiatric Quarterly 64*(2): 151–171.

Krug, E. G., M. Kresnow, J. P. Peddicord, et al. 1999. Retraction: Suicide after natural disasters. *New England Journal of Medicine 340*(2): 148–149.

Lacy, T., and D. M. Benedek. 2003. Terrorism and weapons of mass destruction: Managing the behavioral reaction in primary care. *Southern Medical Journal 96*(4): 394–399.

Latham, A. E., and H. G. Prigerson. 2004. Suicidality and bereavement: Complicated grief as psychiatric disorder presenting greatest risk for suicidality. *Suicide and Life-Threatening Behavior 34*(4): 350–362.

Laudisio, G. 1993. Disaster aftermath: Redefining response—Hurricane Andrew's impact on I & R. *Alliance of Information and Referral Systems 15*: 13–32.

Layne, C. M., J. S. Warren, A. H. Shalev, and P. Watson. 2007. Risk, vulnerability, resistance, and resilience: Towards an integrative model of posttraumatic adaptation. In *Handbook of PTSD: Science and Practice—A Comprehensive Handbook*, eds. M. J. Friedman, T. M. Keane, and P. A. Resick, 497–520. New York: Guilford Press.

Lifton, R. J. 1967. *Death in Life Survivors of Hiroshima*. New York: Random House.

Maes, M., J. Myelle, L. Delmeire, and C. Altamura. 2000. Psychiatric morbidity and comorbidity following accidental man-made traumatic events: Incidence and risk factors. *European Archives of Psychiatry and Clinical Neuroscience 250*(3): 156–162.

Marmar, C. R., T. J. Metzler, C. Otte, and S. McCaslin. 2004. The peritraumatic dissociative experiences questionnaire. In *Accessing Psychological Trauma and PTSD,* eds. J. P. Wilson and T. M. Keane, 197–217. New York: Guilford Press.

Maunder, R., J. Hunter, L. Vincent, et al. 2003. The immediate psychological and occupational impact of the 2003 SARS outbreak in a teaching hospital. *Canadian Medical Association Journal 168*(10): 1245–1251.

McDuff, J., and W. E. Ford. 2005. A report on the post-September 11 State Disaster Relief Grant Program of SAMHSA's Center for Substance Abuse Treatment. DHHS Pub. No. SMA 05-3993. Rockville, MD: Center for Substance Abuse Treatment, Substance Abuse and Mental Health Services Administration.

McEwen, B. S., and E. N. Lasley. 2002. *The End of Stress as We Know It.* Washington, DC: Joseph Henry Press.

McFarlane, A. C. 1988. The phenomenology of posttraumatic stress disorders following a natural disaster. *Journal of Nervous and Mental Disease 176*(1): 22–29.

McFarlane, A. C. 2000. Posttraumatic stress disorder: A model of the longitudinal course and the role of risk factors. *Journal of Clinical Psychiatry 61*(Suppl.5): 15–23.

McKernan, B. 2005. SAMHSA DTAC: *Lessons learned from the 2005 hurricane response.* Substance Abuse and Mental Health Services Administration Disaster Technical Assistance Center. http://www.samhsa. gov/CSATDisasterRecovery/lessons/09-APHA_DisasterSA_11-7-06_CSATCDROM.pdf.

McMillen, J. C., C. S. North, and E. M. Smith. 2000. What parts of PTSD are normal: Intrusion, avoidance, or arousal? Data from the Northridge, California, earthquake. *Journal of Traumatic Stress 13*(1): 57–75.

McNally, R. J., R. A. Bryant, and A. Ehlers. 2001. Does early psychological intervention promote recovery from posttraumatic stress? *Psychological Science in the Public Interest 4*(2): 45–79.

Mezuk, B., G. L. Larkin, M. R. Prescott, et al. 2009. The influence of a major disaster on suicide risk in the population. *Journal of Traumatic Stress 22*(6): 481–488.

Miguel-Tobal, J. J., A. Cano-Vindel, H. Gonzalez-Ordi, et al. 2006. PTSD and depression after the Madrid March 11 train bombings. *Journal of Traumatic Stress 19*(1): 69–80.

Mueser, K. T., L. B. Goodman, S. L. Trumbetta, et al. 1998. Trauma and posttraumatic stress disorder in severe mental illness. *Journal of Consulting and Clinical Psychology 66*(3): 493–499.

National Center for PTSD (NCPTSD). 2005. *Disasters and substance abuse or dependence.* http://www. samhsa.gov/csatdisasterrecovery/outreach/disastersAndSubstanceAbuseOrDependence.pdf.

National Center for PTSD (NCPTSD). 2010. *Effects of traumatic stress after mass violence, terror, or disaster.* http://www.ptsd.va.gov/professional/pages/stress-mv-t-dhtml.asp.

Newman, J. P., and C. Foreman. 1987. The Sun Valley Mall disaster study. Paper presented at the Annual Meeting of International Society for Traumatic Stress Studies, Baltimore, MD.

Norris, F. H. 2005. *Range, magnitude, and duration of the effects of disasters on mental health: Review update.* Research Education Disaster Mental Health: Dartmouth Medical School and National Center for PTSD, 1–23. http://www.katasztrofa.hu/documents/Research_Education_Disaster_Mental_Health.pdf.

Norris, F. H., M. J. Friedman, P. J. Watson, C. M. Byrne, E. Diaz, and K. Kaniasty. 2002. 60,000 disaster victims speak: Part I. An empirical review of the empirical literature, 1981–2001. *Psychiatry 65*(3): 207–239.

Norris, F. H., S. Galea, M. J. Friedman, and P. J. Watson. 2006. Preface. In *Methods for Disaster Mental Health Research*, eds. F. H. Norris, S. Galea, M. J. Friedman, P. J. Watson, xi. New York: The Guilford Press.

Norris, F. H., A. D. Murphy, C. K. Baker, and J. L. Perilla. 2003. Severity, timing and duration of reactions to trauma in the population: An example from Mexico. *Biological Psychiatry 53*(9): 769–778.

Norris, F., J. Perilla, G. Ibanez, and A. D. Murphy. 2001. Sex differences in symptoms of posttraumatic stress: Does culture play a role? *Journal of Traumatic Stress 14*(1): 7–28.

Norris, F. H., J. L. Perilla, J. K. Riad, K. Kaniasty, and E. A. Lavizzo. 1999. Stability and change in stress, resources, and psychological distress following natural disaster: Findings from Hurricane Andrew. *Anxiety, Stress, and Coping 12*(4): 363–396.

North, C. S. 2007. Epidemiology of disaster mental health. In *Textbook of Disaster Psychiatry*, eds. C. S. Fullerton, L. Weisaeth, B. Raphael, 29–47. Cambridge: Cambridge University Press.

North, C. S., S. J. Nixon, S. Shariat, et al. 1999. Psychiatric disorders among survivors of the Oklahoma City bombing. *Journal of the American Medical Association 282*(8): 755–762.

North, C. S., B. Pfefferbaum, L. Tivis, A. Kawasaki, C. Reddy, and E. L. Spitznagel. 2004. The course of post-traumatic stress disorder in a follow-up study of survivors of the Oklahoma City bombing. *Annals of Clinical Psychiatry: Official Journal of the American Academy of Clinical Psychiatrists 16*(4): 209–215.

North, C. S., E. M. Smith, R. E. McCool, and P. E. Lightcap. 1989. Acute post-disaster coping and adjustment. *Journal of Traumatic Stress 2*(3): 353–360.

North, C. S., E. M. Smith, and E. L. Spitznagel. 1994. Posttraumatic stress disorder in survivors of a mass shooting. *American Journal of Psychiatry 151*(1): 82–88.

NSW Institute of Psychiatry and Centre for Mental Health. 2000. *Disaster Mental Health Response Handbook.* North Sydney: NSW Health.

Oquendo, M., D. A. Brent, B. Birmaher, et al. 2005. Posttraumatic stress disorder comorbid with major depression: Factors mediating the association with suicidal behavior. *American Journal of Psychiatry 162*(3): 560–566.

Pandya, A. 2009. Clinical Synthesis. Adult disaster psychiatry. *Focus 7*(2): 155–159.

Perilla, J., F. Norris, and E. Lavizzo. 2002. Ethnicity, culture, and disaster response: Identifying and explaining ethnic differences in PTSD six months after Hurricane Andrew. *Journal of Social and Clinical Psychology 21*(1): 20–45.

Prigerson, H. G., P. K. Maciejewski, and R. A. Rosenheck. 2001. Combat trauma: Trauma with highest risk of delayed onset and unresolved posttraumatic stress disorder symptoms, unemployment, and abuse among men. *Journal of Nervous and Mental Disease 189*(2): 99–108.

Quarantelli, E. L. 1960. Images of withdrawal behavior in disasters: Some basic misconceptions. *Social Problems 8*(1): 68–79.

Rando, T. A. 1996. Complications in mourning traumatic death. In *Living with Grief After Sudden Loss: Suicide, Homicide, Accident, Heart Attack, Stroke*, ed. K. A. Doka, 139–160. Washington, DC: Hospice Foundation of America.

Raphael, B. 2000. *Disaster Mental Health Response Handbook: An Educational Resource for Mental Health Professionals Involved in Disaster Management.* Sydney: NSW Health.

Rasinksi, K. A., J. Berktold, T. W. Smith, and B. L. Albertson. 2002. *America recovers: A follow-up to a national study of public response to the September 11th terrorist attacks.* NORC: University of Chicago. http://www.norc.uchicago.edu.

Reissman, D. B. 2006. Workforce and community resilience: Health protection strategies for emerging public health threats. *Early psychological intervention following mass trauma: The present and future directions.* http://www.nymc.edu/trauma/program.asp.

Rodrigo, A., A. McQullin, and J. Pimm. 2009. Effect of the 2004 tsunami on suicide rates in Sri Lanka. *The Psychiatrist 33*(5): 179–180.

Rothbaum, O., E. B. Foa, D. S. Riggs, and T. Murdock. 1992. A prospective examination of post-traumatic stress disorder in rape victims. *Journal of Traumatic Stress 5*(3): 455–475.

Rubin, G. J., C. R. Brewin, N. Greenberg, J. Simpson, and S. Wessely. 2005. Psychological and behavioural reactions to the bombings in London on 7 July 2005: Cross sectional survey of a representative sample of Londoners. *British Medical Journal 331*: 606–612.

Rundell, J. R. 2007. Assessment and management of medical-surgical disaster casualties. In *Textbook of Disaster Psychiatry*, eds. R. Ursano, C. S. Fullerton, L.Weisaeth, and B. Rapheael, 164–189. Cambridge: Cambridge University Press.

Rundell, J. R., and G. W. Christopher. 2004. Differentiating manifestations of infection from psychiatric disorders and fears of having been exposed to bioterrorism. In *Bioterrorism: Psychological and Public Health Interventions*, eds. R. J. Ursano, A. E. Norwood, and C. S. Fullerton, 88–108. Cambridge: Cambridge University Press, 2004.

Satel, S. 2007. 9/11 mental health in the wake of terrorist attacks. *Psychiatric Services 58*(2): 276–277.

Schuster, M. A., B. D. Stein, L. H. Jaycox, et al. 2001. A national survey of stress reactions after the September 11, 2001, terrorist attack. *New England Journal of Medicine 345*(20): 1507–1512.

Schnurr, P. P., and B. L. Green. 2004. *Trauma and Health: Physical Health Consequences of Exposure to Extreme Stress*. Washington, DC: American Psychological Association.

Shalev, A. Y., R. Adessky, R. Boker, et al. 2003. Clinical intervention for survivors of prolonged adversities. In *Terrorism and Disaster: Individual and Community Mental Health Interventions*, eds. R. J. Ursano, C. S. Fullerton, A. E. Norwood, 162–188. Cambridge: Cambridge University Press.

Shioiri T., A. Nishimura, H. Nushida, Y. Tatsuno, and S. W. Tang. 1999. The Kobe earthquake and reduced suicide in Japanese males. *Archives of General Psychiatry 56*(3): 282–283.

Shultz, J. M, Z. Espinel, R. E. Cohen, R. G. Smith, and B. W. Flynn. 2005. *Disaster Behavioral Health: All-Hazards Training*. Miami: Center for Disaster & Extreme Event Preparedness.

Shultz, J. M., Z. Espinel, R. Cohen, J. Shaw, and B. Flynn. 2003. *Behavioral Health Awareness Training for Terrorism and Disasters*. Miami: Center for Disaster & Extreme Event Preparedness.

Shultz, J. M., Z. Espinel, B. W. Flynn, Y. Hoffman, and R. E. Cohen. 2007. *Deep Prep: All-Hazards Disaster Behavioral Health Training*. Tampa, FL: Disaster Life Support Press.

Shultz, J. M., Z. Espinel, J. L. Hick, S. Galea, J. A. Shaw, and G. T. Miller. 2006. *Surge Sort Support: Disaster Behavioral Health for Health Care Professionals*. Miami: Center for Disaster & Extreme Event Preparedness. http://www.deep.med.miami.edu/documents/Surge-Sort-Support_DBH%20for%20HC%20%28textbook%29.pdf.

Silver, R. C., E. A. Holman, D. N. McIntosh, M. Poulin, and V. Gil-Rivas. 2002. Nationwide longitudinal study of psychological responses to September 11. *Journal of the American Medical Association 288*(10): 1235–1244.

Smith, D. W., E. H. Christiansen, R. Vince, and N. E. Hann. 1999. Population effects of the bombing of Oklahoma City. *Journal of the Oklahoma State Medical Association 92*(4): 193–198.

Solomon, S., and M. Mikulincer. 2006. Trajectories of PTSD: A 20-year longitudinal study. *American Journal of Psychiatry 163*(4): 659–666.

Stein, M. B., J. R. Walker, A. L. Hazen, and D. R. Ford. 1997. Full and partial posttraumatic stress disorder: Findings from a community survey. *American Journal of Psychiatry 154*(8): 1114–1119.

Steury, S., and J. Parks, eds. 2003. State mental health authorities' response to terrorism. Alexandria, VA: National Association of State Mental Health Program Directors (NASMHPD). http://www.nasmhpd.org/general_files/publications/med_directors_pubs/Med%20Dir%20Terrorism%20Rpt%20-%20final.pdf.

Suryani, L. K., A. Page, C. B. Lesmana, M. Jennaway, I. D. Basudewa, and R. Taylor. 2008. Suicide in paradise: Aftermath of the Bali bombings. *Psychological Medicine 39*(8): 1317–1323.

Tedeschi, R. G., and L. G. Calhoun. 1996. The posttraumatic growth inventory: Measuring the positive legacy of trauma. *Journal of Traumatic Stress 9*(3): 455–471.

True, W. R., J. Rice, S. A. Eisen, A. C. Heath, et al. 1993. A twin study of genetic and environmental contributions to liability of posttraumatic stress symptoms. *Archives of General Psychiatry 50*(4): 257–264.

Tucker, J. B. 1996. Chemical/biological terrorism: Coping with a new threat. *Politics & the Life Sciences 15*(2): 167–183.

Tyhurst, J. S. 1951. Individual reactions to community disaster: The natural history of psychiatric phenomena. *American Journal of Psychiatry 107*(10): 764–769.

UCLA Center for Public Health and Disasters. 2009. Psy-START Rapid Mental Health Triage and Incident Management System. http://www.cphd.ucla.edu/pdfs/PsySTART%20Rapid%20Mental%20Health_Web.pdf.

Ursano, R. J., C. Fullerton, L. Weisaeth, and B. Raphael. 2007. *Textbook of Disaster Psychiatry*. Cambridge: Cambridge University Press.

U.S. Department of Health and Human Services (USDHHS). 2004. *Mental Health Response to Mass Violence and Terrorism: A Training Manual*. DHHS Pub. No. SMA 3959. Rockville, MD: Center for Mental Health Services, Substance Abuse and Mental Health Services Administration.

Vazquez, C., P. Perez-Sales, and G. Matt. 2006. Post-traumatic stress reactions following the March 11, 2004, terrorist attacks in a Madrid community sample: A cautionary note about the measurement of psychological trauma. *Spanish Journal of Psychology* 9(1): 61–74.

Vlahov, D., S. Galea, H. Resnick, et al. 2002. Increased use of cigarettes, alcohol, and marijuana among Manhattan, New York, residents after the September 11 terrorist attacks. *American Journal of Epidemiology* 155(11): 988–996.

Warheit, G., R. Zimmerman, E. Khoury, W. Vega, and A. G. Gil. 1996. Disaster related stresses, depressive signs and symptoms, and suicidal ideation among a multi-racial/ethnic sample of adolescents: A longitudinal analysis. *Journal of Child Psychology and Psychiatry* 37(4): 435–444.

Watson, P., and A.Y. Shalev. 2005. Assessment and treatment of adult acute responses to traumatic stress following mass traumatic events. *CNS Spectrums* 10(2): 123–131.

Weisaeth, L., and A. Tønnessen. 2003. Responses of individuals and groups to consequences of technological disasters and radiation exposure. In *Terrorism and Disaster: Individual and Community Mental Health Interventions*, eds. R. J. Ursano, C. S. Fullerton, and A. E. Norwood, 209–235. Cambridge: Cambridge University Press.

Whalley, M. G., and C. R. Brewin. 2007. Mental health following terrorist attacks. *British Journal of Psychiatry* 190: 94–96.

Whitehead, D. L., L. Perkins-Porras, P. C. Strike, and A. Steptoe. 2006. Post-traumatic stress disorder in patients with cardiac disease: Predicting vulnerability from emotional responses during admission for acute coronary syndromes. *Heart* 92(9): 1225–1229.

Wilson, J. P. 2004. PTSD and complex PTSD: Symptoms, syndromes, and diagnoses. In *Assessing Psychological Trauma and PTSD*, eds. J. P. Wilson and T. M. Keane, 7–44. New York: Guilford Press.

World Health Organization (WHO). 2003. *Summary table of SARS cases by country, 1 November 2002–7 August 2003*. http://www.who.int/csr/sars/country/country2003_08_15.pdf.

World Health Organization (WHO). 2005. *Violence and disasters*. http://www.who.int/violence_injury_prevention/publications/violence/violence_disasters.pdf.

Zatzick, D. F., J. Russo, R. K. Pitman, F. Rivara, G. Jurkovich, and P. Roy-Byrne. 2005. Reevaluating the association between emergency department heart rate and the development of posttraumatic stress disorder: A public health approach. *Biological Psychiatry* 57(1): 91–95.

Zlotnick, C., C. L. Franklin, and M. Zimmerman. 2002. Does "subthreshold" posttraumatic stress disorder have any clinical relevance? *Comprehensive Psychiatry* 43(6): 413–419.

Part IV

At-Risk Populations, Disaster Risk Factors, and Individual and Community Vulnerability

8 Disaster Behavioral Health for Children and Adolescents
Best Practices for Preparedness, Response, and Recovery

Melissa J. Brymer, Gilbert Reyes, and Alan M. Steinberg

CONTENTS

In recent years much more attention has focused on the unique needs and services required to assist children and adolescents impacted by disasters. This chapter will review our current understanding of the emotional, behavioral, and cognitive impact on children of different developmental levels and from different cultural backgrounds. It provides an overview of some of the risk and protective factors that influence child, adolescent, and family recovery, and how to establish response and recovery programs that best support their recovery. Finally, the chapter will focus on future directions in the areas of research, services, and policy.

8.1 IMPACT OF DISASTERS ON CHILDREN AND ADOLESCENTS

Parents and societies go to great lengths to promote children's well-being, while providing them with environments that support healthy development. Nevertheless, large numbers of children and adolescents are exposed to many types of adverse events, including disasters that destroy or disrupt systems that normally serve the needs of youth and families. At least since the 1950s (Bloch, Silber, and Perry 1956; Silber, Perry, and Bloch 1958), disasters in the United States have been characterized as a major public health concern with potentially significant negative consequences for children's mental health. These early studies focused on experiences that might render children more susceptible to emotional disturbance after a disaster, with an emphasis on the influences of experiences preceding the disaster, the types and degrees of children's exposure to the disaster, and ways in which the children's families and other significant persons coped with the disaster itself and the children's reactions. Other social factors were also investigated, such as religion and the influences of peers and schools. The investigators attributed the levels of postdisaster disturbance found in children to the degree of their exposure, including severity of threat, injury, and loss, and qualities of the parents' reactions to the disaster that served to either aggravate or palliate the child's distress. This set of early studies indicated the combined importance of exposure factors and family dynamics in understanding the psychological and psychosocial impact of disasters on children.

Subsequent studies have elaborated upon earlier findings, supporting predictive relationships among children's predisaster functioning (Asarnow et al. 1999; La Greca, Silverman, and Wasserstein 1998), parental and family factors (Earls et al. 1988; Norris et al. 2002), mitigating factors in the affected communities (Galante and Foa 1986; Vogel and Vernberg 1993), exposure factors (Anthony, Lonigan, and Hecht 1999; Goenjian et al. 2001), degree of loss (Asarnow et al. 1999; Vogel and Vernberg 1993), being evacuated or displaced (Lonigan et al. 1994; McDermott and Palmer 2002), and postdisaster stresses and adversities (Garrison et al. 1995). Demographic influences on children's reactions and resilience have also been found, including age (Green et al. 1991; Kronenberg et al. 2010), gender (Green et al. 1994; Hoven et al. 2005), and race (Hardin et al. 1994; La Greca, Silverman, and Wasserstein 1998), although these findings are not entirely consistent across studies. An extensive review of empirical studies of disaster psychology found that the young appear to be at elevated risk for negative outcomes across a variety of events (Norris et al. 2002), and thus there is a compelling interest to better protect children from the hazardous effects of disasters and to dedicate adequate resources toward postdisaster support for recovery among children, their families, and their communities.

8.1.1 EMOTIONAL, BEHAVIORAL, AND COGNITIVE IMPACT

In working with children and adolescents affected by disasters, it is important to remember that adverse circumstances present developmental challenges. The most immediate responses of children in disasters comprise a set of emotional, behavioral, and cognitive reactions that motivate and guide attempts to escape and survive threatening situations (Bowlby 1973). Prominent among these reactions is the seeking of support from attachment figures and other persons who might provide protection and a means to securing safety and comfort. The attachment response is likely to include emotions like fear and anxiety, and behaviors designed to establish proximity to caregivers. In the absence of known caregivers, children are likely to seek protection and support from surrogates such as teachers, neighbors, spiritual care providers, first responders, or other adults who appear trustworthy and capable of lending assistance. The most obvious behavioral signs of distress like crying or sobbing may be present, but children may also be worried, frightened, anxious or confused. The level of distress is influenced by the availability of attachment figures that are able to sooth and comfort the child; children who are separated from parents and family may be preoccupied with seeking reunion with their loved ones. For as long as the attachment response is activated, children's emotions, behaviors, and cognitions are likely to revolve around security seeking in general and being reunited with loved ones more specifically. While this theoretical framework has long informed clinical perspectives on the needs of children faced with adversity, recent research has sought to provide empirical support and clarification for how attachment beliefs and parenting are related to children's adaptation and resilience following disasters (e.g., Costa, Weems, and Pina 2009).

As the postdisaster situation evolves, children are likely to experience a range of emotional and cognitive reactions that reflect their immediate social circumstances. Under the best of conditions these would include achieving emotional relief, experiences that support self-efficacy and social connectedness, and a return to a more normal set of goals and behaviors that are less influenced by the disaster. But many children will endure substantial losses of security, social support, and material resources, and may manifest emotions and behaviors that signal problematic adaptations.

Studies of children affected by disasters have found symptoms of somatization (Green et al. 1994), prolonged anxiety, including separation anxiety (Anthony, Lonigan, and Hecht 1999; Asarnow et al. 1999; Earls et al. 1988; Hoven et. al. 2005), anger and/or depression (Goenjian et al. 2001; Hardin et al. 1994; Kronenberg et al. 2010), and posttraumatic stress reactions (Anthony, Lonigan, and Hecht 1999; Asarnow et al. 1999; Garrison et al. 1995; Goenjian et al. 2001; La Greca et al. 1996; Weems et al. 2007).

In addition to the great variety of emotional reactions, children's behavior may also be affected. For example, children might behave in ways that suggest immaturity or developmental regression (Durkin et al. 1993). Some examples of this phenomenon include bedwetting, separation anxiety, school refusal, and nighttime fears that may involve resistance to sleeping alone. Children affected by disasters may also manifest more externalizing behaviors, such as aggression (Durkin et al. 1993), defiance, and other problems with conduct (La Greca, Silverman, and Wasserstein 1998) and social adjustment (Asarnow et al. 1999). Behaviors indicative of posttraumatic stress have also been observed in disaster-affected children, including heightened arousal, avoidance, and intrusive thoughts and ruminations related to their fears and stressful experiences (Anthony, Lonigan, and Hecht 1999; Asarnow et al. 1999; Kronenberg et al. 2010). Many of these reactions and behaviors can contribute to a vicious cycle that undermines children's adaptation after the disaster, academic functioning, and peer and family relationships, and decreases much needed social support. There is also a developing literature on neurobiological alterations among adolescents after disasters (Goenjian et al. 2003) and on disturbances in conscience functioning (Goenjian et al. 1999).

8.1.2 Risk and Protective Factors That Influence Impact

It has long been recognized that characteristics of children exposed to disasters and aspects of their environments tend to raise or lower the probability of resilient outcomes (Lonigan et al. 1994). Children who are more likely to exhibit PTSD and other mental health problems following disasters include those with preexisting anxiety and other mental health conditions (Earls et al. 1988; Nolen-Hoeksema and Morrow 1991; Weems et al. 2007), previous exposure to trauma and disaster (Jaycox et al. 2010; Mullet-Hume et al. 2008; Salloum et al. 2010), as well as those who display negative types of coping (Terranova, Boxer, and Morris 2009). Characteristics of the children's parents and family dynamics that are associated with less favorable outcomes include excessively anxious and overly protective parenting, as well as conflict, irritability, and withdrawal among family members (McFarlane 1987). There are also several studies identifying preexisting mental health issues in one or more parents as a risk factor for children's resilience in the face of disasters (Earls et al. 1988; Green et al. 1991).

Aspects of the child's environment are also altered by the disaster and its effects, and although the most salient stress may be the disaster itself, there are likely to be many aggravating stresses and adversities following the disaster. Adverse postdisaster circumstances may constitute risk factors that exacerbate the effects of the disaster by provoking persistent distress. Examples include being displaced from the predisaster residence, which in turn might lead to loss of social support among familiar teachers, peers, or neighbors, along with the need to adapt to a new dwelling, neighborhood, and school (Asarnow et al. 1999; Garrison et al. 1995; Lonigan et al. 1994; Terranova, Boxer, and Morris 2009). And while peer victimization is a hazard faced by many youths across a variety of circumstances, it has been identified as a risk factor for young people displaced by Hurricane Katrina and should not be overlooked by families and others seeking to assist children after a disaster (Terranova, Boxer, and Morris 2009). Importantly, chronic exposures to trauma and loss reminders in the postdisaster ecology that reactivate fear and distress have been shown to constitute a major source of postdisaster adversity (Pynoos et al. 2006).

A variety of protective factors have also been noted among children who prove more resilient to disasters, and these too are categorized as either personal or environmental attributes. Foremost among resilient children's personal attributes is effective coping ability (La Greca et al. 1996; Lengua, Long, and Meltzoff 2006), meaning coping that is flexible and responsive to the nature of the stress, is effective at regulating emotions and impulses (Terranova, Boxer, and Morris 2009), and that makes effective use of social support while not relying too strongly on avoidance or excessive support seeking (Vernberg et al. 1996). Positive parental and family coping, along with other social support factors, is associated with better postdisaster adjustment among children (Costa, Weems, and Pina 2009; Laor, Wolmer, and Cohen 2001). Thus, it is clear that evaluating and assisting children following a disaster requires attention not only to the means by which the child is coping, what the child is coping with, and what coping support the child is receiving from family and others, but also to any exacerbating factors in the family or community that may need to be addressed to improve the conditions toward those of more optimal development and resilience.

8.1.3 Cultural, Developmental, and Gender Differences

A child's developmental level influences the ability of the child to accurately appraise the disaster and formulate responses that will support effective adaptation. Younger children have fewer formative experiences and a more limited behavioral repertoire to draw upon, and thus will be more dependent upon caregivers to provide safety and support. As children age they make more complex connections among experiences, and thus become increasingly aware of their environments, the expectations and behaviors of others, and the options they have for coping. Disasters, however, can quickly overwhelm the coping capacity of most young people and thus present extreme challenges to coping and adaptation. The observable effects of development on children's reactions to disasters include differences in event appraisal, familiar coping options, means of signaling distress and other emotional reactions, and the types of support that are most likely to produce an effective response.

Few studies of children following disasters have stratified children's reactions according to developmental levels, and much of what is published on this issue reflects well-founded observation from developmentally sensitive clinicians and others. Notably, McDermott and Palmer's (2002) study of children affected by a wildfire suggested the existence of important developmental differences in children's psychological responses to disasters as a function of a child's grade in school. Other studies have examined the relationship between age and the probability of PTSD or other symptoms, although the findings have not been consistent. Some studies found symptoms to be more prominent among younger children (e.g., Kronenberg et al. 2010; Shannon et al. 1994), while others found symptoms to be more prominent among older children (e.g., Garrison et al. 1995), while other studies found little or no evidence of age differences (Anthony, Lonigan, and Hecht 1999; Costa, Weems, and Pina 2009; Green et al. 1991; Lonigan et al. 1994). Future studies are needed to investigate a variety of developmentally sensitive outcome domains to clarify differences across developmental stages.

Gender differences in children's reactions to disasters are more consistent, with most studies reporting higher incidence or elevation of symptoms among girls as compared to boys (e.g., Green et al. 1991; Kronenberg et al. 2010; Goenjian et al. 1995; Weems et al. 2007). It should be noted, however, that some studies find no gender differences (Costa, Weems, and Pina 2009; McDermott and Palmer 2002), and that these seeming differences in findings may reflect differences in samples, circumstances, methodology, metrics, and the nature of the research questions being asked. It is also unclear whether differences that are found are explicable in terms of a greater willingness on the part of girls to endorse symptoms as compared with boys (Vogel and Vernberg 1993). Nevertheless, it is important for those working with children affected by disaster to maintain sensitivity and receptiveness to individual differences among children's disaster experiences, responses, and needs as a function of gender without relying too greatly on gender-based stereotypes or research findings that may not apply to a given child's experience.

Studies reporting differences in experiences related to race, ethnicity, and nationality have transformed the discourse in social sciences and raised sensitivity to the importance of culture in the human experience and the need to better understand the cultural context of psychosocial perception and behavior. As a result, culture has become an overarching rubric for conceptualizing group difference, and is often used interchangeably with race, ethnicity, and nationality, and thus has become difficult to describe or operationalize as a distinct construct. Racial differences found in disaster studies performed in the United States have mostly contrasted whites with African Americans, and findings regarding other racial and/or ethnic groups are less available, especially in regard to children more specifically. A set of studies reviewed for this chapter may help to illustrate the variability of results and the consequent difficulty in drawing general conclusions. Shannon and others (1994) found differences between whites and blacks, but attributed them to differences in risk of exposure, biases in reporting, as well as differences in the relative risk of developing posttraumatic symptoms. Lonigan and others (1991) found higher reports of PTSD symptoms among African American children in contrast to white children, while Hardin and others (1994) found that African American children experienced greater exposure to disaster and negative life events than white children, but reported the least psychological stress, the lowest social support, and the highest self-efficacy. Other researchers, such as Costa, Weems, and Pina (2009), have examined the role of "ethnicity" (rather than race) and found no significant differences. Nevertheless, those who work with disaster survivors tend to recognize the importance of cultural differences, and it is unfortunate that research has lagged behind in the examination of this important aspect of how children and their communities experience and respond to disasters. Rabalais, Ruggiero, and Scotti (2002) have acknowledged and addressed the limitations of this area of disaster literature, with an emphasis on the importance of socioeconomic status and social support. These authors have also highlighted the importance of culture as an aspect of societies designed to serve a protective function, even as it may also constitute a risk factor under some conditions. At present, what seems most prudent is to avoid stereotyped generalizations and to work with culturally proficient consultants to establish means of effectively bridging cultural differences with appropriate sensitivity and respect (Jones et al. 2006).

8.2   A PUBLIC MENTAL HEALTH MODEL OF POSTDISASTER INTERVENTION

To most effectively assist children and adolescents after disasters, a modern public mental health approach to postdisaster recovery needs to be established (Pynoos, Goenjian, and Steinberg 1998). This type of approach recognizes the importance of coordination among governmental and nongovernmental organizations, establishing psychosocial programs in schools to increase access to services for youths, and staging of interventions across phases of recovery (Pynoos, Goenjian, and Steinberg 1998). Interventions and services should be proactive, protective, pragmatic, and principle driven, including providing a sense of safety, promoting calming activities, supporting connectedness, fostering self- and community efficacy, and increasing hope at all stages (Hobfoll et al. 2007; Watson, Thimm, and Santiago 2009). Although the timing, setting, and service providers for response, intermediate recovery, and longer-term recovery will vary by type of disaster and postdisaster ecology, it is generally accepted that different levels of intervention are needed for each of these stages. Tier 1 provides outreach, public health information, needs assessments, and Psychological First Aid (PFA) to the affected population. PFA may include stabilization of the child, family or community milieu; addressing immediate health, mental health, and safety concerns; providing practical assistance; enhancing coping strategies and the use of community and social support resources; providing information on common stress reactions and cautions about risk-related behavior; and linkage with available community support resources. Tier 2 provides more-specialized child and adolescent interventions for those with moderate-to-severe persisting distress and associated impairment, including substance abuse. Tier 3 provides specialized psychiatric services for children and adolescents who require immediate and/or intensive intervention, and may include pharmacological treatment or hospitalization.

8.2.1 PREPAREDNESS

To most effectively support children and adolescents with the behavioral health impact of disasters, planning and allocation of appropriate resources needs to occur prior to a disaster. Preparedness includes developing adequate local, state, national, and international disaster/emergency management plans and disaster/emergency procedures that address the unique needs of children. Planning needs to occur across all child-serving systems, including health, public health, justice, child welfare, foster care, mental health, spiritual care, and education. Interagency agreements or a Memorandum of Understanding (MOU) needs to be established between these systems to ensure continuity of care for children and families. Preparedness activities should include the following:

- *Training* for child-serving systems and childcare facility personnel on the reactions of children with different developmental levels, risk and resilience issues, psychological first aid, bereavement support, resilience-enhancing activities, and knowledge of agencies that provide more-intensive trauma and grief-focused mental health services, psychiatric services, and substance abuse treatment. Training also should include information on emergency management operations (e.g., National Incident Management System, Incident Command System, and National Response Framework).
- *Technical assistance* to child-serving systems to ensure that plans are comprehensive and have an all-hazards approach. Technical assistance includes ensuring that plans enhance the safety and well-being of children of all developmental levels, cultures, and those with special needs. For example, plans need to address the evacuation needs of children with physical disabilities or for children living in a residential facility or in foster care.
- *Identify adequately trained personnel or partners* who can assist in disaster response and recovery activities. Those certified should have proper credentialing, background screening, and clear roles and responsibilities. Trained personnel should be identified who have special expertise, including different linguistic competence, working with children of different ages and with extended families, and experience with different cultures.
- *Practice* of the plan on a regular basis, including the use of drills in various child-serving settings (e.g., Head Start facilities, schools, YMCAs). Evaluation of drills is essential, including identifying lessons learned and adapting existing plans accordingly.
- *Encourage preparedness planning* with families. Preparedness planning includes (1) having families learn about the types of disasters or hazards in their community and evacuation plans in the community and at their children's schools; (2) creating a family emergency plan, including identification of evacuation routes, reunification and communication strategies if separated, and filling out and carrying a Family Preparedness Wallet card; and (3) creating an emergency supply kit. Useful information and resources for family preparedness planning is available at: http://www.nctsn.org or http://www.ready.gov.
- *Be up-to-date* on relevant policies, research, and resources regarding children and families. There are a number of consensus guidelines that provide recommendations on key components of disaster behavioral health care. For example, the *IASC Guidelines on Mental Health and Psychosocial Support in Emergency Settings* (Inter-Agency Standing Committee 2007), *European Network for Traumatic Stress Guidelines* (Bisson and Tavakoly 2008), *Disaster Mental Health Recommendations* of the National Biodefense Science Board (Disaster Mental Health Subcommittee 2009), and the *National Commission on Children and Disasters: 2010 Report to the President and Congress* (National Commission on Children and Disasters 2010). Several organizations provide guidance on the current evidence on treatments and interventions that are appropriate at different phases of recovery for children, adolescents, and families (see http://www.nctsn.org and http://www.istss.org).

Finally, there are several Web sites that have useful resources on supporting children after disasters, including the following:

- National Child Traumatic Stress Network (http://www.nctsn.org and http://learn.nctsn.org)
- Readiness and Emergency Management for Schools Technical Assistance Center (http://rems.ed.gov)
- National Association of School Psychologists (http://nasponline.org/resources/crisis_safety/index.aspx)
- American Psychological Association (http://apa.org/topics/disasters/index.aspx)
- American Academy of Pediatrics (http://www.aap.org/disasters/index.cfm)
- National Association of Child Care Resources & Referral Agencies (http://www.naccrra.org/disaster)

8.2.2 RESPONSE PHASE

The response phase occurs when the disaster starts and can continue for up to a few weeks depending on the extent of community resource loss and threat to human life. The primary goal during the response phase is to assist children, adolescents, their families, and those who work with children to address their current needs and concerns, including calming their fears and anxieties, reestablishing a sense of safety and security, and beginning to restore the environment. The primary activities in the response phase include the following:

- *Identify needs* through the use of a needs assessment to determine the extent of trauma and loss exposure, identify different high-risk exposure groups, the degree of current adverse psychosocial difficulties, and need for and availability of resources. Needs assessments can be community based or carried out within specific settings, such as schools (e.g., Balaban et al. 2005; Brock et al. 2009; Jacobs et al. 2006). Sharing of data from various governmental departments can help promote more judicious allocation of resources and support for intervention efforts (Pynoos, Goenjian, and Steinberg 1998).

  Children and adolescents exhibiting distress, functional or behavioral impairment, in the first few weeks should be more formally assessed. This assessment should include (1) basic trauma and loss exposure information; (2) health and safety needs; (3) specific questions about high-risk experiences, for example, direct life threat, being trapped or injured, witnessing injury or death, and being separated from family members or caregivers; (4) cultural, religious, political, and socioeconomic issues; (5) current adversities; and (6) current behavioral and functional difficulties (Balaban et al. 2005). Trauma and loss exposure questions should not just focus on the current event but also assess for previous trauma (Jaycox et al. 2010; Mullet-Hume et al. 2008; Salloum et al. 2010).

- *Provide outreach and information* to the affected community that includes accurate and sensitive information about the event and its impact on the community, psychoeducation about how children and families may be affected by the disaster, ways that children and families can support one another in this difficult time, and how they can get resources or services. It is critical that multiple outreach mechanisms be used, including face-to-face contacts and the use of print materials, Internet, telephone, text messages, and public service announcements through the media. Providers need to actively outreach to parents and to those serving children. For example, outreach should target health care providers to help them quickly screen for whether a child was impacted by the disaster, provide a description of ways that they can educate children and families about the effects of trauma, and provide a list of resources or available additional services (Cohen, Kelleher, and Mannarino 2008). Ideally, outreach will occur prior to the disaster, but materials can be updated for the current circumstances. Other outreach activities can include holding parent and school staff meetings, circulating educational materials at community events, and hosting of hotlines.

- *Provide psychological first aid (PFA)* to assist children, adults, and families in reducing initial distress; foster short- and long-term adaptive functioning; and to link survivors with additional services. This intervention encourages providers to give pragmatic support in a nonintrusive and compassionate manner and does not force disclosure of traumatic details. One of the most systematic PFA approaches is the National Child Traumatic Stress Network and the National Center for Posttraumatic Stress Disorder's *Psychological First Aid Field Operations Guide,* 2nd ed. (Brymer et al. 2006). This PFA guide is based on a modular approach that has eight core actions (see Table 8.1). It has been adapted for use by religious professionals, the Medical Reserve Corps, schools, universities and colleges, and homeless shelters serving youth and families. It has been translated into many languages. Free online training *(PFA online)* and access to these PFA adaptations are available at http://learn.nctsn.org. Although PFA has not yet been systematically studied, PFA responders reported that it was well received by children and caregivers who were provided PFA services after Hurricanes Gustav and Ike (Allen et al. 2010).
- *Attend to basic needs and support normal routines* in children's lives as soon as possible. This includes resuming school activities, even if in a temporary environment, creating safe play areas, and ensuring that children's safety is continuously monitored. For example, school staff should monitor student conversations and social networking Web sites to identify rumors and concerns of safety. The school needs to provide timely and accurate information to address unnecessary worry or concern and provide additional support to those who may be experiencing extreme distress or suicidal ideation. Providers should encourage parents to maintain, as much as possible, children's routines, such as bedtime rituals, mealtime, and chores.

TABLE 8.1

Psychological First Aid Core Actions

1. Contact and engagement
   Goal: To respond to contacts initiated by survivors, or to initiate contacts in a nonintrusive, compassionate, and helpful manner
2. Safety and comfort
   Goal: To enhance immediate and ongoing safety, and provide physical and emotional comfort
3. Stabilization (if necessary)
   Goal: To calm and orient emotionally overwhelmed or disoriented survivors
4. Information gathering: Current needs and concerns
   Goal: To identify immediate needs and concerns, gather additional information, and tailor Psychological First Aid interventions
5. Practical assistance
   Goal: To offer practical help to survivors in addressing immediate needs and concerns
6. Connection with social supports
   Goal: To help establish brief or ongoing contacts with primary support persons and other sources of support, including family members, friends, and community helping resources
7. Information on coping
   Goal: To provide information about stress reactions and coping to reduce distress and promote adaptive functioning
8. Linkage with collaborative services
   Goal: To link survivors with available services needed at the time or in the future

Source: Adapted from Brymer, M., Jacobs, A., Layne, C., Pynoos, R., Ruzek, J., Steinberg, A., Vernberg, E., and Watson, P., *Psychological First Aid Field Operations Guide*, 2nd ed., National Child Traumatic Stress Network and National Center for PTSD, http://www.nctsn.org and http://www.ncptsd.va.gov, 2006.

These core actions of Psychological First Aid constitute the basic objectives of providing early assistance within days or weeks following an event. Providers should be flexible and base the amount of time they spend on each core action on the survivors' specific needs and concerns.

Example 8.1

Rosalie, a third grader, was in class when the 8.0 earthquake struck the island where she lives. Everyone was frightened as they were concerned that a tsunami might soon strike. Her teacher quickly got word from the principal that they needed to evacuate the building and head up the mountain. As soon as they reached safer grounds, the children saw the ocean waters recede from the shoreline. Then, the tsunami waves came crashing down on their village and school. Rosalie and her classmates were initially concerned that the waves would swallow them up, too. To calm the children, the school officials told the children they were safe and moved them further inland so that they did not have to see the destruction occurring down below.

After the tsunami ended, Rosalie was worried about the safety of her parents and siblings. To provide support, her teacher instructed the class that she and the other school officials would remain with them until a member of their family could come to get them, and others were inform-ing their parents of their current location and that all the children and staff at the school were evacuated safely. She highlighted that she understood how scary this situation was for them, but that everyone was working as quickly as possible to reunite them with their loved ones. To help distract the students, they decided to sing songs that they had learned in church.

After 30 minutes, Rosalie's mother showed up and quickly hugged her. She told Rosalie that the rest of her siblings and her father were safe. However, the village, including their home, was destroyed by the tsunami. Rosalie began to cry as she realized that she had lost everything. Rosalie's mom tried to comfort her but Rosalie became increasingly distressed. A "helper" saw Rosalie crying and asked her mother if she needed help. Her mother told "the helper" that their village was damaged and that they had no place to stay that night. The man informed her that families from her village were going to stay at the nearby field and that supplies would be sent to this location, including food and drink. With her mom's permission, "the helper" bent down and explained to Rosalie what was being done to help her family and the community that night and over the next few days. He also answered her questions about what had just happened and how she could anticipate aftershocks and how to manage her fears when they occurred. With this information, Rosalie calmed down and wanted to go with her mother to find the rest of her family.

SUMMARY

It is important that all individuals involved in a child's life get trained in PFA. These adults practi-cally helped Rosalie with her safety concerns, calmed her, facilitated her connections with loved ones, promoted her sense of self-efficacy, and instilled hope that others would be there to help. They also protected her from unnecessary exposure to additional trauma by moving the class away from seeing the destruction of their village and educated her on the role of reminders and how to manage them. For more information on how to talk with children and adolescents, see Table 8.2.

8.2.3 RECOVERY PHASE

The recovery phase occurs after the acute impact of the disaster and the threat to human life has subsided. The transition from the response to the recovery phase may vary with the type of disaster and community resource loss. Most children in this phase will not need services, as their symptoms will have subsided. Consequently, recovery activities are focused on providing more comprehensive and more in-depth services for those children who continue to experience difficulties weeks to years after a disaster (Pynoos, Steinberg, and Brymer 2007). Although early interventions may be evidence informed, to date there has been insufficient direct evidence for the effectiveness of early interventions for children exposed to disasters in the short-term recov-ery phase and very few controlled outcome studies in the long-term recovery phase (Brymer et al. 2012; La Greca and Silverman 2009). A comprehensive review summarizing the existing evidence on interventions and treatments for children and adolescents postdisaster can be found elsewhere (Brymer et al. 2012; Cohen, Mannarino, Gibson, et al. 2006; La Greca and Silverman

TABLE 8.2
Guidelines for Talking with Children and Adolescents

- For young children, sit or crouch at the child's eye level.
- Speak calmly. Be patient, responsive, and sensitive.
- Help school-age children verbalize their feelings, concerns and questions; provide simple labels for common emotional reactions (e.g., mad, sad, scared, worried). Do not use extreme words like *terrified* or *horrified* because this may increase their distress.
- Listen carefully and check in with the child to make sure you understand him/her.
- Be aware that children may show developmental regression in their behavior and use of language.
- Give information that is accurate and age appropriate. Remember that even very young children need to know what has happened. Tell children the truth, but keep it brief and speak to their developmental level (e.g., avoid discussing details of a death).
- Reassure young children that the adults are there to protect them and keep them safe. Even when adults do not feel safe, young children need to be assured that everything is being done to keep them safe.
- Talk to adolescents "adult-to-adult" so you give the message that you respect their feelings, concerns, and questions.
- Reinforce these techniques with the child's parents/caregivers to help them provide appropriate emotional support to their child.

Source: Adapted from Brymer, M., Jacobs, A., Layne, C., Pynoos, R., Ruzek, J., Steinberg, A., Vernberg, E., and Watson, P., *Psychological First Aid Field Operations Guide*, 2nd ed., National Child Traumatic Stress Network and National Center for PTSD, http://www.nctsn.org and http://www.ncptsd.va.gov, 2006.

2009). Based on the current evidence and evaluations of psychosocial programs, there are some primary considerations in the recovery phase:

- *Conduct periodic screenings/surveillance* to identify the ongoing mental health needs of children and adolescents, monitor the course of recovery to identify current or new adversities or exposures to trauma, and identify the type and quality of services utilized (Balaban et al. 2005). Surveillance can include monitoring of juvenile arrest records, attendance at school, grades, and suicide rates.
- *Be proactive in identifying at-risk children* by continuing outreach and information services, as most children will not seek services on their own. Consider establishing youth leadership or mentorship programs or engage youths in helping to identify others that may have been missed in earlier outreach efforts or have recently experienced adversities that have made them more vulnerable. Be cognizant of "key dates," such as anniversaries, holidays, and criminal and civil proceedings. For example, students who are grieving the death of their best friend may have a harder time on the deceased friend's birthday. A counselor reaching out to these students prior to this day and making sure that each of them has a plan for how to cope could help reduce their distress.
- *Increase children's utilization of services* by implementing psychosocial programs in schools, offering a spectrum of services, and providing culturally and developmentally sound interventions. For example, some programs should be geared to younger children, which are activity or play based, such as *After the Storm* (La Greca, Sevin, and Sevin 2005), *Healing After Trauma Skills* (Gurwitch and Messenbaugh 1998), and *Classroom/Community/Camp-based Intervention* (CBI; Tol et al. 2008; Jordans et al. 2010). Until further evidence is available, cognitive behavioral approaches are recommended for those children and adolescents with moderate to severe symptoms. These approaches utilize components summarized by the acronym PRACTICE, including psychoeducation and parenting skills, relaxation, affective modulation, cognitive coping and processing, trauma narrative, in vivo mastery of trauma reminders, conjoint child-parent

sessions, and enhancement of future safety and development (Cohen, Mannarino, and Deblinger 2006).

- *Offer services that can be implemented in existing systems or programs* to ensure that child and adolescent services are implemented with greatest efficiency and effectiveness. One such promising practice that was developed to meet the specific criteria for the FEMA/SAMHSA Crisis Counseling program is *Skills for Psychological Recovery* (SPR; Berkowitz et al. 2010). SPR assists children, adults, and families with learning and using a set of empirically based interventions, including problem solving, positive activity scheduling, managing reactions, promoting helpful thinking, and rebuilding healthy social connections using a skills-building approach. It was developed to ensure that training and service provision would be feasible in the intermediate phase after a disaster for use by paraprofessionals. Thus, each module begins with a rationale for the importance of the skill, followed by a step-by-step procedure to implement the skill. This intervention has been used in several postdisaster programs, including in Louisiana after Hurricanes Katrina, Rita, and Gustav; in Australia after the 2009 Victorian bushfires; and in American Samoa after the 2009 earthquake/tsunami. Evaluation reports from Louisiana and Australia indicate that the intervention was favorably perceived by providers as an acceptable and useful intervention for disaster survivors and that the intervention was implemented without difficulty, with most reporting that they would use the intervention in the event of a future disaster (Fletcher et al. 2010; Hansel et al. 2011).
- *Provide ongoing consultation and training* throughout the recovery program to address barriers of accessing and implementing services of children, to make sure that services are being implemented flexibly to address the variability of needs of children across developmental stages and cultures, and to ensure fidelity to evidence-based practices (Cohen, Mannarino, Gibson, et al. 2006; Hansel et al. 2011).
- *Encourage prosocial activities* to enhance children's and adolescents' self-efficacy and to promote opportunities for them to contribute to the recovery process.

Example 8.2

Six months after the tsunami/earthquake had struck Rosalie's community, her house was rebuilt, she transitioned to a new school, and she was participating again in dance classes. She hardly thought about the tsunami. However, on one spring day, her new teacher read an announcement that another earthquake struck a different country and there were concerns that tsunami waves might strike her island within the next 12 hours. The school dismissed the students so that they could prepare for a potential evacuation. Despite the media reports indicating that families did not have to seek shelter on higher grounds until the morning, her family immediately fled to the mountains without bringing any supplies or food.

Although no tsunami hit and her family was safely home, Rosalie was still afraid for herself and her family's safety. For days she complained to her mother that she could not fall asleep and wanted to sleep in her parents' bed, she protested that she no longer wanted to go to school as she wanted to stick close to her family, and she became distressed if her father was late getting home from work. When a crisis counselor came to the house to check on Rosalie's family after the recent scare, her mother reported that she was concerned about the recent changes in her daughter's behavior. The counselor explained how an intervention, *Skills for Psychological Recovery,* could help. The counselor further explained that reacting to reminders of the disaster are common and can cause physical reactions (such as stomachaches) or emotional reactions (such as fear and worry). These reactions can cause sleep difficulties and make typically enjoyable activities less fun. The counselor further explained that there were activities that Rosalie could do to help reduce these reactions.

Rosalie and her mother then went through the Managing Reactions module with the counselor. In this module, Rosalie identified when she was being reminded most of the tsunami and the feelings that it provoked. Then they set up a coping plan for how to manage these reactions. In particular, Rosalie discussed being fearful of another tsunami. The counselor and the family discussed that having a disaster kit ready by the door would help if they had to evacuate again. During an evacuation, Rosalie discussed that singing and dancing, being soothed by her mother, and using a breathing technique were all strategies to calm her. She also discussed that when she went to sleep, this was a time when she thought about how scared she was during the evacuation. Her mother agreed to spend more time with Rosalie at bedtime, that they would say a prayer together, and that she would practice her breathing technique. The counselor then asked that Rosalie test out her plan in the next week. When the counselor checked in the following week, Rosalie and her mother reported that she was sleeping better and she was not as moody. The counselor congratulated Rosalie and they then discussed other times when she could practice her new coping plan.

SUMMARY

Active outreach, especially when additional secondary adversities have occurred in a community, helps to increase access to those who may not seek services on their own. Moreover, skills-building approaches, like SPR, have been found to be more effective than supportive counseling (Beutler 2009; Bryant et al. 1998; Bryant et al. 1999).

8.3 CONCLUSION AND FUTURE DIRECTIONS

Increased disaster-related research on risk, vulnerability, and resilience factors for children and adolescents holds promise for the development of knowledge to inform evidence-based acute, intermediate, and long-term postdisaster interventions. For this field of research to progress, an array of psychometrically sound assessment tools will need to be developed and refined, including those for needs assessment, triage, surveillance, clinical assessment, clinical outcome, and program evaluation (Balaban et al. 2005). Findings will also pave the way for the design of intervention strategies that target specific risk factors and adverse outcomes.

Pressing disaster-related research issues can be conceptualized along a continuum of preparedness, and response/recovery. Examples of needed disaster-related research in the area of *preparedness* includes (1) research to develop an evidence base for risk communication and public education strategies; (2) research to identify, develop, and evaluate methods of increasing predisaster parent and family knowledge of disaster preparedness and response plans; and (3) research to evaluate and improve school disaster and safety plans and the extent to which such plans are integrated in community, county, and state disaster plans. Needed *response/recovery* research includes (1) research on the effectiveness of public health and mental health strategies to promote the recovery of communities; (2) research on the psychological and functional impact of disaster on parents, families, schools, and communities; (3) research to identify, develop, and evaluate strategies to improve functioning in school, home, and community; and (4) research to determine psychological responses by specific disaster type (Pynoos et al. 2006).

There is currently a lack of adequate research regarding how disasters affect children with disabilities, as these children may be particularly vulnerable due to higher poverty rates, increased risk of exposure, and greater reliance on caregivers (Peek and Stough 2010). A research agenda in this area should seek to delineate the special risks for children with disabilities, clarify how different types of disability affect child and family preparedness, response, and recovery, and elucidate the role of social stigma in regard to limiting access to sheltering options, interventions, and other disaster-related resources. Finally, studies need to be conducted to determine how best to support the recovery of children with disabilities and their families. Many of these issues need to be addressed for diverse ethnic and cultural groups, as findings have indicated that after disasters African American children experience higher levels of psychological distress as compared with white children (Lonigan et al. 1991) and are less likely to experience declines in levels of PTSD (La Greca et al. 1996). For minority children and those with disabilities, barriers to research, including issues of access, culture, and language, as well as lack of trust, will need to be addressed (Jones et al. 2006). Finally, more research is needed on how best to serve children at different developmental levels, especially infants and preschoolers, and college-age youth.

The success of a disaster response is predicated on preparation that includes building capacity through training and technical assistance at all levels, along with periodic practice employing drills to ensure effective implementation. Such training should include education about the needs of at-risk populations and issues of cultural responsiveness (Disaster Mental Health Subcommittee 2009). In regard to drills, an important area for future research includes the development of setting-related disaster drill protocols and evaluation methods and metrics that can be used to study fidelity in the implementation of interventions by disaster responders and the effectiveness of incident command systems and infrastructure that support disaster response. Importantly for the future, effective policy decisions will be required in regard to the allocation of scarce federal, state, and local resources that are necessary to build and sustain infrastructures that support disaster response and recovery efforts (Osofsky, Osofsky, and Harris 2007).

There are currently a number of different early intervention models for disaster-affected children and adolescents. The NCTSN/NCPTSD *Psychological First Aid* is considered a sound initial early intervention, as it does not assume pathology, assesses current needs and concerns, identifies future service requirements, links with collaborative services, has a cultural and developmental perspective, and identifies the role of parents as a primary source for supporting a child's recovery. There is preliminary evidence of its acceptance by providers (Allen et al. 2010). For children and adolescents needing more in-depth intervention, skill-based and cognitive-behavioral approaches are indicated, including those included in the NCPTSD/NCTSN *Skills for Psychological Recovery* protocol. Establishing the evidence base for acute and intermediate interventions will need to be done in progressive stages that correspond to a number of basic research questions, including (1) the types of training methods and resources that are needed to effectively disseminate these interventions; (2) how best to ensure that providers implement these interventions with fidelity; (3) the extent to which these interventions can be effectively delivered and received by survivors in community settings; (4) whether implementing the intervention leads to improved outcomes as compared to other intervention practices; and (5) whether implementing the intervention in a community setting improves the overall effectiveness and efficiency of the community response. Attention should also be directed toward identifying and assessing intervention components that may be most beneficial for children and their families affected by disaster so that a child and adolescent behavioral health response can be more targeted, to improve the capacities of providers, and to enhance planning (Shoenbaum et al. 2009).

REFERENCES

Allen, B., M. J. Brymer, A. M. Steinberg, E. M. Vernberg, A. Jacobs, A. Speier, and R. S. Pynoos. 2010. Perceptions of psychological first aid among providers responding to Hurricanes Gustav and Ike. *Journal of Traumatic Stress* 23(4): 509–513.

Anthony, J. L., C. J. Lonigan, and S. A. Hecht. 1999. Dimensionality of posttraumatic stress disorder symptoms in children exposed to disaster: Results from confirmatory factor analyses. *Journal of Abnormal Psychology* 108(2): 326–336.

Asarnow, J., S. Glynn, R. S. Pynoos, J. Nahum, D. Guthrie, D. P. Cantwell, and B. Franklin. 1999. When the earth stops shaking: Earthquake sequelae among children diagnosed for pre-earthquake psychopathology. *Journal of the American Academy of Child and Adolescent Psychiatry* 38(8): 1016–1023.

Balaban, V. F., A. M. Steinberg, M. J. Brymer, C. M. Layne, R. T. Jones, and J. A. Fairbank. 2005. Screening and assessment for children's psychosocial needs following war and terrorism. In *Promoting the Psychosocial Well-being of Children Following War and Terrorism*, eds. M. J. Friedman and A. Mikus-Kos, 121–161. Amsterdam: the Netherlands: IOS Press.

Berkowitz, S., R. Bryant, M. Brymer, J. Hamblen, A. Jacobs, C. Layne, R. Macy, H. Osofsky, R. Pynoos, J. Ruzek, A. Steinberg, E. Vernberg, and P. Watson. 2010. *Skills for Psychological Recovery: Field Operations Guide*. Los Angeles, CA: National Child Traumatic Stress Network.

Beutler, L. E. 2009. Making science matter in clinical practice: Redefining psychotherapy. *Clinical Psychology: Science and Practice 16*(3): 301–317.

Bisson, J., and B. Tavakoly. 2008. *The TENTS guidelines.* http://www.tentsprojoct.eu/_site1264/dbfiles/document/_~57~_7eTENTS_Full_guidelines_booklet_A5_FINAL_24-04.pdf.

Bloch, D. A., E. Silber, and S. E. Perry. 1956. Some factors in the emotional reaction of children to disaster. *American Journal of Psychiatry 113*(5): 416–422.

Bowlby, J. 1973. *Attachment and Loss: Vol. 2. Separation, Anxiety and Anger.* New York: Basic Books.

Brock, S. E., A. B. Nickerson, M. A. Reeves, S. R. Jimerson, R. A. Lieberman, and T. A. Feinberg. 2009. *School Crisis Prevention and Intervention: The PREPaRE Model.* Bethesda, MD: NASP Publications.

Bryant, R. A., A. G. Harvey, S. T. Dang, T. Sackville, and C. Basten. 1998. Treatment of acute stress disorder: A comparison of cognitive-behavioral therapy and supportive counseling. *Journal of Consulting and Clinical Psychology 66*(5): 862–866.

Bryant, R. A., T. Sackville, S. T. Dang, M. Moulds, and R. Guthrie. 1999. Treating acute stress disorder: An evaluation of cognitive behavior therapy and supportive counseling. *American Journal of Psychiatry 156*(11): 1780–1786.

Brymer, M., A. Jacobs, C. Layne, R. Pynoos, J. Ruzek, A. Steinberg, E. Vernberg, and P. Watson. 2006. *Psychological First Aid: Field Operations Guide*, 2nd ed. National Child Traumatic Stress Network and National Center for PTSD. http://www.nctsn.org and http://www.ncptsd.va.gov.

Brymer, M. J., A. M. Steinberg, P. J. Watson, and R. S. Pynoos. 2012. Prevention and early intervention programs for children and adolescents. In *The Oxford Handbook of Traumatic Stress Disorders*, eds. J. G. Beck and D. Sloan, 381–392. New York: Oxford University Press.

Cohen, J. A., K. J. Kelleher, and A. P. Mannarino. 2008. Identifying, treating, and referring traumatized children: The role of pediatric providers. *Archives of Pediatric & Adolescent Medicine 162*(5): 447–453.

Cohen, J. A., A. P. Mannarino, and E. Deblinger. 2006a. *Treating Trauma and Traumatic Grief in Children and Adolescents.* New York: Guilford Press.

Cohen, J. A., A. P. Mannarino, L. E. Gibson, S. Cozza, M. J. Brymer, and L. Murray. 2006b. Interventions for children and adolescents following disasters. In *Interventions Following Mass Violence and Disasters: Strategies for Mental Health Practice,* eds. E. C. Ritchie, P. J. Watson, and M. J. Friedman, 227–256. New York: Guilford Press.

Costa, N. M., C. F. Weems, and A. Pina. 2009. Hurricane Katrina and youth anxiety: The role of perceived attachment beliefs and parenting behaviors. *Journal of Anxiety Disorders 23*(7): 935–941.

Disaster Mental Health Subcommittee. 2009. Disaster Mental Health Recommendations: Report of the Disaster Mental Health Subcommittee of the National Biodefense Science Board. http://www.phe.gov/Preparedness/legal/boards/nbsb/Documents/nsbs-dmhreport-final.pdf.

Durkin, M. S., N. Khan, L. L. Davidson, S. S. Zaman, and Z. A. Stein. 1993. The effects of a natural disaster on child behavior: Evidence for posttraumatic stress. *American Journal of Public Health 83*(11): 1549–1553.

Earls, F., E. Smith, W. Reich, and K. G. Jung. 1988. Investigating psychopathological consequences of a disaster in children: A pilot study incorporating a structured diagnostic interview. *Journal of the American Academy of Child & Adolescent Psychiatry 27*(1): 90–95.

Fletcher, S., D. Forbes, B. Wolfgang, T. Varker, M. Creamer, M. Brymer, J. Ruzek, P. Watson, and R. Bryant. 2010. Practitioner perceptions of Skills for Psychological Recovery: A training program for health practitioners in the aftermath of the Victorian bushfires. *Australian and New Zealand Journal of Psychiatry 44:* 1105–1111.

Galante, R., and D. Foa. 1986. An epidemiological study of psychic trauma and treatment effectiveness for children after a natural disaster. *Journal of the American Academy of Child Psychiatry 25*(3): 357–363.

Garrison, C. Z., E. S. Bryant, C. L. Addy, P. G. Spurrier, J. R. Freedy, and D. G. Kilpatrick. 1995. Posttraumatic stress disorder in adolescents after Hurricane Andrew. *Journal of the American Academy of Child & Adolescent Psychiatry 34*(9): 1193–1201.

Goenjian, A. K., L. Molina, A. M. Steinberg, L. A. Fairbanks, M. L. Alvarez, H. A. Goenjian, and R. S. Pynoos. 2001. Posttraumatic stress and depressive reactions among Nicaraguan adolescents after Hurricane Mitch. *American Journal of Psychiatry 158*(5): 788–794.

Goenjian, A. K., R. S. Pynoos, A. M. Steinberg, D. Endres, K. Abraham, M. E. Geffner, and L. A. Fairbanks. 2003. Hypothalamic-pituitary-adrenal activity among Armenian adolescents with PTSD symptoms. *Journal of Traumatic Stress 16*(4): 319–323.

Goenjian, A. K., R. S. Pynoos, A. M. Steinberg, L. M. Najarian, J. R. Asarnow, I. Karayan, M. Ghurabi, and L. A. Fairbanks. 1995. Psychiatric comorbidity in children after the 1988 earthquake in Armenia. *Journal of the American Academy of Child & Adolescent Psychiatry 34*(9): 1174–1184.

Goenjian, A. K., B. M. Stilwell, A. M. Steinberg, L. A. Fairbanks, M. R. Galvin, I. Karayan, and R. S. Pynoos. 1999. Moral development and psychopathological interference with conscience functioning among adolescents after trauma. *Journal of the American Academy of Child and Adolescent Psychiatry 38*(4): 376–384.

Green, B., M. Grace, M. Vary, T. Kramer, G. Gleser, and A. Leonard. 1994. Children of disaster in the second decade: A 17-year follow-up of Buffalo Creek survivors. *Journal of the American Academy of Child and Adolescent Psychiatry 33*(1): 71–79.

Green, B. L., M. Korol, M. C. Grace, M. Vary, A. Leonard, and G. Gleser. 1991. Children and disaster: Age gender and parental effects on PTSD symptoms. *Journal of the American Academy of Child and Adolescent Psychiatry 30*(6): 945–951.

Gurwitch, R.H., and A. K. Messenbaugh. 1998. *Healing after trauma: Skills manual for helping children.* http://www.nctsn.org.

Hansel, T. C., H. J. Osofsky, A. M. Steinberg, M. Brymer, R. Landis, K. S. Riise, S. Gilkey, J. Osofsky, and A. Speier. 2011. Louisiana Spirit Specialized Crisis Counseling: Counselor perceptions of training and services. *Psychological Trauma: Theory, Research, Practice, and Policy 3*: 276–282.

Hardin, S. B., M. Weinrich, S. Weinrich, T. L. Hardin, and C. Garrison. 1994. Psychological distress of adolescents exposed to Hurricane Hugo. *Journal of Traumatic Stress 7*(3): 427–440.

Hobfoll, S. E., P. E. Watson, C. C. Bell, R. A. Bryant, M. J. Brymer, M. J. Friedman, M. Friedman, B. P. R. Gersons, J. T. de Jong, C. M. Layne, S. Maguen, Y. Neria, A. E. Norwood, R. S. Pynoos, D. Reissman, J. I. Ruzek, A. Y. Shalev, Z. Solomon, A. M. Steinberg, and R. J. Ursano. 2007. Five essential elements of immediate and mid-term mass trauma intervention: Empirical evidence. *Psychiatry 70*(4): 283–315.

Hoven, C. W., C. S. Duarte, C. P. Lucas, P. Wu, D. J. Mandell, R. D. Goodwin, M. Cohen, V. Balaban, B. A. Woodruff, F. Bin, G. J. Musa, L. Mei., P. A. Cantor, J. L. Aber, P. Cohen, and E. Susser. 2005. Psychopathology among New York City public school children 6 months after September 11. *Archives of General Psychiatry 62*(5): 545–552.

Inter-Agency Standing Committee (IASC). 2007. IASC guidelines on mental health and psychosocial support in emergency settings. Geneva: IASC. http://www.who.int/mental_health/emergencies/guidelines_iasc_mental_health_psychosocial_june_2007.pdf.

Jacobs, G. A., J. P. Revel, and G. Reyes. 2006. Development of the rapid assessment of mental health: An interventional collaboration. In *Handbook of International Disaster Psychiatry*, eds. G. Reyes and G.A. Jacobs, 129–140. Westport, CT: Praeger Publishers.

Jaycox, L. H., J. A. Cohen, A. P. Mannarino, D. W. Walker, A. K. Langley, K. L. Gegenheimer, M. Scott, and M. Schonlau. 2010. Children's mental health care following Hurricane Katrina: A field trial of trauma-focused psychotherapies. *Journal of Traumatic Stress 23*(2): 223–231.

Jones, R. T., J. M. Hadder, F. Carvajal, S. Chapman, and A. Alexander. 2006. Conducting research in diverse minority and marginalized communities. In *Methods for Disaster Mental Health Research*, eds. F. Norris, M. Friedman, S. Galea, and P. Watson, 265–277. New York: Guilford Press.

Jordans, M. J. D., I. H. Komproe, W. A. Tol, B. A. Kohrt, N. P. Luitel, R. D. Macy, and J. T. de Jong. 2010. Evaluation of a classroom–based psychosocial intervention in conflict-affected Nepal: A cluster randomized controlled trial. *Journal of Child Psychology and Psychiatry 51*(7): 818–826.

Kronenberg, M. E., T. C. Hansel, A. M. Brennan, H. J. Osofsky, J. D. Osofsky, and B. Lawrason. 2010. Children of Katrina: Lessons learned about postdisaster symptoms and recovery patterns. *Child Development 81*(4): 1241–1259.

La Greca, A. M., S. Sevin, and E. Sevin. 2005. *After the storm.* Miami, FL: Sevendippity, Inc. http://www.7-dippity.com/index.html.

La Greca, A. M., and W. K. Silverman. 2009. Treatment and prevention of posttraumatic stress reactions in children and adolescents exposed to disasters and terrorism: What is the evidence? *Child Development Perspectives 3*(1): 4–10.

La Greca, A. M., W. K. Silverman, E. M. Vernberg, and M. J. Prinstein. 1996. Posttraumatic stress symptoms in children after Hurricane Andrew: A prospective study. *Journal of Consulting and Clinical Psychology 64*(4): 712–723.

La Greca, A. M., W. K. Silverman, and S. B. Wasserstein. 1998. Children's predisaster functioning as a predictor of posttraumatic stress following Hurricane Andrew. *Journal of Consulting and Clinical Psychology 66*(6): 883–892.

Laor, N., L. Wolmer, and D. J. Cohen. 2001. Mothers' functioning and children's symptoms five years after a SCUD missile attack. *American Journal of Psychiatry 158*(7): 1020–1026.

Lengua, L. J., A. C. Long, and A. N. Meltzoff. 2006. Pre-attack stress-load, appraisals, and coping in children's responses to the 9/11 terrorist attacks. *Journal of Child Psychology and Psychiatry 47*(12): 1219–1227.

Lonigan, C. J., M. P. Shannon, A. J. Finch, T. K. Daugherty, and C. M. Taylor. 1991. Children's reactions to a natural disaster: Symptom severity and degree of exposure. *Advances in Behavioral Research & Therapy 13*(3): 135–154.

Lonigan, C. J., M. P. Shannon, C. M. Taylor, A. J. Finch, and F. R. Sallee. 1994. Children exposed to disaster: II. Risk factors for the development of post-traumatic symptomatology. *Journal of the American Academy of Child and Adolescent Psychiatry 33*(1): 94–105.

McDermott, B. M., and L. J. Palmer. 2002. Postdisaster emotional distress, depression and event-related variables: Findings across child and adolescent developmental stages. *Australian and New Zealand Journal
of Psychiatry 36*(6): 754–761.

McFarlane, A. 1987. Family functioning and overprotection following a natural disaster. The longitudinal
effects of post-traumatic morbidity. *Australian and New Zealand Journal of Psychiatry 21*(2): 210–218.

Mullet-Hume, E., D. Anshel, V. Guevera, and M. Cloitre. 2008. Cumulative trauma and posttraumatic
stress disorder among children exposed to the 9/11 World Trade Center Attack. *American Journal of
Orthopsychiatry 78*(1): 103–108.

National Commission on Children and Disasters. 2010. National Commission on Children and Disasters: 2010
Report to the President and Congress. http://www.childrenanddisasters.acf.hhs.gov.

Nolen-Hoeksema, S., and J. Morrow. 1991. A prospective study of depression and posttraumatic stress symptoms after a natural disaster: The 1989 Loma Prieta Earthquake. *Journal of Personality and Social
Psychology 61*(1): 115–121.

Norris, F. H., M. J. Friedman, P. J. Watson, C. M. Byrne, E. Diaz, and K. Kaniasty. 2002. 60,000 disaster victims
speak: Part I: An empirical review of the empirical literature, 1981–2001. *Psychiatry 65*(3): 207–239.

Osofsky, J. D., H. J. Osofsky, and W. W. Harris. 2007. Katrina's children: Social policy considerations for children in disasters. *Social Policy Report 21*(1): 3–9.

Peek, L., and L. M. Stough. 2010. Children with disabilities in the context of disaster: A social vulnerability
perspective. *Child Development 81*(4):1260–1270.

Pynoos, R. S., A. K. Goenjian, and A. Steinberg. 1998. A public mental health approach to the post-disaster
treatment of children and adolescents. *Child and Adolescent Psychiatric Clinics of North America 7*(1):
195–210.

Pynoos, R. S., A. M. Steinberg, and M. J. Brymer. 2007. Children and disasters: Public mental health approaches.
In *Textbook of Disaster Psychiatry*, eds. R. J. Ursano, C. S. Fullerton, L. Weisaeth, and B. Raphael,
48–68. Cambridge, UK: Cambridge University Press.

Pynoos, R. S., A. M. Steinberg, M. D. Schreiber, and M. J. Brymer. 2006. Children and families: A new
framework for preparedness and response to danger, terrorism and trauma. In *Psychological Effects of
Catastrophic Disasters: Group Approaches to Treatment*, eds. L. A. Schein, H. I. Spitz, G. M. Burlingame,
and P. R. Mushkin, 83–112. New York: Haworth Press.

Rabalais, A. E., K. J. Ruggiero, and J. R. Scotti. 2002. Multicultural issues in the response of children to disasters. In *Helping Children Cope with Disasters and Terrorism*, eds. A. M. La Greca, W. K. Silverman,
E. M. Vernberg, and M. C. Roberts, 73–99. Washington, DC: American Psychological Association.

Salloum, A., P. Carter, B. Burch, A. Garfinkel, and S. Overstreet. 2010. Impact of exposure to community violence, Hurricane Katrina, and Hurricane Gustav on posttraumatic stress and depressive symptoms among
school-age children. *Anxiety, Stress & Coping 17*: 1–16.

Shannon, M. P., C. J. Lonigan, A. J. Finch, and C. M. Taylor. 1994. Children exposed to disaster: I. Epidemiology
of post-traumatic symptoms and symptom profiles. *Journal of the American Academy of Child and
Adolescent Psychiatry 33*(1): 80–93.

Shoenbaum, M., B. Butler, S. Katoaka, G. Norquist, B. Springgate, G. Sullivan, N. Duan, R. C. Kessler, and
K. Wells. 2009. Promoting mental health recovery after Hurricanes Katrina and Rita. *Archives of General
Psychiatry 66*(8): 906–914.

Silber, E., S. E. Perry, and D. A. Bloch. 1958. Patterns of parent-child interaction in a disaster. *Psychiatry 21*(2):
159–167.

Terranova, A., P. Boxer, and A. Morris. 2009. Factors influencing the course of posttraumatic stress following a natural disaster: Children's reactions to Hurricane Katrina. *Journal of Applied Developmental
Psychology 30*(3): 344–355.

Tol, W. A., I. H. Komproe, D. Susanty, M. J. D. Jordans, R. D. Macy, and J. T. V. M. De Jong. 2008. School-
based mental health intervention for political violence-affected children in Indonesia: A cluster randomized trial. *Journal of the American Medical Association 300*(6): 655–662.

Vernberg, E. M., A. M. La Greca, W. K. Silverman, and M. J. Prinstein. 1996. Prediction of posttraumatic stress
symptoms in children after Hurricane Andrew. *Journal of Abnormal Psychology 105*(2): 237–248.

Vogel, J. M., and E. M. Vernberg. 1993. Task force report part 1: Children's psychological responses to disasters. *Journal of Clinical Child and Adolescent Psychology 22*(4): 464–484.

Watson, P., K. Thimm, and P. Santiago. 2009. CCP model analysis: Informing the program through evidence
and expert consensus. An interdisciplinary taskforce white paper.

Weems, C. F., A. A. Pina, N. M. Costa, S. E. Watts, L. K. Taylor, and M. F. Cannon. 2007. Predisaster trait
anxiety and negative affect predict posttraumatic stress in youths after Hurricane Katrina. *Journal of
Consulting and Clinical Psychology 75*(1): 154–159.

9 Disaster Behavioral Health and Older Adults
American and Canadian Readiness and Response

Lisa M. Brown, Maggie Gibson, and Diane L. Elmore

CONTENTS

9.1 INTRODUCTION

Societies with developed economies, like the United States and Canada, are struggling with how to adequately prepare for the anticipated health care needs of the aging baby boomer generation. Chronic illnesses, including dementia, already dominate the geriatric health care agenda, and a shortage of health care providers with geriatric training, including behavioral health, currently exists. The needs and challenges of caring for an older population are that much greater in societies where economic development is less advanced and the population is aging even faster. Add a catastrophic event and the tenuous status quo becomes dire. Already limited resources needed to facilitate recovery may be destroyed or quickly depleted. Local service providers are often personally affected by the disaster, further hindering their ability to respond to others in need. In this chapter, an overview is provided of the key issues related to disaster behavioral health for older Canadians and Americans. While it is beyond the scope of this chapter to describe the challenges in delivering culturally and linguistically sensitive behavioral health interventions to older adults from an international perspective, related activities undertaken by three major international organizations are highlighted. In conclusion, future directions for programs and policy in Canada and the United States are discussed.

9.2   BACKGROUND

Disasters occur when natural hazards or human-caused events meet vulnerable populations, including but not limited to those with few economic resources, low levels of education, and from culturally and ethnically diverse backgrounds (Brown, Hickling, and Frahm 2010; Wisner et al. 2004). Although older adults may have poorer health and fewer social and economic resources than younger cohorts, they also have a lifetime of experience in coping with stressful events, and often, fewer currently unresolved stressful experiences, both of which promote adaptation to and recovery from disasters (Phifer 1990). Nevertheless, even without known factors associated with increased vulnerability, most older adults require assistance in preparing for, responding to, and recovering from such events. Given the change in American and Canadian demographics, the pressure to provide such assistance is mounting for government agencies responsible for disaster response and relief organizations tasked with providing care and services to affected populations. But are relief workers and disaster responders adequately trained to interact with and provide care to older adults? This critical question should be carefully considered by policy makers, emergency operations managers, public health officials, and other key stakeholders involved in disaster preparedness, planning, and response.

The number of seniors in Canada was projected to increase from 4.2 million to 9.8 million between 2005 and 2036, and seniors' share of the population was expected to almost double, increasing from 13.2 percent to 24.5 percent (Turcotte and Schellenberg 2007). American demographics mirror those of Canada. In 2011, the first wave of baby boomers, people born between 1946 and 1964, reached the age of 65. By the year 2030, 20 percent of the American population will be 65 years of age and older. Although both countries predict population changes whereby a growing number of older people live longer, it is important to reiterate that age alone does not increase vulnerability during disasters. Age-related physiological changes do not necessarily result in disease; however, most older adults have at least one chronic health condition such as diabetes, arthritis, osteoporosis, or chronic obstructive pulmonary disease. In both countries, health care interventions increase the likelihood of reaching old age and living independently with chronic conditions. The growing number of older people who are likely to have one or more chronic health conditions effectively increases the pool of vulnerable people who may be at greater risk for adverse consequences during a disaster because of their health status (Turcotte and Schellenberg 2007; DHHS 2000).

A range of economic, structural, political, historical, and cultural conditions can affect the ability of people to protect themselves, respond effectively, and recover from hazardous events. While environmental risk factors—such as housing and location—are important, social risk factors—such as poverty and isolation—also play a critical role in shaping the overall vulnerability of a group. In general, people who depend on others for assistance with activities of daily living because of physical limitations resulting from mobility, sensory, or cognitive impairment, or those with prior exposure to an extreme or prolonged traumatic stressor, such as refugees or Holocaust survivors, are at greater risk for adverse outcomes. Disasters place a severe strain on both personal well-being and social support networks, and risk profiles differ as a function of circumstances. During a disaster, a physically and mentally healthy, community-dwelling, older adult with an active social network is vulnerable, along with the rest of the general population, but a frail, socially isolated, homebound older person of the same age may be extremely vulnerable.

9.3   SOCIAL NETWORKS AND CAREGIVING ISSUES

Most older adults are well integrated within their communities and have supportive family and peer networks, although family do not necessarily live close by. Unfortunately, some older adults are at significant risk for social isolation due to a combination of circumstances and choices. The term *social isolation* describes a situation in which a person has few interpersonal relationships or social roles (Keefe et al. 2006). Personal factors that can contribute to social isolation include increased likelihood of living alone at older ages, role losses, mobility problems, financial difficulties, and poor health. Social factors include changes in family structure, a highly mobile society, and trends that discourage communal living arrangements for older adults in favor of independent residency. It is essential that emergency preparedness and planning includes a component specifically targeting the minimization of disturbance, confusion, and unfamiliarity, in addition to the usual focus on physical safety, for frail elders.

Informal caregivers, such as family, neighbors, and friends, often play a critical role in helping older adults during all stages of a disaster. The extent of social embeddedness—that is, the number of members, degree of closeness, and level of activity of the older adult's social network—is related to mental health functioning. Social networks can enable practical assistance such as obtaining safe shelter, food, water, and health care. In a disaster situation, local resources, including preexisting social networks, are the first line of defense. Moreover, these social ties buffer or mitigate the negative effects of stressors and are vital to the psychological well-being of older adults. Research indicates that anticipated or perceived support and the belief that significant others care and will provide assistance if required, is predictive of better psychological outcomes following a disaster, rather than the receipt of actual assistance (Cook and Bickman 1990; Krause 2001).

However, these socially protective resources are vulnerable to disruption and decline after a disaster because many in the social network will also be victims of the same incident. Assistance is less available when property is damaged or destroyed, electricity or phone communication is lost, or daily routines are disrupted (Kaniasty and Norris 1999). Social network members may have died, relocated, or be unable to assist because their immediate needs exceed their current resources. Significant deterioration of the social support system can result in adverse short- and long-term psychological consequences (Kaniasty and Norris 1993). Compounding the situation, destruction and disruption of local infrastructure diminishes the availability of social support through religious organizations and community-based services. As a result, the need for support and services for all disaster survivors may surpass availability of existing resources. In the ensuing shortage, support needs of older adults are likely to go unmet. To offset potential mental health problems, provisions for preparing, responding, and recovering from a disaster must be adequate. While social networks are depleted, first responders and relief workers can provide temporary support and assistance in rebuilding informal support systems.

An aging population, strained health care resources, and a preference toward "aging at home" contribute to the trend for increasing numbers of older adults with functional and cognitive impairments to receive community-based care (Markle-Reid et al. 2008). A 2002 Health Canada report stated that approximately 933,000 people in Canada provide care to family members with functional limitations due to disability, or age-related declines in functioning or illness resulting in frailty (Health Canada 2002). The demand on family caregivers, who are predominantly women, will only increase. The implications of this situation for emergency management are multifaceted. For example, assuming the greater response community is representative of the general population, more than 20 percent of health care, public health, and disaster management professionals over age forty-five could have family caregiving responsibilities above and beyond normal demands of day-to-day life (O'Sullivan 2009). Emergency respite care for those with significant supervision and care needs is an important instrumental and emotional support mechanism for families that should be planned in advance of a disaster (O'Sullivan 2009).

For some older adults, acute injuries, dangerous evacuations, unfamiliar surroundings, and altered routines serve as precipitants for a host of adverse physical and mental health outcomes that in many instances hasten death. The fact that only 10 percent of Hurricane Katrina fatalities were 45 years of age and younger, and that the average age of Katrina victims was 69, highlights the increased vulnerability of this population (Brunkard, Namulanda, and Ratard 2008). Many of these survivors experience a lasting legacy of negative social, economic, and mental health consequences. To avoid similar outcomes in future disasters, it is imperative to have policies and programs in place, along with a cadre of well-trained health professionals who are knowledgeable about geriatric issues and disaster behavioral health.

9.4   DISASTER TRAINING AND THE GERIATRIC HEALTH CARE WORKFORCE

Recent reviews, conducted in both Canada and the United States, of the current status and antici-pated need for geriatric health care professionals, reveal a woefully inadequate workforce that is generally not prepared to meet the needs of a growing older adult population. This concern has motivated remedial efforts by the Geriatric Preparedness and Response (GEPR) Collaborative in the United States (Howe 2010) and the Public Health Agency of Canada (PHAC 2008a, 2008b). In 2008, the Institute of Medicine (IOM) Committee on the Future Health Care Workforce for Older Americans released the report, "Retooling for an Aging America: Building the Health Care Workforce." This report documented the health care needs of Americans 65 years of age and older and provided recommendations regarding how best to address these needs through workforce devel-opment, including education and training, models of care, and public and private programs (IOM 2008). The IOM report warned that to maintain the current ratio of providers to elders, by 2030 an additional three and a half million health care workers will be needed—a 35 percent increase from current levels. This report served as a helpful foundation for understanding geriatric health workforce shortages; however, it focused only minimally on the unique aspects of the geriatric mental and behavioral health workforce. In response to this lack of focus on mental health, several organizations, including the American Psychological Association, the American Association for Geriatric Psychiatry, the National Association of Social Workers, and the American Psychiatric Association, joined together to urge policy makers to support a follow-up study related specifically to the geriatric mental health workforce. In 2010, following more than a year of advocacy, Congress designated funds for an IOM study focused on the geriatric mental health workforce. The mental health and aging community is now awaiting official announcement of committee member assign-ments from the IOM.

A number of professional associations are working actively on a variety of additional initiatives to address these concerns. In the United States, psychologists have developed core competencies for geropsychology training and recently established geropsychology as a specialty in professional psy-chology (American Psychological Association 2008). Psychiatrists who wish to be board certified in geriatric psychiatry are required to pass an examination with questions specific to geriatric psy-chiatry (American Association for Geriatric Psychiatry 2004). Nearly one-third (32 percent) of mas-ter's of social work programs offer gerontology specialization (Council on Social Work Education 2007). However, only one percent of all registered nurses are certified as gerontological nurses, and the number of geriatricians continues to slowly decrease as the demand for their services steadily increase (Hartford Geriatric Nursing Initiative nd; American Geriatrics Society 2010).

In Canada, there are limited academic opportunities for geropsychology training (Konnert, Dobson, and Watt 2009). Most schools of social work include education on geriatrics in the cur-riculum. Specialty designation does not apply in professional psychology or social work. Specialty designations are applied in Canada in the fields of geriatric psychiatry (Royal College of Physicians and Surgeons of Canada; http://rcpsc.medical.org) and gerontology nursing (Canadian Nurses Association; http://www.cna-nurses.ca/cna/nursing/certification/specialties/default_e.aspx). In all mental health fields, demand for practitioners with training in care of older adults is significantly greater than supply. Estimates in 2006 called attention to the need for more than 500 geriatricians to meet the existing demand in Canada versus the current availability of fewer than 200 practitioners (Torrible et al. 2006). This gap has not diminished during the past five years and will continue to grow in light of the predicted population changes described earlier in the chapter.

Because nearly all health professionals at some point in their career will provide care to older adults, core competencies should be established for all disciplines, and training in geriatric mental health should be a component of all training programs. It is widely acknowledged that an insufficient number of training programs offer specialized education in geriatrics and gerontology and that relatively small numbers of health care professionals are pursuing careers in this area, resulting in immediate shortages of providers and future shortages of faculty (Eldercare Workforce Alliance 2009). Fortunately, there are an increasing number of professional efforts to educate policy makers, faculty, students, and clinicians about the importance of a well-trained geriatric workforce. Specifically, in the United States, the Eldercare Workforce Alliance (EWA) is a group of 28 organizations that joined together in 2008 to address this concern and other related workforce challenges (Eldercare Workforce Alliance 2009). EWA, which is supported by member contributions and grant funding from the Atlantic Philanthropies and the John A. Hartford Foundation, represents health professionals across disciplines, direct care workers, caregivers, and consumers. EWA partners worked together throughout the health reform legislative process to successfully secure key provisions in the new law to enhance and expand federal geriatric education and training programs. These organizations are continuing to work collaboratively to ensure appropriate implementation of the new law and advocating for additional related policy priorities.

In Canada, the National Initiative for Care of the Elderly (NICE) was funded in 2005 under a grant from the Canadian government's Networks of Centres of Excellence. Through partnerships with universities, industry, the federal government, organizations, and institutions, NICE is facilitating initiatives to improve the image of caring for seniors and to attract people to the field. With a financial contribution from Health Canada on behalf of the Geriatric Education and Recruitment Initiative (GERI), NICE and partners are developing and/or promoting core competencies in the areas of geriatric medicine, psychiatry, nursing, social work, and interdisciplinary practice, which will be distributed to key curriculum-development stakeholders to advocate for the inclusion of these competencies into basic curricula.

Just as there are inadequate numbers of clinicians trained to provide mental health care to older adults, there are even fewer who are also trained to provide disaster mental health care. This is a missed opportunity because the access to patients that health care professionals have across a wide range of health care settings uniquely positions them to contribute to emergency preparedness activities (Markenson, DiMaggio, and Redlener 2005). Although not widely recognized, professional responsibility can include supporting development of contingency plans in the event of the potential loss of critical services (medications, power to run medical equipment, active intervention [e.g., chemotherapy, radiation], health maintenance monitoring) for people who require these services (Buckner 2009).

Supply and demand dictates that a health promotion focus in disaster preparedness is essential to supplement the limited capacity for direct intervention that is available through primary and secondary care (Hobfoll et al. 2007). National organizations with specific health care and/or patient population interests can facilitate this focus. For example, in Canada the National Association for Home Care & Hospice (NAHC) Emergency Preparedness Workgroup was established to develop an all-hazards emergency preparedness plan to be used by home care and hospice providers (NAHC 2008). The Canadian Pharmacists Association notes that pharmacists are among the most accessible health care professionals, and they should capitalize on this attribute to help older adults prepare for the worst (Weir 2007).

In 1991 in the United States, a Statement of Understanding between the American Psychological Association and the American Red Cross established the Disaster Response Network (DRN). State psychological associations manage the local disaster response programs. The purpose of the DRN is to provide a mechanism for psychologists to provide volunteer assistance to relief workers and survivors after disasters in the United States and territories. All DRN psychologists have to complete a series of American Red Cross courses before serving in the field (American Psychological Association nd). In Canada, provincial psychological associations have developed similar initiatives, partnered with the Canadian Red Cross (Ontario Psychological Association nd).

It is increasingly evident that sustainable disaster mitigation requires collaboration among all sectors within the community. The health sector has a significant role to play in directly reducing the risks to its facilities, staff, and patients, as well as in advocating for mitigation efforts in the community that reduce the harmful effects of disasters on the older population (Lindsay 2003). The 2003 severe acute respiratory syndrome (SARS) outbreaks in Canada provided an impetus for research on the emergency preparedness of frontline health care providers (Amaratunga et al. 2008b). Lessons were learned in many aspects of emergency management, including surge capacity, infection control, and risk communication. New knowledge is reflected in the evolution of pandemic response plans at federal, provincial, and local (institutional and community) levels, but gaps persist, warranting ongoing attention and development in this area. For example, 92.9 percent of nurses in one study reported feeling unprepared for another large-scale infectious outbreak (Amaratunga et al. 2008a).

9.4.1 GERONTOLOGICAL TRAINING FOR RELIEF WORKERS AND FIRST RESPONDERS

Currently, there is a need for disaster behavioral health training for relief workers and disaster responders that includes information about the specific needs and concerns of older adults (Brown et. al. 2010). Most important is an increased awareness of the heterogeneity, diversity, and strengths of the older population from a lifespan perspective. This includes understanding how aspects of the social and physical environment can exacerbate or attenuate stress, particularly for the most vulnerable segment of the older adult population—those who are frail and cognitively impaired (Brown, Shiang, and Bongar 2003).

Understanding the heterogeneity of the older population requires recognition that changing social forces and health care advances have improved the overall physical and mental functioning of younger seniors, and successive cohorts are demonstrating health levels that are comparable to that of younger people from earlier cohorts. A growing body of evidence shows that most people maintain their everyday intelligence, learning potential, and language ability while developing wisdom and high levels of emotional intelligence as they age. In addition, a majority of older adults demonstrate self-plasticity in terms of their ability to maintain subjective reports of good physical and mental health in the face of loss and physical decline (Baltes and Smith 2003). Nonetheless, there is considerable evidence that in late old age, people generally experience significant declines in physical and mental health, and in very late old age, declines are almost universal. Dementia becomes increasingly prevalent with increasing age, characterized by significant impairment in a range of cognitive domains, including memory, executive functioning, attention, concentration, and language ability. In addition, previously established stability and gains in emotionality and subjective well-being are shown to decline across the later stages of old age (Baltes and Smith 2003).

Another age-related concept that may be particularly important for responders to understand is that older persons may have a different perception on the relative value of both symbolic and material losses (Cox 2006), including attachment to place (Stefanovic 2003) that can be related to their stage in the life cycle. Relief workers may need education and assistance to combat the common tendency to avoid or minimize end-of-life issues. Time itself is related to this issue. The older one is, the more compressed one's timeline for disaster recovery, often with a reduced set of social and material resources (Gibson 2007). Also critical is an understanding that over time, cumulative challenges—including physical, cognitive, and socioeconomic losses—may progressively deplete the aging person's capacity for resilience. Declines in self-reported psychological distress and self-reported well-being that are observed in younger cohorts of seniors begin to reverse in middle old age (75 years and older) and one's sense of mastery (i.e., the level of control a person feels they have over their life) declines with age (Turcotte and Schellenberg 2007).

An understanding of behavioral health and gerontology is helpful for interpreting the inconclusive evidence about how older adults cope during disasters. Some research suggests that older age may buffer disaster impact (Phillips et al. 2009). The inoculation hypothesis refers to the concept of a lifetime of experience and coping strategies when facing a disaster (Norris et al. 2002; Norris, Friedman, and Watson 2002). In general, research supports the premise that during disasters, older adults typically fare better in terms of emotional and psychological functioning when compared to younger adults (Huerta and Horton 1978; Phifer 1990; Thompson, Norris, and Hanacek 1993; Verger et al. 2004). For example, researchers cited decreased distress and increased protective actions for older adults during the Three Mile Island disaster (Prince-Embury and Rooney 1988, 1990). At the same time, effects are mixed. A World Health Organization (WHO) review of seniors' issues during four Canadian disasters revealed that emotional stress was a major health effect for many older adults and that risky behaviors contributed to injuries (WHO 2008). However, many seniors attributed positive as well as negative outcomes to their disaster experience. In reflecting upon these diverse outcomes older adults report after disasters, it is important to recall the heterogeneity that exists within this population. Sources of resilience and risk factors for disproportionate vulnerability will vary within the population of older adults. Consider that healthy older adults are essentially similar to the general population in terms of needs and resources—community-dwelling older adults with functional needs require assistance in preparing and recovering, and frail, institutionalized older adults with very limited functional reserves depend heavily on existing emergency and health care systems to remain safe and secure.

9.5 DISASTER MENTAL HEALTH INTERVENTION WITH OLDER ADULTS

Geriatric health care providers, relief workers, and first responders are called upon in disasters to meet not only physical but mental health needs of older adults who have been affected by the event. Psychological First Aid (PFA) is a broadly applicable intervention supported by a skill set that should cross disciplinary boundaries. Crisis counseling and clinical intervention has a more circumscribed application. Crisis counseling may be offered to disaster-affected populations who need more than PFA to facilitate their behavioral health recovery. These programs may be offered by state-administered federally funded programs or by nongovernment organizations, such as senior centers, churches, and area agencies on aging. Other organizations, such as the Veterans Health Administration and nursing homes, may elect to augment their existing services with disaster intervention that is tailored to the needs of their clients. Intervention in general should be informed by a sound understanding of how older age and disasters intersect with mental health conditions and disorders, particularly trauma reactions, dementia, and delirium (Rothman and Brown 2007).

9.5.1 PSYCHOLOGICAL FIRST AID

In the United States, PFA is a set of actions that is now widely taught by the American Red Cross (ARC) and the Medical Reserve Corps (MRC) to relief workers who provide care to affected populations in the immediate aftermath of a disaster. Founded in 2002, the MRC, along with the Peace Corps and Citizen Corps, is part of the president's USA Freedom Corps. Each community-based MRC organizes volunteer medical professionals and others related disciplines, including psychology, to prepare for and respond to disasters (Medical Reserve Corps nd). The overarching goal of PFA is to reduce distress and increase adaptive coping. Information about older adults (e.g., potential risk factors, strengths, common health problems) should be included in standard PFA training. PFA training could also provide a forum where stereotypes and myths about old age could be confronted and countered. In fact, it may be the only time when mental health professionals as well as public health and disaster relief workers are educated about common health conditions and issues affecting older adults.

For example, one in three people aged 60 and older and half of those aged 85 and older have hearing loss (National Institute of Deafness and Other Communication Disorders 2001). Relief workers providing PFA should be aware that some older adults may have hearing problems that may adversely affect their ability to benefit from the intervention. Some may require encouragement to use their hearing aids or accept use of a portable amplifying device. Speaking clearly while facing a hearing impaired person will also aid them in reading lips and facial expressions. Additionally, if there are questions about a person's ability to follow directions and receive needed help independently, some older adults may require assessment of cognitive status. A mental status exam or questions to assess orientation may be necessary to detect presence of cognitive impairment. People without preexisting cognitive impairment who show signs of cognitive dysfunction in the aftermath of a disaster should be referred for further evaluation to rule out the presence of medical illness, heat stroke, delirium, drug mismanagement, and other conditions that may require immediate treatment.

Delivery of PFA should be nonintrusive—that is, if done correctly, the person receiving PFA should be unaware that the provider is using PFA techniques to help them maintain function and to foster psychological well-being. Because it is normal for most people to have strong reactions to abnormal events, like a disaster, PFA allows individuals to share as little or as much about the incident and their feelings as they desire. To avoid pathologizing thoughts, feelings, and behaviors in the immediate postdisaster period, no formal psychological assessments are used and people are not diagnosed with mental disorders. In instances where the application of PFA appears inadequate, follow-up evaluation is conducted to determine if there may be an underlying issue, such as a preexisting mental or physical illness, that is contributing to the poor outcome and requires medical or psychiatric intervention.

Although a growing number of relief workers have been trained to use PFA, because disasters are a low base-rate event and learned skills deteriorate over time if not used regularly, it is unknown how PFA skills are actually used after a disaster. Skills that are rarely used, as for nonhealth professionals who are trained in cardiopulmonary resuscitation, often require recertification training. At present, PFA recertification classes are not offered or required. Further, formal studies of PFA with disaster-exposed populations have not been conducted and the efficacy of the intervention has not been scientifically established. What is known is that PFA as an evidenced-based practice differs from crisis counseling in respect to who is treated and type of treatment (Brown et al. 2009). For more information and a description about use of PFA in nursing homes, see Chapter 14, this volume.

9.5.2 Crisis Counseling

Although older adults, like younger adults, benefit from crisis counseling, the attitudes and beliefs of the providers and recipients alike may hinder delivery and acceptance of services. For a comprehensive discussion regarding personal and system barriers and facilitators to use of disaster mental health services, see Chapter 21, this volume on social marketing. Notably, transportation issues are an often-neglected but crucial infrastructure issue for emergencies and disasters (Scanlon 2003), which is uniquely nuanced for both those who live in areas that are underserved by public transit and for health care providers who serve these populations. In damaged communities, older adults may be forced to seek treatment and obtain life-sustaining supplies and medication outside the area. Programs need to be in place to coordinate services among agencies providing care, identify community-dwelling residents who might be in need of such services, and assist with transportation needs. Physical, cognitive, and sensory impairments that impede planning and mobility may adversely affect access to services and material goods, such as food and water, from disaster assistance centers. Lack of transportation is a significant barrier to use of crisis counseling programs. In rural communities or in areas without a well-developed public transportation system, it may be impossible to use services even when offered for free (Brown, Cohen, and Kohlmaier 2007).

In some instances, crisis counseling services may have to be modified to accommodate health and mental health issues (Brown, Rothman, and Norris 2007). For example, older adults who are profoundly depressed may benefit more from behavioral than cognitive intervention in the early stages of treatment. Incorporating pleasant activities into their daily schedule and monitoring mood may be particularly useful. As their cognitive processing becomes more efficient in later sessions, traditional talking therapy approaches can be added. Referral to community providers should be made if the number of sessions provided by the crisis counseling program is inadequate to facilitate recovery.

Additionally, the extent of the intervention in some instances should be shortened or lengthened to accommodate the needs of the older person. For example, residents seen in a nursing home setting may only be able to tolerate brief sessions. Because the clinician comes to the facility to provide treatment, it may be possible to have short, frequent sessions without causing an undue burden on the resident. In situations where transportation is limited, the length of the session might actually be increased depending on the preference and ability of the older person to fully use the session time. To reduce barriers to crisis counseling, some providers have offered intervention in the homes of older adults and in community centers and libraries. Notably, different crisis counseling programs have varying restrictions on the number or length of sessions that can be offered to people affected by a disaster.

9.5.3 MENTAL CONDITIONS AND DISORDERS

There are adults in all age groups for whom health problems and disorders exacerbate life's challenges on an ongoing basis. Exposure to traumatic events, such as disasters, represents a unique stressor that has its impact within the context of a person's ongoing mental health status. In addition, some disorders with significant cognitive and behavioral symptoms become increasingly likely with age, particularly dementia and delirium. It is important that disaster preparedness and planning is informed by at least a basic understanding of each of these issues—trauma, dementia, and delirium—as they present in the older adult population.

9.5.3.1 Trauma Reactions

Trauma reactions may present differently in older adults (Busuttil 2004). More somatic symptoms are common, as are medical and psychological comorbidities. Moreover, there may be salient differences in the natural course of posttraumatic stress disorder (PTSD) in later life (Averill and Beck 2000). Developmental factors (e.g., maturity, perspective, reduced timeline for recovery) can increase resilience as well as vulnerability depending on the context in which a trauma occurs and its aftermath (Averill and Beck 2000). Many people have more than one traumatic experience in the course of a lifetime. Thus, consideration of the impact of trauma on older adults needs to take into account both the cumulative effect of trauma exposure across the lifespan (Busuttil 2004) and the possibility that traumatic experiences may have different effects depending on when they occur during the life course (Krause, Shaw, and Cairney 2004).

9.5.3.2 Delirium

Delirium is a medical emergency (Hogan et al. 2006). It presents as a sudden change in mental function. Persons with delirium may fade in and out of consciousness, have difficulty paying attention, and are disoriented and sometimes delusional. Causes are diverse and include heat stroke, drug interactions, infections, a failure in diabetes management, and uncontrolled pain. Older adults are highly susceptible to delirium when their health status is compromised. Although delirium is treatable, it often goes unrecognized, especially in older adults where the symptoms may be misinterpreted as part of an ongoing dementia. Left untreated, delirium is associated with increased risk of morbidity and mortality. Older adults who do not have a familiar caregiver to advocate for them and identify the sudden onset of cognitive and behavioral changes may be at particular risk of failing to receive appropriate medical attention.

9.5.3.3 Dementia

Dementia is a progressively debilitating neurological syndrome associated with an increasing loss of memory and other intellectual functions that interferes with the ability to perform daily activities and represents a decline from previous functioning (American Psychiatric Association

2000). There are many diseases that result in dementia, the most common of which is Alzheimer's disease. Alzheimer's disease is a progressive, irreversible disease characterized by memory loss and brain degeneration. Worldwide, an estimated 29.8 million people suffer from dementia; by the year 2050, the number is expected to nearly triple to 81.1 million (Alzheimer's Society 2009). Dementia becomes increasingly common with advanced age (Chertkow 2007). Half a million Canadians and as many as 2.4 million to 5.1 million Americans are estimated to have Alzheimer's disease or a related dementia (Alzheimer's Society of Canada 2010; National Institute on Aging nd).

There is substantial literature on dementia care that documents the importance of a supportive physical and social environment to maintain the delicate equilibrium of older adults with dementia. Much is known about how to avoid escalation of problem behaviors, emotional distress, and cognitive deterioration through consistent, responsive care provided by familiar caregivers who are versed in the strategies and nuances of dementia care and psychogeriatrics (Conn and Gibson 2007). Unfortunately, the urgency, unpredictability, and chaos associated with emergencies and disasters create the antithesis of this environment.

9.6 ACTIVITIES OF INTERNATIONAL ORGANIZATIONS

Although our primary focus herein has been on disaster mental health issues in the Canadian and American context, it is important to recognize that there is a growing international concern with the well-being of older adults in disaster situations. Canadian and American interests are interwoven with those of the global community. We highlight the activities of three major international organizations to illustrate this broader context.

According to HelpAge International (HAI), by the year 2045 people aged 60 and older will outnumber children aged 14 and younger worldwide (HAI 2010). HAI was established in 1983 and now has more than 80 affiliates worldwide. Although their general mission is to promote healthy, dignified aging and to ensure that older people have the same right to health care, social services, and economic and physical security as younger adults, a particular focus of the organization is on disasters (HAI 2010). One of the ten actions to end age discrimination identified by HAI is to include and consult older people in emergency aid and rehabilitation planning after disasters and humanitarian crises (HAI 2001). Research by HAI (2006) demonstrates that mainstreaming older adults' distinct issues within emergency management is an essential strategy to combat the systemic neglect of older persons in emergency situations.

The WHO has an increasing focus on older adults in general, including older adults and disasters. Among the many documents available from WHO that reflect this interest, we highlight two recent reports that were developed with support from the Public Health Agency of Canada (PHAC; Hutton 2008; WHO 2008). Hutton (2008) provides a situational analysis of older people in emergencies, leading to recommendations for the development of policies and practices to enhance emergency health planning and programming for older people (Hutton 2008). The WHO (2008) technical report includes an integrated strategy for emergency preparedness and response that is grounded in the WHO Active Ageing Policy Framework (World Health Organization 2002). Recommendations speak to both universal (nonage-specific) and distinct age-related issues in emergency situations. Psychosocial issues are included among other concerns (e.g., nutrition, mobility, livelihoods).

The Inter-Agency Standing Committee (IASC) consists of 21 organizations, including WHO, PHAC, HAI, whose mission is to develop policy and facilitate coordination of humanitarian relief efforts in response to complex disasters. A recent report emphasized the importance of conducting outreach to isolated older people during disasters (IASC 2008). Key barriers to services included limited literacy or language limiting older adults' ability to use available resources and understand public information to avoid risks and access care.

Research suggests that despite international protocols, seniors are given low priority and little attention during emergencies (HAI 2006). Ageism is implicated in this observation. *The*

Encyclopedia of Aging (Maddox 1995, 35) defines ageism as "a process of systematic stereotyping and discrimination against people because they are old, just as racism and sexism accomplish this for skin color and gender." The paradox of ageism is that people have acquired an enduring, prejudicial set of beliefs about a population that most of us are eventually destined to join (Hansson 1989).

Ageism serves to perpetuate stereotypic and negative views of older adults, resulting in inequities in access to opportunities and resources. One result can be that older adults are systematically confronted with greater challenges under adverse circumstances than are younger adults, despite their increased vulnerability due to normal aging processes. For example, if older adults are expected to show poorer recovery after a disaster, they may receive substandard care and fewer resources, resulting in their degree of recovery falling below their potential.

9.7 CONCLUSION

Since the events of September 11, 2001, in the United States, billions of federal dollars have been allocated to enhance the public health infrastructure. The goal has been to develop an agile health care system that is poised to respond appropriately and expeditiously to a spectrum of threats ranging from natural disasters to human-made events. Thus, much of the funding has been directed to efforts focused on improving response of hospital preparedness and traditional emergency response organizations (i.e., police, fire, emergency operation centers), with less consideration given to the development and delivery of evidence-based behavioral health programs. Despite these improvements, as evidenced by recent hurricanes, floods, and tornados, there clearly remain gaps in our ability to effectively respond with and provide needed mental health services to older adults.

The 2005 hurricanes along the gulf coast of the United States left more than 1,500 dead and 780,000 displaced (FEMA, 2010). While these disasters affected people across the lifespan, older adults were disproportionately affected by Hurricane Katrina. In particular, because of the well-publicized deaths of nursing home residents following Hurricanes Katrina and Rita, the general public and key stakeholders are more aware of the challenges encountered by institutionalized older adults during disasters (Elmore and Brown 2007). Carefully framed policies can foster a crucial balance between funding popular initiatives geared toward strengthening systems to enhance homeland security and supporting the needs of organizations responsible for providing direct care, including behavioral health treatment, to vulnerable elders after disasters. Additional policy efforts are necessary to safeguard the health and well-being of older adults who have been adversely affected by disasters.

Recent hurricanes clearly demonstrated that older adults make up the subgroup of our population at greatest risk for increased morbidity and mortality. AARP reported that of the 1,200 deaths associated with Hurricane Katrina, 75 percent were aged 60 years and older. Further, in the year following the storm, overall morbidity in a sample of older adult Katrina survivors increased by 12.6 percent compared to a 3.4 percent increase among a nondisaster-exposed national sample of elders. As compelling as these finding are, the United States lacks a coordinated, federally funded program to address the needs of older adults who have experienced traumatic events, including disasters. Such successful programs have been established in the United States to focus on the needs of children who have experienced trauma, most notably the highly successful National Child Traumatic Stress Initiative. In 2001, more than $30 million was made available by the Center for Mental Health Services, SAMSHA, and the U.S. Department of Health and Human Services to establish the National Child Traumatic Stress Network. The overarching goals of the Network are to "improve access to care, treatment, and services for children and adolescents exposed to traumatic events and to encourage and promote collaboration between service providers in the field" (National Child Traumatic Stress Network 2010). Older adults would benefit from a similar dedicated program focused on aging and disasters.

One relevant legislative proposal that has been developed in the United States is the *Public Mental Health Emergency Preparedness Act of 2007* (S. 1452 – 110th Congress). This legislation recommends the establishment of a National Center for Public Mental Health Emergency Preparedness to prepare for and address the immediate and long-term mental health needs of the general population and potentially vulnerable subgroups, including older adults, children, individuals with disabilities, individuals with preexisting mental health problems, caregivers, and individuals living in poverty. The Center's activities would include developing and disseminating training curricula for emergency mental health professionals, establishing a clearinghouse of mental health emergency resources, organizing an annual national forum on mental health emergency preparedness and response, and ensuring the inclusion of mental health professionals within disaster medical assistance teams (Elmore and Brown 2007).

Rather than solely investing in programs in response to specific disasters, only to discontinue the programmatic activities and marketing of products once a dedicated amount of time or funding is depleted, more benefit may be gained from a sustained investment in public mental health preparedness and response for older adults. Such coordinated initiatives focused on the needs of vulnerable populations, including older adults, would serve as an invaluable resource to policy makers, public health entities, government agencies, nonprofit organizations, and the constituents these entities serve.

The Canadian Disaster Database (http://www.publicsafety.gc.ca) includes information on more than 700 natural, technological, and conflict events (excluding war) that Canada has experienced over the past century. Approximately 80 percent of Canadian disasters are due to weather and weather-related events (Hwacha 2005). Flooding is Canada's most frequently occurring disaster. Canadians' vulnerability to disasters is heightened by the concentration of population in areas of high risk (seismically active regions, on coastal plains and river basins). Because Canada has a relatively small population scattered over a large country, and has fortunately not been subject to events causing extensive loss of life, there is a temptation to ignore predictable risks of potential disasters (Scanlon 2001).

Although relatively few lives have been lost in Canada due to natural disasters, significant costs have been accrued related to personal property and public infrastructure damage (Hwacha 2005). In recent years, the Saguenay River flood (1996), the Red River flood (1997), and the Eastern Canadian Ice Storm (1998) affected approximately 20 percent of the Canadian population, cost the Canadian government approximately $266 million in disaster financial assistance payments, and provided the impetus for the government to embark on a major initiative to reduce vulnerability through an increased focus on disaster mitigation efforts.

While much remains to be done, it is notable that vulnerable populations, including older adults, have been a priority in this effort. Since 2006, the Public Health Agency of Canada (PHAC), Division of Aging and Seniors (DAS), has spearheaded efforts to create new partnerships among the gerontology and emergency management sectors both nationally and internationally. DAS serves as a central coordinating body for three international working groups on older adults and emergency management, focused on seniors and emergency issues in the domains of health care (health professionals and continuity of care), integration (seniors' contributions and seniors' issues in emergency management planning), and policy (age-friendly principles and procedures).

In both the United States and Canada, it remains to be seen to what extent the disaster preparedness, response, recovery, and mitigation issues faced by the aging baby boomer generation can be met through existing initiatives. Significant political will is necessary to move beyond traditional approaches toward genuine mainstreaming of the needs of vulnerable populations within emergency management planning based on principles of inclusion and collaboration. Undoubtedly, important lessons can be learned from international counterparts to help shape the opportunities, challenges, and demand for new policies and programs in North America. A clear need exists to ensure that mental and behavioral health—in particular, the unique needs of older adults—are fully integrated into current and future disaster preparedness and response efforts.

REFERENCES

Alzheimer's Society. 2009. *Statistics.* http://www.alzheimers.org.uk/site/scripts/documents_info.php?category
ID=200120&documentID=341&pageNumber=1.

Alzheimer's Society of Canada. 2010. *Rising tide: The impact of dementia on Canadian society.* http://www.
alzheimer.ca/english/rising_tide/rising_tide_report.htm.

Amaratunga, C. A., M. Carter, T. O'Sullivan, P. Thille, K. Phillips, and R. Saunders. 2008a. *Caring for Nurses in
Public Health Emergencies: Enhancing Capacity for Gender-Based Support Mechanisms in Emergency
Preparedness Planning.* Ottawa: Canadian Policy Research Networks.

Amaratunga, C. A., M. Carter, T. L. O'Sullivan, P. Thille, K. P. Phillips, and R. Saunders. 2008b. *Lessons
Learned from Canada: The Imperative to Build a Culture of Preparedness for Health Care Providers as
First Responders.* Ottawa: Canadian Policy Research Networks.

American Association for Geriatric Psychiatry. 2004. *Health care professionals: Geriatrics and mental health –
the facts.* http://www.aagponline.org/prof/facts_mh.asp.

American Geriatrics Society, Geriatrics Workforce Policy Studies Center. 2010. *Documenting the development
of geriatric medicine.* http://www.adgapstudy.uc.edu/index.cfm.

American Psychiatric Association. 2000. *Diagnostic and Statistical Manual of Mental Disorder,* 4th ed., text
revision. Washington, DC: American Psychiatric Association.

American Psychological Association. 2008. Presidential Task Force on integrated health care for an aging population. *Blueprint for Change: Achieving Integrated Health Care for an Aging Population.* Washington,
DC: Author.

American Psychological Association. nd. *Disaster response network: Helping communities in times of crisis.*
http://www.apa.org/practice/programs/drn/brochure.pdf.

Averill, P. M., and J. G. Beck. 2000. Posttraumatic stress disorder in older adults: A conceptual review. *Journal
of Anxiety Disorders 14*(2): 133–156.

Baltes, P. B., and J. Smith. 2003. New frontiers in the future of aging: From successful aging of the young old
to the dilemmas of the fourth age. *Gerontology 49*(2): 123–135.

Brown, L. M., M. L. Bruce, K. Hyer, W. L. Mills, E. Vongxaiburana, and L. Polivka-West. 2009. A pilot study
evaluating the feasibility of psychological first aid for nursing home residents. *Clinical Gerontologist
32*(3): 293–308.

Brown, L. M., D. Cohen, and J. Kohlmaier. 2007. Older adults and terrorism. In *Psychology of Terrorism*, eds.
B. Bongar, L. M. Brown., L. Beutler, P. Zimbardo, and J. Breckenridge, 288–310. New York: Oxford
University Press.

Brown, L. M., E. Hickling, and K. A. Frahm. 2010. Emergencies, disasters, and catastrophic events: The role
of rehabilitation nurses in preparedness, response and recovery. *Rehabilitation Nursing 35*(6): 236–241.

Brown, L. M., K. Hyer, J. A. Schinka, A. Mando, D. Frazier, and L. Polivka-West. 2010. Use of mental health
services by nursing home residents after hurricanes. *Psychiatric Services 61*(1): 74–77.

Brown, L. M., M. Rothman, and F. Norris. 2007. Issues in mental health care for older adults during disasters.
Generations 31(4): 25–30.

Brown, L. M., J. Shiang, and B. Bongar. 2003. Crisis intervention: Theory and practice. In *Comprehensive
Handbook of Psychology, Volume 8: Clinical Psychology*, eds. G. Stricker and T. A. Widiger, 431–451.
New York: John Wiley & Sons, Inc.

Brunkard, J., G. Namulanda, and R. Ratard. 2008. Hurricane Katrina deaths, Louisiana, 2005.
Louisiana Department of Health and Hospitals. http://www.dhh.louisiana.gov/offices/reports.
asp?ID=192&Detail=207.

Buckner, A. V. 2009. The role of clinicians in preparing patients for disasters. *Medscape Public Health and
Prevention.* http://www.medscape.com/viewarticle/709697_print.

Busuttil, W. 2004. Presentations and management of post traumatic stress disorder and the elderly: A need for
investigation. *International Journal of Geriatric Psychiatry 19*(5): 429–439.

Chertkow, H. 2007. Introduction: The third Canadian consensus conference on the diagnosis and treatment of dementia, 2006. *Alzheimer's & Dementia: The Journal of the Alzheimer's Association 3*(4):
262–265.

Conn, D. K., and M. Gibson. 2007. Guidelines for the assessment and treatment of mental health issues in
long-term care homes. In *Practical Psychiatry in the Long Term Care Home: A Handbook for Staff*, eds.
D. K. Conn, N. Herrmann, A. Kaye, D. Rewilak, and B. Schogt, 3rd ed., 267–278. Toronto: Hogrefe &
Huber.

Cook, J. D., and L. Bickman. 1990. Social support and psychological symptomatology following a natural
disaster. *Journal of Traumatic Stress 3*(4): 541–556.

Council on Social Work Education. 2007. *2006 Statistics on social work education in the United States: A summary.* http://www.eldercareworkforce.org/images/PDF/Fact%20Sheet.pdf.

Cox, R. 2006. Older persons in emergency and disaster situations: A case study of British Columbia's firestorm 2003. Unpublished manuscript.

Eldercare Workforce Alliance. 2009. *Caring for America's growing older adult population: Eldercare workforce facts.* http://www.eldercareworkforce.org/images/PDF/Fact%20Sheet.pdf.

Elmore, D. L., and L. M. Brown. 2007. Emergency preparedness and response: Health and social policy implications for older adults. *Generations 31*(4): 59–67.

Federal Emergency Management Agency. 2010. *Declared disasters by year or state.* http://www.fema.gov/news/disaster_totals_annual.fema.

Gibson, M. 2007. Psychosocial issues pertaining to seniors in emergencies. Unpublished manuscript.

Hansson, R. O. 1989. Old age: Testing the parameters of social psychological assumptions. In *The Social Psychology of Aging*, eds. S. Spacapan, S. Oskamp, and C. A. Newbury, 25–52. Newbury, CA: Sage.

Hartford Geriatric Nursing Initiative. nd. *An aging patient population: The challenge for nursing.* http://www.hgni.org/aging.html.

Health Canada. 2002. *National profile of family caregivers in Canada.* http://www.hc-sc.gc.ca/hcs-sss/pubs/home-domicile/2002-caregiv-interven/index-eng.php.

HelpAge International. 2001. *Equal treatment equal rights: Ten actions to end age discrimination.* http://silverinnings.com/docs/Facts%20n%20Issues/Equal%20Treatment.PDF.

HelpAge International. 2006. Neglect in emergencies. *Ageing and Development 19*(1). http://www.helpage.org/resources/publications/?adv=1&ssearch=&filter=f.yeard&type=&region=&topic=3&language=&page=4.

HelpAge International. 2010. *Strategy to 2015: When older people speak up we listen.* http://www.helpage.org/Resources/AnnualReview/main_content/wz0b/Strategy2015.pdf.

Hobfoll, S. E., P. Watson, C. C. Bell, et al. 2007. Five essential elements of immediate and mid-term mass trauma intervention: Empirical evidence. *Psychiatry 70*(4): 283–315; discussion 316–369.

Hogan, D. B., L. Gage, V. Bruto, et al. 2006. National guidelines for seniors' mental health: The assessment and treatment of delirium. *Canadian Journal of Geriatrics 9*(S2): S42–S51.

Howe, J. L. 2010. The Geriatric Preparedness and Response (GEPR) Collaborative: A successful and productive network. In *Geriatric Mental Health Disaster and Emergency Preparedness*, eds. J. A. Toner, T. M. Mierswa, and J. L. Howe, 47–63. New York: Springer.

Huerta, F., and R. Horton. 1978. Coping behavior of elderly flood victims. *The Gerontologist 18*(6): 541–546.

Hutton, D. 2008. *Older Persons and Emergencies: Considerations for Policy and Action.* Geneva: World Health Organization.

Hwacha, V. 2005. Canada's experience in developing a national disaster mitigation strategy: A deliberative dialogue approach. *Mitigation and Adaptation Strategies for Global Change 10*(3): 507–523.

Institute on Medicine (IOM). 2008. *Retooling for an aging America: Building the health care workforce.* http://www.iom.edu/Reports/2008/Retooling-for-an-Aging-America-Building-the-Health-Care-Workforce.aspx.

Inter-Agency Standing Committee (IASC). 2008. *Humanitarian action and older persons: An essential brief for humanitarian actors.* http://www.humanitarianinfo.org/iasc/pageloader.aspx?page=content-products-common&tempid=94.

Kaniasty, K., and F. H. Norris. 1993. A test of the support deterioration model in the context of natural disaster. *Journal of Personality and Social Psychology 64*: 395–408.

Kaniasty, K. Z., and F. H. Norris. 1999. The experience of disaster: Individuals and communities sharing trauma. In *Response to Disaster: Psychosocial, Community, and Ecological Approaches*, eds. R. Gist and B. Lubin, 25–61. Philadelphia: Brunner/Mazel.

Keefe, J., P. Fancey, M. Andrew, and M. Hall. 2006. *A profile of social isolation in Canada.* http://www.health.gov.bc.ca.proxy2.lib.uwo.ca:2048/library/publications/year/2006/keefe_social_isolation_final_report_may_2006.pdf.

Konnert C., K. S. Dobson, and A. Watt. 2009. Geropsychology training in Canada: A survey of doctoral and internship programs. *Canadian Psychology 50*(4): 255–260.

Krause, N. 2001. Social support. In *Handbook of Aging and the Social Sciences*, eds. R. H. Binstock and L. K. George, 5th ed., 273–294. San Diego: Academic Press.

Krause, N., B. A. Shaw, and J. Cairney. 2004. A descriptive epidemiology of lifetime trauma and the physical health status of older adults. *Psychology and Aging 19*(4): 637–648.

Lindsay, J. R. 2003. The determinants of disaster vulnerability: Achieving sustainable mitigation through popu-lation health. *Natural Hazards 28*(2): 291–304.

Maddox, G. L., ed. 1995. *The Encyclopedia of Aging,* 2nd ed. New York: Springer.

Markenson, D., C. DiMaggio, and I. Redlener. 2005. Preparing health professions students for terrorism, disas-ter, and public health emergencies: Core competencies. *Academic Medicine 80*(6): 517–526.

Markle-Reid, M., G. Browne, R. Weir, A. Gafni, J. Roberts, and S. Henderson. 2008. Seniors at risk: The asso-ciation between the six-month use of publicly funded home support services and quality of life and use of health services for older people. *Canadian Journal on Aging 27*(2): 207–224.

Medical Reserve Corps. nd. *Medical Reserve Corps Fact Sheet.* http://www.medicalreservecorps.gov/File/MediaKit/MediaKit_FactSheet_English_2007.pdf.

National Association for Home Care & Hospice (NAHC). 2008. *Emergency Preparedness Packet for Home Health Agencies.* Washington, DC: NAHCH. http://www.nahc.org/regulatory/EP_Binder.pdf.

National Child Traumatic Stress Network, September 27, 2010. *The history of the NCTSN.* http://www.nctsnet.org/nccts/nav.do?pid=abt_hist.

National Institute of Deafness and Other Communication Disorders, 2001. *Hearing loss and older adults.* NIH Publication No. 01-4913. http://www.nidcd.nih.gov/health/hearing/older.asp.

National Institute on Aging. nd. *About Alzheimer's disease: Alzheimer's basics.* U.S. Department of Health & Human Services. http://www.nia.nih.gov/alzheimers/topics/alzheimers-basics.

Norris, F. H., M. J. Friedman, and P. J. Watson. 2002. 60,000 disaster victims speak: Part II. Summary and implications of the disaster mental health research. *Psychiatry 65*(3): 240–260.

Norris, F. H., M. J. Friedman, P. J. Watson, C. M. Byrne, E. Diaz, and K. Kaniasty. 2002. 60,000 disaster victims speak: Part I. An empirical review of the empirical literature, 1981–2001. *Psychiatry 65*(3): 207–239.

Ontario Psychological Association. nd. http://www.psych.on.ca/?id1=128.

O'Sullivan, T. L. 2009. Support for families coping with stroke or dementia: Special considerations for emer-gency management. *Radiation Protection Dosimetry 134*(3-4): 197–201.

Phifer, J. F. 1990. Psychological distress and somatic symptoms after natural disaster: Differential vulnerability among older adults. *Psychology and Aging 5*(3): 412–420.

Phillips, A. C., G. D. Batty, C. R. Gale, et al. 2009. Generalized anxiety disorder, major depressive disorder, and their comorbidity as predictors of all-cause and cardiovascular mortality: The Vietnam experience study. *Psychosomatic Medicine 71*: 395–403.

Prince-Embury, S., and J. F. Rooney. 1988. Psychological symptoms of residents in the aftermath of the Three Mile Island nuclear accident and restart. *Journal of General Psychology 128*(6): 779–790.

Prince-Embury, S., and J. F. Rooney. 1990. Life stage differences in resident coping with restart of the Three Mile Island nuclear generating facility. *Journal of Social Psychology 130*(6): 771–779.

Public Health Agency of Canada. 2008a. *Building a Global Framework to Address the Needs and Contributions of Older People in Emergencies.* Ottawa: Minister of Public Works and Government Services Canada. http://www.phac-aspc.gc.ca/seniors-aines/publications/pro/emergency-urgence/global-mondial/index-eng.php.

Public Health Agency of Canada. 2008b. *Second International Workshop on Seniors and Emergency Preparedness. Workshop Report.* Ottawa: PHAC. http://www.phac-aspc.gc.ca/seniors-aines/publications/pro/emergency-urgence/workshop-colloque/index-eng.php.

Rothman, M., and Brown, L. M. 2007. The vulnerable geriatric casualty: Medical needs of frail older adults during disasters. *Generations 31*(4): 20–24.

Scanlon, J. 2001. *Lessons Learned or Lessons Forgotten the Canadian Disaster Experience.* London, Ontario, Canada: Institute for Catastrophic Loss Reduction.

Scanlon, J. 2003. Transportation in emergencies: An often neglected story. *Disaster Prevention and Management 12*(5): 428–437.

Stefanovic, I. L. 2003. The contribution of philosophy to hazards assessment and decision making. *Natural Hazards 28*(2): 229–247.

Thompson, M. P., F. H. Norris, and B. Hanacek. 1993. Age differences in the psychological consequences of Hurricane Hugo. *Psychology and Aging 8*: 606–616.

Torrible, S. J., L. L. Diachun, D. B. Rolfson, A. C. Dumbrell, and D. B. Hogan. 2006. Improving recruitment into geriatric medicine in Canada: Findings and recommendations from the geriatric recruitment issues study. *Journal of the American Geriatrics Society 54*(9): 1453–1462. http://resolver.scholarsportal.info/resolve/00028614/v54i0009/1453_irigmiftgris.

Turcotte, M., and G. Schellenberg. 2007. *A Portrait of Seniors in Canada, 2006.* Ottawa: Minister of Industry.

U.S. Department of Health and Human Services (DHHS). 2000. *Healthy People 2010: Understanding and Improving Health.* 2 vols. 2nd ed. Washington, DC: U.S. Government Printing Office.

Verger, P., W. Dab, D. L. Lamping, et al. 2004. The psychological impact of terrorism: An epidemiologic study of posttraumatic stress disorder and associated factors in victims of the 1995–1996 bombings in France. *American Journal of Psychiatry 161*(8): 1384–1389.

Weir, K. 2007. Consider seniors in emergency planning. *Canadian Pharmacists Journal 140*(5): 330–331.

Wisner, B., P. Blaikie, T. Cannon, and I. Davis. 2004. *At Risk: Natural Hazards, People's Vulnerability and Disasters.* 2nd ed. London: Routledge.

World Health Organization. 2002. *Active Ageing: A Policy Framework.* Geneva: World Health Organization.

World Health Organization. 2008. *Older Persons in Emergencies: An Active Ageing Perspective.* Geneva: World Health Organization.

10 Cultural Competence in Behavioral Health Disaster Response
The Challenge, the Opportunity

Kermit A. Crawford, Mari C. Bennasar, and Lauren M. B. Mizock

CONTENTS

10.1 INTRODUCTION

A key question in the behavioral health disaster response area relates to outcome disparities. How effective are current behavioral health disaster response interventions with individuals when compared across different racial, ethnic, and cultural groups? This question emerges in the context of a substantial and developing technology of disaster behavioral health intervention (Bonanno et al. 2006). There is extensive literature on cultural competence and its application across different racial, ethnic, and cultural groups (Hernandez et al. 2009). A significant amount of research highlights a generally accepted base rate for population resilience (>60 percent) supported in the literature (Watson and Ruzek 2009). Given these bodies of work, it would be reasonable to assume that outcome disparities across racial, ethnic, and cultural differences would be negligible or even eliminated, but this is not the case. This chapter will highlight the outcome literature, the documented disparities, and the developing discipline of "cultural competence," and suggest ways to move the "technology" of behavioral health disaster response forward with more effective implementation of the cultural competence approach. It is hoped that this model, based on literature and multiple response experiences by the authors, will lead to significant reductions and/or elimination of outcome disparities for racial, ethnic, and cultural minority groups in the aftermath of disaster.

There have historically been significant disparities across racial, ethnic, and cultural minority groups, and they continue to be measured (Adams and Boscarino 2005; Boscarino, Adams, and Figley 2004; Galea et al. 2004; Norris and Alegria 2006; Sastry and Van Landingham 2009). It is important to acknowledge that disparities are not the sole province of racial and ethnic minority groups in the United States. Outcome disparities exist across many demographic groups (i.e., gender, age, disability status, low income, etc.; Sastry and Van Landingham 2009; Stuber, Resnick, and Galea 2006). While the disparities experienced by any groups are unfortunate and unacceptable, those beyond race, ethnicity, and culture are beyond the scope of this chapter. The reader is referred elsewhere for information on these important topics (Brewin, Andrews, and Valentine 2000; Fernandez et al. 2002; Foa and Street 2001; Green et al. 2000; Yule 2001).

10.2   THE DISPARITIES LITERATURE

Among adult samples, ethnic minority status has been found to be among those factors that most consistently increase the probability of adverse outcomes in the aftermath of disasters (Norris et al. 2002). While some studies countered this assertion, the overwhelming majority validated this finding. Consistent with the differential exposure hypothesis, non-Hispanic blacks and Latinos were more adversely impacted by Hurricane Andrew with higher rates of posttraumatic stress disorder (PTSD) than were non-Hispanic whites (Perilla, Norris, and Lavizzo 2002). In the aftermath of the World Trade Center attacks, African Americans were less likely than whites to utilize mental health services and less likely to utilize medications when prescribed, thereby contributing to disparate outcomes (Boscarino, Adams, and Figley 2004). Other factors also negatively correlated with greater postdisaster distress, including economic status, education (Goltz, Russell, and Bourque 1992), and predisaster functioning (North et al. 1999; Brymer et al. 2006). One review of the literature identified racial and ethnic differences in risk communication, cross-cultural sensitivity, incomes, unemployment, housing and access to resources as barriers to recovery and reconstruction for minority groups (Fothergill, Maestas, and Darlington 1999). This study highlighted the increased vulnerability to disaster among communities of color in the United States, and the importance of decreasing disparities across racial, ethnic, and cultural populations in the aftermath of disaster.

10.3   BEHAVIORAL HEALTH RESPONSE INTERVENTIONS

A substantial body of research and literature has emerged regarding various behavioral health intervention models since the disaster of the World Trade Center attacks on September 11, 2001. Multiple response experiences since that time have demonstrated the need for a greater focus on cultural competence in behavioral health disaster interventions. This chapter is not intended to include a comprehensive discussion of each behavioral health response model. A comprehensive description and comparison of these approaches can be found in Watson and Ruzek (2009). The discussion here will include brief mention of three of what arguably are the "Big Four" behavioral health intervention techniques, which include: Critical Incident Stress Management (CISM; Everly and Mitchell 1997); the Seven-Stage Crisis Intervention Model (Roberts and Ottens 2005); and the Federal Emergency Management Agency (FEMA) Crisis Counseling Assistance and Training Program (CCP) model (Castellano and Plionis 2006). There will be more extensive discussion of the fourth technique, Psychological First Aid (PFA; Brymer et al. 2006).

CISM initially focused on firefighters and law enforcement officers with the intent of providing support so these individuals could continue to do their jobs of "responding to the disaster." This approach was developed for use in the first responder culture and is based on peer support models (Castellano and Plionis 2006). Roberts and Ottens's Seven-Stage Crisis Intervention model was developed for use in psychiatric and community-based clinics. This approach focuses on rapid assessment, collaborative problem solving, coping tools, and developing a strong working alliance. Roberts and Ottens's approach is based on a "client-centered" model. The FEMA-funded CCP model evaluates strengths and resources with the aim of returning individuals to their level of predisaster functioning. The approach is support focused and psychoeducationally oriented.

Finally, the most extensively researched and referenced approach has been PFA. PFA is an evidence-informed modular approach to provide supportive services to individuals in the immediate aftermath of disaster. It was designed to reduce initial and debilitating stress caused by traumatic events and aimed at fostering short-, intermediate-, and long-term recovery. This technique ostensibly has been developed for "response" and aimed at mitigation of psychological, emotional, and social problems after a disaster or emergency and decreasing the probability of PTSD. It has been reported that the term PFA was coined by Von Greyerz, the Chief Medical Officer for the Swedish Civil Defense, in 1962, as he urged his government to prepare for "World War III" (Barbanel and Sternberg 2006). The refinement of this model occurred in a later collaboration between the National Child Traumatic Stress Network, the National Center for Posttraumatic Stress Disorder, and the Substance Abuse and Mental Health Services Administration (SAMSHA) with support of the Robert Wood Johnson Foundation. PFA has been recommended by the World Health Organization, the Institute of Medicine, the International Federation of Red Cross and Red Crescent Societies, the American Psychological Association, and the American Psychiatric Association among others.

10.4   THE CULTURAL COMPETENCE MODEL: STANDARDS AND GUIDELINES

As mentioned previously, the objective of this chapter is to offer suggestions for the response model aimed at decreasing outcome disparities after disaster. This approach is not intended to replace any existing methods, models, or techniques but, rather, is intended to augment their use. This approach integrates a disciplined process with a set of principles, identified in cultural competence guidelines, that will enhance the given intervention models and approaches. This effort is similar to the past marketing and advertising campaign by the giant chemical company BASF that states, "We don't make a lot of the products you buy. We make a lot of the products you buy better" (BASF Corporation 2010). It is the authors' view that cultural competence guidelines do not make the product, like the PFA model, but can make implementation of PFA more effective. A better product theoretically should lead to better outcomes and decreased disparities. The information and insights presented will be based on the authors' experience in responding to multiple human-caused and natural disasters ranging from work with a diverse array of families of the victims on the planes of 9/11, to the aftermath of Hurricanes Katrina, Rita, and Wilma to, recently, the aftermath of the earthquake in Haiti. Further support has been gained from the literature and the developing science of behavioral health disaster response and intervention.

10.4.1   CULTURAL COMPETENCE: STATE OF THE ART, STATE OF THE SCIENCE

There is no single definition of cultural competence (Goode, Dunne, and Bronheim 2006). The authors observed that many conceptualizations of cultural competence in the literature have revolved around the attitude, awareness, knowledge, and skills necessary to work effectively across cultural difference. Cross et al. (1989) further refined this concept by stating that "cultural competence is a set of congruent behaviors, attitudes and policies that come together in a system, agency, or amongst professionals and enables that system, agency, or those professionals to work effectively in cross-cultural situations" (iv–v). In the authors' opinion this perspective is necessary, admirable, and desirable. The notion of cultural competence has been important in promoting effective mental health care for all populations and for establishing guidelines on equitable treatment at the local, state, and national levels (Sue 2006). The notion embodied by the term *cultural competence* gained momentum due to a need to fill significant gaps in the primary health and behavioral health services net for individuals from racial, ethnical, and/or cultural minority groups in the United States (Tyler 2007). At the same time this perspective has notable challenges that seem to limit its practical utility with populations, in general, with individuals in the aftermath of disaster, in particular.

In addition to considerable value and strength, current approaches to cultural competence have noteworthy limitations. The authors view the concept of cultural competence as a necessity for implementation aimed at eliminating disparities. A review of the disaster literature indicates that only a relatively few sources over a number of years have been focused on issues of race, ethnicity, and culture, especially in regard to interventions (Carter 2004). The content focus and discussion in the behavioral health disaster response literature addressing cultural competence has tended to focus mainly on two approaches. The first approach is the "Cultural Competence Continuum" (Cross et al. 1989). The second approach is the "National Standards on Culturally and Linguistically Appropriate Services."

Race can be viewed as classification of people based on identifiable phenotype(s), self-ascribed and/or other sociocultural factors. Ethnicity refers to shared language, activities, beliefs, foods, and so forth that form a common sense of bonding and contribute to a sense of belonging (Sue and Sue 1990). Culture is inclusive of broad patterns of human behavior that include beliefs, customs, norms, thoughts, behaviors, relationships, language, and indigenous traditions. According to the American Psychological Association (APA), reactions to disasters or traumatic events vary due to a number of factors (APA 2010). So, too, do reactions vary as a result of the influence and complexity of culture in the aftermath of disaster. Differences can range from how disasters are viewed, to disaster experience, to how problems are interpreted, to help-seeking behaviors and beyond. Many times these differences can be masked by so-called "proxy variables" that correlate with race, ethnicity, and culture (Carter 2004; Hunt and Megyesi 2008; Putzke, Hicken, and Richards 2002; Lillie-Blanton and Laveist 1996). Even as discussion of the impact of proxy variables raged on, researchers began to report disparities in health care outcomes based on race and ethnicity when other differences (e.g., proxy variables) were controlled (Ford and Cooper 1995; Gornick et al. 1996; Mayberry et al. 1999; Williams 1999).

10.4.2 CULTURAL COMPETENCE CONTINUUM

Perhaps more in-depth examination of the two approaches to cultural competence will highlight their respective benefits and limitations. The best known of the approaches is the Continuum of Cultural Competence (Figure 10.1; Cross et al. 1989).

Figure 10.1 represents the framework and model from the National Center for Cultural Competence at Georgetown University. This model is described as a continuum and developmental process ranging from cultural destructiveness on the negative end (characterized by policies, practices, and procedures in organizations that are destructive to cultural groups) to cultural proficiency on the positive end (characterized by acceptance, respect, valuing, and promoting the benefit of cultural differences). A description of its attempted conceptual application in disaster mental health

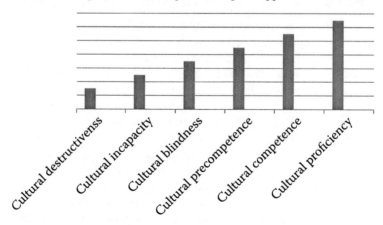

FIGURE 10.1 Cultural competence continuum.

programs can be found in *Developing Cultural Competence in Disaster Mental Health Programs: Guiding Principles and Recommendations* (Athey and Moody-Williams 2003).

While each progressive step from cultural destructiveness to cultural proficiency represents advancement toward culture competence, and beyond to cultural proficiency, the absence of measures or guideposts does not enable criterion-based evaluation of progress or research on the methodology. Categorical descriptions tend to be broad and somewhat undifferentiated. As a result, these descriptions are not quantifiable or sufficiently qualitative to aid in assessment or prediction of cultural competence. The definition of culture provided by Cross and colleagues (1989) is an "integrated pattern of human behavior that includes thoughts, communication, actions, customs, beliefs, values, and institutions of a racial, ethnic, religious, or social group" (iv). In reality, culture is neither monolithic nor static and is therefore ever changing. Given the intersection of multiple cultures, service recipient experiences, multidimensional contexts, and complex nature of "culture" itself, one would be hard-pressed to assume that anyone can gain "competence"—defined as a state of being well qualified—in that framework. Further, given the nature of cultural competence and the multidimensional skill sets and knowledge base required, along with its limitations, the question could emerge of whether cultural competence as a construct is, in fact, achievable. The authors believe that pursuit of cultural competence is a goal. Given the complexities involved, it is not likely to ever be "achieved." It is our opinion that the active and committed process toward achieving cultural competence is equally important (i.e., the journey is as important as the destination). More on this point later.

10.4.3 THE CULTURAL AND LINGUISTIC STANDARDS

The Cultural and Linguistic Standards (CLAS Standards) are a set of mandates, guidelines, and recommendations developed by the Office of Minority Health of the U.S. Department of Health and Human Services. CLAS Standards were designed to ensure compliance with Title VI (Title VI of the Civil Rights Act of 1964, 42 U.S.C. § 2000d et seq.) by federal agencies and other organizations in health care. There are fourteen standards that focus on health care organizations and the provision of health care services to patients, including: standards (1–3), which address culturally competent care; standards (4–7), which relate to language access services; and standards (8–14), which address organizational supports for cultural competence. Standards (4–7) are mandated under Title VI. Standards (1, 2, 3, 8, 9, 10, 11, 12, and 13) are guidelines, while standard 14 is a recommendation (DHHS 2001). The CLAS standards provide helpful guidance for organizations that have the goals of enhancing the quality of cross-culturally appropriate health care. The standards ostensibly specify actions or guidelines that "should" be taken in order to meet the federal mandates, guidelines, and recommendation. These standards are not quantified and do not operationalize terminology related to advancement toward cultural competence. The standards do inform culturally competent practices. They emphasize the importance of access to effective and respectful services, in the appropriate language, at the appropriate literacy level. They also highlight the role of development, implementation, management, and accountability for the mechanisms necessary to provide culturally and linguistically relevant and appropriate services.

While both the Continuum of Cultural Competence and the CLAS Standards have acknowledged limitations, both also have strengths and benefits for providing effective behavioral health disaster response services across culturally different individuals. It is important to keep in mind that both approaches were developed in response to alarming and unacceptable gaps in health care and behavioral health services that resulted in major outcome disparities for racial, ethnic, and cultural minority groups. In addition to the research previously cited, additional findings were that, when compared to whites (generally), racial and ethnic minority groups were likely to receive less accessible services and have them less effectively delivered (Sue et al. 2009). Further, ethnic minority groups were at increased risk for underutilization of services and for premature terminations (Pole, Gone, and Kulkarni 2008). The goal of cultural competence remains critically important for a number of reasons. As Paasche-Orlow (2004) states in her discussion of cultural competence as an ethical imperative, "the essential principles of cultural competence are (1) acknowledgement of the importance of culture in people's lives, (2) respect for cultural differences, and (3) minimization of any negative consequences of cultural differences" (347).

10.4.4 Disaster Behavioral Health Intervention and Cultural Competence

The model of intervention preferred for implementation by the authors is PFA. While CISM and the Seven-Stage Crisis Intervention Model continue to be used (the former among the uniform services, and the latter among school-based providers), PFA remains the standard in the field of behavioral health disaster response. A critical objective of PFA is the promotion of individual coping skills after the impact of disaster. This evidence-informed model of behavioral health provides necessary "tools" to enhance cultural competence in service to the goal of helping disaster-impacted individuals return to "typical" functioning. It is also an iterative process in which the intersection of human resilience and the dynamics of cross-cultural knowledge, sensitivity, and skills can positively influence the effectiveness of PFA. The authors determined that the PFA model is highly compatible with cultural competence and with the philosophy and response practices of the Center for Multicultural Mental Health (CMMH) at the Boston University Medical Campus.

The authors have a wealth of experience responding in the aftermath of large- and small-scale disasters over a number of years, with the most recent being the Haitian earthquake of 2010. The CMMH mission includes a commitment to providing culturally competent training and interventions leading to more cross-culturally appropriate and effective outcomes. CMMH has been able to integrate much of the practices and principles of cultural competence—based on literature, research, and practice—to develop a more cross-culturally effective behavioral health disaster response model despite the limitations of the primary models for achieving cultural competence.

10.4.5 The Approach

As mentioned, the authors view cultural competence as more a process than an endpoint. Sue and colleagues (1996) would agree with this point and compare it to the challenge of cultural competence meeting the standard of a substantive "content area." Sue's work further highlights the value of viewing cultural competence as a journey and not just as a destination.

Sue and colleagues (1996) further proposed a conceptual framework for providing culturally competent care. It remains the most widely recognized framework for conceptualizing the definition of cultural competence. Simply stated, the conceptual framework includes: cultural awareness and beliefs; cultural knowledge; and cultural skills.

First, cultural awareness focuses the provider on her/his own biases, stereotypes, held values and knowledge, and on how these influence her/his perceptions of the service recipient, the service recipient's problem(s) and, ultimately, on the nature of the relationship. Responding effectively to diverse communities requires that training of responders be focused on self-exploration to build awareness of one's own "cultural baggage" to enable the provider to address areas of bias, and stereotype or inflexibility that may be detrimental to individuals receiving behavioral health response services. This has been shown to enhance the provider's ability to work effectively across cultural differences with peers and, more importantly, with service recipients (Carter 2004). In CMMH, responders spend a significant amount of time focusing on this area in group sessions (peer-to-peer) ahead of the disaster event. In these sessions each provider is asked to acknowledge and discuss her/his biases, stereotypes, and personal values that she/he has that may come into conflict with cultural differences of the service recipient (Carter 2004; Dean 2001; DHHS 2003). Sessions are feedback and support oriented. This process is continual and it is perhaps the most important aspect of the three areas of D. W. Sue's schema. Learning about ourselves implies being aware of our own cultural norms, attitudes, values, and communication styles and so forth. This exploration allows us in turn to consider and understand other ways of seeing the world, even a "world" that is familiar. It is vital for each provider to carefully consider how her/his values, beliefs, biases, and/or life experiences shape her/his worldview and influence their understanding of other people and other cultures. Lopez (1997) posits that a necessary component of cultural competence is "the ability of the therapist to move between two cultural perspectives in understanding the culturally based meaning of clients from diverse cultural backgrounds" (573). The authors agree with Lopez's view and consider the self-exploration process as an essential task for "moving between two cultural perspectives." Being aware of one's own cultural biases, stereotypes, and limitations will enhance providers' awareness and openness to other views and ways of life, and therefore will enhance her or his chances of connecting with others in a manner to help their psychosocial and emotional recovery.

The second area identified is cultural knowledge (Sue, Ivey, and Pedersen 1996). In the authors' opinions it is crucial for providers to acquire knowledge across racial, ethnic, and cultural groups they serve. Accumulation of knowledge can be accomplished in a number of ways. Lived experience is always beneficial. The authors have found that it can also be helpful to consider aspects of one's own culture when learning about others. The responder should attempt to actively determine how these aspects are similar or dissimilar to her or his own culture and to assess their relative meaning. Learning about the culture(s) of others should be a deliberate and continuing process with the understanding that one will never learn all there is to know about any group. Learning about traditions, values, language and dialects, communication styles, ways of coping with stress, idioms for illness, gender roles, family dynamics, help-seeking behaviors, and so forth are parts of the "whole" of culture and would be helpful. Reading about different groups and spending time with members of those groups could also be helpful. During this part of the process, researching specific characteristics of the group/community in question, talking with others who are knowledgeable, and maintaining an attitude of humility and openness to learn from others is useful. This was the case as shown in the following example the authors will cite from the aftermath of Hurricane Katrina.

It is generally known that in some cultures members may believe that problems encountered by individuals are the result of wrongdoing in life (DHHS 2003), and, therefore, disasters may be viewed as a "punishment" for what needs to be redeemed. The lead author, while providing behavioral health response intervention in Mississippi, encountered an African American adult male who lived northeast of New Orleans. In referring to Hurricane Katrina, the individual stated: "You know they got what was coming to 'em. I mean Sin City and all." He went on to explain his opinion, rationale, and his stress level in not knowing the location of extended family members. It was helpful for the responder to recognize and acknowledge this gentleman's religious traditions, his ability to cite scripture in the Old Testament of the Bible, his belief in retribution, his belief in family, etc. These were essential components of his self-identity and cultural identity that were important to consider in the formulation of an effective intervention. Regardless of the author's beliefs, practices, and values, any relationship coconstructed with this individual would have to accommodate his cultural beliefs, practices and worldview. It was not the responder's role to agree or disagree with the service recipient's view. It was the responder's responsibility to actively listen to and acknowledge what was said. It was further incumbent on the provider to be aware of and secure in his own cultural beliefs and values, to be aware of his counter-transference, and to manage it in a manner that would not negatively impact the intervention. Listening, in this instance, demonstrated respect, evidenced a genuine interest to engage the individual, and seemed to help promote a sense of comfort and emotional stabilization for the individual to share more deeply the sources of his stress and concern.

When working with racial, ethnic, and cultural minority groups, the responder should keep in mind that exploration of any history of oppression, sociocultural, and the sociopolitical history of the particular group(s). This is particularly important for recent immigrant groups. Studies show that some groups are more susceptible to PTSD due to prior trauma history (e.g., immigrants, low SES). Therefore, responders should consider the effects of prior traumatic events, including experiences related to daily living (such as violence in communities, sudden deaths, and discrimination;

Carter 2004). Individuals belonging to groups and countries with a history of oppression may be apprehensive about obtaining help from certain social and government groups. It is also known that preexisting social problems will be reflected in the interactions between affected individuals and responders (Fothergill, Maestas, and Darlington 1999). For example, the long history of social oppression or underlying tensions in some parts of the country between whites and blacks in the United States may affect the receptiveness of African Americans in seeking and effectively utilizing supports from white responders. After Hurricane Katrina, a number of residents from New Orleans (mostly underserved blacks) were evacuated and sheltered by other states. Many individuals took it upon themselves to help from among the recipient communities in a spirit of generosity. White middle-class communities (e.g., Cape Cod, Massachusetts; Seattle, Washington) embraced evacuees in a wonderful way. At the same time there was not sufficient consideration or discussion of the vast differences between the evacuees' culture(s), practices, and worldviews and those of their recipient communities. Inevitable tensions between these communities developed. Unfortunately, as a result, many individuals from New Orleans expressed feelings of rejection and were reluctant to participate in community activities or engage in conversations about long-term plans. While there were multiple reasons that the rescue and shelter mission did not accomplish all its goals, an ironic consequence of cultural difference was that evacuees by and large seemed unable to fully access the generosity and opportunities offered by recipient communities. Several evacuees stated that this course of events reminded them too much of the oppression and trauma they experienced in New Orleans. To our awareness there was no concerted effort made to bridge and mitigate the effects of the cultural gap. The CMMH response team, in order to avoid a similar outcome in the aftermath of the Haitian earthquake, first sought information from Haitian clinicians and others from or familiar with the Haitian culture, context, and worldview. The responder team also sought information from other sources to inform its interventions in a culturally sensitive manner. One of the manuscripts utilized was a very thorough report, "Mental Health in Haiti: A Literature Review" by the World Health Organization (WHO, 2010), which addressed the complex sociocultural context of this first black republic. Recognizing the team's limitations (language barriers, difficulties with direct access to affected individuals) instead of providing direct assistance, it became clear that a more effective approach would be to train, consult with, and support responders and health providers who spoke Creole and were already immersed in the culture. The feedback from those trained and others among the Haitian community leadership was that the approach and support were very beneficial.

The third area in Sue's conceptual schema is a focus on the provider's cultural skills, or the ability of the provider to function in a culturally sensitive, congruent, and relevant manner. Skill sets are developed over time and based on acquisition of knowledge and experience. The CMMH team shares its collective wisdom with all members and others, as well as learns from each of its members. One instance of utilization of cross-cultural skill sets (e.g., active listening, acknowledgement of differences, management of countertransference, tolerance and objectivity, ability to integrate knowledge of cultural context and literature of behavioral health and PFA) can be seen in the aforementioned example while working with the individual who believed that New Orleans "got what it deserved." Another example was in working with a young African American mother who was transported to Massachusetts in the aftermath of Hurricane Katrina with one of her five children. She and a group of other evacuees were placed on a plane in New Orleans. They were not told where they were being taken until after the plane was airborne. This was her first time on an airplane. Upon arrival she reportedly presented to mental health professionals as depressed and suicidal. Medication and isolation for observation were mentioned. The lead author, whose specialization is in forensic psychology, was asked to interview the young woman and assess the extent of her depression and suicidality. She had no prior history of depression. She reported never having attempted or seriously contemplated harming herself or anyone else. She admitted to being frightened. It quickly became clear that she was worried about the fate of four of her five children. She knew they were with other relatives but did not know how her family fared after the hurricane or where they were relocated to. She did not know any of the people on the evacuation flight. She clearly knew that she had been relocated to "Massachusetts." She expressed as her overriding concern to know where her children were and how they were doing. Second, she wanted them back with her. Having spent time with many evacuees from a natural disaster, this provider knew it was important to listen to her stories and to carefully follow her narration of experiences. She was concerned about the fate of her extended family and her loss of livelihood. She expressed concerns about having been relocated to a new and unfamiliar community with people who "talk funny"—all this for the first time in her life because, with the exception of one other occasion to visit relatives out of state, she reported never having ventured beyond the city limits of New Orleans and never before having been without members of her family. It was clear that her worries and concerns did not meet the criteria for depression and that she was in touch with reality, was not suicidal, and that she needed a great deal of practical support. Much of the information and clarity of her situation came as a result of utilizing cross-cultural skills and sensitivity with this individual as well as respect and appreciation for her plight. Language and its use were also key. She reported being very "nervous" and, with only a high school education and very limited experience beyond her community, did not understand much of what was said to her. In the authors' opinion, this experience demonstrates the advantage for the provider to be able to, as Lopez says, "move [and work] between two cultures."

10.4.6 PROCESS FACTORS

Preparation for behavioral health disaster response should start well before the disaster occurs and continue in the interceding periods. Carter (2004) suggests a "pre-disaster preparation plan" that should include staff training and self-exploration (2). For instance, the authors recognized and incorporated a set of values similar to those identified by the CLAS Standards. Beyond "do no harm" we began with respect (Paasche-Orlow 2004). Respect could be operationalized as a stance of positive regard and/or admiration for the culture of another. This posture recognizes that others are the true "experts" about their own cultures and worldviews. The authors acknowledge and value the cultural difference of others and their abilities to convey what will be helpful for them. Respect for cultural difference, by implication, requires the following: acquisition of knowledge about the culture of others; development of skills in working across those difference; acknowledging one's own culture and how it relates to that of the service recipient; active informed listening; and belief that the individual will have the greatest likelihood of expertise in her or his own culture.

One particular experience illustrates these suggestions. The second author of this chapter was asked to intervene with a multigenerational Puerto Rican family in the aftermath of the 9/11 disaster. As a bilingual Spanish-speaking responder, she was assigned to respond to the family. It was determined that PFA was appropriate for this family as an intervention by which individuals and the family could benefit from validation of feelings, information, a connection with helpful resources, and reinforcement of their ability for coping. As a bicultural responder with awareness and knowledge of similar families, she hypothesized that it was necessary to be invited by the elders to help, rather than being ascribed this "authority" by assignment. She knew that she would have to earn the privilege to serve this family. The family was accompanied by a priest, whom the responder approached. The process of intervention was formal and deliberate. The formality was necessary given the cultural dynamics and fluidity of the situation and the necessity of *respeto* (respect). It was more effective to approach a family/individual in a formal manner first, and then more informally thereafter per invitation/suggestion by the family/individuals. The responder remained physically outside the huddled family group until invited in. The spiritual leader introduced her to the "leaders of the family group," the parents of the victims, as someone who could offer support and guidance in their own language (both literally and in terms of understanding their culture). This was an effective way to gain access to the group in a manner that would be helpful to more globally meet their needs. Her objectives included helping to facilitate individual and group coping. Over the course of several hours, she was accepted, literally, into the middle of the family. It was as if she became a part of the family, which was necessary for her to be of assistance. Once invited in and having restated the purpose of why she was there, she asked for everyone's input, and then remained silent and observant to listen to the family for instructions on how she could be most helpful. A special connection with the father seemed to have the effect of "giving permission" to other males in the group to understand their emotions as "normal" for the circumstances. At the same time, the responder began to assess the needs of all group members. There were no special immigration issues to take into consideration. There were acculturation issues with the older generation that had been born and raised in Puerto Rico and the younger generation that had been born in the United States. On the other hand, different members had different experiences of racism and/or ethnocentrism and therefore were reassured by the process and the willingness of most responders there to assist them regardless of race, ethnicity, and country of origin. Religion was important in their lives and, therefore, would play an integral part in their collective and individual recovery. The responder was comfortable with their praying when needed.

This example highlights several process factors that, according to Sue (2006), underlie cultural competence. First, the provider used "scientific mindedness" (239). Scientific mindedness is the provider's continual effort to formulate, test, confirm, or disconfirm hypotheses about the individual or family, regardless of one's perceived familiarity. This enables the intervention to be data driven and mitigates against inaccurate assumptions or premature conclusions. Although this was known to be a Puerto Rican family and the responder approached the group with in-depth knowledge of Hispanic families in general and with a Hispanic heritage, the responder was aware that she had to continually test her knowledge and assumptions about what was being presented to her. It was the responder's responsibility not to stereotype the family and to look at this family from a scientifically minded perspective, which she accomplished through forming hypotheses, testing hypotheses, participant-observation, acting based on knowledge and experience, and guidance from individuals in the family and informal data sources.

Further, the responder demonstrated the skill of "dynamic sizing." Dynamic sizing relates to the ability to distinguish when to generalize an observation and when to restrain generalization to a single individual or instance. Essentially, dynamic sizing involves a skill set and knowledge base that informs the responder when to broaden conceptions toward a more categorical or group-based perspective, or to constrain conceptions toward a more individual-based perspective. Although having had numerous experiences and having worked with Puerto Rican families on multiple prior occasions, the responder viewed this particular family as a "new encounter" and chose not to generalize from prior contacts to her new experience. A view of a "new encounter" is not to be construed as a *tabula rasa* (clean slate) but, instead, as an approach in which her/his held cultural baggage is continuously challenged by the responder. This process is more challenging in the beginning and gets much easier when practiced over time, especially with the support of colleagues. The benefits accrue to the service recipient almost immediately. The "art" in this approach is to minimize the risk of overgeneralization while fully appreciating cultural differences. This does not mean there were not commonalities observed over multiple instances with the family. It does mean that these perceived commonalities are not overvalued, will not shape her view of the "new encounter," and would be tested through scientific mindedness. It was clear from the beginning that this family was unique in many ways and, although all were of Hispanic heritage, they were nonetheless diverse. One is cautioned to resist the temptation to see "all Hispanics as...." In this instance, some members showed a great deal of emotional distress, while others did not exhibit distress in any overt manner. Some family members quietly sobbed, while others demonstrated verbosity and anger. Still other members were circumspect. It is important to note that those behaviors exhibited by family members were across a range of normal reactions to an abnormal situation.

Finally, an overview of Sue's schema reminds us of the advantage of prior knowledge and expertise in the culture of the individuals who are the focus of the interventions. This process is proposed in the context of scientific mindedness and dynamic sizing. Prior knowledge can represent a significant advantage when working with individuals from the same and from different cultures. In this instance the responder's knowledge of the cultural background of the family was important to acquiring sufficient credibility to be accepted by and to work with the family. She hypothesized, based on experience and continuing acquisition of cross-cultural knowledge, that this Hispanic family would likely have a clearly delineated family structure and hierarchy. She then tested this knowledge through observations and inquiry and found it to be accurate. Knowledge of the culture can include, but is not limited to, the following: awareness of background culture; awareness of the context of the individual's/family's culture; acculturation or immigration history and status; acculturation stress and stressors; self-identification; orientation toward interacting with authority figures; and orientation toward help seeking and receiving help. The assigned responder possessed culture-specific expertise. The intersection of each of these has to also be considered, which highlights the complexity of working across cultural differences. Incorporation of the process factors of scientific mindedness and dynamic sizing, based on utilization of the PFA, yielded a successful intervention in which the members of the family were able to regain emotional stability and were able to more effectively avail themselves of information that would be beneficial to their recovery. These individuals were also able to gain a better understanding of what behavioral health response is about and how they could benefit. They requested, and were provided, follow-up from the responder.

A further technique that the authors have employed is suggested by Sue (2006), called "pretherapy intervention." PFA is not formally viewed as therapy, but has sufficient therapeutic components to make this intervention potentially beneficial. Pretherapy intervention is essentially informing the individual or family beforehand what to expect from the intervention. It is a technique aimed at inducting the individual or family into the intervention in an informed and realistic manner. Specifically, the pretherapy intervention activity would inform the family about the following: the intervention, and the potential benefits and risks (if any); the potential outcomes; the processes used; what they would be asked to do; what would happen with the information; confidentiality requirements; and the projected time frame. At each step along the way, the responder would provide information about the mechanics, process, and potential outcomes of the intervention. The family reported to the responder that this technique was very helpful as they more clearly understood her role and goals in attempting to help. This process seemed to be empowering to the family as they went through the course of the day and more actively sought out available services and information.

10.5   CONCLUSION

Outcomes disparities exist in primary health care and behavioral health care for a number of population groups. Disparities associated with race, ethnicity, and culture in the aftermath of disaster were identified in this chapter. There is a growing body of research documenting disparities and a correspondingly smaller amount of research on ways to mitigate and/or eliminate disparities in this area. The authors view the emerging literature on cultural competence as an important component for decreasing disparities through more effective use of models of behavioral health disaster response. While the two primary models of cultural competence are important, represent significant progress, and are widely recognized, they remain more conceptual than practical. This chapter intended to focus attention on integrating the concepts of cultural competence with applied models to provide more effective intervention to diverse racial, ethnic, and cultural groups in the aftermath of disaster. This approach was based on the use of Psychological First Aid. Experience has helped us become increasingly aware of how race, ethnicity, and culture shape the way in which different communities react, respond, and connect to resources. It is hoped that further research will lead the way to further integration of cultural competence into all models of disaster behavioral health response and intervention, thereby increasing the likelihood for decreasing disparities across racial, ethnic, and cultural differences.

REFERENCES

Adams, R. E., and J. A. Boscarino. 2005. Difference in mental health outcomes among whites, African-Americans, and Hispanics following a community disaster. *Psychiatry 68*(3): 250–265.

American Psychological Association. 2010. *Tips for recovering from disasters and other traumatic events.* http://www.apa.org/helpcenter/recovering-disasters.aspx.

Athey, J., and J. Moody-Williams. 2003. *Developing Cultural Competence in Disaster Mental Health Programs: Guiding Principles and Recommendations.* Rockville, MD: U.S. Department of Health and Human Services.

Barbanel, L., and R. J. Sternberg. 2006. *Psychological Interventions in Times of Crisis.* New York: Springer Publishing Company.

BASF Chemical Company. 2010. *Customer success story.* http://www2.basf.us/corporate/customersuccess/pdfs/Composatron_CSS.pdf.

Bonanno, G. A., S. Galea, A. Bucciarelli, and D. Vlahov. 2006. Psychological resilience after disaster: New York City in the aftermath of the September 11th terrorist attack. *Psychological Science 12*(3): 181–186.

Boscarino, J. A., R. E. Adams, and C. R. Figley. 2004. Mental health service use 1-year after the World Trade Center disaster: Implications for mental health care. *General Hospital Psychiatry 26*(5): 346–358.

Brewin, C. R., B. Andrews, and J. D. Valentine. 2000. Meta-Analysis of risk factors for posttraumatic stress disorder in trauma-exposed adults. *Journal of Consulting and Clinical Psychology 68*(5): 748–766.

Brymer, M., A. Jacobs, C. Layne, R. Pynoos, J. Ruzek, A. Steinberg, E. Vernberg, and P. Watson. 2006. *Psychological First Aid: Field Operations Guide,* 2nd ed. National Child Traumatic Stress Network and National Center for PTSD. http://www.nctsn.org and http://www.ncptsd.va.gov.

Carter, R. T. 2004. *Disaster response to communities of color: Cultural responsive intervention.* Technical report for the Connecticut Department of Mental Health and Addiction (DMHAS). http://www.dmhas.state.ct.us.

Castellano, C., and E. Plionis. 2006. Comparative analysis of three crisis intervention models applied to law enforcement first responders during 9/11 and Hurricane Katrina. *Brief Treatment and Crisis Intervention 64*(4): 326–336.

Cross, T. L., B. J. Bazron, K. W. Dennis, and M. R. Isaacs. 1989. *Towards a Culturally Competent System of Care. Vol. I: A Monograph of Effective Services for Children Who Are Severely Emotionally Disturbed.* Washington, DC: Georgetown University Child Development Center.

Dean, R. G. 2001. The myth of cross-cultural competence. *Families in Society: The Journal of Contemporary Human Services 82*(6): 623–630.

Everly, G. S., and Mitchell, J. T. 1997. *Critical Incident Stress Management (CISM):A New Era and Standard of Care in Crisis Intervention.* Ellicott City, MD: Chevron

Fernandez, L. S., D. Byard, L. C. Lin, S. Benson, and J. A. Barbera. 2002. Frail elderly as disaster victims: Emergency management strategies. *Prehospital and Disaster Medicine 17*(2): 67–74.

Foa, E. B., and G. P. Street. 2001. Women and traumatic events. *Journal of Clinical Psychiatry 62*(17): 29–34.

Ford, E. S., and R. S. Cooper. 1995. Implications of race/ethnicity for health and health care use. *Health Services Research 30*(1): 237–252.

Fothergill A., E. G. Maestas, and J. D. Darlington. 1999. Race, ethnicity and disasters in the United States: A review of the literature. *Disasters 23*(2): 156–173.

Galea, S., D. Vlahov, M. Tracy, D. R. Hoover, H. Resnick, and D. Kilpatrick. 2004. Hispanic ethnicity and post-traumatic stress disorder after disaster: Evidence from a general population survey after September 11, 2001. *Annals of Epidemiology 14*(8): 520–531.

Goltz, J. D., L. A. Russell, and L. Bourque. 1992. Initial behavioral response to a rapid onset disaster: A case study of the October 1, 1987 Whittier Narrows Earthquake. *International Journal of Mass Emergencies and Disasters 10*(1): 43–69.

Goode, T. D., M. C. Dunne, and S. M. Bronheim. 2006. *The Evidence Base for Cultural and Linguistic Competency in Health Care.* New York: Commonwealth Fund.

Gornick, M. E., P. W. Eggers, T. W. Reilly, R. M. Mentnech, L. K. Fitterman, L. E. Kucken, and B. C. Vladeck. 1996. Effects of race and income on mortality and use of services among Medicare beneficiaries. *New England Journal of Medicine 335*(11): 791–799.

Green, B. L., L. A. Goodman, J. L. Krupnick, C. B. Corcoran, R. M. Petty, P. Stockton, and N. M. Stern. 2000. Outcomes of single versus multiple trauma exposure in a screening sample. *Journal of Traumatic Stress 13*(2): 271–286.

Hernandez, M., T. Nesman, D. Mowery, I. D. Acevedo-Polakovich, and L. M. Callejas. 2009. Cultural Competence: A literature review and conceptual model for mental health services. *Psychiatric Services 60*: 1046–1050.

Hunt, L. M., and M. S. Megyesi. 2008. Genes, race, and research ethics: Who's minding the store? *Journal of Medical Ethics 34*(6): 495–500.

Lillie-Blanton, M., and T. Laveist. 1996. Race/ethnicity, the social environment, and health. *Social Science and Medicine 43*(1): 83–91.

López S. R. 1997. Cultural competence in psychotherapy: A guide for clinicians and their supervisors. In *Handbook for Psychotherapy Supervision*, ed. C. E. Watkins Jr., 570–588. Hoboken, NJ: Wiley.

Mayberry, R. M., F. Mili, I. G. M. Vaid, A. Samadi, E. Ofili, M. S. McNeal, P. A. Griffith, and G. LaBrie. 1999. *Racial and Ethnic Differences in Access to Medical Care: A Synthesis of the Literature*. Menlo Park, CA: The Henry J. Kaiser Family Foundation.

Norris, F. H., and M. Alegría. 2006. Promoting disaster recovery in ethnic-minority individuals and communities. In *Intervention Following Mass Violence and Disasters: Strategies for Mental Health Practice*, eds. E. C. Ritchie, P. J. Watson, and M. J. Friedman, 319–342. New York: Guilford Press.

Norris, F. H., M. J. Friedman, P. J. Watson, C. M. Byrne, E. Diaz, and K. Kaniasty. 2002. 60,000 disaster victims speak: Part I. An empirical review of the empirical literature, 1981–2001. *Psychiatry 65*(3): 207–239.

North, C. S., S. J. Nixon, S. Shariat, S. Mallonee, J. C. McMillen, E. L. Spinagel, and E. M. Smith. 1999. Psychiatric disorders among survivors of the Oklahoma City bombing. *JAMA 282*(8): 755–762.

Paasche-Orlow, M. 2004. The ethics of cultural competence. *Academic Medicine 79*(4): 347–350.

Perilla, J., F. Norris, and E. Lavizzo. 2002. Ethnicity, culture, and disaster response: Identifying and explaining ethnic differences in depression and PTSD six months following Hurricane Andrew. *Journal of Social and Clinical Psychology 21*(1): 20–45.

Pole, N., J. P. Gone, and M. Kulkarni. 2008. Posttraumatic stress disorder among ethnoracial minorities in the United States. *Clinical Psychology: Science and Practice 15*(1): 35–61.

Putzke, J. D., B. L. Hicken, and J. S. Richards. 2002. Race: Predictor versus proxy variable? Outcomes after spinal cord injury. *Archives of Physical Medicine and Rehabilitation 83*(11): 1603–1611.

Roberts, A. R., and A. J. Ottens. 2005. The Seven-Stage Crisis Intervention Model: A road map to goal attainment, problem solving, and crisis resolution. *Brief Treatment and Crisis Intervention 5*(4): 329–339.

Sastry, N., and M. Van Landingham. 2009. One year later: Mental illness prevalence and disparities among New Orleans residents displaced by Hurricane Katrina. *American Journal of Public Health 99*(S3): S725–S731.

Stuber, J., H. Resnick, and S. Galea. 2006. Gender disparities in posttraumatic stress disorder after mass trauma. *Gender Medicine 3*(1): 54–67.

Sue, D. W., A. E. Ivey, and P. B. Pedersen. 1996. *A Theory of Multicultural Counseling and Therapy*. San Francisco: Brooks/Cole Publishing.

Sue, D. W., and D. Sue. 1990. *Counseling the Culturally Different: Theory & Practice*. 2nd ed. New York: John Wiley & Sons.

Sue, S. 2006. Cultural competency: From philosophy to research and practice. *Journal of Community Psychology 34*(2): 237–245.

Sue, S., Z. Nolan, G. C. Nagayama Hall, and L. K. Berger. 2009. The case for cultural competency in psychotherapeutic interventions. *Annual Review of Psychology 60*: 525–548.

Tyler, F. B. 2007. *Developing Prosocial Communities across Cultures*. New York: Springer Science and Business Media.

U.S. Department of Health and Human Services (DHHS). 2001. *National Standards for Culturally and Linguistically Appropriate Services in Health Care*. Washington, DC: Office of Minority Health. http://minorityhealth.hhs.gov/assets/pdf/checked/finalreport.pdf

U.S. Department of Health and Human Services (DHHS). 2003. *Developing Cultural Competence in Disaster Mental Health Programs: Guiding Principles and Recommendations*, DHHS Pub. No. SMA 3828. Rockville, MD: Center for Mental Health Services, Substance Abuse and Mental Health Services Administration. http://download.ncadi.samhsa.gov/ken/pdf/SMA03-3828/CulturalCompetence_FINAL withcovers.pdf

Watson, P. J., and J. I. Ruzek. 2009. Academic/state/federal collaborations and the improvement of practices in disaster mental health services and evaluation. *Administration and Policy in Mental Health 36*: 215–220.

Williams, D. R. 1999. Race, socioeconomic status, and health: The added effects of racism and discrimination. *Annals of the New York Academy of Sciences 896*: 173–188.

World Health Organization. 2010. *Mental Health in Haiti: A Literature Review*. http://www.state.nj.us/human services/dmhs/disaster/MH_in_Haiti%20_Literature_Review.pdf

Yule, W. 2001. Posttraumatic stress disorder in the general population and in children. *Journal of Clinical Psychiatry 62*(17): 23–28.

11 Helping the Helpers
Ameliorating Secondary Traumatic Stress in Disaster Workers

April Naturale and Mary L. Pulido

CONTENTS

11.1 BACKGROUND

Over the past two decades, there has been a growing recognition of the fact that persons may manifest symptoms of posttraumatic stress disorder (PTSD), depression, or other serious emotional distress through secondhand or indirect exposure to the traumatic experience of others (Figley 1995). Such cases include Holocaust survivors and their children (Danieli 1985), intimates of rape victims (Kelly 1988), and mental health professionals who work with trauma survivors (Lindy and Wilson 1994; Figley 1995; Stamm 2002). Literature generated from within the field of traumatology has also emphasized the potential for harm to therapists who specialize in trauma therapy (Figley 1995, 1999; Pearlman and MacIan 1995; Wilson 1994). Therapists are exposed to the stressors and psychic pain experienced by their clients. Therapists also carry the professional burden of being expected to remain open and available to their clients on an emotional level. This empathic involvement sets the stage for the potentially deleterious effects of therapy to impact the professional (Pickett 1998).

    This chapter focuses on disaster responders who provide psychosocial support and mental health counseling in the aftermath of natural disasters (e.g., hurricanes, floods) as well as man-made events of mass violence such as terrorism and school shootings. While there is only a small body of research that looks specifically at how trauma work affects the disaster mental health responder, it is sufficient to begin to inform the field and suggest further areas of study.

Hodgkinson and Shepherd (1994) report that disaster workers not only experience high levels of stress at the time of the traumatic event, but also that these elevated levels are still present at the 12-month follow-up. Wee and Meyers (2002) studied mental health workers who responded to the Oklahoma City bombing and found that staff who worked in this disaster over the long term (up to nine months) suffered higher distress levels than any other emergency services workers studied over the prior 16 years. Creamer and Liddle (2005) found that a longer length of assignment in the 9/11 mental health responders resulted in a higher risk of secondary traumatic stress, and Pulido (2005) described the levels of secondary traumatic stress (STS) in social workers who responded to 9/11 as "alarming." Naturale (2007) describes several cases that required personal and professional interventions for STS in workers responding to 9/11, Hurricane Katrina, and a school shooting. These studies support the need for more understanding of the risks that disaster mental health responders face and additional research to inform the process of how to mitigate the development of STS.

11.2 DEFINITIONS

11.2.1 SECONDARY TRAUMATIC STRESS

The experience of trauma symptoms in counselors often mirrors that of their clients and is attributed to hearing their client's trauma (Figley 1999; Cunningham 2003). This distress has been identified as compassion fatigue (CF; Figley 1994, 1999), vicarious trauma (VT; Pearlman and MacIan 1995; Pearlman and McCann 1990), and more recently as *secondary traumatic stress* (STS; Stamm 1999, 2002). Stamm (1999) indicates that STS and CF are alike in meaning, and Figley (1999) uses STS interchangeably with CF. He defines STS as the natural consequent behaviors and emotions resulting from knowledge about a traumatizing event experienced by a significant other or from helping or wanting to help a traumatized person (1999).

In the process of learning about the traumatic material of the client and trying to understand and identify with the experience, the therapist may actually experience emotions and other symptoms that are very similar to that of the victim (Figley 1999; Cunningham 2003). Dutton and Rubinstein (1995) categorize STS reactions/symptoms in three domains: (1) indicators of psychological distress or dysfunction, (2) changes in cognitive schema, and (3) relational disturbances.

Indications of psychological distress or dysfunction in trauma counselors may include distressing emotions such as sadness, grief, depression, anxiety, dread and horror, fear, rage, and shame (Dutton and Rubenstein 1995; Figley 1995; McCann and Pearlman 1990). Other indications of distress may include intrusive imagery, such as nightmares, flooding and flashbacks of images generated during and following the client's recounting of traumatic events (Courtois 1999; Herman 1992; McCann and Pearlman 1990). Numbing or avoidance of efforts to work with traumatic material of the client may also occur (Dutton and Rubenstein 1995; McCann and Pearlman 1990).

Other counselors have discussed the cognitive shifts that sometimes result from STS. These include shifts in the counselors' beliefs, expectations, and assumptions. This is often related to the need to find meaning in trauma, a process that can facilitate healing in many trauma survivors. McCann and Pearlman (1990) note that therapists may find their cognitive schemas altered or disrupted by long-term exposure to the traumatic experiences of their clients. For example, they may view the world as a more dangerous place. This concern could be transferred to their work with clients.

Relational disturbances, both personal and professional, are the final category of STS effects or symptoms. Figley (1995) notes that therapists' personal relationships may suffer due to increased stress, resulting in difficulty with trust and intimacy, or increased sensitivity to relationship dynamics that are similar to those being discussed by a trauma survivor (e.g., exploitation, abuse, or violence). In the professional domain, the counselor's response to the survivor client may be overidentification, detachment, or vacillation between the two (Miller 2000; Dutton and Rubenstein 1995).

Individual, organizational, social, community, and traumatic event factors have the potential to either increase or decrease one's vulnerability to STS. These include, but are not limited to: a history of psychiatric symptoms or a personal traumatic experience; demographic characteristics such as age and ethnicity; level of identification with the victim; organizational influences on the recognition of, and recovery from, on-the-job-trauma; the social support network of the therapist/crisis worker including the availability of professional supervision; and the level of community response/support for the disaster recovery and the characteristics of the traumatic event (Beaton and Murphy 1995; Figley 1995).

11.2.2 VICARIOUS TRAUMA

Vicarious trauma, a term introduced by Laurie Ann Pearlman and Lisa McCann (1990, 133), is identified as the "profound psychological effects ... that can be disruptive and painful for the helper and persist for months or years after work with traumatized persons."

Similar to compassion fatigue and secondary traumatic stress, vicarious trauma itself has not been identified as a diagnosable disorder such as acute stress or posttraumatic stress disorder. However, the concept of indirect trauma arose from the addition of the PTSD diagnosis to the *Diagnostic and Statistical Manual of Mental Disorders III* (APA 1980) by the American Psychiatric Association (Figley 1999). There is recognition that some vicarious trauma symptoms are similar to those seen in persons suffering with acute and posttraumatic stress disorders. Criteria that inform this view include the stipulation that the traumatic event from which the individual is suffering arises from outside the individual rather than an endogenous, individual weakness. These symptoms may emerge from any or all of the domains of PTSD, such as:

- *Intrusion*: The occurrence of memories, nightmares or flashbacks.
- *Avoidance*: Individuals make extensive efforts to go out of their way so as not be exposed to the site of a trauma or no longer even associate with any family or friends that remind them of the resulting pains of the traumatic event.
- *Hypervigilence*: The individual may become oversensitive to sounds around them and be easily frightened or even paranoid.
- *Disassociation*: The affected individual becomes numb, unable to feel emotion, or is distanced from any affect (Eriksson et al. 2001).

The description of vicarious trauma includes a number of symptoms that differ from the PTSD diagnosis and are measured by the Traumatic Stress Institute Belief Scale (TSI-BSL), which Pearlman and MacIan (1995) developed for use in her studies of VT. These symptoms include as examples a loss of sense of personal safety and a questioning of the meaning of events. McCann and Pearlman (1990) specifically note that vicarious trauma is an accumulation of symptoms over time due to multiple exposures to client's trauma material. This is one aspect that differentiates VT from STS as Figley (1999) indicates STS can occur from a single exposure to traumatic material.

11.2.3 BURNOUT

In addition to STS, helping professionals have long been known to experience *burnout*. As opposed to STS that can occur suddenly and without warning, burnout develops gradually due to the accumulation of stress and the erosion of idealism resulting from the combination of intensive contact with clients and the lack of institutional support systems. Burnout can be caused by one or a combination of the following: conflict between a person's values and organizational goals and demands; an overload of responsibility; a sense of having no control over the quality of services provided; awareness of little emotional or financial reward; a sense of loss of community within the work setting; and the existence of inequity or lack of respect at the workplace (Maslach and Leiter 1997).

This outcome can also be caused by continuous conflicts and lack of support from colleagues or supervisors. Freydenberger, who coined the term *burnout* described it as "a depletion or exhaustion of a person's mental and physical resources attributed to his or her prolonged, yet unsuccessful striving toward unrealistic expectations, internally or externally derived" (Wicks 2006, 18).

Many researchers and authors on the topic of burnout have developed their own list of the causes, but there is much overlap. Yet, all seem to point to the problem as being a lack of some type that produces frustration. Causes can include a deficiency, such as the lack of education, opportunity, free time, opportunities to ventilate, institutional power, or professional or personal recognition. Wicks (2006) cites causes that include:

- Inadequate quiet time/physical rest, cultural diversion, and personal psychological replenishment
- Vague criteria for success and/or adequate positive feedback on efforts made
- Guilt over failures and over taking time out to properly nurture oneself
- Unrealistic ideals that are threatening rather than motivating
- Inability to deal with anger or other interpersonal tensions
- Extreme need to be liked by others, prompting unrealistic involvement with others
- Seeing money or resources wasted on projects that do not seem to help people
- Too many clients assigned with too little time to handle their needs
- Serious lack of charity among those with whom we must work
- Significant lack of appreciation by superiors, colleagues, or those whom we are trying to serve
- Extreme powerlessness to effect needed change or being overwhelmed by paperwork and administrative tasks
- Working with people who have burnout

Burnout syndrome is characterized by physical symptoms such as fatigue, sleeplessness, backache, upset stomach, and headaches. Emotional changes may include anxiety, irritability, depression, and hopelessness. These symptoms are similar to STS, and therefore lead some people to confuse the syndromes. The major difference is in behaviors. The behavioral manifestations of burnout include aggression, cynicism, calling in sick, being relieved when clients do not show up for appointments, substandard work performance, and "just getting by." One specific characteristic noted in people who suffer burnout is that of indifference—a lack of caring about their work and even about their clients. Burnout fuels significant attrition among professionals working with traumatized populations (Pulido 2007).

In contrast to burnout, STS behaviors are quite different than those observed most often in disaster responders. The characteristic of indifference is lacking in staff experiencing STS. Instead, the counselor works relentlessly for the survivor, often sacrificing their own health and private life to devote more time to the case or cause. The counselor is passionately involved in her or his work, often stays late on the job, and skips lunch or breaks to continue their efforts to help others. Burnout victims are more often likely to quit the job or leave the profession altogether as opposed to those suffering from STS, who, with proper professional and self-care, will likely experience a quick recovery. Disaster mental health responders, in particular, generally remain working in the field, often moving from one traumatic event to another.

11.3 PSYCHOLOGICAL AND PHYSIOLOGICAL RESPONSES TO TRAUMATIC STRESS

As disaster mental health workers, it is important to help survivors recognize the normalcy of most stress reactions. It is important to recognize this for oneself as well. Mild to moderate stress reactions in the immediate and early postimpact phases of disaster are highly prevalent because survivors (and their families, community members, and rescue workers) accurately recognize the grave danger in disaster (Young et al. 1998). Although stress reactions may seem "extreme," and cause distress, they generally do not remain or become chronic problems. Most people recover fully from even moderate to severe stress reactions within 6 to 16 months (Baum and Fleming 1993; Green and Lindy 1994; La Greca et al. 1996; Steinglass and Gerrity 1990). Physical distress may come and go in rapid intervals depending on the number of hours that the disaster worker continues in the field, their level of stress, the amount of sleep they get, and their general physical health.

A variety of factors have been found to influence the likelihood that an individual within a community will develop serious or lasting psychosocial problems in the wake of disasters or, conversely, serve as a support to aid the individual in recovering from the disaster experience. Gender, age, prior trauma experiences, ethnicity, culture, socioeconomic status, family structure, severity and length of exposure, secondary stressors, predisaster psychiatric history, and a lack of psychosocial resources all appear to play a role. Undoubtedly, these factors work together in complex ways, and in fact may be interactive to either mitigate or exacerbate the effects of the disaster (Norris, Friedman, and Watson 2002a).

The type, size, and scope of a disaster can affect the survivor's mental health. In particular, traumatic events caused by human malevolence are perceived as more stressful than those caused by human error or accident. In general, incidents precipitated by humans are seen as more stressful than natural disasters (Callahan 1998). Some traumatic events appear to be particularly difficult to cope with because of their apparent meaninglessness. Family members of victims who die in transportation disasters (large plane or boat accidents) or terrorist attacks report a meaninglessness about their family member's death that seems to add to their crisis state, possibly because of the rarity of such accidents (Brooks and McKinlay 1992; Dalgliesh et al. 1996; North et al. 1999). Several studies have compared the results across samples experiencing natural disasters, technological disasters, and war/mass violence (Norris et al. 2001; Norris et al. 2002b). The findings regarding the consequences of experiencing disasters caused by malicious human intent were unequivocal. Samples of survivors who experienced mass violence, such as terrorist attacks, were far more likely than other samples to be severely or very severely impaired. From either an information processing or resource loss perspective, disasters of mass violence may be especially difficult for victims to comprehend or assimilate, making intrusion and avoidance symptoms more likely. Because shooting sprees and terrorist attacks tend to be indiscriminate and random (Stern 1999), they create acute helplessness and anxiety and may be more likely than other disasters to shatter beliefs of the self as invulnerable and of the world as a meaningful and just place (Pearlman and MacIan 1995).

Disasters that engender severe, lasting, and pervasive psychological effects are rare, but they do happen. On occasion, even natural disasters may be of sufficient magnitude to produce severe and chronic impairment in a substantial portion of the population (Briere and Elliot 2000; Norris et al. 2001). The literature has indicated that effects were greatest when at least two of the following event-level factors were present: (1) The disaster caused extreme and widespread damage to property; (2) The disaster engendered serious and ongoing financial problems for the community; (3) The disaster was caused by human intent; and (4) The impact was associated with a high prevalence of trauma in the form of injuries, threat to life, and loss of life. When such disasters occur, it appears that the need for professional mental health services will be widespread (Norris 2002a, b; North, Hong, and Pfefferbaum 2002; Pfefferbaum et al. 1999).

There are a number of possible psychological and physiological reactions that are considered within the norm for individuals experiencing traumatic stress following a disaster. The psychological symptoms that align with the DSM-IV (2000) diagnosis of PTSD include intrusiveness, which can take the form of nightmares, flashbacks, sounds, and/or smells that are associated with the event; hypervigilance, which can take the form of a heightened startle response or a false sense of being unsafe; dissociation and/or numbing, which is often described as having observed the traumatic event from outside oneself as if watching a movie and having no feeling related to it; and avoidance, characterized by taking measures to assure that one is not exposed to the people or places that were associated with the traumatic event.

However, while PTSD is a serious and debilitating condition, it is neither the only nor the most common psychological response to a traumatic event. Symptoms of generalized anxiety may actually occur more often than PTSD, taking the form of nervousness or unrealistic and/or unfocused fear. Other psychological effects of trauma include depressive-like symptoms such as feeling down or feeling despair over one's situation. Some disaster workers may experience manic-like symptoms due to the buildup of adrenaline, cortisol, and other hormones that are not discharged properly. This chemical imbalance may present as a sense of fearlessness, overconfidence, or even grandiosity.

As noted in Table 11. 1, the psychological effects of trauma include a list of symptoms that may not create a diagnosis, but rather cause distress and disturbance to the individuals (and their families) as they continue to attempt to move toward recovery. Common complaints include irritability, rage, and feelings of guilt.

The physical effects of trauma can also be extracted from a long list of complaints. Most commonly noted trauma-related physical concerns, including fatigue, headaches, stomachaches, physical pain, insomnia, and loss or gain of appetite, are not associated with any physiological cause. These and other symptoms can occur alone or coincide with other problems listed in the domains located in Table 11.1.

The number of influential factors makes it important for survivors to perform their own self-assessment. They should be encouraged to reflect on what has changed for them since the traumatic event and to determine to what extent their symptoms are bothering them or interfering with their daily functioning. As with any physical complaints that continue for more than two weeks, a physical assessment or medical consultation is recommended. There may be physiological reasons for pain that may be related to or may be a result of the traumatic event. Conversely, the emergence of a physical problem unrelated to but occurring within the same time frame as the traumatic event may be coincidental and should be evaluated. Individuals with chronic medical conditions can suffer an exacerbation or worsening of symptoms during times of high stress. It is important to emphasize that disaster mental health workers may experience similar reactions as the survivors as a result of their exposure to, contact with, and concern for those individuals primarily impacted by the disaster situation. This "secondary" exposure to the grief and loss of others has been found to produce the same physiological and psychological responses among first responders. These symptoms include those listed in Table 11.1 in the emotional, cognitive, physical, social, or spiritual domains. Symptoms may be aggravated by the severity of the traumatic material to which the disaster worker is exposed, such as the direct contact with survivors, listening to their graphic accounts, stories, photos, and other circumstances associated with the traumatic event (Stamm 2002). For example, following the terrorist attacks of 9/11, mental health workers who were responsible for accompanying family members to identify body parts of their loved ones reported experiencing severe STS reactions following their sessions with these clients (Pulido 2005).

Additionally, since many disaster mental health response staffs are from within the affected community and often share the exposure of those they are helping, they may be doubly burdened by experiencing their own direct stress in addition to the stress of helping others. The study results described here are generalizeable to all disaster-response staff and most especially to those with a shared trauma experience (Tosone et al. 2003). Alternately, many staff report some stress relief resulting from their ability to take positive action by participating in the disaster response. In Hudnall-Stamm's Professional Quality of Life Compassion Satisfaction and Fatigue Scales (ProQOL-IV; 2002), she notes that having a sense of work satisfaction can mitigate STS.

Similar to survivors they are helping, disaster mental health response staffs can perform a self-assessment at intervals throughout their work to help them monitor their stress. Evaluating what has changed for them as a result of responding to the disaster as well as utilizing the ProQOL-IV (Stamm 2002) noted previously can assist in this process. This ProQOL-IV (2002) is described in more detail in Section 11.7.

TABLE 11.1

Summary Chart of Common Traumatic Stress Reactions

Emotional Effects	Cognitive Effects
Shock	Impaired concentration
Terror	Impaired decision-making ability
Irritability	Memory impairment
Blame	Disbelief
Anger	Confusion
Guilt	Nightmares
Grief or sadness	Decreased self-esteem
Emotional numbing	Decreased self-efficacy
Helplessness	Self-blame
Loss of pleasure derived from familiar activities	Intrusive thoughts/memories
Difficulty feeling happy	Worry
Difficulty experiencing loving feelings	Dissociation (e.g., tunnel vision, dreamlike or "spacey" feeling)

Physical Effects	Interpersonal Effects
Fatigue, exhaustion	Increased relational conflict
Insomnia	Social withdrawal
Cardiovascular strain	Reduced relational intimacy
Startle response	Alienation
Hyperarousal	Impaired work performance
Increased physical pain	Impaired school performance
Reduced immune response	Decreased satisfaction
Headaches	Distrust
Gastrointestinal upset	Externalization of blame
Decreased appetite	Externalization of vulnerability
Decreased libido	Feeling abandoned/rejected
Vulnerability to illness	Overprotectiveness
Pounding heart, rapid breathing, sweating	

Behavioral Effects	Spiritual Effects
Irritability; outbursts of anger	Questioning values and beliefs
Easily upset or agitated	Experiencing a loss of meaning
Startle response; jumpiness	Becoming cynical
Upset stomach; eating too much or too little; other gastrointestinal problems	Angry that bad things have happened to good people
Alcohol and/or substance abuse	Loss of interest in faith-based activities
Pounding heart, rapid breathing sweating, or severe headache	Directing anger toward God (Shultz et al. 2009)
Sleep problems	
Hypervigilence; constantly alert	
Worsening of medical problems	
Exhaustion	

Source: New South Wales Institute of Psychiatry and Centre for Mental Health, *Disaster Mental Health Response Handbook*, NSW Health, North Sydney, Australia, 2000.

11.4 COGNITIVE AND BEHAVIORAL REACTIONS TO TRAUMA

Individuals affected by trauma often do not make the connection between cognitive and/or behavioral changes in themselves in the immediate or even intermediate aftermath of the event. Most individuals do not see themselves as having reactions to a trauma that require any type of mental health intervention and statistically, they are correct (Galea et al. 2005; CMHS 2001). Generally, people are able to recover over time and return to their predisaster level of functioning or adapt to the change in their environment with no mental health intervention at all. Still, in the time frame between the traumatic event and recovery, many people who have never previously suffered any emotional distress may, in fact, have seriously disturbing symptoms. They may still continue to function and therefore are not diagnosable. These individuals rise every morning and attend to their activities of daily living, get their children off to school, go to work, prepare dinner for the family, and so forth. They just do so while suffering with distress symptoms. During the time of recovery from the shock, grief, fear, anxiety, or other symptoms related to the trauma but before reaching a point where they experience recovery or adaptation, these groups may benefit from help to more easily or quickly work through their distress.

The same is true of disaster mental health response staff who often do not recognize STS symptoms in themselves. Since many responders are mental health professionals, they may feel they are "immune" or "not vulnerable" to the same types of distress experienced by the general population or a high-risk group. Moreover, an underlying sense of incompetency or lack of confidence may add to denying, avoiding, or hiding their symptoms. Cognitive and behavioral reactions to a disaster can appear in the immediate aftermath and can be quite disturbing. Yet, these symptoms are often perceived as unrelated to the trauma. A common cognitive problem reported by disaster-response staffs is memory impairment. This may be due to a combination of physical fatigue and information overload, but can also be a reaction to stress. Additionally, individuals may suffer with confusion or difficulty concentrating. Cognitive problems can also lead to poor judgment, a critically necessary attribute when responding to a disaster.

Responders who begin to realize that they may be having cognitive problems may risk being pulled from their assignment if they report such. Therefore, they may be even more hesitant to let anyone know of the difficulties they are experiencing. This is one of the many reasons why buddy systems work well in disasters and why supervisory supports are so important. There needs to be an agreement between designated buddies that they will trust each other to determine if a serious cognitive problem is evident. Poor judgment on a disaster site can result in high-risk or outright dangerous decisions being made (e.g., walking into a "hot" zone without protection or authorization, driving while impaired, etc.).

Other cognitive problems are closely related to behavioral and other responses (and are therefore listed in more than one domain in Table 11.1). These include nightmares, worrying, and dissociation. Behavioral issues themselves can present as the routine ups and downs that anyone might experience in the course of a few days, weeks, or months. These, too, can be direct stress reactions. Someone who is normally cool under pressure might become irritable or short tempered. A responder who is also a parent trying to manage their intense disaster caseload might become short tempered with her/his spouse or children—losing patience when they had previously shown more understanding and acceptance. Others might begin to use tobacco, alcohol, or illicit substances as a way of self-medicating, numbing, or negative coping. For many years, the excessive use of alcohol in the emergency response professions was accepted as a norm of the culture. Coworkers did not view nightly drinks together or weekend binges as problematic. Increased knowledge about the serious problems that can arise from using alcohol as a coping mechanism has changed this previous norm (SAMHSA 2010). It is no longer acceptable to watch colleagues use alcohol as a numbing agent, drink themselves into a divorce, or lose their profession due to alcohol or substance abuse.

Behavioral responses such as irritability, overworking, and substance abuse bring with them a tendency for isolation. It is worthwhile to note that lack of social supports has been known to increase an individual's risk of experiencing more serious distress symptoms and also that isolation itself is problematic. Connecting survivors with family members, friends, and other supports are primary aspects of helping (NCTSN and NCPTSD 2006).

11.5   RISK FACTORS INHERENT IN DISASTER RESPONSE WORK THAT CONTRIBUTE TO STS RISK

Disaster response workers need the valuable assets of empathy, perseverance, diligence, and the ability to give themselves to their work usually for long periods each day and over time (e.g., weeks and months). These important qualities combined with exposure to the disaster work environment and traumatic client cases may heighten STS symptoms. Empathy is a valuable tool for staff working with traumatized adults and children. Survivors recover with crisis interventions and/or good casework and therapy because staff are there emotionally for them. However, when disaster workers overempathize with survivors or "feel their pain," they become vulnerable to internalizing the survivor's trauma-related pain. Children's trauma is especially difficult and provocative for disaster-response workers. Empathy with a child who has been injured, witnessed violence, become homeless, or has lost a loved one can produce additional stress. In addition to the intense feelings empathy can invoke, the workers often perceive themselves as the caregiver, the one responsible for the safety and well-being of the child, and the one who has somehow failed regardless of the cause of the child's trauma.

Significant disparity between a worker's expectations and the realities of the work can also develop. This may be true especially for newer staff who were not anticipating the intensity of the work and have no previous experience or reference point. Difficulty can arise when taking on the "role" of bearing witness to a survivor's pain and discomfort. Training alone cannot prepare a new recovery worker for this job reality. The combination of being exposed to their client's trauma and the burden of having to achieve results in mental health, legal, or other administrative systems that are not always sympathetic to survivors also cause stress to the disaster worker.

Responding to a large-scale or grievous disaster with a significant number of deaths, exposure to physical injury, and/or massive destruction may evoke in disaster workers feelings of vulnerability, powerlessness, and ineffectiveness. Often workers may be embarrassed to admit that they are having a difficult time emotionally for fear of being perceived as weak or incompetent, and they may deny or try to conceal feelings. Disaster workers may try to make light of a negative experience or joke about it rather than admit to distressing feelings. This type of joking is known as gallows humor and is often seen in fire and police response staff who are trained to be "inoculated" against emotional responses to trauma.

In addition, many disaster workers have experienced prior personal losses or traumas as well as now having a "shared trauma" experience with the survivors. The pain of current or past experiences can resurface during work with disaster survivors, exacerbating the STS impact. Experiences that helpers share with survivors may deepen their understanding of the survivors' material. However, if the helper's trauma history or their own current experience remains unrecognized, unprocessed, or unresolved, helpers may have their own emotions triggered by survivors' stories and be at greater risk for missing or blocking out the survivors' most immediate needs (Rosenbloom, Pratt, and Pearlman 1999). In addition, they may then further bury their own emotions only to have them "triggered" again in another disaster, risking the development of a more serious and/or chronic problem.

Disaster responders may also experience information overload, as a result of interacting with a large number of survivors in a minimal amount of time, often with insufficient regrouping or recovery time. This can occur when the responder takes in a large amount of information quickly and over a short period of time regarding survivors' painful, gruesome, and horrific situations. Staff may be secondarily traumatized by listening to similar stories over and over without adequate time to recover, debrief, or process their cases with peers or supervisors.

The high level of accountability in all areas of disaster work is an additional stressor. Responders often have no control over their work schedule. Documentation of contacts, field reports, and referral tracking are needed, with little time, and inadequate support systems or equipment for timely completion. Disaster survivors with various needs, supervisors, agency demands, and public responsibility all contribute to the stress and unavoidable imbalance often experienced by staff. While these stressors do not often lead to STS, workers need to be aware of potential contributing factors and develop a plan to manage these on both professional and personal levels.

11.6 MONITORING YOUR LEVELS OF STS, BURNOUT, AND SATISFACTION WITH WORK

Detection of secondary stress trauma may require taking a history of exposure to trauma through one's employment (Steinberg 1997). Professionals who work in the disaster-response field may benefit from being able to identify and monitor their levels of STS, potential for burnout, and level of satisfaction with their work life. A scientifically reliable and valid tool that is commonly used for this purpose is the Professional Quality of Life Scale–Revision IV (ProQOL R-IV), developed by traumatologist Charles R. Figley (1996) and revised by B. Hudnall-Stamm (2002). This scale, a self-test, measures three distinct subscales: Compassion Satisfaction, Burnout, and Compassion Fatigue/Secondary Trauma. Hudnall-Stamm (2002) reported that the ProQOL-IV is composed of three discrete scales that do not yield a composite score. Each scale is psychometrically unique and cannot be combined with the other scales.

The first scored scale is Compassion Satisfaction and is designed to identify the pleasure derived from work. For example, an individual may enjoy helping others through their work. They may feel positively about their colleagues and their ability to contribute to the work setting or even the greater good of society. Higher scores on this scale represent a greater satisfaction related to the ability to be an effective caregiver on the job. Compassion Satisfaction is also expected to mitigate the development of STS.

The second scored scale is Burnout. From the research perspective, burnout is associated with feelings of hopelessness and difficulties in dealing with work or in doing one's job effectively. These negative feelings usually have a gradual onset. They can reflect the feeling that an individual's efforts make no difference, or they can be associated with a very high workload or a nonsupportive work environment. It is important for workers to differentiate between burnout and STS, since the interventions differ.

The third scored scale is Compassion Fatigue/Secondary Trauma, which concerns work-related, secondary exposure to extremely stressful events, such as repeatedly hearing disturbing, traumatic stories of what happened to clients or others. Workers exposed to others' trauma experiences in areas such as disaster response, emergency medical care, or child protective services are at risk for suffering secondary traumatic stress. The symptoms of STS are usually rapid in onset and associated with a particular event. They often include excessive fear, difficulty sleeping, seeing mental images of the upsetting event, or avoiding things that remind one of the event.

The entire scale on the ProQOL consists of 30 questions, with 10 questions in each subscale. Respondents are asked to rate the frequency that they have experienced a characteristic or feeling in the last 30 days. Scores are then summed across subscales for three distinct scores. Theoretic cut scores and averages are noted as a reference point and may suggest a follow-up medical or mental health evaluation. Stamm (2002) indicates that these scores are not meant to be diagnostic in nature, but rather to assist in the awareness of STS and to be used as a guide. Disaster response workers can download this scale at the Web site http://www.isu.edu/~bhstamm. The ProQOL is free and should not be modified or sold. The author should be credited.

The ProQOL can be utilized by workers on a routine basis to monitor their compassion satisfaction, burnout, and secondary traumatic stress levels. Supervisors might use the completion of the ProQOL as part of an overall stress management or in-service self-care to assist workers by increasing their awareness and providing education about STS.

11.7 KNOWLEDGE, RECOGNITION, AND RESPONDING

In order to prevent or manage secondary trauma, there are three key prevention practices that disaster responders should know and incorporate into their routine work regime: (1) obtaining knowledge of STS and risk factors; (2) monitoring and recognition of the symptoms of STS should they begin to impact the disaster recovery worker or their peers; and (3) responding to STS symptoms by applying skills to mitigate the effects.

Knowledge of STS is accomplished through the acquisition of information and skills, such as reading this chapter, familiarizing oneself with the personal and professional risk factors, and attending outside training on the subjects of STS and stress management, in general.

Recognition takes place as the worker is able to identify risks and exposure. The worker will notice personal changes that are not attributable to other factors in his or her life and seem to be connected to work with clients. These personal changes can occur in the worker's relationships, or in the worker's physical, emotional, or spiritual life. Sometimes colleagues, supervisors, or friends can play a role in helping one recognize signs of STS. Taking the ProQOL self-assessment can be useful as a guide and an indicator of change. The test should be taken at regular intervals that serve to create baseline and continuous data for comparison. This stage is accomplished with peer support, supervision, and reflection. Recognizing these changes leads to the next step—responding.

Responding is the application of skills, accomplished with organizational support, professional and peer support, and personal self-care. Fortunately, there are ways workers can manage secondary trauma. Secondary trauma can often be prevented, always be addressed, and usually resolved with the practices suggested herein.

11.7.1   INTERVENTIONS THAT HELP

The interventions that can be used to ameliorate the effects of STS are grouped into three main categories; organizational, professional and personal.

11.7.1.1   Organizational Interventions

Agency leaders and those in charge of disaster recovery efforts are responsible for helping prevent and manage STS (Munroe 1999). They need to be aware of the risks inherent in disaster work and address them proactively within the organizational structure and directly with the workforce. Some important responsibilities of management include: providing training and information to workers on handling STS; providing a healthy work setting that makes the environment as supportive as possible; adequate security precautions for workers both in the office and in the field; and instituting a "buddy system" for workers to offset STS reactions. Recognition of STS and "buy-in" from top executives down to managers and supervisors makes a significant difference.

Management must ensure adequate supervision for the staff, particularly in times of emergency/ crisis cases. Supervisors should be trained to recognize and respond to STS among their workers. This skill will enable them not only to validate and normalize the STS reactions that staff are having regarding the disaster work, but can also quicken recovery. Accessibility to supervisors can be difficult in the throes of disaster work, so supervisors must be creative if individual supervisory sessions are not feasible. Managers can try to support their staff via individual telephone or e-mail supervision, or via group supervision, teleconferences or Web-based list serves. The critical component is the regularity of "check-ins" as the workers need to have time to discuss troubling issues that arise while working disaster recovery assignments. Debriefings, supervision, training, and peer support have been shown to be effective methods to ameliorate stress symptoms from traumatic events and hasten recovery (Bell 1995). Pulido (2005) reported that after the terrorist attacks of 9/11, those clinicians who received these services reported they were a benefit and that they appeared to help them reduce stress levels. Clinicians also reported a desire for individual "checking-in" by a supervisor as well as training on how to deal with the complex aspects of providing mental health care after a terrorist attack.

Management should attempt to provide disaster recovery workers with varied activities or caseloads so that certain staff are not always caring for the most traumatized or difficult cases. Scheduling needs to be thoughtful and include mechanisms by which the time that a disaster recovery worker spends at the disaster site, or working directly with disaster victims, is monitored. Alternating case-loads, assigned activities, and site locations can serve to offset STS reactions. Management must also set good practice policies for hiring, compensation, work hours, overtime, and a regular break schedule. Personnel policies that ensure adequate time off, access to medical and mental health care, and solid insurance coverage for staff are also important organizational responsibilities. Munroe (1999) posited that since those who work with trauma survivors are susceptible to suffering effects from their exposure, organizations have a "duty to warn" workers prior to starting their assignments or job. A good time to address these issues is during the recruitment process, allowing the disaster recovery candidate to avoid being blindsided by the types of cases that he or she may encounter in the course of a normal work situation. It is appropriate to describe to the candidate the types of situations, cases, and overall working climate associated with disaster situations. Accessible resources for handling stress should be explored, along with an overview of agency supports available to candidates during assignments.

The organization leading the disaster recovery effort should also provide training for the work-force in logistical issues, standards of practice, and STS. A central repository of training information readily accessible for response to both current and future disaster work should be available. Content should include information on dealing with client reactions, therapeutic interventions, and referral sources. The most comprehensive, evidence-informed manual for immediate disaster mental health response work is the *Psychological First Aid: Field Operations Guide* (NCTSN and NCPTSD 2005). Following 9/11, clinicians expressed a desire for more seminars, training sessions, and workshops dealing specifically with outcomes related to terrorist-inflicted trauma. Trainings should also include information regarding the prevention and management of STS reactions (Pulido 2005).

Supervisors need to be familiar with the mental health supports available to staff and have a comfort level with recommending therapy or other counseling services when warranted. When supervisors and agency heads have a greater recognition and understanding of the impact of STS risks involved in treating trauma survivors, there will likely be a more supportive and encouraging milieu for counselors to utilize therapeutic support for themselves. Administrators should attend training regarding the management and prevention of STS and be prepared to initiate the organizational support for their staff.

Finally, organizations should plan follow-up care for disaster mental health workers once the disaster behavioral response program ends. Disaster recovery workers may have continued posttraumatic and STS responses associated with their own prior trauma history, the disaster that they just encountered, and the cumulative impact of their work with survivors. As a result of 9/11, many clinicians reported they began to experience STS reactions 30 months following the attacks. Unfortunately, this was the time when their contracts to provide services ended. Now unemployed, these workers were left to deal with their reactions on their own, without any organizational or professional support. This scenario was especially evident for many counselors who participated in the 9/11 disaster mental health response called Project Liberty, who were released from their agencies as soon as the contracts to provide this service ended (Pulido 2005). Routine, monthly follow-up programs and activities targeted for these workers should be integrated into the overall framework of terrorist disaster recovery plans as disaster-response programs end.

Forums should be provided as a venue by which counselors can not only talk about their experiences, but also to be recognized for their heroic efforts in helping with the disaster recovery effort. This programming should include the following: an overview of the symptoms of STS explaining why disaster recovery clinicians experience STS; examples of disaster STS reactions and the differences between STS and "burnout"; self-report measures for STS, burnout, and work satisfaction; and an overview of the various types of interventions that can be put in place to prevent and manage STS. Workers should know that STS is an unavoidable, but manageable, aspect of disaster mental health response work.

11.7.1.2 Professional Interventions

Disaster recovery workers can utilize the followings steps to minimize the impact of trauma-related work:

1. *Balancing the number of hours* worked per week as well as the proportion of work that is directly trauma related should be taken into consideration when cases are assigned. Disaster recovery workers should also create a work pace that maximizes emotional and physical health, taking time for breaks, lunch, and vacation. It is also important to set time boundaries that balance work life with personal life. Overworking is common among dedicated professionals. Many assume too many responsibilities, take work home, and subsequently do not allow adequate time to separate from work. Setting limits may be hard, especially in disaster-response settings where long days are expected, but rejuvenation is critical for sustaining the ongoing recovery effort.

2. *Regular supervision* for all staff conducting high-stress work is essential, regardless of their years of experience. Receiving perspective on a case from someone skilled and trusted, or to receive guidance when facing a new challenge, can be most helpful. If supervision is not available at the disaster-recovery site, staff should reach out to a mentor, preferably another professional familiar with the unique stressors of disaster work.

3. *Peer group supervision* used for case consultation is helpful. Such collaboration nurtures collegiality and reduces worker isolation. This worker-team concept can also help staff acknowledge STS reactions as well as recognize the toll that exposure to a survivor's trauma can have on a professional. Colleagues can also help peers arrange particularly complex trauma cases into manageable action steps and reduce the overwhelming quality and disorganizing influence of disaster-recovery work.

4. Staff should try to attend *professional trainings* and subscribe to newsletters or pertinent journals that will enhance knowledge about issues facing disaster survivors, early intervention techniques, treatment modalities, and ongoing research in the area. These formats can be reinvigorating and serve to provide new knowledge in the effort to support survivors' recovery. Disaster-recovery workers should be aware of the impact that their own personal trauma history could have on current work. Some activities may help the worker ameliorate the secondary effects that are related to their trauma histories (e.g., personal therapy or supportive counseling). Awareness of personal "red flags" and even structuring the caseload to avoid certain types of clients or situations may be helpful for both the disaster-recovery worker and the survivor.

5. Finally, all disaster-recovery workers should develop a *workday self-care plan* to aid with coping. Plan for time pre and post contacts with survivors and for emergencies, which may include suicidal ideation or flashbacks. Also, it is important to take breaks throughout the day. Respite should be part of the scheduling process. Depending on the schedule, make time for breakfast, lunch, or dinner. If pressed for time, workers should take mini breaks where they can. Even minimal down time helps keep a positive perspective. Staffs should incorporate replenishment into each workday.

11.7.1.3 Personal Interventions

Personal interventions include aspects of physical, social, and psychological self-care. Maintaining the health of one's body is essential. This includes regular exercise, scheduling and keeping routine medical and dental appointments, and making sure to get adequate sleep and nutrition every day. Workers should try to plan for nutritious meals as best they can under the circumstances. Prepackaged energy or protein snacks can be helpful and are easily transported. Workers should also be aware of how sleeping and eating habits can change under stress and how careful monitoring helps to ensure functioning at full capacity.

As with survivors, social support is essential for disaster mental health response workers. Talking with others can be a stress reliever. Coworkers may share similar feelings, and discussions can serve to normalize and validate staffs' experiences as well as reduce isolation. Therapeutic support from a licensed clinician may also be helpful and, in some situations, recommended.

Social activism may be a restorative activity for some. Connecting with other advocates about issues impacting survivors generates a sense of hope and purpose, and provides a sense of shared mission. Joining professional societies that have an advocacy arm or informative newsletters/mailings can give one a sense of control and purpose.

Maintaining a diversity of activities further strengthens coping capacity. Disaster recovery staff should aim to have a balance of work, outside interests, social contacts, personal time, and recreation. Recommendations include: incorporating relaxation into every day; engaging in pleasurable activities such as having contact with nature; spending time caring for pets or gardening; and engaging in creative expression. This change of view gives one a larger perspective of the world. Recovery workers are so busy they may forget to engage the creative side of themselves. Artistry, baking, cooking, playing a musical instrument, singing, dancing, and playing sports all help mitigate STS reactions.

Practitioners often cite spirituality and meditation as helpful in handling STS (Pulido 2005). The benefits of meditation can include reduced blood pressure, easier breathing, and muscle relaxation. Spirituality can include participating in an organized religion or simply engaging in activities that bolster positive faith in one's self. Some find comfort in religious groups; others may expand their beliefs in new ways.

Humor is a precious commodity. Workers should aim to have a good laugh at least once a day. Laughing can reduce stress and relieve tension, and as a coping strategy, it is priceless.

Finally, disaster recovery workers should be encouraged to develop a self-care protocol. There are basic elements of a self-care protocol that almost everyone needs to renew themselves on a daily basis. It really does not require too much to take a step back from our work routine to become refreshed and regain perspective. Wicks (2006) cited some basic elements that include:

- Quiet walks
- Time and space for meditation
- Spiritual and recreational reading, including the diaries and biographies of others whom you admire
- Exercise
- Opportunities to laugh offered by television, movies, or cheerful friends
- A hobby such as baking, gardening, or painting
- Telephone calls to family and friends who inspire you
- Listening to music

It is most important to recognize the need to intentionally and spontaneously put leisure activities into a schedule so they represent a constant, significant portion of the time that disaster recovery workers have available each day, week, month, and year.

By selecting a few of the interventions from each category, workers can greatly reduce the negative impact of STS while keeping themselves strong and energized so they can continue their important and life-saving work.

11.8   TRAINING

Relevant professional training, education, and supervision can assist staff to develop and improve the skills required to respond appropriately to disaster-affected communities. These are also the supports and structure that most mental health professionals require to perform at their best (Young et al. 1998). In their study of 9/11 responders, which included construction workers, engineers, law enforcement, and other unaffiliated volunteers as well as mental health staffs, higher rates of PTSD were found in those workers with less experience and training (Perrin et al. 2007). The New York Case Study (Norris et al. 2006) found that despite confidence in their clinical skills, most providers felt that additional training was necessary for their mental health response staffs.

These studies support the recommendation that while mental health professionals are involved in disaster-response programs, many of the staffs are paraprofessionals (students, interns, related health professionals) and untrained community workers. Response staffs should all receive disaster training despite varying levels of education. Professional mental health workers may fill roles as supervisors and managers, but should be well informed as to the primary skills being taught to crisis counselors and outreach workers. While many mental health professionals receive crisis intervention and assessment skills training as part of core educational curriculum, disaster-specific education and training is not currently part of required university study. Therefore, it is highly recommended that disaster-specific training be a requirement for all responder staffs. National crisis counseling and training programs authorized as a result of federally declared disasters mandate that all staffs receive basic disaster-response training (SAMHSA 2009). Core trainings include information about what disaster mental health counseling is, and about what it is not. As an example, core training or "just-in-time" training that is offered in the immediate aftermath of a disaster should convey the message that disaster mental health counseling is not office-based, psychoanalytic or psychodynamic psychotherapy that addresses trauma. Moreover, it is not formal mental health treatment for posttraumatic stress disorder or other diagnosable mental illnesses such as anxiety or depression.

In brief, disaster mental health services focus on making a connection that helps to calm and support survivors. While these connections are based in the present time frame, they will assist survivors in planning for the immediate future by helping them remain functional and hopeful. The *Psychological First Aid: Field Operations Guide* (PFA; NCTSN and NCPTSD 2006) is the most current evidence-informed manual that provides detailed instruction for addressing disaster survivors in the immediate phase response. The PFA identifies eight core actions: contact and engagement; safety and comfort; stabilization; information gathering/needs and current concerns; practical assistance; connection with social supports; information on coping; and linkage with collaborative services. Examples of communication with survivors are provided, and as with any type of counseling, flexibility is stressed. The counselor must work with the survivors "where they are at" and recognize that not all survivors will want or need all core actions. Survivors might not be ready to address each of these actions in the allotted time frame.

Psychological First Aid training is recommended as a preparedness measure since the materials can be taught prior to a disaster. The PFA is appropriate as a "just-in-time" training post incident as well. In addition, the PFA training can be offered to community workers, paraprofessionals, and mental health professionals responding to a disaster. One does not need to be a clinician to learn how to deliver psychological first aid.

While PFA is best delivered in the immediate aftermath of an event, it may continue to be offered in circumstances where safety issues remain unresolved (e.g., numerous earthquake aftershocks or continued terrorist activity). PFA may also benefit survivors who have been previously unattended by mental health service providers weeks into the response.

The United States Federal Emergency Management Agency (FEMA) and Substance Abuse and Mental Health Services Administration (SAMHSA) training curricula are available to states requesting such assistance in the event of a federally declared disaster. These trainings are generally provided in the acute phase of the disaster mental health response and aim to assist disaster survivors in returning to their previous level of functioning. The federal Crisis Counseling Assistance and Training Program (CCP) core training covers the topics of active listening, outreach, cultural competence, and provision of education, support, resources, and referral. While only the core training is mandated for federal grantee CCPs, several additional, related trainings are strongly recommended. The content of supplemental training includes transition training, which can assist workers to understand how survivors' needs might be changing. Such changes may be based on the physical status of the affected community, the economic losses, and the level of political attention over time. The mid-phase training is generally offered three to six months post incident. This training addresses the stress survivors may encounter as disaster-related problems continue and new issues—such as health concerns, substance abuse, or serious mental health concerns—emerge. Anniversary training is generally held a few weeks prior to the first-year anniversary of the disaster and assists mental health responders in identifying anticipatory reactions to the anniversary as well as other triggers. Responders learn what kinds of intervention strategies to offer survivors and to assimilate themselves as they move through this time frame with the communities they are assisting. Phase-down and close-out training teaches staff how to turn over any remaining concerns to the community in a way that empowers those affected to manage independently.

Additional training that addresses the needs of high-risk populations, namely, children, frail elderly, immigrants, and those previously traumatized may be helpful. Such training is generally contingent upon how much information the responders already possess and what further needs are indicated (Young et al. 2006). As noted at the beginning of this section, several studies report that staffs have fewer symptoms of distress, report higher levels of confidence, and perform optimally with appropriate training.

Disaster responders who remain working in a response setting with the same survivors for extended periods of time may require special training to address more complex issues such as boundary setting, transference/countertransference, and burn-out. Emergency and disaster situations can decrease the natural defense systems that individuals (and groups) build over the course of their life experience resulting in increased vulnerability. Susceptibility may create a false or temporary character presentation atypical of the person in nonemergency situations. For example, the person may present as more helpless or needy than usual. As a result of needing more help than they would outside of the traumatic circumstances, they may share more personal details or invite a deeper level of intimacy. Disaster mental health counselors need to be highly aware of the appropriate boundaries in such situations to avoid disempowering, infantilizing, or, at worst, becoming personally involved in an inappropriate manner with affected individuals and colleagues. Responders also need to differentiate between crisis counseling and case management so as not to join the survivor in emotional avoidance or using their designated time advocating for physical and economic needs rather than in counseling. Staff who cannot create proper boundaries, or who foster dependency rather than empowering survivors, or who have difficulty realizing that survivors' needs are usually more than any staff can completely address, likely require supervisory intervention rather than training. Such staff should be closely supervised to assure appropriate interactions or, possibly, be removed from the disaster setting as necessary.

In addition to specific training aimed at providing staff with the skills needed to assist community members, stress management training should be offered throughout the response for the workers themselves. If staff are not managing their own distress as it relates to the trauma itself as well as their work, they may be susceptible to secondary traumatic stress. Building stress management training into the formal response program assures that mental health response staff have an opportunity to address their own needs (Pulido and Jacina 2007).

Stress management and secondary traumatic stress trainings have multiple goals, including:

- Educating the staff about the existence of secondary traumatic stress in the responder population
- Providing staff the skills to self assess, or to self-identify
- Destigmatizing secondary traumatic stress responses in the workers; assisting the workers in understanding they are not alone
- Providing a venue where the staff are more comfortable talking about their stress as well as offering an immediate opportunity to interact with colleagues

The psychoeducational materials presented in secondary traumatic stress trainings should include much of what has been presented in this chapter—education about the effects on different domains, namely, the physical, psychological, emotional, behavioral, and spiritual. Just as staff teach disaster survivors about their common responses, STS training should include normalizing details about what symptoms may be observed in the disaster mental health response population. Further, staff should be provided with tools to self-identify and self-assess. Trainings should include recommended interventions for addressing STS on a personal level such as self-care, pleasurable activity scheduling, adequate rest and physical exercise, proper nutrition, and a healthy dose of friends and family.

Staff should also be informed that STS symptoms might appear post deployment. While the Cochrane Review (Rose, Bisson, and Weseley 2001) on Critical Incident Stress Debriefing (CISD) cautions that the model may cause harm, some of the CISD recommendations provide useful and practical information that is harmless. These include reducing alcohol consumption and avoiding overexercising, addressing sleep problems, monitoring one's physical status, seeking spiritual support, and visiting a physician or counselor if any symptoms persist over a two-week period. Staff should avoid overexposure and refrain from participating in any situations where traumatic stress symptoms may be rearoused. Staff are at risk of rearousal or reexperiencing the trauma if they are mandated to give details of their traumatic experiences or witness that of others, especially when they are psychologically unprepared to do so.

Finally, disaster mental health response managers and administrators have a clear responsibility to provide staff with professional supports such as supervision, case conferencing, peer supports, buddy systems, and rotating schedules (Munroe 1999).

The Task Force on International Trauma Training of the International Society for Traumatic Stress Studies (Weine et al. 2002) suggests a supervision structure to support newly trained humanitarian aid workers who are exposed to traumatic stressors. These guidelines are based on a consensus process and state the necessity of monitoring and evaluation for training procedures. Still, empirical research regarding the outcomes of training and supervision has not yet emerged in this developing field (Weine et al. 2002).

Of note is a recommendation from the New York Case Study (Norris et al. 2006) aimed at trainers indicating the need to recognize that trainees are likely to have been affected by the disaster themselves. Norris and her colleagues (2004) note that a trainee's own acute emotions can interfere with the understanding or acceptance of educational materials. Tosone and Bialkin (2003) also note that direct exposure becomes integrated into the professional lives of trauma counselors. Training and supervision are the most responsible ways by which to address these concerns and mitigate the development of secondary traumatic stress in the disaster mental health response population.

11.9   CONCLUSION

In this chapter, we have identified the differences between secondary traumatic stress and other terms that have been used interchangeably. The various domains that secondary traumatic stress can touch have been identified as well as the potential symptoms in each of these domains. Risk factors and ways in which to mitigate the development of secondary traumatic stress emphasizing the need for proper training, supervision, stress management, and self-care have been reviewed. Still, every disaster is as different as it is the same. There will be different types of survivors and communities with varying needs, as there will be different types of staff who participate in the response. When preparing disaster mental health response staff to work in the field, it is important to address the consideration that staff may be stressed in different ways depending on the disaster and the populations they are assigned to assist. Working under certain conditions with specific populations can increase the risk of stress. For example, we know that emergency response workers who are exposed to bodies in water and injured children may be at higher risk of suffering with distress symptoms themselves (Leffler and Dembert 1998).

Also, certain populations that require more attention, or who are physically more frail, or less able to communicate adequately, or unstable emotionally due to previous trauma, can be more demanding on responders. Disaster response managers should not assume that staff know how to properly respond to or how to self-protect against the risk of developing secondary traumatic stress. Staff should not be expected to manage alone. Programs should implement the structures, trainings, and proper oversight that will support both survivors and staffs in addressing their needs in the aftermath of disasters.

REFERENCES

American Psychiatric Association. 1980. *Diagnostic and Statistical Manual of Mental Disorders,* 3rd ed. Washington, DC: Author.

Baum, A. S., and I. Fleming. 1993. Implications of psychological research on stress and technological accidents. *American Psychologist 48*(6): 665–672.

Beaton, R. D., and S. A. Murphy. 1995. Working with people in crisis: Research implications. In *Compassion Fatigue: Coping with Secondary Traumatic Stress Disorder in Those Who Treat the Traumatized*, 51–81, ed. C. R. Figley. New York: Brunner-Routledge.

Bell, J. 1995. Traumatic event debriefing: Service delivery designs and the role of social work. *Social Work 40*(1): 36–43.

Briere, J., and D. Elliot. 2000. Prevalence, characteristics, and long-term sequelae of natural disaster exposure in the general population. *Journal of Traumatic Stress 13*(4): 661–679.

Brooks, N., and W. McKinlay. 1992. Mental health consequences of the Lockerbie disaster. *Journal of Traumatic Stress 5*(4): 537–543.

Callahan, J. 1998. Crisis theory and crisis intervention in emergencies. In *Emergencies in Mental Health Practice: Evaluation and Management*, 22–40. New York: Guilford Press.

Center for Mental Health Services. 2001. *Emergency Mental Health and Traumatic Stress. An Overview of the Crisis Counseling Assistance and Training Program* (CCP-PG-01). Rockville, MD: Center for Mental Health Services.

Courtois, C. A. 1999. *Recollections of Sexual Abuse: Treatment Principles and Guidelines*. New York: Norton.

Creamer, T. L., and B. J. Liddle. 2005. Secondary traumatic stress among disaster mental health workers responding to the September 11 attacks. *Journal of Traumatic Stress 18*(1): 89–96.

Cunningham, M. 2003. Impact of trauma work on social work clinicians: Empirical findings. *Social Work 48*(4): 451–459.

Dalgleish, T., S. Joseph, S. Thrasher, T. Tranah, and W. Yule. 1996. Crisis support following the Herald of Free Enterprise disaster: A longitudinal perspective. *Journal of Traumatic Stress 9*(4): 833–845.

Danieli, Y. 1985. The treatment and prevention of long term effects and intergenerational transmission of victimization: A lesson from Holocaust survivors and their children. In *Trauma and Its Wake: The Study and Treatment of Posttraumatic Stress Disorder*, 295–313, ed. C. R. Figley. New York: Brunner/Mazel.

Dutton, M. A., and F. L. Rubinstein. 1995. Working with people with PTSD: Research implications. In *Compassion Fatigue: Coping with Secondary Traumatic Stress Disorder in Those Who Treat the Traumatized*, ed. C. R. Figley, 82–100. New York: Brunner/Mazel.

Eriksson, C. B., H. Vande Kemp, R. Gorsuch, S. Hoke, and D. W. Foy. 2001. Trauma exposure and PTSD symptoms in international relief and development personnel. *Journal of Traumatic Stress 14*(1): 205–212.

Figley, C. R. 1994. *Compassion Fatigue: The Stress of Caring Too Much.* Panama City, FL: Visionary Productions, Inc.

Figley, C. R. 1995. *Compassion Fatigue: Coping with Secondary Traumatic Stress Disorder in Those Who Treat the Traumatized.* New York: Brunner/Mazel.

Figley, C. R. 1999. Compassion fatigue: Toward a new understanding of the costs of caring. In *Secondary Traumatic Stress. Self Care Issues for Clinicians, Researchers & Educators*, 2nd ed., 3–28, ed. B. H. Stamm, 3–29. Baltimore: Sidran Press.

Galea, S., A. Nandi, J. Stuber, J. Gold, R. Acierno, C. L. Best, M. J. Bucuvalas, S. Rudenstine, J. A. Boscarino, and H. S. Resnick. 2005. Participant reactions to survey research in the general population after terrorist attacks. *Journal of Traumatic Stress 18*(5): 461–465.

Green, B. L., and J. D. Lindy. 1994. Post-traumatic stress disorder in victims of disasters. *Psychiatric Clinics of North America 17*(2): 301–309.

Herman, J. 1992. *Trauma and Recovery*. New York: Basic Books.

Hodgkinson, P. E., and M. A. Shepherd. 1994. The impact of disaster support work. *Journal of Traumatic Stress* 7(4): 587–600.

Hudnall-Stamm, B. 2002. *Professional quality of life: Compassion satisfaction and fatigue subscales IV.* http://www.isu.edu/~bhstamm.

Kelly, L. 1988. *Surviving Sexual Violence.* Minneapolis: University of Minnesota Press.

La Greca, A. M., W. K. Silverman, E. M. Vernberg, and M. J. Prinstein. 1996. Symptoms of posttraumatic stress in children after Hurricane Andrew: A prospective study. *Journal of Consulting and Clinical Psychology* 64(4): 712–723.

Leffler, C. T., and M. L. Dembert, (1998). Posttraumatic stress symptoms among U.S. Navy divers recovering TWA flight 800. *Journal of Nervous and Mental Disease 186*(9): 574–577.

Lindy, J. D., and J. P. Wilson. 1994. Empathic strain and countertransference roles: Case illustrations. In *Countertransference in the Treatment of PTSD*, eds. J. P. Wilson and J. D. Lindy, 62–82. New York: Guilford Press.

Maslach, C., and M. P. Leiter. 1997. *The Truth about Burnout: How Organizations Cause Personnel Stress and What to Do about It.* San Francisco: Jossey-Bass, Inc.

McCann, L., and L. A. Pearlman. 1990. *Psychological trauma and the adult survivor: Theory, therapy and transformation.* New York: Brunner/Mazel.

Miller, L. 2000. Traumatized psychotherapists. In *Cognitive-Behavioral Strategies in Crisis Intervention*, 2nd ed., eds. F. M. Dattilio and A. Freeman, 429–445. New York: Guilford Press.

Munroe, J. F. 1999. Ethical issues associated with secondary trauma in therapists. In *Secondary Traumatic Stress Self Care Issues for Clinicians, Researchers and Educators*, 2nd ed., ed. B. H. Stamm, 211–230. Baltimore: Sidran Press.

National Child Traumatic Stress Network and National Center for Posttraumatic Stress Disorder. 2006. *Psychological First Aid: Field Operations Guide* (2nd edition). http://www.nctpsd.va.gov.

Naturale, A. 2007. Secondary Traumatic Stress in Social Workers: Reports from the field. *Clinical Social Work Journal 35*: 173–181.

New South Wales Institute of Psychiatry and Centre for Mental Health. 2000. *Disaster Mental Health Response Handbook.* North Sydney, Australia: NSW Health.

Norris, F. H, M. J. Friedman, P. J. Watson. 2002a. 60,000 disaster victims speak: Part I. An empirical review of the empirical literature, 1981–2001. *Psychiatry: Interpersonal and Biological Processes* 65(3): 207–239.

Norris, F. H., M. J. Friedman, and P. J. Watson. 2002b. 60,000 disaster victims speak: Part II. Summary and implications of the disaster mental health research. *Psychiatry: Interpersonal and Biological Processes* 65(3): 240–260.

Norris, F. H., J. L. Hamblen, P. J. Watson, J. Ruzek. L. E. Gibson, B. J. Pfefferkaum, J. Price, S. Stevens, B. Young, and M. Friedman. 2006. Toward understanding and creating systems of postdisaster care: A case study of New York's response to the World Trade Center disaster. In *Interventions Following Mass Violence and Disaster*, eds. E. C. Ritchie, P. J. Watson, and M. J. Friedman, 343–365. New York: Guilford Press.

Norris, F. H., J. L. Perilla, G. E. Ibanez, and A. D. Murphy. 2001. Sex differences in symptoms of posttraumatic stress: Does culture play a role? *Journal of Traumatic Stress 14*(1): 7–28.

North, C., B. Hong, and B. Pfefferbaum. 2002. *Project P-FLASH: Practical support for front line assistance & support for healing curriculum.* Published by the September 11th Fund and Washington University, St. Louis, MO.

North, C. S., S. J. Nixon, S. Shariat, S. Mallonee, J. C. McMillen, E. L. Spitznagel, and E. M. Smith. 1999. Psychiatric disorders among survivors of the Oklahoma City bombing. *Journal of the American Medical Association 282*(8): 755–762.

Pearlman, L. A., and P. MacIan. 1995. Vicarious traumatization: An empirical study of the effects of trauma work on trauma therapists. *Professional Psychology: Research and Practice 26*(6): 558–565.

Pearlman, L. A., and L. McCann. 1990. Vicarious traumatization: A framework for understanding the psychological effects of working with victims. *Journal of Traumatic Stress 3*(1): 131–149.

Perrin, M. A., L. DiGrande, K. Wheeler, L. Thorpe, M. Farfel, and M. Brackbill. 2007. Differences in PTSD prevalence and associated risk factors among World Trade Center disaster rescue and recovery workers. *American Journal of Psychiatry 164*(9): 1385–1394.

Pfefferbaum, B., S. J. Nixon, P. H. Tucher, R. D. Tivis, V. L. Moore, R. H. Gurwitch, R. S. Pynoos, and H. K. Geis. 1999. Posttraumatic stress responses in bereaved children after the Oklahoma City bombing. *Journal of the American Academy of Child and Adolescent Psychiatry 38*(11): 1372–1379.

Pickett, G. Y. 1998. Therapists in distress: An integrative look at burnout, secondary traumatic stress and vicarious traumatization. PhD dissertation. University of Missouri–St. Louis, St. Louis, MO.

Pulido, M. L. 2005. The terrorist attacks on the World Trade Center on 9/11: The dimensions of indirect expo-
    sure levels in relation to the development of post traumatic stress symptoms: The ripple effect. PhD dis-
    sertation. City University of New York, New York.
Pulido, M. L. 2007. In their words: Secondary traumatic stress in social workers responding to the 9/11 terrorist
    attacks in New York City. *Social Work 52*(3): 279–281.
Pulido, M., and L. Jacina. June 2007. Report to the NYC Administration for Children's Services,
    "Recommendations/evaluation of the need for crisis debriefing services following a child fatality," New
    York Society for the Prevention of Cruelty to Children.
Rose, S., J. Bisson, and S. Weseley. 2001. Psychological debriefing for prevention: Posttraumatic Stress
    Disorder (PTSD). (Cochrane Review). *The Cochrane Library*, 3.
Rosenbloom, D. J., A. C. Pratt, and L. A. Pearlman. 1999. Helpers' responses to trauma work: Understanding
    and intervening in an organization. In *Secondary Traumatic Stress Self-Care Issues for Clinicians,
    Researchers and Educators*, 2nd ed., ed. B. H. Stamm, 65–79. Baltimore: Sidran Press.
Shultz, J. M., A. Allen, H. Bustamante, and Z. Espinal. 2009. *Safety function action for disaster responders.*
    The Deep Center, Department of Epidemiology & Public Health, University of Miami, Miller School of
    Medicine, Miami, FL.
Stamm, B. H. 1999. Introduction to the second edition. In *Secondary Traumatic Stress: Self-Care Issues for
    Clinicians, Researchers and Educators*, 2nd ed., ed. B. H. Stamm, xix–xxxi. Baltimore: Sidran Press.
Stamm, B.H. 2002. *The helper's power to heal and to be hurt – or helped by trying.* Washington, DC: Register
    Report: A publication of the National Register of Health Service Providers in Psychology.
Steinberg, M. 1997. Assessing posttraumatic dissociation with the structured clinical interview for DSM-IV
    dissociative disorders. In *Assessing Psychological Trauma and PTSD*, eds. J. P. Wilson and T. M. Keane,
    429–447. New York: Guilford Press.
Steinglass, P., and E. T. Gerrity. 1990. Natural disasters and post-traumatic stress disorder: Short-term versus
    long-term recovery in two disaster-affected communities. *Journal of Applied Social Psychology 20*(21):
    Part 1. 1746–1765.
Stern, J. 1999. *The Ultimate Terrorists.* Boston: Harvard University Press.
Substance Abuse and Mental Health Services Administration (SAMHSA). 2009. [Home page]. http://mental-
    health.samhsa.gov/cmhs/EmergencyServices/ccp_pg01.asp.
Substance Abuse and Mental Health Services Administration. 2010. *Tips for managers.* https://store.samhsa.
    gov/shin/content/SMA10-DISASTER/SMA10-DISASTER-06.pdf.
Terr, L., D. Bloch, B. Michel, H. Shi, J. Reinhardt, and S. Metayer. 1997. Children's thinking in the wake of the
    Challenger. *American Journal of Psychiatry 154*(6): 744–751.
Tosone, C., and L. Bialkin. 2003. The impact of mass violence and secondary trauma in clinical practice. In
    Social Work with Victims of Mass Violence, eds. L. A. Straussner and N. Phillips, 157–167. New York:
    Jossey Bass.
Tosone, C., M. Lee, L. Bialkin, A. Martinez, M. Campbell, M. M. Martinez, M. Charters, J. Milich,
    K. Gieri, A. Riofrio, S. Gross, L. Rosenblatt, C. Grounds, J. Sandler, K. Johnson, M. Scali, D. Kitson,
    M. Spiro, S. Lanzo, and A. Stefan. 2003. Shared trauma: Group reflections on the September 11 disaster.
    Psychoanalytic Social Work 10(1): 57–75.
Wee, D. F., and D. Meyers. 2002. Stress response of mental health workers following disaster: The Oklahoma
    City bombing. In *Treating Compassion Fatigue*, ed. C. R. Figley, 57–81. New York: Brunner-Routledge.
Weine, S., Y. Danieli, D. Silove, M. Van Ommeren, J. A. Fairbank, and J. Saul. 2002. Guidelines for interna-
    tional training in mental health and psychosocial interventions for trauma exposed populations in clinical
    and community settings. *Psychiatry 65*(2): 156–164.
Wicks, R. J. 2006. *Overcoming Secondary Stress in Medical and Nursing Practice: A Guide to Professional
    Resilience and Personal Well-Being.* New York: Oxford University Press.
Wilson, J. P. 1994. The historical evolution of PTSD diagnosis criteria: From Freud to DSM-IV. *Journal of
    Traumatic Stress 7*(4): 681–698.
Young, B. H., J. D. Ford, J. I. Ruzek, M. F. Friedman, and F. D. Guzman. 1998. *Disaster Mental Health
    Services: A Guidebook for Clinicians and Administrators.* St. Louis, MO: Department of Veterans Affairs
    Employee Education System.
Young, B. H., J. I. Ruzek, M. Wong, M. S. Salzer, and A. J. Naturale. 2006. Disaster mental health train-
    ing: Guidelines, considerations and recommendations. In *Interventions Following Mass Violence and
    Disaster*, eds. E. C. Ritchie, P. J. Watson, and M. J. Friedman, 55–79. New York: Guilford Press.

12 Understanding Climatic, Geographic, and Topographic Considerations for Assessing Disaster Vulnerability

John C. Pine

CONTENTS

12.1   INTRODUCTION

Disasters of all forms, including those associated with natural events, disease, or human causes, have affected individuals, families, and communities and raise concerns about their sustainability. People are displaced, jobs are lost, and property may be damaged to an extent that recovery takes an extended period. The result is that there are significant human impacts associated with disasters affecting coastal communities. The losses associated with human, social, and cultural impacts from disasters can be mitigated, limited, and in many cases prevented with actions that are based on a sound understanding of vulnerability. A comprehensive hazards analysis forms a basis for sound decision making regarding community hazards and for the development of community risk management and hazard mitigation strategies by individuals, families, and public, private, and nonprofit organizations. Research has revealed that where we understand the hazards that we face, both immediate and long term, conscious decision making can be initiated to prepare, mitigate, respond, and recover from potential disasters. Community planning is critical in ensuring that we have sustainable and resilient organizations and communities.

12.2   VULNERABILITY

Vulnerability refers to the susceptibility or potential for harm that may affect social, built, economic, or natural systems. This susceptibility is the result of a set of conditions and processes that influence the way that we might be harmed by natural or human-caused disaster.

Vulnerability is closely associated with the concept of risk and resilience, which is the capacity of a natural, human, or constructed system to bounce back or adapt to an external shock or extreme event. Risk is thus the result of hazard potential, time, and vulnerability. Vulnerability therefore is central in understanding how communities deal with risks and hazards. Expressed in a different way, vulnerability is the result of our exposure to hazards and our capacity to cope and recover.

Vulnerability to hazards may be examined from several perspectives, including an exposure model, one that emphasizes the social condition of the community or area, and finally an integrated approach that combines an examination of both the exposure of physical and sociocultural conditions.

This exposure model emphasizes the identification of conditions that make people and places vulnerable to disastrous conditions and is related to the relative frequency and intensity of the hazard, risk, or threat. An exposure model would also allow examining the potential for loss associated with constructed systems such as critical infrastructure and facilities. Quantitative approaches in the engineering sciences attempt to assess the infrastructure resilience with the goal of reducing losses through research and the application of advanced technologies that improve engineering, pre-event planning, and postevent recovery strategies (Bruneau et al. 2003). Vulnerability as a hazard exposure includes the distribution of people, economies, and the environment to hazardous conditions. The emphasis here is on the physical occupation of areas that may be prone to hazardous events. Under this view, vulnerability is a result of a physical condition that is associated with place (Cutter 1996).

A second approach views vulnerability as a social condition that measures societal resilience (Blaikie et al. 1994; Hewitt 1997). Vulnerability is an outcome of the relation between a hazard and a social condition, which includes human capacity to respond and recover in a positive manner. This coping capacity is thus inherent within the resilience of human systems, including families, groups of people, or even the community's capacity to respond and cope within a geographic area. A neighborhood, town, or region that has a variety of resources that may be used in a recovery from a disaster inherently has a greater potential to recover than those that have few resources.

Vulnerability includes the comprehensiveness of social networks, the strength of critical infrastructure to hazards, and efforts by a community to mitigate potential losses. Communities with strong social networks, which have adopted sound hazard mitigation strategies and have taken steps to fully prepare the local population, have a greater capacity to cope with disaster.

A community's vulnerability is accordingly filtered through its social fabric, its efforts to strengthen its infrastructure, and business enterprises' initiatives to reduce their exposure and build their capacities to deal with disasters (risk management). Both community mitigation activities as well as organizational risk management initiatives thus affect the social, economic, and ecological exposure to hazards.

Vulnerability is consequently more complex than just the exposure of people to hazards. It is affected by community initiatives to prepare and respond, and by its capacity to absorb the adverse effects of a disaster. Adoption of comprehensive building codes, zoning, construction of seawalls, levees, or stronger highways and bridges all contribute to the community's capacity to respond and cope with disaster events. The fact is that natural, economic, and social systems are deeply integrated and interdependent in many ways, which must be considered to understand why some communities, people, and natural environments are better able to cope and recover from disasters than others.

A third approach in viewing vulnerability suggests that potential exposures and social resilience are interrelated (Kasperson, Kasperson, and Turner 1995; Cutter 1996; Cutter, Mitchell, and Scott 2000). This integrated approach combines risk and exposure with vulnerability as a social response. Cutter (1996) notes problematic issues even in this integrated approach because of its lack of consideration of the underlying causes of social vulnerability and its failure to acknowledge distinct spatial outcomes that may vary over time. Variability of risk over a geographic area is central to Cutter's hazards of place model (Cutter, Boruff, and Shirley 2003). Social and biophysical conditions thus interact to produce an overall place vulnerability. Vulnerability is thus more than just exposure to hazard events; it requires coping strategies by individuals or agencies at multiple spatial and temporal scales.

12.2.1 DIMENSIONS OF VULNERABILITY

Vulnerability consists of three dimensions, including social, economic, and ecologic elements of our communities. Social, economic, and ecologic measures emerged independently during the 1960s and 1970s specifically designed to provide a framework concerning exposures to hazards (Cutter, Boruff, and Shirley 2003). The United Nations Development Program has used socioeconomic indicators to examine social and economic implications of regional partnerships (UNDP 2005). The Coastal Risk Atlas is one of the few attempts to link physical hazards and social vulnerabilities (Boyd 2005). Richmond and colleagues (2001, 32) concluded, "There exists no established methodology for determining the hazardous nature of a coastline," and Cutter et al. (2003) reconfirmed that metric standards do not exist to assess the vulnerability to environmental hazards. Richmond and colleagues quantified the effects of only physical hazards to the Hawaiian Islands by historical records and a ranking scheme based on hazard dynamic and frequency to define an overall hazard assessment to be used for coastal land use planning (Cutter, Boruff, and Shirley 2003).

Environmental degradation can result in health and economic losses, poverty, loss of intellectual property rights, loss of natural heritage, and conflict exposure to extreme events. It also might be related to the root causes of a hazard outcome such as disease. As an example, water supply, air pollution (indoor), and sanitation are all related to the highest level of risk from disease. This would suggest that indicators are therefore related to specific hazards and may be a strong association to some threats while not to others.

All geographic areas are threatened by some hazard such as floods, hurricane storm surge and wind hazards, earthquakes, landslides, volcanoes, drought, lightning, or winter storms. An examination of a local community might suggest that it faces greater exposure to one natural or human-caused hazard than other areas (USAID 1999). A closer look at local geographic features and dynamics could reveal that location matters and that exposure to hazards vary from place to place.

Weather patterns, geographic features, and community assets influence the hazard proneness of an area. As a result, no single set of threats exists for all communities; vulnerability is consequently relative to local and regional conditions.

12.2.1.1 Social and Human Vulnerability

The social dimension of vulnerability arises from the exposure of people, neighborhoods, cities, and rural populations and their capacity to recover from hazard events. The hazards literature has noted that the poor, unemployed, single head of a household, elderly, handicapped, or carless households (Blaikie et al. 1994; Yohe and Tol 2001) are much more likely to suffer the hardest and have more difficulty in restructuring their lives after a disaster than other households that have more resources. The more vulnerable populations take more time than their counterparts to recover following a disaster and as a result suffer to a greater extent. They suggest that vulnerability also involves self-protection actions and access to political networks and institutions. Cutter, Boruff, and Shirley (2003) acknowledges these factors but stresses the geographic dimensions of vulnerability noting that place matters. Too often, the poor and most vulnerable reside in the most hazardous zones in a community.

Social vulnerability suggests a differential capacity of groups and individuals in dealing with the adverse effects of hazards based on their positions within the physical and social world. Historical, cultural, social, and economic processes shape individual or social group coping capacity (Blaikie et al. 1994). Research studies suggest that specific populations are far more vulnerable to the risks from natural and human-caused disasters (Cutter, Boruff, and Shirley 2003; Peacock et al. 2000). These studies also indicate that there is a strong relationship between socioeconomic vulnerability and disasters and that social and economic costs of disasters fall unevenly on these population groups (e.g., Heinz 2000; Cutter, Mitchell, and Scott 1997; Cutter, Mitchell, and Scott 2000; Bolin and Stanford 1991; Blaikie and Brookfield 1987; Mileti 1999; Morrow 1999).

Social vulnerability is influenced by local neighborhood dynamics and family characteristics including a lack of access to information, limited political representation, limited social networks, culture, infrastructure, age, gender, race, socioeconomic status, non-English speaking, and disabilities (Cutter, Boruff, and Shirley 2003). Social vulnerability is considered highly linked to various inequalities, including inequalities of place or location. More valuable homes and higher incomes increase resilience to hazards and reduce risks (Cutter, Mitchell, and Scott 1997). Place and socio-economic characteristics interact to influence hazard potential (Cutter, Mitchell, and Scott 1997). Hazard potential, geography, and infrastructure conditions interface with the social and economic fabric of a region to influence risk (Cutter 1997). The key question raised by these studies centers on the suggestion that some groups are at greater risk than others.

An alternative approach takes a different perspective on social vulnerability, observing that droughts, hurricanes, and other environmental disasters trap the poor and vulnerable populations in many parts of the world into poverty, despair, and dependency. The poorest households struggle to overcome the desperate situation that disaster or shocks deal them. Their short- and long-term well-being and sustainability make it impossible to ever catch up with wealthier households.

A hurricane hazard vulnerability assessment conducted during 2005 for the Mississippi Gulf Coast combined a GIS-based (geographic information system) risk atlas and hurricane simulations (Boyd 2005). Risks were ranked, such as flood zones, and vulnerability was examined using income, age, single parents, education, non-English-speaking, vehicle ownership, home ownership, and type of home to identify populations at risk and hurricane hazards. This study demonstrated that there was a high correlation between low income, single parents, renters, older populations, and non-English-speaking residents and areas at high risk to hazards.

12.2.1.2 Economic Vulnerability

When we look at economic vulnerability, we examine our risk to production, distribution, and consumption of goods and services not only from the private commercial sector but also from the nonprofit and public sectors. The health and vitality of a community's economy is interdependent with the region, nation, and world. Local, regional, national, and international forces influence local wages, production, export volume, unemployment, and the number and types of jobs. There are many linkages in our economies that shape the robustness of our local, regional, and state economic base. Suggesting that we can predict accurately how to establish a highly productive economy is very different from the examination of a set of economic indicators that will imply that a local community could withstand or recover from a natural disaster. Our task then is to identify and examine indicators that will suggest how robust our economy is for a given community and its capacity to contribute in a positive manner to a recovery from a disaster. Economic vulnerability also includes factors that could harm a labor force such as human disease or epidemics. The United Nations World Vulnerability Report (UN Development Program 2000) documents indicators for indexing and monitoring nations in terms of employment, education, health, domestic violence, and potential for disaster recovery.

When we assess the economic vulnerability, we evaluate not only jobs and the nature of the local economy but the status of existing roads, bridges, airports, rail lines, hospitals, prisons, manufacturing plants, shopping areas, utilities, and communication systems to withstand extreme events impacts. It is the potential impact to employee wages, employment, and infrastructure such as electrical, natural gas, and communication sectors that affect our community's capacity to recover from a disaster. As Comfort and colleagues (1999) point out, our vast set of services to our rural and urban communities offer a vital backbone to our commerce and standard of living; the scale of these systems also create dependence and losses that have vast consequences on our economic stability.

The infrastructural and economic vulnerabilities are in fact tightly connected, but can be clearly separated if we consider two aspects: a physical and a nonphysical aspect. While the built environment and its physical resilience against extreme events may be affected by the physical forces of a hazard, economic resilience would deal with pressures and impacts of the global economy. In today's global economy, financial, trade, and policy decisions in other parts of the world may have a significant impact on a local economy.

International agencies judge the size and structure of an economy, exposure to international trade shocks, as well as extreme natural events to justify loan or aid programs (USAID 1999). USAID examined economic vulnerability by determining the frequency and intensity of hazards and conditions such as energy dependency, export characteristics, and destinations and reliance on financing externally (Crowards 1999). Munich Re Group (2002) looked at disasters from an economic perspective including annual per capita income as a reflection of purchasing power. In the agricultural sector of our economy, we can measure the production of various goods. But production is highly affected by external forces such as soil moisture or meteorological forces or geological variables reflecting the hazard itself.

12.2.1.3 Environmental Vulnerability

Ecological dimensions of vulnerability refer to the capacity of our natural systems to bounce back from disaster or their fragility to harm. It is the inability of these natural systems to deal with stress that may evolve over time and space (Williams and Kaputska 2000). Saltwater intrusion into freshwater marshes can cause the impairment and even the loss of breeding grounds for fish and other water creatures, birds, and other coastal animals. Long-term intrusion of saltwater into marsh areas can also affect community surface water systems. Hazardous material contamination that results from flooding, wind, or storm surge can cause immediate and long-term decay of delicate coastal environments (Villa and McLeod 2002).

Environmental systems are also significant to the quality of life for a community and its productivity, as well as its sustainability. Measures that reflect the value of environmental systems to community sustainability include the rate of deforestation, annual water use as a percentage of total water resources, population density, annual use of water by household, volume of recycled materials per household, or the relation of coastline to land area. There could be a relationship between threatened species to land area and the ratio of total number of natural disasters to land area (Patkins, Mazzi, and Easter 2000). The Yale Center for Environmental Law and Policy (YCELP) identified five components for environmental sustainability:

1. The health of environmental systems
2. Environmental stresses and risks
3. Human vulnerability to environmental impacts
4. Social and institutional capacity
5. Global stewardship (World Economic Forum 2000)

Lovins and colleagues (1999) advocate that businesses restore, sustain, and expand our ecosystem so that it can produce vital services and biological resources abundantly. This view suggests that our natural environment as natural capital is to be used, but in a conscious manner so as to reduce waste and expand the productivity of our natural resources. They suggest systems thinking so as to reduce energy costs and waste products. Energy savings can be productivity enhancing. This approach suggests that per capita energy and water consumption is a valid indicator of efficient natural resource allocation and consumption. Further, waste minimization also fits within this model, and thus per capita waste generation and recycling are good indicators of natural systems sustainability. Waste minimization and pollution prevention are also Environmental Protection Agency (EPA)-recommended risk management strategies. Finally, they recommend that we view our natural environment as natural capital, one where we make an investment that will lead to positive return on our investments. A healthy environment provides us with clean air and water, rainfall, productive oceans and water features, fertile soil, and sustainable watersheds. Social economic and environmental sustainability are interdependent, and you cannot have one without the other.

The Commonwealth Secretariat is using indicators to understand environmental sustainability, including annual rate of deforestation, population density, and annual water use (Patkins, Mazzi, and Easter 2000). The World Bank (1999) approach to environmental analysis is based on climate, water, forest, and pollution. Environmental degradation can result in health and economic losses, poverty, loss of intellectual property rights, loss of natural heritage, and conflict exposure to extreme events. It also might be related to the root causes of a hazard outcome such as disease. As an example, water supply, air pollution (indoor), and sanitation are all related to the highest level of risk from disease. This would suggest that indicators are thus related to specific hazards and may be a strong association to some threats, but not to others.

12.2.2 Interdependence of Natural, Human, Economic, and Built Systems

Natural, human-cultural, economic, and constructed systems are interdependent in ways that vulnerability in one can have implications in other systems. Natural disasters reveal that disaster proneness is not just a physical characteristic but one that is also human constructed. Extreme events may be related to geographic features such as high elevations, steep slopes, coastal and river basins, and areas that experience extensive drought. Each can be associated with specific atmospheric, geologic, hydrologic or other hazards and with human inhabitation. The local population may be at great risk simply because of their proximity to a geographic hazard. The literature suggests that many social factors such as age, race, limited income and education, a single head of a household, or a physical disability can create a situation where some social groups experience disasters in ways that make it difficult to cope and recover. Families that have inadequate economic resources, mobility, and capacity to move away from a disaster area; support system for recovery; or job potential may have a limited capacity to cope with the adverse impacts of disasters. The social dynamics of their lives make it very difficult to take advantage of resources in the recovery process. Coping strategies should be included in an integrated vulnerability approach. Vulnerability therefore is integrated into the development of action or coping strategies that can be implemented. These strategies reflect choices or public policies that are made by individuals, families, businesses, and public agencies and models that allow testing. We are interested in who lives in the community and where they reside, but it is the decision that people make on an individual and collective basis that really drives vulnerability.

For example, some communities may adopt land-use planning and comprehensive building codes, which make buildings more resistant in a disaster. For these communities, structures built to the code may be hazard resistant and less likely to be damaged by high wind, floods, storm surge, fire, or other anticipated hazards. Zoning restrictions control building in high-hazard zones either by requiring base elevation for a structure above a specific flood height or setback requirements from coastal zones. Human choices and our policies are part of our examination of vulnerability.

Social, economic, ecological, and constructed systems do not exist independently but in concert with one another. Elements from one system interface and are affected by elements in another. For example, family culture and values influence education expectations and outcomes. Educational attainment also affects employment, income level, and standard of living. Water quality and quantity is part of the ecological system but can also affect local recreation opportunities, quality of life, and human health.

The interrelatedness of these systems also impacts the recovery of a community or organization following a disaster. Resilience is the capacity of the community affected by a disaster to recover quickly. The stronger the social, economic, and environmental capital, the more resources the community has from which to draw for recovery. As an example, low unemployment and a high average weekly wage for the community reflects a stronger economy. Further, if there is a low crime rate, high school dropout rate, or lower percentage of households below the poverty rate, one would suggest that the community is in a better position to recover from a disaster. More resources are available to cope with recovery.

If we represent the three types of capital by a circle, then the size of the capital would represent a stronger robust capacity for dealing with disaster. It might also reflect that one type of capital is stronger than another, such as a vital petro chemical industry might have high wages but have low indicators reflecting the natural environment and higher levels of pollution.

A second view of the relationship between social, economic, and natural environments is their interdependence. A community that relies on the attraction of the natural environment would be drastically affected by a forest fire, hurricane, flood, earthquake, or other disaster. Since each community is unique in its natural, cultural, and economic assets, the overlap between them would vary and influence the community's resilience and sustainability. As leaders in the community examine their social, economic, and natural systems, they should not only determine their robustness but also their interrelatedness. Every community is unique and the interrelatedness of their social, cultural, and natural assets determines the robustness of their assets to deal with disaster (Figure 12.1).

Vulnerability is influenced and dependent on the coping capacity of the social, economic, ecological, and constructed systems. The extent and rate of response and recovery can be measured by monetary resources available, deployment of technology by type, resilience of infrastructure, and capacity of the emergency response system. Per capita income may suggest many things about a community and resilience. The United Nations (UNDP 2003) sees a relationship between per capita income and fatalities by country. Others see a relationship between per capita income and health attainment (level of life expectancy for a country) as measured by Pelling (2004) and UNDP (2003). Per capita income and (unrestricted) access to medical facilities and health care result in a population more resilient against various diseases and therefore longer life expectancy.

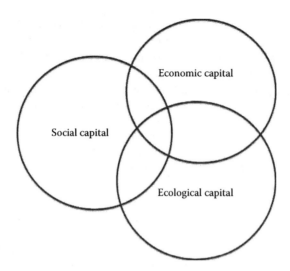

FIGURE 12.1   Interdependence of social, economic, and ecological capital.

12.3   VULNERABILITY AND COMMUNITY PREPAREDNESS, MITIGATION, AND RESILIENCE

12.3.1   HAZARD IDENTIFICATION

Figure 12.2 shows that an understanding of vulnerability is part of risk analysis in the hazards analysis process. In order for communities and organizations to prepare to deal with disasters, and in considering alternative mitigation strategies, a comprehensive understanding of the nature of hazards they may face and just what might be affected in a disaster must be examined. To appreciate the social/cultural, economic, and ecological vulnerability of a geographic area, business, or community, the nature of hazards must be identified and described. With a comprehensive identification of hazards and vulnerability, strategies to reduce or mitigate potential disaster impacts can then be examined.

In order to understand the nature of hazards that might affect an organization or community, we suggest that a profile of the community be prepared. This would include a detailed description of the different forms of local assets or capital, including social/cultural, economic, ecological, and infrastructure resources. Social and cultural capital involves an examination of the local population, including education level, percent of population by age group, cultural diversity, tenure living in the community, percent of population disabled, and premature birth rate or other problem births. Economic assets include the diversity of local businesses, average weekly wage of employees, unemployment rate, housing and commercial building value, level of local investment, number of new businesses, or housing sales. Ecological capital includes public parks and recreation areas, conservancy areas, private, national, or state forests, water features, wetlands, and other natural features including hills, mountains, or plains. A summary of the community assets is prepared to provide a basis for identifying potential disasters that could affect the community.

Understanding hazards in a community or region is based on an examination of the geographic features of the area, including land contour and elevation, water features, and natural areas that might be subject to fires, landslides, or floods. Hazard models can be used to help characterize natural hazards and often are linked to geographic information systems such as ArcGIS. FEMA released HAZUS-MH in 1997 to provide local communities with a tool for characterizing natural and technological hazards. This hazard modeling program is able to describe earthquake, flood, hazardous materials, and hurricane wind hazards. Other natural hazards may also be imported into the program in order to utilize the mapping features of the GIS along with the outputs from a hazard

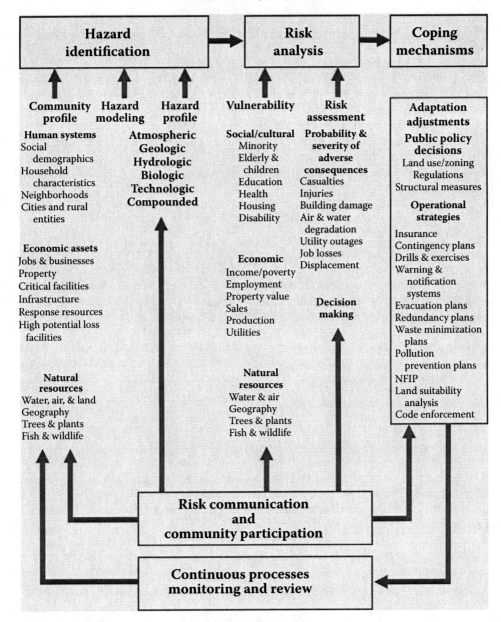

Building community resilience

Hazards analysis process

FIGURE 12.2   Vulnerability and the hazards analysis process (Pine 2009).

model. Hazard profiles then may be prepared for a community, county, or region that outline the nature, extent, and likelihood of a disaster resulting from a potential hazard.

12.3.2   RISK ANALYSIS

The risk assessment process examines the potential impacts from a hazard in a geographic area, including clarifying the potential causalities, injuries, and displaced persons. It also determines number of structures (homes, highways, bridges, businesses, or recreation facilities) damaged, destroyed, or contaminated. During the hazard identification phase of the hazards analysis process, local community assets are described. The description of community assets can be used as a variable to determine the number of shelters that might be needed, debris generated from a disaster, heavy equipment that can be used in a disaster response, and potential shelters for population evacuation.

An understanding of community economic resources allows for a detailed examination of how business and industry might be affected by a disaster. Who is employed in these businesses, what resources do they need to operate, and how might damage on a regional basis affect local business and government operations? What regional response resources could be utilized in the recovery?

A comprehensive hazard identification also provides information on how environmental assets might be adversely affected. Is the community dependent on tourism, and could areas that bring people to the area be affected by a disaster? Would natural areas such as beaches, lakes, rivers, fishing sites, mountains, forests, or wetlands be harmed by a disaster and thus discourage tourists from coming to the area?

12.3.3 COPING MECHANISMS

Strategies to prevent or mitigate the adverse impacts of disasters can be a short- and long-term strategy for a local business or community. Comprehensive initiatives can be undertaken to minimize flooding, prevent fires or explosions, and enable structures to withstand the powerful forces of a natural disaster. Public policies may be adopted to implement a flood insurance program and building codes that would strengthen new homes and businesses.

Emergency preparedness measures are also based on the outputs from the risk analysis and hazard identification. Who should be evacuated and where should they be taken? Can structures be protected in some way that would minimize the adverse impacts?

12.3.4 FACTORS AFFECTING VULNERABILITY

The nature of the disaster event has a major influence on how a local community or region may be affected economically, socially, and ecologically. The size, duration, and intensity of the disaster may determine who is affected and the extent of damage to local and regional infrastructure, businesses, or to the natural environment. Significant damage to local infrastructure, homes, and businesses from Hurricane Katrina extended from the western part of Florida to eastern Texas. Flooding associated with major disasters can extend from the upper reaches of the Mississippi River through the center of the United States. Some events can be limited in their geographic extent and affect a limited number of jurisdictions. Earthquakes or wildfires may affect a geographic area. Atmospheric hazards such as a tornado or a hazardous material spill may also have a limited impact geographically. The vulnerability of a local community to hazards thus depends on the type of hazard that the community faces and can involve very large areas or a disaster that is limited to a small area.

Disasters can last for extended time periods or be limited to just a small time frame. Forest fires can spread rapidly but extend for days. Flooding can affect large areas for several days and gradually flood water levels will reduce. Earthquakes can be limited to a very short time period but also include aftershocks that cause more concern and alarm than serious damage. As for vulnerability, the greater notice that a community has before a disaster, the more likelihood that residents may take actions to facilitate evacuations, sheltering, property protection actions, or warning systems. Individual injuries and loss of life can be greatly reduced through early warning systems. Disasters that give no notice affect residents to a much greater extent than ones that give a longer warning. Emergency preparedness measures can also be adopted to provide residents and businesses with greater notice of a disaster and how they might be affected.

Vulnerability of local communities increases as the intensity of the disaster increases and if the warning is limited. Residents or local businesses may have response plans that could reduce the adverse impacts from a disaster, but without some notice, they may suffer extensive damage. Earthquakes, terrorists' attacks, hazardous chemical spills, or tornadoes can hit a community without notice and with such great intensity that they cause extensive property and environmental damage and many injuries and fatalities.

12.3.5 CLIMATE CHANGE AND VULNERABILITY

The Intergovernmental Panel on Climate Change (IPCC; 2007) reported that long-term climate trends vary around the world, but most regions will experience more extreme weather conditions from longer periods of high temperatures, winds, rain events, or tropical cyclones. These extreme events may occur more often and with greater intensity. The change, however, may be gradual, and local communities likely to be affected by such systems may not recognize their increasing vulnerability. U.S. federal agencies such as the U.S. Environmental Protection Agency, the National Oceanic Atmospheric Administration, U.S. Geological Survey, and U.S. Forest Service have initiated risk communication campaigns to alert specific local areas to their increasing vulnerability to hazards. Future storms and disaster events are likely to be more intense and affect larger geographic areas than past disaster events (Karl et al. 2009). Local communities in both urban and rural settings are now examining how future climate change might affect their community and are adjusting community disaster plans.

The slow pace of climate change may increase our vulnerability simply because we fail to recognize the signals for change that come with a developing hazard. Environmental systems may be altered gradually, allowing an invasive species to move into an area and cause extensive damage to trees or habitat. Longer periods of hot, dry weather can expose areas dependent on agriculture production to suffer from decreased crop productivity. Change may be gradual and expose businesses and families to extensive economic, environmental, and human stressors.

12.3.6 GEOGRAPHIC FEATURES AND VULNERABILITY

Local geographic features and characteristics greatly influence the vulnerability of a local community. Communities with water features that lie within a drainage basin are subject to higher risks from flooding. Those in areas where there are forests or grasslands are subject to wildfires that may be ignited by lightning strikes or campers. Many areas with extensive forests are also subject to winter freeze events that coat tree limbs with ice. Unfortunately, many trees are not capable of holding large amounts of ice and suffer extensive damage from ice storms. Along with the tree damage, the falling trees may also cause extensive property damage and damage power lines. Coastal communities that are in areas with either tidal basins or low-lying areas such as marshlands would be subject to greater flooding from storm surge or other coastal flooding.

12.3.7 NATURE OF THE SOCIAL AND CULTURAL COMMUNITY

The social and cultural nature of the community can influence how the members of the community respond to disaster warnings and how residents and businesses recover from a disaster. For many communities in New Orleans, the period following Hurricane Katrina was stressful and many families were isolated. For Vietnamese residents of eastern New Orleans, the recovery period was supported by a cohesive community—they were linked by common values, religious beliefs, and a common determination to deal with physical, emotional, and political challenges. The Catholic religious leaders provided inspirational support for the community, helped each family find an appropriate role in the community's recovery, and linked the community to local, state, and national relief groups. This tightly linked community took advantage of each offer of support during the recovery and, as a result, was able to deal with the difficult challenges presented by the destruction of Hurricane Katrina. This small, isolated community on the eastern boundary of New Orleans demonstrated what resilience might mean. Older residents of the community had been displaced from Southeast Asia in the 1970s and worked very hard to build a vibrant community in New Orleans. These older residents stressed that they were determined to remain in their New Orleans community and that Hurricane Katrina would not displace them from their homes (Feike 2010).

A different form of social capital in the community is the quality of public and nonprofit organizations that serve the needs of the community. These institutions include city and county governments, public and nonprofit health care, social service systems, emergency services, and the extent of community and civic foundations. The presence of professional city and county management forms of governance, land use and permitting entities, comprehensive emergency response and mitigation plans and systems, and forms of engagement of the greater community all reflect a broader perspective of social capital.

12.3.8 Nature of Economic Resources

Communities that have economic resources in the form of insurance, corporate resources, external aid, or community assets are in a position to recover more quickly and provide the residents and businesses with support (Pine 2009). Families or communities that do not have economic resources are at a much greater disadvantage in the recovery period, and they experience time delays and frustration in dealing with public agency bureaucracy and local public officials. As Feike determined, cultural capital can supplement any economic and financial resources that may be available and often can bridge the gap in getting the right aid to communities (2010). A quick recovery in the City of New Orleans was closely associated with high-income neighborhoods and residents who had flood insurance policies with the National Flood Insurance Program.

Economic capital also includes our community physical infrastructure, including roads, bridges, interstates, airports and airfields, telecommunication systems, and public utilities. These assets reflect an economic capital investment in the community and provide a foundation for businesses and industry.

12.3.9 Nature of Individual, Community, and Regional Preparedness

The quality of public agencies (federal, state, or local) can influence the pace of recovery and thus the exposure of residents as well as government. Communities as well as businesses that do not have comprehensive emergency response plans will be vulnerable to a disaster. Well-managed communities with strong leadership at either the county or municipal level take the appropriate steps to ensure that a capable administration is in place. Qualified public safety personnel along with ones who have other critical skills can be extremely valuable in a disaster response. These local assets can provide the community with skilled resources. Communities that have a comprehensive response plan are in a position to show that preparation pays off. With planning, communities can quickly determine where rebuilding should occur and in what order recovery should proceed. Where preparedness occurs, response is more effective and the recovery process more efficient.

12.4 MEASURING VULNERABILITY

Local community measures help us to appreciate the state of local conditions and what we want to know. They act as a barometer for how well something is doing. Quality indicators reflect existing dynamics and are based on objective data from well-known sources. The indicators measure something that reflects local conditions or assets that are valued by the community.

Damage indicators measure tangible things that are usually built, such as bridges, homes, commercial or industrial buildings, cars and trucks, or communication towers. Coping indicators demonstrate a community's preparedness for a disaster, such as persons evacuated or sheltered. The number of people evacuated or number of established shelters could reflect effective warning systems or procedures to help people get out of harm's way. These indicators may reflect a community's preparedness, the effectiveness of hazard mitigation or response strategies, and could explain why some communities recover more quickly than others, suggesting that they are more resilient.

No set of indicators can be all inclusive. The Dow Jones Industrial Average, a widely respected indicator of stock market performance, does not include every stock traded on the New York Stock Exchange. Nor does the Consumer Price Index measure the prices of all consumer goods. Both indices, like the *Sierra Nevada Wealth Index*, are based on developing and monitoring a sample of indicators that, viewed together, provide a barometer of overall performance. The 60 indicators included in this Web-based version of the *Index* were selected because:

- The indicators are measurable and can be updated with existing and objective data sources.
- The indicators measure the condition of assets of material importance to the Sierra Nevada's wealth.
- The indicators measure the condition of assets where active public interest exists.

12.4.1 Measuring Social Conditions

Many studies have been conducted to identify socioeconomic population characteristics that indicate higher vulnerability (Cutter, Boruff, and Shirley 2003; Pulido 2000; Peacock, Morrow, and Gladwin 2000). High-risk groups, such as those with lower incomes, the very young and elderly, the disabled, women living alone, female-headed households, families with low ratios of adults to dependents, ethnic minorities, renters, recent residents, tourists, and the homeless, are good social vulnerability indicators of risk and show that "social and economic costs of disasters fall unevenly on [these] different classes of victims and stakeholders" (Heinz 2000, 2; Cutter, Mitchell, and Scott 2000; Bolin and Stanford 1991; Blaikie and Brookfield 1987; Morrow 1999; Puente 1999). Lower-income populations are more vulnerable because they do not have the financial resources to recover from disasters (Mileti 1999). Age (younger than 18; older than 65), gender (females), race, and income (mean household value) are viewed as primary social vulnerability indicators (Cutter, Boruff, and Shirley 2003).

Common indicators that reflect a community's vulnerability include nonwhite population, annual household incomes less than $25,000, number of individuals older than age 65, disabled individuals (not including employment disabilities), individuals older than age 25 without a high school diploma, households without a vehicle, renters, single-parent households with children younger than the age of 18, and households without a phone. Where the indicator is expressed by household, the value was then divided by the number of total households in the block group.

- *Households earning less than $25,000 annually*: Percentages of households earning less than $25,000 represent the number of households with earnings less than $25,000 divided by the total number of occupied housing units in the block group (Cutter, Mitchell, and Scott 2000). This indicator was chosen to reflect an income threshold instead of households living at or below poverty. This income value reflects the minimum required to qualify for a home mortgage.
- *No vehicle*: Percentages of households by block group without a vehicle (car, truck, or van) was selected as one of our social vulnerability indicators. The Census Bureau defines household as a housing unit including a house, apartment, mobile home, group of rooms, or a single room that is occupied as separate living quarters.
- *Nonwhite race*: Much of the hazards vulnerability research has suggested that a nonwhite race is usually located in the highest hazard areas (Pulido 2000; Peacock and Ragsdale 1997; Bolin 1993). The percentage of nonwhite population by block group in New Orleans was selected as a social vulnerability indicator and consists of African American, as well

as Asian and Latino, neighborhoods. Howell (2005) noted that African Americans were less likely to have evacuated or retreated to a safer place for Hurricane Georges in 1998 and thus were at a greater risk for Hurricane Katrina. FEMA prioritizes vulnerability in the order of the following: (1) income distribution, (2) elderly populations, (3) disabled populations, (4) children, (5) minority neighborhoods, and (6) language and cultural barriers. FEMA suggests which populations are vulnerable to specific hazards; it is likely that vulnerable populations have similar characteristics.

- *The elderly*: The percentage of persons within a block group over the age of 65 was selected as a social vulnerability indicator. The hazards literature cites numerous studies that suggest that the elderly population is particularly vulnerable to hazards. These studies note that physical, mental, and sensory skills become weaker with age. Age is recognized as an indicator of social vulnerability due to mobility limitations, major dependence on relatives, frequency of respiratory distress, and a lower resilience after the disaster (Mileti 1999; Hewitt 1997; Cutter, Mitchell, and Scott 2000; O'Brien and Mileti 1992). Howell found that individuals older than age 65 were less likely to evacuate or have a plan for evacuation for Hurricane Georges (2005), which threatened New Orleans in September 1998.
- *Disability*: The percentage of noninstitutionalized individuals with a disability includes persons who have sensory, physical, mental, or other self-care limitations that restrict their activities outside the home. This category does not include those with employment disabilities. The percentage is based on the number of disabled individuals in the block group, unlike the other indicators, which use households as the measurement.
- *Education*: This indicator includes the percentage of individuals older than age 25 with no high school diploma. Lower education level has been suggested as a constraint in understanding hazard warnings (Heinz 2000). The indicator reflects the number of people older than age 25 in each block group rather than the number of households.
- *Use of rental housing*: The percentage of rented housing units represents the number of occupied households renting divided by the total number of occupied households in a block group. Several studies suggest that renters are vulnerable because of their lack of finances and/or limitations in transportation (Heinz 2000; Morrow 1999).
- *No phone*: The percentage of housing units without a phone represents all households without a phone divided by the total occupied housing units. Telephone calls are an important means of communication to notify the public of an immediate evacuation. Although phone calling as a means of communication has not yet been documented as a warning tool, access to a phone is an important vulnerability criterion. Automated systems for early hazard warning utilize local phone capabilities (Burby 1998).
- *Single-parent households*: The percentage of single parents who are the head of a household was selected as a social vulnerability indicator. This indicator reflects single parents who are head of a household with children younger than age 18.

The following social indicators provide a closer look at communities and how people may be affected by a disaster (EPA 1999). They are provided as examples of data that might reflect high social vulnerability. Future studies of disasters might examine the relationship between these social indicators and losses:

- Number of persons injured or fatalities
- Number of weeks for injured workers out of work
- Percent of population forced to evacuate
- Duration of displacement
- Percent of population below poverty level displaced by the disaster (personal wealth)
- Duration of population below poverty level displaced

- Crime incidence following a disaster as compared to pre-event levels
- Percent of population living in a high-risk zone (flood zone)
- Number of high school dropouts (annual basis)
- Number of students failing high school exit exam

12.4.2 Indicators of Economic Conditions

Traditional indicators of economic conditions center on employment, housing, business sales, business taxes, and construction. The unemployment rate has been an excellent economic vulnerability indicator as it reflects each of the sectors of the economy, as well as public and private employment. Construction permits have also been used following a disaster to judge the health and vitality of a local economy, separating permits for industrial or commercial operations from either rental or home construction. Examining the number of new housing units over a long-term period is a good way to determine if the present condition is performing at a higher rate. Business taxes are also a good indicator of local economic health, with the number of car sales a steady measure of local conditions.

In selecting economic indicators, the measures should reflect the broad basis of the economy and not heavily focus on a single sector. The number of jobs in each of the major economic categories as measured over a long period provides a comprehensive view of the community. Unemployment rates also provide a broad view of the economy. These indicators include the number of employers and employees (by sector industry), overall unemployment rate (especially small businesses that have 1–5 employees), the percentage of business failures, household population, and the number of students in schools by type of school or college/university.

Zandi and colleagues (2006) also provide a breakdown of volume of production as a key indicator of recovery from a disaster, including: volume of fish caught; volume of chemical extraction (oil or natural gas); and home and rental prices (average home sale price and the fair market rent for a two-bedroom apartment). Comparison of production volume over multiple years is an excellent indicator of the health of the local economy.

Some indicators provide a further view of the local community and the attachment that residents may have to a long-term recovery following a disaster. The percentage of homeowners reflects those residents who have invested economically in the community and when affected by a disaster have an incentive to return and recover. Renters, however, have a more limited investment locally and when displaced may look for employment outside the recovery area.

The extent that a local community is dominated by a single sector of the economy can influence the nature of the impact of a disaster on a community and its ability to recover. Areas that are dominated by tourism could find that the economy is dramatically affected by the destruction of transportation routes including a key corridor, means of transportation, or destruction of a key attraction such as a natural viewshed.

12.4.3 Measures of Ecological Conditions and Services

In a study of the effects of urban design on aquatic ecosystems in the United States, Beach (2002) examined the relationship between land use and the effects of sprawl on both air and water quality. This study demonstrated that as the percent of impervious surfaces increased in a coastal community, the nature of the water runoff into water features changed, causing increased levels of nitrogen, phosphorus, and organic carbon; trace metals such as copper, zinc, and lead; and pesticides (Schueler and Holland 2000). Coastal communities that experience growth of low-density residential and commercial development scattered across large coastal land areas also experience air and water quality issues. Beach characterized this form of development as coastal sprawl. The result was that changes in urban growth patterns affected habitat quality, water temperature, pollutants, and aquatic life. Further, as coastal communities expanded using traditional development patterns of sprawl, drivers were forced into longer trips for work, recreation, or just normal shopping, affecting air quality.

Beach's work centers on a national and even worldwide problem of development patterns in coastal areas. Coastal counties make up 17 percent of the land area in the United States, but just 13 percent of the nation's acreage. Unfortunately, this coastal zone is home to more than half of the U.S. population and is experiencing population increases. We are continuing to put more people in a small area. Pollution and habitat degradation is the end result of this pattern. The population density of a community should be part of an effort to determine the burden that people have on the environment. However, this indicator alone does not reflect the magnitude of human impacts on environmental health. We need further indicators.

Beach cited studies that have demonstrated that when impervious surfaces cover more than 10 percent of a watershed, water features and estuaries become biologically degraded. A key indicator for a community is the percent of the watershed that is composed of impervious surfaces. When it exceeds 10 percent, there will be problems, according to Beach (2002). The fact is that the ecosystem health including streams, marshes, and rivers affected by development results in less diverse, less stable, and less productive watersheds. Walker (1996) examined two streams and compared the effects of development patterns on the ecosystem health. Increases in impervious surfaces led to higher levels of sediments containing higher concentrations of nitrogen, phosphorus, and organic carbon; metals such as copper, zinc, or lead; as well as petroleum hydrocarbons and pesticides (Schueler and Holland 2000). The study found differences in channel erosion, and also in the health of estuaries. Increased levels of nitrogen lead to algal blooms and fish kills. Increases in fertilizer use in watersheds also reduce water clarity, which allows less light to penetrate below the water's surface and affects the health of biologic and aquatic habitats.

The issues related to urban development patterns are not limited to the productivity of watersheds, but also to the changes in the volume of water in streams or the discharge. The fact is that there is an increased threat of flooding as development increases in a watershed and impervious surfaces increase (Booth 1991; Booth and Reinelt 1993). Changes in water feature discharge reflect development patterns and provide a clear indicator for potential flooding problems in a community.

Changes in impervious surfaces also result in the rise of water temperatures in the water (National Research Council 2000). As the percent of impervious surface area increases in a watershed, the water temperature increases (Galli 1991). The result may be decreases in oxygen levels resulting in changes in the marine life and environment.

Hypersprawl is noted as the expansion of residential development with housing densities of one unit on three acres or less. The indicator in this case would be the number of housing units per three acres of land. Measuring housing unit density thus provides us with a means of determining if growth patterns will affect our water features or watershed habitats and whether adjustments should be made to reduce the harmful impacts of urban growth.

Vehicle miles driven by residents also have an impact on environmental health. As the vehicle miles driven per household increases, air quality is affected. Unfortunately, our urban growth patterns require people to drive further so that the average commuter trip increases annually. Many communities have adopted more stringent regulations requiring the use of cleaner gasoline or additional measures to prevent pollutants. One can further measure growing emissions by looking at the average interstate highway travel speed. For the United States, the average speed has dropped from 53 to 41 miles per hour, or a 23 percent decline (Wallis et al. 2001). The result of the decline in the spread is that the average drive takes longer and pollution has increased.

The use of these environmental indicators thus provides a means of assessment and monitoring of our environment so as to determine if we are having a positive or negative impact on water or air quality, aquatic habitat, or the risk of potential flooding in the watershed (Pantin 1997; Figures 12.3 and 12.4).

The EPA has adopted similar measures to determine when water features might be affected negatively from agricultural or related practices (use of fertilizers on commercial or residential

FIGURE 12.3 Environmental capital: healthy forest and clean water and soils that support fish and wildlife (Watauga River, Valle Crucis, NC). (Courtesy of John C. Pine.)

properties). The measure of Total Maximum Daily Loads (TMDLs) is used by the EPA and state regulatory agencies to determine how much pollution a body of water can accept without becoming degraded (EPA 1999). Examples of indicators of environmental conditions include:

- Population density (high density may reflect vulnerability and exposure to specific risks)
- Area contaminated because of hazardous spill and duration of cleanup
- Access to transportation infrastructure
- Amount of rainfall per month/annually
- Per capita water use
- Volume of commercial and or industrial water use
- Deforestation

FIGURE 12.4 Healthy landscapes support tourism and recreation (Elk Knob State Park, Todd, NC). (Courtesy of John C. Pine.)

12.5 COPING MECHANISMS FOR ENSURING SUSTAINABLE COMMUNITIES

Communities may take significant steps in reducing vulnerability by initiating broad-based mitigation plans that not only attempt to reduce the adverse impacts of disasters on homes, businesses, and critical infrastructure, but also ensure that adequate steps are in place so residents and businesses are prepared to respond to a pending disaster. Mitigation steps take the form of both physical measures, such as levees and other flood protection structures, and public policy efforts, such as enhanced building codes and land-use provisions. Together, the structural and nonstructural initiatives provide not only protection to the community but allow residents and businesses to recover more quickly when disaster strikes.

12.5.1 MITIGATION

Godschalk and colleagues (1998) advocate the integration of hazard mitigation and local land use planning. The identification, design, and implementation of hazard mitigation structural measures usually involve numerous local utility, road, and engineering related agencies along with state and federal permitting entities. Protecting vital assets of the community may have an impact on both public and private property, and coordination throughout the design of a project is critical to accomplishing hazard mitigation goals. Local government agencies also need to recognize that uncontrolled development can create or increase local vulnerability. As a result, zoning and other land use decisions must go hand in hand with long-term structural hazard mitigation measures. Hazard mitigation is based on the goal of building a sustainable community that fosters economic elements of the community and acknowledges the role of social and cultural capital. As a result, local governments can take significant steps in utilizing their planning power, as well as their spending and taxing powers, to establish both structural and nonstructural hazard mitigation measures.

12.5.2 COMMUNITY PREPAREDNESS

Community preparedness can provide a basis for ensuring that both property and human capital are protected from adverse impacts from disasters. These preparedness actions can include contingency plans, drills, warning systems, and evacuation initiatives. Emergency planning activities can include the identification of vulnerable populations and geographic areas that would have high impacts from specific hazards, and result in strategies to reduce adverse impacts of specific populations or geographic areas. Despite the terrible property losses, fatalities, and injuries associated with Hurricane Katrina in 2005, community groups were engaged with City of New Orleans emergency management staff and the Center for Hazard Assessment, Response, and Technology at the University of New Orleans to facilitate a plan for the evacuation of vulnerable populations in the event of a hurricane threat. When the evacuation orders were issued prior to the landfall of Hurricane Katrina, these plans were implemented and many citizens were successfully evacuated from the city. Unfortunately, emergency plans do not include enforcement provisions requiring residents to leave and can only facilitate timely and adequate options for transportation from the hazard zone. Residents of New Orleans were well aware of the risks associated with a hurricane such as Katrina and did not conclude that neither they nor their property would be at great risk.

12.5.3 RISK REDUCTION

Perhaps the best illustration of a risk reduction strategy is the National Flood Insurance Program (NFIP), which provides communities with a means of transferring risks associated with flooding from the individual homeowner to the NFIP. The success of this program is the buy-in locally by a local government entity that agrees to establish local land use and building code regulations that limit placement of new structures in flood plains or zones. Permitting of any new structure is required along with enforcement provisions to ensure that residents comply with the public policy goals of the NFIP. Many states that have suffered extensive disasters have gone beyond the provisions of the NFIP and require local governments to follow more stringent building design requirements to deal with high winds that occur in coastal states. Jurisdictions that face other hazards, such as wildfires or landslides, have taken actions to monitor building in hazardous areas and ensure that new construction meets the enhanced building codes.

12.5.4 RISK COMMUNICATION

Local governments may have completed extensive risk assessments and in the process provided a framework for the identification of vulnerable populations. The step that should follow the risk assessment is a concentrated effort to inform the public of local risks that the community faces. Some coastal communities have set up forums in local libraries or community centers to inform citizens of local risks from hazards. Discussions with business leaders and local agency staff also have been useful in getting the word out to the public. Campaigns to inform the public of local risks and the actions that they should take are an effective means of communicating risks to the public and creating a broader awareness of local environmental hazards.

12.6 COMMUNITY VULNERABILITY AND RESILIENCE

Nakagawa and Shaw (2004) note that there are common features that suggest why some communities are more resilient than others. They see that there is a complex mixture of social, economic, religious, and political factors present that influence community resilience to disasters. They found that the resilience of communities to recover following a disaster is based on both social and economic activities that are heavily influenced by social capital or the level of trust present in the community, social norms, degree of community participation, and, finally, the presence of strong community networks.

Risk identification is just the first step in dealing with hazards at the community level. What is needed is a broad-based disaster response and recovery plan and a comprehensive mitigation plan for reducing community vulnerability. More importantly, the community must be engaged throughout this process so they not only see the need for mitigation, but that the steps outlined by local officials are needed and appropriate for the community. Building a resilient community is not just the responsibility of local officials, but also of leaders in neighborhoods, businesses, community groups and agencies, and other local groups.

12.7 CONCLUSIONS

Vulnerability exists in different forms and varies geographically from one region to another. Coastal communities are composed of social, natural, and economic systems that interface to create a unique setting. Gulf coast communities from Texas, Louisiana, Mississippi, Alabama, and Florida are each unique with their coastal environment playing a major role in defining the local economy, history, community culture, and their unique natural resources. Small fishing villages in coastal Louisiana are quite different from the ever-growing resorts in Mississippi, Alabama, and Florida. When and why they were first settled forms a basis for not only their economic assets but also resources that are called on in the recovery from a disaster.

We appreciate the contribution that social, economic, and ecological assets play in the recovery of a coastal community, but now see even more clearly how these systems interface and affect one another. Damage to natural systems as the result of disasters has significant economic impacts and places extensive constraints on families and neighborhoods attempting to recover from disasters. One sees many examples of how physical damage to homes and businesses in greater New Orleans as a result of Hurricane Katrina in 2005 caused the displacement of families into other areas. Despite efforts of the City of New Orleans to bring back its population, many families see that the challenges to rebuilding their homes and thriving neighborhoods, and finding jobs, schools, and day care are just too great. Understanding how social, economic, and natural systems interrelate is critical in appreciating the nature and extent of our vulnerability and how we can cope with threats from natural and human-caused disasters.

Coping mechanisms are key in dealing with coastal community vulnerability. It is critical to understand the nature and extent of threats to a coastal community. We so often fail to appreciate the hidden impacts to disasters and acknowledge the cascading failures that are part of floods, wind, fire or business interruptions, and human displacements. Coping mechanisms include organizing community and neighborhood emergency preparedness, evacuation, or warning plans, business interruption strategies, short-term and long-term sheltering for those evacuated, and an understanding of how structural and nonstructural mitigation strategies can lessen the impacts of disasters. Too often it is not acknowledged how preparedness helped a community to deal with a disaster and avoid being consumed in crisis management. Organizations need to develop a culture of adaptation, but failing to prepare causes unnecessary diversions when responding to a disaster.

It should be acknowledged that the hazards analysis and the vulnerability assessment processes are ongoing. Local emergency preparedness officials review their community assessment of hazards and examine how a disaster might affect neighborhoods and businesses annually to ensure that their awareness of risks to the community are examined to reveal new social, economic, and environmental impacts. As local communities change over time, new threats may emerge along with impacts that affect specific business enterprises, neighborhoods, and preparedness plans. Further, disasters that affect one community can reveal new threats to others and offer lessons learned to expand our appreciation of what could happen. Too often, we do not acknowledge that catastrophes happen and that preparing for the worst-case scenario is not just a bureaucratic requirement. The Deepwater Horizon incident in the Gulf of Mexico (April–May 2010) was considered extremely unlikely and catastrophic plans had not been prepared by British Petroleum. Unfortunately, this approach invites disaster and fails to acknowledge that failures occur and can have impacts that may seem far beyond anything that we might consider. In this incident, very sensitive coastal environments in Louisiana, Mississippi, Alabama, and Florida were threatened by oil leaks that are proving extremely difficult to contain despite the use of the latest technology and coordinated emergency response team efforts. Learning from disasters well outside our own communities enables us to review our hazards assessments and response and recovery plans.

Developing an ability for local officials and communities to assess and monitor a community is critical in identifying problems and issues before a crisis develops. Indicators reflecting the social, economic, and environmental systems can provide local leaders with information on past conditions and current trends. These indicators provide local leaders from public, private, and nonprofit entities with information that can be used to monitor the local conditions and a basis for the identification of emerging issues and problems. Utilizing indicators is a critical element in scanning past and current conditions in order to ensure that as things change in a community, problems are not ignored and do not develop into a crisis. Selecting indicators that are suited for a coastal community is an ongoing process, and changing the indicators may be necessary to ensure that an accurate assessment of local conditions is provided.

Finally, engaging the community in the hazards analysis process and the development of an effective disaster response and recovery plan is critical to community sustainability. Local residents and business leaders appreciate the time-consuming nature of engaging the community and welcome the opportunity to participate in preparing local plans. We have stressed not only the need for engaging the local community but noted also that each community is unique and one approach may not be the best for all. Acknowledging that those outside of the government need to be involved in problem analysis and the development of response and recovery plans is the first step in ensuring that the local community is brought into the response and recovery process.

Coastal communities face unique threats and risks and must approach hazards assessment in a comprehensive effort that engages the community, operates on an ongoing basis, and reflects a broad-based commitment to sustaining their social, economic and natural systems. We appreciate that threats are ever changing and that chronic risks associated with climate change present new challenges to coastal communities. What are needed are processes to allow us to assess current and emerging threats and the development of strategies to cope with these risks today and in the future.

REFERENCES

Beach, D. 2002. *Coastal Sprawl: The Effects of Urban Design on Aquatic Ecosystems in the United States.* Arlington, VA: Pew Oceans Commission.

Blaikie, P., and H. Brookfield. 1987. *Land Degradation and Society.* London, England: Methuen

Blaikie, P., T. Cannon, I. Davis, and B. Wisner. 1994. *At Risk. Natural Hazards, People's Vulnerability and Disasters.* London: Routledge.

Bolin, R. 1993. *Household and Community Recovery after Earthquakes.* Boulder CO: Institute of Behavioral Science, University of Colorado, Boulder.

Bolin, R., and L. Stanford. 1991. Shelter, housing and recovery: A comparison of US Disasters. *Disasters 15*: 24–34.

Booth, D. 1991. Urbanization and the natural drainage system—impacts, solutions, and prognoses. *Northwest Environmental Journal 7*(1): 93–118.

Booth, D., and L. Reinelt. 1993. Consequences of urbanization on aquatic systems: Measured effects, degradation thresholds, and corrective strategies. In *Proceedings of Watershed '93, A National Conference on Watershed Management*, March 21–24, 1993, Alexandria, VA.

Boyd, K. A. 2005. Assessing storm vulnerability using the Coastal Risk Atlas. Presentation to the Southeastern section of the 54th annual meeting of the Geological Society of America, March 17–18, 2005, Biloxi, MS.

Bruneau, M., S. E. Chang, R. T. Eguchi, G. C. Lee, T. D. O'Rourke, A. M. Reinhorn, M. Shinozuka, K. Tierney, W. A. Wallace, and D. von Winterfeldt. 2003. A framework to quantitatively assess and enhance the seismic resilience of communities. *Earthquake Spectra 19*(4): 733–752.

Burby, Raymond J. 1998. *Cooperating with Nature.* Washington, DC: Joseph Henry Press.

Comfort, L., B. Wisner, S. Cutter, R. Pulwarty, K. Hewitt, A. Oliver-Smith, J. Wiener, M. Fordham, W. Peacock, and F. Krimgold. 1999. Reframing disaster policy: The global evolution of vulnerable communities. *Environmental Hazards 1*(1999): 39–44.

Crowards, T. 1999. *An Economic Vulnerability Index for Developing Countries, with Special Reference to the Caribbean.* Barbados: Caribbean Development Bank.

Cutter, S. L. 1996. Vulnerability to environmental hazards. *Progress in Human Geography 20*(4): 529–539.

Cutter, S. L., B. Boruff, and W. L. Shirley. 2003. Social vulnerability to environmental hazards. *Social Science Quarterly 84*(2): 242–261.

Cutter, S. L., J. T. Mitchell, and M. S. Scott. 1997. *Handbook for Conducting a GIS-based Hazards Assessment at the County Level.* Columbia, SC: Hazards Research Lab, Department of Geography, University of South Carolina.

Cutter, S. L., J. T. Mitchell, and M. S. Scott. 2000. Revealing the vulnerability of people and places: A case study of Georgetown County, South Carolina. *Annals of the Association of American Geographers 90*(4): 713–737.

Environmental Protection Agency (EPA). 1999. *Draft guidance for water quality-based decisions: The TMDL process*, 2nd ed. http://www.epa.gov/owow/tmdl/propguid/tmdlguid.pdf.

Feike, M. M. 2010. Revitalizing the suburban dream: Disaster, displacement and resilience in Eastern Orleans Parish. PhD dissertation. Baton Rouge, LA: Louisiana State University.

Galli, J. 1991. *Thermal Impacts Associated with Urbanization and Storm Water Management Best Management Practices.* Washington, DC: Metropolitan Washington Council of Governments, Maryland Department of Environment.

Godschalk, D. R., E. Kaiser, and P. Berke. 1998. Integrating hazard mitigation and local land use planning. In *Cooperating with Nature*, ed. R. J. Burby, 85–118. Washington, DC: Joseph Henry Press.

Heinz III Center for Science, Economics and the Environment. 2000. *The Hidden Costs of Coastal Hazards; Implications for Risk Assessment and Mitigation.* Washington, DC: Islands Press.

Hewitt, K. 1997. *Regions of Risk: A Geographical Introduction to Hazards.* Harlow, Essex, UK: Addison Wesley Longman Limited.

Howell, S. E. 2005. *Citizen hurricane evacuation behavior in southeastern Louisiana: A twelve parish survey.* Survey Research Center, University of New Orleans, New Orleans, LA. http://louisdl.louislibraries.org/CUPA/Pages/repository.html.

Intergovernmental Panel on Climate Change (IPCC). 2007. *Climate change 2007: Synthesis report.* Contribution of Working Groups I, II, and III to the Fourth Assessment Report of the Intergovernmental Panel on Climate Change, eds. Core Writing Team, R. K. Pachauri and A. Reisinger. Geneva, Switzerland.

Karl, T. R., J. M. Melillo, and T. C. Peterson, eds. 2009. *Global Climate Change Impacts in the United States.* Cambridge, UK: Cambridge University Press.

Kasperson, J. X., R. E. Kasperson, and B. L. Turner III, eds. 1995. *Regions at Risk: Comparisons of Threatened Environments.* Tokyo, Japan: United Nations University Press.

Lovins, A. B., L. Lovins, and P. Hawken. 1999. A road map for natural capitalism. *Harvard Business Review* 77(3): 145–158.

Mileti, D. S. 1999. *Disasters by Design.* Washington, DC: Joseph Henry Press.

Morrow, B. H. 1999. Identifying and mapping community vulnerability. *Disasters: The Journal of Disaster Studies, Policy and Management* 23(1): 1–18.

Munich Re Group. 2002. *Topics 2002.* Report of the Geo-Science Research Group. Munich: Munich Reinsurance Company.

Nakagawa, Y., and R. Shaw. 2004. Social capital: A missing link to disaster recovery. *International Journal of Mass Emergencies and Disasters* 22(1): 5–34.

National Research Council. 2000. *Ecological indicators for the nation (2000).* Commission on Geosciences, Environment and Resources. Washington, DC: National Academic Press. http://www.nap.edu/books/0309068452/html.

O'Brien, P., and D. S. Mileti. 1992. Citizen participation in emergency response following the Loma Prieta earthquake. *International Journal of Mass Emergencies and Disasters* 10(1): 71–89.

Pantin, D. 1997. Alternative ecological vulnerability indicators for developing countries with special reference to SIDS. Report prepared for the Expert Group on Vulnerability Index. UN(DESA), December 17–19, 1997.

Patkins, J., S. Mazzi, and C. D. Easter. 2000. *A Commonwealth vulnerability index for developing countries: The position of small states.* Economic Paper 40, Commonwealth Secretariat.

Peacock, W. G., B. H. Morrow, and H. Gladwin, eds. 2000. *Hurricane Andrew and the Reshaping of Miami: Ethnicity, Gender, and the Socio-Political Ecology of Disasters.* Miami: Florida International University, International Hurricane Center.

Peacock, W. G., and A. K. Ragsdale. 1997. Social systems, ecological networks and disasters: Toward a socio-political ecology of disasters. In *Hurricane Andrew,* eds. W. G. Peacock, B. H. Morrow, and H. Gladwin. New York: Routledge.

Pelling, M., ed. 2004. *Reducing Disaster Risk: A Challenge for Development.* New York: United Nations Development Programme, Bureau for Crisis Prevention and Recovery.

Pine, J. C. 2009. *Natural Hazards Analysis: Reducing the Impact of Disasters.* Boca Raton, FL: Taylor & Francis Group.

Puente, S. 1999. Social vulnerability to disaster in Mexico City. In J. K. Mitchell, ed., *Crucibles of Hazard: Mega-Cities and Disasters in Transition,* 295–334. Tokyo, Japan: United Nations University Press.

Pulido, L. 2000. Rethinking environmental racism: White privilege and urban development in Southern California. *Annals of the Association of American Geographers* 90: 12–40.

Richmond, B. M., C. Fletcher, E. Grossman, and A. Gibbs. 2001. Islands at risk: Coastal hazard assessment and mapping in the Hawaiian Islands. *Environmental Geosciences* 8(1): 21–37.

Schueler, T., and H. K. Holland. 2000. *The Practice of Watershed Protection.* Ellicott City, MD: Center for Watershed Protection.

United Nations Development Program (UNDP). 2003. *Human Development Report 2003,* ed. S. Fukoda-Parr. New York: Oxford University Press.

UN Development Program (UNDP). 2005. *Reducing disaster risk. A challenge for development.* United Nations Development Programme, Bureau for Crisis and Recovery.

UN Development Program (UNDP). 2000. *Human Development Report 2000.* New York: Oxford University Press.

USAID. 1999. *Introduction to current vulnerability guidelines.* FEWS current vulnerability assessment guidance manual. http://www.the-ecentre.net/resources/e_library/doc/FEWS.pdf.

Villa, F., and H. McLeod. 2002. Environmental vulnerability indicators for environmental planning and decision-making: Guidelines and applications. *Environmental Management* 29(3): 335–348.

Walker, B. 1996. Community based urban watershed protection: A case study for Atlanta, Georgia of Peavine and South Peachtree Creeks. MS thesis. University of Georgia, Athens, GA.

Wallis, A. D., E. Aguelles, D. Lampe, and M. Meehan. 2001. *Imaging the region: South Florida via indicators and public opinions*. Florida Atlantic University/Florida International University Joint Center for Urban and Environmental Problems, December 20, 2001, Miami, Florida.

Williams, L., and L. Kaputska. 2000. Ecosystem vulnerability: A complex interface with technical components. *Environmental Toxicology and Chemistry 19*(4): 1055–1058.

World Bank. 1999. *Environment Matters. Annual Review 1999*. Washington, DC: World Bank.

World Economic Forum. 2000. *Pilot environmental sustainability index*. An Initiative of the Global Leaders Tomorrow Environment Task Force: Annual meeting 2000, in collaboration with Yale University and Columbia University, Davos, Switzerland.

Yohe, G., and R. S. J. Tol. 2001. Indicators for social and economic coping capacity – moving toward a working definition of adaptive capacity. http://www.aiaccproject.org/resources/ele_lib_docs/gyoheindicators.doc.pdf.

Zandi, M., S. Cochrane, F. Ksiazkiewicz, and R. Sweet (2006). Restarting the economy. In *Rebuilding Urban Places after Disaster: Lessons from Hurricane Katrina*, 103–116, eds. E. Birch and S. Wachter. Philadelphia: University of Pennsylvania Press.

Part V

Addressing Barriers within
Systems of Care

13 Disaster Vulnerability and the School Setting

Understanding Environmental Risk and Implications for Behavioral Health Response

Martell L. Teasley

CONTENTS

13.1 INTRODUCTION

During a disaster occurrence, one of the most pressing concerns for many is the safety of children. When children are in the care of schools, their separation from families becomes an immediate focus during a disaster occurrence, particularly when school settings are involved in the disaster. The United States has approximately 17,000 public schools and 29,000 private schools (Murray et al. 2008). "There are 67 million children in American schools and child care facilities at any given point on a weekday, separate from their families and dependent on school officials and caregivers to provide protection" (Save the Children 2010, 2). Given the increasing frequencies of disasters within the United States (Teasley and Moore 2010) and the high vulnerability of children and youth for problematic behavioral health outcomes, school planning and readiness for a disaster or emergency is of paramount national importance.

Besides obvious potential threats to physical health and psychological well-being, children are also at risk for exploitation, violence, and parental separation, which makes them a highly vulnerable population during and after a disaster occurrence. While it goes without saying that children have a unique set of needs, a host of factors—such as age, level of maturation, and available social support—helps shape their ability to cope and survive a disaster occurrence. Most people have little understanding of the impact of a disaster occurrence on children and their particular needs for supportive measures in the postdisaster environment. "Depending on their age and stage of development, children may require different forms of physical, social, mental, and emotional support than the adults in their lives" (Peek 2008, 4). Peek (2008) explains that children experience three basic categories of vulnerability during a disaster: *psychological* (posttraumatic stress disorder [PTSD], depression, anxiety, sleep disorders, somatic complaints, emotional distress, and behavioral problems), *physical* (injury, death, illness and disease, heat stress, malnutrition, and physical and sexual abuse), and *educational* (missed school, delayed progress, poor academic performance, and failure to complete education). There are multiple pathways in which children are placed at risk for experiencing negative postdisaster outcomes. Normal psychological responses by children who have experienced traumatic events include the development of mood disturbances, depression, PTSD, health and sleep difficulties, anxiety-based problems, sleep problems, anger, substance abuse, and disorientation (Gill and Gershon 2010; Peek 2008). Physical vulnerability is sometimes coupled with postdisaster psychological challenges. There is evidence that some percentage of youth will attempt suicide based on PTSD experiences from the loss and grief over a loved one, particularly parental loss from a disaster occurrence (Weissbecker et al. 2008). Educational challenges are exacerbated by concerns over parental outcomes, low social support, relocation and adjustment, and time away from school (Murray et al. 2008; Peek 2008).

This chapter examines research on school readiness for disaster relief intervention with a particular focus on behavioral health for school-aged children and youth. The author assesses available evidence-based and best practice methods for school-based disaster behavioral health interventions. The school environment is highlighted as a salient factor in disaster vulnerability and readiness. Suggestions are made throughout this review for disaster planning and readiness, and for reducing risk factors that increase problematic behavioral health outcomes for school-aged children and youth. Consistent with the theme of this text, attention is given to understanding cultural competence in school-based disaster readiness and behavioral health interventions.

13.2   SCHOOLS AND DISASTER VULNERABILITY

Recent disaster occurrences both nationally and internationally highlight the need for research on disaster vulnerability for children attending school (Murray et al. 2008; Mitchell et al. 2008; Peek 2008). Assessing the aftermath of the March 2011 earthquake and tsunami that struck Japan's northwest coast, officials estimated that as many as 100,000 school-age children and youth were displaced. In Japan's northeastern Tohoku region, more than 1,000 school teachers and pupils perished. Save the Children, a longtime disaster relief organization, warned that continued housing in makeshift shelters would cause psychological strain and behavioral problems for children. During the aftermath of the 2010 Haitian earthquake, the United Nations estimated that more than 5,000 schools, or 80 percent of all schools, were either damaged or destroyed, leaving 2.5 million children and youth without schooling.

Blamed partially on poor building construction, the Chinese government estimated that more than 7,000 school rooms were collapsed and that some 10,000 children were crushed in their classrooms during the 2008 earthquake in Sichuan, China (Wong 2008). More than 16,000 children died in school buildings that collapsed in the October 2005 earthquake in Pakistan. More than 50 percent of school buildings were destroyed in the New Orleans, Louisiana, public school system during Hurricane Katrina, which left more than 50,000 children out of school during the 2005–2006 school year. Coupled with the displacement of 5,192 children, 37 percent of children from New Orleans post-Katrina experienced clinical depression, increased rates of suicide, anxiety, and behavioral disorders (Save the Children 2010).

The school environment can present multiple challenges during disaster relief and response. Some challenges are related to building design and construction, transportation, relocation, and school size. Special attention to the design and construction of school buildings is needed in order to prepare and reduce disaster vulnerability. The physical school environment must be understood from several vantage points. First, geographical location helps determine environmental susceptibility to a natural disaster occurrence. Schools located in coastal areas with a high risk for hurricanes and floods are obviously vulnerable. To this end, in geographical areas where there is a known history of disaster vulnerability, there tends to be greater local oversight of school building codes and regulations. For example, following the Long Beach earthquake in the 1930s, the state of California passed the Field Act requiring that "public schools be designed by a licensed architect or engineer, their plans checked, and the construction on site inspected by staff of the Department of State of Architecture" (Field Act 1933, 42).

Geographic location of schools is an important factor to contemplate in the development of approaches and strategies for disaster mitigation, preparedness, response, and recovery. "In 2009, of the almost 98,800 public elementary and secondary schools, 31 percent were located in small towns and rural areas and served 43 percent of the students, while 69 percent were located in cities and suburban areas and served 57 percent of the students" (U.S. Department of Education 2009, as cited in Arnold et al. 2010, 40). While urban school systems may be in closer proximity to emergency management operations and services than rural systems, there are alarming challenges that plague many of America's urban school systems. Both state and federal neglect of the nation's urban infrastructure has created areas of high geographic disaster vulnerability. Once well-constructed buildings that were part of a national emergency response system, many urban schools are now characterized by dilapidated buildings in need of major repair or total reconstruction. Many are less than acceptable for school disaster preparation and are part of a deteriorating infrastructure within urban America (Arnold et al. 2010).

Low-income urban communities with blighted infrastructures are more vulnerable to problematic postdisaster outcomes when compared to affluent suburban communities. Many poor children switch schools multiple times after experiencing a disaster occurrence. Research on school attendance for New Orleans children who experienced Hurricane Katrina found that "families were forced to relocate an average of 3.5 times, with some as many as nine times" (Weissbecker et al. 2008). However, the burden of relocation is not totally synonymous with underachievement in schools. For three years, Sacerdote (2008) tracked the academic performance of college-bound public school students affected by Hurricanes Rita and Katrina. Evacuees from suburban locations eventually recovered their lost academic ground from the 2005–2006 school year. Katrina evacuee students from suburban locations experienced a 3.5 percentage point drop in enrollment rates. High school students from New Orleans experienced higher college enrollment rates than high school students from the same school from the previous three years. Sacerdote (2008) concluded that the long-term gain from switching schools may offset early postdisaster disruption.

Important to note is the disaster readiness predicament of marginalized populations, particularly ethnic minorities, who have historically experienced residential segregation and discrimination and subsequently reside in high-risk areas for natural disasters. Families living in such areas have an increased probability of experiencing higher amounts of destruction during a disaster and poor postdisaster recovery outcomes—this was the case for New Orleans prior to and after Hurricanes Katrina and Rita. Children from these families are less likely to return to school after a disaster occurrence and are at greater risk for poor educational outcomes. "Evidence also suggests that both adults and children from ethnic minority groups are more likely to experience increased stress due to relocation, slower recovery and more severe PTSD symptoms following disaster" (Weissbecker et al. 2008, 43). In an assessment of the aftermath of Hurricane Katrina, Vigdor found that "public school enrollment in Orleans Parish fell by slightly more than half between fall 2004 and fall 2007. Private school enrollments declined over the same time period" (Vigdor 2008, 144). It was concluded that, in general, having one's family displaced by a hurricane is likely far more disruptive than a conventional move between schools. Vigdor (2007) estimated that evacuees on average lost three weeks of work, and those evacuees who did not return to the residential address lost closer to 10 weeks of work.

Second, school sizes range from one-room rural schoolhouses to 5,000-student megaschools (Arnold et al. 2010). When rapid evacuation is necessary, children in high-density and high-population schools face greater risk of less-than-desirable outcomes due to increased time to evacuate the premises. Thus, evacuation and relocation plans are highly important for safe outcomes in the advent of school-based emergencies. The average age of a school facility in the United States is over 40 years; thus, it is highly unlikely that older buildings are designed with the same level of protection as newer buildings. Although school building codes dramatically improved during the 1970s, many older urban school buildings were constructed during the 1950s and are two- to three-story buildings with poor space configuration for facilitating evacuation. Urban communities have higher levels of population density and higher-density school systems (Blanco et al. 2009). Moreover, many urban schools are overcrowded and housed in older buildings built in close proximity to other structures.

Third, since various school districts have their own approach to planning and building construction, design and renovation schemes vary from location to location. This has created a situation where there are a variety of structural configurations for school buildings that range from simple to complex. Most are mid-sized structures that are usually built by local governments, but many urban schools are makeshift buildings that were initially designed for other purposes. On the other hand, many modern schools are complex facilities that are configured as multiuse complexes that function as a community resource. Given these dynamics, plans for reducing vulnerability and disaster response in school systems should be individualized for particular building configurations.

Considering these contingencies, it is highly important to engage in the assessment of environmental and structural hazards for disaster vulnerability in school settings. Past lessons on disaster preparation have led to the development of methods of assessing and categorizing school readiness. The Federal Emergency Management Agency (FEMA) developed a comprehensive manual for the purpose of providing guidelines for the protection of school buildings from natural disasters such as floods, earthquakes, and high winds. Focusing on grades K–12, the *Design Guide for Improving School Safety in Earthquakes, Floods, and High Winds* is designed around technical issues facing schools such as financial decision making for school construction, renovation, and repair (Arnold et al. 2010). The manual is a free resource and can be downloaded from http://www.fema.gov/library/viewRecord.do?id=1986.

13.3   DISASTER BEHAVIORAL HEALTH AND SCHOOL CHILDREN

Beyond the inherent vulnerability that the environment can manifest, a focus on training and prevention can help minimize undesirable behavioral health outcomes for children who experience a disaster occurrence. There are three basic areas that help reduce disaster behavioral health challenges: dissemination through education and training, parental integration in disaster education, and preparation for a disaster/emergency occurrence through demonstration and drills (Ronan et al. 2008). Researchers have determined that children who participate in hazard education have less fear of a disaster occurrence than children who do not (Ronan and Johnston 2005). Ronan and Johnston's (2001) study determined that factors linked to increased disaster readiness are (1) increased parent and child interaction concerning hazards programs; (2) particular knowledge of emergency management procedures; (3) use of the most relevant educational materials; and (4) multiple educational opportunities and involvement. Using comparison groups in a follow-up 2005 investigation, Ronan and Johnston confirmed that the value of parental interaction and multiple program involvement were significant factors in predicting hazard adjustment in school children. The author briefly discusses research on each area in the following sections.

13.3.1   Parental Factors

As with adults, most children recover from a disaster occurrence without professional assistance. However, recent trends in school destruction during major disasters have facilitated a surge in the need for research on behavioral health challenges for school children. High resilience in children is associated with a host of indicators, including intelligence, optimism, creativity, an existential belief system, humor, social skills, known coping strategies, and even physical attractiveness (Weissbecker et al. 2008). Existing research demonstrates a host of problematic outcomes after a disaster, such as emotional problems, classroom behavioral and relationship problems, reduced academic effort, and underachievement (Kalantari and Vostanis 2010). Postdisaster family outcomes are a paramount factor in children's behavioral health and can affect school performance in many ways. Parent behaviors, thoughts, and feelings affect children's behavior and outcomes (Ronan et al. 2008). Parents may be so upset that they do not recognize children's distress and need for coping support (Ronan et al. 2008). Therefore, support for both children and family members is needed as part of postdisaster behavioral health screening, assessment, and referral for intervention.

A study by Roll and Payne (2007) demonstrated that children had difficulties in expressing and managing their feelings, fears for the surviving parent, and problems at school (as cited in Kalantari and Vostanis 2010). "Additional long-term stressors can occur as a child mentally re-experiences the disaster, deals with loss of loved ones, relocates, and experiences disruption of routines, or adjustment to new circumstances" (Weissbecker et al. 2008, 35). Four years after the 2003 Iranian earthquake, Kalantari and Vostanis (2010) investigated behavioral and emotional problems in school children who experienced the loss of a parent during the disaster. Eighty-six children ages 7 to 13 participated in the study and were matched with 80 children from intact families in the same schools sampled. "Parental death was found to interact with socioeconomic variables in predicting children's behavioral and emotional problems and surviving parents' mental health problems" (158). Sensitivity to long-term postdisaster behavioral health services for children experiencing bereavement and attention to risk factors, such as family socioeconomic challenges after the lost of a parent, are noted from the study.

In an investigation examining whether family resilience predicted children to have disaster-induced emotional symptoms and PTSD independent of control variables such as previous child mental illness and social connectedness, McDermott and associates (2010) surveyed 568 school children using several disaster-related screening instruments. Results indicate that 11.3 percent of participating children were in the severe to very severe PTSD category, and a low family resilience score was associated with children's emotional problems and "longer duration of previous child mental health difficulties, but not disaster-induced child PTSD or child threat perception …" (384). Also, previous mental health challenges were not significant predictors of PTSD for the sample of children. The authors concluded that for the sample of participants "children with existing mental health problems and those of low-resilience families were not at elevated risk of PTSD" (384).

It is estimated that only one-fourth of children who need behavioral health treatment after a disaster occurrence actually receive it (Murray et al. 2008). This is particularly troubling in many respects since a percentage of children will not initially demonstrate signs of behavioral health problems. To illustrate, Comer and associates (2010) attempted to determine future postdisaster behavioral health intervention efforts by examining the relationship between disaster-related "life disruption" and "children's functioning." Of 8,236 grades 4–12 New York public school children sampled six months after September 11, 2001, one in three children reported that their parent or parents restricted travel post-9/11 and one in five reported that a family member lost his or her job due to the disaster. These instances of disruption found to be "associated with elevated rates of probable posttraumatic stress disorder and other anxiety disorders … indicate that adverse disaster-related experiences extend beyond traumatic exposure and include the prolonged ripple of post-disaster life disruption and economic hardship" (Comer et al. 2010, 460). Comer and associates infer that future disaster-related behavioral health services for "proximally exposed youth" should focus on disrupted life events as a source of psychological distress for school children.

13.3.2 EDUCATIONAL FACTORS

Evidence-based models for behavioral health intervention consist of methods used with families, training, and schools. This model uses sequenced intervention methods consisting of multiple data-gathering assessments, step-by-step intervention, and inherent self-correcting features—monitoring intervention effectiveness and services in response to poor outcomes. The focus on providing children and families basic needs is seen as an important psychological perspective that facilitates "a sense of emotional security and control" (Ronan et al. 2008, 4). Similarly, psychological first aid (PFA) is supported as a method that facilitates a sense of well-being by addressing children's basic needs while simultaneously providing empathetic understanding and emotional support. PFA is designed for individuals who need immediate aid for trauma survival and has demonstrated success in postdisaster contexts. Children who experience trauma due to a disaster occurrence and received PFA by trained practitioners will not need to be referred for further counseling unless they continue to experience problems in functioning. PFA is often all that families need to return to predisaster levels of normalcy (Ronan et al. 2008). Training school administrations, teachers, and other essential personnel is an important step in the reduction of behavioral health challenges for school children. Another proven method is media-driven outreach aimed at providing education and information on what parents and children can do to address issues related to postdisaster stress.

13.3.3 SCHOOL FACTORS

Schools can play a huge role in the cultivation of students for disaster preparation. Although greater study is needed, a school-wide screening has been conducted with large groups and is an empirically supported intervention. This method includes intensive family-focused and individual intervention and emphasizes a cognitive behavioral approach. Techniques such as self-talk, relaxation, problem solving, self-reinforcement, identification of emotional reactions, early cues, and realistic self-evaluation are demonstrated methods of this evidenced-based treatment protocol (Ronan and Johnston 2005). Gradual exposure to disaster conditions during school readiness exercises has been proven useful as a training method. This method includes a combination of having the client directly view the anxiety-provoking situation while simultaneously providing the client with coping skills (Ronan et al. 2008). Group-based intervention in schools has also demonstrated benefits. When school-based interventions are conducted, it is important that parents are aware of and approve of the intervention so that the home environment is consistent with the formal intervention provided at school.

13.4 SCHOOL DISASTER READINESS

During a disaster occurrence, the school administration, teachers, and staff play an important role in assisting children to safety. These individuals and other personnel working in schools must be equipped with the necessary knowledge and training to engage in effective response and risk reduction. Schools can function as de facto mental health facilities during a disaster occurrence (Young et al. 2006). During school-based preparation for a disaster occurrence, the development of a school crisis response team is of the utmost importance; this team should check equipment, review and take action in the amelioration of environmental risk factors, and work with community stakeholders who are involved in crisis planning.

There is no federal law that requires school districts to have emergency management plans; however, 32 states have such plans, and 95 percent of school districts report they have some form of emergency procedure (Murray et al. 2008). Yet, despite opportunities for federal grants for emergency planning and readiness, many schools struggle with balancing funding for educational issues, administrative responsibilities, and activities for emergency management preparation. "Challenges include a lack of emergency equipment, staff training, and expertise in the area of emergency planning" (Murray et al. 2008, 896). A 2004 survey of school superintendents found that 86.3 percent report having a readiness plan, but only 57 percent had prevention plans. While 95.6 percent had evacuation plans, 30 percent reported never conducting an evacuation drill, and 48 percent never met with emergency management services (Murray et al. 2008).

Researchers from the National Center for Disaster Preparedness (Gill and Gershon 2010) reviewed disaster mental health training programs for practitioners administered by professional associations, hospitals, community-based organizations, and government agencies after September 11, 2001. Findings indicate that the quality and effectiveness of programs are difficult to assess because of a wide range of programming and a lack of record keeping and credentialing for trainers. A similar problematic assessment of school disaster readiness comes from Save the Children's *A National Report Card on Protecting Children during Disasters* (2010, 2), which provides a grade for all 50 states on four criteria for disaster/emergency preparation. These criteria consist of the development of a plan for evacuating children in child care facilities; the development of a written plan that notifies parents of an emergency, and contingency plans to reunite parents with children; written and executable plans for children with special needs; and evacuation plans for schools. Findings are cited as follows:

- Less than a quarter of all states and the District of Columbia meet all of four basic preparedness standards.
- Less than half require all licensed child care facilities to have an evacuation and relocation plan.
- Less than half require all licensed child care facilities to have a family reunification plan.
- Less than two-thirds do not require all licensed child care facilities to have a plan that accounts for children with special needs.
- Almost a dozen do not require K–12 schools to have a disaster plan that accounts for multiple types of disasters.

Conversely, there are success stories on the academic outcomes of youth affected by a disaster occurrence. A self-report survey on emergency preparedness for three public school districts in Los Angeles County found that respondents generally felt that the schools were prepared; it also revealed the need for improving the writing of disaster response plans, greater training, and the implementation of a statewide standardized emergency management system. For respondents of this survey, a significant predictor of compliance with emergency management system guidelines is related to having experienced past school emergencies (Kano et al. 2007).

Findings from a review of research indicate that greater attention and planning toward school-based disaster preparedness is needed for the determination of best practices. The Child Safety Care and Education Continuity Act of 2010 will provide counseling and health care coverage to children impacted by disasters and requires child care centers that receive federal funding to comply with the criteria developed to evacuate children in the event of a disaster occurrence.

On August 4, 2009, FEMA announced the creation of the Children's Working Group for the purpose of examining the unique needs of children in community disaster planning and response. Areas of focus of the Children's Working Group will include:

- Child-specific guidance as to evacuation, sheltering, and relocation
- Tracking and reunification of families
- Coordinated case management supports
- Enhanced preparedness for child care centers and schools as well as for children in child welfare and juvenile justice systems
- Enhanced national planning, including incorporation of children into national planning scenarios and exercises
- Incorporation of children's needs into grant guidance
- Improved recovery coordination across the federal family and with state and local partners in support of children's education, health and housing

- Consideration as to how the federal family can help ensure child care centers are able rebuild and restore services more quickly following a disaster
- Increased public awareness efforts to educate families and protect children during disasters (FEMA 2009)

13.4.1 CULTURAL COMPETENCE, SCHOOL READINESS, AND BEHAVIORAL HEALTH

The need for school-based disaster preparation, behavioral health management, and culturally competent practices has received scant attention from disaster researchers. However, in making such a statement, it would be problematic to discount the advocacy for community inclusion, collaboration practice, and local planning with particular attention to geographical location found in many of the documents cited in this chapter. From a review of research literature and scholarly reports, one gains a sense of awareness of methods needed for engaging in strategic approaches to culturally competent disaster readiness planning for schools. While all children have basic survival and safety needs during a disaster occurrence, and are in general considered vulnerable due to their status, there is a plethora of issues related to diversity and disaster relief that should be considered in the planning process that may reduce the onset of postdisaster behavioral health complications for school children and youth. For example, evidence "suggest[s] that both adults and children from ethnic minority groups are more likely to experience increased stress due to relocation, slower recovery and more severe PTSD symptoms following disaster" (Weissbecker et al. 2008, 43).

Research studies are needed that heighten awareness of multicultural issues in the school setting and promote critical thinking and engagement in the knowledge-building process for understanding diversity and school-based disaster planning and behavioral health intervention. Such issues should include information on children with disabilities and special education needs, immigrant populations, minority populations, children from families with limited English proficiency, the plight of gay and lesbian school children, homeless school children, and the growing number of children living with grandparents. Additional considerations are socioeconomic factors, coping skills, and political contingencies that mediate risk and protective factors in pre- and postdisaster recovery environments. For example, recent political trends promoting tougher immigration restrictions voted in by some state legislative bodies—those with increasing illegal immigrant populations—will further exacerbate the challenge of working with noncitizens in the postdisaster environment. Thus, families living and working in the United States as noncitizens and without appropriate identification and other documentation may find it harder to navigate the postdisaster relief and recovery environment.

In addition to crowded schools and infrastructure challenges cited earlier in this chapter, many poorer minority communities are located in closer proximity to toxic waste dumps in comparison to more affluent communities (Morello-Frosch 2002). This situation gets complicated when considering that many poor communities and schools depend on the economic base of industries that pollute their communities. Moreover, in locations where there are higher levels of pollution, rent is usually cheaper, and therefore the poor gravitate to such inexpensive dwellings; they may want to return to such areas in the postdisaster environment in order to stay near other relatives (Weissbecker et al. 2008).

Culturally competent disaster planning for school children and youth means taking into consideration the known and expected health complications of highly vulnerable children within America. Unfortunately, there are disproportionate numbers of some minority children and youth that are predisposed to poor health conditions. For example, because of high levels of community exposure to hazardous waste toxicity, African American and Hispanic children have higher diagnosed rates of respiratory complications when compared to white children (Shalala 2000). Rates are reported as high as 50 percent for respiratory complications, such as asthma, among African American children in New York City. Yet, due to socioeconomic challenges and lower rates of health care coverage, African American and Hispanic children are especially at high risk of not receiving preventive treatment for asthma attacks. According to a May 2000 report by the U.S. Department of Health and Human Services, many inner-city minority children receive inappropriate treatment for asthma

(Shalala 2000). "An analysis of preschool children hospitalized for asthma found that only seven percent of African Americans and two percent of Hispanics, compared with 21 percent of white children, were prescribed routine medication to prevent future asthma exacerbations" (Shalala 2000, 12).

Similarly, in the area of behavioral health challenges and particularly concerning learning disabilities, African Americans and Hispanics are less likely to seek behavioral health services. And when they are seen for services, symptoms are more pronounced, leading to a more severe diagnosis. In many localities, schools are a breeding ground for misappropriate minority mental health diagnosis (Frey 2000); the postdisaster environment will bear no difference if specific preparedness planning measures that provide knowledge of minority mental health research are not part of the training and education of all disaster relief and recovery personnel who come into contact with school-age children and youth.

Although there is no comprehensive manual on school-based behavioral health intervention for disaster planning and preparedness, methods for addressing cultural competence in this area can be found in the *Practical Information on Crisis Planning: A Guide for Schools and Communities* (U.S. Department of Education 2007). Widely used throughout the country, this manual provides a four-phase approach to emergency planning activities and is intended to provide schools and communities with tools for critical thinking and strategies for resource procurement during local crisis planning and disaster preparation. The manual includes promising practices and provides information on behavioral health risk reduction for school disaster preparation and postdisaster recovery. A central theme emphasized throughout the manual is that disaster plans are living documents "that need to be reviewed and revised regularly." Here, the author modifies the guidelines in order to reflect disaster planning strategies for culturally competent school-based behavioral health intervention:

- "School and districts should open the channels of communication well before a crisis," (U.S. Department of Education 2007, 1-10).
- Proactive approaches to cultivating community relations can facilitate the crisis planning process. Essentially, it is a way of reducing the incidence of underserved populations during emergency management disaster relief and recovery efforts.
- "Crisis plans should be developed in partnership with other community groups, including law enforcement, fire officials, emergency medical services, as well as health and mental health professionals" (U.S. Department of Education 2007, 1-10). Particular attention and outreach should take place within communities where minority school children reside. Emergency management professionals and paraprofessionals must understand the demographics and the dynamics of the local neighborhood schools and the communities where they provide services.
- "A common vocabulary is necessary" and must be recognizable by all corners of a given community" (U.S. Department of Education 2007, 1-10). Plain language should be used by disaster personnel as much as possible, particularly in dealing with school children. Appropriate planning that includes strategies to enhance community relationship building and that fosters greater communication among residents may help reduce disaster risk and vulnerability for school children. Emergency management personnel should be familiar with local greeting protocols within their service areas.
- "Schools should tailor district crisis plans to meet individual school needs" (U.S. Department of Education 2007, 1-11). Special consideration and attention should be given during crisis planning so that it reflects the needs of the student population and the school staff. Community members should be familiar with school disaster plans and be given opportunity to make comments.
- "Plan for the diverse needs of children" (U.S. Department of Education 2007, 1-11). Families within the school community need to have meaningful input into the disaster planning process to meet the diverse needs of children. Special attention should be given to students with disabilities and those with limited English proficiency. Emergency relief organizations should anticipate when outreach documents for families may need to be written in several languages.

- "Include all types of schools [in the planning] where appropriate" (U.S. Department of Education 2007, 1-12). Planning should include public and private schools, charter and alternative schools within a given community. Planning should include outreach to affluent as well as poor school districts. School systems can coordinate drills together and engage in lessons learned after action reporting.
- "Provide teachers and staff with ready access to the plan so they can understand its components and act on them" (U.S. Department of Education 2007, 1-12). Ensure that school-based personnel are aware of and understand new information including their respective roles in the event of a disaster occurrence. Panic and anxiety are reduced when school-based personnel are made aware of their roles and responsibilities in advance of a crisis occurrence.
- "Training and practice are essential for the successful implementation of crisis plans" (U.S. Department of Education 2007, 1-12). As much as possible, include all students in drills and evaluate what works and what needs improvement. Pay particular attention to training competencies for dealing with diverse student populations, particularly those with special needs.

13.5 CONCLUSION

The school environment is one of major concern in disaster relief and recovery. Given that school children are highly vulnerable during and after a disaster occurrence, special attention and provisions must be taken to accommodate their needs for safety, health, and psychological well-being. Schools present a host of contingencies that must be considered in planning and preparation by emergency management personnel, including geographical location, school size and density, and infrastructure support. Findings from a review of research studies indicate that greater attention and planning towards school-based disaster preparedness is needed for the determination of best practices. The federal government has prepared a host of resources that can facilitate school disaster readiness. School systems and communities that prepare for a disaster occurrence through planning and school-wide drills help reduce vulnerability and the stigma of experiencing a disaster occurrence, and promote disaster readiness.

Behavioral health concerns for children and youth that experience a disaster occurrence depend on the severity of the experience as well as pre- and postdisaster family and social supports. Research demonstrates a host of behavioral and emotional complications that can manifest in school-aged children and youth. For the most part, childhood resilience depends on a return to normalcy (as much as possible), in which school attendance can play a significant role. For children who experience trauma due to a disaster occurrence or crisis situation, PFA is considered a best practice when it comes to reducing the likelihood or severity of behavioral health complications.

Noting the growing diversification of our nation's school systems, and a host of other issues identified within this chapter, cultural competence is extremely important in disaster training, education, and strategic planning. Children and youth from some minority groups reside in communities with higher levels of vulnerability due to socioeconomic factors, live within poor infrastructure, suffer from health disparities, and have low levels of social support. Poor school systems should not be left out of disaster planning and preparation. There are also special needs populations among school children that merit additional disaster planning considerations. With appropriate planning, education, and training, childhood vulnerability in the face of a disaster occurrence can be minimized.

REFERENCES

Arnold, C., J. Lyons, J. Munger, R. C. Quinn, T. L. Smith, and P. Line. 2010. *Design Guide for Improving School Safety in Earthquakes, Floods, and High Winds. Risk Management Series, FEMA P-424.* Washington, DC: Federal Emergency Management Administration.
Blanco, H., M. Alberti, R. Olshansky, S. Chang, S. M. Wheeler, J. Randolph, J. B. London, J. B. Hollander, K. M. Pallagst, T. Schwarz, F. J. Popper, S. Parnell, E. Pieterse, and V. Watson. 2009. Shaken, shrinking, hot, impoverished and informal: Emerging research agendas in planning. *Progress in Planning* 72(4): 195–250.

Comer, J. S., B. Fan, C. S. Duarte, P. Wu, G. J. Musa, D. J. Mandell, A. M. Albano, and C. W. Hoven. 2010. Attack-related life disruption and child psychopathology in New York City public schoolchildren 6-months post-9/11. *Journal of Clinical Child & Adolescent Psychology 39*(4): 460–469.

Federal Emergency Management Agency. 2009. U.S. Department of Homeland Security. FEMA announces creation of children's working group. http://www.fema.gov/news/newsrelease.fema?id=49221.

Field Act, A.B. 2342 (Ca. 1933).

Frey, A. 2000. Educational placement for children with behavioral and/or emotional disorders: Overlooked variables contribution to placements in restrictive settings. *Journal of School Social Work 11*(1): 51–66.

Gill, K. B., and R. R. Gershon. 2010. Disaster mental health training programmes in New York City following September 11, 2001. *Disaster 34*(3): 608–618.

Kalantari, M., and P. Vostanis. 2010. Behavioural and emotional problems in Iranian children four years after parental death in an earthquake. *International Journal of Social Psychiatry 56*(2): 158–167.

Kano, M., M. Ramirez, W. J. Ybarra, G. Frias, and L. B. Bourque. 2007. Are schools prepared for emergencies? A baseline assessment of emergency preparedness at school sites in three Los Angeles County school districts. *Education and Urban Society 39*(3): 399–422.

McDermott, B. M., V. E. Cobham, H. Berry, and H. M. Stallman. 2010. Vulnerability factors for disaster-induced child post-traumatic stress disorder: The case for low family resilience and previous mental illness. *Australian & New Zealand Journal of Psychiatry 44*(4): 384–389.

Mitchell, T., K. Haynes, W. Choong, N. Hall, and K. Oven. 2008. The role of children and youth in communicating disaster risk. *Children, Youth and Environments 18*(1): 254–279.

Morello-Frosch, R. A. 2002. The political economy of environmental discrimination. *Environment and Planning C, Government and Policy 20*(4): 477–496.

Murray, R. D., R. S. Gereige, L. M. Grant, J. H. Lamont, H. Magalnick, G. J. Monteverdi, E. G. Pattishall III, M. M. Roland, L. S. M. Wheeler, C. DiLaura Devore, and S. E. Barnett. 2008. Disaster planning for schools. *Pediatrics 122*: 895–901. http://healthvermont.gov/local/school/documents/disasterinschool2008.pdf.

Ronan, K. R., K. Crellin, D. M. Johnston, K. Finnis, D. Paton, and J. Becker. 2008. Promoting child and family resilience to disasters: Effects, interventions, and prevention effectiveness. *Children, Youth and Environments 18*(1): 332–353.

Ronan, K. R., and D. Johnston, 2005. Community resilience: The role of schools, youth and families. In *Promoting Community Resilience in Disasters: The Role for Schools, Youth, and Families*, eds. K. R. Ronan and D. Johnston, 49–71. New York: Springer.

Ronan, K. R., and D. M. Johnston. 2001. Correlates of hazard education programs for youth. *Risk Analysis 21*(6): 1055–1063.

Sacerdote, B. 2008. When the saints come marching in: Effects of Hurricanes Katrina and Rita on student evacuees. *National Bureau of Economic Research*. NBER Working Paper No. 14385. http://research.studentclearinghouse.org/content/studies/Saints%20Come%20Marching%20InSacerdote92008.pdf.

Save the Children. 2010. *A national report card on protecting children during disasters*. http://www.savethechildren.org/atf/cf/%7B9DEF2EBE-10AE-432C-9BD0-DF91D2EBA74A%7D/2010-Disaster-Report.pdf.

Shalala, D. 2000. *Priority Area 3: Eliminate the disproportionate burden of asthma in minority populations and those living in poverty. Action against asthma: A strategic plan for the Department of Health and Human Services*. http://aspe.hhs.gov/sp/asthma/overview.htm.

Teasley, M., and J. A. Moore. 2010. Disaster recovery case management: Social work and multicultural education. In *Disaster Concepts and Issues: A Guide for Social Work Education and Practice*, eds. D. F. Gillespie and K. Danso, 241–254. Alexandria, VA: Council on Social Work Education, Inc.

U.S. Department of Education, the Office of Safe and Drug-free Schools. 2007. *Practical Information on Crisis Planning: A Guide for Schools and Communities*. Washington, DC: Author. http://www2.ed.gov/admins/lead/safety/emergencyplan/crisisplanning.pdf.

Vigdor, J. 2008. The economic aftermath of Hurricane Katrina. *Journal of Economic Perspectives 22*(4) 135–154.

Weissbecker, I., S. E. Sephton, M. B. Martin, and D. M. Simpson. 2008. Psychological and physiological correlates of stress in children exposed to disaster: Current research and recommendations for intervention. *Children, Youth and Environments 18*(1): 30–70.

Wong, E. 2008. "How angel of Sichuan saved school in quake." *New York Times*, June 16, 2008. http://www.nytimes.com/2008/06/16/world/asia/16quake.html?_r=1&sq=edward%20wong&st=nyt&oref=slogin&scp=5&pagewanted=print.

Young, B. H., J. I. Ruzek, M. Wong, M. S. Salzer, and A. J. Naturale. 2006. Disaster mental health training: Guidelines, considerations, and recommendations. In *Interventions Following Mass Violence and Disasters*, eds. E. C. Ritchie, P. J. Watson, and M. J. Friedman, 54–79. New York: Guilford Press.

14 Issues in Providing Mental and Medical Health Care in Long-Term Care Settings during Disasters

David Dosa, Kathryn Hyer, and Lisa M. Brown

CONTENTS

14.1 OVERVIEW

Emergency planning for vulnerable populations constitutes a major element of community disaster preparedness and is an area where guidance has historically been sparse (Brodie et al. 2006; Kayman and Ablorh-Odjidja 2006). Citing this lack of information, the Institute of Medicine emphasized the need to conduct multidisciplinary research to protect vulnerable populations in a 2008 report on emergency preparedness research priorities (Altevogt et al. 2008). One high-risk population mentioned in the report is the approximately 2.4 million residents of long-term care facilities (LTCF) such as nursing homes and assisted living facilities. As a group, LTCFs often take care of residents with serious comorbid conditions such as cognitive impairment, functional disability, hearing and visual impairment, mental health concerns (e.g., depression and anxiety), and chronic medical conditions (e.g., diabetes, congestive heart failure, chronic renal insufficiency, and chronic obstructive pulmonary disease). These conditions make this population particularly susceptible to the perils of disasters.

The events that followed Hurricane Katrina, a strong Category 3 storm that made landfall on August 29, 2005, outside of New Orleans, provides compelling evidence of just how long-term care facilities can be affected by disasters. Anecdotally, the loss of life and lack of emergency preparedness at LTCFs in Louisiana and elsewhere were well chronicled in the lay press (Hull and Struck 2005; Harris 2005), research papers (Brodie et al. 2006: Dosa et al. 2007; Franco et al. 2006; Hyer et al. 2006), and in several government reports (Root, Amoozegar, and Bernard 2007; GAO 2006; OIG 2006).

More recently, specific data reference the effects of the hurricane disaster on frail nursing home residents. Using death certificates, Brunkard and colleagues noted that of the 877 confirmed fatalities attributed to Hurricanes Katrina and Rita (also 2005), 103 (12 percent) were believed to be nursing home residents (Brunkard, Namulanda, and Ratard 2008). Work by Dosa, Hyer, and Brown using Medicare data found that the hurricane caused 148 additional nursing home resident deaths in the following 30 days among exposed homes compared to the mean number of deaths at the same homes in the two preceding years (Dosa et al. 2010). This translates to a rate of nearly 16 extra deaths per 1,000 residents. At 90 days, a total of 230 additional lives (an additional 25 deaths per 1,000) had been lost. Hospitalizations were also increased with 204 extra hospitalizations (22 additional hospitalizations per 1,000 residents) at 30 days and 132 extra hospitalizations (14 per 1,000 residents) at 90 days (Dosa et al. 2010).

Given the profound effects of previous disasters on residents of LTCFs, this chapter will explore why they are at heightened risk for morbidity and mortality and provide an overview regarding the care needs of residents with a focus on mental and medical health care needs. Additionally, it will outline how assisted living facilities and nursing homes differ relative to disaster planning. Finally, it will consider lessons learned from disaster situations through two historical case examples of long-term care facilities that have dealt with different disasters.

14.1.1 WHY ARE THE ELDERLY AT RISK IN DISASTERS?

A disaster can be defined as a catastrophic event or series of events that results in societal disruptions with deleterious consequences on a massive scale (Ciottone 2006). Disasters may be categorized broadly by etiology as either naturally occurring, such as weather-related events, pandemic events, or caused either directly or indirectly by human behavior, such as acts of terrorism (Noji 1997). Catastrophic events can be further subclassified based on a variety of factors, including whether they are acute (e.g., hurricanes, floods) or chronic (e.g., global warming) in onset; or based on their level of complexity. For some types of natural disasters there may be forewarning (e.g., hurricanes) while for others there is little to no warning (e.g. tornadoes, earthquakes) so only post-disaster response "planning" is relevant. Many disasters are complex emergencies in which initial events lead, through cause-and-effect mechanisms, to additional layers of disruption in infrastructure and the social fabric that provoke a host of additional negative consequences. Examples of such complex emergencies include the 1994 Northridge Earthquake in California, Hurricane Katrina, and the 2007 tsunami in Southeast Asia. A thread common to all disasters is their effect on human health; they may therefore be defined by their impact on the delivery of health services, their negative effects on healthcare infrastructure, and their potential threats to public health. This view has engendered the adoption by the United States federal government of an "all-hazards approach" to preparedness, whereby disaster response planning incorporates principles common to all events and can thus be readily adapted to specific contingencies (Briggs 2005).

As mentioned in the introduction, long-term care residents represent a major vulnerable group with their susceptibility magnified in the setting of disasters (Eldar 1991; Fernandez et al. 2002; Mudur 2005). Key reasons for their increased susceptibility to disasters rest in a number of factors. First, as people age, the tendency to have comorbid conditions increases. However, it is not the age of an individual that creates vulnerability, but rather a constellation of factors that places people at higher risk for experiencing enduring physiological or psychological problems. Factors that contribute to overall risk include the presence of one or more of the following conditions: frailty, impaired cognition, psychiatric disorders, physical disability, sensory impairment, and medical illness.

Secondly, the presence of physical or mental conditions that require skilled nursing home care increases the risk for adverse outcomes from disasters. Mental disorders and physical health limitations curtail the ability of residents to respond to the chaotic environment of a disaster scenario and exacerbate the impact of disaster on their well-being. Dementia and mental illness also make evacuation more difficult because the residents may not cooperate, have concomitant behavioral issues, and potentially are at higher risk for elopement during an evacuation (Dosa et al. 2008). Furthermore, long-term care staff struggle with behavioral issues under optimal conditions. Mental health issues are often exacerbated by relocation—particularly under disaster circumstances—making response more challenging.

Finally, even among the functionally healthy, the elderly population has decreased functional reserve, meaning that their ability to maintain their normal health status during stressful disaster situations becomes impaired. For example, it is well known that the elderly are at the highest risk for infections, such as pneumonia, influenza, and skin infections, due to waning immunity (Nicole, Strausbaugh, and Garibaldi 1996). This may be further exacerbated during disaster emergencies.

Under nondisaster conditions, transfer trauma occurs when a person is moved from one environment to another because of a change in health status (Capezuti et al. 2006). People who are moved from the community or a hospital to a skilled nursing facility may be placed in a nursing home for a few weeks to receive rehabilitation services or admitted for an extended stay. Regardless of length of stay, stress from moving to a new environment is associated with increased confusion, depression, anxiety, apprehension, and changes in eating and sleeping habits (Thorson and Davis 2000; Farhall and Cotton 2002; Robinson 2002; Mallick and Whipple 2000). Although it is unknown if disaster-related evacuations produce stress that is similar to that resulting from transfer trauma, a growing body of evidence suggests that evacuation is physically and emotionally stressful and results in increased rates of morbidity and mortality. A report published by the Office of the Inspector General noted that nursing home (NH) residents exhibited disaster-related symptoms of depression and that "evacuation was psychologically difficult" (OIG 2006).

14.1.2 Special Medical and Mental Health Considerations for Long-Term Care Patients

Given that the focus of this chapter is on institutionalized residents, it should be noted that residents of nursing homes are perhaps the frailest subset of the elderly population (Morrow 1999). The majority of residents in these facilities are institutionalized because of physical or cognitive impairments that make it impossible for them to live and function independently. Almost two-thirds of NH residents (66.5 percent) are reported to have impaired mobility, more than one-third have impaired hearing (35.6 percent) or vision (39.2 percent), and more than half (60.1 percent) have a significant communication problem (i.e., problems being understood or understanding others; AHRQ 2004). In regards to mental health, the baseline prevalence of major depression for NH residents is 12 to 16 percent, less acute depressive disorders range between 30 and 35 percent, and more than 50 percent report some symptoms of depression (Rovner et al. 1986; Rosen, Mulsant, and Pollock 2000; Parmelee, Katz, and Lawton 1989; Weissman, Joranson, and Hopwood 1991). Prevalence estimates for anxiety disorders vary from 1 to 20 percent (Parmelee, Katz, and Lawton 1989; Cheok et al. 1996; Pearson 1998; Smalbrugge et al. 2005). More than 70 percent of NH residents are noted to have some type of cognitive impairment, and approximately 47 percent of NH residents carry a diagnosis of Alzheimer's disease (Alzheimer's Association 2010). These conditions impede residents' ability to comprehend and easily respond to an evolving and often chaotic environment, exacerbate existing mental and medical conditions, and adversely affect well-being.

Most nursing home residents also have significant functional limitations, requiring assistance with their activities of daily living (ADLs). Still others have significant vision/hearing impairments that potentially compromise their ability to respond appropriately during emergencies (Root, Amoozegar, and Bernard 2007; Fernandez et al. 2002; Jones 2002; Shaughnessy and Kramer 1990). Many nursing homes and assisted living residents have complicated medication regimens that require nursing oversight. In the 1990s, the average NH resident was exposed to greater than six medications, with 20 percent receiving more than 10 medications (Bernabei et al. 1999).

Studies of racial and ethnic differences in nursing homes reveal that nursing homes are segregated by race and ethnicity; nonwhites are concentrated in poorer-quality nursing homes as measured by lower staffing levels, higher percentage of Medicaid residents, and higher numbers of deficiency citations (Mor et al. 2004; Smith et al. 2007). A recent study of elderly Hispanics finds that a growing number of Hispanic residents are also concentrated in poorer-quality homes (Fennell et al. 2010). The residents most at risk are those who are poorer and dependent on Medicaid for payment. Facilities highly dependent upon Medicaid for revenue appear least likely to have adequate resources to care for residents and far fewer staff, which increases the likelihood of lower quality of care because staffing is critical to quality of care.

The frailty and limited functional ability of long-term care residents requires nursing homes to hire direct care workers to assist residents with the labor-intensive tasks of dressing, bathing, toileting, and helping residents eat. About 70 percent of the nursing home budget is spent on the estimated 1.47 million direct care workers employed in nursing homes (PHI 2010) who work for an hourly wage. Required training is minimal; federal standards mandate 75 hours of training prior to working at the nursing home. Probst, Baek, and Laditka (2009), using data from the 2004 National Nursing Assistant Survey, report that nursing home staff are overwhelmingly female (92 percent), with an average age of 39 years, and with limited education (45.6 percent report earning a high school diploma and 29.5 percent report less than 12 years of education). Consistent with low education, 37.5 percent report a yearly household income of less than $20,000, another 28 percent report income between $20,000 and $30,000, and only 20 percent report household income greater than $40,000. Multiple studies of direct care workers report physically and emotionally demanding work, poor benefits, and high turnover. Yet, qualitative studies indicate many Certified Nursing Assistants (CNAs) take great pride in their work and want to spend time responding to residents' emotional as well as physical needs (Bowers, Esmond, and Jacobson 2003; Hyer, Temple, and Johnson 2009). A second reason for concern is the increased acuity found in today's LTCFs. As length of stay has decreased in acute care hospitals, nursing homes have increasingly been given the responsibility for caring for complicated postacute patients with hospitalization diagnoses ranging from severe orthopedic injuries to cardiovascular events (Dosa et al. 2008). The Center for Medicare and Medicaid Services (CMS) has revealed a steady increase in acuity since the mid-1990s such that today's nursing homes look very much like yesterday's acute hospitals, and today's assisted living facilities look like yesterday's nursing homes (Feng et al. 2006).

A third reason for the added risk of institutionalized elders lies in simple geography and exposure risk. Almost one-half of the adults living in U.S. nursing homes today reside in one of the 18 hurricane-prone Gulf and Atlantic coast states (Harrington, Carillo, and LaCava 2006). Many more live in the earthquake and wildfire prone regions of California. This simple fact almost ensures that LTCF residents will be involved in disaster situations requiring the competent oversight of public health and emergency preparedness personnel (Dosa et al. 2008).

In a qualitative study of four nursing homes in Mississippi that sheltered residents after Hurricane Katrina, Laditka and colleagues (2009) found that nurses, social workers, and direct care staff provided emotional support to residents who were frightened, displaced, and uncomfortable as the nursing homes without electricity and adequate supplies coped to maintain safe conditions for residents. Reports of nursing staff challenges and exhaustion after evacuation are consistent with Hyer, Brown, et al.'s (2009) findings after the 2004 hurricanes in Florida. Laditka and colleagues recommend long-term care workers receive training that emphasizes "emotional support" as well as physical care of residents because of the anxiety residents and staff feel after disasters strike.

14.1.3 MENTAL HEALTH NEEDS DURING DISASTERS

There are a number of reasons why NH residents may have limited access to disaster mental health care. Despite growing acknowledgment of the unique mental health needs of NH residents, few resources are devoted to addressing these needs under nondisaster conditions (Burns et al. 1993). Most NH staff receive minimal mental health training, and usual care in NH facilities does not adequately address residents' mental health problems (Norris, Molinari, and Ogland-Hand 2002).

Detection of changes in residents' functional status may be particularly challenging for NH staff during an unfolding disaster. For residents with disabilities, medical or mental illness, or cognitive impairment, the act of being transferred to a different facility or disruption to their daily schedule can intensify symptoms of existing conditions and further impair functioning (Mallick and Whipple 2000). At present, an estimated 47 percent of nursing home residents carry a diagnosis of Alzheimer's disease, and approximately 70 percent have a diagnosis of cognitive impairment noted in their medical records (Alzheimer's Association 2010). Traditional approaches, such as Psychological First Aid (PFA), crisis counseling, and cognitive behavioral therapy (CBT), may not be effective with cognitively impaired residents during disaster situations. These talking therapies require an ability to learn and recall new information, such as psychoeducation and relaxation techniques.

Logistically, the expertise needed to provide individualized psychiatric services may not be present during an evacuation. Evacuated nursing home residents may very well be relocated to a school gymnasium or other nonmedical facility where mental health services are absent. Even when the location of transfer is to another nursing home or health care facility, the existing resources at the host site may be stretched beyond their ability to accommodate an influx of potentially distressed residents. Finally, the focus during evacuation is usually placed on the physical health needs of residents to ensure their safety and physical well-being rather than their mental health needs.

It is also noteworthy that the delivery of services during disasters differs in significant ways from traditional psychotherapy. When it is available, an initial mental health screening during a disaster is usually conducted in conjunction with the provision of PFA by first responders who are assisting in the relief effort. Typically these providers are caseworkers and health care clinicians— often without formal mental health training. The objective of PFA is not to make a diagnosis, but to address the symptoms that are most distressing. Although it is normal for people to have strong reactions to a disaster, it is important to identify those who may need additional intervention based on the presence of three prognostic conditions for long-term adverse psychological consequences: flashbacks, derealization, and feelings of disembodiment and depersonalization (Marmar, Weiss, and Metzler 1997). Staff providing PFA should be instructed to obtain a formal evaluation from a clinician if they encounter a situation where the person does not benefit from the PFA intervention or if their reaction to the disaster seems beyond a typical response to an atypical situation. In the days and weeks after a disaster, crisis counseling may be offered to those who need more than PFA. Formal assessment and treatment (e.g., CBT) only occurs if PFA and crisis counseling have not sufficiently ameliorated the symptoms.

14.2 IMPROVING MENTAL HEALTH DELIVERY DURING DISASTER SITUATIONS

PFA is an evidence-based intervention used in the immediate aftermath of a disaster to reduce distress and promote adaptive functioning and coping. PFA, like medical first aid, does not have to be delivered by highly trained licensed mental health clinicians. Because recent research indicated that CNAs could be trained to evaluate cognitive status, manage pain, and deliver interventions to reduce agitation and behavioral disturbance in nursing home residents (Burgio et al. 2002; Fisher et al. 2002; Fitzwater and Gates 2002; Hutt et al. 2006; Mentes, Teer, and Cadogan 2004), a psychological first aid guide was developed for use by NH care providers with residents (Brown et al. 2009).

It is advantageous to train CNAs and nurses to provide PFA for a variety of reasons. They are knowledgeable about the residents' existing mental and physical conditions and can recognize changes in mood or affect. Importantly, they remain with the residents and continue to provide direct care whether they are sheltering in place or evacuating. Moreover, after a disaster, emergency mental health services may not be immediately available. Community-based disaster mental health services are typically not initiated immediately after an event, depending on travel issues and safety concerns (Laditka et al. 2008). PFA-trained NH staff would be able to immediately intervene and provide PFA to disaster-distressed residents. Finally, using community volunteers to provide disaster mental health intervention would require training in geriatric clinical issues and NH regulations in addition to PFA.

Training in PFA should be offered to nursing home staff predisaster. In a survey of 194 NHs in 30 states, Mather LifeWays Institute on Aging found that 91 percent of the long-term care health professionals felt they were "ill prepared to deal with public health emergencies" and that "their workforce lacks the knowledge, skills, and abilities to recognize the impact of a disaster on residents' mental or emotional health" (Mather LifeWays Institute on Aging 2005). Although 80 percent had received some type of disaster-related training, only 10 percent endorsed that they learned how to deal with cognitively impaired residents in emergency situations, and only 8 percent were taught strategies to help residents cope.

PFA was designed to be used in the immediate aftermath of a disaster to reduce initial distress and promote adaptive functioning and coping. The PFA intervention is based on research that demonstrates that disaster survivors experience a broad range of physical, psychological, behavioral, and spiritual reactions that have the potential to interfere with adaptive coping and impede the recovery process. Each of the eight modules that comprise PFA is evidenced-based or informed. The guide describes the basic objectives of early assistance, detailed background information about each of the eight modules, and instruction about how to implement each of the core actions of the intervention. At present, PFA is supported by disaster mental health experts as the *acute intervention of choice* when responding to the psychosocial needs of children, adults and families affected by disaster and terrorism (NCTSN/NCPTSD 2006).

The existing PFA guide for NHs should be modified further to meet the needs of those with moderate Alzheimer's disease. Verbal therapy has been reported to increase agitated behaviors when the level of communication exceeds the person's level of comprehension (Hart and Wells 1997). A modified version of PFA that includes behavioral interventions, such as techniques for soothing distressed residents, would enhance the quality of mental health care provided to people with Alzheimer's disease who have been adversely affected by a disaster.

In most cases, existing NH staff will be both survivors of the event and providers of disaster mental health intervention (Brown et al. 2010). Psychoeducation about the range of normal responses to an abnormal event and information about various strategies to deal with the distressing mental and behavioral effects should be provided to those who are affected by the event. Crisis counseling services should be made available to residents and staff who require additional assistance in recovering from a disaster. Nursing home staff should be aware of the symptoms that suggest psychological distress from exposure to the disaster.

Given the high prevalence of psychiatric comorbidity, assessment for depression, in addition to anxiety, and acute stress disorder may also be warranted. Residents with preexisting mood or psychiatric illness may experience an exacerbation of symptoms during the recovery phase. Somatic symptoms associated with PTSD, depression, and anxiety may motivate some residents to request medication or medical treatment. Given that psychological effects exceed physical injury or illnesses that directly result from disasters, effort should be made to address the mental health needs of NH residents and provide intervention to disaster-affected populations.

14.2.1 THE INTEGRATION OF VARIOUS LONG-TERM CARE FACILITIES INTO STATE AND LOCAL EMERGENCY RESPONSE

Increasing age is a risk factor for institutional placement. While the vast majority (78 percent) of older adults remains independent in the community, among those ages 85 and older, 7 percent live in a housing unit with some communal services and 15 percent live in nursing homes (AOA 2009). The "housing with services" category ranges broadly from independent apartments in a senior community where communal meals or transportation services are available, to an assisted living facility where residents generally have meals prepared, laundry services, transportation, and assitance with medication adminsitration.

Nationally, about one million Americans consider the estimated 38,000 assisted living facilities their home (AAHSA et al. 2009). The regulation of assisted living facilities varies by state because the assisted living market has evolved in response to consumers' preferences for supportive services with more independence, choice, and lower costs than nursing homes. With both consumer preference for assisted living and state efforts to reduce Medicaid nursing home expenditures, approximately 13 percent of residents in assisted living receive Medicaid reimbursement for their stay. Because Medicaid reimbursement is generally available for those individuals who would otherwise qualify for nursing homes, assisted living residents have increasingly had higher levels of functional dependency and cognitive disabilities.

Assisted living facilities can range from new, multiple-story residences with single apartments complete with sprinkler systems, to retrofitted single-room-occupancy buildings without sprinkler systems and alarms (AAHSA et al. 2009). From an emergency preparedness perspective, the physical structure of the residences and the fact that 77 percent of residents require either a wheelchair or assistive device (walker or cane) create challenges to timely evacuation (AAHSA et al. 2009). Beyond timely evacuation, the rules requiring supplies of food, water, medical supplies, and backup generators are far more lax for assisted living facilities than for nursing homes. Finally, few assisted living facilities are integrated into the emergency preparedness infrastructure within a county or state, potentially making assisted living residents vulnerable to adverse outcomes during emergencies. A uniform set of regulations for emergency preparedness, like other aspects of assisted living operations, do not exist despite the increasing number of states that use federal Medicaid funds to pay for assisted living residents.

Staffing requirements and training in assisted living vary; 95 percent of all assisted living facilities require one staff member to be on-site and awake at all times (AAHSA et al. 2009). On average, assisted living facilities have approximately 15 staff members working during a 24-hour period, but the training regulations for staff are minimal. Few states require staff training beyond first aid skills and cardiopulmonary resuscitation. Consequently, the ability of assisted living residents and staff to respond to emegencies or disasters can vary dramatically by the state staffing and training requirements and by the practices of specific facilities. With a population of residents physically frail and cognitively imparied, staff need disaster training in skills such as PFA to keep a highly vulnerable population calm and safe during emergencies.

Unlike assisted living facilities, the 16,000 nursing homes accepting Medicaid and Medicare payment for services (classified as "certified facilities") and caring for approximately 1.5 million residents yearly, nursing homes are required to have well-developed disaster preparedness plans and to train staff for disasters. Despite the requirements for evacuation planning, Castro reported that nursing homes' evacuation plans are not well developed (Castro et al. 2008). Unfortunately, Hurricane Katrina also highlighted the health care consequences to nursing home residents when nursing homes were not helped by the state and local emergency response entities (Castro et al. 2008; Hyer et al. 2010; Laditka et al. 2008).

After Hurricane Katrina, as part of the review of operational problems, the federal government revised its approach to managing natural and man-made disasters. The Department of Homeland Security's publication *National Response Framework* (CMS 2008) outlines how all entities involved in preparing for, responding to, and helping with recovery efforts (local, state, and federal government, agency and nongovernmental organizations) should work together during disasters. This document depicts the FEMA-recommended approach to managing "incidents" and provides specific terminology and structure (further information about the structure and organization of the national incident management system (NIMS) can be found at FEMA). We recommend that all leaders of organizations providing services to vulnerable elders and disabled become familiar with NIMS.

Emergency management presumes the management of an incident remains a local issue unless a jurisdiction's capabilities are overwhelmed and local officials request county or state assistance.

Two emergency support functions (ESFs) are especially important to institutionalized elders and disabled residents; ESF-8 supports Public Health and Medical Services, and ESF-6 supports Mass Care, Emergency Assistance, Housing, and Human Services. These support functions work at the state and local levels to access all other services such as transportation, police help, and restoration of phone and electricity. Under the 2008 National Response Framework, ESF-8s are encouraged to incorporate nursing homes into the network of health care providers. ESF-6s, responsible for mass care, generally operate the general shelters and special need shelters (SNS) but these rules vary by state; for example, Florida established ESF-18 for SNS. Some assisted living facilities, depending upon the state regulations, may rely on special need shelters to house residents during or after a disaster.

Prior to Hurricane Katrina, most federal, state, and local emergency management offices generally treated nursing homes and assisted living facilities as private businesses, ignoring the health care needs of these vulnerable residents during all phases of the disaster. Before Florida's 2004 and 2005 hurricane seasons, some nursing homes and assisted living facilities reported difficulty accessing ambulances and buses to evacuate residents despite signed contracts with the ambulance company to evacuate residents during an emergency. In fact, emergency management offices commandeered ambulances as "assets" and refused to let those assets leave the county even though nursing homes needed the vehicles to evacuate residents (Brown, Hyer, and Polivka-West 2007; Hyer, Polivka-West, and Brown 2007). Because nursing homes take 12–36 hours to evacuate residents and moving residents is not trivial, there are important risks to evacuations (Franco et al. 2006; Hyer et al. 2009).

Since the OIG report of the problems nursing homes faced after the hurricanes, nursing homes have increasingly been recognized as health care providers. The stories of nurses passing medications with flashlights and caring for multiple residents on mattresses in large common areas have helped nursing facilities and assisted living residences, at least in the Gulf-coast states, to receive priority status for rapid restoration of electrical power and telephone (Hyer et al. 2009). A study by Blanchard and Dosa (2009) after Hurricane Gustav indicated that 73 percent of New Orleans nursing home administrators reported improved collaboration with state officials as compared to the situation of feeling abandoned during Hurricane Katrina in 2005.

The Florida Health Care Association (FHCA) has been a national leader in improving disaster preparedness for all long-term care providers. Both the long-term care association and the state are recognized for exemplary emergency preparedness practices by the federal government (CMS 2009). *The Emergency Management Guide for Nursing Homes* (FHCA 2008) and a similar guide for assisted living have been developed and promulgated nationally with generous support from the John A. Hartford Foundation. In addition to manuals providing a comprehensive set of emergency response tools for all hazards, FHCA in partnership with the University of South Florida has also developed drills to encourage long-term care facilities to practice disaster preparedness skills and plans.

Emergency management's recognition of long-term care as health care providers, although critical, is not guaranteed. Despite the CMS (CMS 2009) recommendation that all health care providers "collaborate with their local emergency management agency to ensure the development of an effective plan," nursing homes remain in second-class status to hospitals in the emergency preparedness system (Hyer et al. 2006; Root, Amoozegar, and Bernard 2007). The decision to evacuate is difficult considering the risks and costs associated with moving sick and frail people; as a result, sheltering in place is the preferred alternative to evacuation (Dosa et al. 2008; Thomas et al. 2010).

14.3 CONCLUSION

Residents of LTCFs are at heightened risk for mortality and morbidity during disaster situations. Given the high impact of disasters on this frail population, greater attention to disaster planning on the part of the facilities and to integrating these facilities into federal, state, and local emergency planning is critical to improved outcomes.

CASE VIGNETTE 14.1   Nursing Home Case Study
of Evacuation: Flooding in North Dakota

Evacuation can occur before or after a disaster. Warning time is often a marker for the type of disaster. Many times facilities have limited advance warning such as in the case of a tornado or an earthquake. Even when advance warning is available, as in the following vignette, there are many issues that complicate an evacuation. Issues such as the availability of transportation and the logistics of moving frail residents, staff, medications, and medical equipment become critically important to a successful evacuation. In 2009, record snowfall in North Dakota prompted legitimate concerns for subsequent flooding along the banks of local rivers. In the ensuing months, a total of 1,624 people from 18 health care and medical facilities were evacuated. A time line of the North Dakota events illustrates the complexities inherent in mounting a successful regional evacuation (ND DOH 2009):

- February 24, 2009
  Flooding is predicted in North Dakota due to record snowfall. North Dakota Department of Health (HEALTH) holds a situational briefing with the Department Operations Center staff to discuss response plans.
- March 13, 2009
  The governor of North Dakota issues a statewide Emergency Flood Disaster Declaration.
- March 20, 2009
  Health and medical partners review evacuation plans and preidentify ambulances to transport evacuees. Bed census is collected from health care facilities.
- March 21, 2009
  Medical equipment and emergency medical services (EMS) surge supplies from the state medical cache are prepositioned with Fargo Cass Public Health. A state HEALTH communications trailer is placed in Fargo and a Health Alert message is sent out to volunteer medical personnel.
- March 23, 2009
  Flooding commences and the state HEALTH Incident Command Center is activated. Twice daily video conference briefings are held.
- March 24, 2009
  A presidential disaster area is declared with major sandbagging efforts in Fargo. Elsewhere, the flood intensifies as Beulah and Hazen battle flood waters. In Linton people are forced from their homes.
- March 25, 2009
  The Red River crest is predicted at 39 to 42 feet, raising concerns for a breach at the river's 43-foot reinforced dike. Evacuation plans for local elder care facilities are coordinated through state and local public health and medical incident command.
- March 26, 2009
  News reports announce that the Red River flood will top barriers. Local nursing home residents are evacuated using area hospitals. Eight hundred National Guard troops are utilized to provide assistance and leadership.
- March 27, 2009
  The University of Mary in Bismarck is set up as a staging area for arriving nursing home residents with ages ranging from 70 to 103. Evacuated residents carry medical records in pillow cases. As space becomes available, residents are then transported to other nonthreatened long-term care facilities. Delta Airlines provides free Boeing 757 and DC 9 aircraft to move residents from Fargo to Bismarck.
- March 28, 2009

The Red River crests at 40.82 feet while the state prepares for another blizzard. HEALTH reports on area casualties: 2 cardiac-related deaths, 50 flood-related injuries, and 11 illnesses.

- March 30, 2009

  The blizzard and flooding continue. However the majority of the dikes in Fargo hold, and most of the city remains undamaged and dry.

- April 1, 2009

  Evacuated Fargo residents start returning home. HEALTH starts discussions for moving nursing home residents back to Fargo.

- April 6, 2009

  North Dakota HEALTH, Department Operations Center (DOC) discontinues 24-hour operation.

CASE VIGNETTE 14.2   A Louisiana Nursing Home's Experiences with Hurricane Katrina

Nursing Home X, a 270-bed nursing home in Jefferson Parish, was one of many facilities that weathered Hurricane Katrina but was forced to evacuate in the days after the storm. This case vignette is based on an interview with the facility's administrator that occurred in the months following the storm as part of research conducted by Dosa and colleagues for the Kaiser Family Foundation (Dosa et al. 2007). The interview illustrates some of the difficulties encountered at the facility prior to the storm:

Researcher: Did you evacuate before or after the storm?

Director: We were unable to evacuate before the hurricane. We evacuated post hurricane.

Researcher: Why were you unable to evacuate before?

Director: The companies that we had bus contracts with were not able to fulfill the contracts. They had no drivers.

Researcher: Was there damage to your facility?

Director: We had some superficial damage—there was a little damage to our roof but it wasn't a big deal. We lost power during the storm but we had a generator. We did not flood.

Researcher: What sorts of problems did you encounter during the storm?

Director: We had some anxiety but the residents really toughened up. ... I think they really understood that we were short [of staff] and they understood the magnitude of the issue.

Researcher: Did you have enough food, water, and supplies?

Director: We stocked up, so yes. We even had a city of Kenner truck pull up and give us water and ice in the days after the storm. We never actually needed it but it was nice to have.

Researcher: Why did you leave?

Director: Our generator ran out of gas. We lost power eventually.

Researcher: When did you evacuate?

Director: We got about 175 people out by bus on Thursday after the storm [4 days post landfall]. The rest left by ambulance on Friday and were turned over to FEMA at the airport.

Researcher: Did you encounter difficulties?

Director: Well let me preface by saying this. It's an experience that every politician ought to go through ... We had several false starts as either state or federal officials kept diverting our buses away from us. Once we finally got to load the patients, we realized how difficult it is to move patients into coach buses [that are not designed to accommodate the elderly].

Researcher: And how far did you have to go?

Administrator: One of the things Katrina taught us is that there are not enough empty beds in the state to accommodate the evacuation of a city like New Orleans ... We ended up sending our residents to Texas and they ended up anywhere from Houston to Corpus Christi, San Antonio to Longview. The folks that ended up on the FEMA planes went all over.

Researcher: And how long were they there for?

Administrator: Anywhere from six to eight months, depending. We did not reopen our building until early November ... and we started repopulating it as staffing allowed.... I had 270 residents before the storm, now I have 131.

Researcher: What did you learn from the experience?

Administrator: Hindsight is 20/20 but the decision to evacuate is a dilemma. You have to understand that if you evacuate nursing home residents, some people are not going to make it. And you don't get a lot of help from local or state officials in making the decision. There are a couple things I've learned though ... (1) We would never have a contract with a local bus company. We would only work with out-of-state bus contracts. (2) We've also required families to bring in evacuation bags with at least 3 changes of clothes. (3) Finally, we are putting in a new generator that will power our building [for more than a few days].

REFERENCES

AAHSA, ASHA, ALFA, NCAL, and NIC. 2009. *Overview of Assisted Living: 2009*. Washington, DC: Assisted Living Federation of America.

Agency for Healthcare Research and Quality (AHRQ). 2004. *Research Findings #5: Characteristics of Nursing Home Residents, 1996*. Rockville, MD: AHRQ. http://www.meps.ahrq.gov/data_files/publications/rf5/rf5.shtml.

Altevogt, B., A. Pope, M. Hill, and K. Shine, eds. 2008. *Research Priorities in Emergency Preparedness and Response for Public Health Systems: A Letter Report*. Washington, DC: National Academies Press.

Alzheimer's Association. 2010. 2010 Alzheimer's disease facts and figures. *Alzheimer's & Dementia* 6(2): 158–194. http://www.alz.org/documents_custom/report_alzfactsfigures2010.pdf.

Bernabei, R., G. Gambassi, K. Lapane, A. Sqadari, F. Landi, C. Gatsonis, L. Lipsitz, and V. Mor. 1999. Characteristics of the SAGE database: A new resource for research on outcomes in long-term care. *Journals of Gerontology Series A: Biological Sciences and Medical Sciences* 54(1): M25–M33.

Blanchard, G., and D. Dosa. 2009. A comparison of the nursing home evacuation experience between Hurricanes Katrina (2005) and Gustav (2008). *Journal of the American Medical Directors Association* 10(9): 639–643.

Bowers, B. J., S. Esmond, and N. Jacobson. 2003. Turnover reinterpreted, CNAs talk about why they leave. *Journal of Gerontological Nursing* 29(3): 36–43.

Briggs, S. M. 2005. Disaster management teams. *Current Opinion in Critical Care* 11(6): 585–589.

Brodie, M., E. Weltzien, D. Altman, R. J. Blendon, and J. M. Benson. 2006. Experiences of Hurricane Katrina evacuees in Houston shelters: Implications for future planning. *American Journal of Public Health* 96(8): 1402–1408.

Brown, L. M., M. L. Bruce, K. Hyer, W. L. Mills, E. Vongxaiburana, and L. Polivka-West. 2009. A pilot study evaluating the feasibility of psychological first aid for nursing home residents. *Clinical Gerontologist* 32(3): 293–308.

Brown, L. M., K. Hyer, and L. Polivka-West. 2007. A comparative study of federal and state laws, rules, codes and other influences on nursing homes' disaster preparedness in the Gulf Coast states. *Behavioral Sciences & the Law* 25(5): 655–675.

Brown, L. M., K. Hyer, J. A. Schinka, A. Mando, D. Frazier, and L. Polivka-West. 2010. Use of mental health services by nursing home residents after hurricanes. *Psychiatric Services* 61(1): 74–77.

Brunkard, J., G. Namulanda, and R. Ratard. 2008. Hurricane Katrina deaths, Louisiana, 2005. *Disaster Medicine and Public Health Preparedness*. 2(4): 215–223.

Burgio, L. D., A. Stevens, K. L. Burgio, D. L. Roth, P. Paul, and J. Gerstle. 2002. Teaching and maintaining behavior management skills in the nursing home. *The Gerontologist* 42(4): 487–496.

Burns, B. J., H. R. Wagner, J. E. Taube, J. Magaziner, T. Permutt, and L. R. Landerman. 1993. Mental health service use by the elderly in nursing homes. *American Journal of Public Health* 83(3): 331–337.

Capezuti, E., M. Boltz, S. Renz, D. Hoffman, and R. G. Norman. 2006. Nursing home involuntary relocation: Clinical outcomes and perceptions of residents and families. *Journal of the American Medical Directors Association* 7(8): 486–492.

Castro, C., D. Persson, N. Bergstrom, and S. Cron. 2008. Surviving the storms: Emergency preparedness in Texas nursing facilities and assisted living facilities. *Journal of Gerontological Nursing* 34(8): 9–16.

Cheok, A., J. Snowdon, R. Miller, and R. Vaughan. 1996. The prevalence of anxiety disorders in nursing homes. *International Journal of Geriatric Psychiatry 11*(5): 405–410.

Ciottone, G. 2006. Introduction to disaster medicine. In *Disaster Medicine*, ed. G. R. Ciottone, P. D. Anderson, E. Auf der Heide, R. G. Darling, I. Jacoby, E. Noji, and S. Suner, 3–6. Philadelphia: Mosby.

Dosa, D., Z. Feng, K. Hyer, L. M. Brown, K. Thomas, and V. Mor. 2010. The effects of Hurricane Katrina on nursing home facility resident mortality, hospitalizations and functional decline. *Disaster Medicine and Public Health Preparedness 4*(S1): S28–S32.

Dosa, D. M., N. Grossman, T. Wetle, and V. Mor. 2007. To evacuate or not to evacuate: Lessons learned from Louisiana nursing home administrators following Hurricanes Katrina and Rita. *Journal of the American Medical Directors Association 8*(3): 142–149.

Dosa, D., K. Hyer, L. Brown, A. Artenstein, L. Polivka-West, and V. Mor. 2008. The controversy inherent in managing frail nursing home residents during complex hurricane emergencies. *Journal of the American Medical Directors Association 9*(8): 599–604.

Eldar, R. 1991. Vulnerability of disabled and elderly in disasters: Case-study of Israel during 'Desert Storm.' *Medicine & War 7*(4): 269–274.

Farhall, J., and S. Cotton. 2002. Implementing psychological treatment for symptoms of psychosis in an area mental health service: The response of patients, therapists and managers. *Journal of Mental Health 11*(5): 511–522.

Feng, Z., D. Grabowski, O. Intrator, and V. Mor. 2006. The effect of state Medicaid case-mix payment on nursing home resident acuity. *Health Services Research 41*(4): 1317–1336.

Fennell, M. L., Z. Feng, M. Clark, and V. Mor. 2010. Elderly Hispanics more likely to reside in poor-quality nursing homes. *Health Affairs 29*(1): 65–73.

Fernandez, L. S., D. Byard, C. C. Lin, S. Benson, and J. A. Barbera. 2002. Frail elderly as disaster victims: Emergency management strategies. *Prehospital & Disaster Medicine 17*(2): 67–74.

Fisher, S., L. D. Burgio, B. E. Thorn, R. Allen-Burge, J. Gerstle, D. L. Roth, and S. J. Allen. 2002. Pain assessment and management in cognitively impaired nursing home residents: Association of Certified Nursing Assistant pain report, Minimum Data Set pain report, and analgesic medication use. *Journal of the American Geriatrics Society 50*(1): 152–156.

Fitzwater, E. L., and D. M. Gates. 2002. Testing an intervention to reduce assaults on nursing assistants in nursing homes: A pilot project. *Geriatric Nursing 23*(1): 18–23.

Florida Health Care Association (FHCA). 2008. *Emergency management Guide for Nursing Homes.* Tallahassee, FL: FHCA. http://www.fhca.org/emerprep/guide.php.

Franco, C., E. Toner, R. Waldhorn, B. Maldin, T. O'Toole, and T. V. Inglesby. 2006. Systemic collapse: Medical care in the aftermath of Hurricane Katrina. *Biosecurity and Bioterrorism: Biodefense Strategy, Practice, and Science 4*(2): 135–146.

Harrington, C., H. Carillo, and C. LaCava. 2006. *Nursing Facilities, Staffing, Residents and Facility Deficiencies, 1999 through 2005.* San Francisco: University of California.

Harris, G. 2005. "Nursing home, a fight lost to rising waters." *New York Times*, September 7: A1.

Hart, B. D., and D. L. Wells. 1997. The effects of language used by caregivers on agitation in residents with dementia. *Clinical Nurse Specialist 11*(1): 20–23.

Hull, A., and D. Struck. 2005. "At nursing home, Katrina dealt only the first blow." *Washington Post*, September 23: A01.

Hutt, E., G. A. Pepper, C. Vojir, R. Fink, and K. R. Jones. 2006. Assessing the appropriateness of pain medication prescribing practices in nursing homes. *Journal of the American Geriatrics Society 54*(2): 231–239.

Hyer, K., L. M. Brown, A. Berman, and L. Polivka-West. 2006. Establishing and refining hurricane response systems for long-term care facilities. *Health Affairs 25*(5): w407–w411.

Hyer, K., L. M. Brown, J. J. Christensen, and K. Thomas. 2009. Weathering the storm: Challenges to nurses providing care to nursing home residents during hurricanes. *Applied Nursing Research 22*(4): e9–e14.

Hyer, K., L. M. Brown, K. S. Thomas, D. Dosa, J. Bond, L. Polivka-West, and J. A. Schinka. 2010. Improving relations between emergency management offices and nursing homes during hurricane-related disasters. *Journal of Emergency Management 8*(1): 57–66.

Hyer, K., L. Polivka-West, and L. M. Brown. 2007. Nursing homes and assisted living facilities: Planning and decision making for sheltering in place or evacuation. *Generations 31*(4): 29–33.

Hyer, K., A. Temple, and C. E. Johnson. 2009. Florida's efforts to improve quality of nursing home care through nurse staffing mandates, regulation, and Medicaid reimbursement. *Journal of Aging and Social Policy 21*(4): 318–337.

Jones, A. 2002. The National Nursing Home Survey: 1999 summary. National Center for Health Statistics. *Vital and Health Statistics 13*(152): 1–116.

Kayman, H., and A. Ablorh-Odjidja. 2006. Revisiting public health preparedness: Incorporating social justice principles into pandemic preparedness planning for influenza. *Journal of Public Health Management & Practice 12*(4): 373–380.

Laditka, S. B., J. N. Laditka, C. B. Cornman, C. B. Davis, and J. V. Richter. 2009. Resilience and challenges among staff of Gulf Coast nursing homes sheltering frail evacuees following Hurricane Katrina, 2005: Implications for planning and training. *Prehospital and Disaster Medicine 24*(1): 54–62.

Laditka, S.B., J. N. Laditka, S. Xirasagar, C. B. Cornman, C. B. Davis, and J. V. Richter. 2008. Providing shelter to nursing home evacuees in disasters: Lessons from Hurricane Katrina. *American Journal of Public Health 98*(7): 1288–1293.

Mallick, M. J., and T. W. Whipple. 2000. Validity of the nursing diagnosis of relocation stress syndrome. *Nursing Research 49*(2): 97–100.

Marmar, C. R., D. Weiss, and T. J. Metzler. 1997. The Peritraumatic Dissociative Experiences Questionnaire in assessing psychological trauma and PTSD. In *A Handbook for Practitioners*, 412–428, eds. J. P. Wilson and T. M. Keane. New York: Guilford Press.

Mather LifeWays Institute on Aging. 2005. *Prepare: Learning modules & teacher's guide to prepare specialists.* http://www.matherlifeways.com/re_prepare.asp.

Mentes, J. C., J. Teer, and M. P. Cadogan. 2004. The pain experience of cognitively impaired nursing home residents: Perceptions of family members and certified nursing assistants. *Pain Management Nursing 5*(3): 118–125.

Mor, V., J. Zinn, J. Angelelli., J. Teno, and S. C. Miller. 2004. Driven to tiers: Socioeconomic and racial disparities in the quality of nursing home care. *Milbank Quarterly 82*(2): 227–256.

Morrow, B. H. 1999. Identifying and mapping community vulnerability. *Disasters 23*(1): 1–18.

Mudur, G. 2005. Aid agencies ignored special needs of elderly people after tsunami. *British Medical Journal 331*(7514): 422.

National Child Traumatic Stress Network and National Center for PTSD (NCTSN/NCPTSD). 2006. *Psychological First Aid: Field Operations Guide*, 2nd ed. http://www.nctsn.org and http://www.ncptsd.va.gov.

Nicole, L. E., L. J. Strausbaugh, and R. A. Garibaldi. 1996. Infections and antibiotic resistance in nursing homes. *Clinical Microbiology Reviews 9*(1): 1–17.

Noji, E. 1997. The nature of disaster: General characteristics and public health effects. In *The Public Health Consequences of Disasters*, ed. E. Noji, 3–20. New York: Oxford University Press.

Norris, M., V. Molinari, and S. Ogland-Hand, eds. 2002. *Emerging Practices for Psychologists in Long Term Care.* Binghamton, NY: Hayworth Press, Inc.

North Dakota Department of Health (ND DOH). 2009. *2009 North Dakota Floods.* Video recording, transcribed excerpt. Produced by the North Dakota Department of Health.

Paraprofessional Healthcare Institute (PHI). 2010. Who are direct-care workers? The PHI National Clearinghouse on the Direct Care Workforce 2004–2008, PHI Facts #3 February 2010 Update. http://directcareclearinghouse.org/download/NCDCW%20Fact%20Sheet-1.pdf.

Parmelee, P., I. Katz, and M. Lawton. 1989. Depression among institutionalized aged: Assessment and prevalence estimation. *Journal of Gerontology 44*(1): M22–M29.

Pearson, J. 1998. Research in late-life anxiety: Summary of a National Institute of Mental Health workshop on late-life anxiety. *Psychopharmacology Bulletin 34*: 127–138.

Probst, J. C., J. Baek, and S. B. Laditka. 2009. Characteristics and recruitment paths of certified nursing assistants in rural and urban nursing homes. *Journal of Rural Health 25*(3): 267–275.

Robinson, V. 2002. *A brief literature review of the effect of relocation on the elderly. British Columbia, Canada: The Hospital Employees' Union of British Columbia.* http://www.heu.org/~DOCUMENTS/import/2002/HEU_Literature_Review_Sept23.pdf.

Root, E. D., J. B. Amoozegar, and S. Bernard. 2007. *Nursing Homes in Public Health Emergencies: Special Needs and Potential Roles.* Agency for Healthcare Research and Quality (AHRQ) Publication No. 07-0029-1. Rockville, MD: AHRQ. http://www.ahrq.gov/prep/nursinghomes/nhomerep.pdf.

Rosen, J., B. Mulsant, and B. Pollock. 2000. Sertraline in the treatment of minor depression in nursing home residents: A pilot study. *International Journal of Geriatric Psychiatry 15*(2): 177–180.

Rovner, B. W., S. Kafonek, L. Filipp, M. J. Lucas, and M. F. Folstein. 1986. Prevalence of mental illness in a community nursing home. *American Journal of Psychiatry 143*(11): 1446–1449.

Shaughnessy, P. W., and A. M. Kramer. 1990. The increased needs of patients in nursing homes and patients receiving home health care. *New England Journal of Medicine 322*(1): 21–27.

Smalbrugge, M., A. Pot, K. Jongenelis, A. Beekman, and J. Eefsting. 2005. Prevalence and correlates of anxiety among nursing home patients. *Journal of Affective Disorders 88*(2): 145–153.

. Smith, D. B., Z. Feng, M. L. Fennell, J. Zinn, and V. Mor. 2007. Separate and unequal: Racial segregation and disparities in quality across US nursing homes. *Health Affairs 26*(5): 1448–1458.

Thomas, K. S., K. Hyer, L. M. Brown, L. Polivka-West, and L. G. Branch. 2010. Florida's model of nursing home Medicaid reimbursement for disaster-related expenses. *The Gerontologist 50*(2): 263–270.

Thorson, J. A., and R. E. Davis. 2000. Relocation of the institutionalized aged. *Journal of Clinical Psychology 56*(1): 131–138.

U.S. Department of Health and Human Services, Administration on Aging (AOA). 2009. *A Profile of Older Americans: 2009.* Washington, DC: DHHS/AOA. http://www.aoa.gov/AoAroot/Aging_Statistics/Profile/index.aspx.

U.S. Department of Health and Human Services, Centers for Medicare and Medicaid Services (CMS). 2008. *Promising practices in State Survey Agencies: Emergency Preparedness Practices—Florida.* Washington, DC: DHHS/CMS. http://www.cms.gov/SurvCertPromPractProj/Downloads/emerg-prep_Florida.pdf.

U.S. Department of Health and Human Services, Centers for Medicare and Medicaid Services (CMS). 2009. *Survey & Certification Emergency Preparedness Checklist – Recommended Tool for Effective Health Care Facility Planning.* Washington, DC: DHHS/CMS. http://www.cms.gov/SurveyCertEmergPrep/downloads/S&C_EPChecklist_Provider.pdf.

U.S. Department of Health and Human Services, Office of Inspector General (OIG). August 2006. Nursing home emergency preparedness and response during recent hurricanes. Report No.: OEI-06-06-00020.

U.S. Government Accountability Office (GAO). 2006. Disaster preparedness: Limitations in federal evacuation assistance for health facilities should be addressed. Report to Congressional Committees: GAO-06-826: 1–52.

Weissman, D., D. Joranson, and M. Hopwood. 1991. Wisconsin physicians' knowledge and attitudes about opioid analgesic regulations. *Wisconsin Medical Journal 90*(12): 671–675.

15 Delivery of Behavioral Health Services in General Population Shelters

Brenda D. Phillips, Elizabeth Harris, Elizabeth A. Davis, Rebecca Hansen, Kelly Rouba, and Jessica Love

CONTENTS

15.1 OVERVIEW

This chapter provides an operationally realistic overview of emergency sheltering in a disaster context in the United States. Emergency managers, shelter providers, health care agencies, and others coordinate and collaborate before, during, and after a disaster to provide appropriate locations and care for a diverse set of potential shelter residents. Normally, emergency managers expect that between 10 and 20 percent of the evacuating public will need shelter. Most of those individuals will go to general population shelters while others stay with friends or family or in hotels. During the massive Hurricane Katrina evacuation, millions left the Gulf Coast and demonstrated that the number in need of shelter can swell well past the 20 percent mark.

Historically, many jurisdictions planned and provided a multi-tiered level of sheltering. This would, for example, result in a first aid level of care at the general population shelter and increased specialized supports and/or medical care in what were known as the "special needs" or "medical" or other such shelter tier. This was done in order to best utilize limited resources and focus efforts. However, by late 2010 the conventionally accepted shelter model had shifted to a consolidation of support into general population shelters, thus enabling all access and functional needs to be provided without a separate facility. This is codified in the Functional Needs and Support Services Guidance (FNSS; FEMA 2010) and reinforced from a rights-based perspective for those with disabilities in the U.S. Department of Justice Toolkit (U.S. Department of Justice 2007a). This being the case, the Emergency Support Function (ESF) 6 Annex refers to "nonconventional," "specialized," and "medical" shelters, but these are beyond the scope of this chapter (FEMA, 2008). To best appreciate the current modeling, it is still helpful to have reviewed the evolution of the issues still being settled today.

This chapter, therefore, is organized into two major parts. The first part offers a basic overview of sheltering in general: identifying appropriate locations to designate; some set-up logistics; operations; partners, and so forth. The second part identifies ways to integrate more complex issues pertaining to people with disabilities and access and functional needs into sheltering operations, thus predicting needs of the community and having the ability to appropriately respond and accommodate diverse needs. Integration is the result when a shelter environment has been made least restrictive and provides for the greatest level of independence by those using it. Optimally, this reflects dignity and self-determination for disaster survivors while simultaneously enabling responders to most economically dedicate resources and personnel.

While reading this chapter, it is important to recognize the shifts not only in operational models that are underway but also acknowledge the changes in terminology. Terms such as *special needs, access and functional needs, vulnerable populations, disability,* and so forth will all be used within the context of the time the reference or quote occurs in the chapter.

As behavioral health practitioners and other professionals, this chapter will be helpful in laying out the emergency sheltering concepts such that you are able to find ways to fit them into existing and emerging processes. This results in the best use of your knowledge, skills, and expertise to benefit those in need during disaster sheltering operations.

15.1.1 Conceptual Definitions of Shelter

Sheltering is conceptualized as one phase in the overall process from displacement to relocation (Quarantellli 1982). Sheltering manifests in two main ways, as emergency shelter or as temporary shelter. Emergency shelter occurs in rather ephemeral, short-lived settings that may include vehicles, lawns, underpasses, bridges, and other locations of brief respite. Temporary shelter usually lasts longer and is typically offered by a traditional provider, such as the American Red Cross (ARC), or through the efforts of governmental or nongovernmental organizations and agencies. (Nigg, Barnshaw, and Torres 2006; Quarantelli 1991; Quarantelli 1995). See Box 15.1 to test commonly held assumptions about shelters.

BOX 15.1

MYTH OR REALITY

- All preidentified, preplanned, and publically announced shelters are run by the American Red Cross (ARC).
    - False. While ARC is very seasoned in mass shelter operations and is listed as having a support role under the National Response Framework Emergency Support Function 6, government authorities may have agreements and arrangements with other voluntary organizations such as the Salvation Army, Baptist Family Services, or Church World Service, for example, to act in that capacity. Still other jurisdictions run and manage shelters, evacuation centers, and the like with government employees. It is also important to realize that not all facilities used as a shelter will have been preselected as such or may not be announced until it is known that they are capable of operating for the public's well-being in a particular emergency.
- All shelters open in a disaster are fully equipped and capable of being a long-term operational facility for those displaced by an event.
    - False. Many facilities available for use in mass sheltering can only really be considered for short-term options during the immediate time of need when it comes to providing the most basic safe environment for the public. A school gym, for example, needs to be ready to be a school asset again as soon as possible; otherwise, the school is impacted long term. As another example, a local church assembly hall may not be equipped with shower facilities, continuous and uninterrupted power supplies, and other necessities for long-term sustainability.
- People receiving home-based care on a regular basis will have that provided for them at a publically opened emergency shelter.
    - To a point. Actually, under U.S. Department of Justice guidance, an individual in need of some basic assistance may request and should be provided that help in all shelters (U.S. Department of Justice 2007a and 2007b). However, for planning purposes, we each must assume that if we receive regular services—or supply deliveries for that matter—that the typical routine will likely be disrupted by an emergency. Many home-based care services are specifically assigned to that location and the transfer of care to another location is not possible. From a practical perspective, a specific care provider may need to attend to the disaster impact on his/her own family before being able to resume care for a full caseload of consumers. It is for all these reasons that individuals need to know what to expect at a shelter and, if at all possible, plan to bring someone (be it professional paid services, a friend, or a family member) to assist with the activities of daily living so they can remain independent and comfortable with a regular routine.
- A shelter is like a life boat not a cruise ship.
    - True. The public needs to realize that whatever entity is operating the officially sanctioned shelter operations, to the best of their ability, safety will come first and comforts as available and possible. The best planning is still to have family and friends out of the disaster area as an option when it comes to finding somewhere to stay, and the emergency shelters as a second choice, if no friends or family are available at that point.

15.1.2 OPERATIONAL DEFINITIONS OF SHELTER

Temporary sheltering may appear in several forms. The bulk of temporary shelters provide for the general population (GP). Depending on the need, GP shelters could offer refuge to small numbers or, at times, up to thousands of temporary residents. U.S. Department of Justice guidelines call for the inclusion of people with disabilities, and their service animals, in GP shelters. FEMA's release of the FNSS offers guidance on integrating disability and access and functional needs within general population shelters. Historically, some GP shelters have experienced difficulty in providing adequate accommodations for people with disabilities or those with medical needs and in some cases have sent people with disabilities incorrectly to higher-level shelters. Doing so is not only inappropriate and a violation of the rights of people with disabilities, but unnecessarily increases the workload of those operating higher-level shelters. In recent years, increasing numbers of GP shelters have provided accessible locations for people with disabilities, as well as for those with minimal levels of medical support or specific dietary needs. The content in this section aims to provide an overview of sheltering concepts, partnering strategies, and usage of shelters. The chapter subsequently addresses higher level of care in general population shelters, and issues ranging from facility management and staffing, to how shelter residents are cared for from initial triage through discharge.

15.1.3 SHELTERING AND PUBLIC EXPECTATIONS

Research indicates that 10 to 20 percent of a disaster-affected population may arrive in a shelter location (Drabek 1986), a standard number that emergency managers, public health officials, voluntary organizations, and others use to determine capacity needs in a given number of shelters. Anticipating that a population with 10,000 people will have 1,000 in need of shelter allows for planners to train staff, amass inventory, prestage resources, and be ready to receive evacuees. The bulk of those in need of shelter typically go to the homes of family or friends or to hotels, which require personal relationships and financial resources, respectively. A population that utilizes a GP shelter will often lack considerable resources and social networks. Coping skills may be compromised, ranging from depleted funds that prevent movement to temporary or permanent housing to persons who may experience withdrawal from prescriptions or addictions.

15.1.4 THE IMPACT OF DISASTERS ON SHELTER PROVISION

Certainly some kinds of disasters challenge shelter provision. Rapid-onset events like tornadoes or wildfires demand that providers set up a shelter after a hazard has already impacted a population. Doing so may mean scrambling for a safe and appropriate location and moving resources and personnel quickly into place. Slow-onset, predictable events like hurricanes usually allow time to prestage assets, move personnel into position, evacuate in an orderly manner, and host shelter residents more effectively. The size of an event matters too. Recently, Hurricane Katrina in 2005 and the Haiti earthquake in 2010 demonstrated how shelters can be quickly overrun in a catastrophic event. In both instances, massive numbers evacuated from large urban areas. While the areas and states around the affected U.S. Gulf Coast were able to open shelters, many locations were overwhelmed with evacuees requiring governmental support to reach shelters via bus, train, and airplane. General population shelters were not always ready to receive evacuees with medical conditions or disabilities (National Organization on Disability 2005). Functional needs shelters, which were established as part of the plan to address people with medical or other issues who require a higher level of care than available at a general population shelter, were also overrun, and a number of emergent locations opened, staffed by nursing students, volunteer medical professionals, and others.

Some disasters, such as Hurricane Ike in 2008, may generate conditions that make sheltering evacuees particularly challenging. Ike impacted the coastline and immediate inland areas near

Galveston, Texas. As residents returned from shelters further inland, they moved into Houston shelters to be closer to their homes. Hurricane Ike was so powerful that the city of Houston and many shelters remained without power for several weeks. The same challenges occur in ice storms when power and heat can be lost. Knowing the type of hazard that may affect an area, as well as the past history of such hazards, can help with planning and organizing shelter efforts.

15.2   GENERAL POPULATION SHELTERS

This section provides an overview of GP shelters and the delivery of relevant behavioral health services. We learn that usually only a small portion of the population moves into GP shelters and that preplanning for establishing, operating and managing behavioral health services makes for a better residential and managerial experience for all. To start this section, we first review the terms used to understand GP shelters and then discuss the array of partnerships required to offer respite. In the aftermath of Hurricane Katrina, new shelter models emerged that increasingly incorporated new and stronger collaborative partnerships. That emerging model is presented in part as a means to encapsulate the array of partners likely to participate in sheltering efforts. A discussion of the populations likely to use public shelters follows. A concluding section explains the importance of being prepared to shelter pets and accommodate service animals.

15.2.1   Definitions and Terms

As noted, a GP shelter is the term used to describe the facilities for the majority of the evacuating population in need of a safe haven. A GP shelter is also the type described previously by Quarantelli as a "temporary shelter" that provides some degree of social, psychological, nutritional, and medical services. At its most basic level, a GP shelter is intended to give evacuees a (typically) indoor location where they are either (1) safe from an impending hazard, such as a hurricane, or (2) able to access basic survival resources and other relief. Although indoor locations are preferred, outdoor tent cities have been opened. For example, the U.S. military established a tent city for 2,000 survivors after Hurricane Andrew impacted Homestead, Florida, in 1992. And, though not a desired location, the ARC also assumed operations for an outdoor tent city after the Watsonville, California, area experienced a 7.1 magnitude earthquake in 1989 (Phillips 1993) where local citizens with prior earthquake experience feared aftershocks inside buildings. Outdoor locations are not ideal, as they remain subject to weather conditions that may cause rapid deterioration of the shelter environment or expose residents to dangers from high winds, lightning, and heavy rain.

Indoor facilities vary from giving the basics of a roof over one's head to those that include cots, blankets, food, or well-developed amenities. Ideally, a shelter should offer registration, bathroom and bathing facilities, and general information regarding the disaster. First aid and mental health support should be made available as well, but only by qualified, credentialed staff or authorized volunteers. Some shelters are able to bring in entertainment, movies, televisions, and games as a means to pass the time. Depending on how long the shelter is open and what resources are at hand, providers may also create a daily schedule to allow children to attend school or go to child care, set up computers so that residents can apply for assistance and communicate with family members, and/or bring in prospective employers, social service workers, worship services, and more.

15.2.2   Shelter Partnerships

Clearly a shelter that offers more than basic survival resources requires that a number of community agencies, organizations, and volunteers assist. Preplanning is thus essential and can vary by location and level. Local ARC chapters may take on the task for shelter planning, or that effort may be led by a committee or a local emergency management agency. Regardless, a number of partners must become involved in setting up a shelter plan. Basic questions and logistical coordination need to be undertaken to insure that the shelter is open before evacuees arrive. At a minimum, cots, bedding, and toiletries must be on hand. Food arrangements need to be negotiated, cooks brought in, and custodial staff identified. Staff and volunteers need to be trained on what to do, who to expect as arrivals, and how to manage a variety of situations—from an evacuee arriving with a pet to someone going through a drug withdrawal. For a wider array of services, other partners need to be integrated into planning efforts. When large groups of people gather and remain under the same roof, contagious illnesses may spread more rapidly. Public health officials should be tapped to provide basic guidance from sanitary procedures to immunizations. Organizations that provide child care can be included, but contact with children needs to be through well-trained, preferably certified individuals. For example, the Church of the Brethren puts their disaster child care teams through extensive training along with a "rigorous screening check" (see http://www.brethren.org/site/PageServer?pagename=serve_childrens_disaster_services). The shelter will reflect the predisaster community both in terms of residents but also partner groups available for support.

15.2.3 General Population Shelter Management Models

Hurricane Katrina produced changes in how we offer public shelters. See Box 15.2 to learn about the National Organization on Disability's Special Needs Assessment for Katrina Evacuees (SNAKE) report. The largest evacuation in U.S. history required extensive efforts and ushered in a wide array of nontraditional locations and related partners, including faith-based facilities, massive convention centers, city auditoriums, motels, cruise ships, and private homes. In the aftermath, it became clear that this broad set of locations and partners be recognized in order to offer adequate, appropriate, and coordinated levels of support, deliver supplies, and meet basic human needs. To do so, the American Red Cross identifies four general types of shelters that are increasingly recognized across the United States. Many jurisdictions use at least one of these models to manage shelters. However, a point to keep in mind is that in addition to these models, many jurisdictions are utilizing government assets to establish and manage shelters, secure needed resources, and rely on the American Red Cross or another nongovernmental agency to support these locations.

BOX 15.2

SPECIAL NEEDS ASSESSMENT FOR KATRINA EVACUEES (SNAKE) REPORT

Just weeks after Hurricane Katrina devastated the Gulf Region in August 2005, the National Organization on Disability deployed teams to carry out assessments in Louisiana, Mississippi, Alabama, and Texas. This effort was designed and coordinated under contract by EAD & Associates, LLC. The goal of the assessment was to "capture time-sensitive data on the impact and service delivery to those with disabilities, seniors, and medically managed persons affected by Hurricane Katrina" (NOD 2005). In the interest of getting the results published quickly, the assessments and data gathered were sent to a research team, which then published the SNAKE report by early October. The report reflects a "representative sampling of experience and observation on the ground ... not meant to be a comprehensive review or study" (NOD 2005).

The assessment teams were sent to major shelters and operations centers servicing those impacted by the storm. Teams gathered data pertaining to short-term response efforts and long-term recovery planning efforts capturing creative solutions and problem solving as well as existing gaps. There were a total of 18 shelters visited in the four states managed by different entities (some American Red Cross [ARC], others nonaffiliated with ARC). The report describes the quality of the shelters spanning the "continuum of models from good practices to unorganized and chaotic" (NOD 2005).

The "good practices" that are highlighted in the report take into consideration safety, medical needs, and comfort. One facility, an abandoned school, was restored to code by a cadre of local volunteers to safely accommodate evacuees. This shelter, as well as another highlighted in the report, also provided extensive medical services and care on the premises to evacuees and staff. Other aspects of the shelters highlighted in the report that benefited evacuees included day care services on the premises, recreation rooms, a Deaf Center with interpreters, accessible shuttle service, library, TV rooms, post office, snack areas, separate sleeping areas, computer/Internet access, chapel, and on-site representatives from community services (employment, housing, etc.).

Other shelters were described with "poor living conditions" with a "paucity of services and amenities." Poor conditions such as lack of space and overcrowding, lack of food and drink, unsafe play areas, no privacy areas, no mental health or social services on-site, created an unsafe and uncomfortable environment for evacuees.

The report also highlighted specific aspects that were lacking or detrimental specifically to people with disabilities. This included an intake process that only minimally indentifies specific needs of people with disabilities and the aging. The report also indicates that those who are deaf or hard of hearing were identified as the most underserved group with a lack of services and support. Lastly, the lack of personnel who were experienced working with people with disabilities was detrimental in that it resulted in unnecessary transfer of individuals to medical shelters or nursing homes and separation from family and/or support network.

Some of the recommendations offered in the report that pertain specifically to shelters include:

- Integrate into sheltering operations the expertise that disability-specific and aging organizations provide.
- Train staff and volunteers to increase awareness of disability-related shelter issues and concerns.
- Improve the intake process with the addition of questions to identify needs.
- Conduct an inventory of facilities, prior to an emergency, to identify facilities with the most accessible elements available to be used as shelters.
- Improve communication and coordination among shelters.

The report covers other topic areas such as management, coordination, and service provision, and provides recommendations regarding use of disability and aging organizations, disaster recovery centers, emergency information, service coordination, cross-training, and durable medical equipment, among others.

The first is an ARC-Managed shelter, which is set up, staffed, and managed by trained and certified ARC staff and volunteers. Typically, the ARC-Managed shelter is the most likely type of general population shelter that an evacuee would enter. ARC-Managed shelters are operated by ARC staff and credentialed volunteers.

A second type of shelter is called an ARC Partner that has a formal arrangement with the ARC to provide shelter. The partner could be a school or church that operates independently, but with ARC logistical and resource support. This type of agreement should result in a preestablished flow of resources from the ARC and/or host state into the shelter location. Preplanning is necessary for this type of shelter, and the benefit is clear—being able to deliver key assets to shelters in a timely manner and organically within the community.

The third type of shelter is termed ARC Supported. In this kind, a local provider usually opens and operates the shelter and will have a varying degree of ARC support from minimal to maximal.

There is usually no formal agreement between the provider and the ARC. These kinds of locations may shelter evacuees or those who arrive to assist, such as volunteer medical teams, first responders, or relief workers. The support typically arrives after the disaster as a result of a request made to the ARC. Depending on the scope, magnitude, and extent of the disaster, the ARC and/or the host state may not be able to provide resources.

Finally, independent shelter locations nearly always appear after a disaster. Such locations are best characterized as emergent or spontaneous, meaning that they appear in the aftermath of a disaster out of the compassion and caring of a local provider. These locations tend to have the least degree of formal training among the shelter managers and volunteers. Independent shelters tend to face the most significant challenges in establishing and operating shelters because they tend to lack experience.

15.2.4 SHELTER MANAGEMENT

Shelter managers run the facility. Prior to doing so, decisions must be made about where to open the shelter. Typically, emergency managers communicate with shelter providers such as the ARC regarding the best locations given the particular triggering event. Preidentified sites within those locations are usually opened, personnel and volunteers travel to operate the shelter, and evacuees arrive. The next section describes basic protocol for shelters followed by a discussion of the populations likely to arrive and some of their behavioral health service needs.

15.2.4.1 Shelter Siting and Establishment

Any disaster shelter should be sited in a place that is away from an impending threat, including storm surge, hazardous materials, and seismic risk. The secondary effects of disasters, such as tornadoes spawned by hurricanes or landslides caused by heavy rain or wildfire, should also be sized up prior to establishing a shelter. In most instances, local jurisdictions should have conducted a basic hazard analysis, determined the probability of hazardous events occurring in a given location, and made recommendations to local shelter providers.

Further guidance directs shelter providers to avoid certain locations. For example, the American Red Cross Standards for Hurricane Evacuation Selection (ARC4496; see http://www.floridadisaster. org/Response/engineers/documents/newarc4496.pdf) require that shelters be located outside of the 100-year floodplain and encourage avoiding even a 500-year floodplain. The area around a shelter should be considered as well, such as the potential for river flooding that could inundate roadways and impede access to shelters. Facilities should also be able to bear certain wind loads that can tear the roof from a building or cause projectiles to penetrate the interior. The Federal Emergency Management Agency (FEMA) also recommends selecting a site that is away from large objects such as light towers, antennas, roof-mounted mechanical equipment, and other structures that could fall on the shelter.

Shelters should be situated in locations that allow for easy access from multiple transportation sources and offer accessibility to people with disabilities. The U.S. Department of Justice offers the Title II Checklist to guide planners through the evaluation and selection process (U.S. Department of Justice, 2007b). In addition, working with local disability organizations and experts can help to ensure maximum accessibility of a shelter site. Parking spaces for both residents and shelter staff, including those that are designated for people with disabilities, should be included in a chosen site. Ideally, a shelter will be close enough to allow for emergency transportation of people who become ill or otherwise deteriorate during a shelter stay, including both ground and air ambulance services. This is particularly important, as residents may deteriorate from "transfer trauma" where health decline and/or death occurs from being moved, a particular problem for frail elderly (Fernandez et al. 2002; U.S. Federal Highway Administration 2009). Proximity to cancer care, dialysis, and other health care facilities are considered ideal. Pet shelters should be co-located where at all possible and are discussed further in an upcoming section. Service animals must always be admitted to any shelter per federal law.

A trend in recent years has been to "harden" shelter facilities. The more common form of hardening is to construct a community facility sufficient to shelter at least 100 people and built to FEMA 361 standards for wind resistance (see http://www.fema.gov/plan/prevent/saferoom/fema361.shtm). Also called "safe rooms," such locations offer resistance to wind-borne hazards but may not have sufficient space for larger numbers of evacuees, particularly for a long shelter stay. Some states are working to harden shelters but such efforts are costly, usually require a combination of federal and state funds, and are consequently slow to appear. As described later, the "Safe Center/Senior Center" is an alternative approach under way.

15.2.4.1.1 Location Options

Location matters in establishing any kind of a shelter. Historically, shelters tend to be located in schools or faith-based facilities because they offer large spaces, are in well-known locations, and connect to social networks with resources. Careful consideration should be made, however, for several reasons. First, once the emergency response period has passed and it is time to launch the recovery, the location may be needed to help establish normalcy. Schools, for example, will probably need to reopen. By resuming schools, children return to a secure facility and a familiar routine that enables parents to go about the business of cleaning up, applying for aid, and moving on (Peek 2010). Second, given that education typically represents a significant portion of local employment, reopening schools also allows people to earn a paycheck, which facilitates family and economic recovery. Faith-based locations are also often used as shelter facilities. These locations also need to reopen to hold weekly religious education classes, as well as weekly services and other activities. Although faith-based locations represent logical locations for compassionate outreach, they also need to return to normal routines. A third reason to reconsider these kinds of facilities then is to allow a major social institution, religion, to assist the community with funeral services, grief management, relief efforts, rebuilding assistance, and more. Fourth, facilities may not have the necessary amenities (such as showers, or a means to feed large numbers of people) to stay open for an extended period of time. Finally, the shelter location may not be in the place where it is actually needed given where the disaster occurred.

It is likely that anyone involved in establishing shelters will need to assess and reassess shelter locations. Facilities change over time and may not be available the next time they are needed. An empty or underused facility may fill in the next disaster. The ARC typically engages in preestablished, written agreements that are evaluated on a regular basis and conducts annual assessments of shelter locations and agreements. Working with an organization such as the ARC is advisable since it is likely to lead and/or support in operating GP shelters. Some locations are beginning to utilize community-based sites (such as a senior center) and either retrofit or design these sites so that they can also be used as emergency shelters. See Box 15.3 for an example of this practice.

BOX 15.3

SAFE CENTER/SENIOR CENTER

In 2006, the Alabama Department of Senior Services (ADSS) created a successful and creative model for sheltering known as the "Senior Center/Safe Center" model based on a concept outlined in 2005. The concept is that a senior center is either built or retrofitted to serve dual purposes—support everyday activities for seniors and serve as a shelter during emergencies.

The facilities are hardened so that they are less vulnerable to different hazards. For example, facilities are located outside the flood plain and can withstand hurricane- and tornado-force winds. They are also equipped with a generator, extra wall outlets, and satellite phones. Furthermore, the facilities are accessible and can accommodate seniors and others with disabilities. In order to help emergency officials locate the facility during an emergency event, the roofs are painted bright colors, allowing for easy recognition during flyovers and rescue operations.

There are many benefits to the Safe Center/Senior Center model as the facility is already part of the everyday community fabric and serves the aging community. Because of their familiarity with the facility, and knowing that it can support their needs, it is more likely that seniors will evacuate to the facilities. For the community, this model is a sound investment in that it provides services every day for community members and also provides a safe haven during emergencies.

The ADSS has carried out this concept to creation in partnership with the Alabama Emergency Management Agency, Alabama Department of Economic and Community Affairs, and the U.S. Administration on Aging (AoA). Since the first Safe Center was built in 2006, there have been several more completed and even more in development. The model has also carried over to Florida, where several Safe Centers are in place and in progress.

There are two more important aspects to also highlight. First, mitigation funds through the state can be accessed to provide the matching dollars for a project such as this, thus making it an affordable option that actually pays for itself after the initial investment. Second, while senior centers are the type of facility currently used in this concept, it would work equally well in a community to consider parks and recreation facilities or other municipal service delivery centers. Several locations have been completed and others are under construction or awaiting approval. This trend toward using and hardening locations familiar to populations at risk is expected to heighten compliance with evacuation messages, as well as to increase use of postdisaster relief and recovery efforts among the elderly.

15.2.4.1.2 Mega-Shelters

The term *mega-shelter* initially described logistical planning for an event of significant scale predicted to result in thousands of evacuees. To illustrate, the threat of Hurricane Ivan off the Gulf Coast of Florida in 2004 elevated Florida's emergency operations. Due to the projected path of the storm, a statewide mega-shelter opened in Orlando specifically to care for individuals with access and functional needs. This decision to open a shelter to accommodate up to 8,000 persons and caregivers was made within the highest levels of state and federal government. Mega-shelter, however, did not become a familiar term until 2005 when Louisiana and Texas opened large facilities to house Hurricane Katrina evacuees in the Superdome, the Cajun Dome, Reunion Arena, and the Dallas Convention Center (IAAM 2006). The concept of a mega-shelter has gained popularity since Hurricane Katrina in the emergency planning sector, with even more states in the process of identifying or planning for mega-shelters. The most significant benefit to the mega-shelter model is that it allows for the consolidation and concentration of specialized and possibly limited resources in one location. This was the reason, for example, why San Antonio actually closed its smaller shelters and opened larger centers following Katrina (San Antonio Office of Emergency Management nd). Providing logistical support across dozens of smaller shelters dispersed throughout a region can be time consuming and ineffective.

Some of the greatest challenges to operating a mega-shelter are ensuring that adequate planning is dedicated to the task. Planning must include training staff, educating the public, and amassing necessary supplies and resources for potentially thousands of people in or near to a disaster-stricken area. Consider that the Cajun Dome in Lafayette, Louisiana, housed 18,500 evacuees for 58 days while Houston's Reliant Park sheltered 27,100 evacuees for 22 days. The Cajun Dome served 409,000 meals to evacuees and responders alone (IAAM 2006). Provision of other services included access to medical services, working bathroom facilities and showers, safety, water issues, cleanliness, preventing spread of disease, and children's needs.

Another challenge in planning for the mega-shelter is identifying suitable locations. While the mega-shelter may ease some of the logistical burden, some evacuees may have to travel considerable distances. This can be especially problematic for people with disabilities, older adults, and those who are transportation disadvantaged. The risk is that people may not actually use the facility. This became a problem in Florida in 2004 when the Orlando Convention Center was made into a special needs mega-shelter. The facility was meant to accommodate 8,000 people with special needs and their caregivers. Resources to support the facility, such as supplies and personnel, were pulled from other places. In total, only 127 evacuees went to the shelter at great expense to the state. Furthermore, another complication emerged as the discharge planning process became complicated because some evacuees were more than a hundred miles away from home.

There are both advantages and disadvantages to using such large facilities as shelters. Immediately following Katrina, the International Association of Assembly Managers, Inc. partnered with the ARC to gather information on the mega-shelters that were used during the aftermath. In July 2006, they released *Mega-Shelter: A Best Practices for Planning, Activation, and Operations* with guidance on various aspects of mega-shelters, including classification of shelters (six are identified), definitions, and standards, as well as operational systems such as command and control, administration, food services, medical services, safety, and security. IAAM and ARC also signed a Memorandum of Understanding (MOU) stating that the two organizations with members in every state will work cooperatively with local officials to establish procedures and protocols to open mega shelters during a disaster (GOVPRO 2007). As this is a fairly new practice, more research on mega-shelters should be conducted to continue to build off of the work already accomplished and provide information and guidance to help localities assess the feasibility and benefits of using a mega-shelter, as well as all of the operational components that are needed to operate a facility of this magnitude.

15.2.4.2 General Population Shelter Operations

Shelter operations can be divided into two basic areas: facility management and taking care of the residents. For the purposes of this chapter, we focus on taking care of residents and meeting the needs of the populations most likely to use the shelter. As noted earlier, less than 20 percent of the evacuating public will go to a shelter. Among those that do, it is likely that socioeconomic circumstances will influence who uses a public shelter. Experienced shelter managers know to expect that the majority of their residents will be lower income and may arrive with meager resources for daily survival, let alone the return home.

Poverty: Income is often associated with other demographic characteristics. For example, many elderly persons live on low and/or fixed incomes. Though older adults tend to be reluctant to move away from familiar locations, they do respond to warning messages when they are reached (Perry and Lindell 1997) and when resources facilitate their evacuation. Because they tend to experience problems with both colder and hotter temperatures (Fernandez et al. 2002), they may also be among those most likely to need cooling centers during heat waves (Klinenberg 2002) or shelters open during winter weather power outages. As we age, the prevalence of disability also increases, which suggests that shelter providers should be ready to assist not only with issues associated with low income but the interactive effects of age and disability. Older residents who are immigrants are also less likely to fluently speak and/or read English and thus may require translation services as well. As can be seen in this section, shelter providers need to be ready to meet the needs of not just a specific population like the elderly, but to understand and prepare for the diversity found within any population.

Elderly: Recommendations for sheltering the elderly include assisting them with navigating unfamiliar locations and ensuring that basic supplies such as hearing aid batteries, eyeglass providers, and medical staff are in place (Peek 2010). Special concern should also be taken with case management to help the elderly with applications for assistance, as they tend to underutilize aid packages out of independent spirit and fear of being seen as vulnerable (Huerta and Horton 1978). Older adults report higher losses, so care to replace lost resources is likely to be needed prior to discharge from a shelter (Ngo 2001). Distress associated with such loss is a concern for those providing mental health care for the elderly as well (Peek 2010; Norris et al. 2002a, 2002b).

Children: Age also matters in the case of children. Rather than being simply a "below 18" group, children should be viewed as equally diverse. Age matters in understanding how a shelter resident may respond to being away from home. Small children seem to be more adaptable, in part because they are usually cared for closely by a responsible adult. School-age children seem to adapt more readily when a routine is established, particularly if they can return to school even while in the shelter. Older adolescents and teens may need something specific to occupy their time besides schooling, including help with homework, time for recreation, opportunities to reconnect with now-distant friends, and even the chance to help with the disaster recovery (Peek 2010; Fothergill and Peek 2006). Hurricane Katrina shelter providers gave critical support to children through such opportunities, helping to alleviate distress and provide structure to children whose lives had been uprooted. Researchers have found that particular attention needs to be paid to issues of culture, race, and language as shelter workers may not be adequately trained to assist children of color. Inappropriate and insensitive response furthers childhood distress (Fothergill and Peek 2006).

Disabilities: The National Council on Disability (2009, 2010) recognizes that shelters have not been ready to assist people with disabilities at an adequate level. After Hurricane Katrina, the National Organization on Disability (NOD) conducted a rapid study of shelters, determining that even when staff asked questions about disability during intake, appropriate services and resources were often not made available. The vast majority of shelters did little to offer standard communications resources including teletype machines (TTY), closed-captioned television, or even written message boards. Shelters received evacuees with disabilities who had lost their mobility devices, hearing aids, durable medical equipment, and other critical resources. In many cases, people with disabilities were forcibly separated from their resources and arrived in shelters without a means to move about, use the bathrooms, or communicate. Unfortunately, many shelter providers do not train staff or volunteers in how to make accommodations or in basic disability etiquette (for a guide, see Oklahoma Able Tech, nd).

Shelters should accommodate people with disabilities and not reroute them to medical shelters or hospitals unless they meet eligibility requirements based on technical medical needs. As mentioned earlier in the chapter, the U.S. Department of Justice (2008) currently offers a "Best Practices Toolkit for State and Local Governments" that outlines basic accessibility requirements of shelter elements. These include advanced planning that includes people with disabilities on the shelter planning committee. The committee should ensure accessibility of entrances, restrooms, sleeping, and dining areas. Further, the shelter must provide assistance with learning to navigate the new environment, accept service animals, and store medical equipment, medicine, and nutritional supplies (National Council on Disability 2009, 2010).

Nutritional needs: Nutrition in itself can present an operational challenge. While it is tempting to provide bulk foods for a massive number of people, the reality is that food truly matters to shelter residents. Not everyone can eat the same foods, and for very good reasons. First, people have allergies to some foods and can become quite ill or even die from eating the wrong foods. Second, medical conditions, such as diabetes, require that we know the ingredients contained within the food to avoid negative health consequences (Cefalu et al. 2006). Third, some people may not be able to consume food as prepared, from small children to an individual who needs food delivered in liquefied form. Fourth, some residents will need to eat at specific intervals in order to manage a medical condition or because of their age. Fifth, shelter managers may need to offer specific foods, such as infant formula. Finally, food is a source of physical and emotional comfort. By cooking food that is regionally and/or culturally familiar, residents may feel more comfortable in the shelter. Culturally familiar food is especially important for children who may refuse to eat otherwise (Phillips 1993).

In short, food is a means to help the resident population not only meet nutritional requirements but to dwell more comfortably, happily, and healthily in the shelter. In a major disaster, it is not unusual for people to hoard food under their cots to provide psychological safety, and people should be allowed to do so (Pike, Phillips, and Reeves 2006).

Cultural needs: Food is an important element of one's culture, one that reflects regionally available foods as well as the identity and legacy of a community or people. Travelers well know the Cajun cuisine of the Louisiana coast, fried chicken of the Deep South, fresh salmon of the Pacific Northwest, the cheese of Wisconsin, shoofly pie from Pennsylvania, or the homemade sausages of the Midwest. By providing a means to deliver familiar food, a shelter manager acknowledges the heart of a community and its people—their culture and their way of life. There are other ways to honor cultural heritage, too, including holding cultural events that feature a community's music, poetry, dance, and art through movies, talent nights, live performances, and art sessions. Not only do such shelter events recognize local culture but they also provide for momentary escape as well as help people regain what they may have thought they lost.

Mental health: In most disasters, people respond well in terms of their mental health. Posttraumatic stress disorder is typically low in most disasters, except for cases of extreme exposure, loss of social networks, and trauma previous to the disaster (Norris et al. 2002a, 2002b; Coker et al. 2006). After Hurricane Katrina, North (2008, 112) noted that "disaster managers planning for shelter resources should expect a significant prevalence of both acute and longstanding mental health problems that will require significant resources including psychiatrists and other mental health professionals, psychotropic medications, and addiction treatment resources." Mental health support must be offered by qualified, trained, and certified professionals who can be preidentified by the shelter planning team. In the immediate aftermath, residents may benefit from simply being able to share their story (Pennebaker 1997). Again, the diversity of the shelter must be considered by providing opportunities that address ages, cultures, and accessibility. Some options might include play therapy, art therapy, storytelling, arts and crafts, group discussion, and even individual therapy sessions. Organizations like the ARC train and credential mental health providers and supply materials like children's coloring books that help kids work through their experience. Shelters can also generate opportunities to release stress, including recreation, games, movies, and fun times that meet the needs of all ages, languages, literacy levels, and abilities, and are accessible to all.

Pregnant women: A group that may require special attention in the shelter, and can be subject to significant effects from stress, is pregnant women. High-risk pregnancies are a particular concern and should be identified during registration by asking residents if they have any medical conditions that require monitoring or assistance. Some pregnancies may require movement to a medical shelter or hospital to insure a safe delivery for both mother and child. In non-high-risk pregnancies, shelter providers should ask what would make the expectant mother more comfortable to sleep or rest and what kinds of food may be needed, including food and vitamin supplements. In addition to pregnant women, women who are nursing should be permitted to do so in the shelter although they may prefer a private location to do so. Because disasters may disrupt a woman's ability to nurse, shelter providers need to preidentify a local group or agency that can provide breast milk, lactation support, and/or formula (Enarson 2005).

Addiction: Drug and alcohol addiction represent a group of people who may suffer terribly during an evacuation. Withdrawal from substances can range from making people considerably distressed to violent or even suicidal. In most states, shelters arrange with state agencies tasked with mental health to care for those experiencing symptoms ranging from addiction to withdrawal from either substances or treatment protocol.

Criminal behavior: Safety and security may become a concern in a shelter. While the vast majority of shelters report minimal problems, there are some issues of concern. Domestic violence and child abuse may become an issue, and shelter workers should be trained to observe signs of possible violence and how to report it (Phillips, Jenkins, and Enarson 2010). Recently, the state of Louisiana decided to segregate sex offenders into separate hurricane shelters. While sex offenders should self-identify, they may not do so, and shelter workers should receive training from law enforcement staff on how to recognize situations that can arise and how to report concerns to police. During mass evacuations, it may also be possible that gang members travel together and arrive in a shelter. Once again, involving local police in planning how to manage possible criminal behavior in a shelter is highly recommended.

15.2.4.3 Animals

Animals represent a concern that has been increasingly addressed. Two animal populations, pets and service animals, represent the majority of those in need of shelter. Concern with livestock and the possible damage to not only the animal but to individual farms and local economies is also appropriate although not possible to cover here in detail. Moving livestock can be difficult to impossible, thus mitigating farm buildings from local hazards or moving animals to a facility outside the immediate area (such as a fairground location) may be an option. This section focuses on pets and service animals, which should always be treated as separate groups.

15.2.4.3.1 Pets

An increasing trend, especially since Hurricane Katrina, is to assist with pet transportation and pet sheltering. Public Law 109-308, the Pet Evacuation and Transportation Act, requires states to assist pet owners. Accordingly, a number of Gulf Coast states, such as Alabama and Texas, have organized efforts to educate the public on pet preparedness and to offer transportation assistance. In Texas, hurricane evacuees may board designated buses along with their pets and move inland to shelter. A common strategy is to co-locate pet shelters close to human shelters in order to facilitate pet visitation and to encourage pet owners to care for their animals. States usually organize pet assistance efforts under Emergency Support Function #11 of their state emergency operations plan by incorporating veterinary organizations, animal welfare organizations, and state animal welfare officials into their efforts. A State Animal Response Team (SART) may participate, too. Pet shelters may be set up by local or state officials or by organizations like the local humane society or animal shelter.

Why evacuate pets? By accommodating pets, the number of those evacuating is likely to increase (Heath et al. 2001; Heath and Beck 2001). Noncompliance with evacuation orders is believed to be higher among the elderly who are reluctant to leave a critical companion behind. Children may become distraught in a shelter, begging parents to reenter hazardous areas to retrieve a beloved friend. By accommodating animals, it is thus possible to encourage compliance with protective action directions and to reduce stress. Encouraging owners to care for pets is also believed to enhance mental health for both the owner and the animals. In short, accommodating pets in an appropriate location is increasingly an expectation of shelter providers. Because people are likely to show up with animals regardless of an available pet shelter, it is important for shelter providers to be ready for everything from a dog to an iguana to a horse.

Animals may also expose shelter residents to some degree of risk. Accordingly, it is typically necessary to shelter animals separately from humans to reduce the risk of allergic reactions, asthma, fear of animals, and the possibility of an animal biting someone or becoming injured themselves. FEMA offers additional resources to learn more about animals in disasters, including two free, online, independent study courses (http://training.fema.gov/IS/crslist.asp); the American Veterinary Medical Association offers downloadable guides as well (http://www.avma.org). The U.S. Federal Highway Administration (2009) also offers general information on how to accommodate pets from preparedness through transportation and sheltering.

15.2.4.3.2 Service Animals

Service animals are not the same as pets. Service animals are highly trained, specialized working animals that assist people with disabilities, medical conditions, and/or psychological needs in their daily lives. The Americans with Disabilities Act of 1990 (ADA) enforced by the U.S. Department of Justice require that service animals are accommodated in all shelter locations. Typically, a service animal will present with its human handler wearing some kind of identification designating its status. However, that may not always be the case, and it is important to remember that if an individual tells you the animal in question is a working animal, it must be accommodated. Bear in mind that an emergency evacuation may mean that not all animals have been able to leave with proper identification.

15.3 INCLUSION OF DISABILITY AND ACCESS AND FUNCTIONAL NEEDS IN SHELTERS

Hurricane Katrina served as a watershed moment in sheltering history. The simple reality was that many people could not evacuate without transportation, specialized resources, durable medical equipment, family, or caregivers. As we all watched on television, people died in nursing homes and hospitals and faced sweltering heat on overpasses and impromptu shelters. A mass medical evacuation through the New Orleans airport transported thousands of people to safety, many in poor and deteriorating medical condition. Triage personnel "experienced substantial challenges in making triage and treatment decisions for residents whose numbers far exceeded supplies and personnel" (Klein and Nagel 2007, 56). This section focuses on inclusionary practices in shelters to accommodate needs of people with disabilities and other access and functional needs. We first look at recent trends in terminology and then move into operational concerns and recommendations for practice in shelters. See Box 15.4, which offers practical quick fixes for accommodating needs in shelters.

BOX 15.4

QUICK FIXES IN SHELTERS: MEETING NEEDS OF PEOPLE WITH DISABILITIES AND ACCESS AND FUNCTIONAL NEEDS

- If there are no TTY/TTD phones or phone banks in the facility, bring in a portable TTY and make it known how to request its use.
- If drinking fountains are not working or are not accessible, bring in bottled water.
- Always have bendy straws in the equipment cache as they can be used for someone to independently drink bottled water if they have limited range of motion or upper body strength; a toddler or small child can also be hydrated without sippy cups in stock.
- If there are not separate male and female accessible restrooms, turn the one accessible restroom into a unisex facility, and if it doesn't lock from the inside, then assign a staff person to enforce the use of that restroom. The provision of a unisex bathroom may also be helpful if persons require assistance from a caregiver of the opposite sex (this includes showers, if possible).
- When setting up the special arrangements for sleeping space, take into account the proximity to the restroom for older persons and/or people with mobility disabilities. Be sure to offer to place these persons closer to the restrooms. While it is not legal to segregate any set of persons based on a perceived function or lack thereof, it is wise to be flexible to ensure the most independent outcomes under the circumstances.
- Identify safe areas or private areas for shelter residents. As shelters can be chaotic and overwhelming, the identification of quiet locations so people can "get away" can be extremely useful in managing anxiety or the sense of losing control. Further, identifying private space for nursing mothers or others who may need assistance or require more space in daily activities, such as dressing, can help to maintain a sense of privacy and dignity. For example, it may also be useful to set aside specific areas for those under extreme care circumstances, such persons with Alzheimer's disease

or those who require hospice services. If it is not possible to use separate rooms due to space restrictions, partitions can be added for privacy around cot areas.

- Often adults and children become bored or restless in shelters. Identify ways to engage shelter residents. For example, offer recreation space and activities—separate from the dormitory or eating spaces—for adults and children. Activities, such as watching television and movies (adult and child appropriate programs), playing games, giving out newspapers, and so forth, are often made available in shelters. In fact, Save the Children (http://www.savethechildren.org) offers shelter kits for children. Another approach is to engage the shelter residents as volunteers to help out around the shelter.
- Work with disability organizations, human services agencies, and local businesses to identify resources that are short in supply. For example, engage disability groups to identify supplies, such as wheelchairs, walkers, transfer boards, hearing aids, TTYs, sign language interpreters, transportation services, and other resources, that are needed.
- Incorporate input from people with disabilities and access and functional needs to help identify solutions and meet needs. Most people are experts in identifying what solutions (permanent or temporary) will best meet their own needs.

15.3.1 Terms and Definitions

The term *people with disabilities and access and functional needs* is the latest favored terminology. It is intended to include people with disabilities (as protected by the ADA) and people with access and functional needs, which may include communication, transportation, medical or nutritional support, supervision, or assistance with activities of daily living. Currently this is the preferred term by FEMA. Often, other terms such as special needs have been used in the past and still continue to be used in different sectors.

15.3.2 Spatial Arrangement

The spatial arrangement for shelter is critical and will impact the residents and staff greatly. The shelter should have areas for registration, staff, nursing, and medical support, pharmacy, food preparation and dining, supplies, and administration. Resident areas should be designated, including areas for sleeping, treatment, and quarantine. Isolation may be needed if residents develop contagious illnesses, and/or for those with allergies or chemical sensitivities and/or with asthma. If space allows, ambulatory and nonambulatory areas should be designated. Locations for providing various therapies (e.g., respiratory, physical, occupational, mental health) may be offered although residents may also be transported to off-site locations for these services. Areas for privacy should be provided for personal hygiene (Deal et al. 2006).

Depending on the populations that arrive at the shelter, it may be wise to establish separate areas for pediatric and geriatric care, as well as a location for child care as they may arrive with a resident and/or caregivers. Service animals should remain with the resident, and resources for their bedding, eating, and relief should be designated. The Baylor College of Medicine and the American Medical Association (2006) recommend that specific areas for frail elders and adults who may be vulnerable should be created. Any area may need to be further divided by gender to afford privacy. Because residents may arrive with caregivers and/or family, it is a good idea to include sleeping areas in the shelter for their use as well (Missouri 2008).

Accessibility—both architectural and programmatic—must be considered carefully. The U.S. Department of Justice offers an ADA checklist with specific measurements and guidance on site accessibility. These include a reception center that is accessible for people who use mobility devices, a minimum of 36 inches above the floor with a usable table or clip board (for more specific details, see the U.S. Department of Justice 2007b). Sleeping areas need to consider disability issues as well and allow for access into and out of the sleeping area with a minimum 36-inch-wide area for movement. Cots must be accessible and at least 17–19 inches above the floor to allow for transfer from a mobility device and back. Alternative sleeping support may be needed for residents with paraplegia or quadriplegia because of circulation issues; bariatric residents also require different types of beds (Mental Health Association of San Francisco 2007). Other best practices may include providing for a quiet, private space for people to use in order to avoid stress. An individual with an anxiety disorder or a child with autism, for example, may require a quieter environment to reduce tension and anxiety.

15.3.3 STAFFING

Staff patterns vary among jurisdictions, but the goal is to have teams fully trained and ready to deploy. A list compiled from publicly available plans in Georgia, North Carolina, New York, Alabama, Missouri, and Kansas indicates that the recommended staff include:

- *Management*: A shelter manager, a medical director, a nurse supervisor.
- *Medical staff*: An onsite physician, nurses (RPN, LPN), and nursing aides and access to physical, respiratory, and occupational therapy as needed.
- *Support staff*: Clerical, admissions and registration specialists, janitors, and security personnel.
- *Health and well-being*: Nutritional staff and pharmacy/medications coordinator and a disease intervention specialist, biohazard specialist, and environmental scientist.
- *Social workers*: A discharge coordinator and case managers.
- *Disability support*: It is advisable to retain personnel able to communicate with people experiencing a range of disabilities and to provide advice on alternative designs and accessible accommodations.
- *Other key personnel*: Additional personnel may include an animal coordinator, grief workers, spiritual care, mental health workers, child care specialists, and transportation and evacuation staff.
- *Caregivers*: Family, friends, and others involved in routine support of an individual with medical, disability, or other needs should be integrated into the care of the resident as they can provide important information, as well as emotional and psychological support to the resident.

In addition to ensuring that a cadre of experienced, well-prepared staff is available, care should be taken to provide staff in appropriate ratios to the numbers of residents. Most states use a 12-hour rotation broken into day and night shifts. In Missouri, for example, a day shift requires one RN manager and one RN/LPN per every 25 residents. One additional caregiver (other than family or friend) is included per every 15 residents, as well as one mental health worker for every 75 residents. The night shift reduces the RN/LPN to 40 residents, a reduction in staff that is fairly typical across other states.

Personnel may come from existing agencies, including public health departments, home health care agencies, hospitals, and nursing homes. Some states prefer to contract with medical care agencies to ensure a ready force able to deploy on quick notice. Another recent trend has been the establishment of Federal Medical Stations (FMS). The FMS includes about 100 personnel provided through the U.S. Public Health Service with a three-day supply of critical medical and pharmaceutical supplies. An FMS can support up to 250 residents. Other units that may provide support include the Medical Reserve Corps, which includes trained and credentialed volunteers, and the Disaster

Medical Assistance Team, which typically supports rapid assessment, triage, and routing of residents to proper facilities.

15.3.4 SECURITY

Security issues also need to be considered carefully. In the latter, security to safeguard medical and pharmaceutical supplies should be in place. Standard protocol includes careful monitoring of who enters and exits the facility in order to prevent unauthorized entry. In many settings, a photograph is taken of residents in addition to staff credentialing. Family, particularly those involved in caregiver roles, may also be provided with a photo identification card.

Additional security concerns resident safety. Special care must be taken to protect those with dementia, for example; security is tasked with implementing emergency procedures in the event that someone does exit the facility. Security procedures may also involve providing color-coded identification bracelets so that staff can easily recognize an individual with dementia or another condition that may put the resident at risk. Typically, such measures take place during registration and intake, often using standardized forms. Security should also be concerned with the protection of residents who may not be able to protect themselves from interpersonal violence, particularly individuals with cognitive disabilities (Phillips, Jenkins, and Enarson 2010).

More generally, security may involve checking for unauthorized weapons, alcohol, or drugs (Orange County 2005). Further, security and/or safety personnel may be tasked with fire evacuation planning, marking and maintaining the integrity of fire exits, checking smoke detectors, and conducting fire drills (Pitt County 2008). A final task may require security and/or safety personnel to manage traffic ingress and egress and to monitor parking lots.

15.3.5 TRANSPORTATION

Transportation into and out of a shelter can become extraordinarily challenging to organize and manage because of the diverse array of residents as well as the ways in which they may arrive. Increasingly, jurisdictions preplan transportation in order to estimate the numbers of kinds of residents that will need assistance. Residents may arrive through personally owned vehicles, with family or friends, in an ambulance or ambulette, or via mass transportation such as a bus, plane, or train. As noted before, the security role becomes particularly important as arrivals are routed into the shelter facility. The U.S. Department of Justice requires certain standards per the ADA for ramps, curbs, and slopes, as well as an available number of accessible parking spaces for vans and other vehicles (for details, see U.S. Department of Justice 2007a).

Transportation must be linked to knowing where the resident is physically located at all times. Some states use bar-coded bracelets that can be scanned and uploaded via GPS for tracking purposes. Simply knowing where the resident is located, however, does not mean that their medical records, prescription drugs, durable medical equipment, assistive devices, or other medical supplies traveled with them. Accordingly, transportation procedures need to make every effort to keep residents with their medical records and resources. Because family and friends may not be able to travel with the resident, a means to communicate with loved ones should be in place as well so that trailing caregivers can arrive at the facility at some point in time.

Transportation involves movement into and out of a facility. Movement out of a facility may occur when a resident is discharged to go home or is transferred to a different location. The latter involves emergency situations where ambulances, helicopters, or airplanes may be needed to move an individual to a hospital or other location. Such movement, which requires rapid response and organization, must also be linked to administrative and clerical personnel who track movement of residents.

Finally, transportation of shelter staff may require support. Medical personnel, communications staff, volunteers, and others may not be able to move easily from their homes into shelter sites. In such circumstances, law enforcement personnel, the military, and even volunteer drivers have been used. Minnesota, for example, uses volunteers who own Humvees to transport key shelter personnel.

15.3.6 ORGANIZATIONAL PARTNERS

Setting up a shelter requires the contributions of a large cadre of planning partners. While each state varies to some degree in how they manage this, there are a number of key partners that should be involved. Increasingly, public health departments are playing a key role in supporting shelters. Public health departments may roster a team of medical personnel to support the shelter and/or use contractual partners to support the shelter. In the aftermath of Hurricane Katrina, calls for medical personnel ultimately involved nursing students and faculty, first responders, and a wide array of community-based physical and mental health services. To illustrate, the University of Texas at Austin sent more than one hundred nursing students and faculty to assist in various locations (for more, see http://www.utexas.edu/katrina/nursing.html). Personnel are only a portion of what is required, however. Locations must be preidentified and agreements must be written regarding use of the facility. Across the Gulf Coast, for example, locations that vary from schools to university arenas to community college gymnasiums have been used. While it might be ideal to have a facility designated for shelters, it is simply not financially feasible for most jurisdictions to build a shelter that might go unused for years. Accordingly, partners must be involved in shelter siting and establishment.

Besides the medical personnel mentioned earlier in this chapter, other planning partners would include ambulance services, dialysis care units, cancer treatment centers, and hospice (for an example on dialysis, see Kenney 2007). Because of the potential for a shelteree to be moved because of an emergency or through routine discharge, it would be necessary to also include nursing homes and area medical facilities from hospitals to veterans' administration locations. Aging organizations should also be included, as well as providers familiar with conditions that require special expertise such as dementia care. Facility managers at the desired location should be involved throughout the planning process in order to understand the potential impact on their facilities and how to best prepare for and recover from facility use.

People with disabilities in the shelter would benefit from planning that included representatives from the disability community, which could range from individuals to organizations and/or agencies. Their perspectives provide valuable insights that might not be considered otherwise. To support such planning and to ensure a good shelter experience, it would also be necessary to include people with expertise in making accommodations for a range of disabilities from mobility to communication needs. On a related note, having preplanned agreements with sign language interpreters and/or video relay and language banks and Assistive Technology Centers will prove to be helpful assets and connections to much needed resources (see Box 15.5). Finally, service animals may arrive stressed, injured, or ill and should be supported through veterinarian partners.

BOX 15.5

WHAT IS ASSISTIVE TECHNOLOGY?

Assistive technology is technology used by individuals with disabilities in order to perform functions that might otherwise be difficult or impossible. Assistive technology can include mobility devices such as crutches, walkers, and wheelchairs, which is also classified as durable medical equipment or "DME." It can also include various forms of portable ramps to assist in making parts of a nonaccessible environment accessible such as folding ramps that could be placed over several steps or a threshold of door so someone in a wheelchair could enter or exit a room or building.

Assistive technology also includes hardware, software, and peripherals that assist people with disabilities in accessing computers or other information technologies. For example, people with limited hand function may use a keyboard with large keys or a special mouse to operate a computer, people who are blind may use software that reads text on the screen in a computer-generated voice, people with low vision may use software that enlarges screen content, people who are deaf may use a TTY (text telephone), or people with speech impairments may use a device that speaks out loud as they enter text via a keyboard. This is extremely important in a shelter because the three ways of processing a FEMA claim for assistance are by phone, computer, or interacting with a person representing FEMA.

The need for assistive technology within our emergency sheltering system is critical. Information during a crisis or disaster is important to everyone. Whether it is news about status of the disaster itself, finding family members, pets, loved ones who might be in another shelter, assistive technology for many people with disabilities allows them to have a voice to communicate what their needs are, access information and their environment around them, and allow them maintain their independence.

George Heake (personal communication, March 15, 2010)

Another population that requires specialized understanding is people with mental health needs that may include psychiatric disorders and alcohol or drug addictions. Because disasters have the potential to disrupt medication protocols and daily routines, mental health needs may escalate especially as people move through withdrawal from a medication or from drugs or alcohol and are exposed to a new, often chaotic, environment.

To ensure a secure facility, careful coordination with law enforcement is advised. While uniforms may cause distress to some populations, the presence of identifiable security typically reassures most residents. Further, the participation of law enforcement is crucial because of the resources they provide, including communications, integration with other first responders, and expertise in supporting the populations likely to be in the shelter.

15.3.7 SHELTER MANAGEMENT

This section reviews basic shelter management and addresses ways to integrate people with disabilities and access and functional needs.

15.3.7.1 Triage

Triage is the first step that will occur prior to intake in the shelter. It is an immediate, quick evaluation to be certain that the person who is entering the shelter is not in need of acute medical care or does not have a communicable disease and requires hospital care instead. Triage should be conducted by medical personnel.

15.3.7.2 Intake

The intake process at any shelter should be as efficient and secure as possible under the circumstances. The specific procedures to be used during the intake process will vary depending on the jurisdiction, but the process should be standardized from shelter to shelter within the same jurisdiction. Many jurisdictions use standardized forms and protocols to achieve this. In Pitt County, North Carolina (2008), residents fill out medical release forms, as well as lists for valuables and durable medical equipment; they are given shelter rules, information about privacy practices, and shelter identification.

Another consideration is how to secure medical records and prescriptions. Each jurisdiction and shelter should follow all federal, state, and local laws, such as the Health Insurance Portability and

Accountability Act (HIPAA), when handling medical records. The types of records that should be secured include individual medical records, residential group tracking records, medication dispensing records, medical equipment tracking records, and confidentiality/release forms (National Capital Region nd). These documents and prescriptions should be kept in a secured area with limited access, such as the shelter manager's office or another separate area.

15.3.7.3 Communication

Communication within a shelter is very important. Within the shelter there are residents that may be blind, deaf, do not speak English, or unable to communicate due to a medical issue. Accordingly, shelter planners and staff must make accommodations to provide those residents with the same quality and quantity of information as those residents who are able to communicate without assistance. There are several strategies to increase the flow of information. All of these strategies must meet the minimum standards set by not only the U.S. Department of Justice and Americans with Disabilities Act (ADA) but also any state and local guidance.

The U.S. Department of Justice (2007b) has laid out several steps that should be taken to provide an accessible shelter. The first step is to adopt procedures, such as exchanging notes or posting written announcements, to enhance communication (U.S. Department of Justice 2007a). Staff should also be trained to implement these procedures. Each shelter should be equipped with at least one TTY (text telephone) (U.S. Department of Justice 2007a, 2007b; National Capital Region nd). Each shelter should also have access to interpreters for not only those with communication disabilities, but also for those who speak only limited English (U.S. Department of Homeland Security Office for Civil Rights and Civil Liberties 2008; U.S. Department of Justice 2007b; National Capital Region nd).

Providing accessible communication is only the first step in providing quality communications. Shelter planners and staff must also consider how to provide an environment conducive to open communications between shelter staff and residents. Meeting the legal minimums set by the local, state, and federal governments will help, but may not provide all the tools necessary. Creating an environment that encourages open communications begins before the shelter is even open. Shelter planners should utilize organizations in their communities to reach out to potential residents prior to an event in order to share information about where shelters will be located, how shelters will be operated, and how to be prepared for staying in a shelter (U.S. Department of Homeland Security Office for Civil Rights and Civil Liberties 2008). This same technique can be used to locate and secure translators and volunteers.

In addition to communicating within the shelter, planners and managers must also consider how they will communicate with partners outside of the shelter. The two most important features of this communication system are redundancy and interoperability (National Capital Region nd; New York 2008; Waushara County Wisconsin nd).

Redundancy helps to ensure that communication will not break down if one piece of the communication system is not functional. Redundancy can be achieved through backup systems or having different technologies available. Waushara County, Wisconsin, recommends the use of hard line phones, e-mail, cell phones, satellite phones, handheld radios, and runners to provide redundant communications under different types of situations. Shelters will need to communicate with central command officials, transportation officials, hospitals and health agencies, and other community agencies, so it is very important that each of these entity's communication systems are compatible and will work together.

Some general guidelines for more effective communication in shelters include:

- Establish a predictable and regularly scheduled time, location, and means to provide information updates and situational awareness to all those in the shelter. Additionally, post information on meal times, snacks, coffee areas, shower schedules, lights out, and so forth. Be sure to repeat schedule announcements and post schedules in multiple locations. This will go a long way in controlling rumors, empowering people to make safe decisions for themselves, and managing stress and anxiety.

- Always be sure information is provided in multiple formats, modalities, and languages. If not perfect under the emergency situation, be creative but be sure to provide information. Use audible reports, written reports, and pictorials or graphics to represent information; also, look to bridge gaps while getting more appropriate solutions in place as quickly as possible.
- It is often helpful to provide a quiet, private space in which to communicate with some shelter residents. For some, the shelter environment may make it difficult to hear or process audible or written announcements, so communicating in a more private space and/or one-on-one and/or at a slower pace may help some shelter residents receive and process information. This is often dependent on space allocation and allowances. Some facilities are open fully to shelter staff while others clearly designate only a few areas to the shelter.
- Offer opportunities for residents to self-identify communication needs to shelter staff. This should happen during registration, but also at other times during their stay at the shelter.

15.3.7.4 Case Management

Case management means that an individual or team is assigned to work with a shelter resident to ensure that needs are met in the shelter and that the resident begins planning for discharge from the shelter. In a disaster context, discharge can become quite problematic as people may not be able to return home any time soon. Even before formal case management is available, shelter staff can facilitate a resident's recovery in a number of ways:

- Have staff engage shelterees in conversation. Allow them to talk about their fears, plans, and their next steps.
- Keep shelterees informed on all aspects of the disaster, any plans for the shelter they are in, and options for temporary housing upon discharge.
- Tie in local social services providers, especially those serving populations with disabilities and/or other access and functional needs: organizations serving people with disabilities, seniors, immigrant populations, people who are homeless, those with mental illness, dementia patients, veterans and others who are familiar to and trusted by the resident. Although these organizations are sometimes brought in for large-scale disasters, they are often overlooked for smaller events. They can add great value to the process of delivering services either as case managers and/or by serving in advisory capacities and should be considered critical partners in case management services.

For larger disasters, multiple organizations besides the American Red Cross will be providing disaster services and resources. These include traditional social services providers, such as Catholic Charities, as well as local state and federal agencies. Formal case management structures may also be established within local long-term recovery committees. It may be wise to connect shelter case managers to these emerging structures that will coordinate the delivery of postdisaster resources, including reconstruction of damaged homes, as well as clothing and other basic resources.

Transition to longer-term or permanent housing can be complex for all shelterees, but especially for those with functional needs. Some of the challenges that often arise include:

- Lack of suitable housing within their community, including the lack of accessible housing
- The loss of or slow recovery of infrastructure in the community, including hospitals, health clinics, schools, dialysis centers, home health agencies, grocery stores, electricity, and so forth
- Not knowing where to secure resources that will allow individuals to transition to a setting where they can maintain the greatest level of independence
- The transition from a shelter back into the community with the appropriate care/services in place

Effective case management in a shelter follows the resident from intake through discharge, ensuring that evacuees' complete set of needs are addressed. Residents cannot be discharged if roads remain impassable to their homes, or if their homes, assisted living centers or group homes have been damaged. Case managers may need to identify alternative locations where residents can return safely into a set of services that can address their functional needs. After a major disaster, those services may not be available from home health agencies to the availability of a general or specialized medical practitioner. Case managers need to advocate for client needs and coordinate with those stepping up to assist a resident after the disaster. It may be necessary to find families able to take in a resident or to locate an alternate group setting. Such locations can be temporary or permanent and the case manager bears responsibility for ensuring that the transition to either location represents an appropriate choice. An excellent option is to partner with linking organizations prior to disasters in order to provide services to discharged evacuees postdisaster.

15.3.7.5 Discharge

Discharging shelter residents should take place in an orderly and efficient manner. One way to help ensure order and efficiency is to have a discharge plan in place prior to even opening the shelter (Jefferson County Emergency Management Agency and Jefferson County Department of Health nd). This plan should set forth general guidelines for shelter managers and staff to follow during discharge. Its goals should be to make sure the needs of residents after leaving the shelter are considered prior to them returning home (U.S. Department of Justice 2008). The State of New York (2008) calls for the restoration of case management and medical services to predisaster levels, which can be achieved through planning and cooperation between various agencies. Cooperation between agencies is especially important when the disaster is very large or of catastrophic levels because agencies that do not normally work together will be forced to do so (New York 2008). The shelter discharge plan should also include information about when and how to inform residents that the shelter will be closing. The National Capital Region (nd) recommends that shelter residents in an extended-stay shelter (more than four days) should be informed of shelter closure no less than 48 hours prior to closure (National Capital Region nd). Another way to help ensure orderly and efficient discharge procedures is to include those procedures in any shelter training and simulations that occur prior to an event.

There are some general procedures that should be implemented in every jurisdiction. The first is to discharge shelter residents according to the plan (Jefferson County Emergency Management Agency and Jefferson County Department of Health nd). Next, shelter staff should ensure that residents can exit the shelter safely. Third, staff must collect and return all assistive equipment and durable medical equipment. Any equipment brought to the shelter by a resident should be returned to the resident before discharge. Other durable medical equipment should be returned to the agency, business, or individual from which it originated. Similarly, all nondurable medical supplies should be collected, packaged, and stored for future use. These procedures will be aided by logging all durable and nondurable medical supplies. This includes not only logging the medical supplies brought by each resident, but also the equipment and supplies donated by different entities.

The discharge process should also include the completion of all paperwork. This will include registration and discharge logs, equipment and supply logs, staff logs, and all other paperwork linked to shelter operations. Once all paperwork has been completed, the staff should participate in a debriefing prior to leaving the shelter. This debriefing should include information about what went well in the shelter and how to improve the sheltering experience in the next disaster. The final general discharge procedure that should be included in all jurisdictions is to have all shelter staff sign out of the shelter as they leave. These general procedures, in conjunction with jurisdictional and event-specific procedures, should help shelter management provide an orderly and efficient discharge process.

15.3.7.6   Reunification

Reunification of families following a disaster is a crucial step toward long-term recovery. Depending on the jurisdiction, the reunification process falls under the purview of many different agencies. In Missouri (2008), the Department of Health and Senior Services and the Department of Social Services are involved in the process. In Florida (2005), the Department of Children and Families supports reunification. No matter the agency involved, there are some basic needs that must be met during reunification. Residents must be safe and supported during the reunification and recovery process. The process must also be efficient and well documented to ensure that no resident gets "lost in the system." Many state guidance documents recommend employing caseworkers, mental health workers, and home health agency workers to carry out the reunification process (New York 2008; Jefferson County Emergency Management Agency nd; Pitt County North Carolina 2008; Missouri 2008). Caseworkers can be extremely helpful because they understand the resources available within the community they serve. Mental health nurses are useful because they are trained to notice the signs of mental distress, which can be common after a disaster. They are also able to make referrals that are outside the scope of training of caseworkers and other shelter staff. Home health agencies, in addition to caseworkers and mental health workers, will be vital after reunification occurs because they help the shelter residents and their families begin to heal and cope with the effects of the disaster.

In order to make the reunification process more efficient, it is helpful to log information about the shelter resident from intake to discharge. During the intake process, the shelter resident or their representative should have been asked to provide information regarding the resident's identification, medical diagnosis, any personal property, medical equipment, and medication brought by the resident and their intended departure plans. A number of shelters use ambulance services, military resources, and private vehicles to support transportation efforts that return shelter residents to their homes and families. The costs of the transportation can be reimbursed by FEMA, but care must be taken to do so in accordance with current requirements for documentation of costs.

15.3.7.7   Deactivation

Once all shelter residents have been discharged, the shelter can be deactivated. Deactivation procedures begin with the collection of all durable medical equipment. The equipment will be reused or returned to its source. Next, nondurable medical supplies will be inventoried and stored. After all supplies are stored or returned, the shelter staff will complete all paperwork associated with deactivation and should participate in a debriefing session. The debriefing should cover shelter performance and what can be improved before the next sheltering situation. Discussing "lessons learned" serves as one of the best ways to improve shelter future performance. After the debriefing, all shelter staff will sign out, which signifies the completion of shelter deactivation (Jefferson County nd).

15.4   SUMMARY

This chapter has provided an overview of general population shelters and the integration of people with disabilities and access and functional needs. The delivery of behavioral health services requires an understanding of the overall approach to and structure of shelters, the types of populations likely to be present in each, and the extent of planning required for both. Shelter planners and providers must ensure that locations are appropriately sited in order to ensure the highest levels of safety and security for residents. Further, attending to the diverse array of needs likely to be present in both shelters requires a strong, collaborative, and well-trained set of partners from across a jurisdiction. In the worst of times, shelter providers represent the best of what our communities can provide: a safe haven, compassionate staff and volunteers, and a transition into a postdisaster recovery environment. Those who step up to deliver behavioral health services in a shelter are advised to secure extensive training and experience. Further, it is important to understand that shelter staff and volunteers rank among those who literally make the difference between being on the street and being able to eat, sleep, and obtain critically needed resources in a major emergency or disaster.

REFERENCES

Area Agency on Aging of Pasco-Pinellas Counties. nd. *Disaster preparedness for those with special needs.* http://www.agingcarefl.org/aging/disaster.

Baylor College of Medicine and American Medical Association. 2006. *Recommendations for best practices in the management of elderly disaster victims.* http://www.bcm.edu/pdf/bestpractices.pdf.

Burnett, J., Dyer, C. B., and S. Pickens. 2008. Rapid needs assessments for older adults in disasters. *Generations 31*(4): 10–15.

Cefalu, W. T., L. Bonde, S. R. Smith, and V. Fonseca. 2006. The Hurricane Katrina aftermath and its impact on diabetes care. *Diabetes Care 29*(1): 158–160.

Coker, A. L., J. S. Hanks, K. S. Eggleston, J. Risser, P. G. Tee, K. J. Chronister, C. L. Troisi, R. Arafat, and L. Franzini. 2006. Social and mental health needs of Katrina evacuees. *Disaster Management & Response 4*(3): 88–94.

Deal, B. J., R. A. Fountain, C. A. Russell-Broaddus, and M. Stanley-Hermanns. 2006. Challenges and opportunities of nursing care in special-needs shelters. *Disaster Management & Response 4*(4): 100–105.

Drabek, T. E. 1986. *Human System Response To Disaster: An Inventory of Sociological Findings.* New York: Springer-Verlag.

Enarson, E. 2005. *Gender note 1: Response.* http://www.gdnonline.org/resources/GDN_hardlessons-gendernote1. pdf.

FEMA. 2008. *ESF #6—Mass care, emergency assistance, housing, and human services annex.* http://www .fema.gov/pdf/emergency/nrf/nrf-esf-06.pdf.

FEMA, 2010. *Guidance for planning for integration of functional needs support services in general population shelters.* http://www.fema.gov/pdf/about/odic/fnss_guidance.pdf.

Fernandez, L. S., D. Byard, C.-C. Lin, S. Benson, and J. A. Barbera. 2002. Frail elderly as disaster victims. *Prehospital Disaster Medicine 17*(2): 67–74.

Florida, State of. 2005. *Special needs shelter protocols.* http://www.doh.state.fl.us/PHNursing/SpNS/ SpecialNeedsShelter.html.

Fothergill, A., and L. Peek. 2006. Surviving catastrophe: A study of children in Hurricane Katrina. In *Learning from Catastrophe*, ed. J. Monday, 97–130. Boulder, CO: Institute of Behavioral Science, University of Colorado. http://www.colorado.edu/hazards/resources/socy4037/FothergillandPeek2006-1.pdf.

GOVPRO. 2007. *Red Cross partners with IAAM for mega shelters.* http://govpro.com/public_safety/ emergency_response/gov_imp_45545/index.html.

Heath, S. E., and A. M. Beck. 2001. Risk factors for pet evacuation failure after a slow-onset disaster. *Journal of the American Veterinary Medical Association 218*(12): 1905–1910.

Heath, S. E., P. H. Kass, A. M. Beck, and L. T. Glickman. 2001. Human and pet-related risk factors for household evacuation failure during a natural disaster. *American Journal of Epidemiology 153*(7): 659–665.

Huerta, F., and R. Horton. 1978. Coping behavior of elderly flood victims. *The Gerontologist 18*(6): 541–546.

International Association of Assembly Managers, Inc. (IAAM). 2006. *Mega-shelter: A best practice for planning, activation and operations.* http://www.fema.gov/pdf/emergency/disasterhousing/MegaShelter PlanningActivation.pdf.

Jefferson County Emergency Management Agency and Jefferson County Department of Health. nd. *Attachment 1: Medical needs shelter operating guide.* https://www.jeffcoema.org/documents/CEMP%202008/04%20 Response%20Functions/04.B.11.1%20Medical%20Needs%20Shelter%20Operating%20Guide.doc.

Kailes, J., and A. Enders. 2007. Moving beyond special needs. *Journal of Disability Policy Studies 17*(4): 230–237.

Kenney, R. J. 2007. Emergency preparedness concepts for dialysis facilities: Reawakened after Hurricane Katrina. *Clinical Journal of the American Society of Nephrology 2*: 809–813.

Klein, K. R., and N. E. Nagel. 2007. Mass medical evacuation: Hurricane Katrina and nursing experiences at the New Orleans airport. *Disaster Management and Response 5*(2): 56–61.

Klinenberg, E. 2002. *Heat wave: A social autopsy of disaster in Chicago.* Chicago: University of Chicago Press.

Mental Health Association of San Francisco. 2007. *Tips for assisting people with disabilities.* http://www. nmha.org/emergencyresponse/Shelter_Tips_for_Assisting_People_with_Disabilities.pdf.

Missouri, State of. 2008. *Special needs sheltering standard operating guide for local and county levels emergency management.* http://www.dhss.mo.gov/BT_Response/SpecialNeedsResources.html.

National Capital Region. nd. *NCR mass care standards.* http://www.mwcog.org/committee/committee/login. asp?COMMITTEE_ID=40&id=do.

National Council on Disability. 2009. *Effective Emergency Management: Making Improvements for Communities and People with Disabilities.* Washington, DC: National Council on Disability.

National Council on Disability. 2010. *The State of Housing in America in the 21st century: A Disability Perspective*. Washington, DC: National Council on Disability.

National Organization on Disability. 2005. *Report on Special Needs Assessment for Katrina Evacuees (SNAKE) Project*. http://www.nod.org/index.cfm?fuseaction=Feature.showFeature&FeatureID=1588.

New York, State of. 2008. *Draft New York State Medical and Functional Needs Sheltering Plan*. Albany, NY: Department of Health and Human Services.

Ngo, E. B. 2001. When disasters and age collide: Reviewing vulnerability of the elderly. *Natural Hazards Review* 2(2): 80–89.

Nigg, J. M., J. Barnshaw, and M. R. Torres. 2006. Hurricane Katrina and the flooding of New Orleans: Emergent issues in sheltering and temporary housing. *Annals of the American Academy of Political and Social Science* 604(1): 113–128.

Norris, F. H., M. J. Friedman, and P. J. Watson. 2002a. 60,000 disaster victims speak: Part II. Summary and implications of the disaster mental health research. *Psychiatry* 65(3): 240–260.

Norris, F. H., M. J. Friedman, P. J. Watson, C. M. Byrne, E. Diaz, and K. Kaniasty. 2002b. 60,000 disaster victims speak: Part I. An empirical review of the empirical literature, 1981–2001. *Psychiatry* 65(3): 207–239.

North, C. S. 2008. Psychiatric disorders among transported hurricane evacuees: Acute-phase findings in a large receiving shelter site. *Psychiatric Annals* 38(2): 104–113.

Oklahoma Able Tech. nd. *Social etiquette guide*. http://www.ok.gov/abletech/Fire_Safety/Fire_Safety_Solutions_Grant_Etiquette_Guide.html.

Orange County Florida Department of Health. 2005. *Emergency operations plan, Annex B, Appendix B1, Special needs shelter*. http://www.nmmems.org/pdfs/FlaSpecialNeedsShel.pdf.

Peek, L. 2010. Age. In *Social Vulnerability to Disasters*, eds. B. Phillips, D. Thomas, A. Fothergill, and L. Blinn-Pike. Boca Raton, FL: CRC Press.

Pennebaker, J. W. 1997. *Opening Up*. New York: Guilford Press.

Perry, R. W., and M. K. Lindell. 1997. Aged citizens in the warning phase of disasters: Re-examining the evidence. *International Journal of Aging and Human Development* 44(4): 257–267.

Pike, L., B. Phillips, and P. Reeves. 2006. Shelter life after Katrina: A visual analysis of evacuee perspectives. *International Journal of Mass Emergencies and Disasters* 24(3): 303–330.

Phillips, B. 1993. Cultural diversity in disasters: Sheltering, housing, and long term recovery. *International Journal of Mass Emergencies and Disasters* 11(1): 99–110.

Phillips, B., P. Jenkins, and E. Enarson. 2010. Violence and Disaster Vulnerability. In *Social Vulnerability to Disasters*, eds. B. Phillips, D. Thomas, A. Fothergill, and L. Blinn-Pike. Boca Raton, FL: CRC Press.

Pitt County, North Carolina. 2008. *Pitt County disaster plan for populations with special medical needs*. http://www.co.pitt.nc.us/formslib/emergserv/disaster_plan_special_needs.pdf.

Quarantelli, E. L. 1982. *Sheltering and Housing after Major Community Disasters: Case Studies and General Observations*. Newark, DE: Disaster Research Center, University of Delaware.

Quarantelli, E. L. 1991. Patterns of sheltering and housing in American disasters. Preliminary Paper no. 170. Newark: Disaster Research Center, University of Delaware.

Quarantelli, E. L. 1995. Patterns of sheltering and housing in United States disasters. *Disaster Prevention and Management* 4: 43–53.

San Antonio Office of Emergency Management. nd. *Local hazard response plans*. http://www.sanantonio.gov/emergency/local_plans.asp?res=1280&ver=true.

Seattle Children's Hospital and Regional Medical Center. 2007. *Emergency preparedness for children with special needs*. http://www.cshcn.org/resources/emergencypreparedness.cfm.

U.S. Department of Homeland Security Office for Civil Rights and Civil Liberties. 2008. *Hurricane Ike impact report: Special needs populations impact assessment source document*. http://www.disabilitypreparedness.gov/pdf/ike_snp.pdf.

U.S. Department of Justice. 2007a. *Seventh installment of the toolkit. ADA best practices toolkit for state and local governments*. http://www.ada.gov/pcatoolkit/toolkitmain.htm.

U.S. Department of Justice. 2007b. *Chapter 7 Addendum 1: Title II checklist (emergency management)*. http://www.ada.gov/pcatoolkit/chap7emergencymgmtadd1.htm.

U.S. Department of Justice. 2008. *An ADA guide for local governments: Making community emergency preparedness and response programs accessible to people with disabilities*. http://www.ada.gov/emergencyprepguide.htm.

U.S. Federal Highway Administration. 2009. *Evacuating populations with special needs*. Washington, DC: U.S. Federal Highway Administration.

Waushara County Wisconsin. nd. *Waushara County Human Services: Disaster response plan*. http://www.co.waushara.wi.us/images/DHS%20Disaster%20Response%20Plan.pdf.

Part VI

Disaster Behavioral Health Interventions

16 Initial Behavioral Health Response

The Conundrums of a State Crisis Counseling Program

Julie L. Framingham

CONTENTS

> And I saw Sisyphus in agonising torment trying to roll a huge stone to the top of a hill. He would brace himself, and push it towards the summit with both hands, but just as he was about to heave it over the crest its weight overcame him, and then down again to the plain came bounding that pitiless boulder. He would wrestle again, and lever it back, while the sweat poured from his limbs, and the dust swirled round his head.

> **Bk XI: 593–640**
> *The Odyssey*

16.1 INTRODUCTION

In the wake of disaster, state agencies frequently play a crucial role in the immediate response to impacted communities by determining if a need for behavioral health services exists, and by designing, implementing, and managing behavioral health programs. State behavioral health agencies have access to certain federal funding resources that are unavailable to other organizations involved in disaster response. This chapter will focus on one particular federal funding resource, the Federal Emergency Management Agency's Crisis Counseling Program, and discuss some of the challenges encountered in designing, implementing, and administering the program. In illustration, the experiences of state behavioral health agency staff in Florida as related to programs developed around Hurricane Charley and subsequent disasters that followed from the period of 2004 to 2007 will be examined.[a] Therefore, select issues such as state agency funding, program continuity, grants administration, and jurisdictional concerns encountered by program staff in Florida are addressed, as well as some of the solutions applied. Some of the challenges described are not unique to Florida, however, but have been experienced by other state behavioral health agencies as well. Therefore, it is hoped that this chapter will not only offer some insight on the Crisis Counseling Program's potential obstacles, but encourage other state behavioral health agencies to find creative means to resolve the potential barriers to administering future programs.

16.2   THE CRISIS COUNSELING PROGRAM

The Crisis Counseling Assistance and Training Program (CCP or the Crisis Counseling Program) was first authorized by the Disaster Relief Act of 1974 (Pub. L. 93-288), later amended by Section 416 of the Robert T. Stafford Disaster Relief and Emergency Assistance Act of 1988 (Stafford Act; Pub. L. 100-707). The Stafford Act authorizes the president of the United States, through a disaster declaration, to provide states and U.S. territories with a wide array of public and individual assistance program funds. Pursuant to Title 42, Chapter 68, Subchapter IV, Section 5183:

> The President is authorized to provide professional counseling services, including financial assistance to State or local agencies or private mental health organizations to provide such services or training of disaster workers, to victims of major disasters in order to relieve mental health problems caused or aggravated by such major disaster or its aftermath.

The CCP is jointly administered by the Federal Emergency Management Agency (FEMA) and the U.S. Department of Health and Human Services (HHS), Substance Abuse and Mental Health Services Administration (SAMHSA), Center for Mental Health Services (CMHS), through an interagency agreement (FEMA *Crisis Counseling* nd; SAMHSA nd). CMHS provides training and program oversight, as well as monitoring for Regular Services Programs, for State Mental Health Authorities (SMHA; 42 U.S.C. § 201). In Florida, the SMHA is the Florida Department of Children and Families (DCF). DCF has the responsibility to administer mental health and substance abuse services within the state and is eligible to request grant funding from FEMA for disaster crisis counseling services.

Given the chronic under-funding of many state mental health and substance abuse services, the CCP is an essential resource for SMHAs to assist large numbers of survivors experiencing psychological distress postdisaster. Sanctioned CCP activities include outreach, counseling, public education, and referrals to community resources. Activities are intended to assist survivors to understand their situations and the physical, cognitive, and behavioral reactions that can result, including anxiety, fear, anger, grief, hopelessness, and changes in sleep patterns or appetite. Crisis counselors, sometimes called outreach workers, attempt to alleviate adverse stress reactions in survivors by providing emotional support. Using active listening, they help validate the survivors' reactions and assist them to understand that they are reacting normally to an abnormal event (SAMHSA CCP Program Guidance nd). Psychoeducation is a key component of the CCP and has been demonstrated to be effective in a number of trauma contexts. Psychoeducation can assist individuals, families, and communities by normalizing stress reactions and ameliorating distress, and encourage support seeking, resilience, and community cooperation (Layne et al. 2008; Jacobs, Vernberg, and Lee 2008; Marbley 2007; Naturale 2007; Fremont 2004; AACAP 2007).

Crisis counselors also help survivors review their recovery options and teach coping skills and relaxation techniques, among other nonclinical interventions. Crisis counseling activities are short term and community based and occur at survivors' homes, schools, places of employment, senior centers, and community centers, among other sites (SAMHSA CCP Program Guidance nd). Research suggests that community outreach may be especially helpful for reaching out to and empowering certain vulnerable groups after disaster. These groups include ethnic minorities, older adults, individuals with mental illness, or others who lack social support systems and services, especially when delivered by indigenous, trained workers (Norris and Alegria 2005; Elmore and Brown 2007; Person and Fuller 2007; Hardiman and Jaffee 2008). Further, communications with diverse populations in the community assist outreach workers to overcome biases and become more culturally aware (Goodman and West-Olatunji 2009). CMHS expects SMHAs to develop CCPs that acknowledge the diversity of the communities served by targeting ethnic and racial minorities and hiring indigenous workers who reflect the community's demographic makeup whenever possible (SAMHSA CCP Program Guidance nd).

16.3   ASSESSING THE NEED FOR CRISIS COUNSELING PROGRAM SERVICES

Two funding mechanisms are available to SMHAs through the CCP: (1) the Immediate Services Program, which provides up to 60 days of funding for disaster crisis counseling services, and (2) the Regular Services Program, which provides for an additional nine months of funding (FEMA *Crisis Counseling* nd; SAMHSA nd). The date of the presidential disaster declaration is the start date for both the Immediate Services Program and Regular Services Program (SAMHSA CCP Program Guidance nd). Between 2004 and 2007, Florida's Immediate Services Program grant applications were approved quickly, whereas Regular Services Program grant applications averaged between 8 and 22 weeks for review and approval (Kimber 2007). Requests for no-cost extensions (to extend the program end date without additional funding) or additional-cost extensions of Immediate Services Programs were therefore necessary to avoid services disruption.

Given the copious amount of information that needs to be included in the grant applications, this generally means weeks to months of extended workdays for SMHA staff assessing the needs of the affected communities, gathering the data, and developing the plan of services and the budget. CMHS requires SMHAs to complete the CMHS Needs Assessment Formula for Estimating Disaster Mental Health Needs (CMHS Needs Assessment; included in the grant applications) when calculating the numbers of survivors who might benefit from crisis counseling. The CMHS Needs Assessment follows the FEMA damage assessment concept and includes loss categories of numbers of dead, hospitalized, or otherwise reported injured; homes with minor and major damages, or totally destroyed; and numbers of survivors who became unemployed as a result of the disaster. Each CCP grant application was developed in close consultation with FEMA and CMHS project officers because FEMA damage assessments were not always completed for each county, or they were completed under very difficult conditions, making it impossible to obtain more than a superficial estimate of damages. FEMA Individual Assistance applications for each county are also helpful data for assessing crisis counseling needs, but CMHS discouraged use of these data if using the FEMA damage assessment methodology due to the potential for duplication.

Consequently, DCF program staff had to be resourceful to find ways to include other loss categories or data sources in the formula that would be acceptable to CMHS and FEMA in order to provide more realistic numbers of individuals likely to benefit from crisis counseling. Negotiation was also necessary since the numbers of teams and team members, as well as ratios of crisis counselors to team leaders, were prescribed based on the numbers of survivors calculated to benefit from services in the CMHS Needs Assessment. With each grant application, DCF presented the unique aspects of the impacted counties and the service districts responding to the disaster by highlighting conditions that made the use of standardized staffing formulas problematic. For instance, are the impacted counties mostly urban or rural? In the latter case, teams may have to travel much greater distances to reach survivors. Population density or large cultural groups could also be reasonable grounds to deviate from expected staffing formulas. While the state may include special populations or other circumstances in other sections of the grant application, the CMHS Needs Assessment is given significant weight during the application review.

16.4   THE STATE MENTAL HEALTH AUTHORITY'S RESPONSE TO HURRICANE CHARLEY

In the days leading up to the landfall of Hurricane Charley in August 2004, personnel in the Mental Health Program Office at DCF were busy preparing for the storm's arrival. The National Hurricane Center's tracking and prediction graphic models suggested that the hurricane would strike Florida's Gulf Coast somewhere between the Fort Myers and the Tampa Bay areas with initial reports predicting the latter being the most likely point of landfall (NOAA 2006). In anticipation of Hurricane Charley's arrival, then Governor Jeb Bush executed Executive Order #04-182 on August 11 declaring a State of Emergency (SLAF nd).

On Friday, August 13, 2004, Hurricane Charley, with little warning, turned suddenly from its greatly anticipated landfall near Tampa Bay and slammed into the southwest coast of Florida at Captiva Island, and then Port Charlotte, as a Category 4 storm with winds approaching 150 mph (NOAA 2006). It was the strongest hurricane to hit the United States since Hurricane Andrew in 1992 (FDEP nd). It was also the first time Florida had been struck by two major storms in less than 36 hours (Tropical Storm Bonnie struck northwest Florida on August 12; Avila 2004; FDEP nd). The storm then continued diagonally, north by northeast, across the state, before exiting near Daytona Beach as a Category 2 hurricane. Almost 1.5 million people evacuated their homes. Tens of thousands of homes and businesses were damaged or totally destroyed and more than 2 million residents were left without electricity. Damages exceeded $11 billion. There were 24 hurricane-related deaths and 792 injuries (NOAA nd). Due to the enormity of the disaster, Governor Bush requested federal assistance from the president, who issued a Federal Disaster Declaration, FEMA-1539, the same day (FEMA *Major Disaster* nd). Of Florida's 67 counties, 26 were declared disaster areas eligible for Individual Assistance funding, including the CCP.

It had been several years since the state of Florida had experienced a major disaster or had the need to provide crisis counseling for survivors trying to cope with the emotional aftermath of a storm. Nevertheless, anticipating there would be a need for such a response to Hurricane Charley, the Disaster Behavioral Health Coordinator and other key DCF leaders began discussions about how to prepare a response ahead of the storm's arrival. They formed a small team of workers consisting of several permanent and temporary staff[b] to develop the response.

Fortunately, there were a few team members who had developed CCP grant applications for prior disasters. DCF was also contacted by federal project officers with offers of guidance for developing the grant application. The Disaster Behavioral Health Coordinator[c] had been making preparations throughout the preceding year by obtaining support from the department's senior management should the need arise to provide a behavioral health response to a disaster. He also cultivated useful contacts at other state agencies and nonprofit organizations that could offer assistance during or postdisaster, including the Florida Department of Health, the Department of Elder Affairs, the State Emergency Operations Center, the National Organization for Victim Assistance (NOVA), and Florida Interfaith Networking in Disasters (FIND). FIND played a prominent role in the Department's response as this organization was able to put the DCF in contact with Lutheran Disaster Response and other helpful nongovernmental organizations. Lutheran Disaster Response offered to host daily conference calls for Florida's state agencies and voluntary organizations to help the state provide an adequate level of coverage for behavioral health services in the impacted communities while avoiding duplication. These calls helped establish lasting collaborative partnerships by fostering candid discussion and the sharing of information and resources among the participating agencies.

Before Hurricane Charley, DCF endeavored to increase its capacity to respond to disasters by developing and training a volunteer cadre. Long experience had made DCF's leadership realize that each time a disaster was over and the impacted communities had returned to "normal," the staff who had gained experience working in the disaster drifted away for various reasons. New employment opportunities, relocation, burnout, or disillusionment after prior disaster work, or lack of supervisory support, were recurring grounds for later nonparticipation and contributed to a chronic loss of institutional memory. The agency was also hamstrung by the fact that disaster behavioral health preparedness funding from the Centers for Disease Control and Prevention (CDC) and the Office of the Assistant Secretary for Preparedness and Response (ASPR) is earmarked for ESF 8, Public Health and Medical, agencies. Under the National Response Framework,[d] ESF 8 agencies are tasked to provide disaster behavioral health services.[e] In Florida, however, the ESF 8 agency is the Department of Health, whereas DCF is designated as an ESF 6, Mass Care, agency. ESF 6 agencies are responsible for providing disaster crisis counseling (Sundararaman, Lister, and Williams 2006).[f]

Without preparedness funding, DCF did not have the resources to maintain sufficient staff year-round to prepare for future disasters and sustain its knowledge base. The sustainment problem was not, however, limited to headquarters staff. It was common throughout the DCF system, including its contracted community agencies. Thus, when Hurricane Charley arrived, DCF found itself in the same predicament as before. In fact, the department was to reexperience this same dilemma and others with each succeeding hurricane as Hurricane Charley was quickly followed by Hurricanes Jeanne, Francis, and Ivan in 2004, and Hurricanes Dennis, Wilma, and Katrina[g] in 2005.

DCF distributed its disaster cadre at Disaster Recovery Centers,[h] DCF emergency food stamp locations,[i] comfort stations, or other designated sites established within the impacted areas. The cadre and DCF's disaster partners provided immediate assistance for survivors and freed SMHA staff to develop the grant applications to secure sufficient federal funding for recovery services. Cadre members brought educational materials and set up information tables within the sites. They provided emotional support, listened to the survivors' disaster experiences, provided them with guidance in completing FEMA or other applications for assistance, and steered them to helping resources. One colleague described her first experience as a crisis counselor in a Disaster Recovery Center. She stated a male survivor approached her while she was standing at her information table:

> She asked, "How may I help you sir?" The man immediately exploded into a tirade concerning his frustrations with the disaster, the response process, and the bureaucratic "red tape" that impeded obtaining the assistance that he desperately needed. The crisis counselor's eyes opened wide and she froze in fear. After a couple of minutes, however, she plucked up her nerve and repeated her question.
>
> "Sir, how can I help you?"
>
> Suddenly, the survivor ceased his tirade, took a deep breath and looked at her and said, "I feel much better now. Thank you!" He then walked off without asking for any other assistance or information.[j]

The point illustrated here is that crisis counselors provide a great deal of emotional support simply by listening to survivors' stories. Survivors may not need much more than having someone listen to them and/or some informational materials to help them understand their reactions to the disaster and learn more adaptive ways to cope with current stressors.

16.5 PUBLIC MISCONCEPTIONS

In fact, the term *crisis counseling* is somewhat misleading since all CCP services, even when delivered by licensed behavioral health specialists, are nonclinical in nature. However, the disaster literature suggests that the majority of survivors do not develop long-term posttraumatic psychopathology (Gray, Litz, and Maguen 2004; Davidson and McFarlane 2006), especially in the absence of extensive property damage, injuries and loss of life, or human-caused incidents (Norris et al. 2001). Consequently, no clinical services are authorized under the CCP (SAMHSA CCP Program

Guidance nd). Crisis counselors are expected to refer individuals in need of clinical mental health or substance abuse treatment to preexisting community behavioral health agencies, which frequently have long waiting lists for Medicaid-funded services. An unfortunate consequence of failing to authorize clinical services is that, of those individuals who do go on to develop long-term psychological or substance use disorders, the uninsured and under-insured suffer the most (Sundararaman, Lister, and Williams 2006).

The fact that no clinical services are offered in the CCP appears to contradict the Stafford Act's language, which states that "professional counseling" may be offered to survivors experiencing psychological distress postdisaster (42 U.S.C. § 5183). However, it has been left up to CMHS to determine what constitutes professional counseling (Drury, Scheeringa, and Zeanah 2008). The FEMA CCP instead relies on many of the same principles used in the Psychological First Aid model developed by the National Child Traumatic Stress Network (NCTSN) and the National Center for Posttraumatic Stress Disorder (NCPTSD), which many organizations have endorsed as a preferred intervention for response to emergencies or disasters (Chapter 10, this volume). Similar to the CCP, Psychological First Aid is used in diverse community settings and is designed to provide disaster survivors with nonclinical assistance. Core components of Psychological First Aid involve engaging, comforting, and stabilizing survivors; gathering information about their needs or concerns and offering practical help to satisfy those needs; connecting survivors to social support systems and community resources; and providing information on stress reactions and coping (Brymer et al. 2006).

Misconceptions about what the CCP has to offer survivors has led to a number of misunderstandings with the media and, consequently, with the public. This has at times occurred with painful results, not just for Florida's DCF, but also for other SMHAs that have implemented CCPs. The media have sometimes assumed that crisis counseling refers to clinical counseling, and various news stories have criticized CCPs for failing to provide clinical services. For example, in October 2006, the *New Orleans Times-Picayune* published a news story (Varney 2006) about the SMHA's Louisiana Spirit[k] wherein it criticized FEMA for not allowing CCP funding to be spent on "medical doctors" and instead implied it was being spent on "muffins and coffee." The article further stated that research concerning the CCP's effectiveness is lacking and an expert source was quoted as suggesting that the program possibly causes more harm than good (Varney 2006). The fact that the trauma expert cited in the story referred to the CCP's intervention as "psychological debriefing"[l] suggests he was unaware that the CCP does not permit use of psychological debriefing (SAMHSA CCP Program Guidance nd, 14), which indeed has come under fire as a means of assisting disaster survivors and has been discouraged from practice by some researchers (Rose et al. 1999; Mayou, Ehlers, and Hobbs 2000; Rose et al. 2001; Litz et al. 2002; NIMH 2002).

It is true, however, that there have been few studies of the CCP that sought to examine the program's effectiveness (Elrod, Hamblen, and Norris 2006; Norris, Hamblen, and Rosen 2009; Drury, Scheeringa, and Zeanah 2008). Evaluating the CCP's effectiveness has been difficult because, unlike clients in traditional mental health systems, crisis counseling services are short term (CMHS recommends assessment and referral after three visits; SAMHSA CCP Program Guidance nd, 19) and no personally identifying information is retained. Therefore, it is not possible to obtain pre- and posttest measures of the program's efficacy in ameliorating post-disaster distress (Norris, Hamblen, and Rosen 2009; Drury, Scheeringa, and Zeanah 2008). It is also true that FEMA and CMHS have allowed SMHAs wide latitude in administering CCPs. CCPs use a wide variety of outreach and engagement strategies to identify survivors who might benefit from services. In October 2006, Florida's Hurricane Wilma and Hurricane Katrina Regular Services Programs were criticized by the Fort Lauderdale *Sun-Sentinel* (Kestin 2006a) as a ridiculous waste of taxpayer money because of the staff time expended on what the paper alleged to be frivolous, ineffective strategies to identify and engage survivors. These strategies included dressing in costume and singing songs for preschoolers. The news story featured a performance by crisis counselors dressed in costumes at a preschool where they sang, "Windy

Biggie is our friend. Windy Biggie is strong wind. She turns, turns, turns, turns around. She's knocking things to the ground."

The story also discussed how CCP funds were expended on staff organizing hurricane bingo, puppet shows, and yoga for various organizations as a way to try to identify and reach out to survivors. The crisis counselors interviewed admitted that finding survivors who might really benefit from the CCP was difficult because, despite the fact that the program is FEMA funded, FEMA would not share the names and addresses of FEMA aid registrants due to privacy concerns (Kestin 2006a). This was not always the case, however, but transpired after FEMA instituted a policy change in the late 1990s due to privacy concerns (Elrod, Hamblen, and Norris 2006).

Following the *Sun-Sentinel*'s report, The Honorable Susan M. Collins, Chairman of the Committee on Homeland Security and Governmental Affairs, requested both FEMA and HHS to investigate Project H.O.P.E.'s Hurricane Wilma and Katrina programs to determine if federal funding was being wasted (Department of Homeland Security 2008).[m] The *Sun-Sentinel* continued publishing articles critical of Florida's CCPs over the next few months. In December 2006, the newspaper reported CCPs administered in states other than Florida had also engaged in allegedly inappropriate activities (Kestin 2006b). The article referred to other CCPs (California, Virginia, Wisconsin, and Colorado) offering classes on crafts, martial arts, canning and freezing foods, providing massages, haircuts, and gumbo cook-offs, among other engagement strategies, to identify survivors and offer crisis counseling services (Kestin 2006b). Later, in January 2007, the *Sun-Sentinel* (Kestin 2007) reported that Rep. Tom Feeney, R-Oviedo, and Rep. Mario Diaz-Balart, R-Miami, intended to file a bill to prevent future federal disaster funding from being spent on crisis counseling activities ensuring that "no disaster relief funds are used for any type of crisis counseling, recreation or self-esteem building classes or instruction, including but not limited to dance and exercise classes, bingo, gardening workshops, puppet shows or theater productions." FEMA's initial response to Sen. Collins in December 2008 found that Project H.O.P.E. was spending its funding on "reasonable and approved items and activities" under federal guidelines (Kestin 2007; Department of Homeland Security 2008). FEMA's final report of its findings was not released until September 2008 (Department of Homeland Security 2008). Suffice it to say that there is a genuine need to create a more realistic public perception of crisis counseling.

16.6 TEMPORARY DISASTER EMPLOYMENT

From 2004 to 2007, DCF had to overcome many challenges to the program, and the unfavorable media coverage of the Fort Lauderdale *Sun-Sentinel* was just one head of the hydra. Other barriers to the CCP included the use of temporary disaster workers and unemployment compensation issues. Until 2006, DCF used two options for hiring disaster teams: the teams were either contracted through community behavioral health agencies, or they were hired directly as temporary departmental staff by the service districts in the impacted areas. Contracting through a community agency meant the workers could receive certain fringe benefits that temporary departmental disaster staff members were not given. No line item expenses for vacation or sick leave, pension or unemployment benefits were included in the CCP budgets for temporary departmental workers.

The decision to hire teams as temporary departmental staff or on contract was left up to individual DCF service district managers. Some of the service districts elected to hire CCP teams directly rather than contract them out to community behavioral health agencies. A disadvantage to this hiring method was that the district supervisors were then responsible for supervising many more staff, which could be quite challenging. Direct control and close monitoring of team activities by the DCF service districts, and a relatively quick hiring process, on the other hand, were distinct advantages to hiring temporary departmental workers. Even when there is a gubernatorial declaration of emergency, which waives normal state procurement regulations (F.S. 252.36), the contract execution process can be very time consuming. Further, some service districts did not have any providers that were willing or had the capacity to host large teams of disaster outreach workers.

16.7   PROVIDER AGENCY CAPACITY

Since no indirect costs are permitted in the CCP (SAMHSA CCP Program Guidance nd), contracting CCP teams can present a significant hardship on community agencies that are already financially strained. Contracted community agencies are therefore forced to provide supervision, financial management, and frequently, office space, free of charge. Nevertheless, a number of agencies agreed to host teams citing reasons such as goodwill for their communities and concern that untreated postdisaster distress can develop into long-term mental illness. In the latter instance, this means that more people might eventually become long-term clients of an already beleaguered and overburdened health care system. Some of Florida's contracted agencies, however, simply did not have the capacity to sustain teams, which DCF discovered in a very painful circumstance.

In 2006, DCF's contract with a small agency in southwest Florida had to be terminated abruptly because it could not handle the expenses for the large number of CCP staff on its payroll. Unable to meet its payroll obligations, the agency reached a point where it was giving staff only half of their paychecks or no paychecks at all. The team members were understandably anxious and alarmed. The funding shortfall was attributed in large part to the agency's cost reimbursement-based contracts, the payment methodology used by DCF to ensure compliance with the CCP prohibition on indirect costs. The state's cost reimbursement[n] methodology, however, can seem bewildering since it requires copious amounts of documentation to demonstrate that monies were spent on approved items and activities. It was sometimes several months before providers were reimbursed for their CCP expenses. The service district eventually hired the teams directly as temporary departmental staff. Thus, Florida joined ranks with other states that have experienced similar reimbursement problems according to one study of state disaster crisis counseling programs (Elrod, Hamblin, and Norris 2006).

16.8   UNEMPLOYMENT COMPENSATION

As temporary departmental workers, the staff from the aforementioned agency were paid wages but no fringe benefits, including unemployment compensation, because, under Florida law, employees hired to serve on a temporary basis "in case of fire, storm, snow, earthquake, flood, or similar emergency" are exempt [F.S. 443.1216 (4)(c)3]. At that time, almost half of the CCP's 450 workers were hired as temporary departmental staff. Despite awareness of the temporary nature of the work, some of these temporary staff submitted claims for benefits to the state's employment security agency after the grants ended. DCF service districts fought these claims, and at least some of the cases were denied on appeal by state employment security adjudicators.[o] Consequently, it came as quite a shock when DCF discovered that federal law did not exclude its temporary departmental workers from unemployment benefits. In fact, only very short-term and immediate activities such as firefighting, storm debris removal, public works, and similar activities that must be performed to avoid further harm to individuals, property, or the environment, meet the exclusion. Disasters, on the other hand, suggest extensive devastation and suffering, which require services long after the need for immediate action has ceased. Therefore, personnel engaged in such activities may not be excluded from unemployment compensation benefits (Kilbane 1997).

Consequently, DCF had to request permission from FEMA and CMHS to allow grant budget adjustments to accommodate unemployment compensation for temporary disaster workers. Due to DCF's unemployment compensation rate setting methodology, however, forecasting these expenses accurately was very difficult. As a "reimbursing" employer (F.S. 443.1313), the Department had to reimburse the state employment security agency dollar for dollar on all actual individual claims paid. In contrast, most community agencies have established unemployment tax rates that could be easily budgeted into the CCP grants for reimbursement of claims.[p] Fortunately, there were sufficient unspent grant funds available to cover all of the estimated claims and DCF received approval from FEMA and CMHS to adjust CCP budgets accordingly. There was, however, the possibility that individual unemployment compensation expenses could arise after the end of the grants' service period, a circumstance that would unlikely be remedied by FEMA and CMHS, and had to receive approval from the Florida Legislative Budget Commission (LBC; F.S. 11.90). This is necessary because the Florida Appropriations Act (Chapter 216, F.S.) provides funding for state agencies to pay routine expenses only and does not anticipate special funding for infrequent programs like the CCP. Needless to say, after the turmoil and frustration of dealing with the unemployment compensation issue, DCF elected to contract all field-based CCP services from that point forward.

Indeed, the very existence of the CCP hinged on the Department's ability to obtain spending authority because each Notice of Grant Award (NOGA) required approval from either the state legislature, which convenes annually in the spring, or the LBC, which typically meets only a few times each year (Kimber 2007, 7). Since the statutory exemption from state procurement regulations in a state of emergency expires after 60 days (F.S. 252.36), DCF frequently required urgent assistance from the state emergency management agency and the governor's office to ensure the CCP was explicitly authorized in any extended executive orders. Further, receipt of a Regular Services Program NOGA requires the state to terminate its Immediate Services Program right away (SAMHSA CCP Program Guidance nd). This requirement poses another conundrum since budget authority requests must be presented to the LBC at least one month before it convenes, accompanied by substantiating documentation of need (i.e., the NOGA or other official federal communication of grant approval; Kimber 2007). Consequently, DCF personnel were often in a state of panic to get budget authority requests for new Regular Services Programs to the LBC before the Immediate Services Programs ended. The absence of budget authority would have forced DCF to stop the CCP at a crucial time in the postdisaster recovery period and deprive survivors of the emotional and educational supports they needed to deal with the disaster's aftermath (Kimber 2007, 7).

16.9 CONCLUSION

The issues discussed in this chapter represent a sampling of those experienced by Florida's SMHA staff as they were attempting to develop and manage CCPs during the 2004–2007 hurricane seasons. Since then, Florida's SMHA has developed zero-dollar funded contracts within a provider network consisting of 12 community behavioral health agencies (DCF nd). This network now covers 62 of Florida's 67 counties. The zero-dollar contracts can be easily amended after the state receives a grant award following a major disaster declaration to immediately begin implementing a CCP, thereby substantially reducing the time needed to execute contracts. This development was largely due to the ingenuity and technical skills of the current Disaster Behavioral Health Coordinator. The SMHA still endeavors to maintain a functional disaster cadre for immediate response.

Beginning with Tropical Storm Fay in 2007, Florida's DCF and other state SMHAs have been granted limited access to FEMA's disaster assistance registry. This has allowed CCP teams to focus their outreach during the Immediate Services Program with known survivors potentially in need of crisis counseling. During the Regular Services Programs, the teams can attempt contact with any survivors missed previously or recontact other registrants who may still need crisis counseling or referrals to recovery resources.[q] Without confirmation, it is difficult to determine if this change in information sharing is due to the negative media publicity mentioned earlier or if it is the result of resourceful individuals who have learned ways to work with existing policies and regulations.

There are several lessons to take away from this chapter to inform future crisis counseling programs. First, personnel tasked with implementing disaster crisis counseling services should expect delays and recognize that there may be "extra costs" to administering crisis counseling programs. SMHAs need to ensure disaster cadres are maintained and trained, and that cooperative relationships with disaster partners are in place before a disaster occurs because federal assistance may be delayed or difficult to obtain. State behavioral health agencies should also maintain records, current disaster plans, standard operating procedures and checklists, and conduct disaster exercises to mitigate against institutional memory loss. Furthermore, program advertising should include funding for public "attitude shaping" to explain not only how behavioral health services can assist survivors in postdisaster recovery, but provide a rationale for services limitations. Finally, while state statutes and agency policies may differ, the solutions to program challenges often lay hidden within them. It sometimes takes resourceful and dedicated personnel to tease out the solutions in order to overcome program barriers.

NOTES

a. As Director of Federal Disaster Behavioral Health Projects with the Florida Department of Children and Families from 2005 through 2008, the author managed the Crisis Counseling Program grants and Project Recovery, a program funded by the Substance Abuse and Mental Health Services Administration.

b. These temporary disaster staff included contract and Other-Personal-Services (OPS) workers. Pursuant to Florida Statutes (F.S.), Chapter 110.131, OPS staff may be hired by state agencies to work on a temporary basis and are not entitled to the benefits of permanent state employees.

c. Charles M. Kimber served as the Disaster Behavioral Health coordinator at the Florida Department of Children and Families until his death in August 2007.

d. Homeland Security Presidential Directive 5, Management of Domestic Incidents, established the National Response Plan on February 28, 2003. It was amended on March 22, 2008, and renamed the National Response Framework. See http://www.fema.gov/emergency/nrf/ for additional information.

e. See the Florida Comprehensive Emergency Management Plan, Appendix VIII, at http://www.floridadisaster.org/documents/CEMP/2010/ESF%208.pdf.

f. See the Florida Comprehensive Emergency Management Plan, Appendix VI, at http://www.floridadisaster.org/documents/CEMP/2010/ESF%206.pdf.

g. The department operated a Katrina Evacuee CCP (Immediate Services Program, with extension, and Regular Services Program) from September 2005 to December 2006.

h. See FEMA's web page, *About DRCs*, at http://www.fema.gov/assistance/opendrcs.shtm.

i. Besides being the SMHA, the department is also responsible for administering the Temporary Assistance for Needy Families (TANF) program. See the U.S. Department of Health and Human Services, Administration for Children & Families for more information about this federally funded program at http://www.acf.hhs.gov/programs/ofa/.

j. Thanks to Marilyn Juengst, former CCP program manager, who shared this experience with the author.

k. The Louisiana SMHA's name for the CCP; each state brands its CCP differently.

l. Psychological debriefing generally refers to Critical Incident Stress Debriefing (CISD; Mitchell 1983), which was initially designed to ameliorate adverse psychological sequelae in "first responders" after traumatic events. It was designed to diffuse the intensity of acute stress reactions, which, in turn, reduces the risk of long-term mental disorders.

m. Florida's CCP is branded under the name of Project H.O.P.E. ("Helping Our People in Emergencies").

n. Cost reimbursement allows the state to reimburse providers for actual expenditures incurred, based on a line item budget, which makes it possible to demonstrate that all expenditures were allowable expenses.

o. The author spoke with several adjudication officers in 2006 who heard the appeals of temporary departmental staff employed in the department's CCPs. These officers cited Florida Statute 443.1216 (4)(c)3 as the basis for the exclusion.

p. Nevertheless, laying off numerous contracted staff at the end of a CCP may negatively impact the contributing employer's unemployment compensation tax rate in future quarters.

q. A heartfelt thanks to James (Jimmers) Micallef, DCF's current Disaster Behavioral Health Coordinator, for sharing information about recent developments in Florida's CCPs.

REFERENCES

American Academy of Child and Adolescent Psychiatry (AACAP), Work Group on Quality Issues. 2007. Practice parameter for the assessment and treatment of children and adolescents with anxiety disorders. *Journal of the American Academy of Child and Adolescent Psychiatry 46*(2): 267–283 F.

Avila, L. A. 2004. *Tropical Cyclone Report: Tropical Storm Bonnie 3-13, August 2004.* National Hurricane Center. http://www.nhc.noaa.gov/2004bonnie.shtml.

Brymer M., A. Jacobs, C. Layne, R. Pynoos, J. Ruzek, A. Steinberg, E. Vernberg, and P. Watson. 2006. *Psychological First Aid: Field Operations Guide*, 2nd ed. National Child Traumatic Stress Network and National Center for PTSD. July, 2006. http://www.ptsd.va.gov/professional/manuals/manual-pdf/pfa/PFA_V2.pdf.

Davidson, J., and A. C. McFarlane. 2006. The extent and impact of mental health problems after disaster. *Journal of Clinical Psychiatry 67*(S2): 9–14.

Department of Homeland Security, Office of Inspector General. 2008. *FEMA's Crisis Counseling Assistance and Training Program: State of Florida's Project H.O.P.E.* OIG-08-96. http://www.dhs.gov/xoig/assets/mgmtrpts/OIG_08-96_Sep08.pdf.

Drury, S. S., M. S. Scheeringa, and C. H. Zeanah. 2008. The traumatic impact of Hurricane Katrina on children in New Orleans. *Child Adolescent Psychiatric Clinics of North America 17*(3): 685–702.

Elmore, D. L., and Brown, L. M. 2007. Emergency preparedness and response: Health and social policy implications for older adults. *Generations 31*(4): 66–74.

Elrod, C. L., J. L. Hamblen, and F. H. Norris. 2006. Challenges in implementing disaster mental health programs: State program directors' perspectives. *Annals of the American Academy of Political and Social Science 604*: 152–170.

Federal Emergency Management Agency (FEMA *Crisis Counseling*). nd. *Crisis Counseling Assistance and Training Program.* http://www.fema.gov/assistance/process/additional.shtm#0.

Federal Emergency Management Agency (FEMA *Major Disaster*). nd. *Florida Hurricane Charley and Tropical Storm Bonnie: Major disaster declared August 13, 2004 (DR-1539).* http://www.fema.gov/news/eventcounties.fema?id=3455.

Florida Department of Children and Families (DCF). nd. *Mental Health Services: Disaster behavioral health.* http://www.dcf.state.fl.us/programs/samh/mentalhealth/dbhealth.shtml.

Florida Department of Environmental Protection (FDEP). nd. *Hurricane Charley.* http://www.dep.state.fl.us/beaches/charley.htm.

Fremont, W. P. 2004. Childhood reactions to terrorism-induced trauma: A review of the past 10 years. *Journal of the American Academy of Child and Adolescent Psychiatry 43*(4): 381–92.

Goodman, R. D., and C. A. West-Olatunji. 2009. Applying critical consciousness: Culturally competent disaster response outcomes. *Journal of Counseling and Development 87*(4): 458–465.

Gray, M. J., B. Litz, and S. Maguen. 2004. The acute psychological impact of disaster and large-scale trauma: Limitations of traditional interventions and future practice recommendations. *Prehospital Disaster Medicine 19*(1): 64–72.

Hardiman, E. R., and E. M. Jaffee. 2008. Outreach and peer-delivered mental health services in New York City following September 11, 2001. *Psychiatric Rehabilitation Journal 32*(2): 117–123.

Jacobs, A. K., E. Vernberg, and S. J. Lee. 2008. Supporting adolescents exposed to disasters. *The Prevention Researcher 15*(3): 7–10.

Kestin, S. 2006a. "Fema spends millions on puppet shows, bingo & yoga." *Sun-Sentinel*, October 8. http://articles.sun-sentinel.com/2006-10-08/news/0610070535_1_hurricane-bingo-windy-biggie-project-hope-wilma.

Kestin, S. 2006b. "Disaster grants 'national problem': Florida not alone in using FEMA aid on puppet shows." *Sun-Sentinel*, December 31. http://articles.sun-sentinel.com/2006-12-31/news/0612300349_1_counseling-grants.

Kestin, S. 2007. "Bill to control FEMA spending: Money for puppet shows, dance lessons, massage therapies may be banned." *Sun-Sentinel*, January 6. http://articles.sun-sentinel.com/2007-01-06/news/0701060073_1_hurricane-bingo-crisis-counseling-puppet.

Kilbane, G. A. 1997. *Unemployment Insurance Program Letter No. 22-97.* U.S. Department of Labor. http://wdr.doleta.gov/directives/attach/UIPL22-97.cfm.

Kimber, C. 2007. *Disaster behavioral health: A special report to William Janes, Assistant Secretary of Mental Health and Substance Abuse*. Tallahassee, FL: Florida Department of Children and Families.

Layne, C. M., W. R. Saltzman, L. Poppleton, G. M. Burlingame, A. Pasalić, E. Duraković, M. Musić, N. Campara, N. Dapo, B. Arslanagić, A. M. Steinberg, and R. S. Pynoos. 2008. Effectiveness of a school-based group psychotherapy program for war-exposed adolescents: A randomized controlled trial. *Journal of the American Academy of Child and Adolescent Psychiatry 47*(9): 1048–1062.

Litz, B., M. Gray, R. Bryant, and A. Adler. 2002. Early intervention for trauma: Current status and future directions. *Clinical Psychology: Science and Practice 9*(2): 112–134.

Marbley, A. F. 2007. In the wake of Hurricane Katrina: Delivering crisis mental health services to host communities. *Multicultural Education 15*(2): 17–23.

Mayou, R., A. Ehlers, and M. Hobbs. 2000. Psychological debriefing for road traffic accident victims. *British Journal of Psychiatry 176*: 589–593.

Mitchell, J. 1983. When disaster strikes: The critical incident stress debriefing process. *Journal of Emergency Medical Services 8*: 36–39.

National Institute of Mental Health (NIMH). 2002. Mental Health and Mass Violence: *Evidence-Based Early Psychological Intervention for Victims/Survivors of Mass Violence*. A Workshop to Reach Consensus on Best Practices. NIH Publication No. 02-5138, Washington, DC: U.S. Government Printing Office. http://www.nimh.nih.gov/health/publications/massviolence.pdf.

National Oceanic and Atmospheric Administration (NOAA), National Climatic Data Center. nd. *Event record details*. http://www4.ncdc.noaa.gov/cgi-win/wwcgi.dll?wwevent~ShowEvent~529299.

National Oceanic and Atmospheric Administration (NOAA). 2006. *Service Assessment: Hurricane Charley, August 9–15, 2004*. Silver Spring, MD: U.S. Department of Commerce, National Oceanic and Atmospheric Administration, National Weather Service.

Naturale, A. 2007. Secondary traumatic stress in social workers responding to disasters: Reports from the field. *Clinical Social Work Journal 35*(3):173–181.

Norris, F. H., and M. Alegria. 2005. Mental health care for ethnic minority individuals and communities in the aftermath of disasters and mass violence. *CNS Spectrums 10*(2): 132–140.

Norris, F. H., C. M. Byrne, E. Diaz, and K. Kaniasty. 2001. *50,000 disaster victims speak: An empirical review of the empirical literature, 1981–2001*. Report for the National Center for PTSD and the Center for Mental Health Services (SAMHSA). http://obssr.od.nih.gov/pdf/disaster-impact.pdf.

Norris, F. H., J. L. Hamblen, and C. S. Rosen. 2009. Service characteristics and counseling outcomes: Lessons from a cross-site evaluation of crisis counseling after Hurricanes Katrina, Rita and Wilma. *Administration and Policy in Mental Health 36*(3):176–185.

Person, C., and E. J. Fuller. 2007. Disaster care for persons with psychiatric disabilities. *Journal of Disability Policy Studies 17*(4): 238–248.

Poetry in Translation. 2004. *The Odyssey by Homer*. http://www.poetryintranslation.com/PITBR/Greek/Odhome.htm.

Rose, S. C., J. Bisson, R. Churchill, and S. Wessely. 2001. Psychological debriefing for preventing post traumatic stress disorder (PTSD). *Cochrane Database of Systematic Reviews*, Issue 2. Art. No.: CD000560. DOI: 10.1002/14651858.CD000560.

Rose, S., C. Brewin, B. Andrews, and M. Kirk. 1999. A randomized controlled trial of individual psychological debriefing for victims of violent crime. *Psychological Medicine 29*(4): 793–799.

State Library and Archives of Florida (SLAF), Florida Public Documents Collection. nd. *Executive Order 04-182*. http://edocs.dlis.state.fl.us/fldocs/governor/orders/2004/04-182.pdf.

Substance Abuse and Mental Health Services Administration (SAMHSA) nd. *Crisis Counseling Assistance and Training Program*. http://www.samhsa.gov/dtac/proguide.asp.

Substance Abuse and Mental Health Services Administration (SAMHSA CCP Program Guidance). nd. *Federal Emergency Management Agency Crisis Counseling Assistance and Training Program guidance*. http://www.samhsa.gov/dtac/CCPtoolkit/pdf/CCP_Program_Guidance.pdf.

Sundararaman, R., S. A. Lister, and E. D. Williams. 2006. *Gulf Coast Hurricanes: Addressing Survivors' Mental Health and Substance Abuse Treatment Needs*. Report RL33738, ed. Congressional Research Service. Washington, DC: The Library of Congress. http://stuff.mit.edu/afs/sipb/contrib/wikileaks-crs/wikileaks-crs-reports/RL33738.pdf.

Varney, J. 2006. "Post-storm mental health plan comes with a catch: Critic says program is not likely to help." *Times-Picayune*, October 2. http://www.nola.com/news/t-p/frontpage/index.ssf?/base/news-6/115976875190040.xml&coll=1&thImmediate Services Programage=1.

17 Long-Term Mental Health Treatment for Adult Disaster Survivors

Jessica L. Hamblen, Erin Barnett, and Fran H. Norris

CONTENTS

17.1 INTRODUCTION

The impact of major disasters on mental health is well understood. Posttraumatic stress disorder (PTSD) is the most commonly studied mental health problem observed in these studies (Norris and Elrod 2006; Norris et al. 2002). Prevalence rates range from 30 percent to 40 percent among direct victims, 10 percent to 20 percent among rescue workers, and 5 percent to 10 percent among the general population (Galea, Nandi, and Vlahov 2005).

In this chapter we review long-term mental health treatments for adult disaster survivors. Bryant and Litz (2009) distinguished intermediate or long-term interventions designed to prevent or treat psychopathological responses from immediate or short-term interventions designed to promote safety and stabilization. They made the important point that the decision about which intervention to implement is not based on the amount of time that has passed, but rather on the degree of ongoing threat and stability (Bryant and Litz 2009). A survivor who is worried about the life of a loved one, caring for an injured family member, homelessness, or being unemployed cannot focus on his or her own mental health needs. Thus, a World Trade Center survivor might be ready for long-term treatment several months after the attack while a Katrina survivor might not be ready for close to a year because the infrastructure in Louisiana was severely disrupted due to the massive flooding after Katrina.

The best information on effective treatments for disaster comes from the strong treatment outcome literature on PTSD. Although only a minority of these studies include disaster samples, this broader literature has been shown to generalize across trauma types. Additional information comes from the small but emerging literature on disaster-specific treatments. We review each of these areas with a focus on interventions appropriate for long-term recovery. We consider issues of comorbidity and how conditions such as depression, substance abuse, and grief can be addressed. We end with a review of barriers to care and what factors might prevent survivors from utilizing effective treatments and clinicians from delivering them. We pay specific attention to cultural and socioeconomic barriers.

17.2 LONG-TERM TREATMENTS

17.2.1 PTSD TREATMENT

Several clinical practice guidelines from different federal agencies, professional organizations, and countries offer recommendations for the treatment of PTSD (Australian Centre for Posttraumatic Mental Health 2007; Foa, Keane, and Friedman 2009; National Collaborating Centre for Mental Health 2005; Ursano et al. 2004; VA/DoD Clinical Practice Guideline Working Group 2003). The Institute of Medicine (IOM) also recently published a report evaluating the evidence on PTSD treatment (Institute of Medicine 2008). The guidelines unanimously recommend cognitive behavioral therapies as the most effective treatment for PTSD.

Cognitive behavioral treatments (CBTs) typically include a number of components, including psychoeducation, anxiety management, exposure, and cognitive strategies. Exposure and cognitive restructuring are thought to be the most effective components. Exposure involves having survivors repeatedly reexperience their traumatic event by confronting feared situations by imagining their traumatic event (imaginal exposure) and/or by entering previously avoided situations that elicit fear (*in vivo* exposure). Cognitive strategies have a primary focus on challenging and modifying maladaptive beliefs related to the trauma. We will review exposure interventions first, followed by the cognitive ones. Many cognitive behavioral treatments include both components or aspects of both components.

There is strong evidence for exposure therapy's effectiveness in a wide range of populations, including those who have experienced sexual assault, childhood sexual abuse, motor vehicle accidents, crime, and mixed trauma samples (e.g., Bryant et al. 2003; Cloitre et al. 2002; Foa et al. 1999; Foa et al. 2005; Blanchard et al. 2003; Marks et al. 1998; Schnurr et al. 2007). Further, although study samples have included mainly middle-aged survivors, exposure therapies have been found to be effective in women and men of various racial backgrounds (Cloitre et al. 2002; Foa et al. 1999; Foa et al. 2005; Schnurr et al. 2007). Of these various approaches, prolonged exposure (PE), developed by Edna Foa, has received the most attention. In Foa's first trial, PE, stress inoculation training (SIT), and to a lesser extent supportive counseling were all more effective in reducing PTSD, rape-related distress, anxiety, and depression than a waitlist control in a small sample of 45 female sexual assault survivors (Foa et al. 1991).

In an attempt to optimize the effects of exposure, PE was combined with other effective treatments in the next two trials. Unexpectedly, the combined treatments fared worse. In the first, PE alone was more effective than the combination of PE plus SIT, SIT alone, or a waitlist control (Foa et al. 1999) on symptoms of PTSD, depression, and anxiety. The authors concluded that the combination of PE plus SIT, which was expected to be superior, may have overloaded the client with techniques since SIT included a variety of techniques.

In response to the previous study, in the next trial a single technique, cognitive restructuring (CR), was added. One hundred seventy-one female survivors of sexual assault, physical assault, or childhood sexual abuse were randomized to PE alone, PE plus CR, or waitlist (Foa et al. 2005). While both active treatments were superior to waitlist on PTSD and depression, again the combined treatment was no more effective than PE alone. The authors offered two possible explanations (Foa et al. 2005). The first was that the effect of equating treatments reduced the necessary dose of PE. That is, in order to equate the amount of time in the two active treatments the dose of PE was reduced and may not have reached a therapeutic level. A second suggestion was that the approaches included similar elements, and therefore the effect of combining elements amounts to switching one effective element for another.

Other investigators who have added a novel component to an exposure treatment in an effort to optimize the treatment have found similar results (e.g., Arntz, Tiesema, and Kindt 2007; Cloitre et al. 2002; Falsetti, Resnick, and Davis 2008; Glynn et al. 1999). For example, behavioral family therapy following exposure therapy added nothing to exposure therapy alone in terms of PTSD improvement (Glynn et al. 1999). In addition, imagery rescripting (or modifying an image to decrease distress), in conjunction with imaginal exposure, added nothing to imaginal exposure alone (Arntz et al. 2007). These findings suggest that the novel components were not necessary.

Several others have evaluated PE and found it effective (e.g., Schnurr et al. 2007; Taylor et al. 2003). For example, in a recent multisite randomized controlled trial of PE with female veterans and active-duty personnel with PTSD, women who received PE experienced a greater reduction of PTSD symptoms and were less likely to meet diagnostic criteria for PTSD relative to women who received present-centered therapy (Schnurr et al. 2007). In another investigation (Resick et al. 2002), PE alone was compared to a cognitive intervention, Cognitive Processing Therapy (CPT), and a waitlist control. Both PE and CPT were superior to waitlist, but there were few differences between the active treatments.

Exposure has also been compared to eye movement desensitization and reprocessing (EMDR), a CBT that involves engaging in imaginal exposure to a trauma while simultaneously performing saccadic eye movements. Several clinical practice guidelines list EMDR as an effective treatment. Two well-controlled studies compared EMDR to PE. One study (Rothbaum, Astin, and Marsteller 2005) found equivalent results while the other found PE to be superior (Taylor et al. 2003). However, although studies support the effectiveness of EMDR, additional research has raised questions about the mechanism of action. There is growing evidence that the theorized eye movements are an unnecessary component (Davidson and Parker 2001), which suggests that the mechanism for action might be the exposure component.

Although widely researched, prolonged exposure is not the only form of exposure therapy. Others have used imaginal and in vivo exposure with and without cognitive components with equal success (e.g., Arntz et al. 2007; Blanchard et al. 2003; Glynn et al. 1999; Marks et al. 1998). Thus, exposure is effective in various forms and with a range of trauma types. Exposure therapy for PTSD also seems to have a significant effect on reducing comorbid depression and anxiety. However, add-ons to exposure do not appear to boost its effectiveness.

Cognitive interventions also are widely supported in treatment guidelines (Duffy, Gillespie, and Clark 2007; Ehlers et al. 2005; Marks et al. 1998; Mueser et al. 2008). CPT (Resick and Schnicke 1996), one of the most well-researched cognitive approaches, has a primary focus on challenging and modifying maladaptive beliefs related to the trauma, but also includes a written exposure component. Developed by Patricia Resick, CPT was initially shown to be as effective as PE and more effective in treating PTSD, depression, and guilt than a minimal attention control condition in a study of 171 female sexual assault survivors (Resick et al. 2002). CPT has also been shown to be effective for male and female veterans with military-related PTSD (Monson et al. 2006). Sixty veterans were randomized to CPT or a waitlist. Intention-to-treat analyses revealed significant improvements in PTSD and comorbid symptoms in the CPT condition compared with the waitlist condition. After treatment, 40 percent of the CPT group no longer met criteria for PTSD.

In contrast to the study of PE, once CPT was shown to be effective, the treatment developers conducted a dismantling study to determine the relative utility of the full protocol compared with its components: cognitive therapy and written exposure (Resick et al. 2008). All three treatments resulted in significant improvement in PTSD. However, cognitive therapy alone resulted in faster improvement than written exposure, with the effects of the full protocol falling in between (Resick et al. 2008).

Just as there are various approaches to exposure, there are also different forms of cognitive therapy. For example, Ehlers and Clark developed a cognitive therapy for PTSD that involves three goals: (1) modifying excessively negative appraisals, (2) correcting disturbances in autobiographical memory, and (3) removing problematic behavioral and cognitive strategies (Ehlers and Clark 2000). In a small, randomized controlled trial, 28 survivors of accident, assault, or witnessing death improved significantly more on PTSD, depression, and anxiety in cognitive therapy compared to waitlist (Ehlers et al. 2005). Mueser and Rosenberg (Mueser et al. 2004) developed a CR for PTSD program that includes education, breathing retraining, and CR taught as a general self-management skill for dealing with any negative feeling rather than solely using it to target trauma-related cognitions. Results showed that CR was more effective than usual care for treating PTSD, depression, and anxiety in people with severe mental illness, including borderline personality disorder and psychotic disorders (Mueser et al. 2008).

In sum, like exposure-based treatments, there is strong support for the effectiveness of cognitive therapy. Cognitive interventions have been evaluated in women and men, sexual assault survivors, veterans, people with severe mental illness, and mixed trauma samples, and with a variety of approaches. However, aside from the CPT dismantling study (Resick et al. 2008), racial diversity has been limited, and each study sample consists primarily of middle-aged survivors. Nevertheless, these treatments appear to target depression and anxiety in addition to PTSD.

Currently, there is more consistent support for CBT than for medications in the treatment of PTSD. In fact, there is some disagreement among the clinical practice guidelines as to whether pharmacotherapy should be considered a frontline treatment for PTSD (see Friedman 2008). However, at times survivors may choose a medication over psychotherapy or may want a combination of both. Two selective serotonin reuptake inhibitors (SSRIs), sertraline and paroxetine, have been approved by the U.S. Food and Drug Administration for the treatment of PTSD. Both have been evaluated in multisite randomized controlled trials with survivors (Brady et al. 2000; Davidson, Pearlstein, et al. 2001; Davidson, Rothbaum, et al. 2001; Marshall et al. 2001) with positive results. There is also a positive trial of the SSRI fluoxetine (Martenyi et al. 2002). However, negative trials have been reported as well (Friedman et al. 2007; Martenyi, Brown, and Caldwell 2007) and the results for medications are typically less impressive than those found with CBT (see Friedman, Davidson, and Stein 2009 for a review of medications for PTSD).

17.2.2 CBT for Disaster-Related PTSD

A few studies have evaluated treatment for disaster-related PTSD. In early studies with earthquake survivors in Turkey, Basoglu and colleagues found that one to two sessions of CBT or exposure to artificial tremors in an earthquake simulator significantly reduced PTSD symptoms (Basoglu, Livanou, and Salcioglu 2003; Basoglu et al. 2003). Two later randomized controlled trials involved a single-session exposure intervention compared to either a wait-list control or repeated assessment (Basoglu, Salcioglu, and Livanou 2007; Basoglu et al. 2005). Findings suggested the single-session behavioral treatment given approximately three years post-disaster produced a substantial decrease in PTSD symptoms. Given the promising implications of this trial for expedient and cost-effective treatment, these results are in need of replication.

In other preliminary work, Gillespie and colleagues (Gillespie et al. 2002) studied the effectiveness of Ehlers and Clark's cognitive therapy in 91 survivors of a bombing in Northern Ireland 10 months post-bombing. All survivors had PTSD related to the bombing. After treatment, the survivors had significant improvement in PTSD, depression, and general health. In response to these promising results, the research team randomized 58 survivors of terrorism and other civil conflict to either cognitive therapy or waitlist (Duffy et al. 2007). At posttreatment, participants in cognitive therapy demonstrated significantly greater improvement in self-reported PTSD, depression, and functioning than those in the waitlist with continued improvement in those who received additional sessions (Duffy et al. 2007)

A third research team focused on providing treatment to survivors and disaster workers from the World Trade Center. One study utilized a quasi-experimental design in which survivors were assigned to a virtual reality or a matched waitlist control group. Results indicated significant improvement in PTSD in the virtual reality group compared to waitlist (Difede, Cukor et al. 2007). In the other study, 31 disaster workers were randomized to CBT or "treatment as usual" (TAU; Difede, Malta et al. 2007). CBT included psychoeducation, breathing retraining, imaginal and in vivo exposure, cognitive reprocessing, and relapse prevention. TAU included an assessment with referral for PTSD treatment with a community provider. Over half of the CBT and an eighth of the TAU participants dropped out of treatment. For those who completed treatment, participants in CBT showed significant improvement in PTSD relative to those in TAU, although no participants followed through on the referral. Intention-to-treat analyses yielded no significant effects, likely because of the high dropout rate.

In another study of World Trade Center victims, therapists at an outpatient clinic were taught Skills Training in Affective and Interpersonal Regulation/Modified Prolonged Exposure (STAIR/MPE), a CBT that adds affect regulation and interpersonal skills into a prolonged exposure treatment. Significant decreases in PTSD, depression, and social adjustment were observed and were similar to results found in a randomized controlled trial of the same treatment (Levitt et al. 2007).

One other study is worth mentioning for its novelty in responding to disaster. The study involved a public mental health program initiated in response to the London bombings. The program involved two components, screening and treatment (Brewin et al. 2008). Extensive efforts were made to identify and screen individuals involved in the bombings to identify either preexisting mental health problems or mental health problems stemming from the bombings. If new problems were identified, individuals could either be referred for immediate trauma-focused treatment or monitored to determine if the problem would resolve on its own and then referred if necessary. Treatment resources included existing programs that utilized licensed clinical psychologists offering trauma-focused CBT or EMDR. Therapists were supervised by specialists, and treatment and travel costs were reimbursed.

The program screened 596 individuals, 346 of whom received a more-detailed assessment to determine whether a referral was indicated. PTSD was the predominant diagnosis. Seventy-four percent were referred for treatment, while 26 percent were judged to require monitoring only. Preliminary outcome data were available for 82 individuals, 72 of whom completed treatment. Treatment yielded large-effect sizes for PTSD and depression (Brewin et al. 2008).

Overall, there is a strong and growing literature supporting the use of cognitive behavioral treatments for disaster-related PTSD. These treatments have been used with survivors of terrorism and natural disaster. In each trial, survivors who receive CBT improve relative to waitlist conditions. Importantly, improvements are regularly seen in depression, anxiety, and functioning in addition to PTSD. These findings do, however, need to be extended to diverse populations, as most of the survivors studied were middle-aged women (Basoglu et al. 2007; Basoglu et al. 2005; Brewin et al. 2008; Gillespie et al. 2002; Levitt et al. 2007). Many authors did not report racial/ethnic backgrounds of their samples.

17.2.3 Disaster-Specific Treatments

To our knowledge, our Hamblen and colleagues (Hamblen et al. 2006) are the only ones to develop a treatment for the long-term response that is focused more broadly on postdisaster distress rather than PTSD specifically. Postdisaster distress encompasses a range of cognitive, emotional, and behavioral reactions to disaster, including symptoms of PTSD, depression, stress vulnerability, and functional difficulties. Postdisaster distress is not a psychiatric diagnosis. Within certain limits, distress is perfectly natural and normal and can be expected to improve on its own. Sometimes, however, this distress becomes severe and/or prolonged enough to interfere with quality of life.

There are several advantages to this approach (Hamblen et al. 2006). First, it could assist individuals who present with other primary reactions, such as depression, mixed conditions, or subclinical conditions. Although the PTSD treatment studies reviewed previously demonstrate effects beyond PTSD, disaster survivors without a primary PTSD diagnosis are excluded from these treatments. Second, a treatment focused on postdisaster distress or stress is potentially more acceptable to survivors who may be suffering from mental health problems for the first time. Finally, a single treatment focused on distress as opposed to diagnosis reduces the need for extensive assessment and can be disseminated to community clinicians through a single training (rather than through multiple trainings for disorders) and increases the feasibility of the treatment's use in community settings.

Cognitive Behavioral Therapy for Postdisaster Distress (CBT-PD; Hamblen et al. 2006) is a manualized disaster-specific intervention that has a primary focus on identifying and challenging maladaptive disaster-related beliefs. It includes psychoeducation, breathing retraining, behavioral activation, and cognitive restructuring. Evaluation was minimal in the first pilots of the approach, taking place in New York after the World Trade Center bombings (Donahue et al. 2006) and in Florida after the 2004 Hurricanes Bonnie, Charley, Frances, Ivan, and Jeanne (Hamblen and Norris 2007), but preliminary results were promising. In a subsequent study employing a quasi-experimental repeated measures design, 88 racially diverse adult survivors of Hurricane Katrina were given CBT-PD and were assessed at referral, pretreatment, intermediate treatment, and posttreatment (Hamblen et al. 2009). The overall pre-posteffect size was 1.4 in intention-to-treat analyses, demonstrating CBT-PD resulted in large and significant improvements in distress. Benefits were maintained at five-month follow-up.

17.2.4 CONSIDERING COMORBIDITY

Although PTSD is the most common mental health problem after disaster, depression, anxiety, and increased substance use are frequent as well. Depending on the nature of the disaster, prolonged grief can also be an area of concern if there was significant loss of life. In our opinion, depression and anxiety can often be addressed as part of the PTSD treatment. As reviewed before, most CBTs for PTSD also significantly reduce depression and anxiety. Similarly, medications effective for PTSD also target symptoms of anxiety and depression.

Substance abuse problems are another area of concern after disaster (see Chapter 18, this volume, for more on this topic). After a disaster, survivors may relapse or use more heavily than before the disaster, but new onset substance abuse problems are rare (North et al. 1999). A series of studies on the use of cigarettes, alcohol, and marijuana among New York City residents after the World Trade Center attack demonstrated an increase in substance use immediately following the attack (Vlahov et al. 2002); however, it was still true that the percentage of new onset cases was relatively small (2.2 percent) compared to the number of new onset cases of PTSD (Vlahov et al. 2006).

Few treatments exist to treat comorbid PTSD and substance use. The most popular treatment is Seeking Safety (SS). SS is a present-focused therapy that focuses on teaching coping skills that are relevant to both PTSD and substance use. There are 25 topics that address cognitive, behavioral, interpersonal, and case management issues. Data from two large randomized controlled trials of SS both demonstrated significant reductions in PTSD symptoms, but SS was no more effective than either active control condition (relapse prevention or women's health education) in reducing PTSD symptoms. Outcomes related to substance use were inconsistent. While both SS and relapse prevention resulted in improved substance outcomes in the first study, there was no effect of SS or women's health education on substance use in the second study (Hien et al. 2004; Hien et al. 2009). Thus, at this point the literature does not support its use as a PTSD or substance abuse treatment, although it may be an effective treatment engagement strategy.

Two models have been proposed to account for the association between PTSD and SUD (Jacobsen, Southwick, and Kosten 2001). In one case, the PTSD is primary and patients drink to cope with PTSD symptoms. In the other case, SUD is primary and patients' substance use places them in risky environments where they are more likely to be traumatized. Data support the first model (Chilcoat and Breslau 1998a, 1998b), sometimes called the self-medication theory, where patients use substances to manage their PTSD symptoms. Given the state of the literature and the proposed relationship between PTSD and substance use, our current recommendation is that when possible, individuals with substance abuse problems should be included in cognitive behavioral treatments for PTSD. Pilot work under way suggests that both PE and CPT can be effective in treating PTSD in people with the comorbid condition and may reduce substance use as well (E. Foa personal communication, October 14, 2009; K. Chard personal communication, October 6, 2009).

Prolonged grief is a condition that can be observed after trauma when there is a major loss, such as the death of a spouse or child. Prolonged grief has also been called complicated grief or traumatic grief (Prigerson et al. 2009). Prolonged grief is more persistent, consuming, and debilitating than is normal grief. Now under evaluation for inclusion in the *Diagnostic and Statistical Manual*, 5th ed. (APA, in press), prolonged grief disorder describes a severe condition wherein the bereaved person has experienced both separation distress, characterized as an intense yearning for the deceased person, and a high co-occurring frequency of cognitive, emotional, or behavioral symptoms such as avoidance, shock, confusion, trouble accepting loss, difficulty trusting others, bitterness, difficulty moving on, emotional numbness, and sense of meaninglessness. Symptoms must persist for at least six months and result in significant functional impairment (Prigerson et al. 2009).

Although prolonged grief disorder shares some symptoms with depression and anxiety (most notably PTSD), it has repeatedly been shown to differentiate from the two (Prigerson et al. 2009). Few treatments exist for prolonged grief; we were able to identify only one randomized controlled trial. Shear and colleagues developed a complicated grief treatment that includes both interpersonal psychotherapy (IPT) components for the depressive symptoms and cognitive behavioral therapy components for the intrusive and avoidant symptoms (Shear et al. 2005). IPT focuses on helping patients arrive at a more realistic assessment of the relationship with the deceased and identifying positive and negative aspects of the relationship. Cognitive behavioral therapy includes both in vivo and imaginal exposure. The patient is asked to complete a "revisiting" exercise in which they tell the story of the deceased's death. They are also asked to have an imaginary conversation with the deceased in which the patient asks questions and then takes on the role of the deceased to answer. In a randomized controlled trial comparing the complicated grief treatment to IPT alone, 51 percent of participants in the complicated grief treatment responded to the treatment compared to 28 percent of participants in IPT alone (Shear et al. 2005).

While the results of the trial were promising, more than half of participants in the grief treatment continued to present with symptoms following the treatment. In addition, only a minority of deaths were from unnatural causes such as a natural disaster or terrorism. Thus, it is not clear whether participants who were grieving from "traumatic" deaths would respond similarly. Another limitation was that while almost half of participants had current PTSD, PTSD was not assessed as an outcome measure. Thus, it is impossible to determine if the grief treatment targeted the PTSD symptoms as well. It may be that when loss of life is due to a traumatic event, a PTSD-specific treatment may be indicated.

17.2.5 TREATMENT SUMMARY

The previous treatment review should help inform clinicians and policy makers on the range of treatments that are available following disaster. There is a strong evidence base for using cognitive behavioral treatments for PTSD and a growing one in support of their use with disaster survivors, although findings need to be extended to diverse populations, particularly to the young, the elderly, and members of racial minority groups. These treatments are highly effective for PTSD, but also often treat comorbid problems. Novel treatment approaches are also in development for use with survivors with postdisaster distress who may either not have PTSD or may be resistant to being labeled with a mental disorder. Finally, researchers are starting to consider how to provide more integrated care for some conditions such as substance abuse and prolonged grief.

17.3 BARRIERS TO CARE

In the second half of the chapter, we turn to barriers to care. Even if we can identify the best treatments for the long-term response to disaster, they are only effective if survivors access them and providers deliver them with efficacy. We begin by defining the relevant concepts. By utilization, we mean connecting with and using available services; retention refers to completing an adequate "dose" of an intervention so improvements are possible. Other important concepts include "need" and "demand" for mental health services. We believe that at times these constructs are used interchangeably when they really should be considered distinct. At the population level, need can be defined as the number of individuals directly affected by a disaster who could benefit from receiving mental health services. However, it has repeatedly been shown that not all people who *need* services seek them. Thus, we define demand as those individuals who actually seek mental health care.

The distinction between need and demand is important because some researchers have asserted that mental health "needs" following disasters often exceed the services available in a community (Marshall et al. 2006). Some researchers have also predicted that optimal mental health response programs, those predicted to have high recovery rates and avert long-term public health costs, would exceed available providers (Schoenbaum et al. 2009). However, the ways in which need has been defined in the literature likely includes many individuals who will neither desire nor seek care. In our experience, demand is rarely equivalent to need, and only a small portion of those who may need services ever demand them. However, there are many barriers to utilization.

17.3.1 UTILIZATION OF MENTAL HEALTH SERVICES

17.3.1.1 Utilization Rates

It is no surprise that disasters are followed by increases in psychological symptoms (Norris et al. 2002) and that many who likely need or demand services do not receive care. For example, researchers estimated that six months after Hurricane Katrina, 31 percent of individuals living in the areas affected by the hurricane acquired mental health disorders (need); yet only one-third (32 percent) of these individuals had utilized services (Wang et al. 2007). Following the 9/11 terrorist attacks, estimates of between 11 percent and 36 percent of those with mental health disorders sought mental health care (DeLisi et al. 2003; Stuber et al. 2006). Further, among individuals who do demand and enroll in services, retention rates are poor. Wang et al. reported that 64 percent attended only one or two visits to health or mental health care agencies following Hurricane Katrina. Similarly, 55 percent of those enrolled in a cognitive-behavioral treatment study following Hurricane Katrina did not complete treatment (Hamblen et al. 2009), even thought the treatment was free and offered in many convenient locations. The high proportion of individuals who need care yet do not seek or receive it is alarming considering the public health relevance of psychiatric conditions after disasters, such as PTSD, major depression, and anxiety (Norris et al. 2002).

17.3.1.2 Variables Related to Utilization

Recent investigations in postdisaster contexts have begun to uncover factors that relate to utilization. Because the literature often does not distinguish between need and demand, we will attempt to disentangle these concepts throughout our discussion. Anderson's Behavioral Model of health care utilization (Andersen and Newman 1973) has been applied and validated in numerous studies of trauma and disaster victims (Anderson 1995; Elhai and Ford 2009; Koenen et al. 2003). The model outlines three factors that impact utilization: need, predisposing factors, and enabling factors. In this model, need refers to both perceived need for help and severity of symptoms. Predisposing factors include historical or sociodemographic characteristics. Enabling factors encompass access to resources and availability of interventions. In a recent meta-analysis of 25 studies investigating utilization of mental health services after disasters, Elhai and Ford (2009) found that the need variables of severity of PTSD, depression, and anxiety had the largest bearings on utilization. The predisposing variables of more stressful life events, more exposure to trauma and disaster, and being middle-aged were also positively related to utilization. Enabling factors were not strongly related to utilization, although, notably, these variables were the least likely to be included in studies.

Although enabling factors did not strongly relate to utilization in the meta-analysis, raising awareness and increasing availability of psychological care is an obvious important step following disasters. Survivors cannot utilize treatment unless they are aware of it and it is available to them. To this end, large-scale mental health response programs have been implemented in the wake of disasters. One such program following the 9/11 World Trade Center attacks, Project Liberty, spent $9.4 million on marketing in the three months following the event (Frank et al. 2006). Researchers reported that 24 percent of New York City inhabitants were aware of the project. However, awareness was not enough to improve utilization. Of those who were aware, 67 percent had a good impression of the project, yet only 23 percent reported they would call the hotline for services (estimate of demand; Rudenstine et al. 2003). Higher socioeconomic status was related to awareness of the program, whereas indications of underprivileged status (e.g., racial minority, lower income, immigrant), as well as severity of PTSD symptoms (need), were positively related to estimated demand.

In an effort to further assess whether mental health needs were met following the 9/11 World Trade Center attacks, a random digit dial phone survey was initiated in the NYC metropolitan area six months following the attack (Stuber et al. 2006). Seventeen percent of those with probable PTSD or depression (need) considered mental health treatment. Of those with probable diagnoses who considered but did not seek care, the most frequently reported barriers included believing that other people needed the help more than they did (58 percent), perceptions of not having enough time (42 percent) and money (39 percent), perceived stigma associated with having a mental illness (27 percent), lack of knowledge of services (17 percent), and preferences to take care of the problems on their own or with the help of family (14 percent). Prior emotional problems and sexual abuse, previous mental health services, and current physical health problems increased the likelihood of utilization (Stuber et al. 2006).

Other investigators have found that many people who need mental health care do not utilize services because they do not know or do not believe that effective treatments are available (Pietrzak et al. 2009). In our experience, the competing demands and stressors that accompany disasters, such as property damage, displacement, and financial and resource loss, also serve as significant barriers to mental health care utilization.

17.3.1.3 Utilization of At-Risk Groups

Although being a member of an underprivileged or minority group (racial minority, physical disability, etc.) did not significantly relate to utilization in Elhai and Ford's (2009) meta-analysis, much attention has been focused on the vulnerability of at-risk groups. Some research has shown that not only are marginalized groups at greater risk for psychiatric problems following disasters than nonmarginalized groups, they also have unequal access to information about impending disasters and are treated differently during relief efforts (Stough 2009). For example, statistics show that the elderly and persons with disabilities in institutions are overrepresented among disaster fatalities (Cook and Elmore 2009). As a result, recent attention has been given to the complexities of disaster preparedness, response, and recovery for long-term care facilities (Dosa et al. 2008; Hyer et al. 2006).

In addition, professionals argue that members of marginalized groups have more barriers to recovery than do able-bodied and able-minded persons and are at higher risk for postdisaster psychiatric problems (Hawkins et al. 2009; Stough 2009). Researchers assert that this increased risk is accounted for by an interaction of various pre-, peri-, and postdisaster factors, including important socioeconomic and sociocultural variables (Hawkins et al. 2009). For example, key differences between groups exist in terms of risk perceptions, disaster preparation, prior traumatic experiences, cultural beliefs (e.g., external locus of control, mistrust of professionals), and help-seeking behaviors (e.g., use of family or kin rather than professionals). Taken together with the reality that marginalized communities often have weaker infrastructures to support interventions and less access to culturally competent interventions and resources (e.g., documents and services only provided in English), we can glean a clearer picture of why these groups might not utilize mental health services (Hawkins et al. 2009).

17.3.1.4   Recommendations for Improving Utilization

It is our belief that it is not enough just to set up a disaster treatment program and hope that survivors will access it. Even the most expensive media campaigns fail to enroll the majority of survivors in need of treatment. Special attention must be paid to identifying those survivors in the greatest need of services and finding ways of making the treatments more acceptable to these groups. We suggest that disaster treatment programs work with social service and crisis agencies to determine: the groups most in need, appropriate outreach strategies to reach these groups, and unique barriers to care for these groups. Marketing and recruitment should also aim to make individuals aware that there are enough services to go around and that they personally deserve treatment. Individuals also need to be informed that mental health care is often of no cost to them following disasters; government and grant-funded programs are put into place due to the expected mental health problems that can occur.

The needs of special populations should be considered as well. For example, following the World Trade Center attack, a special effort was made to reach out to undocumented workers who may have been working in the World Trade Center. In addition, materials had to be translated into multiple languages in order to make the treatments acceptable to non-English-speaking survivors. Similarly, in Florida the elderly were a population of concern after the 2004 hurricanes. Older adults are often not able to come to the therapist for an office visit and may require more time to comprehend the treatment material. More generally as a field, we need to understand more about why individuals underutilize and drop out of treatment. Investigators are encouraged to consider this research question when designing studies and analyzing outcomes.

17.3.2   Treatment Dissemination

Even if effective treatments exist and survivors want to access them, both systemic and clinician barriers may exist. Several unique systemic issues arise when attempting to disseminate effective treatments in the wake of disaster (see Marshall et al. 2006 for review). Treatments are often implemented through a community response, which brings with it distinctive systems issues regarding referral and treatment delivery. Training programs often need to be implemented quickly, inexpensively, and to many providers with a range of backgrounds. There is often less time to offer comprehensive didactics and supervision to providers than in other training contexts. Further, effective treatments compete with other types of interventions, and service planners and organizations may fail to work together, experience communication problems, feel ambivalent toward trainers who might be considered "outsiders," and have limited funding and resources (Norris et al. 2005).

Clinician barriers can exist both in terms of training needs and in terms of resistance to delivering the identified treatments. With respect to training, a review of the CBT dissemination literature in- and outside of the postdisaster context indicates that community-based therapists can be trained to implement effective treatments in local crisis and community agencies. Rape crisis counselors, community mental health clinicians, and school-based counselors have been shown to be able to learn specific CBT interventions and to provide them with good outcome (Foa et al. 2005; Gillespie et al. 2002; Stein et al. 2003). Together these studies indicate that it may be possible to train clinicians in a variety of nonacademic settings to provide effective manualized CBT treatments for PTSD.

Only two studies report on training therapists to provide CBT following a disaster. The first involved a two-day training of PE to more than 100 frontline clinicians following the 9/11 World Trade Center attacks (Marshall et al. 2006). Results from the pretraining assessment indicated that therapists were moderately favorable regarding the active components of the treatment, but felt that they lacked the skill to adequately deliver the exposure treatment. No posttraining assessment was completed.

The second study involved a two-day training of community clinicians in Baton Rouge, Louisiana, to deliver CBT-PD following Hurricane Katrina (Hamblen et al. 2010). Results indicated that the training was effective in educating therapists about CBT-PD. Therapists, especially those who were not already at the maximum score at pretraining, showed significant improvements in their ratings of the importance of various elements of CBT in therapy, their knowledge and understanding of those elements, and their confidence that they could use them effectively.

These studies indicate that it may be possible to train community-based clinicians in manualized interventions for PTSD or postdisaster distress. A large number of therapists from different agencies were taught to deliver these interventions with relatively little training and significantly less intensive supervision than in a typical randomized controlled trial. The two disaster studies also support the success of "just-in-time" trainings of evidence-based CBT interventions that can be implemented in the aftermath of a disaster (Hamblen et al. 2010; Marshall et al. 2006).

Another barrier to treatment can be resistance on the part of the clinician. Many clinicians are reluctant to delivering manualized treatments, either because they think they do not "fit" their clients or they believe that their clinical techniques and interventions are more effective (Addis, Wade, and Hatgis 1999). Therefore, a training goal should be helping clinicians understand that most CBTs are quite adaptive to specific client presentations and can be tailored to meet the specific client needs. The cognitive and behavioral components of the treatments are focused on the unique issues of the client. No two clients will ever receive the exact same treatment because it is their own values, beliefs, and fears that shape the treatment. It may also be that manuals can be used more flexibly than once thought. Two disaster treatment models have been used flexibly with success. One such model is specialized crisis counseling services (SCCS), a team-based program that was implemented as part of Project Recovery following Hurricane Katrina (Jones et al. 2009). SCCS is a blend of CBT, solution-focused, and person-centered approaches that involves flexible, stand-alone sessions. Clinicians could identify what techniques they wanted to implement in each session. Not only were satisfaction ratings high and outcomes promising, researchers found that master's level clinicians with various backgrounds could be effectively trained in the approach.

The other model is a flexible application of STAIR/MPE (reviewed previously; Levitt et al. 2007). In this model, therapists received limited training and had little or no CBT experience. They were encouraged to follow the manual, but to use it flexibly as determined by their judgment. This included skipping sessions, repeating sessions, ending before the full 16 sessions, and adding nonprotocol sessions if a crisis needed to be addressed. On average, therapists delivered one extra session of STAIR and one extra session of MPE, with one additional nonprotocol session (Levitt et al. 2007). This study suggests that strict adherence to manuals may not be necessary and that training should help clinicians understand the rationale for each treatment component so that they can determine the best pacing of the intervention.

17.3.2.1 Recommendations for Improving Dissemination

Lack of training is one barrier to care that can be overcome. Evidence suggests that community clinicians can learn to deliver these treatments, but most will require training. While training clinicians in advance of a disaster has advantages, we believe this is not realistic. First, community mental health centers do not have the resources to send clinicians to trainings if they may not be needed. Second, clinicians' skills will likely deteriorate if they do not have the option to treat clients immediately after the training. Therefore, we recommend "just-in-time" training. We also suggest that there may be some advantages to training clinicians in a model like CBT-PD that requires only a single training but is effective for a range of postdisaster responses and disorders, rather than taking the time to train clinicians in two or more effective treatments, such as one for PTSD and one for depression.

Finally, it is important for administrators to understand that just because clinicians receive training in effective treatments, this does not ensure that they will utilize those treatments. Significant attention must be directed at helping clinicians understand how these treatments can be specifically tailored to respond to their client's unique needs while still keeping faithful to the manual. A remaining empirical question is the extent to which clinicians can go off protocol without reducing treatment effectiveness.

17.4   SUMMARY AND CONCLUSIONS

In this chapter we reviewed the literature on the range of long-term treatments available after a disaster and on issues that may prevent survivors from receiving these treatments. There is a substantial literature supporting the use of CBT for PTSD, the condition most commonly observed after a disaster. These studies include a few studies of CBT for disaster-related PTSD. We also reviewed the literature on CBT-PD, a treatment that can be delivered more broadly to survivors with postdisaster distress. The ultimate decision regarding which treatment to choose may depend most on a program's specific goals or needs. For example, a statewide crisis counseling program may well want to treat everyone who is significantly upset by the disaster. Therefore, CBT-PD may be the right choice. Conversely, a local treatment center or program may want to offer services to only those who are most severely impaired and may therefore choose a PTSD treatment.

The review on barriers to care reveals a complex literature. There are many factors and levels to contend with. We focused primarily on survivor-level barriers and clinician barriers. For survivors to seek care, they must first recognize they have a problem; second, know that help is available; and third, access the help. We suggest that it is critical to provide outreach to at-risk groups and to specifically address unique barriers to care for these groups.

With respect to clinician barriers, we focused on training and resistance. It appears that clinicians can be trained to use these interventions. The bigger question is how to most efficiently conduct the training. It is likely that large-scale trainings in advance of a disaster are not feasible and clinicians would likely need a refresher course just prior to delivering them. Thus we recommend just-in-time training and raise the issue whether it is necessary to train clinicians in more than one approach. Obtaining trainers may be another barrier. One possible solution is to provide the training over the Internet or by video- or teleconferencing.

A more radical suggestion is to provide the therapy itself over the Internet. These options are low cost, have the potential to reach large numbers of survivors, and can be interactive and personalized (Ruggiero et al. 2006). Moreover, individuals may be more apt to use the Internet than a therapist due to stigma associated with seeking therapy. These programs can also be easily revised, may reduce the burden on CBT clinicians, gain high satisfaction ratings, and obtain successful outcomes (Litz et al. 2007; Ruggiero et al. 2006). However, currently there is not enough data to recommend this option as a primary treatment strategy.

Finally, clinicians' resistance to providing these treatments must be addressed. The goal of dissemination is to change clinicians' behaviors in order to effectively implement treatments (Marshall et al. 2006). Training research has shown that targeting clinicians' expected values of the outcome, beliefs about existing norms, and self-efficacy through didactics, demonstrations, and role-playing is crucial (Marshall et al. 2006). This research also demonstrates low favorability ratings toward using a manual, as well as fears that clients will decompensate in trauma-focused models (Marshall et al. 2006; Cahill et al. 2006; Becker et al. 2004). Thus these specific points must be addressed as part of the training.

To convey the importance of using treatments that are supported by science, administrators and trainers could use a metaphor from the medical field to emphasize the importance of using effective treatments: "If your loved one was ill and research showed that one medication was more helpful than another, would you choose the less effective one?" Finally, to motivate clinicians to use effective treatments, some have advocated for policy change in managed health care organizations such that effective treatments are reimbursed at a higher rate than interventions without an evidence base (K. Mueser, personal communications, November 20, 2009).

A final clinician barrier unique to disasters is that clinicians are likely to share in the experience of the disaster with the survivor seeking care, which we have found to create special issues in training and implementation (Hamblen et al. 2009). Although these collective experiences might increase empathy, it might decrease clinician objectivity. For example, local clinicians might have difficulty challenging distorted beliefs around the likelihood of future disasters or whether things will ever improve because they may struggle with these very same beliefs. When they have shared the client's experience, clinicians are more likely to engage in self-disclosure and are more easily led off topic during sessions. These issues can be addressed effectively if they are acknowledged in training. In conclusion, effective long-term treatments exist for disaster survivors. However, to optimize these treatments we need to make sure that survivors are aware of them and that they are delivered in ways that make them accessible and acceptable. Special attention must be paid to at-risk or marginalized groups. Finally, training considerations should include when and how to train clinicians, as well as how best to reduce resistance to delivering the treatments.

REFERENCES

Addis, M. E., W. A. Wade, and C. Hatgis. 1999. Barriers to dissemination of evidence-based practices: Addressing practitioners' concerns about manual-based psychotherapies. *Clinical Psychology: Science and Practice 6*: 430–441.

American Psychiatric Association. In press. *Diagnostic and Statistical Manual of Mental Disorders* (5th Edition). Washington DC: American Psychiatric Association.

Anderson, R. M. 1995. Revisiting the behavioral model and access to medical care: Does it matter? *Journal of Health and Social Behavior 36*: 1–10.

Andersen, R. M., and J. F. Newman. 1973. Social and individual determinants of medical care utilization in the United States. *Milbank Quarterly 51*: 95–124.

Arntz, A., M. Tiesema, and M. Kindt. 2007. Treatment of PTSD: A comparison of imaginal exposure with and without imagery rescripting. *Journal of Behavior Therapy and Experimental Psychiatry 38*(4): 345–370.

Australian Centre for Posttraumatic Mental Health. 2007. *Australian Guidelines for the Treatment of Adults with Acute Stress Disorder and Posttraumatic Stress Disorder*. Melbourne, Victoria: Australian Centre for Posttraumatic Mental Health.

Basoglu, M., M. Livanou, and E. Salcioglu. 2003. A single session with an earthquake simulator for traumatic stress in earthquake survivors. *American Journal of Psychiatry 160*(4): 788–790.

Basoglu, M., M. Livanou, E. Salcioglu, and D. Kalender. 2003. A brief behavioural treatment of chronic post-traumatic stress disorder in earthquake survivors: Results from an open clinical trial. *Psychological Medicine 33*(4): 647–654.

Basoglu, M., E. Salcioglu, and M. Livanou. 2007. A randomized controlled study of single-session behavioural treatment of earthquake-related post-traumatic stress disorder using an earthquake simulator. *Psychological Medicine 37*(2): 203–213.

Basoglu, M., E. Salcioglu, M. Livanou, D. Kalender, and G. Acar. 2005. Single-session behavioral treatment of earthquake-related posttraumatic stress disorder: A randomized waiting list controlled trial. *Journal of Traumatic Stress 18*(1): 1–11.

Becker, C. B., C. Zayfert, and E. Anderson. 2004. A survey of psychologists' attitudes towards and utilization of exposure therapy for PTSD. *Behavior Research and Therapy 42*(3), 277–292.

Blanchard, E. B., E. J. Hickling, T. Devineni, C. Veazey, T. E. Galovski, E. Mundy, L. S. Malta, and T. C. Buckley. 2003. A controlled evaluation of cognitive behavioural therapy for posttraumatic stress in motor vehicle accident survivors. *Behaviour Research and Therapy 41*(1): 79–96.

Brady, K., T. Pearlstein, G. M. Asnis, D. Baker, B. Rothbaum, C. R. Sikes, and G. M. Farfell. 2000. Efficacy and safety of sertraline treatment of posttraumatic stress disorder: A randomized controlled trial. *Journal of the American Medical Association 283*(14): 1837–1844.

Brewin, C. R., P. Scragg, M. Robertson, M. Thompson, P. d'Ardenne, and A. Ehlers. 2008. Promoting mental health following the London bombings: A screen and treat approach. *Journal of Traumatic Stress 21*(1): 3–8.

Bryant, R. A., and B. T. Litz. 2009. Mental health treatments in the wake of disaster. In *Mental Health and Disasters*, eds. Y. Neria, S. Galea, and F. H. Norris, 321–335. New York: Cambridge University Press.

Bryant, R. A., M. L. Moulds, R. M. Guthrie, S. T. Dang, and R. D. Nixon. 2003. Imaginal exposure alone and imaginal exposure with cognitive restructuring in treatment of posttraumatic stress disorder. *Journal of Consulting and Clinical Psychology 71*(4): 706–712.

Cahill, S. P., E. A. Hembree, and E. B. Foa. 2006. Dissemination of prolonged exposure therapy for posttraumatic stress disorder: Successes and challenges. In *9/11: Mental Health in the Wake of Terrorist Attacks*, eds Y. Neria, R. Gross, R. Marshall, 475–495. Cambridge, England: Cambridge University Press.

Chilcoat, H. D., and N. Breslau. 1998a. Investigations of causal pathways between PTSD and drug use disorders. *Addictive Behaviors 23*(6): 827–840.

Chilcoat, H. D., and N. Breslau. 1998b. Posttraumatic stress disorder and drug disorders: Testing causal pathways. *Archives of General Psychiatry 55*(10): 913–917.

Cloitre, M., K. C. Koenen, L. R. Cohen, and H. Han. 2002. Skills training in affective and interpersonal regulation followed by exposure: A phase-based treatment for PTSD related to childhood abuse. *Journal of Consulting and Clinical Psychology 70*(5): 1067–1074.

Cook, J. M., and D. L. Elmore. 2009. Disaster mental health in older adults: Symptoms, policy, and planning. In *Mental Health and Disasters*, eds. Y. Neria, S. Galea, and F. H. Norris, 233–263. New York: Cambridge University Press.

Davidson, J., T. Pearlstein, P. Londborg, K. T. Brady, B. Rothbaum, J. Bell, R. Maddock, M. T. Hegel, and G. Farfel. 2001. Efficacy of sertraline in preventing relapse of posttraumatic stress disorder: Results of a 28-week double-blind, placebo-controlled study. *American Journal of Psychiatry 158*(12): 1974–1981.

Davidson, J. R., B. O. Rothbaum, B.A van der Kolk, C. R. Sikes, and G. M. Farfel. 2001. Multicenter, double-blind comparison of sertraline and placebo in the treatment of posttraumatic stress disorder. *Archives of General Psychiatry 58*(5): 485–492.

Davidson, P. R., and K. C. Parker. 2001. Eye movement desensitization and reprocessing (EMDR): A meta-analysis. *Journal of Consulting and Clinical Psychology 69*(2): 305–316.

DeLisi, L. E., A. Maurizio, M. Yost, C. F. Papparozzi, C. Fulchino, C. L. Katz, J. Altesman, M. Biel, J. Lee, and P. Stevens. 2003. A survey of New Yorkers after the Sept. 11, 2001, terrorist attacks. *American Journal of Psychiatry 160*(4): 780–783.

Difede, J., J. Cukor, N. Jayasinghe, I. Patt, S. Jedel, L. Spielman, C. Giosan, and H. G. Hoffman. 2007. Virtual reality exposure therapy for the treatment of posttraumatic stress disorder following September 11, 2001. *Journal of Clinical Psychiatry 68*(11): 1639–1647.

Difede, J., L. S. Malta, S. Best, C. Henn-Haase, T. Metzler, R. Bryant, and C. Marmar. 2007. A randomized controlled clinical treatment trial for World Trade Center attack-related PTSD in disaster workers. *Journal of Nervous and Mental Disease 195*(10): 861–865.

Donahue, S. A., C. T. Jackson, M. K. Shear, C. J. Felton, and S. M. Essock. 2006. Outcomes of enhanced counseling services provided to adults through Project Liberty. *Psychiatric Services 57*(9): 1298–1303.

Dosa, D. M., K. Hyer, L. M. Brown, A. W. Artenstein, L. Polivka-West, and V. Mor. 2008. The controversy inherent in managing frail nursing home residents during complex hurricane emergencies. *Journal of the American Medical Directors Association 9*(8): 599–604.

Duffy, M., K. Gillespie, and D. M. Clark. 2007. Post-traumatic stress disorder in the context of terrorism and other civil conflict in Northern Ireland: Randomised controlled trial. *British Medical Journal 334*(7604): 1147–1150.

Ehlers, A., and D. M. Clark. 2000. A cognitive model of posttraumatic stress disorder. *Behaviour Research and Therapy* 38(4): 319–345.

Ehlers, A., D. M. Clark, A. Hackmann, F. McManus, and M. Fennell. 2005. Cognitive therapy for post-traumatic stress disorder: Development and evaluation. *Behaviour Research and Therapy* 43(4): 413–431.

Elhai, J. D., and J. D. Ford. 2009. Utilization of mental health services after disasters. In *Mental Health and Disasters*, eds. Y. Neria, S. Galea, and F. H. Norris, 366–386. New York: Cambridge University Press.

Falsetti, S. A., H. S. Resnick, and J. L. Davis. 2008. Multiple channel exposure therapy for women with PTSD and comorbid panic attacks. *Cognitive Behaviour Therapy* 37(2): 117–130.

Foa, E. B., C. V. Dancu, E. A. Hembree, L. H. Jaycox, E. A. Meadows, and G. P. Street. 1999. A comparison of exposure therapy, stress inoculation training, and their combination for reducing posttraumatic stress disorder in female assault victims. *Journal of Consulting and Clinical Psychology* 67(2): 194–200.

Foa, E. B., E. A. Hembree, S. P. Cahill, S. A. M. Rausch, D. S. Riggs, N. C. Feeny, and E. Yadin. 2005. Randomized trial of prolonged exposure for posttraumatic stress disorder with and without cognitive restructuring: Outcome at academic and community clinics. *Journal of Consulting and Clinical Psychology* 73(5): 953–964.

Foa, E. B., T. M. Keane, and M. J. Friedman, eds. 2009. *Effective Treatments for PTSD*. New York: Guilford Press.

Foa, E. B., B. O. Rothbaum, D. S. Riggs, and T. B. Murdock. 1991. Treatment of posttraumatic stress disorder in rape victims: A comparison between cognitive-behavioral procedures and counseling. *Journal of Consulting and Clinical Psychology* 59(5): 715–723.

Frank, R. G., T. Pindyck, S. A. Donahue, E. A. Pease, M. J. Euster, C. J. Felton, and S. M. Essock. 2006. Impact of a media campaign for disaster mental health counseling in post-September 11 New York. *Psychiatric Services* 57(9): 1304–1308.

Friedman, M. J. 2008. Treatments for PTSD: Understanding the evidence: Pharmacotherapy. *PTSD Research Quarterly* 19(3): 6–11.

Friedman, M. J., J. R. T. Davidson, and D. J. Stein. 2009. Psychopharmacotherapy for adults. In *Effective Treatment for PTSD: Practice Guidelines from the International Society for Traumatic Stress Studies*, eds. E. Foa, T. M. Keane, M. J. Friedman, and J. A. Cohen, 245–268. New York: Guilford Press.

Friedman, M. J., C. R. Marmar, D. G. Baker, C. R. Sikes, and G. M. Farfel. 2007. Randomized, double-blind comparison of sertraline and placebo for posttraumatic stress disorder in a Department of Veterans Affairs setting. *Journal of Clinical Psychiatry* 68(5): 711–720.

Galea, S., A. K. Nandi, and D. Vlahov. 2005. The epidemiology of post-traumatic stress disorder after disasters. *Epidemiologic Reviews* 27: 78–91.

Gillespie, K., M. Duffy, A. Hackmann, and D. M. Clark. 2002. Community based cognitive therapy in the treatment of posttraumatic stress disorder following the Omagh bomb. *Behaviour Research and Therapy* 40(4): 345–357.

Glynn, S. M., S. Eth, E. T. Randolph, D. W. Foy, M. Urbaitis, L. Boxer, G. G. Paz, G. B. Leong, G. Firman, J. D. Salk, J. W. Katzman, and J. Crothers. 1999. A test of behavioral family therapy to augment exposure for combat-related posttraumatic stress disorder. *Journal of Consulting and Clinical Psychology* 67(2): 243–251.

Hamblen, J., F. H. Norris, L. E. Gibson, and L. Lee. 2010. Training community therapists to deliver cognitive behavioral therapy in the aftermath of disaster. *International Journal of Emergency Mental Health* 12: 33–44.

Hamblen, J. L., L. E. Gibson, K. T. Mueser, and Norris, F. H. 2006. Cognitive behavioral therapy for prolonged postdisaster distress. *Journal of Clinical Psychology* 62(8): 1043–1052.

Hamblen, J. L., and F. Norris. 2007. *Project Recovery Evaluation: CBT for Postdisaster Distress*. White River Junction, VT: National Center for PTSD.

Hamblen, J. L., F. H. Norris, S. Pietruszkiewicz, L. E. Gibson, A. Naturale, and C. Louis. 2009. Cognitive behavioral therapy for postdisaster distress: A community based treatment program for survivors of Hurricane Katrina. *Administration and Policy in Mental Health and Mental Health Services Research* 36(3): 206–214.

Hawkins, A. O., H. M. Zinzow, A. B. Amstadter, C. K. Danielson, and K. J. Ruggiero. 2009. Factors associated with exposure and response to disasters among marginalized populations. In *Mental Health and Disasters*, eds. Y. Neria, S. Galea, and F. H. Norris, 277–290. New York: Cambridge University Press.

Hien, D. A., L. R. Cohen, G. M. Miele, L. C. Litt, and C. Capstick. 2004. Promising treatments for women with comorbid PTSD and substance use disorders. *American Journal of Psychiatry* 161(8): 1426–1432.

Hien, D. A., E. A. Wells, H. Jiang, L. Suarez-Morales, A. N. Campbell, L. R. Cohen, G. M. Miele, T. Killeen, G. S. Brigham, Y. Zhang, C. Hansen, C. Hodgkins, M. Hatch-Maillette, C. Brown, A. Kulage, A. Kristman-Valente, M. Chu, R. Sage, J. A, Robinson, D. Liu, and E. Nunes. 2009. Multisite randomized trial of behavioral interventions for women with co-occurring PTSD and substance use disorders. *Journal of Consulting and Clinical Psychology* 77(4): 607–619.

Hyer, K., L. M. Brown, A. Berman, and L. Polivka-West. 2006. Establishing and refining hurricane response systems for long-term care facilities. *Health Affairs (Millwood)* 25(5): 407–411.

Institute of Medicine. 2008. *Treatment of Posttraumatic Stress Disorder: An Assessment of the Evidence.* Washington, DC: The National Academies Press.

Jacobsen, L. K., S. M. Southwick, and T. R. Kosten. 2001. Substance use disorders in patients with posttraumatic stress disorder: A review of the literature. *American Journal of Psychiatry* 158(8): 1184–1190.

Jones, K., M. Allen, F. H. Norris, and C. Miller. 2009. Piloting a new model of crisis counseling: Specialized crisis counseling services in Mississippi after Hurricane Katrina. *Administration and Policy in Mental Health* 36(3): 195–205.

Koenen, K. C., R. Goodwin, E. Struening, F. Hellman, and M. Guardino. 2003. Posttraumatic stress disorder and treatment seeking in a national screening sample. *Journal of Traumatic Stress* 16(1): 5–16.

Levitt, J. T., L. S. Malta, A. Martin, L. Davis, and M. Cloitre. 2007. The flexible application of a manualized treatment for PTSD symptoms and functional impairment related to the 9/11 World Trade Center attack. *Behaviour Research and Therapy* 45(7): 1419–1433.

Litz, B. T., C. C. Engel, R. A. Bryant, and A. Papa. 2007. A randomized, controlled proof-of-concept trial of an Internet-based, therapist-assisted self-management treatment for posttraumatic stress disorder. *American Journal of Psychiatry* 164(11): 1676–1683.

Marks, I., K. Lovell, H. Noshirvani, M. Livanou, and S. Thrasher. 1998. Treatment of posttraumatic stress disorder by exposure and/or cognitive restructuring: A controlled study. *Archives of General Psychiatry* 55(4): 317–325.

Marshall, R. D., L. Amsel, Y. Neria, and E. Jung Suh. 2006. Strategies for determination of evidence-based treatments: Training clinicians after large-scale disasters. In *Methods for Disasters Mental Health Research,* eds. F. H. Norris, S. Galea, M. J. Friedman, and P. J. Watson, 226–242. New York: Guilford Press.

Marshall, R. D., K. L. Beebe, M. Oldham, and R. Zaninelli. 2001. Efficacy and safety of paroxetine treatment for chronic PTSD: A fixed-dose, placebo-controlled study. *American Journal of Psychiatry* 158(12): 1982–1988.

Martenyi, F., E. B. Brown, and C. D. Caldwell. 2007. Failed efficacy of fluoxetine in the treatment of posttraumatic stress disorder: Results of a fixed-dose, placebo-controlled study. *Journal of Clinical Psychopharmacology* 27(2): 166–170.

Martenyi, F., E. B. Brown, H. Zhang, S. C. Koke, and A. Prakash, 2002. Fluoxetine v. placebo in prevention of relapse in post-traumatic stress disorder. *British Journal of Psychiatry* 181: 315–320.

Monson, C. M., P. P. Schnurr, P. A. Resick, M. J. Friedman, Y. Young-Xu, and S. P. Stevens. 2006. Cognitive processing therapy for veterans with military-related posttraumatic stress disorder. *Journal of Consulting and Clinical Psychology* 74(5): 898–907.

Mueser, K. M., S. D. Rosenberg, M. K. Jankowski, J. L. Hamblen, and M. Descamps. 2004. A cognitive-behavioral treatment program for posttraumatic stress disorder in persons with severe mental illness. *American Journal of Psychiatric Rehabilitation* 7(2): 107–146.

Mueser, K. T., S. D. Rosenberg, H. Xie, M. K. Jankowski, E. E. Bolton, J. L. Hamblen, H. J. Rosenberg, G. J. McHugo, and R. Wolfe. 2008. A randomized controlled trial of cognitive-behavioral treatment for posttraumatic stress disorder in severe mental illness. *Journal of Consulting and Clinical Psychology* 76(2): 259–271.

National Collaborating Centre for Mental Health. 2005. *Post-traumatic Stress Disorder: The Management of PTSD in Adults and Children in Primary and Secondary Care.* London: Gaskell and the British Psychological Society.

Norris, F. H., and C. L. Elrod. 2006. Psychosocial consequences of disaster: A review of past research. In *Methods for Disaster Mental Health Research,* eds. F. H. Norris, S. Galea, M. Friedman, and P. J. Watson, 20–42. New York: Guilford Press.

Norris, F. H., M. J. Friedman, P. J. Watson, C. M. Byrne, E. Diaz, and K. Kaniasty. 2002. 60,000 disaster victims speak: Part I. An empirical review of the empirical literature, 1981–2001. *Psychiatry* 65(3): 207–239.

Norris, F. H., P. J. Watson, J. L. Hamblen, and B. J. Pfefferbaum. 2005. Provider perspectives on disaster mental health services in Oklahoma City. In *The Trauma of Terrorism: Sharing Knowledge and Shared Care, an International Handbook,* eds. Y. Danieli, D. Brom, and J. B. Sills, 649–662. Binghamton: NY: Haworth Press.

North, C. S., S. J. Nixon, S. Shariat, S. Mallone, J. C. McMillen, E. L. Spitznagel, and E. M Smith. 1999. Psychiatric disorders among survivors of the Oklahoma City bombing. *Journal of the American Medical Association* 282(8): 755–762.

Pietrzak, R. H., D. C. Johnson, M. B. Goldstein, J. C. Malley, and S. M. Southwick. 2009. Perceived stigma and barriers to mental health care utilization among OEF-OIF veterans. *Psychiatric Services* 60(8): 1118–1122.

Prigerson, H. G., M. J. Horowitz, S. C. Jacobs, C. M. Parkes, M. Asian, K. Goodkin, B. Raphael, S. J. Marwit, C. Wortman, R. A. Neimeyer, G. Bonanno, S. D. Block, D. Kissane, P. Boelen, A. Maercker, B. T. Litz, J. G. Johnson, M. B. First, and P. K. Maciejewski. 2009. Prolonged grief disorder: Psychometric validation of criteria proposed for DSM-V and ICD-11. *PLoS Medicine* 6(8). http://www.plosmedicine.org/article/info:doi%2F10.1371%2Fjournal.pmed.1000121.

Resick, P. A., T. E. Galovski, M. O'Brien Uhlmansiek, C. D. Scher, G. A. Clum, and Y. Young-Xu. 2008. A randomized clinical trial to dismantle components of cognitive processing therapy for posttraumatic stress disorder in female victims of interpersonal violence. *Journal of Consulting and Clinical Psychology* 76(2): 243–258.

Resick, P. A., P. Nishith, T. L. Weaver, M. C. Astin, and C. A. Feuer. 2002. A comparison of cognitive-processing therapy with prolonged exposure and a waiting condition for the treatment of chronic posttraumatic stress disorder in female rape victims. *Journal of Consulting and Clinical Psychology* 70(4): 867–879.

Resick, P. A., and M. Schnicke. 1996. *Cognitive Processing Therapy for Rape Victims: A Treatment Manual.* Newbury Park, CA: Sage Publications.

Rothbaum, B. O., M. C. Astin, and F. Marsteller. 2005. Prolonged Exposure versus Eye Movement Desensitization and Reprocessing (EMDR) for PTSD rape victims. *Journal of Traumatic Stress* 18(6): 607–616.

Rudenstine, S., S. Galea, J. Ahern, C. Felton, and D. Vlahov. 2003. Awareness and perceptions of a communitywide mental health program in New York City after September 11. *Psychiatric Services* 54(10): 1404–1406.

Ruggiero, K. J., H. S. Resnick, R. Acierno, M. J. Carpenter, D. G. Kilpatrick, S. F. Coffey, A. M. Ruscio, R. S. Stephens, P. R. Stasiewicz, R. A. Roffman, M. Bucuvales, and S. Galea. 2006. Internet-based intervention for mental health and substance use problems in disaster-affected populations: A pilot feasibility study. *Behavior Therapy* 37(2): 190–205.

Schnurr, P. P., M. J. Friedman, C. C. Engel, E. B. Foa, M. T. Shea, B. K. Chow, P. A. Resick, V. Thurston, S. M. Orsillo, R. Haug, C. Turner, and N. Bernardy. 2007. Cognitive behavioral therapy for posttraumatic stress disorder in women: A randomized controlled trial. *Journal of the American Medical Association* 297(8): 820–830.

Schoenbaum, M., B. Butler, S. Kataoka, B. Nordquist, G. Springgate, G. Sullivan, N. Duan, R. C. Kessler, and K. Wells. 2009. Promoting mental health recovery after hurricanes Katrina and Rita: What can be done at what cost. *Archives of General Psychiatry* 66(8): 906–914.

Shear, K., E. Frank, P. R. Houck, and C. F. Reynolds. 2005. Treatment of complicated grief: A randomized controlled trial, 3rd ed. *Journal of the American Medical Association* 293(21): 2601–2608.

Stein, B. D., L. H. Jaycox, S. H. Kataoka, M. Wong, W. Tu, M. N. Elliott, and A. Fink. 2003. A mental health intervention for school children exposed to violence: A randomized controlled trial. *Journal of the American Medical Association* 290(5): 603–611.

Stough, L. M. 2009. The effects of disaster on the mental health of individuals with disabilities. In *Mental Health and Disasters*, eds. Y. Neria, S. Galea, and F. H. Norris, 264–276. New York: Cambridge University Press.

Stuber, J., S. Galea, J. A. Boscarino, and M. Schlesinger. 2006. Was there unmet mental health need after the September 11, 2001 terrorist attacks? *Social Psychiatry and Psychiatric Epidemiology* 41(3): 230–240.

Taylor, S., D. S. Thordarson, L. Maxfield, I. C Fedoroff, K. Lovell, and J. Ogrodniczuk. 2003. Comparative efficacy, speed, and adverse effects of three PTSD treatments: Exposure therapy, EMDR, and relaxation training. *Journal of Consulting and Clinical Psychology* 71 (2): 330–338.

Ursano, R. J., C. C. Bell, S. Eth, M. J. Friedman, A. E. Norwood, B. G. Pfefferbaum, R. S. Pynoos, D. F. Zatzick, D. M. Benedek, J. S. McIntyre, S. C. Charles, K. H. Altshuler, I. Cook, C. D. Cross, L. Mellman, L. A. Moench, G. S. H. Norquist, S. W. Twemlow, S. Woods, J. Yager, American Psychiatric Association Work Group on ASD and PTSD, and American Psychiatric Association Steering Committee on Practice Guidelines. 2004. *Practice Guidelines for the Treatment of Acute Stress and Posttraumatic Stress Disorder.* Washington, DC: American Psychiatric Association.

VA/DoD Clinical Practice Guideline Working Group. 2003. Management of post-traumatic stress. In *Office of Quality and Performance 10Q-CPG/PTSD-03, 10.* Washington, DC: Veterans Health Administration, Department of Veterans Affairs and Health Affairs, Department of Defense.

Vlahov, D., S. Galea, J. Ahern, S. Rudenstein, H. Resnick, D. Kilpatrick, and R. M. Crum. 2006. Alcohol drinking problems among New York City residents after the September 11 terrorist attacks. *Substance Use & Misuse 41*(9): 1295–1311.

Vlahov, D., S. Galea, H. Resnick, J. Ahern, J. A. Boscarino, M. J. Bucuvales, J. Gold, and D. G. Kilpatrick. 2002. Increased use of cigarettes, alcohol, and marijuana among Manhattan, New York, residents after the September 11th terrorist attacks. *American Journal of Epidemiology 155*(11): 988–996.

Wang, P., M. Gruber, R. Powers, M. Schoenbaum, A. H. Speir, K. B. Wells, and R. C. Kessler. 2007. Mental health service use among Hurricane Katrina survivors in the eight months after the disaster. *Psychiatric Services 58*: 1403–1411.

18 Disaster and Substance Abuse Services

Dee S. Owens, Brian McKernan, and Julie L. Framingham

CONTENTS

18.1 INTRODUCTION

This chapter will use a multifaceted approach to bring the reader up to date with recent research on the effects of disaster on survivors with substance use problems. The subject of substance abuse has been the focus of relatively few empirical studies in comparison to other areas of disaster research, including disaster mental health, which is also a burgeoning field of study. Much of the serious research on substance use postdisaster occurred within the past decade, since the terrorist attacks of September 11, 2001 (9/11), and again after observing the devastating impacts of Hurricane Katrina on August 29, 2005, along the U.S. Gulf Coast. Some of these research findings are discussed within this chapter. Additionally, the field observations of three different states' substance abuse responses to disasters are presented. Together, both the scholarly studies and the anecdotal state reports yield a number of considerations for disaster planners and responders. We will discuss some of these considerations and how they informed several important state and federal disaster substance abuse initiatives during the past several years. While the precise relationship between disasters and substance use is still not fully understood, the topic nevertheless merits more serious consideration and should be addressed in the local or state jurisdiction's overall behavioral health planning and response to disasters.

18.2 LITERATURE REVIEW OF THE EPIDEMIOLOGY OF SUBSTANCE USE, ABUSE, AND DEPENDENCE POSTDISASTER

As the study of alcohol and other drug use after disaster is an emergent field, there is growing evidence that survivors of disaster increase use of alcohol and/or other drugs, and that, for certain populations, this phenomenon is especially ill advised. While many survivors may "go to the bars" more and drink to relieve stress, those who have existing substance use disorders are making potentially life-threatening choices by doing so. Most methodologically sound studies about alcohol and other drug use have shown some increase or deviance in use after a disaster. For example, almost 30 percent of 988 New York City residents surveyed reported an increase in the use of alcohol, cigarettes, and marijuana soon after the 9/11 attack on the World Trade Center. Alcohol consumption reported the largest increase with 24.6 percent, followed by cigarettes at 9.7 percent, and 3.2 percent for marijuana (Vlahov et al. 2002). Other studies of 2,368 and 1,681 New York City adults conducted at one and two years, respectively, after the World Trade Center attack, report sustained increases in alcohol consumption (10 percent) and alcohol dependence after disaster exposure, while an increase in binge drinking was observed at one year postdisaster (Boscarino, Adams, and Galea 2006; Adams, Boscarino, and Galea 2006). Wu and colleagues (2006) demonstrate that of 2,731 New York City public high school students surveyed, 10.9 percent increased their consumption of alcohol. Although 5.4 percent also reported an increase in cigarette smoking after 9/11, this increase was attributed more to the students' self-reports of past trauma experiences and posttraumatic stress disorder than to disaster exposure (Wu et al. 2006). Increased alcohol consumption is noted among 13 percent of the survivors of the attack on the Pentagon as well ($n = 77$; Grieger, Fullerton, and Ursano 2003).

The effects of terrorism on drinking are also noted by researchers who find that binge/intoxication drinking postdisaster is increased not only by a lack of social-bonding variables, such as parenthood, but even political factors, such as higher alerts for terrorism (Richman et al. 2009). Furthermore, a meta-analysis by Dimaggio, Galea, and Li (2009) supports that terrorism influences substance use and abuse by survivors and other groups affected. Specifically, and using Bayesian techniques, this analysis of 31 population-based studies finds that in the first two years after a terrorist event, 7.3 percent of a population will increase alcohol use, with a 20 percent probability that at least 14 percent of that population will increase use. Similarly, 6.8 percent of an affected group will increase smoking behaviors, while drug use (including prescriptions and illicit substances) will rise 16.3 percent.

Studies of adolescent survivors of Hurricanes Katrina and Rita also demonstrated a connection between disaster exposure and increased substance use and abuse (Flory et al. 2009; Rohrbach et al. 2009). Furthermore, other types of disasters, such as the 1998 Swissair Flight 111 disaster in Saint Margaret's Bay, Nova Scotia, Canada, the Mount St. Helens volcanic eruption in 1980, and the Herald of Free Enterprise disaster in 1987, demonstrated similar increases in substance use and abuse (Stewart et al. 2004; Adams and Adams 1984; Joseph et al. 1993).

Although these studies support that disaster survivors may increase their consumption of alcohol, tobacco, and other substances, not all do. One study of the Great Hanshin Earthquake in Japan, for instance, found that alcohol use was 10–20 percent lower than anticipated postdisaster (Shimizu et al. 2000). Some research (Valdez et al. 2009) seems to demonstrate a lower immediate use of illicit drugs but higher alcohol sales, indicating a likely disruption of drug-supply networks after disaster. These seeming disparities are replicated by other disaster studies, such as those about first responders, where some are seen to be resilient while others are "more symptomatic than unexposed comparison groups" (North et al. 2002a, 172). In fact, studies have found higher rates of predisaster alcohol-use disorder among firefighters, a population that self-selects for traumatic work but that seems to cope by drinking alcohol (Boxer and Wild 1993; North et al. 2002b). While these studies are more equivocal concerning the increase of substance use postdisaster, they nevertheless illustrate that disaster services should include substance abuse as an important portion of behavioral health planning and response.

18.3 DYNAMICS OF SUBSTANCE ABUSE POSTDISASTER

18.3.1 INCREASE OF SUBSTANCE USE IN THE GENERAL POPULATION TO COPE WITH STRESS

A meta-analysis was conducted by Fran Norris (2005) including not only United States data, but also research from 34 other countries, developing and developed, and including 132 natural and human-caused disasters. The study shows that some populations do increase the use of alcohol, other drugs, and cigarettes, especially those who demonstrate comorbidity with other disorders. Fifteen percent of survivors of a 1994 shooting in a Texas cafeteria said they used alcohol to cope with stress (North et al. 1994), but the extent to which alcohol is used as self-medication can be difficult to determine, as can the relationship between alcohol use and stressors in general.

18.3.2 PERSONS NEARING SUBSTANCE ABUSE OR DEPENDENCE CROSS THE LINE

In New York City after 9/11, a constant refrain was that many who were borderline alcoholics had "crossed the line," drinking to excess to cope and then becoming dependent upon alcohol for daily functioning (Frank and Owens 2002). This area deserves more research so core indicators of addiction following disaster can be identified.

18.3.3   Persons in Active Addiction Increase Use of Substances

A characteristic of addiction is an increase in use of the substance over time, until such time as either recovery or early death or disability occurs. There is no reason to believe that a stressor the size of a disaster, be it natural or human caused, would be any different in its outcomes. Frank and Owens (2002) found that 9/11 New York City street survivors and clients were requesting more benzodiazepines from their doctors (50), while Stewart (1996) and Adams and Adams (1984) found that driving-while-intoxicated (DWI) rates rise after disaster.

18.3.4   Persons in Recovery Experience Relapse

Relapse, a clinical worsening of symptoms (Norris 2005, 3), increases upon exposure to disaster. After 9/11 in New York City, staff of substance abuse treatment facilities who were in recovery sometimes relapsed, and many left their jobs entirely (Frank and Owens 2002, 19), while police, firefighters, and other responders, such as teachers in affected schools, in recovery were relapsing (18). A focus group of providers conducted by Rowe and Liddle (2008) found that, of Hurricane Katrina adolescent disaster survivors, over half of the youth in drug-abuse-treatment programs had relapsed during the hurricane and evacuation. The Midwestern floods of 1993 caused 20 percent of those who were in recovery from alcohol-use disorders to use alcohol to cope after the floods (North et al. 2004). Zywiak and colleagues reported in 2003 that relapse among patients who were detoxified prior to 9/11 increased by 42 percent, while a recent analysis by North and colleagues (2011) found that survivors of disaster in recovery were four times more likely to drink than were survivors without a previous addiction. Clearly, persons in recovery, especially those in early recovery, are in danger of relapsing back to the addictive substance after disaster.

18.3.5   Persons Experiencing Posttraumatic Stress Disorder or Depressive Symptoms Increase Use of Substances

Posttraumatic stress disorder (PTSD) is a known outcome in disasters, but how this diagnosis relates to substance use deserves further study. In Oklahoma City, alcohol-use disorder among firefighters was correlated with less satisfaction at work, higher PTSD-related impairment in job performance and personal relationships, and use of alcohol as a coping mechanism after the bombing (North et al. 2002a). Vlahov and colleagues (2002) postulate that substance use after disaster may rise for several reasons, including the increase in need to cope with stress or relax; nervousness from withdrawal symptoms or self-medication, especially by those with PTSD; and a vicious cycle of substance use to treat symptoms, which in fact exacerbates them and prolongs use. Norris (2005) notes that the most observed condition after disaster is PTSD, followed by depression, and these are made worse by proximity of exposure to the disaster and by the disaster type, with mass violence causing the most severe impairment. Norris also discusses substance use in this context as possibly increased because those affected already had substance use disorders or other psychological disorders (3). It is clear that PTSD and substance use are related; exactly what that relationship might be is yet to be fully determined by research. According to Adams and colleagues (2006), understanding the relationship between substance use and PTSD is crucial because substance use "may hinder the resolution of psychological distress and the treatment of psychological problems" (205).

18.3.6   Persons in Other At-Risk Groups, Such as First Responders, Increase Use of Substances

Frank and Owens (2002) found that police and fire recovery workers were noted by treatment providers to be increasing alcohol use, in part due to survivor guilt (50–51). Before and after Oklahoma

City, there is a body of literature that documents the resilience of first responders, who "self-select" for this work (Boxer and Wild 1993; North 2002a and 2002b; Frank and Owens 2002) along with an admonition that drinking as a coping mechanism is significantly associated with poor outcomes. For example, those Oklahoma City firefighters who drank to cope had four times the alcohol-use disorders than did others (North et al. 2002a, 174; see Section 18.5.3 for further information).

18.3.7   COMPLEX DYNAMICS

18.3.7.1   National Survey on Drug Use and Health Shows Increase in Use among Hurricane Katrina and Rita Evacuees Compared to Those Who Remained

The National Survey on Drug Use and Health reported on January 31, 2008, that although there were no significant overall increases in illicit drug use or binge alcohol use (and an actual decrease in marijuana use) among the Gulf Coast areas that were hit by Hurricanes Katrina and then Rita, there were higher rates of use in all categories for adults who were displaced from their homes for at least two weeks (SAMHSA 2008, 1). Female caregivers who were living in Federal Emergency Management Agency (FEMA) trailers or hotels reported depression and anxiety (68 percent); they were some of the 1.5 million people who were displaced for longer than two weeks (SAMHSA 2008, 2). Clearly, loss of residence is a major stressor that is related to substance use.

18.3.7.2   Changes in Drug Distribution Networks Postdisaster

Valdez and colleagues (2009) demonstrate that patterns of drug use by the population studied (poverty, minority race, previous substance use, displaced to Houston from New Orleans) were disrupted because the usual illicit drug markets were destroyed or inaccessible, and new markets in Houston supplied different drugs. As a result, overall use of illicit drugs dropped, despite an overall increase in substance use (Valdez et al. 2009, 23). The NSDUH Report (SAMHSA 2008) shows that, although use continued to rise in other areas of the country, the Gulf states showed decreases in the use of illicit drugs, marijuana, illegal use of prescriptions, binge alcohol use, and cigarette use (Tables 5 and 6, p. 6). Lack of availability of all drugs certainly played into these numbers, as there was no electricity or automobile gas in much of the region for weeks, so stores that sell legal drugs were generally not open.

18.3.7.3   Localized versus Regional Devastation

Because there was widespread and total hurricane destruction in many of the Gulf Coast areas, but especially from Biloxi, Mississippi, to beyond New Orleans, Louisiana, by Katrina, and from Lake Charles, Louisiana, past Beaumont, Texas, by Rita, no local help was available for immediate call-out (SAMHSA 2008, 3). Interstates in Mississippi all the way north to Jackson were covered with trees, gas was unavailable, and cell towers were toppled or overloaded. Disaster planning ought to take these considerations into account when devising plans for agencies and clients, especially in areas prone to natural disaster.

18.4   DISASTER IMPACT ON SUBSTANCE ABUSE AND PREVENTION TREATMENT INFRASTRUCTURE

New York City substance abuse treatment systems experienced extraordinary breaks in service delivery after the attacks of 9/11. For example, everything below 14th and Houston Streets was closed to all clients and residents—everyone except responders—for a long period of time; those providers who did not have their offices destroyed outright were nonetheless faced with cremains and ash six inches deep, with elevators that would not work, and with respiratory issues upon return. The Frank and Owens (2002) report available from the SAMHSA Center for Substance Abuse Treatment entitled "The Impact of the World Trade Center Disaster on Treatment and

Prevention Services for Alcohol and Other Drug Abuse in New York" is a lengthy report that describes what it is like to have infrastructure destroyed or so ruined that it takes three months to even consider moving back in. What about records? Communication with staff? Client services? The report, complete with focus group results, describes lessons learned for providers and programs, for state/counties/cities, and makes recommendations for the future. Examples include provision of alternative communication systems; cross-disciplinary, comprehensive planning; fiscal rules for quick resource allocation; and specialized disaster and response training for all behavioral health providers.

18.4.1   Impact of 9/11 Attack on Lower Manhattan Opioid Treatment Providers

As noted in the previously mentioned report, lower Manhattan opioid treatment providers were either inaccessible or wiped out by the collapse of the twin towers. Those who would normally provide services ran for their lives, often alongside their clients, and they would not be allowed back for a long time. Clients were not required to carry identification so were technically unable to get "guest" doses of their medicine at other clinics—but these were extraordinary times. The state agency quickly told remaining providers to guest-dose these clients after asking the client how much the dosage was to be, which they did, and there was not one documented case of abuse of this guest-dosing privilege, which is extraordinary in itself. This gap in the system was quickly studied and filled; there are now protocols for guest-dosing that were shared nationally so that others could benefit from the experience of the New York City providers.

18.4.1.1   Impact of Hurricane Katrina on Methadone Provision in the South

With the mental health and substance abuse treatment systems destroyed along the Gulf Coast, provision of methadone medication proved to be difficult, at best. Many displaced persons in Louisiana went to Baton Rouge, where Tulane Medical School staff also relocated. These staff provided doses to clients, but only after reassessing their needs, as most clients did not know or have their dosage amounts, and records were nonexistent (Winstead and Legeai 2007). In fact, at eight months after the disaster, only 1 percent of evacuees to Houston were found to use methadone as a street drug, with 19 percent preferring marijuana to relieve physical and emotional pain (Valdez et al. 2009, 19). The systems were not set up to deal with total displacement for many months—few are.

18.4.2   Impact of 2005 Hurricanes on Gulf Coast Substance
Abuse Prevention and Treatment Providers

Mental health and substance abuse services to veterans were significantly disrupted due to destruction of Veterans Affairs facilities in Gulfport, Mississippi, and the closing of the facility in New Orleans after Katrina; interestingly, the Biloxi, Mississippi, facility remained open, despite the utter destruction in that area (Druss, Henderson, and Rosenheck 2007, 155), and provided services to the Gulfport displaced veterans.

The Gulf Coast Mental Health Center system in southern Mississippi was destroyed by the storm, and a team of Indiana state police, conservation officers (complete with swamp buggies), National Guard (including gasoline and MREs[a]), and medical and mental health professionals was deployed to Biloxi within four days of the hit by Hurricane Katrina under a state-to-state emergency management assistance compact (EMAC[b]). The mental health professionals functioned as a temporary replacement for the community mental health center, providing resources and helping clients to obtain service when possible. The Indiana group changed its personnel every two weeks to avoid burnout, for a period of six weeks, until the system could resume functionality. In this way, clients were able to access some services, and medications could be obtained for those who needed them.

18.4.3 Loss or Disruption of Recovery Networks

In New York City, many lower Manhattan Alcoholics Anonymous (AA) and other peers-in-recovery meetings were lost, both people and places, but the Ground Zero workers set up two daily meetings that people could attend (see Section 18.5.3 for more information). In Biloxi, Mississippi, personnel on the ground within one week, this author included, were told that the recovery network pulled together, went out to find its members, and reestablished meetings as it could. This was self-help in the truest sense of the term. Since these meetings are set up by members, the recovery networks, although lost, seemed to reestablish themselves quickly. The offices of Alcoholics Anonymous are in New York City, and, while not displaced, the staff there were affected like anyone else. The *AA Grapevine*, the international publication of AA, discussed the story in January 2002, and talked about the hardhats and boots at the Group at Ground Zero (S., Richard 2002). These informal networks were disrupted or lost, but the spirit of self-help caused them to regroup and come together again in support of members who needed ongoing support.

18.5 AT-RISK POPULATIONS

While most at-risk populations have been discussed in a general manner, certain of these deserve special mention.

18.5.1 Disaster Survivors Who Are in Early Recovery

From a substance abuse treatment perspective, those who are in the first six months of recovery from substance use disorders are very vulnerable to relapse, or the reinitiation of use of the particular addictive substance. Disasters, especially those that are human caused and have culpability associated with them, can and do push those newly in recovery to relapse, or "go back out" (Frank and Owens 2002). These persons will need extra attention and care following any disaster to help them preserve their sobriety.

18.5.2 Survivors Experiencing Disaster-Related Mental Health Symptoms

Mental health diagnoses including PTSD are infrequently studied in relation to postdisaster substance use disorders, but it again goes without saying that these people need special care and patience as they process what healthy people have difficulty handling themselves. Clients who are displaced from their service providers, as when the mental health centers in lower Mississippi and in New Orleans were completely wiped out after Katrina, may be without a trusted therapist, or without medication (see Section 18.4.1.1), and most psychotropic medications are not in a push pack that will come from the Strategic National Stockpile (SNS).[c] Setting up redundant provision of these services will go a long way toward reducing anxiety for both the client and the provider, in the event of disaster.

18.5.3 First Responders

Police and firefighters and other responders are trained in many areas of trauma response, but there is no one who can mentally digest dealing with body parts of children, for example. Oklahoma City firefighters had 25 percent current alcohol-use disorder and reported using alcohol to cope (North et al. 2002a, 174) after doing recovery work at the Murrah Federal Building site. Additionally, these responders come from what is termed a "closed shop"—those who come from the outside are often viewed with suspicion. Frank and Owens (2002) found that police officers in New York City who would talk with them were resentful when they were required to go through stress debriefings at their precincts; a recent court case had revealed that an officer was alcoholic, and no one then trusted the confidentiality of services provided to them (13). It is important to work with the Employee Assistance Programs that are usually in place for first responders; it is here that they will often turn.

Self-help groups for first responders and others make sense when near a site as enormous as that in New York City. The officers and NYFD firefighters who were in recovery found that the self-help groups set up at Ground Zero were lifesaving for them (Frank and Owens 2002, 12). Helping to find sites so that these groups can form is one way to assist first responders and to help avoid relapse for those in recovery.

18.5.4 ADOLESCENT YOUTH

Youth who are displaced or whose lives change drastically due to disaster are finally being examined from a substance abuse perspective, as youth are the most vulnerable to early onset of use. Rohrbach and colleagues (2009) were already studying a group of Lake Charles, Louisiana, youth just before Hurricane Katrina hit, so baseline data were established. While Katrina spared Lake Charles, Hurricane Rita arrived 28 days later, and this time it did not bypass the area, but devastated it. Youth here were evacuated (87 percent), while 6 percent of these students were themselves hurt, 7 percent saw others hurt, 2 percent saw someone die, and 38 percent lost their homes. Surveys administered at 7 and 19 months post-Rita showed increased use of marijuana that was directly related to exposure to the hurricane as well as an increase in all alcohol and other drug use as a result of negative life events caused by the hurricane (222).

Following a café fire in Volendam, the Netherlands, in 2001, a survey of adolescent survivors by Reijneveld and colleagues (2003) found a significant increase in alcohol consumption, with corresponding increases in anxiety, depression, and aggressive behavior. Prior to these studies, we are aware of only one other study that has specifically examined adolescent alcohol use, especially binge drinking, in relation to disaster. In 1998, several devastating tornadoes tore through Minnesota, and researchers found that adolescents increased drinking, especially those who were older, who had previous trauma history, and who already had started drinking. PTSD symptoms correlated with higher levels of binge drinking in this sample (Schroeder and Polusny 2004).

18.6 CASE STUDIES

The following disaster responses by three different states that assisted survivors with substance abuse problems both support the lessons learned through the cited empirical studies and offer additional lessons for future reflection. The state field reports discuss substance abuse services both within and outside the FEMA-funded Crisis Counseling Assistance and Training Program (CCP). The CCP is a supplemental disaster behavioral health response and recovery grant for eligible states, territories, and tribes and is administered through an interagency agreement with the Substance Abuse and Mental Health Services Administration, Center for Mental Health Services. The CCP is unique in that it focuses on both individual and community recovery and relies on a strengths-based, outreach-oriented, public health model for the provision of crisis counseling services. The CCP funds individual crisis counseling; group crisis counseling; basic supportive contacts; public education; community networking; assessment, referral, and resource linkage; development and distribution of educational materials; and media messaging (SAMHSA nd). CCP services are typically provided by paraprofessionals who are supervised by master's level team leaders. Once grant funding is received, the State Mental Health Authority[d] typically contracts with local community mental health centers that have experience with crisis counseling and the CCP model. Since the CCP is the "primary mechanism for the federal government to authorize the delivery of behavioral health services to disaster-affected communities and individuals" (Chapter 3, this volume), addressing disaster-related substance abuse through the CCP should be a key objective for state agencies.

18.6.1 Iowa Disaster Response

The following disaster substance abuse response field report is based in part on a questionnaire sent to Karen Hyatt, Emergency Mental Health Specialist for the Iowa Department of Human Services, Division of Mental Health and Disability Services and a follow-up interview, as well as the state's final CCP program report. The report describes the experiences of incorporating disaster substance abuse services into a CCP that was implemented in response to widespread flooding in 2008. Although the CCP can address both disaster-related mental health and substance abuse issues, it has been a challenge to consistently address disaster-related substance abuse within CCPs. State mental health authorities infrequently contract with substance abuse providers to offer CCP services. Further, ambiguity in federal legislation concerning crisis counseling and inconsistent integration of state public mental health and substance abuse prevention and treatment systems has contributed to a misconception that the CCP cannot address substance abuse. Just as disaster-related mental health issues are addressed through the parameters of the CCP, disaster substance abuse can be addressed through the provision of psychoeducation, supportive interventions, substance abuse screenings, referrals to traditional substance abuse treatment when indicated, and networking with community recovery support systems.

18.6.1.1 2008: Catastrophic Floods

During the summer of 2008, catastrophic storms caused widespread flooding across most of Iowa, resulting in significant devastation to many communities and a subsequent presidential disaster declaration (FEMA-DR-1763; FEMA 2010). Ultimately, 78 of Iowa's 99 counties were declared for Individual Assistance leading to the largest Crisis Counseling Assistance and Training Program (CCP) in the state's history. This program was known as Project Recovery Iowa and came to provide both disaster mental health and substance abuse services to 31 counties.

In the past, the State relied on a single health provider to offer statewide crisis counseling services, which sometimes resulted in services being offered by a provider that was not indigenous to the communities being served. Project Recovery Iowa, however, utilized a different service delivery strategy based on disaster behavioral health service provision by six local mental health and substance abuse providers, in addition to the Iowa Concern Hotline. One provider, in particular, was known for traditionally offering a wide range of substance abuse prevention and treatment services, including services for adolescents.

The establishment of community-based partnerships was critical to the success of Project Recovery Iowa and helped to provide additional disaster substance abuse outreach. Providers networked with groups such as public libraries, farm associations, and faith-based organizations. One provider, in particular, established community-based partnerships with local substance abuse service centers well known in several communities (Iowa Department of Human Services 2009). The State noted the success of this new model in its final program report. "The Project Recovery Iowa model that was developed by the MHDS staff was clearly a best practice for the State of Iowa. For the first time in Iowa's CCP grant history, community mental health and substance abuse providers were contracted with to provide the grant services. Their knowledge and history assisted in the needs assessment necessary for outreach work, in the projection of the needs of people who had experienced the disaster events and in the recruitment of people to hire for Project Recovery Iowa who were indigenous to the communities served" (Iowa Department of Human Services 2009, 35). The strategy to utilize a variety of behavioral health providers supported both the needs of local communities, as well as fostered the delivery of CCP disaster substance abuse services.

Disaster substance abuse services benefited greatly from Project Recovery Iowa's use of staff with professional substance abuse treatment backgrounds. All of the CCP team leaders at one provider had professional substance abuse treatment backgrounds. These team leaders provided supportive substance abuse interventions and referrals when needed and provided project-wide trainings on substance abuse issues. "As staff identified the training needs of their Crisis Counselors, Team Leaders developed and provided additional in-services. For example, instruction was provided on how to conduct an educational presentation, facilitate support groups, and assess for substance abuse and mental health risk factors" (Iowa Department of Human Services 2009, 68).[e] In addition, some of the outreach workers also had paraprofessional substance abuse experience.

Project Recovery Iowa's crisis counselors offered impacted communities a wide assortment of educational presentations and support groups, often targeting specific at-risk populations for additional support during the recovery process. For instance, they used a variety of activities to engage students in age-appropriate discussions of feelings associated with the flooding and the impact on their current lives. In the following example, issues of substance abuse in the family were addressed, which led to a discussion of the student's hopes for the family. "Students made family crests. One student drew a beer bottle, and explained that after the flood his dad was stressed out and began drinking heavily. The student explained that this caused a lot of arguing and fighting in the home and how he hopes for peace because his dad is going to AA meetings. This opened a discussion about alcoholism, and other students related and shared their experiences with this student" (Iowa Department of Human Services 2009, 290).

Of the many CCP services provided by Project Recovery Iowa, the consistent administration of substance abuse screenings across providers was a strength of the program. Project Recovery Iowa crisis counselors and team leaders implemented alcohol abuse screenings for adults, along with the adult mental health screenings, and adolescents. However, challenges accompanied the introduction of the CAGE Questionnaire for adults (Ewing 1984) and the CRAFFT for adolescents (Knight et al. 1999). "Initially, the crisis counseling staff was hesitant to use the screening tools; however, with further training on how to make an appropriate referral, staff started to use the tools. The overall feedback from staff was that the screening tools gave them a comfort level in asking questions they were not otherwise comfortable asking. Once the screening tools were in place, there was a positive increase in referrals to substance abuse treatment services. The data [do] not show, however, whether the increase in referrals was because more people screened high on the questions or whether staff became more comfortable referring to substance abuse treatment services based on the new training and the screening tool" (Iowa Department of Human Services 2009, 43). It is notable that staff across all Project Recovery Iowa providers was trained in the use of these tools. In addition, all Iowa Concern Hotline counselors received training in listening for potential clues of substance abuse and how to appropriately respond when disaster survivors presented with substance abuse issues.

The Iowa Concern Hotline was instrumental in the state's substance abuse response to the floods. In illustration, "Iowa Concern received a call from a man with a history of substance abuse. He stated that he has been working on his house but it has become an emotional burden. He is having trouble sleeping and concentrating, and has had memory loss, admitting to 'falling off the wagon.' He found a PRI brochure in his door and called Iowa Concern for help. He said he was relieved to find the brochure; it was the answer he had been looking for" (Iowa Department of Human Services 2009, 292).

Another programmatic element that facilitated the provision of disaster substance abuse services was the importance given to ongoing needs assessment. Early in the program, Project Recovery Iowa used a "pyramid diagram" to target services in which about 80 percent of a community benefited from services that were preventive and psychoeducational in nature, about 15 percent of a community benefited from services targeted to at-risk populations, and about 5 percent of community members required more intensive services based on significant behavioral health adjustment needs (Iowa Department of Human Services 2009). Community and at-risk population needs were continually assessed throughout the life of the program, leading to observed variances over time as well as differences from one community to another. Such ongoing needs assessment activities helped to ensure that individuals with substance abuse issues continued to be among those who merited special consideration throughout the program.

Project Recovery Iowa's experience illustrates several important ways disaster substance abuse services can be effectively incorporated into a large-scale disaster behavioral health response and recovery program. First, disaster substance abuse services fit nicely within the service parameters of the CCP and should be viewed as a critical partner of mental health services. Second, valid and reliable substance abuse screening tools for both adults and youth should be completed whenever mental health screening tools are used and at other times as indicated. Third, crisis counselors should receive appropriate substance abuse training at the beginning of a CCP to assist them to identify individuals with substance abuse problems. And, finally, state disaster mental health and disaster substance abuse coordinators should be encouraged to collaborate during the writing of the CCP application in order to maximize effective behavioral health outreach efforts, as well as develop a program responsive to both disaster mental health and substance abuse needs.

As a disaster behavioral health response and recovery program that has evolved over the course of its 35-plus-year history, the CCP is increasingly addressing disaster-related substance abuse issues. State public mental health and substance abuse prevention and treatment systems, which have often operated independently of each other, have continued to move toward a unified behavioral health model in recent years. As a result, CCPs will most likely continue to engage providers with substance abuse expertise. The Project Recovery Iowa CCP demonstrated that disaster-related substance abuse issues can be addressed through the inclusion of substance abuse providers, as well as the incorporation of substance abuse trainings, screenings, supportive services, partnerships, and referrals across CCP service providers.

18.6.2 COLORADO DISASTER RESPONSE

The following disaster substance abuse field reports are based on a questionnaire sent to Katie Wells, Disaster Response Coordinator for Substance Abuse with the Colorado Department of Human Services, Division of Behavioral Health, and a follow-up interview. The Colorado reports highlight how substance abuse professionals can make important contributions to the local or state jurisdiction's disaster behavioral health response; how collaborative education and cross-training of mental health and other partner organizations' workers can raise awareness of the effects of disaster on substance use and abuse; and the special role and utilization of peers in recovery and 12-step programs in disaster response. The importance of outreach to at-risk populations, the building of rapport and trust with survivors with substance use problems, and the need to address psychological triggers that can threaten recovery and sobriety are also discussed.

18.6.2.1 2008: Severe Storms and Tornadoes

After a powerful tornado struck north-central Colorado in May 2008 (FEMA-1762-DR-CO; FEMA 2009), efforts were made to link the Crisis Counseling Assistance and Training Program (CCP) with a local substance abuse prevention coalition, with an increased focus on helping youth in school settings. The response consisted mostly of information sharing on the location of providers, crisis intervention for individuals who were struggling with relapse and trauma, and basic supportive services for those in varying stages of recovery. For individuals requiring substance abuse treatment, referrals and assessments were provided, and collaborative partnerships helped to provide transportation to treatment providers. Many survivors were very reluctant to identify their need for substance abuse services, so it was a slow process. Psychological First Aid was provided by mental health staff, and substance abuse providers were consulted when a substance use issue was discovered. Many substance abuse professionals helped by listening and providing simple, supportive interventions.

18.6.2.2 2005: Hurricane Katrina

Colorado was one of many states that received Hurricane Katrina evacuees, under a program entitled Colorado Safe Haven. Although the state administered a CCP for the Katrina evacuees, a substantial portion of the substance abuse services provided was outside the CCP. Evacuees began arriving in Colorado on September 4, 2005; some arrived by plane and were assisted by the Federal Emergency Management Agency, and others came on their own using different modes of transportation. The state provided dormitory housing, medical services, services for pets, crisis counseling, and all other necessities for the evacuees in a 550-room dormitory on Lowry Air Force Base. Evacuees were not allowed to use alcohol or other drugs while at the base.

In addition to certified addiction counselors at the site to provide support and guidance for those seeking treatment services or access to recovery support meetings, the participation of recovering individuals from 12-Step programs was a key factor in the substance abuse response to support Hurricane Katrina evacuees. Approximately 10–12 substance abuse responders from local provider agencies and 25–30 individuals from Alcoholics Anonymous and Narcotics Anonymous provided outreach, support, screenings and assessment, and referrals to community services for substance abuse treatment. Outreach included literature distribution; brochures were left at the site for families who needed referrals for medication-assisted therapy, detoxification, or ongoing substance abuse treatment services. Educational materials were also distributed to local schools where adolescent evacuees attended to raise awareness of substance abuse problems and community resources. It was expected that the first 6–12 months after relocation would be the most challenging time for evacuees with substance abuse problems.

Substance abuse professionals and paraprofessionals integrated their services within the larger disaster response effort and worked effectively alongside other behavioral health response partners such as the American Red Cross and the Colorado Organization for Victim Assistance. Substance abuse workers explained the services that recovering individuals would need and their own roles and responsibilities. They were especially helpful with the referral process due to their expertise and knowledge of community substance abuse treatment and detoxification services. Having peers-in-recovery onsite was invaluable, as they provided an important support role as evacuees made the transition to their new location. They provided trucks to help evacuees move, donated items evacuees needed in order to get settled, and provided transportation to 12-Step recovery support meetings.

18.6.2.3 2002: Wildfires

In Colorado's 2002 wildfire disaster (FEMA-1421-DR-CO; FEMA 2004), a substance abuse treatment provider participated in the CCP to help the families impacted by the disaster. One of the program's crisis counselors reported conversations with different survivors with substance use disorders after the fires. One of these survivors had lost everything and was living in a tent. Each time the crisis counselor spoke to him he was intoxicated and refused help. Consequently, behavioral health workers must face the fact that survivors with substance abuse or mental health issues do not always seek nor will they accept help. However, outreach workers can sometimes motivate such individuals to seek help by providing supportive interventions, which contribute to relationships of trust in which confidentiality and safety are assured.

For the survivors who needed medication-assisted therapies, the substance abuse-funded providers, known as the Managed Service Organizations, offered the assessments and services required outside the CCP. There was significant outreach, including door-to-door canvassing, to older adults and non-English-speaking populations after the fires. Workers provided information in both English and Spanish regarding disaster preparedness and stress management, including how to deal with painful reminders such as the disaster's anniversary. Such trigger events can test the resolve of individuals in recovery.

The Division of Behavioral Health discovered that both large-and small-scale disaster substance abuse responses include the importance of planning ahead of time and knowledge of services available in any given community. Whatever can be done to elevate the need for an awareness of the role substance abuse can have on survivors would be helpful. Due to lack of training and awareness, nonbehavioral health emergency responders do not often consider the mental health and substance abuse issues with which some survivors struggle. Therefore, there is a need to train nonbehavioral health workers in other disaster response agencies to increase their knowledge of the potential impact of disaster on people in recovery or in active addiction. Interagency collaborations and trainings should occur regularly so that in the future, no matter what the disaster, a community response team would know immediately if substance abuse services have been interrupted and to ensure a substance abuse professional is always available and involved in the disaster response. Distributing literature to help responders and survivors alike recognize when an individual's use is becoming problematic is an important aspect of outreach education. Furthermore, there is greater recognition of the necessity for mental health services postdisaster than substance abuse services. Training on the stigma of substance abuse is important to help mental health outreach workers to talk confidently about the subject of substance use and abuse with disaster survivors.

18.6.3 Massachusetts Disaster Response

The following disaster substance abuse response field report is based on a questionnaire sent to Rodrigo Monterrey, All-Hazards Coordinator for the Massachusetts Department of Public Health, Bureau of Substance Abuse Services (BSAS), and a follow-up interview. The field report describes the experiences of substance abuse workers who assisted Hurricane Katrina evacuees who relocated to Massachusetts after the storm. Their experiences illustrate the importance of effective substance abuse screening and referral of survivors; interagency collaboration and cross-training; medication maintenance; surge capacity and worker stress issues. Furthermore, the provision of disaster behavioral health services must occur within the context of the local or state jurisdiction's overall response to disaster. Contrary to posing a barrier to substance abuse workers, such collaborative efforts provide opportunities to raise awareness of survivor substance abuse problems.

18.6.3.1 2008: Hurricane Katrina Evacuees and Response

On August 29, 2005, Hurricane Katrina impacted the southeast Louisiana coast with severe flooding, damaged levees, and, ultimately, causing flooding and loss of life in New Orleans. Assisted by the Federal Emergency Management Agency, approximately 200 evacuees from the greater New Orleans area began arriving in Massachusetts by plane on September 8, 2005. Another 100 evacuees arrived by other means of transportation. Under a program entitled Operation Helping Hands, the state welcomed, triaged, and temporarily housed the evacuees at Otis Air National Guard Base on Cape Cod, with the BSAS playing an integral role in the effort. The newcomers were referred to as "guests" instead of the more impersonal term "evacuees."

All guests arriving at Otis Air National Guard Base were given a brief substance abuse screening. The screening documented substance use history with a focus on current withdrawal risks. It included simple, straightforward questions about medications guests were taking or typical alcohol and other drug intake, in order to prevent survivors from experiencing withdrawal symptoms while at the base. Drinking or illegal drug use was not allowed "on campus." Guests were instructed on the rules of conduct, compliance with which was a prerequisite for remaining in the shelter.

BSAS substance abuse outreach workers primarily provided interventions consistent with Psychological First Aid, in addition to ongoing recovery support and relapse prevention interventions for evacuees in recovery. However, substance abuse education, screenings, and referrals, as well as transportation to and from formal treatment, were also part of their roles. Specific tools were developed for Department of Mental Health staff to conduct substance abuse assessments effectively. Based on the substance abuse screenings, three guests were immediately referred to the State's Acute Treatment Services (ATS) or a detoxification facility following arrival. Others were monitored and offered support throughout their stay by substance abuse outreach workers who were trained to engage clients who are homeless or otherwise unable or unwilling to access traditional office-based services. A number of other guests were subsequently referred to substance abuse treatment during the course of their stay. Additionally, Alcoholics Anonymous was invited to establish regular meetings on campus.

Guests on medication-assisted therapy for opioid dependence were identified through the initial medical screening given to all guests upon their arrival at the base and referred to a substance abuse provider for an assessment to ensure treatment continuity. BSAS arranged for a licensed opioid treatment provider to be on the base during the first 24 hours of guest intake to take referrals if needed. Methadone was not available on the base, but several times a day, shuttle buses took guests off the base to collect their medications or other needs. There was also a medical station on the base where guests could collect their prescription medications as needed. After-action reports noted staff concerns about medication dosages as guests' preexisting diagnoses and medical histories were typically inaccessible after the disaster.

Although the Massachusetts substance abuse prevention and treatment infrastructure did not suffer physical damage due to Hurricane Katrina, the influx of guests with substance abuse treatment needs tested the state's surge capacity. To mitigate against secondary traumatic stress, the outreach workers were offered counseling. They were also briefed and then debriefed at the beginning and end of their shifts as part of the clinical supervision and self-care support to ensure work continuity and worker effectiveness.[f]

The guests came from a very different culture, in many cases without any local support networks such as family, friends, neighbors, spiritual advisors, or work colleagues. Consequently, the BSAS deployed a number of bilingual substance abuse outreach workers. Additional interpreters were also available on campus and on call, if needed. Older adults were accommodated on the ground floors of the residences and provided with wheelchairs and canes, as well as other assistive devices. Many guests brought their pets and, with the exception of certain exotic pets, most were allowed to keep them in the residences. Families with children were kept together in a separate building. Sexual offender/criminal background checks were completed to ensure guest safety.

The Massachusetts BSAS operated within the state's Incident Command System in response to receiving evacuees. Most of the nonbehavioral health disaster agency workers had little knowledge of substance abuse problems and services. Many of them saw the BSAS as the "alcohol or drug police." Much education was necessary as the response was taking place with nearly every entity involved with the response and recovery coordination effort. These collaborations, however, raised awareness of substance abuse, typical signs and symptoms of use or abuse, and available community resources, which contributed to greater resilience within the emergency management community for future disaster response.

18.7   LESSONS LEARNED

There are a number of important takeaway points for individuals involved in disaster substance abuse planning and response. Research to date and anecdotal field observations support that the issue of substance abuse should be included in any jurisdiction's overall behavioral health response to disaster. Individuals in recovery, especially early recovery, may relapse after disaster and need supportive interventions to maintain their sobriety. Additionally, survivors who are borderline addicts or individuals in active addiction may increase their consumption of substances after disaster, sometimes with life-threatening results. Since it appears that loss of residence and lack of social support are significantly related to substance use problems, the homeless may need extra support to prevent substance use from spiraling out of control. Likewise, disaster response should incorporate measures to mitigate against trigger events that may impede the best efforts of individuals in recovery to preserve their sobriety.

Substance abuse professionals and paraprofessionals should be included in both the jurisdictional disaster behavioral health response and preparedness efforts because they are trained to provide initial screenings and assessments to identify addiction issues and will be the most familiar with available resources in the impacted community. Their actions should reflect an appreciation for cultural diversity and how culture can impact survivors' response to disaster. Substance abuse workers should also be proactive in reaching out to and collaborating with other partner organizations active in the response, including providing education and training to mental health workers and nonbehavioral health partners on the effects of stigma, recognizing signs and symptoms of substance abuse, and building rapport and trust with survivors who may be struggling with addiction.

Further, the demonstrated ability of peers-in-recovery to regroup quickly after disaster and their willingness to provide support to survivors facing similar issues should not be overlooked. Disaster planners would be wise to engage in discussion with groups such as Alcoholics Anonymous or Narcotics Anonymous and to augment the jurisdictional disaster response and develop Memoranda of Understanding with other recovery support organizations.

Catastrophic disasters pose special concerns because they can destroy or indefinitely delay substance abuse infrastructure and services. Even when disasters do not destroy or delay use of the substance abuse infrastructure, providers need to have surge capacity and sufficient ability to continue medication-assisted therapies to avoid dangerous consequences for survivors. Therefore, the emergency planning needs of opioid treatment providers should be factored into local and state preparedness activities. Further, opioid treatment providers need to have protocols for guest-dosing in place prior to disaster because medical records may be unavailable afterwards.

18.8 NATIONAL DEVELOPMENTS

Fortunately, some of the disaster substance abuse lessons learned are being applied on the national level. Since the events of 9/11, disaster substance abuse responses benefited from several initiatives and developments. State and territory planning for the substance abuse impact of disasters increased and is becoming more integrated with mental health, emergency management, and public health planning. In addition, experience with the impact of terrorism and large-scale disasters led to efforts to ensure that patients receiving medication-assisted therapy can get medication safely and effectively after a disaster. Finally, there is a substantial increase in the number of identified state and territory disaster substance abuse or behavioral health coordinators over the last several years.

18.8.1 DISASTER SUBSTANCE ABUSE PLANNING

Effective response to the substance abuse impact of disasters depends, in large part, on best practice disaster substance abuse preparedness and planning efforts at the state, territory, and local levels. This promotes further integration of disaster substance abuse planning with overall state and territory disaster mental health, emergency management, and public health plans. One important catalyst for increased and coordinated disaster substance abuse planning was the SAMHSA Targeted Capacity Expansion Grants to Enhance State Capacity for Emergency Mental Health and Substance Abuse Response, also known as the State Capacity Expansion (SCE) grants, which were initiated in 2003 and ended in 2006 for most states participating in the initiative. These grants were a direct outgrowth of the 9/11 terrorist attacks, which highlighted the need for coordinated mental health and substance abuse responses to disasters that are integrated with the larger emergency management and public health responses. Thirty-four states and the District of Columbia received the grants, a primary deliverable of which was the development of a state all-hazards plan that required "coordinated mental health and substance abuse emergency planning and capacity development activities" (Donato and Mosser nd, 2).

Prior to the SCE grants, only four states participating in the SCE grant initiative had a unified disaster behavioral health plan that addressed both disaster mental health and substance abuse preparedness, with an additional three states holding a disaster substance abuse plan that also addressed mental health concerns. A final review of the state all-hazards plans submitted under the grants indicated improved disaster substance abuse planning evidenced by 26 states with a unified disaster behavioral health plan, two states with separate disaster mental health and substance abuse plans, four states with disaster mental health plans that also addressed substance abuse, and one state with a disaster substance abuse plan that also addressed mental health (Donato and Mosser nd). SAMHSA is continuing to promote integrated best-practice disaster substance abuse all-hazards planning for states and territories that is compliant with the National Incident Management System.[g]

18.8.2 DIGITAL ACCESS TO MEDICATION

One important program that resulted from lessons learned from the 9/11 terrorist attacks is the SAMHSA Center for Substance Abuse Treatment's (CSAT) Digital Access to Medication, or D-ATM initiative. The attacks led to the destruction of one opioid treatment provider (OTP) and the closure of several others in lower Manhattan. The disruption in medication-assisted therapies and the subsequent impact on roughly 1,000 patients is well documented in the Frank and Owens (2002) report mentioned earlier in this chapter. As a result, SAMHSA CSAT collaborated with stakeholders, including the Committee of Methadone Program Administrators and patient representatives, to plan for a secure, Web-based database that would allow a patient to be effectively and safely guest-dosed at an OTP other than their home clinic in an emergency. Later, the arrival of Hurricane Katrina evacuees at guest OTPs, many of whom came with no identification, reinforced the need for both effective guest-dosing protocols and the development of the D-ATM project, which was initiated in the fall of 2005. D-ATM utilizes a biometric identifier based on a patient's finger scan so that a guest OTP can verify that the patient is in treatment at another D-ATM participating OTP and can receive information on the patient's medicinal history. The home OTP is also notified of the patient's request for guest dosing, the dosage provided, and the frequency of guest dosing. Patient participation in D-ATM is strictly voluntary and the system is designed with a high degree of security to protect the patient's personal information, which is only accessed at the request of the patient. Currently, D-ATM is in phase III pilot testing with plans to eventually make the project available to OTPs nationwide.[h]

18.8.3 DISASTER SUBSTANCE ABUSE PREPAREDNESS AND RESPONSE COORDINATION

Many states and territories have increased their personnel resources devoted to the coordination of disaster substance abuse preparedness and response. Known as disaster substance abuse coordinators, virtually no states or territories held such a position before 9/11. However, by 2006, at least six states had coordinators serving in this role, and as of this writing, 17 state or territory disaster substance abuse coordinators were identified by the SAMHSA Disaster Technical Assistance Center, with an additional 29 state or territory disaster behavioral health coordinators holding responsibilities for both mental health and substance abuse disaster preparedness and response.

18.9 CONCLUSION

This chapter used several methods to raise awareness of disaster substance abuse including a review of recent literature, field observations from several state responses to disaster, and discussion of several important state and federal initiatives that incorporated some of the lessons learned from prior disasters. Although the practice of disaster substance abuse is a relatively new field of study, current research suggests that use of substances after disaster increases and survivors in recovery may be at greater risk of relapse. We believe the information presented in this chapter will stimulate the appetites of both readers and behavioral health researchers. Much more research, including longitudinal studies in particular, is needed to understand the relationship between disasters and substance use and abuse. It is our hope that, having shed light on disaster substance abuse, others will continue to refine interventions and practices that will improve the health and well-being of disaster survivors with substance use problems.

NOTES

a. Meals Ready to Eat (MREs) are prepackaged, individual meals bought by the U.S. military for use in combat and other field deployments where food facilities may be unavailable.

b. PL-104-321; see http://www.fema.gov/pdf/emergency/nrf/EMACoverviewForNRF.pdf for additional information about the EMAC.

c. See the Centers for Disease Control (CDC) Web site at http://www.cdc.gov/phpr/stockpile.htm for information about the Strategic National Stockpile (SNS).

d. State Mental Health Authority (SMHA), 42 U.S.C. § 201.

e. The term *in-services* refers to intraorganizational trainings offered by CCP staff.

f. The debriefings were not based on Critical Incident Stress Debriefing, however (see Mitchell 1983).

g. Information concerning the National Incident Management System can be found at http://www.fema.gov/emergency/nims/.

h. See the SAMHSA D-ATM Web site for additional information on this important project: http://datm.samhsa.gov.

REFERENCES

Adams, P. R., and G. R. Adams. 1984. Mount Saint Helens' ashfall: Evidence for disaster stress reaction. *American Psychologist 39*(3): 252–260.

Adams, R. E., J. A. Boscarino, and S. Galea. 2006. Alcohol use, mental health status and psychological well-being 2 years after the World Trade Center attacks in New York City. *American Journal of Drug and Alcohol Abuse 32*(2): 203–224.

Boscarino, J. A., R. E. Adams, and S. Galea. 2006. Alcohol use in New York after the terrorist attacks: A study of the effects of psychological trauma on drinking behavior. *Addictive Behaviors 31*(4): 606–621.

Boxer, P., and D. Wild. 1993. Psychological distress and alcohol use among firefighters. *Scandinavian Journal of Work and Environmental Health 19*(2): 121–125.

Dimaggio, C., S. Galea, and G. Li. 2009. Substance use and misuse in the aftermath of terrorism. A Bayesian meta-analysis. *Addiction 104*(6): 894–904.

Donato, D., and C. Mosser. nd. *State Behavioral Health All-Hazards Disaster Plan Review Report.* Rockville, MD: Substance Abuse and Mental Health Services Administration.

Druss, B., K. Henderson, and R. Rosenheck. 2007. Swept away: Use of general medical and mental health services among veterans displaced by Hurricane Katrina. *American Journal of Psychiatry 164*(1): 154–156. http://www.ncbi.nlm.nih.gov/pmc/articles/PMC1868551/pdf/nihms20835.pdf.

Ewing, J. A. 1984. Detecting alcoholism: The CAGE questionnaire. *Journal of the American Medical Association 252*(14): 1905–1907.

Federal Emergency Management Agency (FEMA). 2004. *Colorado Wildfires: Major Disaster Declared June 19, 2002 (DR-1421).* Last modified November 15, 2004. http://www.fema.gov/news/event.fema?id=84.

Federal Emergency Management Agency (FEMA). 2009. *Colorado Severe Storms and Tornadoes: Major Disaster Declared May 26, 2008 (DR-1762).* Last modified February 17, 2009. http://www.fema.gov/news/event.fema?id=9866.

Federal Emergency Management Agency (FEMA). 2010. *Iowa Severe Storms, Tornadoes, and Flooding: Major Disaster Declared May 27, 2008 (DR-1763).* Last modified September 20, 2010. http://www.fema.gov/news/event.fema?id=9867.

Flory, K., B. L. Hankin, B. Kloos, C. Cheely, and G. Turecki. 2009. Alcohol and cigarette use and misuse among Hurricane Katrina survivors: Psychosocial risk and protective factors. *Substance Use & Misuse 44*(12): 1711–1724.

Frank, B., and D. Owens. 2002. *The Impact of the World Trade Center Disaster on Treatment and Prevention Services for Alcohol and Other Drug Abuse in New York: Immediate Effects, Lingering Problems, and Lessons Learned.* Rockville, MD: Center for Substance Abuse Treatment, SAMHSA. http://www.samhsa.gov/csatdisasterrecovery/lessons/impactWTCtreatment.pdf.

Grieger, T. A., C. S. Fullerton, and R. J. Ursano. 2003. Posttraumatic stress disorder, alcohol use, and perceived safety after the terrorist attack on the Pentagon. *Psychiatric Services 54*(10): 1380–1382. http://www.ps.psychiatryonline.org/cgi/reprint/54/10/1380.

Iowa Department of Human Services, Division of Mental Health and Disability Services. 2009. *FEMA-DR-1763-IA, Regular Services Crisis Counseling Assistance and Training Program Final Program Report.* Des Moines, IA: Iowa Department of Human Services.

Joseph, S., W. Yule, R. Williams, and P. Hodgkinson. 1993. Increased substance use in survivors of the Herald of Free Enterprise disaster. *British Journal of Medical Psychology 66*(2): 185–191.

Knight, J. R., L. A. Shrier, T. D. Bravender, M. Farrell, J. Vander Bilt, and H. J. Shaffer. 1999. A new brief screen for adolescent substance abuse. *Archives of Pediatrics and Adolescent Medicine 153*(6): 591–596.

Mitchell, J. T. 1983. When disaster strikes ... The Critical Incident Stress Debriefing process. *Journal of Emergency Medical Services 8*: 36–39.

Norris, F. H. 2005. *Range, Magnitude, and Duration of the Effects of Disasters on Mental Health: Review Update 2005*. Hanover, NH: Dartmouth College. http://www.katasztrofa.hu/documents/Research_Education_Disaster_Mental_Health.pdf.

North, C., A. Kawasaki, E. Spitznagel, and B. Hong. 2004. The course of PTSD, major depression, substance abuse, and somatization after a natural disaster. *Journal of Nervous and Mental Disease 192*(12): 823–829.

North, C., C. Ringwalt, D. Downs, J. Derzon, and D. Galvin. 2011. Postdisaster course of alcohol use disorders in systematically studied survivors of 10 disasters. *Archives of General Psychiatry 68*(2): 173–180.

North, C., E. Smith, and E. Spitznagel. 1994. Posttraumatic stress disorder in survivors of a mass shooting. *American Journal of Psychiatry 151*(1): 82–88.

North, C., L. Tivis, J. McMillen, B. Pfefferbaum, J. Cox, E. L. Spitznagel, K. P. Bunch, J. Schorr, and E. M. Smith. 2002a. Coping, functioning, and adjustment of rescue workers after the Oklahoma City bombing. *Journal of Traumatic Stress 15*(3): 171–175.

North, C., L. Tivis, J. McMillen, B. Pfefferbaum, E. L. Spitznagel, J. Cox, K. P. Bunch, E. M. Smith, and S. J. Nixon. 2002b. Psychiatric disorders in rescue workers after the Oklahoma City bombing. *American Journal of Psychiatry 159*(5): 857–859.

Reijneveld, S. A., M. R. Crone, F. C. Verhulst, and S. P. Verloove-Vanhorick. 2003. The effect of a severe disaster on the mental health of adolescents: A controlled study. *The Lancet 362*: 691–696.

Richman, J. A., C. A. Shannon, K. M. Rospenda, J. A. Flaherty, and M. Fendrich. 2009. *Substance Use & Misuse 44*(12): 1665–1680.

Rohrbach, L. A., R. Grana, E. Vernberg, S. Sussman, and P. Sun. 2009. Impact of Hurricane Rita on adolescent substance use. *Psychiatry 72*(3): 222–237.

Rowe, C. L, and H. A. Liddle, 2008. When the levee breaks: Treating adolescent families in the aftermath of Hurricane Katrina. *Journal of Marital Family Therapy 34*(2): 132–148.

S., Richard. 2002. The Group at Ground Zero. *AA Grapevine* (January). http://www.aagrapevine.org.

Schroeder, J., and M. Polusny. 2004. Risk factors for adolescent alcohol use following a natural disaster. *Prehospital and Disaster Medicine 19*(1): 122–127.

Shimizu, S., K. Aso, T. Nota, S. Ryukei, Y. Kochi, and N. Yamamoto. 2000. Natural disasters and alcohol consumption in a cultural context: The Great Hanshin Earthquake in Japan. *Addiction 95*(4): 529–536.

Stewart, S. H. 1996. Alcohol abuse in individuals exposed to trauma: A critical review. *Psychological Bulletin 120*: 83–112.

Stewart, S. H., T. L. Mitchell, K. D. Wright, and P. Loba. 2004. The relations of PTSD symptoms to alcohol use and coping drinking in volunteers who responded to the Swissair Flight 111 airline disaster. *Anxiety Disorders 18*(1): 51–68. http://alcoholresearchlab.psychology.dal.ca/documents/publications/2004/Stewart%20Mitchell%20%20et%20al%202004.pdf.

Substance Abuse and Mental Health Services Administration (SAMHSA). 2008. *The NSDUH Report, January 31, 2008: Impact of Hurricanes Katrina and Rita on Substance Use and Mental Health*. Rockville, MD: Office of Applied Studies, SAMHSA. http://www.oas.samhsa.gov/2k8/katrina/katrina.pdf.

Substance Abuse and Mental Health Services Administration (SAMHSA). nd. *Federal Emergency Management Agency Crisis Counseling Assistance and Training Program Guidance, Version 3.0*. http://www.samhsa.gov/dtac/CCPtoolkit/pdf/CCP_Program_Guidance.pdf.

Valdez, A., A. Cepeda, A. Canga, K. Nowotny, and J. Onge. 2009. Substance use and other health consequences among Hurricane Katrina evacuees in Houston: A community report. R01 NIH Monograph. Center for Drug and Social Policy Research, University of Houston. http://www.uh.edu/cdspr/NEWSITE/KatrinaCommunityReport.pdf.

Vlahov, D., S. Galea, H. Resnick, J. Ahern, J. A. Boscarino, M. Bucuvalas, J. Gold, and D. Kilpatrick. 2002. Increased use of cigarettes, alcohol, and marijuana among Manhattan residents after the September 11th terrorist attacks. *American Journal of Epidemiology 155*(11): 988–996.

Winstead, D., and C. Legeai. 2007. Lessons learned from Katrina: One department's perspective. *Academic Psychiatry 31*(3): 190–193.

Wu, P., C. S. Duarte, D. J. Mandell, B. Fan, X. Liu, C. J. Fuller, G. Musa, M. Cohen, P. Cohen, and C. W. Hoven. 2006. Exposure to the World Trade Center attack and the use of cigarettes and alcohol among New York City public high-school students. *American Journal of Public Health 96*(5): 804–807.

Zywiak, W. M., R. L. Stout, W. B. Trefry, J. E. LaGrutta, and C. C. Lawson. 2003. Alcohol relapses associated with September 11, 2001: A case report. *Substance Abuse 24*(2): 123–128.

19 Understanding Disaster Recovery Case Management and Behavioral Health

A Review of Research

Martell L. Teasley

CONTENTS

19.1 INTRODUCTION

Disaster response consists of governmental and social services, humanitarian aid, and the appropriate allocation of resources, including the deployment of designated personnel and volunteers for crisis intervention that is life preserving in the promotion of health and well-being. A major challenge for state and local governments, including disaster relief organizations, is the identification and mobilization of disaster case managers after a disaster occurrence. This challenge is elevated by the fact that there are competing definitions of what skills constitute being a disaster case manager and who qualifies as one.

This chapter provides an overview of research on disaster case management and its role in assessment, referral, and treatment of behavioral health challenges related to a disaster occurrence. First, an examination of the role and functioning of disaster case management in the organizational scheme of federal and state emergency management agencies is discussed. Next, related definitions and the reality of case management practices during the aftermath of a disaster are discussed along with research that informs approaches to disaster case management (DCM). A definition of culturally competent DCM is provided along with a review of its necessity in DCM practices. The last section of this chapter briefly deals with the role of faith-based organizations in disaster relief and recovery.

19.2 DEFINING DISASTER CASE MANAGEMENT

Exact definitions of DCM vary and depend on professional disciplines, paraprofessional participation, and organization or agency mission (COA 2008). For this reason, there has been no past interdisciplinary consensus on what constitutes DCM and subsequently no past comprehensive framework on DCM. As such, the term *disaster case management* has had multiple meanings and professional interpretations depending on the goals and objectives of a given organization or agency. Problems with this set of circumstances became increasingly evident particularly during Hurricanes Katrina and Rita in 2005. During the aftermath of these disasters the volume of individuals and communities needing services compromised normative state and local services and resources for disaster response and their ability to timely implement case management services (GAO 2008a). The challenges that these events posed led to concerted efforts by government agency representatives, scholars, and experienced professionals in the field of disaster relief and recovery to research and define the meaning and function of disaster case management. Within this effort is a specific emphasis on identifying evidence-based practices as the underlying rationale for designing a DCM framework. Recent attempts at these efforts are discussed within this chapter.

During the aftermath of Hurricane Katrina in October 2005, the State Department authorized the transfer of $66 million from international donations to FEMA for the purpose of financing DCM (GAO 2009). As an amendment to the Robert T. Stafford Disaster Relief and Emergency Assistance Act in 2006, Congress passed the Post-Katrina Emergency Management Reform Act (PKEMRA) that "grants the President authority to provide case-management services, including financial assistance to state or local government agencies or private organizations to provide such services, to victims of major disasters" (Lavin and Menifee 2009, 4). This gave birth to the federal government's participation in DCM to include assessment and oversight compliance. Given the broad spectrum and array of circumstances in which the federal government may participate in DCM, the Stafford Act necessitated the need for a comprehensive framework that defines and outlines the roles and responsibilities of disaster case managers (see GAO 2008b).

Based on the large-scale intervention during relief and recovery following the 2005 Gulf Coast hurricanes, there was also the launch of four demonstration projects for the purpose of evaluating DCM practices. This led to a series of forums, discussion panels, and the search for best practices among subject matter experts in both the public and private sectors toward the development of DCM standards of practice. Many experts from various organizations were involved in the initial DCM best practices review panels in Washington, DC, in 2007 and 2008. They were from the American Red Cross, the Salvation Army, Catholic Charities, U.S. Refugee & Immigration, and Florida's Department of Children and Families, among others. In a more recent phase, individuals from academia participated in review panels for the purpose of examining the framework and proposed guidelines for DCM. An important outcome of the pilot DCM projects and expert forums was the publication of the *Disaster Case Management: Implementation Guide*. The Implementation Guide was published by the U.S. Department of Health and Human Services, Administration for Children and Families, Office of Human Services Emergency Preparedness and Response (OHSEPR). This guide states:

> Disaster Case Management is the process of organizing a providing a timely, coordinated approach to assess disaster-related needs including healthcare, mental health and human services needs that were caused or exacerbated by the event and may adversely impact an individual's recovery if not addressed. Disaster case management facilitates the delivery of appropriate resources and services, works with a client to implement a recovery plan and advocates for the client's needs to assist him/her in returning to a pre-disaster status while respecting human dignity. If necessary, disaster case management helps transition the client with pre-existing needs to existing case management providers after disaster-related needs are addressed. This is facilitated through the provision of a single point of contact for disaster

assistance applicants who need a wide variety of services that may be provided by many different organizations …. The purpose of disaster case management is to rapidly return individuals and families who have survived a disaster to a state of self-sufficiency. (Lavin and Menifee 2009, 6–7)

While the document goes into greater details in defining the parameters and context in which case management occurs, it further states that DCM "is based on the principles of *self-sufficiency* [restoring adversely impacted lives to predisaster status], *federalism* [federal enhancement and support of state and local government recovery efforts], flexibility and speed, and support to states" (Lavin and Menifee 2009, 7).

The Implementation Guide by OHSEPR is not the only framework for approaching DCM services. The Council on Accreditation (COA; 2008) has developed a framework outlining disaster recovery case management too. Although this framework is inclusive of many case management practices outlined in the OHSEPR Implementation Guide, it focuses on DCM standards within the context of communities and families, client personal responsibility and self-determination; it includes a focus on the principles of cultural competence, intervention with individuals with psychiatric disabilities, and practice with older adults and those with substance abuse conditions. Moreover, it emphasizes community partnerships as a method of reducing unmet needs and the duplication of services. The COA adds that DCM includes not only the immediate short-term needs of disaster survivors such as employment, housing, health care, and other social services, but also the long-term "unmet needs" that extend beyond the initial response and recovery efforts. Thus, based on recovery plans, long-term disaster case managers coordinate services to advocate for clients' unmet needs, and help clients procure resources when other resources are inadequate or exhausted (De Vita and Morley 2007).

Federally-funded DCM projects work in tandem with long-term recovery committees (GAO 2009). Long-term DCM has been endorsed by FEMA and picks up after formal short-term disaster recovery programs have run their course (usually from an exhaustion of federal funding) and are primarily operated by nonprofit and community-based organizations to include VOAD agencies, and civic organizations (De Vita and Morley 2007; GAO 2009). Funding for long-term DCM depends on the coffers and ability to attract funding by agencies involved. Research after Hurricanes Katrina and Rita on long-term recovery by George Washington University scholars "found many remaining challenges" at the end of federally funded services, "including cases tabled because of missing information, no guidance for case managers to obtain needed information, and social service systems still in disarray and unable to provide direct services and financial assistance" (De Vita and Morley 2007, 61). Upon this finding, the Greater New Orleans Disaster Recovery Partnership developed a single presentation package for funders resulting in a dramatic increase in case closures.

Because of a lack of accountability for many VOADs, researchers concluded that it was extremely difficult to determine the efficacy of long-term DCM after Hurricanes Katrina and Rita. Yet, research by the Urban Institute on long-term DCM during Hurricanes Katrina and Rita indicates a clear need for such interventions; those with legal and family problems, extended health care needs, public housing needs, previous connection to the penal system, mental health issues caused by the disaster, and victims of crimes and recovery construction fraud required new levels of DCM and support services after short-term recovery programs were exhausted (De Vita and Morley 2007).

19.3 RESEARCH ON DISASTER CASE MANAGEMENT

Given the many challenges in evaluating DCM, research on the topic heavily focuses on specific populations or tasks. One obstacle to research investigations is that there are numerous models and competing definitions of what constitutes case management (COA 2008). Because of this, there are few empirical investigations that provide insight into the efficacy and efficiency of DCM practices and outcomes. Additionally, there is a lack of research on the development of psychometric instruments used to assess disaster case management practices. Second, and to the point, "Circumstances under which disaster recovery case management service[s] are delivered create challenges for research and evaluation, for example, control or comparison group studies would be difficult to conceptualize and implement" (COA 2008, 1). Third, the largest database of client information to track resources and client outcomes based on participation in coordinated DCM programming is within the Coordinated Assistance Network (CAN). Developed by charitable organizations, CAN has been off limits to research for FEMA officials and other government agencies due to client confidentiality regulations. Third-party reports contend that CAN has been instrumental in facilitating interagency communication and generating progress reports; this includes tracking client services and reducing client service duplication (GAO 2009). Research investigation challenges with CAN are noted as missing data from large segments of client cases and a lack of consistent information across cases in terms of the data collected. As such, although it has the largest array of data on DCM practices, CAN has not been a user-friendly resource for research.

Notwithstanding these limitations, there are empirical studies on tasks and responsibilities related to DCM. The most comprehensive and large-scale study on DCM comes from the Government Accounting Office (GAO 2009). In a report detailing the outcomes of implementing case management programs during the aftermath of Hurricanes Katrina and Rita, the GAO was tasked to report on (1) steps the federal government took to support DCM programs, (2) implementation of DCM programs, (3) challenges that DCM agencies experienced in the delivery of services, and (4) the utility of past federal DCM programs in forming the future of federally sponsored DCM programming. Methods used for this study consisted of qualitative inquiries via site visits, the use of telephone interviews to key personnel to include members of Katrina Aid Today, and a review of case management data. The study was part of the federal government's state-managed Disaster Case Management Pilot (DCM-P) program in Louisiana and Mississippi.

Unfortunately, findings from this study leave more questions concerning the reality of evaluating large-scale case management programs than questions that were answered. Data compared from three federally sponsored programs—Katrina Aid Today, the Louisiana Family Recovery Corps, and the Disaster Housing Assistance Program (DHAP)—were found to be incompatible, with limited access and unreliable in some cases. The report provides useful information on problematic occurrences within the DCM programs, such as tardy program implementation, the overwhelming number of survivors in need of DCM services due to the magnitude of the disaster, and unmanageable client-case manager ratios. Such issues reduced the capacity of case managers to establish rapport and client confidence in the case management process. Housing was a major issue for clients, and the challenges with CAN, as posited by program personnel interviewed for the investigation, may have caused some clients to miss housing program opportunities prior to the closing of the DHAP. As a whole, "The Mississippi DCM-P program officials considered this process inefficient" (GAO 2009, 21).

Scholars from the Urban Institute have engaged in research studies on DCM. During the aftermath of 9/11, government agency representatives and members of nonprofit organizations developed a plan to facilitate the coordination of services for future emergencies in the Washington, DC, region. "As a result of these efforts, the D.C. region now has a model for case management with established standards for participation and guidelines for sharing data that is accepted by five major social service agencies, a plan for scaling up volunteer efforts when needed, and clear standards for soliciting and handling monetary and in-kind donations" (De Vita 2007, 28). Key to the success of this model is the development of a coordinated response effort to include information sharing between agencies small and large, secular and faith based.

19.4 BEHAVIORAL HEALTH AND DISASTER CASE MANAGEMENT

Disaster case managers are not mental health providers but do have the responsibility of initial assessment and triage in referring clients for mental health services (GAO 2008a). It is a given that issues related to client mental health needs will emerge for some percentage of clients during case management practices. Therefore, it is highly important that disaster case managers understand risk factors for poor mental health outcomes as they relate to a pre- and postdisaster occurrence. Research demonstrates that both short-term and long-term behavioral health interventions are needed following a major disaster occurrence. As De Vita and colleagues (2008, 73) note:

> Experts who worked with Katrina victims described the particular needs of traumatized populations for systematic screening and assessment, to establish a baseline of psychological status, and to respond to an inevitable spiral of challenges—high rates of school truancy, high rates of parental depression, and post-traumatic stress disorder (PTSD), which fuels children's difficulties, all of which must be followed by long-term treatment. One expert suggested that nearly everyone in the FEMA trailer park had some measure of PTSD.

Short-term disaster-related mental health intervention concerns the removal of individuals from hazardous environments and the attempt to return them to a sense of equilibrium. Traditionally, nongovernmental agencies, particularly charitable and faith-based organizations, have played an important role in providing short-term recovery mental health services.

Best practices for facilitating client resilience from the stress of disaster point to the use of Psychological First Aid (PFA). Physiological and psychological responses to trauma often trigger biological cues, which may result in situational fight or flight and the associated cognitive stressors involved. "PFA strategies are intended to help survivors begin the process of deactivating these physiological responses and accompanying psychological repercussions as quickly as possible once imminent threat has passed" (Vernberg et al. 2008, 383). There are five basic tenets of PFA strategies and techniques that are empirically supported and should be stressed as a part of DCM: "(a) promoting sense of safety, (b) promoting calming, (c) promoting sense of self- and community efficacy, (d) promoting connectedness, and (e) instilling hope" (Vernberg et al. 2008, 383). Core principles of PFA include providing practical assistance, safety and comfort; collecting ongoing information gathering, as well as monitoring postevent risk and resilience factors; connecting disaster survivors with social supports; and linking individuals with collaborative services (Vernberg et al. 2008). For these reasons, disaster case managers should have training in PFA as a method for understanding how its core principles can facilitate the DCM process.

Despite the need, there appear to be few programs that offer longer-term disaster mental health services. Longer-term disaster mental health intervention focuses on restoring individuals to their normative state of cognitive and behavioral functioning prior to the emergency/disaster. Other than the federally funded Crisis Counseling Assistance and Training Program (FEMA 2010), which can provide services for up to one year postdisaster, there have been relatively few programs that provide longer-term disaster mental health services. Therefore, there is concern for how disaster survivors will continue to progress in their recovery once such programs discontinue. Among recent disaster mental health initiatives, however, the National Child Traumatic Stress Network and the National Center for Posttraumatic Stress have developed the Skills for Psychological Recovery (SPR). SPR is "an evidence-informed intervention ... intended to foster short- and long-term adaptive coping by offering simplified, brief application of interventions found effective in other service contexts: problem-solving training, positive activity scheduling, skills training in management of intrusive thoughts and emotional distress, cognitive reframing, and social support" (Watson and Ruzek 2009, 218). Designed to help disaster survivors develop coping skills for their most pressing concerns, SPR is well received by disaster counselors but will need to establish its effectiveness.

Not to be confused with Skills for Psychological Recovery (SPR), the September 11 Recovery Program (SRP) was established by the American Red Cross to provide long-term assistance to those who continued to experience 9/11-related needs. A survey of 1,501 individuals who received

SRP services post-9/11 from the Red Cross indicated that service recipients continued to have emotional issues and service needs long after the disaster; this finding underscored the need for behavioral health and longer-term recovery services. Approximately four years after 9/11, 43 percent of respondents stated that family members were still in need of recovery services. Mental health services were the most frequently requested, with 63 percent of service recipients requesting services. Despite these findings, 79 percent of the respondees indicated that they felt "somewhat" or "much better off" as a result of receiving SRP services (Morley et al. 2006).

19.5 CULTURAL COMPETENCE AND DISASTER CASE MANAGEMENT

Beyond the general task of facilitating client self-sufficiency, evidence for the need for culturally competent DCM continues to mount. Individual and group response to crises/disasters varies by beliefs, cultural traditions, and economic and social status. When cultural norms, mores, and values are neglected in the consideration of approaches to client services, there is the risk of less-than-optimal case management rapport building, and often problems with trust and other barriers to intervention in the promotion of client self-sufficiency (Athey and Moody-Williams 2003).

Culturally sensitive disaster case management is the process of establishing culturally acceptable approaches to intervention through education, training, knowledge, and skill development for the purpose of providing culturally acceptable and effective methods of intervention. On the one hand, it might involve transforming the given meaning of a particular behavior or social practice in order to instill a new meaning toward desirable behaviors or practices. On the other hand, it may involve the practice of transforming organizations and agencies and their management structures to engaging in the development of personnel, programming, and practices for the purpose of achieving specific objectives and mission mandates through culturally acceptable services for specific client populations. "An effective case manager is more of an entrepreneur on behalf of his or her clients than a cog in a well-oiled rational delivery system" (National Human Services Assembly nd, 1).

Cultural competence during client assessment is an important component of effective DCM. When client assessment is completed in a culturally responsive manner, it helps in the identification of resources that can increase service participation and foster agreed-upon goals for achievement. Factors such as traditional values and beliefs, geographic location, age, gender, religious and spiritual preferences, race, and ethnicity are all important considerations (COA 2008).

Culturally competent disaster case managers are those that are familiar with local communities, including formal and informal leaders, and communication channels. Understanding informal community contacts often helps determine how resources are allocated (De Vita and Morley 2007). Puig and Glynn (2003, 57) suggest that "effective relief efforts include having emergency personnel who are familiar with local authorities, customs, and norms and who can strengthen and sustain natural support networks." Culturally competent disaster relief and recovery practitioners are those who transition specific knowledge of their own racial/ethnic cultural histories, beliefs, values, and biases in order to understand and gain awareness, knowledge, and skills for effective intervention in a cross-cultural encounter.

While empirical studies on culturally competent DCM are missing from the research literature, there are studies that delineate the need for this approach. The culturally competent disaster case manager must consider a broad swath of risk factors that impact client well-being both prior to and after a disaster occurrence. Some of these considerations are discussed in the following sections.

19.5.1 INCREASED VULNERABILITY AND DISCRIMINATION

Recent trends in disaster outcomes demonstrate the need to place considerable attention on at-risk and vulnerable populations as a component of DCM training and practice. In the disaster planning process, many poor and vulnerable populations and communities are given less-than-appropriate consideration. First, the poor, particularly minority groups, reside in the more vulnerable geographic areas of a given vicinity, often with high population density. Such was the case in the Lower Ninth Ward (9 feet below sea level with a 40 percent poverty rate and more than 90 percent of residents identifying as African American) of New Orleans, Louisiana. Second, many impoverished communities are beset by high levels of risk (e.g., drug abuse, alcoholism, domestic and criminal violence) that contribute to poor behavioral health outcomes in a postdisaster environment. Third, discriminatory practices pre- and postdisaster come in a variety of forms and increase disaster vulnerability. The *World Disaster Report 2007* points out that the impact of disasters on many indigenous and minority populations are often exacerbated by the shortage of disaggregated information that is normally obtained during disaster mitigation and planning. For example, during Hurricane Katrina in 2005, the county's emergency warming system was activated in the Gulfport, Mississippi, community informing local residents of the need to evacuate prior to the storm; however, the communication system did not include the message in Vietnamese, and thus, many non-English-speaking Vietnamese, who work in the shrimp fishing industry, did not receive the warning and subsequently did not evacuate prior to the hurricane.

Fothergill and Peek's (2004) review of disaster outcomes demonstrates how low-income minority populations with low political clout are often neglected in the planning and relief phases of a disaster occurrence. Dyson (2006) notes that during the immediate aftermath of Hurricane Katrina, white residents from St. Bernard Parish (five miles southeast of New Orleans) passed a city ordinance that prohibited rental housing to anyone who was a nonblood relative of residents of the area. While this ordinance was rescinded with the threat of a housing discrimination lawsuit, by default its enactment would have meant that nonwhites would have been ineligible to rent housing in the area. Another example concerns a little-known story related to Hurricane Katrina and the displacement of nearly 40,000 Mexicans in the Gulf Coast working in the service and construction industries (Dyson 2006). These families received little to no assistance from the U.S. government for disaster relief. Admittedly, while there were illegal immigrants residing in the area, there were likewise many low-income Latino families with legal status; however, their less-than-optimal past experiences with traditional services contributed to their decision not to place themselves in situations where this could reoccur. Moreover, although many Native American tribes were impacted by Katrina, state and federal government officials made little contact with affected tribes. "In the immediate aftermath of Katrina, there was little information about the death tolls among the six federally recognized Native American tribes in Alabama, Louisiana, and Mississippi" (Dyson 2006, 143).

19.5.2 Differences in Perceptions

Despite the collective empathy that is expressed during the postdisaster period, ethnic and racial perceptions and attitudes toward disaster relief and recovery are in many ways similar to those found prior to a heightened disaster period. "The general lack of accountability during the crisis and its aftermath can be seen in the conflicting stories of acts of generosity and potential underlying discrimination" (De Vita et al. 2008, 80). A study by the University of Chicago's Center for the Study of Race, Politics and Culture (Dawson, Lacewell, and Cohen 2006) found gross disparities in perceptions and opinions among African Americans and whites concerning lessons learned from Hurricane Katrina. Using survey research methods, the random sample of New Orleans residents included 703 whites and 487 African Americans. Dawson and colleagues found that African Americans have vastly different perceptions about Hurricane Katrina when compared to whites. For example, when asked if the "federal government should spend whatever's necessary to rebuild and restore people to their homes in Katina's aftermath," 79 percent of African Americans agreed while only 33 percent of whites agreed. When presented with the statement that "people trapped didn't have resources to leave," 89 percent of African Americans agreed while only 57 percent of whites agreed. Similar disparities in perceptions and opinions were identified in the areas of media reporting (African Americans were reported as "displaced refugees" whereas whites were reported as "displaced Americans") and attitudes of Katrina survivors concerning the cause of the disaster.

19.5.2.1 Ageism

Along with prejudicial attitudes, disaster vulnerability is often heightened for older adults. Despite the expanding numbers of persons aged 60 and above, many humanitarian agencies lack a clear rationale for reaching older populations during a disaster occurrence. "Between 2005 and 2050, the global population aged 60 or above will triple from 673 million to over 2 billion, while the number of children (0–14 years of age) will remain largely static at around 1.8 billion" (Klynman, Kouppari, and Mukhier 2007, 67). Disaster population displacement is greater among older people and there are many stigmas and false misperceptions concerning older people during disaster planning, relief, and recovery. The 2007 *World Disasters Report* (Klynman, Kouppari, and Mukhier 2007) cites six common misperceptions concerning older people in emergencies: (1) The extended family and community will help and protect them at all times; (2) an agency will look out for them; (3) their needs can easily be covered by general aid distribution; (4) they only have to worry about themselves; (5) they are waiting to be helped; and (6) they are too old to work.

19.5.2.2 Disability Bias

Another group that is highly susceptible to enhanced risk for poor disaster relief and recovery outcomes are those living with a disability. "Disability is an evolving concept and results from the interaction between a person's impairment and obstacles such as physical barriers and prevailing attitudes that prevent their participation in society" (Klynman, Kouppari, and Mukhier 2007, 88). Across the world, living with a disability is linked to poverty, barriers, discrimination, marginalization, and therefore, increased risk for poor outcomes after experiencing a disaster occurrence.

In addition, case managers monitor and evaluate the options and services available to clients. They are the link between traumatized disaster victims, who are often confused and caught in a disturbing, chaotic situation, and the resources that nonprofit organizations and the government make available to such victims. DCM should consist of a trusting relationship between the case manager and the client. Ideally, a partnership is formed with the client, helping the individual feel empowered (less helpless) when presented with the options available for obtaining resources and, hopefully, improving the clients' situation. When case managers make their decisions and recommendations after carefully listening to the client, and considering their input, disaster survivors may feel even more empowered.

Training for disaster case managers should include a systematic approach for developing skills toward culturally competent DCM practice. Such methods must include ways of "making sense" of the depth and breadth of knowledge needed for culturally competent disaster relief and recovery intervention. One example comes from the documented international experiences of graduate social work students providing disaster relief services in Honduras after Hurricane Mitch in 1998. Puig and Glynn (2003) cite several approaches to knowledge development for cross-cultural international social work practice based on their qualitative research findings: (1) understanding of personal prejudices, biases, attitudes, and beliefs and how these influence personal professional interactions; (2) understanding and awareness of socioeconomic and political factors and how they bias international relationships; (3) awareness and understanding about the people or groups of people with whom they work within a particular country; (4) awareness of personal views toward local helping practices and whether one values intrinsic methods of indigenous populations for helping others; (5) knowledge of culturally specific family structures, social hierarchies, beliefs, and values that affect community characteristics; (6) awareness of discriminatory and oppressive practices by existing social and political structures in the host country/community; and (7) awareness of the personal limitations, skills, and competencies for providing disaster relief and recovery services. Should education and training for DCM include these elements, the challenges that cultural differences present in disaster relief and recovery will be minimized.

19.6 COLLABORATION WITH FAITH-BASED ORGANIZATIONS

Central to DCM are volunteers and faith-based organizations (FBOs). In many ways, the future success and recognition of DCM is related to collaboration with FBOs (White House Office of Faith-Based and Community Initiatives 2008). As stated earlier, FEMA is now authorized to fund DCM services in a declared disaster zone. What the federal government has recognized is the fundamental role that FBOs continue to play and the importance of their role in community social service provisions, particularly during disaster recovery and specifically for underserved and highly vulnerable populations. For example, approximately 10,000 Vietnamese Americans were settled in Houston, Texas, during the aftermath of Hurricane Katrina. Like many Latino hurricane survivors, Asian Americans faced difficulties in accessing services from FEMA and the American Red Cross due to language and cultural differences; some did not know they were eligible for services and others were unfairly denied (Dyson 2006). Because of their expertise and existing relationships, community and faith-based organizations responded to the needs of the Asian American community through short- and long-term DCM.

The central role that many FBOs played in the aftermath of Hurricanes Katrina and Rita are spelled out in recent federal government reports such as *The Federal Response to Hurricane Katrina: Lessons Learned* (Townsend 2006). Moreover, this document advises the U.S. Department of Homeland Security (DHS) to designate more responsibility to many faith-based and community organizations for disaster relief and recovery intervention. As such, the DHS has held conferences around the country promoting governmental partnerships and greater collaboration with FBOs. Perhaps the most tangible product of such a partnership was Katrina Aid Today—a consortium of 10 social service organizations headed by the United Methodist Committee on Relief that ended in March 2008. It received international funding, as well as funding from FEMA in the amount of $66 million for long-term case management services. Katrina Aid Today processed and served more than 10,000 clients during its existence (GAO 2009).

19.7 CONCLUSION

The development of disaster case management standards is an ongoing process that will continue to unfold as researchers and interested professionals continue to investigate and identify standards for practice based on available evidence. The federal government has funded several projects aimed at identifying response to client needs and outcomes based on case management intervention. These efforts demonstrate the difficulty that is commonplace in attempting to investigate the DCM process. Many of the recent documents and standards for DCM developed by interested emergency management organizations and agencies can be found on the Internet and downloaded for review.

In terms of behavioral health, it is important that disaster case managers understand the potential, as well as clear-and-present risk and vulnerability, for client trauma-induced behavioral health outcomes. While disaster case managers are not necessarily behavioral health counselors, they will become gatekeepers to behavioral health resources within the impacted communities and instrumental in the referral process. Some familiarity with best practice intervention methods for addressing client behavioral health challenges is necessary given the veracity of contextual narratives in which DCM takes place. Of equal importance is the need for culturally sensitive case management practice, as well as the need for cultural competence throughout the relief and recovery process because these are essential to client resilience, cooperation, and collaboration in the DCM process.

REFERENCES

Athey, J., and J. Moody-Williams. 2003. *Developing Cultural Competence in Disaster Mental Health Programs: Guiding Principles and Recommendations.* DHHS Pub. No. SMA 3828. Rockville, MD: U.S. Department of Health and Human Services, Substance Abuse and Mental Health Services Administration, Center for Mental Health Services. http://store.samhsa.gov/shin/content//SMA03-3828/SMA03-3828.pdf.

Council on Accreditation (COA). 2008. *Council on Accreditation Standards: Eighth Edition/Private Standards, August 2008.* http://www.coastandards.org.

Dawson, M., M. H. Lacewell, and C. Cohen. 2006. 2005 Racial attitudes and the Katrina disaster study. University of Chicago Center for the Study of Race Politics and Culture, Initial Report January 2006. http://melissaharrislacewell.com/docs/Katrina_Initial_Report.doc.

De Vita, C. J. 2007. Preparing for the next disaster. In *After Katrina: Shared Challenges for Rebuilding Communities.* Louisiana Association of Nonprofit Organizations, ed. C. J. De Vita, 27–31. Washington, DC: Urban Institute. http://www.urban.org/UploadedPDF/311440_After_Katrina.pdf

De Vita, C. J., F. D. Kramer, L. Eyster, S. Hall, P. Kehayova, and T. Triplett. 2008. *The Role of Faith-Based and Community Organizations in Post-Hurricane Human Service Relief Efforts.* Washington, DC: Urban Institute. http://www.urban.org/UploadedPDF/1001245_hurricane_relief_recovery_full_report.pdf.

De Vita, C. J., and E. Morley. 2007. *Providing Long-Term Services after Major Disasters.* Washington, DC: Urban Institute. http://www.urban.org/UploadedPDF/411519_major_disasters.pdf.

Dyson, M. E. 2006. *Come Hell or High Water: Hurricane Katrina and the Color of Disaster.* New York: Basic Civitas Books.

Federal Emergency Management Agency (FEMA). 2010. *Additional assistance: Crisis counseling assistance and training program.* http://www.fema.gov/assistance/process/additional.shtm.

Fothergill, A., and L. Peek. 2004. Poverty and disasters in the United States: A review of recent sociological Findings. *Natural Hazards 32*(1): 89–110.

Klynman, Y., N. Kouppari, and M., Mukhier, eds. 2007. World disaster report: Focus on discrimination (2007). International Federation of Red Cross and Red Crescent Societies. http://www.ifrc.org/Docs/pubs/disasters/wdr2007/WDR2007-English.pdf.

Lavin, R., and S. Menifee, eds. 2009. *Disaster Case Management: Implementation Guide.* Washington, DC: Administration for Children and Families.

Morley, E., J. De Vita, N. Pindus, and J. Auer. 2006. An assessment of services provided under the American Red Cross September 11 recovery grants program. Final Report June 2006. http://www.urban.org/UploadedPDF/411346_Redcross_RGP.pdf.

National Human Services Assembly. nd. Re-establishing normalcy: Helping families address the long-range effects of disaster through case management. http://www.nationalassembly.org/Publications/documents/casemanagementbrief.pdf.

The Nonprofit Roundtable of Greater Washington. 2005. *Working Together When the Worst Happens: Nonprofit Emergency Preparedness in the National Capital Region.* Washington, DC: The Nonprofit Roundtable of Greater Washington.

Puig, M. E., and J. B. Glynn 2003. Disaster responders: A cross-cultural approach to recovery and relief work. *Journal of Social Service Research, 30*(2): 55–66.

Townsend, F. F. 2006. *The federal response to Hurricane Katrina: Lessons learned.* http://library.stmarytx.edu/acadlib/edocs/katrinawh.pdf.

United States Government Accountability Office (GAO). 2008a. Report to Congressional requesters: FEMA should more fully assess organizations' mass care capabilities and update the Red Cross role in catastrophic events, GAO-08-823 (Washington, DC: September 18, 2008).

United States Government Accountability Office (GAO), 2008b. National disaster response: FEMA should take action to improve capacity and coordination between government and voluntary sectors, GAO-08-369 (Washington, DC: Feb. 27, 2008).

United States Government Accountability Office (GAO). 2009. Report to Congressional requesters: Greater coordination and an evaluation of programs' outcomes could improve disaster case management. (Washington, DC: July 8, 2009). http://www.gao.gov/new.items/d09561.pdf.

Vernberg, E. M., A. M. Steinberg, A. K. Jacobs, M. J. Brymer, P. J. Watson, J. D. Osofsky, C. M. Layne, R. S. Pynoos, and J. I. Ruzek. 2008. Innovations in disaster mental health: Psychological first aid. *Professional Psychology: Research and Practice, 39*(4): 381–388.

Watson, P. J., and J. I. Ruzek. 2009. Academic/state/federal collaborations and the improvement of practices in disaster mental health services and evaluation. *Administration and Policy in Mental Health 36*: 215–220.

Part VII

Leaving a Legacy

Training and Community Empowerment

20 Disaster Behavioral Health Services

Implementation, Training, and Sustainability

Bruce H. Young and Josef I. Ruzek

CONTENTS

20.1 INTRODUCTION

Disasters and other potentially traumatic events can adversely affect the mental health of those exposed. In order to minimize the negative psychosocial consequences of these events, it is important for certain health care organizations and institutions of higher learning to operate disaster behavioral health (DBH) services. This chapter clarifies important considerations related to services implementation; delineates content and processes in the training of managers, supervisors, service practitioners, and teams; and identifies strategies for achieving program sustainability. Discussion is organized around two primary phases of disaster response in which teams are likely to be deployed: the immediate hours and days following an event, and the weeks and months later when many survivors may benefit from brief crisis counseling.

20.2 ESTABLISHMENT OF DBH SERVICES WITHIN AN ORGANIZATION: THE IMPLEMENTATION PROCESS

The implementation of DBH services within an organization[a] often begins as a response to legislative mandates, new funding/training resources, executive decisions, or simply the perceived need to participate and contribute help during the immediate phase of disaster. Paraphrasing Andreasen (1995), the "DBH exploration process" requires knowing the needs of those affected by the event and matching interventions and creating services to meet those needs. Typically, as a first step, a disaster behavioral health steering committee is formed to develop and adopt a policy defining the following:

- Mission
- Funding sources, human resources, structural supports
- Start-up and operational procedures
- Staffing
- Training
- Program evaluation

20.2.1 MISSION

Whether it is per legislative mandate or another process, the operational definition of the mission (e.g., purpose and scope of services) will shape and define all aspects of the operation, including administrative structure, populations served, structuring of the team, roles and responsibilities of team members, and internal and external operational procedures. Mission statements generally consider addressing scalable response capability, that is, responses ranging from circumscribed incidents to community-wide events.

How does an organization determine its mission? Answers to the following questions will go a long way to helping clarify and define guidance policies and the mission of the DBH service:

- *Who are the populations to be served?* Will services be primarily directed to staff impacted by an event, staff responding to an external event, clients/patients of the host organization who are affected, community members, or all of these groups?
- *What authority might DBH services operate under?* Whether the response team will operate as part of a county, state, or national Incident Management System, or whether solely its own management system will affect operational planning.
- *What is the scope of services?* What types of resources and services will be made available (e.g., crisis intervention, case management, brief intervention, medication management, other services) given the capacity and structure of the host organization?
- *How long will services be provided?* Is the intention to make DBH services available for two weeks, a period of months, or until no longer needed?
- *Where will services be provided?* Will the program be mobile or be offered only within the host facility?
- *Who will provide the services?* Which helping disciplines will be represented?
- *How will authority be structured?* Who will task the DBH team, and who will be in charge? What will be the lines of communication?
- *How will services be funded?* Who pays to launch the services, for potential costs related to salaries, overtime pay, extra hires, travel, lodging, communication equipment, Internet fees, materials, safety equipment, and so on? What, if any, mutual aid, will be involved (e.g., organizations' participation in a network made up of many organizations agreeing to offer services outside of each one's catchment area to increase each organization's assets in emergencies)?

20.2.2 START-UP AND OPERATIONAL PROCEDURES

Initial implementation of a DBH service inescapably affects the organizational environment in which it operates. Such changes may include long employee absences or personnel reassignment, temporary crossover of authority lines (e.g., a social worker having temporary supervisory responsibility over a psychologist), and realignment of employee counseling services to support the DBH mission. If initiated in the immediate aftermath of a disaster, the start-up program may lead to inter-professional rivalry and unanticipated interpersonal stressors; senior management may experience additional pressures to soothe the fears of staff members and patients who are adapting to changes in practice patterns.

Operational procedures are largely defined by the mission and size of the DBH service. Considerations include the process of tasking declarations, lines of authority, creating a logistical infrastructure, establishing communication protocols involving notification of staff and support of staff in the field, deployment protocols, field operations, return of staff members to normal operations, and documentation and program evaluation. Describing each of these procedures in detail is beyond the scope of this chapter. But how the service operates depends to a large degree on the answers to the questions posed. At the point when DBH services become more routine and the service is integrated into the organization, they can be considered to be fully operational. Ideally, over time, new evidence-based or empirically defensible practices are regularly integrated, and service innovation becomes the norm.

20.2.3 STAFFING

There are no evidenced-based findings to guide selection of personnel for disaster behavioral health services. It is generally advisable to include representation of a range of behavioral health disciplines (psychology, social work, psychiatry, nursing), in addition to chaplaincy, with a reasonable ratio of senior management or supervisors included. Common sense and experience suggests that, to the degree possible, the cultural diversity of the DBH team should be matched reasonably to the population it serves. As it is, in racially and ethnically diverse communities, minorities are more likely to be less prepared for disasters and experience prolonged and more challenging recoveries in part due to greater unemployment, low incomes, fewer savings, less insurance, poorer access to information, and bias in search for replacement housing (USDHHS, Office of Minority Affairs 2009). When considering size of the team, it is important to take into account that not everyone selected will be available for every deployment and to ensure that backfill members are included and that there is adequate capacity to support staff rotations. The size of the team should also allow team members to work in pairs or in small subgroups. Pairing team members and creating subgroups fosters mutual support between members. Ideally, team composition should allow the pairing of males with females, and of members with different cultural backgrounds or bilingual capacities, age differences, and high and low degrees of disaster response experience. Providers' knowledge, skills, and attitudes must also take into consideration the defined scope of DBH services. If long-term agency response is within the scope of services, staffing considerations involve the use of practitioners who are trained to administer evidence-based treatments for PTSD. New brief CBT-oriented models are emerging, e.g., "Skills for Psychological Recovery" (Brymer et al. 2008); however, PTSD evidence-based treatments, e.g., prolonged exposure (Foa et al. 2005; Foa et al. 1999), cognitive processing therapy (Resick et al. 2002; Resick and Schnicke 1992) are more likely to fall within the service domain of the Employee Assistance Program. Each case calls for training consideration by agency administrators.

20.3 TRAINING

To date, few empirical studies have investigated outcomes associated with the first response, the FEMA-funded Crisis Counseling Programs, or other community services that survivors commonly receive (Rosen, Young, and Norris 2006; Rosen and Young 2005), and virtually none has established the effectiveness of preparedness training for organizations, stand-alone DBH teams, or individual DBH providers before disaster strikes. An initial study examining a "Train-the-Trainer" (TTT) program (Cross et al. 2010) analyzed variables likely to predict dissemination of DBT training across the state of New York three years after 9/11. Sixty percent of second generation trainees

BOX 20.1   DBH PRACTITIONER KNOWLEDGE AND COMPETENCIES

- All hazards systems (e.g. National Incident Command System), plans (National Response Framework), and key concepts
- Rapid assessment and triage
- Disaster-related stress reactions: survivors, responders, colleagues, and self
- Evidence-based disaster behavioral health risk factors
- Crisis intervention
- Psychological first aid
- Psychoeducation
- Cross-cultural considerations
- Traumatic grief and loss
- Management of substance abuse
- Problem solving and conflict resolution
- Information and referral process considerations
- Advocacy
- Evidence-based stress-related treatments
- Working in disaster behavioral health settings/altered environments (e.g., shelters, relief centers, unconventional intervention settings)
- Concepts of risk communication
- Field safety considerations
- Provider self-care issues

provided DBH training. Members of this group were likely to have the most DBH training prior to the TTT program they participated in. Until a stronger research evidence base is developed, we necessarily look to synthesize knowledge used to form the content of and processes of training from four primary sources: existing DBH research; studies of early posttrauma interventions conducted in other trauma survivor populations; practitioner experience reported in the nonscientific anecdotal "gray" literature; and formal consensus development processes.

20.3.1 TRAINING CONTENT

DBH response team members require knowledge about a range of issues related to their role, including team operations, the larger organizational contexts of their deployments, specific skills for helping related to phase of disaster response, populations served and self-care. What trainees are expected to learn will depend as well on the needs of the trainees, when the training takes place, time allotted for training, and resources available for training. Box 20.1 lists the range of core knowledge and skill competencies needed by DBH practitioners to begin working with survivors in the immediate postdisaster phase.

Training may be offered to the range of helpers commonly represented in disaster response efforts: behavioral health and medical professionals, clergy, emergency and police personnel, school personnel, and paraprofessionals. Those who lead the behavioral health response teams should receive training in the management of teams and in methods and strategies of supporting team members.

It is also important to provide training for senior management and supervisors in the organization from which responders are drawn. Managers play key roles in supporting disaster workers. They are well placed to monitor employee job performance and aspects of interpersonal and emotional functioning, problems that can signal a need for help. They are also important sources of support to the individual worker. Content of managerial training can include an overview of the workplace DBH policy, ways of supporting affected employees, the nature of acute stress responses, indicators

BOX 20.2   SENIOR MANAGEMENT AND SUPERVISORY ACTIVITIES POSTDISASTER

- Briefing workers about the incident (including regular briefings if incident is ongoing)
- Informing workers about available mechanisms of support
- Destigmatizing seeking social and behavioral health support
- Encourage the view that help-seeking is a practical and proactive approach to coping
- Attending to rumor control
- Informing disaster behavioral health services about effectiveness of actions or gaps in services
- Helping to educate workers about the nature of traumatic stress (e.g., via informal conversations and written handouts)
- Encouraging sharing of information with families
- Walking through facility or unit to hold informal conversations and to inquire (in general) how staff are doing

Ongoing supervisory tasks include:

- Monitoring affected individuals for signs and symptoms of continuing distress as evidenced by changes in job performance, attendance, and interpersonal and emotional functioning
- Being aware of workers who may be at elevated risk for posttrauma problems (e.g., workers with high levels of exposure or personal loss, workers with a personal history of trauma, workers with preexisting vulnerabilities)
- Referring employees to DBH services or EAP/other behavioral health support as appropriate
- Attending to needs of workers who may be returning to work after the incident (e.g., granting time off as necessary, offering flexibility regarding work schedules, discussing return with employee, preparing coworkers if necessary)
- Paying attention to conflicts that may emerge
- Defusing turf battles and efforts to cast blame
- Fostering natural support mechanisms (e.g., social support is key in recovery and the workplace is an important means of this support for a number of workers)
- Seeking guidance/training as needed from DBH members

when behavioral health referral may be warranted, the nature of available helping services, self-care for supervisors and staff (including monitoring for secondary traumatic stress), sources of consultation, and ways of supporting the deployment mission (e.g., adapting work schedules so that impacted staff can participate; see Box 20.2).

Perhaps most important to training efforts is providing helpers with the specific helping skills needed in their direct work with survivors. Those organizing training programs in immediate response must first decide what skills are to be taught. As research on stress debriefing interventions has demonstrated that they do not prevent development of PTSD (e.g., Roberts et al. 2009; Bisson et al. 2009; Rose, Bisson, and Wesseley 2001), emergency outreach guidelines for working in large group settings (Young 2002), and methods of providing Psychological First Aid (PFA; see Section 20.3.2 for more detail) have received more attention (Parker et al. 2006; Young 2006; Young et al. 2006; NCTSN and NCPTSD 2006) and have increasingly been endorsed via expert consensus processes (National Institute of Mental Health 2002; Hobfoll et al. 2007) until empirical research yields a stronger base on which to select practices. PFA has been manualized in a *PFA*

BOX 20.3   PFA CORE HELPING ACTIONS

1. Contact and engagement
2. Providing safety and comfort
3. Helping to achieve stabilization (if necessary)
4. Information gathering
5. Practical assistance
6. Connection with social supports
7. Information on coping and support
8. Linkage to collaborative services

Field Operations Guide (NCTSN and NCPTSD 2006; http://www.ncptsd.va.gov/pfa/PFA.html), and, in this version, it is comprised of eight core helping actions (Box 20.3) and a wide range of knowledge and skills.

Online training in this model is available (http://learn.nctsn.org), but, as noted before, such training must be supplemented by additional training procedures. We recommend that processes of training on PFA include formal instruction in the intervention via hands-on workshops in which all participants practice key elements of the intervention via role play and receive individual feedback and coaching related to their performance. Following this, participants are encouraged to receive regular supervision. Research indicates that, to be maximally effective, this supervision should include actual observation of skills participants have been taught to deliver by trainers (Miller et al. 2004)—in this case, either by directly observing trainees conduct PFA with survivors or by listening to recorded tapes of PFA sessions (if formal consent for this activity has been obtained from PFA recipients). This supervision can be provided in weekly or biweekly face-to-face meetings, or via scheduled telephone supervision sessions. When organizations conduct disaster exercises, care should be taken to include opportunities to observe providers as they deliver PFA, and to present individualized feedback following the exercise. After training takes place, along with supervision, it is important to establish "communities of practice" that provide opportunities for trained providers to share experiences with the new interventions and problem-solve issues that arise during its implementation.

The interpersonal support, stress-related education, and normalization of acute stress responses that take place under the label of PFA are much needed but unlikely to address the full range of survivor needs, especially following events characterized by high-intensity individual exposure to potentially traumatic events. That is, many individuals will require more than PFA, and many community members will never receive PFA despite experiencing problems.

During the first days, weeks, and months, most of those distressed by their disaster experiences will recover, via personal coping efforts, natural social support, or simply the passage of time. But some persons will continue to experience distress and some may develop posttraumatic stress disorder, other anxiety disorders, depression, or other significant postdisaster problems. Many of these individuals may benefit from relatively brief culturally appropriate counseling efforts that are offered to natural disaster and terrorism survivors who continue to experience distress in the first months following a disaster. This requires a different skill set than PFA. Typically, services include individual, family, and small-group counseling focused on providing emotional support, education, and referral, as needed, and behavioral health treatment resources in the community. Such counseling appropriately seeks to be nonstigmatizing by avoiding processes of diagnosis and labels associated with psychopathology.

Research on early interventions to prevent development of trauma-related problems in those exposed to other kinds of traumatic events represents an important source of information that can inform selection of which brief counseling skills will be selected for training. Unfortunately, there is little evidence that simple provision of education and support is effective in preventing PTSD and other behavioral health problems in trauma survivors. Reviews of early preventive interventions instead indicate that specific brief (4–5 sessions) cognitive-behavioral interventions can effectively reduce posttraumatic stress reactions and prevent development of PTSD when they are delivered starting as early as two weeks posttrauma. These interventions have included several helping components, including education, breathing training/relaxation, imaginal and in vivo exposure, and cognitive restructuring. When interventions have been targeted at all trauma survivors, regardless of levels of stress reaction, they have not been found to effectively reduce and prevent posttraumatic stress symptoms. It is when trauma-focused CBT has been targeted at those with significant symptom levels, especially those meeting criteria for acute stress disorder, that intervention has been effective (Roberts et al. 2009). Many individuals requesting counseling for postdisaster problems will experience such symptoms.

At present, the cognitive-behavioral interventions that have been tested in other service contexts have some potential limitations in the context of disaster counseling. They have not been researched with disaster survivors, may be inappropriate for some survivors, and have been delivered by well-qualified and trained behavioral health professionals rather than the paraprofessionals and non-specialist health care providers who may be called upon to provide postdisaster counseling. Such interventions are now being adapted for disasters (cf., Ruzek 2006; Ruzek et al. 2008). For example, Hamblen and others (2009) developed Cognitive Behavior Therapy for Postdisaster Distress (CBT-PD), a 10-session manualized intervention designed to address a range of cognitive, emotional, and behavioral reactions to disaster. Trained community-based therapists provided CBT-PD for 88 adult survivors of Hurricane Katrina, and participants showed significant improvements on the 12-item Short Post-Traumatic Stress Disorder Rating Interview–Expanded (Sprint-E; Norris et al. 2006), a composite measure of disaster-related PTSD symptoms, depression, stress vulnerability, and functional impairment.

Other development efforts are under way. NCPTSD has collaborated with NCTSN and Dr. Richard Bryant to manualize "Skills for Psychological Recovery" (SPR), an evidence-informed counseling approach that is comprised of simplified, brief application of interventions found effective in other service contexts: problem-solving training, positive activity scheduling, skills training in management of trauma reminders and emotional distress, cognitive reframing, and social support. SPR is intended to help survivors identify their most pressing current needs and concerns, and teach and support them as they master skills to address those needs. While formal evaluation will be necessary to establish the effectiveness of SPR (and the manual is designed to facilitate evaluation efforts), training in SPR has been extremely well received by counselors working in the Louisiana Spirit (Katrina) Specialized Crisis Counseling Services; they reported that the skills were highly practical and improved their ability to serve their clients.

Improving services for disaster-impacted minorities is critical. U.S. Census data indicate that minorities represent nearly one-third of the U.S. population. Cultural competency, defined as a set of congruent behaviors, attitudes, and policies enabling a system, agency, or group of professionals to effectively work in cross-cultural situations (Cross 1989), is one of the primary means to closing the disparities gap in disaster preparedness, intervention, and all of health care. DBH-related training content must incorporate cultural competency principles into preparedness plans and interventions. Training that addresses how to provide culturally sensitive care, how to work with an interpreter, negotiating cultural differences, and implementing culturally and linguistic-appropriate services will better serve the increasingly diverse population of the United States. The Office of Minority Mental Health offers online disaster-related cultural competency training for physicians, nurses, social workers, emergency first responders, and others. In addition, a "Health Care Language Services Implementation Guide" is available online. These training modules can all be found at http://www.thinkculturalhealth.org.

20.3.2 Training Processes

Training in DBH is widespread among helping organizations. But up to the present time there has been little effort to evaluate DBH training programs and dissemination initiatives. To ensure that resources expended on training are well used, and that training results in improved skills among DBH workers, it will be increasingly important that training programs learn from other fields and begin to incorporate principles of effective training and implementation. Although it is not a surprise that passive communication of best practices can be expected to have little impact on the actual behavior of DBH providers, it is unfortunately also true that traditional training workshops often fail to change practices (Jensen-Doss, Cusack, and de Arellano 2008). Recognition of the limitations of traditional training methods (which form the basis of most current training in the disaster field) is important if the situation is to be reversed. To be effective, workshops must include demonstration of skills and give significant opportunities for behavior rehearsal (Fixsen et al. 2005) and interactive participation via discussion, peer performance feedback, and group planning (Grol and Grimshaw 2003). Such workshop training must then be followed by a period of coaching/supervision. Skills are consolidated via consultation/coaching on the job as workers seek to apply their new abilities (Fixsen et al. 2005). At present, however, few educational activities offered for DBH providers incorporate these crucial elements of active, ongoing practice under supervision.

There is growing evidence that training that includes workshops and continuing supervision can enable practitioners to deliver effective treatment services to those affected by terrorist attacks (Gillespie et al. 2002; Duffy, Gillespie, and Clark 2007; Levitt et al. 2007; Brewin et al. 2008; CATS Consortium 2007). For example, in the context of implementation of a centralized public health program to assist survivors of the 2005 terrorist bombing attack on the London transportation system, Brewin and others (2008) trained clinicians to provide trauma-focused cognitive-behavioral therapy and eye movement desensitization and reprocessing to individuals needing such services. Clinician trainees received ongoing supervision from experienced clinicians within their individual treatment centers. Preliminary outcome data on 82 individuals meeting criteria for PTSD diagnosis indicated significant reductions in PTSD symptoms, with a large effect size. The Child and Adolescent Trauma Treatments and Services (CATS) Project (CATS Consortium 2007) similarly trained providers to deliver two evidence-based cognitive-behavioral therapy interventions to children and adolescents who were experiencing problems related to the 9/11 terrorist attacks. Training included direct training workshops, telephone consultation, and on-site consultation. By the end of the project, 173 clinical staff, primarily social workers and master's-level psychologists, had been trained in one of the two interventions. Seven hundred youth clients participated in the evaluation arm of the project, and 385 received CBT treatment (1–36 sessions). Although these research demonstrations were organized well beyond the time period during which most disaster response occurs, they do begin to demonstrate that practitioners can be trained to deliver best practice interventions for disaster survivors.

Interactivity can help keep trainees engaged with the training experience and can be introduced into training activities in a variety of ways (via use of short film clips and live demonstrations of key skills, short lectures and discussions, large-group role plays, group problem-solving exercises, and skill exercises with embedded constructive feedback). We recommend that trainers create exercises that include aspects of the organization's working environment and realistic scenarios specific to settings in which trainees may work. Two such examples of interactive exercises are given in the Exercise Appendix at the end of this chapter. The first exercise involves a work-related environment and its staff, while the second exercise concerns community citizens and agencies.

20.4 SUSTAINABILITY OF SERVICES

After DBH services are established and implemented, it will be important to sustain their availability and set up evaluation and training strategies designed to improve operational effectiveness and service efficacy. Program evaluation standards have been articulated by several researchers (Fleischman and

Wood 2002; Patton 1978; Rosen, Young, and Norris 2006; University of Kansas Work Group 2004). These include utility (how useful), feasibility (can it be accomplished), ethics (regard for the right and welfare of all involved), and accuracy (results have integrity). Rosen, Young, and Norris (2006) describe DBH program evaluation strategies to improve processes and outcomes. While a DBH program is operating, monitoring of important aspects of services (e.g., wait-time) may be used to make program adjustments to improve functioning or outcomes. At the conclusion of services, a postprogram evaluation should be used to gather information that may help guide and improve future programs.

Other sustainability strategies include implementation of ongoing education, marketing activities, and regularly held training. Education and marketing involve the DBH team presenting on its activities and methods to the leaders and staff members of the organization in which it is embedded, and to the communities it is designed to serve. This may help maintain leader and organizational support for the operation and increase visibility of services. Ongoing training, including exercises (e.g., virtual online, tabletop, and real world), is necessary to ensure that the team maintains skills and changes its repertoire as new ideas enter the DBH field.

20.5   CONCLUSION

DBH is a relatively young field looking to become more evidence based. Until there is an empirical knowledge base, extant DBH-related research, evidence-based findings in the successful treatment of other trauma survivors, and the grey literature are best integrated and used to guide implementation, training, and sustainability of an organization's DBH services. This necessarily involves a complex planning effort to meet the array of needs of the populations served. This chapter delineates important considerations in view of the processes and elements involved with establishing disaster behavioral health services, it describes related DBH training content and processes, and, lastly, identifies key issues associated with the need for continuous quality improvement and sustainability of services.

EXERCISE APPENDIX

Exercise A20.1: Instructions for 1:1 Skill-Building Exercise (Brief Supportive Counseling)

HANDOUT: ATTEMPTED SHOOTING AT A COMMUNITY HOSPITAL EMERGENCY ROOM

The Event

Yesterday afternoon, a 49-year-old male veteran walked up to the reception desk of the community hospital emergency room (ER) stating that he had been sent away by his doctor in the ambulatory care clinic *without* the medications he needed for severe headaches. When the receptionist asked for his name and the name of his doctor, he replied angrily that he was not going to put up with another "run around," and that he wanted to be seen immediately by a doctor to give him his medications. He then pulled out a semiautomatic and began yelling that he might as well shoot everyone.

Alarmed, the receptionist instinctively told him that he could not see a doctor right away. The patient then pointed his gun at her, and screamed for her to get up, find him a doctor or he would kill her and everyone else in the waiting room. The receptionist froze from fright while some other people in the waiting room tried to slip out the door unnoticed. Seeing people attempting to escape, the patient turned and fired his gun in their direction, hitting and shattering a glass door. A hospital security officer, stationed nearby and wearing a holstered pistol, asked the patient to put down his weapon, pleading with him to not shoot anyone. This only further enraged the man, and he began to claim that he knew that cops wanted to kill him.

While the patient was distracted, a doctor who came out to the reception desk lunged toward the patient and knocked him down. A nurse appeared and kicked the gun out of the patient's hand. The doctor and nurse then restrained the man as local police arrived and handcuffed him and took him to the county jail. No one was injured.

Exercise Instructions

Form a group of four. Pair off into two dyads. In the first dyad, one person is the disaster behavioral health team responder, the other is one of the eight hospital staff members listed below. The two people of the second dyad observe the role play. After seven minutes, all four of you discuss role play, for example, what seemed to work well, what did not, how it might be done differently. Then switch roles and repeat the process until each member of the group has had a chance to be the disaster behavioral health responder providing the brief supportive counseling and a staff member receiving the counseling. The person playing the part of a staff member can pick one of the eight roles described below.

Roles

(1) Hospital disaster behavioral health responder
(8) Hospital staff
Receptionist   Security Officer   ER Physician #1 ER Physician #2
Nurse #1   Nurse #2   Orderly Psychiatrist

Hospital Disaster Behavioral Health Responder

The medical center director is looking to provide support for employees immediately following the incident, and calls upon the disaster behavioral health response team to meet with the staff who were directly involved. The day following the incident, you are requested by the medical center's disaster behavioral health team leader to meet with individual employees who were either present during the incident or who had been previously involved with the treatment of the pistol-bearing man. For purposes of the role play, you have seven minutes to conduct an intervention.

Receptionist

You are a new employee who was assigned a week ago to be the ER receptionist while the permanent receptionist is out on medical leave. You were working in a quiet setting as receptionist for the Women's Health Clinic, and you have found the ER setting to be chaotic and stressful. You have a baby and toddler at home, and your spouse is a police officer. Your spouse told you stories about violent patients coming into ERs and warned you that you would not be safe there.

Security Police Officer

You are a Vietnam veteran who was deployed from 1968 through 1969 as a warehouse truck loader at a large air base just outside of Saigon. You have been a security officer for 26 years and are planning to retire later this year. You heard yelling in the ER in the corridor while on your regular rounds, and arrived just as gun shots echoed in the corridor and the glass door shattered. You recognized the patient because you saw him storm out of the ambulatory care clinic earlier and you wondered then if you should do something to calm or restrain him. After you arrived, you tried to reason with the patient, and you told the other people in the area to stay put and not make any sudden moves.

ER Physician #1

You were suturing a superficial but bloody arm wound sustained by a psychiatric patient who had punched out a window earlier that day. The patient was sedated, but uncooperative and disoriented, and became more distressed when yelling could be heard from the waiting room. You felt in conflict as to whether you should stay with the patient or go out to assist in the waiting room, but when you asked the nurse to watch the patient after you heard gun shots, she looked confused and terrified. You felt that you could not leave the patient, but felt guilty that you did not go out to protect the people in the waiting room.

ER Physician #2

You were on break after working 36 hours straight, and tried to ignore the sounds of yelling that you heard out in the waiting room. When you heard gun shots, you rushed out to the waiting room, saw the man looking at the door with a pistol in his hand, and lunged to knock him down. You do not remember much until you saw the police rush in and handcuff the man, roughly pulling him out from under you and the nurse who was helping to restrain the gunman.

Nurse #1

You were in the ER assisting with suturing the arm of a patient who was sedated but uncooperative and disoriented. The patient became more distressed when yelling could be heard from the waiting room. You were feeling very uneasy because you had been assaulted and beaten by a similarly agitated psychiatric patient a year ago. You heard yelling in the waiting room, and the next thing you recall was the physician having told you to watch the patient while he left toward the waiting room. You felt dazed and terrified, and felt unable to move or respond. The physician looked very angry, and brushed you aside saying that you should get yourself back together in case you have to clean up a "real mess" out there.

Nurse #2

You were the second nurse in the ER assisting with the suturing of the arm of a patient who was sedated but uncooperative and disoriented. The yelling you heard reminded you of how soldiers erupted when they were over the edge in the casualty staging area you supervised in Vietnam. You knew that the receptionist was new and inexperienced, so you immediately told the other nurse to handle the patient for the physician and went out to the waiting area. When you heard the gunshots you reflexively fell to the floor, and you thought "Oh, no!" when you saw a physician rush out toward the man with the gun. You jumped up and went for the gun, kicking it out of the man's hand just as he was about to turn it on the physician who had jumped on him. You tried to apply physical restraint, but kept getting knocked around by the doctor who was trying to restrain the gunman as well.

Orderly

You were putting supplies away in the storage area at the back of the ER when you heard two sharp loud noises. You wondered if one of the doctors or nurses had knocked over some of the expensive equipment and felt annoyed that you would probably have to clean up their mess. You continued to work in the storage area until you were surprised to see a mental health "type" come back and ask if you were all right. When the disaster behavioral health person told you there had been a shooting incident, you felt guilty, but mostly concerned you would be in trouble for not helping.

Psychiatrist

You have been treating the man with the gun for a bipolar illness for six years, primarily doing medication maintenance on a bimonthly basis. You recently met with the patient on an unscheduled visit because he came in agitated, demanding Demerol for pain. You tried to convince the patient to attend the pain management program to which you had referred him, and considered hospitalizing him because of what appeared to be an acute increase in mania. However, the patient reported taking his medications and you had seen him regain his composure after similar episodes of agitation. Before you could make a decision, the patient walked out in a huff, so you decided to evaluate further when he would return for his regular appointment next week.

Before this particular exercise is put into motion, a brief lecture is provided to guide participants as the exercise takes place (Table A20.1).

TABLE A20.1

Disaster Behavioral Health Services Clinic-Based 1:1 Brief Supportive Counseling Model for Clinic Staff

This table summarizes the steps of a 15-minute meeting to offer support, screen for risk, facilitate resilience, and refer if appropriate. Unlike one-off encounters, a setting with DBH services allows for follow-up and more immediate referral resources. Summarize (in context of survivor's presenting information) common stress reactions, vulnerabilities, warning signs, self-care strategies, and when and where to seek additional help.

1. Introduction and explanation of rationale (objectives) for meeting
   - Provide staff support
   - Inform staff about common stress reactions
   - Inform staff about potentially useful stress management strategies
   - Inform staff of other resources
   - Review confidentiality
2. Screen for risk factors associated with adverse behavioral health outcomes
   - "Where were you when it happened?"
   - "What kind of reactions did you have?"
   - "What concerns you most about what happened?"
   - "Is there anything in particular you keep thinking about over and over?"
3. Discuss coping and stress management strategies
   - "How have you been coping with what happened?"
   - "What do you ordinarily do to manage stress?"
   - "Is there anyone in particular you turn to for support?"
4. Discuss pertinent risk factors
   - Degree of exposure
   - Severe acute stress reactions
   - Previous trauma
   - Preexisting psychopathology
   - Current life stressors (health, legal, employment, family and relationships, etc.)
5. Discuss follow-up and/or referral

Exercise A20.2 Disaster Role Play: Mass Casualties Scenario

TRAINER NOTE #1

This scalable role play is for use with 8 or more trainees. It has been used with 110 trainees and requires 60–90 minutes, depending on the number of trainees and training assistants. Use assistants to help hand out role play instructions.

The role play may be placed on the training agenda before much DBH-related information or skills training is delivered, with the rationale that in doing so, it will help to create added interest in learning new skills. Alternatively, it may be placed toward the end of the agenda to give trainees an opportunity to practice or observe DBH-related skills taught beforehand during the training.

TRAINER NOTE #2

Using the "Role Play Assignment Sheet," identify training participants' roles. Divide the total number of training participants into three roughly equal-sized groups and select one of the three groups to populate the three response teams, distributing team members as equally as possible. The remaining two groups of trainees will role play survivors (with the exception of two trainees discreetly given the roles of security guard and journalist). For example, if the total number of trainees is 47, divide by three and use a group of 15 to create three disaster behavioral health response teams of 5 members each. Thirty trainees will role play survivors and two others will role play the security guard and journalist, respectively.

ROLE PLAY ASSIGNMENT SHEET

Disaster Behavioral Health Teams

DBHT responders Disaster Team 1 members
DBHT responders Disaster Team 2 members
DBHT responders Disaster Team 3 members

Other Roles

Journalist (1)
Security guard (1)
Survivors

TRAINER NOTE #3

Have blank name tags to distribute to DBHT team members. Have name for security guard (or child's "sheriff" badge). Instructions and blank name tags are given to DBHT team members inside the primary training room that, for purposes of the role play, serves as a service center for survivors and those who have experienced a loss.

HANDOUT: ROLE PLAY INSTRUCTIONS FOR DISASTER BEHAVIORAL HEALTH TEAM #1

Background Information

Yesterday, two commercial planes collided over (use name of a local geographical area), resulting in nearly 70 fatalities, including individuals who were inside their homes.

Shortly after the crash, the National Transportation Safety Board (NTSB) secured the area. Since then, residents whose homes were red-tagged unsafe have been temporarily sheltered at a large nearby hotel. As per 1997 Congressional legislation, the American Red Cross and the airlines involved have set up a family service center to begin the process of providing resources and information about long-term replacement housing, rebuilding, refurnishing, and so forth. This room (training facility room) serves as the service center where those who have losses are gathering.

You are members of an ad hoc (name a local county community behavioral health agency) disaster behavioral health response team and have been detailed to the conference room to provide mental health support.

DBH Team #1 Role

Put on ID tags. Elect a team leader. Your role playing begins inside the conference room where family members are gathered.

TRAINER NOTE #4

The instructions below are given to the participants volunteering for DBHT #2 outside of the room serving as the service center. You may opt to have someone assisting with the training hand these instructions out. No ID tags are given.

HANDOUT: ROLE PLAY INSTRUCTIONS FOR DISASTER BEHAVIORAL HEALTH TEAM #2

Background Information

Yesterday, two commercial planes collided over a suburban area over _____, resulting in nearly 70 fatalities, including individuals who were inside their homes.

Shortly after the crash, NTSB secured the area. Since then, residents whose homes were red-tagged unsafe have been temporarily sheltered at a large nearby hotel. A Red Cross/airline service center has been set up in a hotel conference room to begin the process of providing resources and information about long-term replacement housing, rebuilding, refurnishing, and so forth. Residents are gathered in the conference room waiting to talk to airline representatives about their losses and the airline's responsibilities.

You are members of the county triage hospital's disaster behavioral health response team and have been detailed to the hotel to provide behavioral health support.

DBH Team #2 Role

Elect a team leader. Report to the security guard stationed at the door to the entrance of the conference room.

TRAINER NOTE #5

The instructions below are given to the participants volunteering for DBHT #3 outside of the room serving as the service center. You may opt to have someone assisting with the training hand these instructions out. No ID tags are given.

HANDOUT: ROLE PLAY INSTRUCTIONS FOR DISASTER BEHAVIORAL HEALTH TEAM #3

Background Information

Yesterday, two commercial planes collided over a suburban area over _____, resulting in nearly 70 fatalities, including individuals who were inside their homes.

Shortly after the crash, NTSB secured the area. Since then, residents whose homes were red- tagged unsafe have been temporarily sheltered at a large nearby hotel. A Red Cross/airline service center has been set up in a hotel conference room to begin the process of providing resources and information about long-term replacement housing, rebuilding, refurnishing, and so forth. Residents are in the conference room waiting to talk to airline representatives about their losses and the airline's responsibilities.

You are members of the local University Medical Center's disaster behavioral health response team and have been detailed to the conference room to provide behavioral health support.

DBHT #3 Role

Elect a team leader. Report to the security guard stationed at the door to the entrance of the conference room.

TRAINER NOTE #6

The instructions below are given to someone you have selected beforehand as a confederate. The volunteer for this role is best played by an assistant to the training rather than a trainee.

HANDOUT: ROLE PLAY INSTRUCTIONS FOR JOURNALIST

Background Information

Yesterday, two commercial planes collided over a suburban area over _____, resulting in nearly 70 fatalities, including individuals who were inside their homes.

Shortly after the crash, the National Traffic and Safety Board (NTSB) secured the area. Since then, residents whose homes were red-tagged unsafe have been temporarily sheltered at a large nearby hotel. A Red Cross/airline service center has been set up in a hotel conference room to begin the process of providing resources and information about long-term replacement housing, rebuilding, refurnishing, and so forth. Residents are in the conference room waiting to talk to airline representatives about their losses and the airline's responsibilities.

Your Role

You are a journalist with a widely distributed newspaper. After having learned that residents of the crash area are housed at a local hotel, you try to get a story. Posing as a behavioral health professional (having used phony ID to gain entrance to the conference room), you circulate among the survivors and ask intrusive and inflammatory questions, for example:

"How do you feel about the way the airlines are handling the situation?"
"Did you ever think anything like this could happen to you?"
"Was anyone you know injured or killed?"
"Who's to blame here?"

TRAINER NOTE #7

The instructions below are given to someone you have selected beforehand as a confederate. The volunteer for this role is best played by an assistant to the training rather than a trainee. He or she is told who the "journalist" is before the role play begins.

HANDOUT: ROLE PLAY INSTRUCTIONS FOR HOTEL SECURITY GUARD

Background Information

Yesterday, two commercial planes collided over a suburban area over _____, resulting in nearly 70 fatalities, including individuals who were inside their homes.

Shortly after the crash, the NTSB secured the area. Since then, residents whose homes were red-tagged unsafe have been temporarily sheltered at a large nearby hotel. A Red Cross/airline service center has been set up in a hotel conference room to begin the process of providing resources and information about long-term replacement housing, rebuilding, refurnishing, and so forth. Residents are in the conference room waiting to talk to airline representatives about their losses and the airline's responsibilities.

The conference room has been designated as an emergency Red Cross/airline service center for individuals in need of information about family members residing in the neighborhood where two airlines have crashed earlier in the day.

Your Role

You have been assigned to guard the entrance to the conference room and have been instructed not to let anyone in without asking who they are. If people identify themselves as behavioral health professionals, they must show you ID. For purposes of the role play, some behavioral health professionals will not have ID. Give them a difficult time, and don't let them in at first. After a few minutes, let them in.

If family members arrive late, ask them for ID. Of course, they won't have any. Just let them in. A journalist will pose as a behavioral health professional. For purposes of the role play, let him or her in immediately.

TRAINER NOTE #8

The instructions below are given to the trainees who have not volunteered for the DBHTs. In short, everyone at the training is involved with the role play. Divide the number of trainees by 5 and use the resulting number to determine how many trainees to choose for each of the five survivor scenarios. For example, if you have 20 trainees remaining after trainees have volunteered for one of the DBHTs, you can assign four of the remaining trainees to each role below.

Have some trainees pose as married to each other; have one or two survivors not speak English, have another speak limited English.

HANDOUT: FAMILY MEMBERS: INSTRUCTIONS
FOR INDIVIDUALS AND COUPLES

Background Information

Yesterday, two commercial planes collided over (name of geographical area), resulting in nearly 70 fatalities, including individuals who were inside their homes.

Shortly after the crash, NTSB secured the area. Since then, residents whose homes were red- tagged unsafe have been temporarily sheltered at a large nearby hotel. A Red Cross/airline service center has been set up in a hotel conference room to begin the process of providing resources and information about long-term replacement housing, rebuilding, refurnishing, and so forth. Residents are in the conference room waiting to talk to airline representatives about their losses and the airline's responsibilities.

Your Role

You (or you and your spouse) are in the conference room waiting to speak to an airline representative to discuss your losses and what you can expect from the airlines.
Choose one or two of the following scenarios to role play:

1. You weren't home at the time of the crash. You are upset because the fire that destroyed your home destroyed many irreplaceable items (e.g., picture of your grandmother, childhood pictures, family heirlooms).
2. You weren't home at the time of the crash. You are upset because the fire destroyed your new home built to specifications after 18 months of planning, permit seeking, obtaining hard-to-find building materials, and struggles with the building contractor. You and your spouse just moved in last month.
3. You weren't home at the time of the crash as you were shopping at the _____ Mall. Your neighbor, who was also a good friend, was home and was killed along with her two young daughters. You had thought to ask her (and the two girls) to go shopping with you, but didn't because you had been feeling overwhelmed the days just before the crash and wanted some time to yourself. When you exited the mall, you could see the smoke above the mountains.
4. You weren't home at the time of crash. Five years ago, you were in a severe car crash in which you received relatively minor injuries; however, a close friend died in the crash. You find that you keep thinking about the crash and the loss of your friend. Even though you hold common the loss of your home, you feel somewhat distant from the other neighborhood residents/victims.
5. You were home at the time of the crash and heard the unbelievable sounds of the crash racing through the neighborhood. Your home was a block away from the first wave of destruction. You ran to help, but the smoke and debris left you disoriented. You heard people yelling for help, but didn't know exactly where the voices were coming from and didn't know what to do. A policeman saw you and took you to his squad car for safety.
6. When the fire spread, your home was unable to be saved. You have been distraught over the deaths in the neighborhood and unable to sleep more than three hours a night.

In addition to the scenarios described above, please choose from any of the following stress reactions to portray:

Severe anxiety	Grief	Anger	Emotional numbing
Disbelief	Guilt	Impaired concentration	Impaired decision-making ability

If you are in the role of a couple, find time to verbalize your lack of support toward your spouse's emotional reaction when a mental health professional speaks with you.

Do not use anger or rage to the point of disrupting the role play or to the degree that it limits the learning experience of others.

MASS CASUALTIES ROLE: ADDITIONAL TRAINER FACILITATION NOTES

1. After all the trainees have received instructions and are ready to begin, run role play for 20 minutes.
2. If available, use television to cause unnecessary noise.
3. If a trainee asks you questions during the role play, respond that you are with housekeeping and do not know the answers to their questions.
4. Move around to make observations and mental notes.
5. When role play is over, lead discussion.

Beginning with DBHT #1, ask those who were in the role of responders to share what seemed to work for them and what circumstances they felt challenged or confused by. Ask what goals they had and how they related to the other teams in the room. Ask about any cross-cultural issues they faced and how they tried to resolve them. Proceed to do the same with Teams 2 and 3.

Next, ask the trainees in the role of survivors what they appreciated most from the responders. Ask if there were any behavioral exchanges that were not helpful, were confusing, or caused discomfort or frustration.

Next, have the individual posing as the journalist share his or her experience. Ask trainees for their impression of the journalist and whether anyone guessed that he or she was not a behavioral health professional.

Ask the assistant in the role of the security guard to share his or her experience.

In the course of this discussion, look for opportunities to interject key teaching points related to strategies for working in large-group settings, behavioral health service objectives, engagement strategies, PFA core actions, and cross-cultural issues.

Finally, encourage trainees to express appreciation for each other's efforts in the role play.

NOTE

a. The term *organization* includes similar terms, e.g., *agency, institution, department.*

REFERENCES

Andreasen, A. R. 1995. *Marketing Social Change.* San Francisco: Jossey-Bass Publishers.
Bisson, J. C., A. I. McFarlane, S. Rose, J. I. Ruzek, and P. J. Watson. 2009. Psychological debriefing for adults. In *Effective Treatments for PTSD: Practice Guidelines from the International Society for Traumatic Stress Studies*, eds. E. B. Foa, T. M. Keane, M. J. Friedman, and J. Cohen, 83–105. New York: Guilford Press.
Brewin, C. R., P. Scragg, M. Robertson, M. Thompson, P. d'Ardenne, and A. Ehlers. 2008. Promoting mental health following the London bombings: A screen and treat approach. *Journal of Traumatic Stress 21*: 3–8.
Brymer, M. J., A. M. Steinberg, J. A. Sornborger, C. M. Layne, and R. S. Pynoos. 2008. Acute interventions for refugee children and families. *Child and Adolescent Psychiatric Clinics of North America 17*: 625–640.
CATS Consortium. 2007. Implementing CBT for traumatized children and adolescents after September 11: Lessons learned from the Child and Adolescent Trauma Treatments and Services (CATS) Project. *Journal of Clinical Child and Adolescent Psychology 36*: 581–592.
Cross, T. 1989. *Towards a Culturally Competent System of Care: A Monograph on Effective Services for Minority Children Who Are Severely Emotionally Disturbed.* Washington, DC: CASSP Technical Assistance Center, Georgetown University.
Cross, W., C. Cerulli, H. Richards, H. He, and J. Hermann. 2010. Predicting dissemination of a disaster mental health "Train-the-Trainer" program. *Disaster Medicine and Public Health Preparedness 4*: 339–343.
Duffy, M., K. Gillespie, and D. M. Clark. 2007. Post-traumatic stress disorder in the context of terrorism and other civil conflict in Northern Ireland: Randomised controlled trial. *British Medical Journal 334*: DOI: 10.1136/bmj/39021.846852.BE.
Fixsen, D. L., S. F. Naoom, K. A. Blase, R. M. Friedman, and F. Wallace 2005. *Implementation Research: A Synthesis of the Literature.* Tampa, FL: University of South Florida, Louis de la Parte Florida Mental Health Institute, The National Implementation Research Network (FMHI Publication #231).

Fleischman, A. R., and E. B. Wood. 2002. Ethical issues in research involving victims of terror. *Journal of Urban Health 79*: 315–321.

Foa, E. B., C. V. Dancu, E. A. Hembree, L. H. Jaycox, E. A. Meadows, and G. P. Street. 1999. A comparison of exposure therapy, stress inoculation training, and their combination for reducing posttraumatic stress disorder in female assault victims. *Journal of Consulting and Clinical Psychology 67*: 194–200.

Foa, E. B., E. A. Hembree, S. P. Cahill, S. A. Rauch, D. S. Riggs, N. C. Feeny, and E. Yadin. 2005. Randomized trial of prolonged exposure for posttraumatic stress disorder with and without cognitive restructuring: Outcome at academic and community clinics. *Journal of Consulting and Clinical Psychology 73*: 953–964.

Gillespie, K., M. Duffy, A. Hackmann, and D. M. Clark. 2002. Community based cognitive therapy in the treatment of post-traumatic stress disorder following the Omagh bomb. *Behaviour Research and Therapy 40*: 345–357.

Grol, R., and J. Grimshaw. 2003. From best evidence to best practice: Effective implementation of change in patients' care. *Lancet 362*: 1225–1230.

Hamblen, J. L, F. H. Norris, S. Pietruszkiewicz, L. E. Gibson, A. Naturale, and C. Louis. 2009. Cognitive Behavioral Therapy for Postdisaster Distress: A community based treatment program for survivors of Hurricane Katrina. *Administration and Policy in Mental Health and Mental Health Services Research 36*: 206–214.

Hobfall, S. E., P. Watson, C. C. Bell, R. A. Bryant, M. J. Brymer, M. J. Friedman, M. Friedman, B. P. R. Gersons, J. T. V. M. de Jong, C. M. Layne, S. Maguen, Y. Neria, A. E. Norwood, R. S. Pynoos, D. Reissman, J. I. Ruzek, A. Y. Shalev, Z. Solomon, A. M. Steinberg, and R. J. Ursano. 2007. Five essential elements of immediate and mid-term mass trauma intervention: Empirical evidence. *Psychiatry 70*: 283–315.

Jensen-Doss, A., K. J. Cusack, and M. A. de Arellano. 2008. Workshop-based training in trauma-focused CBT: An in-depth analysis of impact on provider practices. *Community Mental Health Journal 44*: 227–244.

Levitt, J. T., L. S. Malta, A. Martin, L. Davis, and M. Cloitre. 2007. The flexible application of a manualized treatment for PTSD symptoms and functional impairment related to the 9/11 World Trade Center attack. *Behaviour Research and Therapy 45*: 1419–1433.

Miller, W. R., C. E. Yahne, T. B. Moyers, J. Martinez, and M. Pirritano. 2004. A randomized controlled trial of methods to help clinicians learn motivational interviewing. *Journal of Consulting and Clinical Psychology 72*: 1050–1062.

National Child Traumatic Stress Network and National Center for PTSD. 2006. *Psychological first aid: Field operations guide,* 2nd ed. http://www.nctsn.org and http://www.ncptsd.va.gov.

National Institute of Mental Health. 2002. *Mental Health and Mass Violence: Evidenced-Based Early Psychological Intervention for Victims/Survivors of Mass Violence. A Workshop to Reach Consensus on Best Practices.* NIH publication No. 02-5138. Washington, DC: U.S. Government Printing Office.

Norris, F., S. Donahue, C. Felton, P. Watson, J. Hamblen, and R. Marshall. 2006. Psychometric analysis of Project Liberty's adult enhanced services referral tool. *Psychiatric Services 57*: 1328–1334.

Parker, C. L., G. S. Everly, D. J. Barnett, and J. M. Links. 2006. Establishing evidence-informed core intervention competencies in psychological first aid for public health personnel. *International Journal of Emergency Mental Health 8*: 83–92.

Patton, M. Q. 1978. *Utilization-Focused Evaluation.* Beverly Hills, CA: Sage.

Resick, P. A., P. Nishith, T. L. Weaver, M. C. Astin, and C. A. Feuer. 2002. A comparison of cognitive processing therapy, prolonged exposure, and a waiting condition for the treatment of posttraumatic stress disorder in female rape victims. *Journal of Consulting and Clinical Psychology 70:* 867–879.

Resick, P. A., and M. K. Schnicke. 1992. Cognitive processing therapy for sexual assault victims. *Journal of Consulting and Clinical Psychology 60*(5): 748–756.

Roberts, N. P., N. J. Kitchiner, J. Kenardy, and J. I. Bisson. 2009. Multiple session early psychological interventions for the prevention of post-traumatic stress disorder. Cochrane Database of Systematic Reviews 2009, Issue 3, Art. No.: CD006869. DOI: 10.1002/14651858.CD006869.pub2.

Rose, S., J. Bisson, and S. Wesseley. 2001. A systematic review of single psychological interventions ("debriefing") following trauma. Updating the Cochrane review and implications for good practice. In *Reconstructing Early Intervention after Trauma: Innovations in the Care of Survivor,* eds. R. Orner and U. Schnyder, 24–39. Oxford, England: Oxford University Press

Rosen, C., and H. Young. 2005. Quantitative analysis of archival data from crisis counseling grants. In *Retrospective 5 Year Evaluation of the Crisis Counseling Program,* eds. F. Norris, C. Rosen, C. Elrod, H. Young, L. Gibson, and J. Hamblen, B9–B42. White River Junction, VT: National Center for PTSD.

Rosen, C., H. Young, and F. Norris. 2006. On a road paved with good intentions, you still need a compass: Monitoring and evaluating disaster mental health services. In *Mental Health Intervention Following Disasters or Mass Violence*, eds. C. Ritchie, P. J. Watson, and M. J. Friedman, 206–226. New York: Guilford Press.

Ruzek, J. I., R. D. Walser, A. E. Naugle, B. Litz, D. S. Mennin, M. A. Polusny, D. M. Ronell, K. J. Ruggiero, R. Yehuda, and J. R. Scotti. 2008. Cognitive-behavioral psychology: Implications for disaster and terrorism response. *Prehospital and Disaster Medicine 23:* 397–410.

United States Department of Health & Human Services (USDHHS), Office of Minority Affairs. 2009. The cultural competency curriculum for disaster preparedness and crisis response. http://www.thinkcultural-health.org/ccdpcr.

University of Kansas Work Group on Health Promotion and Community Development. 2004. *Community toolbox.* http://www.ctb.ku.edu.

Young, B. H. 2002. Emergency outreach: Navigational and brief screening guidelines for working in large group settings following catastrophic events. *NCPTSD Clinical Quarterly 11*(1): 3–7.

Young, B. H. 2006. The immediate response to disaster: Guidelines for adult psychological first aid. In *Interventions Following Mass Violence and Disasters*, eds. E. C. Ritchie, P. J. Watson, and M. J. Friedman, 134–154. New York: Guilford Press.

Young, B. H., J. I. Ruzek, M. Wong, M. Salzer, and A. Naturale. 2006. Disaster mental health training: Guidelines, considerations, and recommendations. In *Interventions Following Mass Violence and Disasters*, eds. E. C. Ritchie, P. J. Watson, and M. J. Friedman, 54–79. New York: Guilford Press.

21 The Role of Social Marketing in Developing Disaster Behavioral Health Programs

Lisa M. Brown, Christine Haley, and Carol Bryant

CONTENTS

21.1   INTRODUCTION

Agencies responsible for crisis counseling programs in the aftermath of nationally declared disasters have encountered significant challenges delivering disaster behavioral health services. When a disaster has been federally declared, the state can apply for a Federal Emergency Management Agency (FEMA) Crisis Counseling and Assistance Program (CCP) Grant to deliver disaster behavioral health services in eligible counties. The purpose of the CCP is

> to provide short-term interventions with individuals and groups experiencing psychological sequelae to large-scale disasters. These interventions involve the counseling goals of assisting disaster survivors in understanding their current situation and reactions, mitigating additional stress, assisting survivors in reviewing their options, promoting the use of or development of coping strategies, providing emotional support, and encouraging linkages with other individuals and agencies who may help survivors recover to their pre-disaster level of functioning. While always cognizant of those with special needs, the thrust of the Crisis Counseling Program since its inception has been to serve people responding normally to an abnormal experience. (U.S. Department of Health and Human Services, nd, b)

In general, these federally funded programs have not reached many of the people they were intended to serve (Amaya-Jackson et al. 1999; Kessler 2000; Weisler, Barbee, and Townsend 2006; Sundararaman, Lister, and Williams 2006). While the use of evidence-based practices shows great promise in improving survivors' mental health outcomes (Hamblen et al. 2006; Wilson, Friedman, and Lindy 2001), most people who would benefit from intervention have not accepted services (Connor, Foa, and Davidson 2006; Covell et al. 2006; Davidson and McFarlane 2006; Donahue et al. 2006; Galea et al. 2007; Wang et al. 2007). Under-usage of CCP services can be attributed to a variety of institutional factors related to methods for outreach, delivery, and packaging of services.

At present, the approach used to deliver disaster behavioral health services is based on a traditional service-centered model. In effect, this model represents an "if you build it, they will come" approach in which management's faith in the unique value of their services creates an assumption that people will seek treatment when needed. Service-centered programs focus on designing services and facilities that the providers consider effective, while devoting little attention to designing, packaging, marketing, or placing services to fit the wants and needs of their consumers (Cooper 1994; Arnold 1994). Unfortunately, this expert-driven or service-oriented approach of mental health service delivery has not proven particularly effective after disasters.

Culture not only influences how disaster-affected populations understand and respond to outreach and mental health intervention, it also influences how program administrators and clinicians interact with the public. Traditional models of mental health service delivery may not be appropriate for survivors of disasters (Silk 2006; Substance Abuse and Mental Health Services Administration 2000). Traditional mental health intervention differs from disaster crisis counseling in that the former suggests the delivery of psychological treatment to people with existing pathological conditions or disorders, whereas the latter assumes that people are able to resume their predisaster level of functioning if provided support, information, and assistance in a timely fashion that is appropriate to the clients' culture, education, developmental stage, and previous life experiences. Disaster survivors who use crisis counseling services have been called "accidental clients" because an external event (i.e., disaster) as opposed to an intra- or interpersonal issue resulted in their use of services (Silk 2006). Further, language that is commonly used by administrators and clinicians in a professional work environment may not be readily understood by the intended audience. For example, use of mental health terminology may deter some from using services because the message is not understood, culturally relevant, or appropriate. Factors that affect disaster literacy include age, culture, education, language, and access to resources. Those at high risk for low disaster literacy include older adults, racial and ethnic minorities, nonnative speakers of English, low income levels, and poor physical health (National Center for Education Statistics 2006).

People from different cultural backgrounds or with limited knowledge of mental illnesses are likely to misattribute their lingering postdisaster mood disorder, anxiety, or other psychological symptoms (Chiriboga 2007). Not only will many ascribe their poor mood and emotional problems as a normal reaction to the disaster, but few will understand that crisis counseling could alleviate their distress, enhance their ability to cope, and help facilitate the recovery process. In fact, some survivors will present to primary care physicians with somatic complaints for their disaster-induced psychological symptoms. Others may refuse treatment to avoid the stigma of being labeled as mentally ill. Understandably, disaster survivors are unlikely to self-identify as having a mental health problem or illness. Because most people do not appreciate how crisis counseling differs from traditional psychotherapy, and current outreach practices and promotion efforts do not well articulate this difference, a mismatch exists between client needs and wants and how disaster mental health services are currently marketed and delivered. As a result, when offered crisis counseling, many who would benefit from treatment decline intervention.

In contrast to the wealth of studies examining the mental health consequences of disasters, comparatively little attention has been focused on methods for increasing service utilization and improving delivery systems. As a result, little is known about the reasons people in need of counseling services do not seek or use them after a disaster, or the best methods for conducting outreach. Social marketing offers a valuable planning framework for enhancing service utilization and service outcomes. This approach has proven effective in marketing many hospital and health care organization services, as well as other health care programs and healthy behaviors (Arnold 1994).

This chapter describes how social marketing can be used to create a comprehensive, systematic outreach plan to market mental health services to disaster-affected people. First, we provide an overview of the distinctive elements of the social marketing framework. Next, we outline how social marketing could be used to promote disaster-related mental health services, and highlight two case studies in which social marketing was successfully used to enhance service delivery and change select behaviors. Resources that can be used to develop a plan are provided at the end of the chapter.

21.2 SOCIAL MARKETING: WHAT IT IS ... AND ISN'T

Social marketing is "a process that applies marketing principles and techniques to create, communicate, and deliver value in order to influence target audience behaviors that benefit society (public health, safety, the environment, and communities) as well as the target audience" (Kotler and Lee 2008). As a framework for planning new or improving existing programs and services, social marketing differs from other approaches in its (1) passionate commitment to understand and respond to the wants and needs of consumers, (2) recognition of the need to segment target populations into distinct audience segments and develop services and outreach approaches for each, (3) reliance on marketing's conceptual framework to design or improve products and services, and (4) continuous monitoring and revision of products and services. Each of these distinguishing features and their implications for disaster-related mental health service delivery are discussed in greater detail in this chapter.

21.2.1 Social Marketing's Distinguishing Features

21.2.1.1 Consumer Orientation

A commitment to understand and respect consumers' wants and needs lies at the very heart of social marketing's approach to service design and delivery. All planning decisions (e.g., what to offer, how to structure provider-patient interaction, plans for promoting services) are based on information about consumers' values, expectations, beliefs, and perceptions. Insights gained from secondary and primary consumer data are used to build a long-term relationship with clients. Service administrators' willingness to invest the time and resources to understand consumers is an essential ingredient in the social marketing approach. Unfortunately, it also makes social marketing more difficult to apply than expert-driven planning approaches in which a small number of people make these decisions based on their experience, expertise, and intuition.

21.2.1.2 Audience Segmentation

Another distinguishing feature of social marketing is its reliance on audience segmentation in selecting target audiences to give the greatest priority in program planning. Audience segmentation refers to the process of dividing a population into distinct segments based on characteristics that influence their responsiveness to marketing interventions, such as the price they are willing to pay for services or the spokespersons they trust most when deciding to seek care. Social marketers segment a potential target population for several reasons. First, segmentation allows program planners to identify subgroups that give them the opportunity to do the most good with the resources they have available to them, for example, by giving greatest priority to people who are both receptive to seeking services and who will benefit greatly from treatment. Second, because each segment has distinct needs and preferences, segmentation reminds program administrators that "one size" service does not fit everyone's needs very well and underscores the need to either plan for the highest priority segments or offer service options to meet multiple segments' needs and expectations. For example, mental health service administrators may want to continue offering the services valued by their loyal consumers, while changing procedures that alienated clients who have stopped using services and offering alternative clinic hours to attract new clients.

21.2.1.3 Marketing's Conceptual Framework

Marketing's conceptual framework views consumers at the center of an exchange process in which they attempt to maximize their ability to satisfy wants and needs and minimize what they must sacrifice to obtain them (Kotler and Zaltman 1971). In commercial transactions, consumers typically exchange money for tangible products or services. In disaster mental health settings, people more often sacrifice comfort, time, and effort for the value gained from mental health treatment. Social marketing uses a set of conceptual tools that are consumer driven to guide development of a comprehensive, integrated plan for designing, delivering, and communication value. In commercial and social marketing, these concepts include marketing's 4 P's: product, price, place, and promotion. In service marketing, it also includes people, physical evidence, and process (Zeithaml, Bitner, and Gremler 2008).

Product refers to disaster mental health service utilization. While keeping their eye on the behavioral goal—service utilization—they know that the essence of the product strategy is to offer consumers the right benefit package, such as a solution to a problem, ability to realize an aspiration, and/or other valuable advantages. Typically, consumer research is undertaken to gain insight into consumers' aspirations, preferences, and other desires in order to discover what appeals to them most, even if it does not relate directly to their mental health needs. Thus, people who have been forced to relocate after a disaster may seek services to remedy their employment, social, and financial losses and not treatment for symptoms of depression and anxiety, although many may meet full diagnostic criteria for a mental health disorder. It may be useful to consider packaging mental health services with other needed products (i.e., financial compensation, employment services) that address pressing concerns.

Price encompasses tangible costs (fees, travel expenses, time off from work) and intangible costs (e.g., embarrassment, time, hassle, and stigma) that are exchanged for product benefits. Unless costs for disaster mental health services are priced correctly, even people who value treatment may consider services too expensive to use. For this reason, it is vital for program planners to have a clear picture of clients' perceptions of costs and benefits and develop strategies to either lower the costs and barriers or make them more acceptable.

It is worth noting that while social marketers attempt to make services appear affordable, it is possible to devalue a product by setting its price too low. This is particularly true when "free" is equated with welfare and service users are stigmatized for accepting help. In pricing mental health services, a careful balance must be achieved between minimizing costs and maximizing the perceived value.

Place refers to the locations and times clients can use mental health services. It also can be used to encompass the *physical evidence* or *facilities* where services are provided, including signage, ease of parking, waiting area comfort, and overall clinic appearance.

People are another important component in the service marketing mix (Zeithaml, Bitner, and Gremler 2008). Employees play a major role in how services are delivered; in fact, in mental health services, the provider is the service. Even clerical staff members contribute to the service outcome and influence consumer perceptions of the service through their dress, personal appearance, and relationship with consumers.

Another variable in the service marketing mix is *process*—procedures, mechanisms, and flow of activities for delivering mental health services. Eligibility requirements, enrollment procedures, the perceived logic of steps involved in appointment scheduling, and the patient-flow system are important parts of a mental health services marketing plan.

Finally, *promotion* includes an integrated set of activities intended to encourage use of disaster mental health services. Customer service training, service delivery enhancements, and community-based activities are often combined with more traditional communications (e.g., client education and advertising). Research and pretesting messages are critical to determine the most efficient and effective methods to reach the target audience to increase use of disaster mental health services. Promotional activities are carefully designed to reinforce other elements of the marketing mix. The promotional strategy is crafted to ensure that consumers know and value the benefits being offered, believe the product is "affordable," and are inspired to act (Kotler and Lee 2008).

Whereas promotional activities are often the most visible component of a marketing intervention, it should be obvious that social marketing extends well beyond media messages and other forms of persuasive communications. For that reason, it is important to distinguish between social advertising and media campaigns that rely on communications to bring about the desired change and social marketing interventions that are based on a comprehensive, consumer-oriented marketing plan.

21.2.1.4 Continuous Monitoring and Improvement

Social marketing relies on ongoing research to monitor consumer perceptions of service delivery and identify ways to improve service outcomes. Consumer feedback can identify gaps between their expectations and service experience and uncover strategies for increasing consumer retention and consumer satisfaction.

In the next section, we describe how social marketing can be used to increase mental health service utilization. The terms *crisis counseling* and *disaster mental health services* are used interchangeably throughout the chapter to refer to a variety of interventions that may be offered by a federally funded crisis counseling program. The types of treatment provided (i.e., counseling, case management, cognitive behavioral therapy, substance abuse treatment, etc.) vary depending on the requirements established by the funding agency, availability of trained clinicians, and client needs. Because most disaster mental health services are delivered by crisis counseling programs, we have elected to call our target population *clients* instead of patients (the term used in traditional psychotherapy settings).

21.2.2 APPLYING A SOCIAL MARKETING APPROACH TO DISASTER MENTAL HEALTH SERVICES

Analogous to the four phases of disaster planning—mitigation, preparedness, response, and recovery—effective marketing of disaster mental health services can also be divided into phases.

This process includes: (1) formative research; (2) strategic program planning and implementation; (3) program development; and (4) program monitoring, evaluation and modification. Note that while each phase is distinct in its purpose and objectives, the phases may overlap, with one beginning while the previous is ongoing or revisiting an earlier phase after new information is learned in a later phase.

21.2.2.1 Phase 1: Formative Research

The first step in developing a social marketing plan is to conduct formative research. Formative research is designed to gain insights into consumer expectations, aspirations, needs, and perceptions of mental health services. Situational factors affecting the project are considered, and formative research is conducted to understand the issue from the clients' viewpoint. Of special interest are clients' perceptions of service benefits, costs, placement, and potential promotional strategies, and the factors that influence their decision to seek care.

Whenever possible, marketers rely on existing data or secondary data sources, such as census track information, administrative data sets, scientific and technical journals, existing disaster mental health service utilization data, and program evaluations. Other rich sources of information are online listservs, the Centers for Disease Control and Prevention audience research Web site, and, often, peers and colleagues. The latter group may include both disaster and mental health professionals, as well as those involved in similar types of social marketing efforts. A useful benefit social marketers enjoy that commercial marketers typically do not is that of a spirit of collaboration amongst those in the field. Those who employ social marketing techniques to advance a social cause are usually willing to share their research findings, planning strategies, implementation experiences, and lessons learned.

Often primary data collection is needed to learn more about the specific target audience. These data are gathered from key informants and the target audience via individual interviews, focus groups, and survey instruments. Formative research is essential in determining the knowledge, attitudes, and beliefs of the target audience that influence behavioral decisions. Understanding these determinants enables identification of those audience segments most likely to need and accept disaster mental health services, as well as paint a picture of the target audiences' perceptions of desirable mental health service products, pricing, places, and promotions.

21.2.2.2 Phase 2: Strategic Program Planning and Implementation

As alluded to before, formative research findings are used to make key marketing decisions and to develop a blueprint or marketing plan to guide program development, such as audience segments to target, strategies for determining costs or making services acceptable, places to offer services, partners to support delivery of services, and ways to promote disaster mental health services to select audience segments.

Kotler and Lee (2008) have developed a 10-step model for creating a strategic marketing plan. It begins with describing the background, purpose, and focus of the plan and concludes with a plan for implementation. The plan serves as a detailed roadmap to reaching the final destination, which, for most readers, will be disaster mental health service utilization. The 10 steps are outlined in greater detail in the next section.

Comparable to disaster response, implementation of the strategic marketing plan is where the rubber meets the road, so to speak. The execution of carefully researched and formulated strategies and tactics finally occurs, ideally putting into play a series of orchestrated events designed to heighten client response to disaster mental health services.

21.2.2.3 Phase 3: Program Development

This phase involves the development of program materials and tactics. Often an advertising agency or other creative team is hired to design messages and prepare communication materials. Instructional designers and professional trainers develop new products, curricula, campaign messages and materials, and public relations activities. Program strategies, campaign messages and materials, and other products are pretested and revised.

Many social marketing projects do not reach the implementation phase until after months of planning. Although coordination is important for any program, social marketing projects typically require managers to balance an unusually large number of staff, consultants or subcontractors, and manage multiple activities, each of which requires careful timing. Proper sequencing of organizational policy and procedural enhancements, professional training, materials distribution, public relations, and public policy formation are essential to the success of a project. It is especially important to have service delivery enhancements in place and customer service training completed before advertising a new, improved program.

21.2.2.4 Phase 4: Program Monitoring, Evaluation, and Modification

This section presents how to determine what, how, and when monitoring and evaluation will take place. Program monitoring is a continuous process that typically occurs at predetermined intervals throughout the implementation phase. The purpose is to measure both process and outcome objectives and to determine if program modification (altering the course of action in some way) is necessary. Process and objectives measures simply assess whether the program output is what was intended. Assessing outcome objectives involves determining if the course of action is yielding the desired knowledge, attitude, belief, and behavioral responses.

Program evaluation is performed to measure the effectiveness of a social marketing plan. It differs from monitoring in that it normally occurs at the conclusion of a program. The program endpoint is determined during the strategic planning phase and is influenced by the specific program goals/objectives and most likely the nature and intensity of the disaster. For example, outreach and delivery of crisis counseling services after a hurricane would differ from those provided during a moderate or severe flu pandemic. Thus, the program lengths and evaluation points may vary. In the same way monitoring provides information about required course correction for the current program, evaluation results are used to make strategic planning decisions in future programs.

21.2.3 10-STEP STRATEGIC MARKETING PLANNING PROCESS (ADAPTED FROM KOTLER AND LEE 2008)

21.2.3.1 Step 1: Background, Purpose, and Focus Statement

The first step in the planning process is to develop a background statement to frame, within a historical and current context, the status of disaster survivors' mental health. The background statement will also paint a clear picture of the role of disaster mental health services and why they are worthy of promoting to survivors. You may begin by explaining the need for disaster crisis counseling—both in general, and with respect to the current situation—and go on to describe past utilization of such services, the result of low utilization rates, and evidence for a positive social outcome associated with disaster mental health services.

Stating the purpose is simply saying what it is you hope to accomplish. The purpose is broad and general and does not need to be quantifiable. For many reading this text, the purpose will be something akin to, "Increase crisis counseling service utilization following a disaster." Developing a focus involves determining what approach will be taken to achieve the stated purpose, and may be centered on the product, a population, or a behavior. For example, your focus may be addressing the needs of a vulnerable population such as the homeless. Or, you might elect to focus your efforts on increasing mental health screening rates (behavior). A slightly different approach would be to center the program on a mobile disaster crisis counseling service (product). The remaining steps in the planning process would differ depending on the purpose and focus selected. Thus, it is important to select a focus that takes into account the potential for realizing increases in service utilization, the capacity of the agent of change (and its partners) to carry out required campaign activities, as well as what available or potential opportunities for funding exist to support the effort.

21.2.3.2 Step 2: SWOT Analysis

A SWOT analysis is an assessment of how disaster mental health is situated in the current environment. SWOT is an acronym for strengths, weaknesses, opportunities, and threats. Analysis enables identification of factors, both internal and external to the sponsoring organization (agency of change), that may have some influence on campaign efforts, either positive or negative. Strengths and weaknesses are relative to the internal or microenvironment, while opportunities and threats refer to macroenvironmental factors, or those external to the agency of change/sponsoring organization. Begin assessing the situation by taking inventory of internal strengths that may advance campaign efforts and weaknesses that may need to be addressed to minimize potentially adverse consequences. These may relate to fiscal, personnel, and other organizational service delivery resources, support of management and other internal publics, existing partnerships/alliances, current organizational priorities, or past performance with similar projects.

Opportunities and threats are features of the macroenvironment, over which the sponsoring organization has no control. Opportunities may be leveraged to bolster the project, while threats have the potential to hinder efforts. As with strengths and weaknesses, thoughtful inventory of opportunities and threats will provide an arsenal of factors that may be used to your advantage in determining project strategies, while allowing action to mitigate potentially destructive forces. Forces to examine include demographic trends, cultural and economic dynamics, technological advancements (or specific to disasters, damage to technology infrastructure), related political or legislative action, and influential external public stakeholders.

21.2.3.3 Step 3: Target Audiences

Selecting one or more target audiences is a key step in maximizing the project's return on investment. Ideally, a project will beget maximum behavior change for any given quantity of resources used. Target audience selection begins with segmenting the market into smaller, more homogenous groups. Groups may be segmented in many ways, including geographic, demographic, psychographic (psychological), or behavior characteristics. More complex methods of segmenting are rooted in theoretical models of behavior change, and often more than one method of segmentation is used to identify potential target markets.

One common way of segmenting audiences on the basis of behavior change is the Transtheoretical Model of Behavior Change, also referred to as the Stages of Change model (Prochaska and DiClemente 1983). The Stages of Change model is based on the premise that the likelihood of adopting a new behavior is dependent on one's position along a continuum of readiness for change. This continuum as related to disaster mental health service utilization would begin with precontemplation, in which an individual doesn't even realize there is a problem. The survivor may ignore or attribute any physical or psychological symptoms to other causes. Contemplation is next on the continuum. In this stage, the survivor may recognize there is a problem and begin to think about ways to solve it. The solution options considered may or may not involve mental health service utilization, depending on the individual's knowledge, attitudes, and beliefs. The next stage, preparation, involves actively planning to address the problem. At this point, disaster survivors still may or may not be planning to address the appropriate problem. It will depend on whether identification of the problem (mental health problems related to the disaster) was accurate. The fourth stage is that of action. Individuals in the action stage will engage in behavior(s) to address the problem. This may include going to see a general practitioner, seeking out mental health services, taking substances, or engaging in other activities perceived as beneficial in addressing the problem. Individuals in the maintenance phase have successfully engaged in behaviors to correct the problem. In the context of disaster mental health services, this may involve keeping regular counseling appointments, support group attendance, medication compliance, or other activities related to restoring psychological well being.

Note that Stages of Change is but one method used to segment audiences. Other approaches may be more effective given the specific situation, or a combination of methods may be used to further refine market segments. In addition to distinguishing consumer market segments, upstream market segments should also be identified. Upstream targets are those who have influence over mental health service consumer behavior. Some examples are general practitioners, employers, employee assistance programs, and health insurers, to name a few.

Once the audience has been segmented, each segment must be evaluated to determine the viability of selection for the campaign target audience. Criteria to consider when determining which segment to target are the size of the segment, degree to which the segment has been affected by disaster-related mental health problems, accessibility of the audience, current behaviors and attitudes toward mental health services, the extent to which the audience appears ready to engage in disaster crisis counseling, and the degree to which the segment can influence other segments to engage in crisis counseling. In mathematical terms, final selection should reflect a target audience that results in a high value for maximum impact (I), where $I = U$ (service utilization)/R (resources spent).

21.2.3.4   Step 4: Goals and Objectives

After identifying the purpose, focus, and target audience, campaign goals and objectives can be determined. Goals and objectives are related to the project's purpose and focus, but are distinct in that they are specific, measureable, attainable, relevant, and time sensitive (SMART). Objectives may be oriented to knowledge, beliefs, attitudes, or behaviors. Most social marketing campaigns will have a specific behavioral objective, or what you wish to influence the target audience to do. An example of a behavioral objective for a specific audience segment affected by disaster is to be screened for depression. Knowledge objectives would then be related to what the target audience needs to know in order to get screened. Do they need to know how to identify symptoms of disaster-related depression? Do they need to know where to get screened? What else do they need to know? Belief objectives are what you need the audience to believe in order to get screened. Perhaps they know that services exist, how to access them, and that they are experiencing some of the symptoms of depression. What then do you need for them to believe to get screened? Do they need to believe that getting screened may lead to an intervention that will make them feel better and foster recovery? Do they need to believe that seeking services is easy and convenient? That depression is not a sign of character weakness?

At present, little is known about the determinants of disaster mental health service use, in general, and in racially and ethnically diverse populations, in particular. In addition to the primary determinants of intention to perform a given behavior (i.e., beliefs, attitudes, ability, motivation), personal variables specific to the priority population are indirect factors that are reflected in the underlying belief structure. It is noteworthy that these determinants are specific to the behavior and population. Thus, it is crucial to determine the degree to which the intention to use disaster mental health services is under attitudinal or normative control with regard to the selected population in addition to understanding salient beliefs *prior* to developing programs to deliver disaster mental health services.

Most plans incorporate knowledge, belief, and behavior objectives. Understanding the target audience is a crucial element in setting your plan objectives. If you are not aware of what they know, believe, and do, it will be nearly impossible to recognize what you need them to know and believe in order to utilize mental health services. Also, determining where you are starting relative to these objectives will allow for a quantifiable means of monitoring and evaluating objectives outcomes.

Program goals, in addition to being quantifiable and measurable, establish a specific level of desired behavior change that occurs as a result of the campaign efforts, among the target audience, within a specified amount of time. This requires the ability to quantify current rates of the desired behavior. In some cases, current behavior rates are not known—either due to the lack of data and/or constraints to collecting data (lack of time or financial resources, for example). When this occurs, proxies or alternatives can be used to measure goal attainment. Some commonly used proxies include measurements of campaign awareness, campaign response, process outcomes and/or increases in disaster-related mental health knowledge, beliefs, or intention to utilize services.

21.2.3.5 Step 5: Competition and Perceived Barriers and Benefits

At this phase, insights gained when segmenting and prioritizing audience populations are explored in greater depth. Formative research is conducted to understand consumers' perceptions of barriers and benefits to mental health service utilization. Consistent with marketing's exchange theory, the goal is to identify benefits that far outweigh the costs or barriers of using disaster mental health services. In some cases, the most attractive benefits may not be the mental health treatment delivered by the providers. For example, people with disaster-related emotional problems may perceive newfound support when others offer encouragement and provide tangible means (e.g., providing transportation to an appointment). Conversely, families who feel shame about the expression of mental health problems may hinder use of services through their words and actions. Social marketers strive to understand the barriers that exist for target audiences and systematically work to eliminate or minimize them through strategic program planning, while simultaneously underscoring the benefits.

Identification of the costs and benefits associated with competing behaviors can also be used to develop effective marketing strategies. Exploiting the costs of engaging in competing behaviors may accompany reducing the costs of the desired behavior. Sometimes, as in the case of laws and policies designed to discourage competing behaviors through punitive measures, upstream marketing is used to actually raise the costs of competing behaviors rather than just bring to light the negative aspects.

It is worth noting that barriers and benefits of the desired and competing behaviors may be real or perceived. Real or not, however, they are what the consumer believes to be true, and as such have to be acknowledged and properly addressed to elicit desired campaign outcomes.

21.2.3.6 Step 6: Product Positioning

Product positioning refers to how the sponsoring organization wants the product to be perceived by the target audience. Positioning, or repositioning when there is a current ineffectual product position, may be oriented to behaviors, benefits, barriers or the competition.

When pondering product positioning, it is helpful to think for a moment about the commercial realm. What comes to mind when you think of Subway restaurants? For many, eating at Subway has come to be equated with healthful fast food, and this was no accident. The organization deliberately set out to position their product in this fashion through a variety of campaign strategies and tactics, and has undoubtedly achieved success in positioning the product in a specific way in the minds of consumers.

Now, think about what is known about how disaster mental health services are viewed at present. What comes to the mind of the average consumer (or, more specifically, your target consumer) when this product is mentioned? Anything? How does this compare with the desired image of your product? Using what is now known about your target audience, Kotler and Lee (2008) suggest developing a position statement by completing the blanks in the following phrase:

We want [TARGET AUDIENCE] to see DISASTER CRISIS COUNSELING
[or other desired behavior] as [DESCRIPTIVE PHRASE] and as more important and beneficial than
[COMPETITION]. (187)

21.2.3.7   Step 7: Marketing Mix

Formative research results are used to create a comprehensive, integrated marketing plan. In addition to product benefits and costs discussed previously, strategies are developed for the other elements of the marketing mix—placement, people, processes, and promotion. This plan serves as the blueprint for developing program materials and activities.

21.2.3.8   Step 8: Monitoring and Evaluation Plan

A plan for monitoring and evaluation will encompass both campaign outputs and outcomes. Outputs are simply measures of what has been produced by the campaign. For example, the plan may include airing public service announcements on a local radio station. An output measure would be the number of media announcements aired during a specific time period or number of consumers those ads reached. Outcome measures, on the other hand, attempt to capture and quantify consumer response to campaign output. They relate to your goals and objectives determined in Step 4. Referring back to the radio public service announcement (PSA) example, one possible outcome measure would be how many people in a surveyed group of the target audience were able to recall the radio PSA, indicating an awareness of the campaign.

The monitoring and evaluation plan should incorporate details about what you are measuring and why, how the assessments will be performed, when (at what intervals) measurements will be taken, and the cost of measurements. From the standpoint of fiscal efficiency, consideration should be given to whether the benefits of specific measures outweigh the costs of performing them.

21.2.3.9   Step 9: Budgets and Funding Sources

In a perfect world, there would be unlimited means to enact the plan. Unfortunately, most organizations have finite resources to allocate to any given project. Thus, budget constraints are inevitable. A simple way to begin is to list all of the planned campaign activities (including formative research, monitoring, and evaluation) and determine the costs associated with each. Ideally, the total costs will not exceed the project budget, but in reality they often do. If this is the case, alternate sources of campaign monies can often be generated through grants or partnerships with various types of organizations. If budget requirements still are not met after other options for funding have been exhausted, cost-reducing measures may be explored. Reduced expenses can be achieved by implementing the campaign in multiple phases, eliminating or cutting back on those activities deemed to have a lower yield relative to cost outlay, or narrowing the goals and objectives of the campaign.

21.2.3.10   Step 10: Implementation Plan

The implementation plan specifies the overall time frame for project execution. It details exactly what, when, and how campaign activities will take place, as well as who is responsible for each activity. Establishing regular meeting intervals for key project personnel and stakeholders may also be helpful to include in the implementation plan, thus promoting communication and facilitating course changes as deemed necessary through regular program monitoring.

21.3   SOCIAL MARKETING WORKS—TWO CASE STUDIES

The Centers for Disease Control and Prevention, the National Institute of Mental Health, AARP, and other governmental and nonprofit organizations at the national, state, and local levels have successfully used social marketing to increase the number of people using a variety of health services and social programs (i.e., nutrition programs, immunizations, cancer screenings) and to promote health behavior change with older adults (i.e., physical activity, diabetes prevention, dietary practices, arthritis diagnosis and treatment). Environmental agencies have utilized social marketing techniques to encourage behaviors, such as recycling and reducing water usage to conserve resources. Next, two case studies are presented to illustrate how social marketing has been used successfully to enhance preparedness for a bioterrorism event and as a means to decrease stigma associated with severe and persistent mental illness.

21.3.1 RHODE ISLAND CASE STUDY

Social marketing can be used during all phases of a disaster—from preparation to response and recovery. At the present time, the only known example of such is an effort by the Rhode Island Department of Health (DOH). The DOH used a social marketing approach to enhance residents' level of disaster preparedness for bioterrorism events (Marshall et al. 2007). The program was implemented over the course of several years "in three distinct phases: initial planning and formative research—including focus groups and key informant interviews; strategy development and program implementation—involving an emergency preparedness product; and finally, tracking, monitoring, and evaluation." Results from the formative research revealed that people felt overwhelmed by the number of directives, desired less technical language in messaging, and wanted more emphasis placed on the availability of free services regardless of ability to pay.

A press conference held by the DOH and partner organizations, Boy Scouts of America, United States Postal Service, and supermarket sponsors to kick off the campaign resulted in widespread media coverage. To generate awareness and break through the direct mail clutter, postcard-sized announcements were distributed by the Boy Scouts at high-volume grocery stores the weekend prior to the bulk mailing. A pre- and postintervention evaluation was conducted by telephone survey to measure key behavioral change outcomes: (1) knowledge of assembling an emergency kit; (2) activities to assemble an emergency kit; (3) knowledge of developing a plan to stay in contact with family and friends; (4) activities to develop a plan to stay in contact with family and friends; and (5) establishing a way to stay informed by the media during an emergency. Though there was no significant change in residents' self-reported knowledge about biological, chemical, or radiological emergencies, the percentage of participants who reported being aware of emergency kits and emergency plans increased significantly postintervention. The number of people who indicated they assembled partial or complete emergency kits increased significantly as well. The investigators reported that "formative research to design the product made a real difference in the public's behavioral response" (Marshall et al. 2007, 60). They noted that a commercial undertaking of the same magnitude would have cost "hundreds of thousands, perhaps even millions of dollars in research, development, advertising, placement, and sales effort. Clearly, some of the fiscal deficit in the project was offset by news coverage and the cooperation of multiple organizations that played a key role in its success" (Marshall et al. 2007, 60).

Two reported limitations were that the project relied primarily on focus groups and that adults were grouped into a single audience segment. The authors noted an approach including both quantitative and qualitative data would have better targeted their efforts and products. Second, they indicated that by grouping all adults as a single audience they were unable to identify potential "differences in the factors that influence emergency behaviors between younger adults with small children compared to older adults with grown children or grandchildren" (Marshall et al. 2007, 61).

21.3.2 WORLD PSYCHIATRIC ASSOCIATION CASE STUDY

As noted earlier in this chapter, stigma adversely affects use of disaster mental health services. Stigma not only results in decreased diagnosis of disorders, but also in worse outcomes (Link et al. 1997). The following case study illustrates how social marketing was used to reduce stigma and improve care of people with schizophrenia. In 1996, the World Psychiatric Association (WPA) developed a social marketing plan to implement its *Programme to Reduce Stigma and Discrimination because of Schizophrenia* in 20 countries (Warner 2005). Each project was established using the same basic formula for program design: (1) form a local action committee, (2) conduct a survey to identify sources of stigma, (3) select target audiences, (4) select messages and communication channels, and (5) continuously evaluate the effectiveness of the interventions and refine the program accordingly.

The local action committee members were volunteers who were selected in an effort to have a diverse representation from all potential target audiences. The WPA recommended inviting prominent members of the community to serve on the committee as a means to gain prestige and attention from media and form alliances with potential partner organizations. Once the committee was established, a survey was administered locally to identify sources of stigma and determine target audiences.

An example of one of the projects is an antistigma program that was established in Boulder, Colorado. High school students were selected as a target audience because of their ability to shape the beliefs, attitudes, and behaviors of an up-and-coming cohort of young adults. Police, jail and probation officers, and judges were chosen as a second target audience because they often encounter challenging situations with offenders who have mental illness. Moreover, judges are commonly faced with the arduous task of determining appropriate sentences (or alternatives to incarceration) for offenders with mental illness. Despite the frequency with which criminal justice personnel encounter mentally ill offenders, there were no programs in place to provide these professionals with the tools necessary to effectively work with this population.

Key messages, goals, and process and outcome objectives were developed for each specific target audience. Messages that were targeted to high school students were delivered by speakers with mental illness, the WPA Web site, a teaching guide on schizophrenia, a juried art show with monetary prizes, public transit, and local cinema screens. The art contest called for artwork related to stigma and mental illness. Also geared to high school students were ads with antistigma messages displayed on the interiors of public transit buses. One featured student artwork with the message, "Sometimes those that are different are the most amazing." Because these ads were considered public service announcements, they were displayed at no cost. Antistigma messages were displayed in slides that ran prior to a feature movie at local theaters. At least one of the three messages addressed negative stereotypes of individuals with mental illness who were depicted in movies. Exit interviews revealed that 18 percent of the moviegoers remembered at least one of the messages shown. This translated to more than 10,000 people recalling an antistigma message two hours after initial exposure.

A training course in mental illness developed by mental health professionals, consumers, and police officers was pilot tested on police officers in the county's largest city. Pre- and post-evaluation of this day long course led to a refined course, which was offered to officers in the county's second-largest city. The course, facilitated by psychiatrists, consumers, and their family members, demonstrated a 48 percent improvement in scores related to knowledge of adult and child mental disorders. Also promising was that the percentage of officers who held inaccurate beliefs about the causes of schizophrenia dropped from 24 percent to 3 percent. Unfortunately, the progress seen in these specific knowledge and beliefs did not translate into an improvement in attitudes toward people with psychosis or the inaccurate perceptions about the usual behavior of people with schizophrenia. The program evaluation revealed this finding was the result of previous police interactions with people with psychosis. Rather than having an opportunity to observe those with mental illness in stable life situations, police were most commonly in contact with those who were acutely disturbed. To change inaccurate beliefs and perceptions about people with mental illness, future training should involve exposure to consumers who have recovered from psychosis.

Three training sessions on adult mental disorders and one on child disorders were provided for judges, attorneys, and probation officers. Results of pre- and posttesting indicated a 27 percent increase in knowledge of schizophrenia amongst judges, with some reporting changes in sentencing practices. Also noteworthy was that the judges requested additional training related to child disorders following the four initial sessions.

A separate, but key, component of the Boulder and other WPA antistigma projects was the establishment of media-watch groups to lobby news and entertainment media to stop perpetuating stigma through negative depictions of mentally ill people. The use of a volunteer action committee and strategically targeted audiences, interventions, and messages allowed the Boulder project to be conducted over a three-year period for under $10,000. Similar programs could be developed to counter stigma associated with use of disaster mental health services.

21.4 PRODUCING WRITTEN SOCIAL MARKETING MATERIALS USING HEALTH LITERACY CRITERIA

Print materials produced for any social marketing campaign should adhere to good design guidelines and health literacy criteria (U.S. Department of Health and Human Services nd, a; Plain Language Action and Information Network 2005). Nearly half of the U.S. adult population has trouble understanding and acting on health information (Institute of Medicine 2004). Many health materials are written at reading levels higher than the reading comprehension levels of most patients. Poor health literacy is associated with delays in accessing and using services, adherence to instructions, and compromised self-care.

Irrespective of their educational level, most people prefer simple-to-read, culturally appropriate materials. Print materials should recognize the cultural beliefs, traditions, language preferences, and health practices of the intended audience (U.S. Department of Health and Human Services 2001). Most people find it easier to comprehend and act correctly on short, straightforward messages than on more complex ones (Wallace 2006; Wolf, Gazmararian, and Baker 2005). It is highly advantageous to use a plain language strategy when developing written materials for outreach, psychoeducation, treatment, and referral. Key elements of plain language include organizing information so that the most important points are presented first, presenting complex information simply and clearly, defining technical terms, and using an active voice (Plain Language Action and Information Network 2005). Because language that is plain to one audience segment may not be plain to others, materials should be pilot tested with participants who represent the targeted population and provide an appropriate mix of sex, age, ethnic, and race characteristics.

21.5 CONCLUSION

In this chapter we describe how a social marketing approach could be implemented to enhance outreach and increase acceptance of disaster mental health services. A social marketing approach strives to elucidate how attitudes, beliefs, norms, and motivation influence whether, where, why, how, and when people seek and use disaster mental health services. The chances for increased mental health service utilization are far greater if a match exists between client wants or needs and the treatment that is offered.

RESOURCES

NONPROFIT AND FOR-PROFIT AGENCIES

Center for Social Marketing and Behavior Change
Academy for Educational Development
1825 Connecticut Ave.
Washington, DC 20009-5721
Phone: (202) 884-8902
Fax: (202) 884-8713
E-mail: csmbcinfo@aed.org
Online: http://csmbc.aed.org

Florida Prevention Research Center
Mailing address
USF Health College of Public Health
13201 Bruce B Downs Blvd. MDC056
Tampa, FL 33612
Physical address
1441 E Fletcher Ave., Suite 204
Tampa, FL 33612
Phone: (813) 983-3216
Fax: (813) 983-3217
E-mail: lphilli1@health.usf.edu
Online: http://health.usf.edu/nocms/publichealth/prc

Kirby Marketing Solutions
12887 Caminito Del Canto
Del Mar, CA 92014
Phone: (858) 245-2456
Fax: (858) 769-4481
Online: http://www.kirbyms.com

Social Marketing Institute
1825 Connecticut Ave. NW, Suite S-852
Washington, DC 20009
Online: http://www.social-marketing.org

Uncommon Insights, LLC
4201 Wilson Blvd. #110-101
Arlington, VA 22203
Phone: (703) 254-6515
Online: http://www.uncommoninsights.com

Winthrop Morgan
6414 Hollins Dr.
Bethesda, MD 20817
Online: http://www.winthropmorgan.com

INTERNET RESOURCES

Agency for Healthcare Research and Quality Health Literacy and Cultural Competency
Online: http://www.ahrq.gov/browse/hlitix.htm

Centers for Disease Control and Prevention
1600 Clifton Rd.
Atlanta, GA 30333
Phone: (800) CDC-INFO (800-232-4636)
TTY: (888) 232-6348
E-mail: cdcinfo@cdc.gov
Emergency Preparedness and Response
Online: http://emergency.cdc.gov
Mental Health Work Group
Online: http://www.cdc.gov/mentalhealth

Social Marketing Resources
Online: http://www.cdc.gov/nccdphp/dnpao/socialmarketing/index.html

Plain Language Action and Information Network (PLAIN)
Online: http://www.plainlanguage.gov

Social Marketing Institute
1825 Connecticut Ave. NW
Suite S-852
Washington, DC 20009
Online: http://www.social-marketing.org

Social Marketing Listserv
The listserv is a forum for talking about social marketing research, practice, and teaching via
e-mail. It was founded by Dr. Alan Andreasen at Georgetown University, one of the leaders in the
area of social marketing. People participate from across the United States and many other countries
and represent a variety of disciplines. To subscribe, send an e-mail message to listproc@listproc.
georgetown.edu. In the body of the message write "subscribe SOC-MKTG [your name]" and type
your actual name in place of "your name."

The Social Marketing Place
Weinreich Communications
Phone: (310) 286-2721
Fax: (310) 553-5496
Online: http://social-marketing.org

Turning Point
Turning Point, which was open from 1997 to 2006, was an initiative of the Robert Wood Johnson
Foundation and the W. K. Kellogg Foundation. Its mission was to transform and strengthen the
public health system in the United States by making it more community based and collaborative.
The initial idea for Turning Point came from the foundations' concerns about the capacity of the
public health system to respond to emerging challenges in public health, specifically the system's
capacity to work with people from many sectors to improve the health status of all people in a
community.
Online: http://www.turningpointprogram.org/Pages/socialmkt.html
Resource guide: http://www.turningpointprogram.org/Pages/pdfs/social_market/social_marketing_
101.pdf

U.S. Department of Health and Human Services
Office of Disease Prevention and Health Promotion – Health Literacy Improvement
Phone: (240) 453-8280
Fax: (240) 453-8282
Online: http://www.health.gov/communication/literacy/default.htm

BOOKS

Andreasen, A. R. 1995. *Marketing Social Change.* San Francisco: Jossey-Bass.
Institute of Medicine. 2004. *Health Literacy: A Prescription to End Confusion*, eds. L. Nielsen-Bohlman, A. M.
    Panzer, and D. A. Kindig. Washington, DC: National Academies Press.
Siegel, M., and L. Donner. 1998. *Marketing Public Health.* 1998. Gaithersburg, MD: Aspen Publishers, Inc.
Weinreich, N. K. 1999. *Hands-On Social Marketing: A Step-by-Step Guide.* Thousand Oaks, CA: Sage
    Publications.

JOURNALS

Journal of Health Communication
Taylor & Francis
1900 Frost Rd., Suite 101
Bristol, PA 19007-1598
Social Marketing Quarterly
c/o Best Start, Inc.
3500 E. Fletcher Ave., Suite 519
Tampa, FL 33613

TRAINING

CDC Professional Development Resources Directory
Online: http://www.cdc.gov/healthmarketing/training.htm

Florida Prevention Research Center
See listing under "Nonprofit and For-Profit Agencies" above for contact information.

Opportunities
Online: http://health.usf.edu/publichealth/prc/training.html
Examples: Social Marketing Conference, Certificate Program, Field School

REFERENCES

Amaya-Jackson, L., J. R. T. Davidson, D. C. Hughes, M. S. Swartz, V. Reynolds, L. K. George, and D. G. Blazer 1999. Functional impairment and utilization of services associated with posttraumatic stress in the community. *Journal of Traumatic Stress 12*: 709–724.

Arnold, A. 1994. The "Big Bang" theory of competition in health care. In *Health Care Marketing. A Foundation for Managed Quality,* 3rd ed., ed. P. D. Cooper. Gaithersburg, MD: Aspen Publishers, Inc.

Chiriboga, D. A. 2007. Cultural considerations: Caring for culturally diverse communities in the aftermath of terrorist attacks. In *Psychology of Terrorism*, eds. B. Bongar, L. M. Brown, L. Beutler, J. Breckenridge, and P. Zimbardo, 338–356. New York: Oxford University Press.

Connor, K. M., E. B. Foa, and J. R. Davidson. 2006. Practical assessment and evaluation of mental health problems following a mass disaster. *Journal of Clinical Psychiatry 67*(S2): 26–33.

Cooper, P. D. 1994. *Health Care Marketing. A Foundation for Managed Quality*, 3rd ed. Gaithersburg, MD: Aspen Publishers, Inc.

Covell, N. H., S. A. Donahue, W. R. Ulaszek, L. Dunakin, S. M. Essock, and C. J. Felton. 2006. Effectiveness of two methods of obtaining feedback on mental health services provided to anonymous recipients. *Psychiatric Services 57*(9): 1324–1327.

Davidson, J. R., and A. C. McFarlane. 2006. The extent and impact of mental health problems after disaster. *Journal of Clinical Psychiatry 67*(S2): 9–14.

Donahue, S. A., C. T. Jackson, K. M. Shear, C. J. Felton, and S. M. Essock. 2006. Outcomes of enhanced counseling services provided to adults through Project Liberty. *Psychiatric Services 57*(9): 1298–1303.

Galea, S., C. R. Brewin, M. Gruber, R. T. Jones, D. W. King, L. A. King, R. J. McNally, R. J. Ursano, M. Petukhova, and R. C. Kessler. 2007. Exposure to hurricane-related stressors and mental illness after Hurricane Katrina. *Archives of General Psychiatry 64*(12): 1427–1434.

Hamblen, J. L., L. E. Gibson, K. T. Mueser, and F. H. Norris. 2006. Cognitive behavioral therapy for prolonged postdisaster distress. *Journal of Clinical Psychology: In Session 62*: 1043–1052.

Institute of Medicine. 2004. *Health Literacy: A Prescription to End Confusion*, eds. L. Nielsen-Bohlman, A. M. Panzer, and D. A. Kindig. Washington, DC: National Academies Press.

Kessler, R. C. 2000. Posttraumatic stress disorder: The burden to the individual and to society. *Journal of Clinical Psychiatry 61*(S5): 4–12.

Kotler, P., and N. R. Lee. 2008. *Social Marketing: Influencing Behaviors for Good*, 3rd ed. Thousand Oaks, CA: Sage Publications.

Kotler, P., and P. Zaltman. 1971. Social marketing: An approach to planned social change. *Journal of Marketing* *35*(3): 3–12.

Link, B. G., E. L. Struening, M. Rahav, J. C. Phelan, and L. Nuttbrock. 1997. On stigma and its consequences: Evidence from a longitudinal study of men with dual diagnoses of mental illness and substance abuse. *Journal of Health and Social Behavior 38*(2): 177–190.

Marshall, R. J., L. Petrone, M. J. Takach, S. Sansonetti, M. Wah-Fitta, A. Bagnall-Degos, and A. Novais. 2007. Make a kit, make a plan, stay informed: Using social marketing to change the population's emergency preparedness behavior. *Social Marketing Quarterly 13*(4): 47–64.

National Center for Education Statistics. 2006. *The Health Literacy of America's Adults: Results From the 2003 National Assessment of Adult Literacy.* Washington, DC: U.S. Department of Education.

Plain Language Action and Information Network. 2005. *What is plain language?* http://www.plainlanguage. gov.

Prochaska, J. O., and C. C. DiClemente. 1983. Stages and processes of self-change of smoking: Toward an integrative model of change. *Journal of Consulting and Clinical Psychology 51*: 390–395.

Silk, S. 2006. Preparing psychologists for the reality of disaster work: Distinctions between traditional psychotherapy and disaster mental health. 114th Annual Convention of the American Psychological Association. New Orleans, Louisiana.

Substance Abuse and Mental Health Services Administration. 2000. *Emergency mental health and traumatic stress: Crisis counseling and mental health treatment similarities and differences.* http://mentalhealth. samhsa.gov/cmhs/EmergencyServices/ccp_pg02.asp.

Sundararaman, R., S. A. Lister, and E. D. Williams. 2006. Gulf Coast hurricanes: Addressing survivors' mental health and substance abuse treatment needs (Rep. RL33738). CRS Report for Congress.

U.S. Department of Health and Human Services. 2001. *National Standards for Culturally and Linguistically Appropriate Services in Health Care.* Washington, DC: Office of Minority Health.

U.S. Department of Health and Human Services, Office of Disease Prevention and Health Promotion. nd, a. *Quick guide to health literacy: Fact sheet.* http://www.health.gov/communication/literacy/quickguide/ factsbasic.htm.

U.S. Department of Health and Human Services, Substance Abuse and Mental Health Services Administration, Center for Mental Health Services. nd, b. *An overview of the Crisis Counseling Assistance and Training Program (CCP-PG-01).* http://www.fema.gov/pdf/media/2006/ccp_over.pdf.

Wallace, L. 2006. Patients' health literacy skills: The missing demographic variable in primary care research. *Annals of Family Medicine 4*(1): 85–86.

Wang, P. S., M. J. Gruber, R. E. Powers, M. Schoenbaum, A. H. Speier, K. B. Wells, and R. C. Kessler. 2007. Mental health service use among Hurricane Katrina survivors in the eight months after the disaster. *Psychiatric Services 58*(11): 1403–1411.

Warner, R. 2005. Local projects of the World Psychiatric Association programme to reduce stigma and discrimination. *Psychiatric Services 56*: 570–575.

Weisler, R. H., J. G. Barbee IV, and M. H. Townsend. 2006. Mental health and recovery in the Gulf Coast after Hurricanes Katrina and Rita. *Journal of the American Medical Association 296*: 585–588.

Wilson, J. P., M. J. Friedman, and J. D. Lindy. 2001. *Treating Psychological Trauma & PTSD.* New York: Guilford Press.

Wolf, M. S., J. A. Gazmararian, and D. W. Baker. 2005. Health literacy and functional health status among older adults. *Archives of Internal Medicine 165*(17): 1946–1952.

Zeithaml, V. A., M. J. Bitner, and D. D. Gremler. 2008. *Services Marketing*, 5th ed. New York: McGraw-Hill/ Irwin.

22 Planning for Disaster
A Behavioral Health Perspective

Raymond Runo and Julie L. Framingham

CONTENTS

22.1 INTRODUCTION

Since 2004, there have been a large number of high-profile disasters and catastrophic incidents, both within the United States and around the world. In the United States, we have been largely subjected to natural disasters in the form of hurricanes and tornadoes, as well as human-caused environmental disasters, including a significant oil spill in the Gulf of Mexico in 2010. Internationally, there was the 2004 tsunami in the Pacific Rim and the catastrophic 2011 event in Japan combining an earthquake, tsunami, and subsequent nuclear power plant radiation release. There is no question that the recent disasters have been long-term, dynamic, and complex events resulting in significant loss of life and property.

As individuals and communities face imminent dangers, they may experience a wide range of negative cognitions and feelings, including stress, anxiety, fear, horror, sadness, anger, and helplessness. These can lead to long-term dysfunction, including interpersonal problems, sleeplessness, depression, prolonged grief, social withdrawal, increased consumption of legal or illegal substances, as well as acute stress and posttraumatic stress disorders (DeWolfe 2000; Compton et al. 2005). More than other feelings, fear, especially when combined with disaster-related physical injury, is significantly associated with anxiety, depression, and posttraumatic stress disorder (Norris, Sherrieb, and Galea 2010).

Disasters also affect the environmental, economic, and social infrastructures of communities. Postdisaster environmental conditions frequently bring numerous changes for survivors, which can be difficult to negotiate. Loss of employment, transportation, quality housing, and social support networks heighten distress (Norris et al. 2002; Acierno et al. 2007). Evacuation resulting in either short- or long-term displacement from one's personal residence and support networks is particularly adverse to mental health (Norris, Sherrieb, and Galea 2010).

22.2   DISASTER PREPAREDNESS AND THE ROLE OF PLANNING

Given the adverse physical, psychological, and social impacts of disaster, individual and community preparedness is critical. Preparedness may be defined as proactively engaging in activities that increase the capabilities of a community or jurisdiction to respond effectively to disaster (McEntire and Myers 2004; Henstra 2010). Preparedness helps save lives, prevents injuries, and protects communities through organized, concerted efforts of involved stakeholders. Preparedness activities include resource identification, training and exercises for disaster responders, developing warning systems, communicating to the public about disaster impacts and how to take protective actions, and creating emergency response plans and procedures. Such activities are essential to saving lives, lessening the risk of personal injuries and property damages, abbreviating disruption to community infrastructures, and handling unexpected circumstances successfully (McEntire and Myers 2004).

Planning is one of the most important aspects of disaster preparedness. Planning has been defined as "a systematic way to anticipate the entire life cycle of a potential event and/or incident. Effective planning will translate policy, strategy, doctrine, and capabilities into specific tasks and courses of action to be undertaken. . . . Planning is a part of the preparedness cycle that also includes training, exercising, evaluating, and incorporating of after action reviews and lessons learned" (FDOH 2010, 5). Planning includes analyses of vulnerability to potential hazards, identification of resources that can assist in preparedness and response, and collaboration with community partners. While the responsibility for disaster planning is shared by federal, state, and local jurisdictions, we posit that planning is, in fact, the responsibility of every individual, discipline, organization, facility, or jurisdiction that may experience negative disaster outcomes or become involved in disaster response. Since 1974, the Disaster Relief Act (Pub. L. 93-288), later amended by Section 416 of the Robert T. Stafford Disaster Relief and Emergency Assistance Act of 1988 (Stafford Act; Pub. L. 100-707), has required states to maintain disaster plans. However, planning for behavioral health needs postdisaster was often overlooked until the last decade despite requirements of the Stafford Act (U.S. DHHS 2003). Developing a disaster plan and procedures for each planning entity is essential to the preparedness process since these will serve as a guide for coordinating and executing response activities, as well as designating authority and responsibility for emergency decision making (Henstra 2010).

22.3   BENEFITS OF PLANNING

While written plans are critical to preparedness, the process of planning is as vital to successful preparedness and response as are the products that evolve from the planning process (U.S. DHHS 2003; Compton et al. 2005). Effective disaster response depends on the availability of financial and human resources; therefore, planning efforts must include an assessment of the jurisdiction's abilities to effectively prepare for and respond to disaster (U.S. DHHS 2003). The benefits of the planning process are manifold. The planning process is where key disaster partners and community stakeholders are identified and relationships created or strengthened, important functions and stakeholder responsibilities essential to disaster preparedness and response are determined, community resources that can be leveraged in response are assessed, and gaps in requisite capabilities and resources are identified (McEntire and Myers 2004). It is important to include stakeholders with decision-making authority at all jurisdictional levels to identify and deploy assets in response to event needs expeditiously. Furthermore, obtaining support for planning from the highest departmental and governmental levels is critical to formal acceptance of a final plan for the jurisdiction (U.S. DHHS 2003). Additional planning process benefits include strengthened communications and responder relationships, improved individual responder and interorganizational coordination, and heightened stakeholder cognizance of problems that will likely be encountered during disasters (Henstra 2010; Quarantelli 1988; U.S. DHHS 2003). These activities ultimately contribute to the protection of critical infrastructures and the maintenance of governmental and other public services after disaster. They minimize disruptions of basic services and lessen financial losses and the potential for widespread panic, confusion, and chaos.

22.4 COLLABORATION AND COORDINATION OF STAKEHOLDERS

Disaster planning is also essential to minimizing the adverse psychological consequences of a disaster occurrence and to assist disaster survivors to return to predisaster levels of functioning. Effective planning helps identify and coordinate the key agencies and organizations that will be needed to provide a behavioral health response to disaster. Their respective responsibilities for disaster preparedness, response, and recovery will be decided. State and local behavioral health planners should involve representatives of local government, particularly local emergency management agencies, since they are delegated responsibility for public health and safety before, during, and after disaster (Henstra 2010). Key leadership from faith-based organizations, nonprofit agencies, schools, local community behavioral health centers and institutions, crisis hotlines, mobile crisis units and crisis stabilization units, public health authorities, law enforcement agencies, organizations that serve older adults and individuals with disabilities, academic institutions, private industry, and services in external jurisdictions that may augment the response, among other groups, also have valuable experience and capabilities that will inform and enhance disaster behavioral health planning (U.S. DHHS 2003; Compton et al. 2005). In some instances, it is advisable to develop memoranda of understanding between the behavioral health agency and other disaster partners to shore up new relationships and agreed-upon support (U.S. DHHS 2003). Adopting a "systems perspective" in local planning is critical because "what happens in one organization or locality can often influence what happens in another" (Auf der Heide 2006, 35). Further, this kind of approach to planning facilitates the stakeholders' ability to envision common goals and objectives and devise strategies to accomplish them (Auf der Heide 2006).

22.5 PLANNING CHALLENGES

Planning is not without its share of challenges. Lack of prior knowledge of or experience with disasters, low probability of a disaster occurrence in some parts of the country making plan activation unlikely, and the difficulty of measuring performance can lead to apathy in communities (McEntire and Myers 2004; Henstra 2010). In state and local behavioral health agencies, there are the additional constraints of limited financial and human resources; insufficient community understanding of postdisaster behavioral health consequences; in some states, organizational separation from the public health agency that could provide invaluable assistance in preparedness and response; insufficient collaboration among federal, state, and local entities receiving disaster funding; and problems identifying evidence-based or evidence-informed services that can be implemented quickly in a behavioral health response to disaster (U.S. DHHS 2003, 7–8).

Although there may appear to be little time for planning, involved stakeholders should be reminded of the benefits, which are numerous (U.S. DHHS 2003). Through the planning process, human and physical assets necessary for preparedness and response actions are identified, behavioral health services and the organizations capable of providing them are selected, and funding sources for services are considered. This is also the time when a written plan will be developed and integrated with the state's emergency operations plan; this will facilitate a coordinated and integrative approach to the efforts of other departmental and jurisdictional partners in disaster response (U.S. DHHS 2003). Coordination and integration strengthen response efforts by allowing emergency managers to address challenges such as absorbing responders from other communities and jurisdictions seamlessly (Auf der Heide 2006). Planning actions serve to improve the health and mental health of individuals, speed disaster recovery, and enhance community resilience (U.S. DHHS 2003; Nelson, Lurie, and Wasserman 2007). Nevertheless, the patience of involved stakeholders will be taxed if their planning efforts are not realistic in terms of timelines, activities, and expectations (McEntire and Myers 2004; Harrald 2006; U.S. DHHS 2003).

When planning participants base their efforts on impractical goals and objectives, planning outcomes will fail to measure up to expectations. According to Quarantelli (1988), "there's often a big gap between what was planned and what actually happens in a major disaster crisis" (46). Reasons for the gap vary, but include failing to train staff and conduct disaster drills to test planned functions and activities, plans are overly specific or segmented, plans have left out important functions or disciplines, lack of dedicated personnel to conduct planning and maintain written plans, and the fact that disaster response is often performed by workers from other communities (McEntire and Myers 2004; Quarentelli 1988; U.S. DHHS 2003; Auf der Heide 2006). In the last instance, planning at an interjurisdictional level is advisable to improve performance outcomes postdisaster (Auf der Heide 2006). Moreover, much of disaster planning has been conducted without adequate knowledge of empirical and historical disaster data or appreciation of the complexity of consequence management. These factors have limited planners in their ability to identify likely threats and plan adequately for impact contingencies, which ought to have been foreseeable. Therefore, in many cases, disaster response has been reactive rather than proactive.

In disaster behavioral health planning, chronic lack of funding has made it difficult for state behavioral health agencies to hire full-time staff to develop and maintain disaster plans and train agency personnel. Disaster plan format and content varies considerably state to state, which is inconsistent with other federal and state all-hazards plans, and at times has resulted in delays in receiving federal funding (U.S. DHHS 2003). Inadequate integration has also resulted in the jurisdiction's inability to effectively meet the demands of disaster response.

22.6 INTEGRATION WITH LOCAL, STATE, AND FEDERAL RESPONSE AGENCIES

Integration with local and state emergency management agencies and adoption of the core concepts, terminology, and principles used by them can enhance the planning efforts of behavioral health agencies. Common administrative and operational terminology for disaster response, command and control functions, and other activities facilitate collaboration with other agencies and help build rapport and trust (U.S. DHHS 2003). Since September 11, 2001, the federal government has undertaken several major initiatives to ensure more consistent, comprehensive, and integrated incident management, including the National Incident Management System (NIMS),[a] the National Response Framework (NRF),[b] and the Comprehensive Preparedness Guide 101 (FEMA CPG 101; FEMA 2010 V.2).[c] Both the NIMS and NRF support interdisciplinary, intersector, and jurisdictional collaboration to provide a comprehensive, national all-hazards approach to disaster response. The NRF provides a uniform foundation and direction for conducting all-hazards response for every kind of emergency and established Emergency Support Functions (ESF), which play a significant support role in disaster response operations. Behavioral health is included in ESF #8 (Public Health and Medical). ESF #8 may request assistance from partner organizations in assessing behavioral health needs, providing disaster behavioral health training and resources for workers; federal, state, tribal, or local program development; and providing additional consultation as needed (DHS 2008). The CPG 101 was issued by the Federal Emergency Management Agency (FEMA) in November 2010 and offers guidance about disaster planning to state, territorial, tribal, and local governments and discusses the steps used to produce disaster plans that are adaptable to the requirements of evolving incidents. It is the foundation for state and local planning in the United States. Behavioral health agencies should be familiar with all three of these important initiatives to understand the current culture and expectations of emergency management.

22.7   THE NEED FOR FLEXIBILITY AND CREATIVITY

While federal endeavors like the NIMS and NRF have made major contributions to improving integration of response efforts at all jurisdictional levels and have reconfirmed the federal commitment to the concept of all-hazards planning, it has also been criticized as being too "top-down" in its approach to state incident management and overly structured at the expense of flexibility and creativity (Harrald 2006; Birkland 2009). Clearly, disaster planning and response should be flexible enough to deal with urgent needs precipitated by unexpected circumstances. Addressing this concern, the CPG 101 states:

> **Time, uncertainty, risk, and experience influence planning.** These factors define the starting point where planners apply appropriate concepts and methods to create solutions to particular problems. Planning is, therefore, often considered to be both an art and a science in that successful planners are able to draw from both operational experience and an understanding of emergency management principles, but also are intuitive, creative, and have the ability to anticipate the unexpected. While the science and fundamental principles of planning can be learned through training and experience, the art of planning requires an understanding of the dynamic relationships among stakeholders, of special political considerations, and of the complexity imposed by the situation. Because this activity involves judgment and the balancing of competing demands, plans should not be overly detailed—to be followed by the letter—or so general that they provide insufficient direction. Mastering the balance of art and science is the most challenging aspect of becoming a successful planner. (1-4)

Thus, stakeholders need to exercise common sense when they incorporate structural and organizational processes and procedures into disaster plans. Recognizing the complex, dynamic, and interactive relationships of individuals within their community systems is an important aspect of planning, which enhances preparing for and responding to contingencies that may arise in disaster response. This understanding will enhance decision making and meeting community needs in a more timely and effective manner.

22.8   ALL-HAZARDS PLANNING

At present, behavioral health agencies are not required to use the same template for creating disaster plans, nor are they required to have a single plan that addresses all types of hazards. In fact, states have often developed separate plans to respond to different kinds of events (U.S. DHHS 2003). However, behavioral health agencies would be wise to design plans that are consistent with other federal, state, and local agencies. Most agencies currently use the FEMA all-hazards model for planning, which is flexible enough to address a wide range of natural or human-caused disasters and uses the core concepts, terminologies, and principles espoused by the NIMS and the NRF. An all-hazards plan will establish lines of authority, identify human and physical resources, assign roles and responsibilities, and, importantly, facilitate integration of stakeholders and their resources to provide a more coordinated, effective, and efficient response (U.S. DHHS 2003).

22.9   PLAN FORMAT AND CONTENT

Developing a written plan is a crucial activity during the planning process. Written plans and standard operating procedures serve as confirmation of agreed-upon functions, roles, and responsibilities of the involved agencies and organizations that helped to create them. They form a roadmap for prepared-ness, response, recovery, and mitigation activities, and, when experienced agency personnel are absent or relocated, they help preserve institutional memory for effective approaches to disaster response. Effective plans are concise, containing only those elements deemed necessary to be understood and followed. The following sections describe how disaster behavioral health functions and activities can be incorporated into the various common components of emergency operations plans and related protocols.

22.9.1 Basic Plan: Front Matter, Legal Authorities, and Purpose

Disaster behavioral health plans, like other emergency operations plans, should have three core components—the basic plan, annexes, and appendices. The basic plan should address how the com-munity or jurisdiction will provide a behavioral health response to disasters. The basic plan's front matter materials should include a signature page, a dated title page with a record of changes, and a plan distribution page. These documents are necessary to demonstrate to readers that the document is official, the plan is maintained and updated regularly, and that individuals who are supposed to be familiar with the plan have received a copy (U.S. DHHS 2003). A table of contents and an executive summary, if needed, should also be included in front matter. Specific legal authorities for disaster planning and response should be cited to demonstrate that the behavioral health agency has the authority to fulfill the functions and activities outlined in the plan (McEntire and Myers 2004; U.S. DHHS 2003). The first section of the plan should include a statement of the plan's general purpose. The purpose segment of a disaster behavioral health plan addresses the planners' objectives for writing the plan such as to preserve lives and protect property and the environment to the greatest extent possible from a disaster occurrence; to provide guidance to responders on reducing adverse postdisaster sequelae and returning survivors and communities to predisaster levels of psychologi-cal functioning; to facilitate a collaborative, effective, and efficient behavioral health response to disaster during all types of emergencies; to identify specific roles, responsibilities, and relation-ships between local, state, and federal entities during each phase of disaster; among other purposes (McEntire and Myers 2004; U.S. DHHS 2003).

22.9.2 Situations: Hazards Analysis

An all-hazards plan includes an analysis of the situations that the plan addresses. The situation portion of the basic plan includes a hazards assessment, vulnerabilities analysis, and determina-tion of risks posed to the community or jurisdiction, including the types of hazards that might occur and their potential for causing mortalities, morbidities, property damages, and disruption to infrastructures (McEntire and Myers 2004). Hazards are classified as natural events, including earthquakes, floods, hurricanes, and tornadoes, and human-caused incidents. Human-caused inci-dents may be broken down into technological hazards such as nuclear accidents or chemical spills; civil incidents such as terrorism, war, or riots; and biological incidents such as disease outbreaks or the spread of dangerous toxins (McEntire and Myers 2004; Allen and Katz 2010). In the latter case, biological hazards may be caused intentionally or unintentionally. Hazards clearly vary by location since not all parts of the country are likely to be impacted by hurricanes or earthquakes. However, many regions may be impacted by tornadoes or floods. Nevertheless, disaster plans should acknowledge that while some disasters are not likely to occur, they are still possible (McEntire and Myers 2004). The fact that emergencies and disasters have the potential to create extensive harm to people, property, and the environment is reason enough for emergency managers to create plans and procedures to deal with all types of disasters and take steps to mitigate their effects by reducing the community's vulnerabilities (Henstra 2010). Hazard factors such as speed of onset, scope, intensity, warning time, and destructive potential, which are data that can be gleaned from public records and disaster partners, must be assessed and included in the plans' general situations. Additionally, envisioning a disaster's impacts can help planners anticipate potential problems and determine disaster consequences (McEntire and Myers 2004). Terrorist incidents like the 2002 Washington, DC, sniper shootings, which was a prolonged event, caused extreme fear and psychological distress in more individuals than those who were actually harmed. Moreover, biological weapons can cause surges to a community's health care facilities due to heightened levels of fear and anxiety regardless of actual exposure (Stein et al. 2004). Disasters can exhaust a community's capacities; therefore, behavioral health agencies should pragmatically assess their resources to deal with disasters' psychological and social consequences (U.S. DHHS 2003).

22.9.3 SITUATIONS: VULNERABILITIES ASSESSMENT

Examining the community's vulnerability to potential hazards is also critical to the plan's contents. The community's vulnerability may be defined as how susceptible it is—physically, socially, environmentally, and economically—to injuries or damages from the hazard and can be evaluated by examining such factors as where the community is situated geographically, established building codes, the community's ability to deal with disaster impacts, and so forth (McEntire and Myers 2004, 144; Henstra 2010). In terms of behavioral health, planners must assess the needs of at-risk groups within the community who may be especially vulnerable to disaster. At-risk groups include older adults, people with disabilities, minorities and ethnic populations, and individuals with low socioeconomic status. Studies have shown that older adults may recover from the effects of disaster more slowly; people with limited vision or hearing, or members of certain ethnic/cultural groups may have difficulty understanding hazard warning information and instructions; and people with insufficient means may have difficulty evacuating without assistance (Henstra 2010; Allen and Katz 2010). In illustration of the last example, the City of New Orleans' disaster plan assumed that evacuation in the event of a major disaster might be warranted, but it failed to provide transportation for the more than 100,000 residents who lacked their own means of transportation (Col 2007). Major disasters such as Hurricane Katrina demonstrate that communities with underserved groups may suffer greater physical and psychological consequences and require additional or specialized care after disaster (Allen and Katz 2010). Therefore, the planning process should involve representatives of these populations or the organizations that serve them to adequately address their unique needs in the disaster response plan. Some plans, in fact, identify specific groups who must be served after a disaster occurrence, such as people with severe mental illness or children with severe emotional disturbances, and other groups as mission parameters and resources permit (U.S. DHHS 2003).

22.9.4 PLANNING ASSUMPTIONS

Besides the situations that a jurisdiction may face, planning assumptions are a fundamental and crucial component of disaster planning. Planning assumptions concern how people will react to disasters and potential problems or benefits of a well-coordinated response (McEntire and Myers 2004). They are developed by the consensus of involved stakeholders; their creation is a thought-provoking process. Planning assumptions anticipate the potential consequences of disaster, limit the conditions that the plan addresses, and help planners formulate realistic remedies for those potential problems. Behavioral health planning may include the following assumptions:

- All people involved in a disaster will be affected by it in some way, which could adversely affect people's ability to respond and function.
- The size, scope, and intensity of events affect individual and community response and recovery.
- Individual recovery from disaster is influenced by prior trauma history, health status, culture, beliefs, social support systems, and personal resiliency. Cognitive, emotional, physical, behavioral, and social reactions may develop immediately or have delayed onset.

- During disasters, people will seek safety, stability, order, structure and support, and a return to a predisaster level of functioning.
- At-risk groups such as individuals with severe mental illness or substance use disorders, older individuals, children, or people with disabilities may be more likely to experience traumatic stress.
- Services and continuity of care may be disrupted after a disaster for an indefinite period because facilities may sustain extensive damages or be destroyed, and staff may not be available.

These are some of the common assumptions found in disaster behavioral health plans, but others also may be considered appropriate to include. The importance of formulating sound assumptions as a basis for plan functions and activities cannot be overemphasized. As Erik Auf der Heide (2006) states, "Disaster planning is only as good as the assumptions on which they are based" (34). Misleading or false planning assumptions about human or organizational behaviors can cause problems for agencies attempting to execute an effective and efficient response to disaster (McEntire and Myers 2004). For instance, contrary to what some individuals might believe, survivors will not normally abandon others after a disaster, but will most likely have a desire to help out by conducting search and rescue work. Additionally, many survivors will be able to obtain, food, clothing, shelter, and other basic living necessities without the assistance of disaster response agencies (McEntire and Myers 2004). Evacuation assumptions can be misleading since predicting how, when, why, and if people will evacuate a disaster area may depend on socioeconomic status, health status, or other factors that planners may find difficult to fathom. Some disaster plans assume that there will be insufficient resources after a disaster occurrence and, thus, the focus of the plan is on how to deploy human and material resources instead of establishing mechanisms to integrate external resources upon arrival (Auf der Heide 2006). Many false planning assumptions can be averted, however, if planners base their assumptions on empirical research findings about individual and organizational behavior in disasters instead of on "conventional wisdom" (Birkland 2009; Auf der Heide 2006, 34).

22.9.5 CONCEPT OF OPERATIONS

The "concept of operations" portion of the plan determines who will be responsible for coordinating the preparation, response, sheltering, and recovery of survivors. Actions necessary to ameliorate adverse postdisaster psychological sequelae in individuals, families, communities, and first responders are described. Additionally, the roles of government agencies and community-based organizations are described and are based on their normal daily functions in the community, which give them the unique expertise required during a disaster (McEntire and Myers 2004). The concept of operations section describes actions that will occur during the four phases of the emergency management cycle—preparedness, response, recovery, and mitigation—which will assist the agencies and organizations involved to conduct a more efficient and effective behavioral health response to disaster (U.S. DHHS 2003).

The concept of operations section should make clear the kinds of services that participating organizations will provide individuals, families, responders, and communities as a whole during and after a disaster. After a major disaster, individuals and families will need assurances of safety and support. Many people may need assistance obtaining food, shelter, clothing, or other basic human needs. These needs must be met before survivors can really reflect on and come to terms with their emotional needs. Therefore, all organizations and functions that are necessary to meet these basic needs should be involved in the planning process. Psychological and behavioral consequences of disaster may range from mild distress and anxiety to psychiatric disorders such as posttraumatic stress disorder, or displays of psychiatric symptoms that do not meet clinical diagnostic criteria. Additionally, survivors may increase their use of tobacco, alcohol, and other substances, or seek unnecessary medical attention (this last example will be especially evident after a biological or terrorist incident; Stein et al. 2004; Compton et al. 2005).

Another consideration is the extent of exposure. Research suggests that survivors who are seriously injured, and bereaved family members of individuals who died as a result of a disaster or its effects, will have greater needs for services (U.S. DHHS 2003). Therefore, the plan should include the organizations that are responsible for providing the care that survivors will require to return to predisaster levels of functioning. Behavioral health services will typically include outreach and information dissemination, psychological first aid, assessment and triage of survivors with presenting needs, as well as referrals to formal behavioral health services if indicated. Common concerns such as confidentiality, informed consent, and recordkeeping should be addressed in the plan (U.S. DHHS 2003). Technical assistance, consultation, and training will help reduce the risk of traumatic stress and improve individual and community coping and resiliency. Services should be culturally sensitive to the various groups that reside in the community or they are less likely to be effective. Further, at-risk groups such as children, non-English-speaking individuals or others of limited literacy, isolated older adults, people with disabilities, and homeless individuals should be targeted during outreach to ensure their needs are being met. Behavioral health agencies must also be able to perform ongoing needs assessment and establish mechanisms to determine changing community needs, identify new individuals or groups who need assistance, or the need for new interventions to facilitate individual and community recovery. Notwithstanding, behavioral health agencies and partner disaster organizations should take stock of their resources and capabilities to provide disaster services, as well as their ability to absorb additional individuals into care when resources may already be stretched. Consequently, there may be eligibility requirements to determine who may be served, the types of events or circumstances that trigger disaster services, and the organizations that will provide the services, depending on the funding source and organization (U.S. DHHS 2003).

22.9.6 ORGANIZATION AND ASSIGNMENT OF RESPONSIBILITIES

This portion of the plan specifically outlines agency tasks, including the provision of resources and information, identification of the need for services, and coordination and integration of disaster activities. Primary and secondary agencies responsible for each task should be identified. The behavioral health agency should train staff on the incident command structure and to have representation at the local or state emergency operations center to help emergency managers assess the need for behavioral health services after disaster. Agency tasks will include many of the following efforts: assessing community needs; coordinating disaster behavioral health services for disaster survivors and responders; coordinating the efforts of external behavioral health organizations; training disaster behavioral health response teams; arranging accommodations, supplies, and equipment for responders; ensuring behavioral health responders have access to disaster areas by issuing them official identification and credentials; providing public information on dealing with disaster-related trauma; and maintaining standard operating procedures.

22.9.7 DIRECTION AND CONTROL

This element of the plan outlines the jurisdiction's or agency's disaster response operations, how the functions will be managed, and the responsible parties (McEntire and Myers 2004). Direction and control of behavioral health operations should be performed by the community agencies that normally provide such services. Plans should reflect consideration of how the behavioral health agency will coordinate and execute its activities across multiple jurisdictions and how it will fit into other county, state, and federal jurisdictional response structures. Behavioral health agencies and other governmental and nongovernmental partners during emergencies should work within the jurisdiction's incident command structure and perform assignments at the request of the local or state ESF-8 desk.

22.9.8 Administration and Support

This final section of the basic emergency operations plan will address reporting requirements, including costs-tracking reports, incident action plans, and situation reports; responsibility for modifying, updating, and maintaining the plan; after-action reporting to determine successes and failures during response efforts; and exercises to test the functions and capabilities of responders. Exercises include tabletop (group problem solving of disaster scenarios), functional (testing functional parts of the plan in a field setting), and full-scale events (where all jurisdictional partners participate in a simulated disaster) and should be conducted regularly during nondisaster periods. They will enhance individual and organizational relationships and improve coordination of efforts and teamwork. Further, exercises assist agencies to identify problems in planning, staffing, and equipment (McEntire and Myers 2004, 148).

22.9.9 Annexes and Appendices

Annexes and appendices are additional to the emergency operations plan. Annexes are essentially supplemental plans that go into greater detail of major emergency functions and the departments or agencies responsible for them, including communications, public information, evacuation, mass care, staffing (including volunteer management), and training (Henstra 2010; McEntire and Myers 2004; U.S. DHHS 2003). Functional annexes are organized in the same manner as the basic plan, that is, they include the functions' authorities, purpose, situation and assumptions, concept of operations, and so forth. Appendices provide supplemental information and direction for responders that the basic plans and annexes do not (McEntire and Myers 2004). For instance, many appendices concern additional directions for dealing with serious hazards such as terrorist events, chemical spills, biological hazards, or adverse weather events. They may also provide maps, standard operating procedures, checklists, and resource lists.

22.10 CONCLUSION

Clearly, disasters require rapid, coordinated responses to lessen the devastating physical, economic, social, and psychological consequences for individuals, families, and communities. Disaster response will not likely be efficient and effective without good planning. Therefore, behavioral health agencies must plan for how they will address the diverse needs of survivors postdisaster. Otherwise, unmitigated disaster-related distress can lead to the development of psychiatric disorders that require long-term community treatment. The ability of community behavioral health agencies to absorb additional clients is generally a contentious issue. Furthermore, planning in itself is a complex and dynamic process. While behavioral health agencies will have specific disaster response goals and objectives to accomplish, they must recognize that the synergies created through the planning process may radically change planning and response decisions and approaches. Thus, maintaining flexibility and creativity during the planning process is essential to creating realistic behavioral health plans for responding to disaster.

NOTES

a NIMS was established on February 28, 2003, by Homeland Security Presidential Directive (HSPD)-5. See the Federal Emergency Management Agency's Web site for additional information about NIMS at http://www.fema.gov/emergency/nims.
b FEMA published the NRF in January 2003 to replace the National Response Plan. Additional information about the National Response Framework is available at http://www.fema.gov/emergency/nrf/.
c Version 2 (November 2010) of the CPG 101 is now available for viewing at http://www.fema.gov/pdf/about/divisions/npd/CPG_101_V2.pdf.

REFERENCES

Acierno, R., K. J. Ruggiero, S. Galea, H. S. Resnick, K. Koenen, J. Roitzsch, M. de Arellano, J. Boyle, and D. G. Kilpatrick. 2007. Psychological sequelae resulting from the 2004 Florida hurricanes: Implications for postdisaster intervention. *American Journal of Public Health 97*(S1): S103–S108.

Allen, H., and R. Katz. 2010. Demography and public health emergency preparedness: Making the connection. *Population Research and Policy Review 29*: 527–539.

Auf der Heide, E. 2006. The importance of evidence-based disaster planning. *Annals of Emergency Medicine 47*(1): 34–47.

Birkland, T. A. 2009. Disasters, catastrophes, and policy failure in the homeland security era. *Review of Policy Research 26*(4): 423–438.

Col, J.-M. 2007. Managing disasters: The role of local government. *Public Administration Review 67*(Supp. D): 114–124.

Compton, M. T., R. J. Kotwicki, N. J. Kaslow, D. B. Reissman, and S. F. Wetterhall. 2005. Incorporating mental health into bioterrorism response planning. *Public Health Reports 120*(S1): 16–19.

DeWolfe, D. J. 2000. *Training Manual for Mental Health and Human Service Workers in Major Disasters* (2nd ed.). Rockville, MD: U.S. Department of Health and Human Services, Substance Abuse and Mental Health Services Administration, Center for Mental Health Services.

Federal Emergency Management Agency (FEMA). 2010. *Developing and maintaining Emergency Operations Plans: Comprehensive Preparedness Guide (CPG) 101 Version 2.0 state, territorial, and tribal, and local government emergency plans.* http://www.fema.gov/pdf/about/divisions/npd/CPG_101_V2. pdf.

Florida Department of Health (FDOH), Bureau of Preparedness and Response. 2010. *Public Health and Medical Preparedness, Version 2.2. Plan Development Guide for State-Level Operational Plans.* Tallahassee, FL: Florida Department of Health. http://www.doh.state.fl.us/demo/bpr/PDFs/State-levelOpPlanDevelopmentGuideV2.pdf.

Harrald, J. R. 2006. Agility and discipline: Critical success factors for disaster response. *Annals of the American Academy of Political and Social Science 604*: 256–272.

Henstra, D. 2010. Evaluating local government emergency management programs: What framework should public managers adopt? *Public Administration Review 70*(2): 236–246.

McEntire, D., and A Myers. 2004. Preparing communities for disasters: Issues and processes for government readiness. *Disaster Prevention and Management 13*(2): 140–152.

Nelson, C., N. Lurie, and J. Wasserman. 2007. Conceptualizing and defining public health emergency preparedness. *American Journal of Public Health 97*(S1): S9–11.

Norris, F. H., M. J. Friedman, P. J. Watson, C. M. Byrne, E. Diaz, and K. Kaniasty. 2002. 60,000 disaster victims speak: Part I. An empirical review of the empirical literature, 1981–2001. *Psychiatry 65*(3): 207–239.

Norris, F. H., K. Sherrieb, and S. Galea. 2010. Prevalence and consequences of disaster-related illness and injury from Hurricane Ike. *Rehabilitation Psychology 55*(3): 221–230.

Quarantelli, E. L. 1988. Disaster crisis management: A summary of research findings. *Journal of Management Studies 25*(4): 373–385.

Stein, B. D., T. L. Tanielian, D. P. Eisenman, D. J. Keyser, M. A. Burnam, and H.A. Pincus. 2004. Emotional and behavioral consequences of bioterrorism: Planning a public health response. *The Milbank Quarterly 82*(3): 413–455.

U.S. Department of Health and Human Services. 2003. *Mental Health All-Hazards Disaster Planning Guidance.* DHHS Pub. No. SMA 3829. Rockville, MD: Center for Mental Health Services, Substance Abuse and Mental Health Services Administration.

U.S. Department of Homeland Security (DHS). 2008. *Emergency Support Function #8 – Public Health and Medical Services Annex.* Washington, DC: U.S. Department of Homeland Security. http://www.fema. gov/pdf/emergency/nrf/nrf-esf-08.pdf

U.S. Department of Homeland Security. 2009. *Homeland Security Presidential Directive 5: Management of Domestic Incidents.* http://www.dhs.gov/xabout/laws/gc_1214592333605.shtm.

Index

Note: Page numbers followed by *A* refer to appendixes, *b* refer to boxes, *f* refer to figures, and *t* refer to tables.